THE OXFORD HANDBOOK OF

SYMBOLIC INTERACTIONISM

THE OXFORD HANDBOOK OF

SYMBOLIC INTERACTIONISM

Edited by
WAYNE H. BREKHUS, THOMAS DEGLOMA,
and
WILLIAM RYAN FORCE

Oxford University Press is a department of the University of Oxford. It furthers the University's objective of excellence in research, scholarship, and education by publishing worldwide. Oxford is a registered trade mark of Oxford University Press in the UK and certain other countries.

Published in the United States of America by Oxford University Press
198 Madison Avenue, New York, NY 10016, United States of America.

© Oxford University Press 2024

All rights reserved. No part of this publication may be reproduced, stored in a retrieval system, or transmitted, in any form or by any means, without the prior permission in writing of Oxford University Press, or as expressly permitted by law, by license, or under terms agreed with the appropriate reproduction rights organization. Inquiries concerning reproduction outside the scope of the above should be sent to the Rights Department, Oxford University Press, at the address above.

You must not circulate this work in any other form
and you must impose this same condition on any acquirer.

CIP data is on file at the Library of Congress

ISBN 978–0–19–008216–1

DOI: 10.1093/oxfordhb/9780190082161.001.0001

Printed by Sheridan Books, Inc., United States of America

Contents

Acknowledgments	ix
About the Editors	xi
Contributors	xiii

1. Introduction: On the Wonderful Complexities and Varied Directions
   of Symbolic Interactionism in the Twenty-First Century   1
   THOMAS DEGLOMA, WAYNE H. BREKHUS, AND WILLIAM RYAN FORCE

PART I: THEORETICAL AND METHODOLOGICAL ORIENTATIONS

2. The Historical Foundations of Symbolic Interactionism   27
   ROBERT DINGWALL

3. Symbolic Interactionism and Social Research   49
   ANDREA SALVINI

4. Toward a Concept-Driven Sociology: Sensitizing Concepts and the
   Prepared Mind   70
   EVIATAR ZERUBAVEL

5. De-realization and Infra-humanization: A Theory of Symbolic
   Interaction with Digital Technologies   81
   SIMON GOTTSCHALK AND CELENE FULLER

6. Quantitative Measurement and the Production of Meaning   104
   HÉCTOR VERA

7. Social Organization, Macro Phenomena, and Symbolic
   Interactionism   122
   PATRICK J. W. MCGINTY

8. Dramaturgical Traditions: Performance and Interaction   146
   SUSIE SCOTT

vi   CONTENTS

9. Social Constructionism in the Symbolic Interactionist Tradition   162
   ARA A. FRANCIS

10. The Narrative Study of Self and Society   175
    AMIR B. MARVASTI AND JABER F. GUBRIUM

PART II: CULTURE, CONTEXT, AND SYMBOLIC INTERACTION

11. Culture, or the Meaning of Meaning Making   195
    MICHAEL IAN BORER

12. Subcultures   207
    WILLIAM RYAN FORCE

13. Interactionist Theories of Emotion: From G. H. Mead to
    Culture Theory   221
    E. DOYLE MCCARTHY

14. Shopping, Identity, and Place   241
    ENRICO CAMPO

15. Symbolic Interaction and Music   258
    JOSEPH A. KOTARBA

16. Sociology of Mass and New Media through an Interactionist Lens   275
    JULIE B. WIEST

17. The Presence, Performance, and Publics of Online Interactions   296
    QIAN LI AND XIAOLI TIAN

18. Symbolic Interactionism and Religion   314
    ANDREA SALVINI AND IRENE PSAROUDAKIS

PART III: POWER AND INEQUALITIES

19. Markedness and Unmarkedness in Identities and Social Interaction   335
    WAYNE H. BREKHUS

20. The Appearance of Nothingness: Concealed Strategic Actions   350
    CARMELO LOMBARDO AND LORENZO SABETTA

CONTENTS vii

21. Power and Interaction 368
MICHAEL L. SCHWALBE AND KELSEY MISCHKE

22. Racial Socialization and Racism 386
MARGARET A. HAGERMAN

23. Gender and Embodiment as Negotiated Relations 402
S. L. CRAWLEY AND ASHLEY GREEN

24. Sex and Sexuality 425
CIRUS RINALDI

25. Deviant Selves, Transgressive Acts, and Moral Narratives: The
Symbolic-Interactionist Field of Transgression, Crime, and Justice 446
THADDEUS MÜLLER

26. Medicine, Health, and Illness 468
GIUSEPPINA CERSOSIMO

PART IV: ENVIRONMENT, DISASTERS, AND RISK

27. Interactionist Tools for Assessing Community Resilience 493
BRADEN LEAP

28. Eco-uncertainty as a Frame and Way of Life 512
DAINA CHEYENNE HARVEY

29. Disasters 529
MARGARETHE KUSENBACH AND GABRIELA B. CHRISTMANN

Index 549

ACKNOWLEDGMENTS

OUR acknowledgments are, like the rest of this book, a bit unconventional. We would like to thank all of the members and affiliates of the Society for the Study of Symbolic Interaction (SSSI) and the European Society for the Study of Symbolic Interaction (EUSSSI) for their dedication to building and maintaining a global community of interactionist scholars. Due to the work of many people in this diverse and evolving community, scholars with various interests and concerns have had space to gather and share ideas related to the broad perspective of symbolic interactionism. We have benefited greatly from the fellowship and the many scholarly conversations that have unfolded in these spaces, without which no handbook of symbolic interactionism would be possible. We also wish to specifically thank Eviatar Zerubavel, Doni Loseke, Jay Gubrium, and the late Spencer Cahill, who were mentors who introduced us to symbolic interactionism and its wonderful complexities.

ABOUT THE EDITORS

Wayne H. Brekhus is Chair and Professor of Sociology at the University of Missouri. His research interests include the sociology of identities, the cultural sociology of cognition, social markedness and unmarkedness, and developing sociological theory to analyze constructions of social difference. He is the author of *The Sociology of Identity: Authenticity, Multidimensionality, and Mobility*; *Culture and Cognition: Patterns in the Social Construction of Reality*; *Sociologia dell'inavvertito* (translated into Italian by Lorenzo Sabetta); and *Peacocks, Chameleons, Centaurs: Gay Suburbia and the Grammar of Social Identity*—and coeditor of *The Oxford Handbook of Cognitive Sociology* (with Gabe Ignatow).

Thomas DeGloma is Associate Professor of Sociology at Hunter College and the Graduate Center of the City University of New York (CUNY). He specializes in the areas of culture, cognition, memory, symbolic interaction, and sociological theory. His research interests also include the sociology of time, knowledge, autobiography, identity, and trauma. He is the author of *Anonymous: The Performance of Hidden Identities* and *Seeing the Light: The Social Logic of Personal Discovery*, which received the 2015 Charles Horton Cooley Book Award from the Society for the Study of Symbolic Interaction. He is also coeditor of *Interpreting Contentious Memory: Countermemories and Social Conflicts over the Past* (with Janet Jacobs) and the *Interpretive Lenses in Sociology* series (with Julie B. Wiest). DeGloma served as President of the Society for the Study of Symbolic Interaction in 2017–2018.

William Ryan Force is a student of social life and Assistant Professor of Sociology at California State University, Fresno. His research and teaching explore the accomplishment of identity at the intersection of language, power, and culture. He has studied a variety of empirical contexts: tattoo culture, punk/indie rock, transgressive TV, bar culture, trick-or-treating, and the supernatural. Dr. Force's work has appeared as book chapters and in journals including *Deviant Behavior*, *Symbolic Interaction*, and *Crime, Media, Culture*. His current projects include a book examining the influence of social media on the tattoo subculture, and a critical interactionist analysis of the relationship between gangsta rap and outlaw country music.

Contributors

Michael Ian Borer is Professor of Sociology at the University of Nevada, Las Vegas. His main research and teaching interests include culture, urban life, spirituality, and the everyday. He is the author of *Faithful to Fenway: Believing in Boston, Baseball, and America's Most Beloved Ballpark* (NYU Press, 2008) and *Vegas Brews: Craft Beer and the Birth of a Local Scene* (NYU Press, 2019). He also co-authored *Urban People and Places: The Sociology of Cities, Suburbs, and Towns* (SAGE, 2014) and *Sociology in Everyday Life* (Waveland, 2016). Borer served as the 2021–2022 President of the Society for the Study of Symbolic Interaction.

Enrico Campo is a research fellow of Sociology at the Department of Philosophy, University of Milan (Italy). His research interests include sociological theory, the sociology of knowledge, and the study of the relations among culture, technology, and cognition. He is the author of *Attention and its Crisis in Digital Society* (Routledge, 2022; Italian edition Donzelli, 2020) and editor, with Andrea Borghini, of *Exploring the Crisis: Theoretical Perspectives and Empirical Investigations* (Pisa University Press, 2015).

Giuseppina Cersosimo is Professor of Sociology at the University of Salerno. Her research interests include sociological theory, qualitative methods, symbolic interactionism, and sociology of health and medicine. She is specialized in health promotion, wellbeing, doctor-patient interaction, health care and emotions, obesity, identity, gender, and violence. She is the author of books, book chapters, and papers in journals, among these: Cersosimo G. (ed.) *Park and Burgess's Sociology: Creation, Evolution and Legacy; The Making of William I. Thomas: Women, Work and Urban Inclusion; Interactionist Colloquies; Women and Health Promotion: Implications for Obesity Prevention in the Family and Beyond; Pragmatism; Narrated Communication; Applications and Developments of Visual Techniques.* She introduced and translated *Mirrors and Masks: The Search for Identity* by Anselm Strauss into Italian for the first time in 2017.

Gabriela B. Christmann is Deputy Director of the Leibniz Institute for Research on Society and Space (IRS), Erkner (near Berlin), Germany; Head of the Research Unit "Social innovations in rural spaces" at the IRS; and Adjunct Professor at the Technische Universität Berlin (Department of Sociology). Her research interests include urban and regional sociology, social innovation, social aspects of climate change, and constructions of vulnerability and resilience. She is the editor of the special issue "Struggling with Innovations" 28:3 (2020) (in *European Planning Studies*) and co-editor of *Climate*

Cultures in Europe and North America (with Thorsten Heimann, Jamie Sommer, and Margarthe Kusenbach) as well as of *Communicative Constructions and the Refiguration of Spaces* (with Hubert Knoblauch and Martina Löw).

S. L. Crawley is Associate Professor of Sociology and Interdisciplinary Social Sciences at the University of South Florida and is broadly interested in identity work and embodiment of gender, race, and sexualities; pragmatism and ethnomethodology; feminist and queer theories and methods; and comparative epistemologies within social science. In addition to publishing several invited chapters for handbooks and edited collections, Crawley has published in scholarly journals including *Gender & Society; Sexualities; Sociological Theory; Journal of Lesbian Studies; The American Sociologist; Journal of Contemporary Ethnography; The Sociological Quarterly; Feminism and Psychology; Cultural Studies←→Critical Methodologies;* and *Hypatia* and co-authored the book *Gendering Bodies*. Following a project with post-Soviet scholars, some of Crawley's work has been translated into Russian and Ukrainian.

Robert Dingwall is Emeritus Professor of Sociology at Nottingham Trent University and a consulting sociologist at Dingwall Enterprises Ltd. He has over fifty years research experience investigating a wide range of topics in medicine, law, science, and technology. He has been particularly interested in studying professional cultures, the ways in which these shape organizations, and the consequences for both individual clients or patients and the wider society. He has also made contributions to the development of qualitative methods and the critical appraisal of research ethics and governance. His main publications include a translation of *Howard S. Becker: Sociology and Music in the Chicago School* by Jean Peneff, *Essays on Professions*, and *The Protection of Children: State Intervention and Family Life* (with J. M. Eekelaar and T. Murray). He has served as editor-in-chief of *Sociology of Health and Illness* and *Symbolic Interaction*. He is a Fellow of the UK Academy of Social Sciences, an Honorary Member of the UK Faculty of Public Health, and a recipient of the Mead Award from the Society for the Study of Symbolic Interaction.

Ara A. Francis is Associate Professor of Sociology at College of the Holy Cross. She is a microsociologist with interests in social disruption, death and dying, emotion, and stigma. Her work has been published in journals such as *Journal of Contemporary Ethnography* and *Sociology of Health and Illness*. She is the author of *Family Trouble: Middle-Class Parents, Children's Problems, and The Disruption of Everyday Life.*

Celene Fuller is a doctoral candidate at the University of Nevada, Las Vegas who specializes in the sociological subfields of gender and sexuality and social psychology, emphasizing stigmatized sexual and gender identities. Celene's dissertation research centers on the experiences of sexual and reproductive health stigma surrounding access to abortion and reproductive healthcare in Nevada.

Simon Gottschalk is Professor Emeritus of Sociology at the University of Nevada, Las Vegas. As a critical social psychologist, he has published on topics as diverse as terrorism, commercial ads, countercultural youth, environmental identity, acceleration, the senses, Las Vegas, the transmission of trauma, ethnography in virtual spaces, and qualitative research methods, among others. He is the co-author (with Phillip Vannini and Dennis Waskul) of *The Senses in Self, Society, and Culture: A Sociology of the Senses*. His most recent book, *The Terminal Self*, explores how interactions with digital technologies shape our everyday lives and experiences, and his most recent research analyzes emotions on white supremacist websites.

Ashley Green is Visiting Assistant Professor of Sociology at Central Connecticut State University. Her research examines experiences of gender, sexuality, space, and community through interactionist and feminist theoretical frameworks. Green's work has been published in the edited collection *Expanding the Rainbow: Exploring the Relationships of Bi+, Polyamorous, Kinky, Ace, Intersex, and Trans People*.

Jaber F. Gubrium is Emeritus Professor of Sociology at the University of Missouri, previously Professor at the University of Florida and Marquette University. Applying a constructionist form of symbolic interactionism, the goal of his research has been to ethnographically discover and make visible assemblages of meaning that rationalization erases. Results initially were presented in a series of monographs including *Living and Dying at Murray Manor* (1975), *Caretakers: Treating Emotionally Disturbed Children* (1979), *Describing Care: Image and Practice in Rehabilitation* (1982), *Oldtimers and Alzheimer's: The Descriptive Organization of Senility* (1986), and *Speaking of Life: Horizons of Meaning for Nursing Home Residents* (1993). Centered on the comparative ethnography of everyday life, Gubrium continues to explore and document novelty and pattern in discursive practice, most recently in collaboration with Professor Amir B. Marvasti in their (2023) edited book *Crafting Ethnographic Fieldwork: Sites, Selves, and Social Worlds*.

Margaret A. Hagerman is Associate Professor of Sociology at Mississippi State University. Her research interests include racial learning/socialization, the sociology of race and racism, the sociology of children and youth, the sociology of education, the sociology of families, privilege, and qualitative methods. She is the author of *White Kids: Growing Up with Privilege in a Racially Divided America* (NYU Press, 2018).

Daina Cheyenne Harvey is Chair and Associate Professor of Sociology at the College of the Holy Cross. He specializes in the areas of social disruption/dislocation; social suffering; agrarianism, the post-pastoral, and food geographies; the environmental precariat; and critical race studies. He is the co-editor of *Beer Places: The Microgeographies of Craft Beer*. His current projects include a book on white allyship in the long-term aftermath of Hurricane Katrina and a book on the colonization of wealth, which looks at the myriad causes and reasons for the racial wealth gap in the United States.

Joseph A. Kotarba is Professor of Sociology at Texas State University, where he directs the Music Across the Course of Life project. He also serves as lead ethnographer and medical sociologist for the Institute for Translational Sciences at the University of Texas Medical Branch in Galveston. His areas of interest include culture, science, health, qualitative research methods, everyday life social theory, and applied/policy sociology. Dr. Kotarba received the George Herbert Mead Award for Lifetime Achievement from the Society for the Study of Symbolic Interaction, and the Society's Charles Horton Cooley Award for Best Book in the Symbolic Interactionist Tradition for *Baby Boomer Rock 'n' Roll Fans*. He served as President of the Society for the Study of Symbolic Interaction in 1998–1999. Dr. Kotarba is currently studying the experience of music in aging and during the COVID-19 pandemic, and the culture of the translational science movement. His most recent book is *Music in the Course of Life* (Routledge, 2023).

Margarethe Kusenbach is Professor of Sociology and Graduate Director at the University of South Florida (USF). Her areas of interest are cities and communities, identities, emotions, disasters, environment, interpretive theory, and qualitative research methods. She has published many articles and chapters, as well as two edited books, on a variety of topics within these areas. Her current research is an international comparison of street art cultures, festivals, and urban politics in North American and European cities. Kusenbach served as President of the Society for the Study of Symbolic Interaction (SSSI) in 2014–2015.

Braden Leap is Associate Professor of Sociology at Mississippi State University. He studies the gendered dynamics of sociological transformations, disruptions, and disasters. He is the author of *Gone Goose: The Remaking of an American Town in the Age of Climate Change*. His work can also be read in outlets such as *Antipode*; *Gender, Work & Organization*; *Men & Masculinities*; *Rural Sociology*; *Social Currents*; and *Sociological Inquiry*.

Qian Li is a PhD candidate in the Department of Sociology at the University of Hong Kong. Her research interests include media and culture, online fandom, and mediated interaction. She is now working on her thesis about the online fandom of Chinese mobile game players and wants to explore how players generate meanings and identities through their gaming experiences, their online interaction, and the social-cultural structures in which they are embedded.

Carmelo Lombardo is Professor of Sociology at Sapienza-University of Rome. He mainly works on questions related to micro-macro transitions, generative models, multi-agents simulation, and theory-research connection. Recent publications include "Subjects of Objectivation: Exercises in Reflexive Socioanalysis" [Special issue] (edited with G. Ienna, L. Sabetta, M. Santoro, *Sociologia e Ricerca Sociale*, 2022) and *Against the Background of Social Reality* (with L. Sabetta, Routledge, forthcoming).

Amir B. Marvasti is Professor of Sociology at Penn State Altoona. His research focuses on identity management in everyday encounters and institutional settings. Marvasti also has an active publication record on the pedagogy of qualitative research. His work in this area provides an overview of qualitative methods from data collection to analysis and writing. His books in this area include *Researching Social Problems* (co-edited with Javier

Trevino, Routledge, 2020), *The Handbook of Interview Research: The Complexity of the Craft*, 2nd edition (co-edited with Jaber Gubrium, James Holstein, and Karyn McKinney, SAGE, 2012); *Doing Qualitative Research: A Comprehensive Guide* (co-authored with David Silverman, SAGE, 2008); and *Qualitative Research in Sociology* (SAGE, 2004). He also is the author of *Being Homeless: Textual and Narrative Constructions* (Lexington Books, 2003) and *Middle Eastern Lives in America* (with Karyn McKinney, Rowman & Littlefield, 2004).

E. Doyle McCarthy is Professor Emerita of Sociology and American Studies at Fordham University in New York City. Her principal areas of research and writing are social and political theories of modernity, sociology of knowledge, and emotion studies. Her interdisciplinary work in emotion studies was published in the monograph *Emotional Lives: Dramas of Identity in an Age of Mass Media* (Cambridge, 2017). This book explores both the long history of today's emotional culture as well as its most recent changes of the last half century. In 2021 she published "Culture and Emotion: Interactionist Perspectives" in *The Routledge International Handbook of Interactionism*, edited by Dirk vom Lehn, Will Gilson, and Natalia Ruiz-Junco. In that same year, McCarthy received the George Herbert Mead Lifetime Achievement Award from the Society for the Study of Symbolic Interaction.

Patrick J. W. McGinty is Professor of Sociology at Western Illinois University. A past president of the Society for the Study of Symbolic Interaction (SSSI) and current labor union leader, his research interests include organizational and institutional change and the relational, processual, enactment of power. The author or co-author of numerous articles attending to the sociology of symbolic interactionism and the implications of interactionist thought for sociological theorizing, his current project (with Natalia Ruiz-Junco and Daniel Morrison) brings each of these themes together in an effort to further unpack the implications of pragmatist thought for sociological theorizing.

Kelsey Mischke is a PhD candidate in sociology at North Carolina State University. Her research interests include inequalities (gender, race, and class), the body, emotions, self and identity, and health. Her research on body dissatisfaction and remedial body projects has appeared in *Journal of Contemporary Ethnography*. Her dissertation examines how people use intuitive eating to manage body-related feelings and form new identities.

Thaddeus Müller is Reader at the Law School of Lancaster University (criminology). He is incoming President of the Society for the Study of Symbolic Interaction (2023) and the current President of its European counterpart. He has researched a range of topics within the symbolic interactionist field of culture, crime, and transgression such as the criminalization and normalization of drugs, the social construction of young men hanging around in public spaces, and defaulting homeowners facing stigma. Within these themes, he focuses on the effects of stigma/labeling, and resisting stigma/labeling (and its effects) through the (collective) construction of empowering (counter-) narratives. He has published in a wide range of journals, such as *Symbolic Interaction*,

Qualitative Sociology Review, *Critical Criminology*, *Deviant Behavior*, and *The British Journal of Criminology*.

Irene Psaroudakis is Assistant Professor of Sociology at the University of Pisa. Her interests mainly deal with the theoretical and methodological perspective of symbolic interactionism, and the processes of data analysis, especially in qualitative methods and constructivist grounded theory. They also include sociology of the third sector, and the application of social network analysis and mixed methods. She is the author of books and papers; among others, she is the co-editor of the volume *Dealing with Grounded Theory: Discussing, Learning, and Practice* (with Thaddeus Müller and Andrea Salvini, 2021), and *La sfida pandemica per il Terzo settore: L'impatto del Covid-19 in un'analisi qualitativa* (2021). She is a member of the European Board of the Society for the Study of Symbolic Interaction (SSSI), and the scientific supervisor (with Andrea Salvini) of the International Summer School on Grounded Theory and Qualitative Methods of the University of Pisa.

Cirus Rinaldi (he/him/his) is Associate Professor of Sociology of Law, Deviance, and Social Change in the Department of Cultures and Societies of University of Palermo (Italy), where he coordinates the lab on "Bodies, Rights and Conflicts." His research areas cover deviance theory, sociological theories of sexuality, male sex work, and LGBTQI+ issues, and he has also introduced the debate on sexual scripts theory into the Italian academic community. He is author of *Sesso, Sè e Società. Per una sociologia delle sessualità* (*Sex, Self, and Society: For a Sociology of Sexualities*) and *Uomini che si fanno pagare. Genere, identità e sessualità nel sex work maschile tra devianza e nuove forme di normalizzazione* (*Men Who Get Paid: Gender, Identity and Sexuality in Male Sex Work between Deviance and New Forms of Normalization*).

Lorenzo Sabetta is Assistant Professor of Sociology at Sapienza-University of Rome. He has held various visiting and postdoc positions in the United States, Sweden, England, and Poland. He works on social theory, cognitive sociology, everyday life, and theories of knowledge. Recent publications include *The Anthem Companion to Robert K. Merton* (with C. Crothers, Anthem Press, 2022) and *What People Leave Behind: Marks, Traces, Footprints and their Relevance to Knowledge Society* (with F. Comunello and F. Martire, Springer, 2022).

Andrea Salvini is Professor of Sociology and Methodology of Social Research at the University of Pisa. His research interests include the relationship among symbolic interactionism and constructivist grounded theory, sociology of the third sector, sociology of religion, and social network analysis. He is the co-editor of *The Present and Future of Symbolic Interactionism* (volume 1 with Joseph Kotarba and Bryce Merril; volume 2 with David Altheide and Carolina Nuti) and *Symbolic Interactionism and Social Network Analysis: An Uncertain Encounter* and editor of *Interazioni inclusive. L'Interazionismo Simbolico tra teoria, ricerca e intervento sociale*. He is also the co-editor of the volume *Dealing with Grounded Theory* (with Thaddeus Müller and Irene Psaroudakis).

Michael L. Schwalbe is Professor Emeritus of Sociology at North Carolina State University. He is the author of *Unlocking the Iron Cage: The Men's Movement, Gender Politics, and American Culture*; *The Sociologically Examined Life: Pieces of the Conversation*; *Rigging the Game: How Inequality Is Reproduced in Everyday Life*; and *Making a Difference: Using Sociology to Create a Better World*; among other books.

Susie Scott is Professor of Sociology at the University of Sussex. Her research interests include micro-sociological theory (symbolic interactionism, dramaturgy, and phenomenology), the work of Erving Goffman, self-identity, emotions and mental health, narratives, and life-stories. She has conducted studies of shyness, swimming, asexuality, performance art, and total institutions. Susie is the author of *Shyness and Society: The Illusion of Competence* (Palgrave, 2007), *Making Sense of Everyday Life* (Polity, 2009), *Total Institutions and Reinvented Identities* (Palgrave, 2011), *Negotiating Identity: Symbolic Interactionist Approaches to Social Identity* (Polity, 2015), *The Social Life of Nothing: Silence, Invisibility and Emptiness in Tales of Lost Experience* (Routledge, 2019), and (co-edited with James Hardie-Bick) *Extreme Identities and Transitions out of Extraordinary Roles* (Palgrave, 2022).

Xiaoli Tian is Associate Professor in the Department of Sociology at the University of Hong Kong. She received her PhD from Department of Sociology, the University of Chicago. She has written extensively on various forms of online interactions, including emails, blogs, online literature websites in China, and social media. Her writings have been published in *American Journal of Sociology*; *Sociological Forum*; *Qualitative Sociology*; *Journal of Contemporary China*; *Information, Communication and Society*; *Symbolic Interaction*; *Journal of Contemporary Ethnography*; *Media, Culture and Society*; *Modern China*; *Chinese Sociological Review*; and *Journal of Social and Personal Relationships*, among others.

Héctor Vera is Researcher at the Instituto de Investigaciones sobre la Universidad y la Educación at Mexico's National University (UNAM). He received a PhD in sociology and historical studies from the New School for Social Research. His research interests include sociology of knowledge, historical sociology, social theory, and sociology of education. Among his recent publications are "Norbert Elias and Emile Durkheim: Seeds of a Historical Sociology of Knowledge," in Depelteau and Landini (eds.), *Norbert Elias and Social Theory* (2013); "The Social Construction of Units of Measurement: Institutionalization, Legitimation and Maintenance in Metrology," in Huber and Schlaudt (eds.), *Standardization in Measurement: Philosophical and Sociological Issues* (2015); "Rebuilding a Classic: The Social Construction of Reality at 50," *Cultural Sociology* (2016); "Weights and Measures," in Lightman (ed.), *Blackwell Companion to the History of Science* (2016); and "Breaking Global Standards: The Anti-Metric Crusade of American Engineers," in Pretel and Camprubí (eds.), *Technology and Globalisation: Networks of Experts in World History* (2018).

Julie B. Wiest is Professor of Sociology at West Chester University of Pennsylvania. Her research focuses on the sociocultural contexts of mass media, new media technologies, and violence. She authored *Creating Cultural Monsters: Serial Murder in America* and co-authored *The Allure of Premeditated Murder: Why Some People Plan to Kill*, as well as scholarly articles published in journals including *American Behavioral Scientist, Criminal Justice Studies, First Monday, Howard Journal of Communications*, and *International Journal of Communication*. Wiest co-edits the *Interpretive Lenses in Sociology* book series and is Senior Crime and Media Editor for the *Studies in Media and Communications* book series, for which she edited two volumes, *Theorizing Criminality and Policing in the Digital Media Age* and *Mass Media Representations of Crime and Criminality*.

Eviatar Zerubavel is Board of Governors Distinguished Professor of Sociology, Emeritus, at Rutgers University–New Brunswick. His publications include *Hidden in Plain Sight* (Oxford University Press, 2015), *Taken for Granted* (Princeton University Press, 2018; winner of the Charles Horton Cooley Award for Best Book by the Society for the Study of Symbolic Interaction as well as the Susanne K. Langer Award for Outstanding Scholarship in the Ecology of Symbolic Form by the Media Ecology Association), and *Generally Speaking* (Oxford University Press, 2021). He served from 1992 to 2001 and from 2006 to 2009 as the director of the Rutgers sociology graduate program. In 2000–2001 he served as Chair of the Culture Section of the American Sociological Association. In 2003 he was awarded a Guggenheim Fellowship. In 2016 he received the Rutgers University Faculty Scholar-Teacher Award, in 2017 he received the Society for the Study of Symbolic Interaction's Helena Lopata Mentor Excellence Award, and in 2022 he was awarded the Society for the Study of Social Interaction's George Herbert Mead Lifetime Achievement Award. He has recently completed the book *Don't Take It Personally* (Oxford University Press, forthcoming).

CHAPTER 1

INTRODUCTION

On the Wonderful Complexities and Varied Directions of Symbolic Interactionism in the Twenty-First Century

THOMAS DEGLOMA, WAYNE H. BREKHUS,
AND WILLIAM RYAN FORCE

SYMBOLIC interactionism (SI) is an entrenched and broadly influential perspective in the field of sociology, one that has had a profound impact on our qualitative and ethnographic traditions. There is now a familiar narrative about the origins and history of SI, as well as new interpretations that complicate and enhance the traditional story (Huebner 2014; Ruiz-Junco and Brossard 2019; Dingwall this volume). However, we still lack a clear understanding, let alone agreement, on the current status and definition of this rich tradition. While it continues to bear plenty of fruit, many have trouble identifying the tree. In no small part, such an understanding is elusive because SI is no longer a coherent intellectual camp, if it ever was. Many scholars inspired by the interactionist perspective remain "intellectually promiscuous" and "blend" SI with other traditions to address new topics in a wide variety of areas, as Gary Alan Fine (1993:64–65) so insightfully recognized approximately three decades ago. To understand what SI is today, and more importantly what scholars who use the theoretical and methodological tools of SI do, we need to embrace the wonderful complexities and varied directions of SI in a multifaceted matrix of sociological research and theory.

Developing out of the social and political pragmatism centered at the University of Chicago in the early twentieth century—what is famously known as the "Chicago school" of social theory and research—SI evolved as an alternative to the structural-functionalist paradigm that dominated US sociology throughout the mid-twentieth century. From its inception, SI took form with a polemical tone that defined its relation to the rest of the field, a tone that continues to characterize the statements of many who opine about the status of SI today. Structural-functionalist sociologists emphasized a holistic view of society as a *sui generis* entity and the source of social norms, institutional structures, and durable social roles. Its most distinguished proponent, Talcott Parsons (1937, 1951/1991), sought to bridge a macro-structural analysis of society and its most basic functions (drawing from the earlier work of Emile Durkheim) with a theory of human action (drawing from Max Weber's *verstehen* sociology) and psychic motivation (drawing from psychoanalysis and other sources), all while viewing society as an integrated entity and the source of normative values and orientations at all levels of analysis. As an alternative to this grand and imperialistic theoretical vision, one that skirted the nuances and contingencies of human relationships and failed to consider the local dynamics of experience, symbolic interactionist sociologists stressed that meanings *emerge* from our interactions—from a blend of learned routine and creative human activity in specific situations, communities, and contexts. Meanings are not externally molded norms, but *co-constructed* in the everyday activity of human social life. This theoretical orientation carries strong methodological implications: one should observe these interactive processes *in situ* and gather data in and from the contexts in which they unfold if one wishes to really know the core fabric of social life.

Positioning himself polemically against the macro-deterministic biases of structural-functionalism and the positivist quantitative approaches then dominating mainstream US sociological thought, as well as against the methodological individualism of mainstream psychology, Herbert Blumer coined the term "symbolic interaction" in 1937 and later made it famous when he explicitly outlined the "perspective and method" of symbolic interactionism and laid out its well-known and oft-cited "three simple premises" (1969:2). Following Blumer, early proponents of this vision drew heavily on the sociology of George Herbert Mead, as well as the writings of Charles Horton Cooley and Chicago school sociologists such as Robert Park, W. I. Thomas, Ernest W. Burgess, Everett Hughes, and others (see Fine 1993:62; Dingwall 2001, this volume). In its traditional manifestation, SI consisted primarily of attention to a few basic social processes such as interpersonal behavior and coordination, symbolic exchange or communication, and the situated emergence of meaning. In line with these concerns, SI scholars viewed the self as a social, reflexive, and dialogical process. With regard to the last point—the self as a reflexive social process—Mead developed ideas previously introduced by William James, Charles H. Cooley, and Charles Sanders Peirce, all of whom conceptualized the self as some sort of inner conversation, but in different ways (see Wiley 2006). Mead (1934/2015) put forth a thoroughly sociological theory of the reflexive self by more carefully linking the component parts of the self to the "social act" (p. 7), which at a ground level is a process of "communication involving participation in the other" (p. 253) and, on a broader level, requires society as a symbolic "system of common or social meanings" (p. 156). Building on this paradigm, Blumer also "focused on how the individual interacts with others in interpersonal relations to formulate a sense of self" (Brekhus 2008:1060). This approach emphasized the social foundations of psychology and established part of the groundwork for a multifaceted sociology of identity as we know it today (see Brekhus 2020 for a contemporary statement).

While a focus on interpersonal coordination and on the social constitution of the self characterizes the early SI perspective, many who inspired this tradition were also trailblazers in urban ethnography and in the study of subculture. Chicago School researchers approached the city of Chicago as an urban laboratory well suited to study social life in its dynamic complexities. Among the most influential were Ernest Burgess and Robert Park, both of whom stressed the importance of the environments and contexts of social interaction. Sociologists of deviant affiliation and subcultural formation also developed this perspective, including Frederic Thrasher (1927) and Donald Cressey (1932), and later Edwin Sutherland (1939) and Albert Cohen (1955) (see Force, this volume). A general emphasis on context and ecology is also evident in the work of Everett Hughes and his students who stressed the importance of social organization to the extent of deemphasizing the self (see Fine 1993:77; Dingwall 2001:238), along with others among the second generation of Chicago scholars who analyzed the environments or ecologies of social life. All of this work paved the way for contemporary interactionist positions that regard selves as inseparably linked to situated concerns rooted in contexts, communities, and institutions of various types, not just interpersonal interactions (see, for example, Becker 1963; Gubrium and Holstein 2000).

The push to emphasize social contexts and situations was further advanced by Erving Goffman (1959, 1961, 1974/1986), who was particularly interested in "the structures within which interactions were framed" (Dingwall, this volume) and on the ways that settings shape the performance of self and meaning more broadly. For Goffman, people bring their selves to life in situated attempts to manage the impressions of others while adapting to the constraints of their social circumstances and the expectations of their contextualized audiences. Furthermore, institutions (1961) and normative structures of communication, such as "episoding conventions" (1974/1986:251), are not simply passive surrounding elements. Rather, they serve as both tools and constraints that social actors use to give meaning to human experiences. Goffman's dramaturgical perspective, wherein the world is composed of multiple performance stages and the individual is a social actor on these stages, has influenced a great deal of ethnographic work in the contemporary SI arena (see, for example, Edgley 2013). Susie Scott (this volume) provides an overview of this rich dramaturgical tradition. Goffman draws from orthodox SI in that "the dramaturgical performer epitomizes Mead's (1934) concept of the reflexive social self" (Scott, this volume), yet he created a new lens with which to analyze human action, interpersonal behavior, and the self. While some (e.g., Benzecry and Winchester 2017) distinguish the Goffmanian dramaturgical perspective from SI proper, we see dramaturgy as a perspective that has merged with the SI family of scholarship, one that shapes how contemporary SI scholars see the worlds they study. Many such scholars have blended Goffman's dramaturgical vision with their analyses of situated cultures of interaction, developing new cultural-interactionist approaches to performance and meaning-making work.

While some SI scholars focused more on the development of selves and identities in their social contexts, and others took a broader view of social ecology or the environment and its impact on group experiences, SI held closely to a central claim that human beings construct meaning through social interaction (the core point of Blumer's three premises). Given Blumer's work to define and defend the parameters of a Meadian social psychology, his positioning of this Meadian approach as the prime alternative to other paradigms that mostly ignored the dynamic interactive dimensions of social life, and his somewhat accidental coining of the term "symbolic interaction," in its beginnings SI theories characteristically traced their lineage back to Mead via Blumer. Despite the fact that SI scholars cited various other sources of influence, to be a symbolic interactionist was ultimately to be a part of a community with a collective identity and a specifically Blumerian/Meadian lineage and Chicago heritage within sociology. This traditionalist core version of SI lives on in many textbook and anthology portrayals of what symbolic interactionism is today. However, it also feeds scholarly attempts to define the "proper" or "true" version of SI and distinguish it from the rest of sociology. While such heritage narratives and typologies might make for useful heuristics, we see contemporary SI as a rich and varied field of scholarship, and those who use SI as scholars who draw inspiration from multiple influences, blending them into new lenses with which to study the emergence or creative performance of meaning in a diverse variety of situated symbolic interactions.

Intellectual Sectarianism and Theoretical Expansion

Throughout the latter half of the twentieth century, in the wake of Blumer's strong claim on the history and trajectory of pragmatism, many of the scholars who wielded the banner of symbolic interactionism saw themselves as the "opposition" to mainstream sociology (see Fine 1993)—a proud sect of pariah sociologists who cut against the grain of the discipline with their bottom-up qualitative and interpretivist approach to social meaning. This sectarian positioning fueled squabbles about the definition of "proper" SI. It also fed a mythical narrative shared among some members of the Society for the Study of Symbolic Interaction that they were somehow more radical and free in their thinking, while the mainstream of the discipline was conservative and constraining. While these interrelated notions—that SI is somehow separate from, and more radical than, mainstream sociology—allowed for a tightknit interactionist community to be maintained, they ultimately became more misleading and intellectually problematic over time.[1]

Meanwhile, the pragmatist tradition and the principal tenets of symbolic interactionism were becoming more influential throughout the discipline of sociology (Fine 1993:65–68). Many notable scholars who did not explicitly identify with the consolidating SI camp nevertheless incorporated SI perspectives and themes in their work. Furthermore, many were developing new interpretive theories and qualitative research agendas that directly addressed vital social questions at multiple levels of analysis, from the interpersonal and biographical to the macro-structural and cultural. Take C. Wright Mills as one example. Not only did Mills, who critically engaged with classical pragmatism early in his career (1966), address power and inequality in ways that were absent in much of traditional SI theory and research, he also began to develop and connect new ideas about biography, language and narrative, motive, action and agency, community, and social structure, linking micro and macro levels of analysis in new and creative ways. Moreover, Mills's work was widely influential, inspiring new generations of scholars and activists who sought to tackle social problems in the world, and to better understand the impact of social forces on their lives and communities. Likewise, as new critical feminist scholars began to challenge the especially conservative assumptions of Parsonian structural-functionalism with regard to gender roles and the family, many bridged interpersonal/interactionist and political frameworks to challenge the basic notion that status quo institutions, which perpetuate all kinds of inequalities, are "functional." In short, as some scholars worked to consolidate SI into an orthodox and sectarian camp, the perspective at the heart of SI was evolving as an interpretive framework and influencing scholars in new ways, reaching into multiple areas of social research and theory (Fine 1993; DeGloma 2019:165).

Even when the renowned critical theorist Jürgen Habermas (1987) made the core tenets of symbolic interactionism a central part of his theory of communicative action and the public sphere, or when Anthony Giddens (1991) later developed themes at the core of interactionism and pragmatism to advance a general theory of late-modern identity, some continued to act as if SI stood outside the gates of mainstream sociology. More accurately, however, scholars who were outsiders to the SI orthodoxy were adapting interactionist ideas and integrating them with new and broadly applicable theories. In our current era, researchers have used symbolic interactionist ideas to develop new theories and methods of interpretive ethnography.[2] Additionally, SI has also become a core part of new approaches to micro and meso cultural sociology. Yet, attending a symbolic interactionist conference in 2019, one would be struck by how some participants continue to define themselves in sectarian terms, and proudly in radical opposition to the "mainstream," especially (in the North American context) to the American Sociological Association (ASA). Such a partisan narrative seems increasingly out of place considering the program of the ASA conference that year was full of qualitative and interactionist studies presented by a diverse range of speakers. Furthermore, the conference theme, "Engaging Social Justice for a Better World," expresses the association's commitment to engaging important issues and making positive social change. The same holds for the conference of the British Sociological Association (its theme was "Challenging Social Hierarchies and Inequalities") and the 2018 International Sociological Association World Congress of Sociology (where the theme was "Power, Violence and Justice: Reflections, Responses and Responsibilities"). While the positivist and quantitative approaches of "mainstream" sociology to which SI formed in opposition are still present, much of so-called mainstream sociology has become both more implicitly interactionist in its range of qualitative research *and* more critically attuned to addressing social problems at the same time. Many who present work at our "mainstream" conferences focus on issues of power and inequality and are (or can be) informed by interactionist lines of thinking.

The old sectarian and oppositional vision of SI is tired and increasingly irrelevant. Symbolic interactionists who insist on standing against the rest of the discipline will fail to provide tools and perspectives for interpreting a multicultural world racked with social inequalities and significant structural issues with which we must contend (see also Fine and Tavory 2019). Today, it is even clearer how much conventional SI missed or excluded because of the sectarian character of its cannon. W. E. B. Du Bois, a scholar who linked theories of self and identity with macro-historical political critique very early in the twentieth century, laying the groundwork for critical identity theory as we know it, was marginalized by much of mainstream sociology, including symbolic interactionism (Morris 2015). However, more flexible interpretations and applications of SI, those that combine the foundational tenets of pragmatism and interactionism with new analytic visions and a sensitivity toward contemporary and historical structures and dynamics of power and inequality, can offer important tools with which to study the wide diversity of topics and questions in the field of sociology and beyond.

An Expansive Vision of Symbolic Interactionism

The vision of symbolic interactionism that we hope to advance with this volume welcomes, indeed celebrates, building connections with other approaches and frameworks of analysis. We recognize that the perspective of symbolic interactionism is, as it should be, increasingly at the center of multiple efforts to address neglected issues and ongoing problems in the world today. Thus, we embrace what one might call the *expansive* rather than the traditional or *orthodox* definition of symbolic interactionism. This view is inclusive in its reach, "big tent" rather than sectarian, and engages multiple other camps and problems in the field (see also Dingwall, DeGloma, and Newmahr 2012; Fine and Tavory 2019). The scholars featured in this handbook merge traditional SI concepts and perspectives with a range of other influences and traditions in order to bring SI to bear on various areas of research and to address a variety of new and interesting questions, problems, and issues. Many of these scholars are situated at the intersection of multiple areas of research and theory, as their chapters will show, but all make use of, and develop, the method and perspective of symbolic interactionism in innovative ways.

Ours is not a conventional approach, but we believe it offers valuable insight into the work that scholars in the expansive world of SI are actually doing, and a helpful take on what others can do with a symbolic interactionist perspective today. To this end, we will now outline and briefly discuss four important developments that are reshaping the broad and varied field of contemporary symbolic interactionist scholarship. There are other important developments as well, but these four are especially significant. They are:

- A shift away from social psychology to a cultural constructionist sociology.
- A renewed engagement with pragmatist ideas.
- A bridging of Simmelian formal sociology with theoretically-informed qualitative research.
- A strong emphasis on power and inequalities as aspects of social identity and social interaction.

We describe and address these four developments in the following sections, emphasizing that a thorough understanding of symbolic interactionism today ought to take them into account.

Culture and Symbolic Interaction

Much of contemporary symbolic interactionism takes form as what we might call a micro or meso constructionist cultural sociology. Attention to culture is certainly not new to the interactionist tradition. Mead's notion of the "generalized other" is an early conceptualization of culture in the American pragmatist framework and social psychological tradition that continues to inspire interactionist scholars.[3] For Mead (1934/2015:154–58) the generalized other is an imagined observer who stands as proxy for the "whole community" and for the "social meanings" and moral order rooted in society, as well as an authoritative voice that we internalize as we think and act (Athens 1994; Wiley 2006:11). Mead's formulation is similar to Emile Durkheim's view of society as both conscience and consciousness, deposited into the minds of individuals, and both were inspired by the German philosophical tradition and especially the philosophy of Immanuel Kant (see Dingwall, this volume, for a brief discussion of Kant's influence on sociology). However, Mead, more than Durkheim, stressed inherently interactive processes and ongoing socialization as the means by which we continually acquire moral, cognitive, and behavioral norms (by which we acquire *society* itself and thus become social beings). Later, Peter L. Berger and Thomas Luckmann (1966) made the symbolic and interactive mechanisms of socialization (primary and secondary) a key launching point for their foundational and widely influential treatise of social constructionism, *The Social Construction of Reality*. Beyond this theoretical framework, which links the phenomenon of symbolic interaction to culture in a foundational and encompassing sense, the Chicago School emphasis on urban settings and subcultures highlighted the importance of particular contexts to culture, linking the topography of the individual's mind to bounded cultural environments.

In recent decades, many scholars have made important contributions that bridge the concerns of cultural sociology and symbolic interactionism. We will mention only a few prominent examples here. Gary Alan Fine (1979, 2021), for example, introduced the concept of the "idioculture" which he defined as "a system of knowledge, beliefs, behaviors, and customs shared by members of an interacting group to which members can refer and employ as the basis of further interaction" (1979:734). In their important contribution based on ethnographies of two localized groups (activists and bar patrons), Nina Eliasoph and Paul Lichterman (2003) show how these communities develop distinctive "group styles" that are "recurrent patterns of interaction that arise from a group's shared assumptions about what constitutes good or adequate participation in the group setting" (p. 737). In both of their cases, group members "filter collective representations" through shared local processes, which shows the importance of understanding "culture in interaction" (p. 782). Additionally, Jeffrey C. Alexander (2004, 2017) has developed the concept of "cultural pragmatics" to stress the ways that social actors must effectively incorporate deep-seated culture structures and other entrenched background aspects of culture with their particular performances in order to effectively bring meanings to life in ways that win the hearts and minds of their audiences. Michael Ian Borer (this volume) builds on this seminal work to highlight the important links between SI and cultural sociology. Cultural sociology, Borer notes, is an area that shares a similar set of concerns and a fair amount of common theoretical ground with SI. "Taking the local context seriously," he argues, "makes the 'generalized other' more tangible and empirical and, in effect, grounds studies of culture in real spaces and places with real people interacting with others." Thus, studying the unique attributes and localized processes of a group or community while also highlighting more broadly relevant culture structures is the main task of an SI-influenced cultural sociology, according to Borer. With this framework, he highlights an important path for future scholars to blend the tools of SI with other traditions of cultural sociology and analysis.

With a growing interest in culture and cultural analysis, SI scholars have also engaged the perspectives of performance theory and social constructionism in a number of ways. Performance theorists and social constructionists share a common root in the famous theoretical claim by W. I. and Dorothy Swaine Thomas (1928:572), "If [people] define situations as real, they are real in their consequences." In demonstrating how actors manage the impressions of others in their particular contexts and settings, Erving Goffman (1959) treated localized performances of the self and situation as cultural forces that shape shared meanings. Goffman's insights spurred broader interest in the ways that actors perform both personal and collective identities, as well as in the ways that people perform gender, sexuality, race, and other attributes to define, challenge, or reproduce inequalities and power relations. Many others (e.g., Best 1987, 1997; Loseke 1992, 1999, 2019; Best and Bogle 2014) have combined interactionist and cultural lenses to elucidate the social construction of social problems. Ara A. Francis (this volume) gives us an important overview of the relationship between SI and social constructionism.

All of the scholars featured in section two of this volume, and many of the others as well, blend the tools of SI and cultural sociology in various ways to engage important issues. For example, by focusing on spaces of consumption, Enrico Campo links the social contexts and interactive processes of shopping to cultural processes of identity construction. William Ryan Force illuminates various interactionist perspectives on subcultural communities and Joseph A. Kotarba blends SI with cultural analysis to show the rich importance of music to people's lives. Julie B. Wiest shows that SI can help us to see how mass and new media facilitate the construction of shared sociocultural meanings, and Qian Li and Xiaoli Tian link interactionist and cultural concerns to show how online interactions lead to "unique intersubjectivities." These are just a handful of examples of those who link symbolic interactionism with the analysis of culture in this volume.

A Renewed Engagement with Pragmatism

Pragmatism has influenced sociological research and theory since it took root at the University of Chicago in the early twentieth century. However, since the dawn of the twenty-first century, there has been a renewed and growing interest in bringing classical pragmatist perspectives to bear on major themes of sociological concern, including agency and social action, qualitative analysis, and self-consciousness and reflexivity, among several others. In August of 2015, speakers at the "Pragmatism and Sociology Conference," hosted at the University of Chicago in conjunction with the annual meeting of the American Sociological Association, presented various perspectives on the current value of the pragmatist classics (Owens 2015). While many of the participants may not explicitly identify as symbolic interactionists, this supposed rediscovery of the foundations of SI thinking signals the continual vitality of this area of thought, as well as new opportunities for dialogue about the reach of SI into various areas of sociology. For some, the conference also signified rifts in the field between different camps of scholars that each claim similar traditions while ignoring one another, and perhaps some confusion concerning how we ought to understand the legacies of pragmatism. In this section, we will sidestep many nuances, controversies, and current debates to briefly touch upon just a few examples of contemporary scholarship that applies classical pragmatism to important topics in sociology. While this is a very selective discussion and limited review, all of the examples we reference here point to open questions and areas with which contemporary SI scholars should engage.

Approaching the turn of the century, Mustafa Emirbayer and Ann Mische (1998), drawing inspiration from the work of G. H. Mead and John Dewey along with several others, developed a theoretical view of human agency as rooted in specific contexts and situated in time. Building on Mead's ideas about the situated and emergent experience of time and the social-relational character of human consciousness (pp. 968–69), they outlined a theory of agency as "intrinsically social and relational" involving "the engagement (and disengagement) by actors of the different contextual environments that constitute their own structured yet flexible social universes" (p. 973). For Emirbayer and Mische, as human beings navigate their present circumstances, their agency is informed by past actions and experiences as well as a projective anticipation of future outcomes. The entire process, with regard to both thought and action as well as the links between them, is rooted in one's present social situation and symbolic interactive relations to others—what these scholars call "the temporal-relational contexts of action" (pp. 970,

1002). At the core of this pragmatic perspective is attention to the ways human beings are both motivated by routines *and* driven to engage in creative innovative action to solve situated problems. Such a dualistic vision is rooted in Mead's concepts of the "me" and the "I" (and evokes the temporal structure of an actor's internal conversation) as well as Dewey's (1922) attention to habit and creativity (see also Joas 1996; Gross 2018:91–92).

Developing related perspectives on human action and interpretation, some scholars have applied the principles of pragmatism to macro-level events, structures, and other phenomena (McGinty 2014, this volume; Gross 2018), power (Schwalbe and Mischke, this volume), causality and causal mechanisms (Gross 2009), temporarily and the future (Tavory and Eliasoph 2013), and history (Huebner 2016). Others have brought pragmatist theory to bear on methods of social research and interpretation. Iddo Tavory and Stefan Timmermans (2014), building on the philosophy of Charles Sanders Peirce, recently developed the theory and method of "abductive analysis" to apply the tenets of pragmatism to qualitative research and theory construction. Developing Peirce's ideas about semiotics and signification, Tavory and Timmermans see research as a process of meaning-making in which researchers develop their ideas while working to make sense of the ways their subjects make sense of their situations. These "interpretant" experiences are then carried into the next "iteration of meaning-making," which is always "a highly contingent and interactional [. . .] process" at both levels (p. 24). The surprises generated over the course of this process allow the researcher to develop new theories where established models do not fit (see pp. 39–42, 71–72, 122–24). Taking another angle, Andrea Salvini (this volume) shows how classical pragmatist ideas and core SI concepts, as reconstructed and consolidated in the work of Herbert Blumer, have influenced three important contemporary frameworks for qualitative analysis and interpretation: ethnography, grounded theory, and postmodernism. As Salvini addresses these different methodological and analytic approaches, he shows how various scholars working in the SI tradition have blended ideas rooted in pragmatism with new and evolving ideas about the nature of the social world. In these cases and others, scholars apply pragmatist theory to the processes and contexts under investigation as well as the processes and contexts of social analysis itself. While sometimes distinguishing their work from what they conceive to be SI proper (see Gross 2009:374n13), such research and theory is entirely compatible with the expansive vision of SI we feature, and advocate, with this handbook.

Considering another avenue of social research, Norbert Wiley (1994, 2006, 2016), synthesizing the ideas of William James, C. S. Peirce, G. H. Mead, and John Dewey, links the pragmatist theory of a "dialogical self" to an interactionist theory of meaning, a link expressed in his concept of a "semiotic self." Wiley stresses that "inner speech is the key to the human semiotic or symbolic ability, itself the means of inventing culture" (2006:5). Thus, for Wiley, the pragmatists give us a means of linking the depths of inner meaning and thought to both social relationships and cultural systems, as the various voices of our inner dialogues reflect and express our relationships to other people as well as to the situations we encounter and the communities with which we affiliate. Others (Ezzy 1998; DeGloma 2014; DeGloma and Johnston 2019; Marvasti and Gubrium, this volume) have extended the pragmatist emphasis on reflexive inner dialogue to develop a cultural theory of narrative identity. Combining this foundational pragmatist theory with the insights of Erving Goffman (1961), Paul Ricoeur (1988, 1991), and others who address biographical construction, they have shown how individuals develop their self-reflexive accounts to navigate their particular situations, emplotting their selves and personal identities in ways that express the logics and tensions of social institutions and community affiliations in the world. Still others (McCarthy 2017, this volume; Ruiz-Junco 2017) bring pragmatist ideas about identity and reflexivity to bear on the sociology of emotions.

As this brief discussion shows, classical pragmatism is alive and well in contemporary sociology. Many of the scholars featured in this volume work with and develop pragmatist ideas to advance theoretical, methodological, and substantive arguments. Our hope is that dialogue and constructive debate around such issues will grow among the various scholars working with this broad and multifaceted tradition, and that this handbook will help bring that about.

Formal Interactionism

Several in the broad and evolving camp of symbolic interactionism have been inspired by Georg Simmel's emphasis on patterned forms of interaction. Researchers and theorists in this tradition often use a Simmelian emphasis on social forms and patterns to compare situated interactions across multiple contexts and settings. Others have adapted this formal approach to analyze the plot structure of narratives (drawing inspiration from the classical literary analyses of Northrop Frye and Vladimir Propp, the critical historiography of Hayden White, and others). By elucidating the social forms that undergird our interactions and the stories we tell about our lives and our situations, formal interactionists have advanced our understanding of the self and identity, time and memory, and emotion, along with performance and the dynamics of our social relationships with others in a wide variety of settings. Eviatar Zerubavel's formal culturalist cognitive sociology is one notable example of this kind of approach to SI. In his pioneering article "If Simmel Were a Fieldworker," Zerubavel (1980) established the parameters of a distinctly Simmelian ethnographic method attentive to issues of patterned human associations. Zerubavel (2021, this volume) relates formal sociology back to Blumer's idea of sensitizing concepts and explains how they work to draw the researcher's attention to the formal structural features of the empirical cases that they study. Developing the concept of "generic social processes," Robert Prus (1987) also stressed general patterns and forms of symbolic interaction as the primary lens through which to conceptualize social interaction and symbolic processes. Both Zerubavel and Prus give us a foundation with which to approach social analysis with a "thematic lens," looking for patterns of interaction and common underlying cultural codes that apply to sets of otherwise different cases (DeGloma and Papadantonakis 2020).

Gary Alan Fine (2003) also opens the door to a formal symbolic interactionist sociology when arguing for what he terms a "peopled" ethnographic approach. Central to Fine's approach is the notion that scholars can develop generalizable theories from ethnographic observations and analysis, theories that transcend any particular research site, and that these generalizations allow for interactional data gathered in specific groups and settings to be brought to bear on larger macro-sociological issues of concern (Brekhus 2020:26; see also Lofland's (1995) notion of "analytic ethnography"). In his own ethnographic studies, which are focused on a broad range of topics and many different communities, from little leaguers to chess players, from mushroom collectors to Dungeons and Dragons players, Fine develops generalizable concepts about group behavior and "tiny publics." Fine's (2021) recent work draws on several otherwise different cases to show how meso-level communities provide crucial "hinges" between micro and macro dimensions of social life, a formal similarity (and generic structural property) that unites his disparate cases under a single theme.

In this volume, Héctor Vera unpacks the symbolic significance of "different forms of measurements" that communities of researchers use to create shared meaning in their work. For Vera, quantitative measurement is a formal sociocognitive process that allows people in different times and places to share a common language of analysis and shared stock of knowledge. Likewise, Michael Schwalbe and Kelsey Mischke (this volume) show how power manifests as "five forms of action through which the cooperation of others is elicited." Developing a formal theory of power in this way indeed invites application to a wide diversity of cases. All of these approaches represent ways that SI has moved away from a strict focus on particular situated interactions and a social psychology of the self and toward more broadly relevant and applicable social theory. They also represent a shift from site-particular ethnographic traditions rooted in a Chicago School ecological perspective to a more comparative multi-case formal interactionist and cultural theory (see DeGloma and Papadantonakis 2020).

Power, Inequalities, and Intersectionality in Contemporary Symbolic Interactionism

A common criticism of symbolic interactionism has been that proponents lack adequate concern with issues of social power and structural inequality. In some ways, this criticism may be valid. However, as Patrick J. W. McGinty as well as Wayne Brekhus, Michael Schwalbe and Kelsey Mischke, Margaret A. Hagerman, Thaddeus Müller, Giuseppina Cersosimo, Daina Cheyenne Harvey, and several others argue in this volume, we can use foundational SI perspectives to address and understand power and structural inequalities in important and illuminating ways. In recent decades, we have witnessed a proliferation of SI scholarship that takes a critical perspective or involves a power-focused lens. Many scholars have worked to link SI with critical theories, such as Marxism and critical postmodernism, and to align SI with social standpoint and intersectional feminist theories concerned with issues of power and inequalities. Of these developments, we focus particularly on the links with social standpoint theories as this is an especially promising avenue of future SI research, one that represents a direction in the field that grapples with important macro sociological issues, as well one that allows us to revive marginalized perspectives of the past.

Increasingly, interactionist scholars have become interested in the importance of raced, gendered, and classed social structures for understanding identity and meaning, as well as the role of marginalized epistemological standpoints in generating knowledge and theory. An array of recent work by scholars advancing different theoretical perspectives can inform these efforts. For example, Brekhus (1998) argues that we should not develop group-specific theories from marginalized populations and thus relegate marginalized people to "epistemological ghettos," but rather that ethnographies of the marked and marginalized should be a part of general, generic theorizing (see also Brekhus 2003). Julian Go (2020:84) argues that the epistemic structures of sociology have long considered general sociological theorizing as the province of white, male colonizers and have excluded Black, Indigenous, and subaltern scholars from a kind of full theory citizenship. In challenging the imperial biases of the canon, Go (2020:93) asserts that "canonization is but the universalization of the provincial," and argues for greater recognition of the particularized standpoints of all theoretical traditions, an argument that lends itself well to the development of reflexive standpoint ethnographies. Symbolic interactionism, in many ways, is a natural fit for applying standpoint theories that call attention to difference, inequality, and power at the micro and meso levels of analysis.[4] All identities are intricately linked by axes of social difference (e.g., race, gender, class). The establishment of these patterns of social difference, as Goffman (1979) and, later, Judith Butler (1990) pointed out with regard to gender, may be the goal of very few interactions but are a byproduct of all. Identities are accomplished through carefully managed social performances (Goffman 1959, 1963) that require human actors to succumb to social categories in order to live within a society (West and Fenstermaker 1995; West and Zimmerman 1987), thus linking acts of identity categorization with the expression and maintenance of power.

S. L. Crawley and Ashley Green (this volume) point out that "some of the most productive early critiques of androcentric and individualist gender theory" were put forth by interactionist microsociologists. Although neither Goffman nor Garfinkel approached gender with a feminist lens, they nevertheless located gender as a part of the socially constructed interaction order and thus provided important foundations for others to show it to be an ongoing accomplishment. West and Zimmerman (1987) and West and Fenstermaker (1995) further demonstrated that gender is a pervasive interactional accomplishment, while Butler (1990, 1991) illustrated gender as the "continual repetition of [performative] acts and the citing of such acts as 'naturally' binary," producing the illusion of gender as natural and innate (Crawley and Green, this volume). Crawley and Green urge us to "re-focus on identities as negotiated social relations" and remind us that "identities do not denote types of people but, rather, comprise relational organizing practices of meaning-making in specific historical moments constantly produced between and among us—which can be normalizing or resistant." In their call to see identities as interrelational practices of meaning-making, they highlight power and difference construction as central to interactionist perspectives on identity.

Margaret Hagerman (this volume) demonstrates how focusing on the micro-level dynamics and processes of "racial socialization" helps us to see how people are socialized into racial and racist understandings, and thus how such interactive socialization processes undergird macro-level structures of race in society. Hagerman argues that "understanding how children learn about race requires taking into account how this learning process is shaped by both micro-level meaning making and macro-level structures. And this is a key theoretical principle of symbolic interactionism." Illustrating "how people develop 'common-sense' understandings of race" over the course of their everyday interactions and daily lives, and how this racial socialization shapes "the prevailing racial order," Hagerman demonstrates how racial power can be both reproduced and challenged at the level of social and symbolic interaction.

The work of intersectional (or "third wave") feminists like bell hooks (1984) and Patricia Hill Collins (1990/2000, 2019) complicate the story further by reminding scholars to be wary of all efforts to coerce myriad, fractured experiences under a single signifier or identity. Interlocking signifying systems of race, class, gender, and sexuality (among others) intertwine to create a complex interplay of influences and narratives through which individuals navigate to construct identity and make sense of lived experience. Symbolic interactionism, with its attention to how meaning is experienced, used, and (re)produced in everyday life, offers a conceptual model ideal for grappling with multiple dimensions of inequality and power as sociological phenomena. SI and its related theories (like constructionism, ethnomethodology, and formal sociology) demonstrate the constructedness of everyday life—especially its most time-honored and supposedly "natural" aspects like gender or race—in a way that tugs at the seams of our reality and demonstrates the complexities and fluidity of identity.

As sociologists continue to study inequalities, symbolic interactionism, with its focus on identities and daily life, ought to be central to these concerns (as many scholars make it to be), not a peripheral theory. In today's varied terrain, many still draw from Blumer and Mead, but interactionist scholars should also recognize important classical work that advances core SI themes but has also been marginalized through historical processes of epistemic exclusion. Hagerman highlights, for example, that W. E. B. Du Bois developed empirically grounded theories that stressed the social construction of race and racism long before this now essential sociological idea made it into the mainstream of sociological thought. Furthermore, Du Bois theorized the inner dialogue of identity by describing how a "double consciousness" of self reflects broadly relevant inequalities and imbalances of power. All SI scholars (not just those who study race) need to take Du Bois's work seriously and give his scholarship the recognition it deserves. Blumer's observation that people actively produce the meanings of their situations and the world around them, including the meanings that define and sustain relations of power (Hagerman, this volume), becomes increasingly important to research when it is combined with the critical insights that Du Bois and intersectional standpoint scholars bring to the table. Thus, it is important to broaden the canon of SI to align with sociology's multifaceted critical orientation toward power and inequalities. In the section of this volume on power and inequalities, we highlight work that moves SI further into the critical realm of inquiry and theory.

A Brief Overview of the Book

This volume is organized into four parts. The first of these four parts highlights our interest in the wonderful complexities and varied directions of symbolic interactionism in the twenty-first century by featuring several theoretical and methodological orientations that shape modern SI scholarship. Our hope is that this collection will stimulate dialogue within the tradition and provide researchers with a range of avenues to pursue symbolic interactionist interests. The second part of the volume features various contributors who emphasize the link between culture and symbolic interaction as they explore different topics and institutions, showing how interactionist and cultural perspectives complement and reinforce one another in important ways. Then, in part three, we provide a series of chapters that show how SI theory and research can illuminate the social dynamics of power and the foundations of enduring social inequalities. Finally, as an example of how scholars commonly use an interactionist framework to tackle the big problems of our time, we offer a section on environment, disasters, and risk. Each of these parts and the chapters comprising them are discussed in more detail below.

In part I we highlight several of the major theoretical and methodological orientations that shape contemporary symbolic interactionism. The reader may find the merging of theory and method unusual, but theory and method are intertwined in the SI tradition, as is evident in the work of the pragmatists as well as in Blumer's (1969) seminal essay. Theoretical choices often carry methodological implications and vice versa, so the clean division between theory and method often proposed in graduate school courses and curriculums is a kind of normative rigid analytic fiction (see Zerubavel this volume). To highlight some important facets of the broadening range of theoretical and methodological perspectives in the expansive field of SI, we provide a sampling of various lenses including historical, formal, constructionist, cognitive, postmodern, dramaturgical, macrosocial organizational, and narrative approaches.

First, Robert Dingwall provides an invaluable interpretation of the historical foundations of symbolic interactionism, addressing Hebert Blumer's "invention of symbolic interactionism," but then complicating this invention with a far more comprehensive look at the array of influences that have shaped the diverse world of interactionist theory and research today. Following Dingwall's historical overview, Andrea Salvini demonstrates how symbolic interactionism has become a central framework for consolidating a varied range of qualitative research approaches. Salvini devotes particular attention to "how the interactionist perspective has changed the understanding of the research process" and how it has shaped and influenced three widely relevant qualitative traditions: ethnography, grounded theory, and postmodernism.

Outlining a theory-driven symbolic interactionism that varies significantly from the data-driven approaches of grounded theory and ethnography that Salvini discusses, Eviatar Zerubavel illustrates the "theoretico-methodological" uses of symbolic interactionism for producing a concept-driven sociology. Bringing Herbert Blumer's notion of a "sensitizing concept" into new light, Zerubavel highlights the methodological perspective and analytic strengths of a formal symbolic interactionist approach. In contrast to grounded theory, Zerubavel shows how scholars can focus their research around broadly relevant themes, using sensitizing concepts to illuminate patterns and homologies across otherwise different cases. Such a vision of interactionist scholarship breaks free of many constraints that stem from a more narrow and bounded vision of the symbolic interactionist agenda in sociology.

Simon Gottschalk and Celene Fuller then emphasize the importance of symbolic interactionism for understanding digitally mediated interactions with both human and non-human agents. These scholars indeed advance a twenty-first-century symbolic interactionism to demonstrate how our late "hypermodern" era has influenced our experiences of self and our daily routines, stressing the various impacts of new technologies, including the increasingly rapid pace of social life, the ephemeral character of many experiences, and the changing nature of time and space. Following Gottschalk and Fuller, Héctor Vera uses the perspective of symbolic interactionism to "interrogate underlying assumptions of quantitative measurement [and] show how researchers work to assign meaning to [such] measures" and methods just as actors assign meaning to the rest of the world around them. Quantitative measurement, Vera demonstrates, is "an intersubjective—cooperative and social—accomplishment."

In a critical engagement with the field, Patrick McGinty shows how symbolic interactionism can be used to analyze social organization and macrosocial phenomena, arguing that SI has been reified in the popular imagination of sociologists as an exclusively micro perspective. McGinty demonstrates that the use of an interactionist framework to address "social structure and macro phenomena" is "a historically conditioned pursuit" but also relatively unacknowledged in the field. His chapter is a call for interactionists to realize the potential of this underdeveloped dimension of SI research and theory. In the following chapter, Susie Scott highlights the dramaturgical traditions and perspectives on social performance that have increasingly become associated with symbolic interactionism since the work of Erving Goffman. Scott carefully outlines the contributions of dramaturgical theory to unpack the ways that people work to define the world around them, cooperating to perform their selves and their situations.

Bringing another important perspective to light, Ara Francis explores the centrality of social constructionism and its significance to SI theory and research. She outlines the key tenets of the social constructionist framework while emphasizing its deep connection to SI, considering important critiques, debates, and contemporary issues in the field while arguing for more reflexive scholarly attention "to the lived experiences of social constructions." Finally, Amir B. Marvasti and Jaber F. Gubrium address the central significance of narrative to our understanding of both self and society, focusing on "three forms of narrative study [. . .]—ethnographic, strategic, and conversational." Narrative studies, they demonstrate, developed out of the interactionist tradition beginning with the Chicago school focus on everyday life and were later advanced by Goffman's important contributions. Narrative study now encompasses several domains including "the narrative construction of selves," narrative environments, and "narrative power and practice." Marvasti and Gubrium expand symbolic interactionst perspectives and methods to include focused attention on stories and storytelling as important modes of self construction, and on narrative environments as important contexts for interaction.

In Part II of the volume, contributors explore the links between symbolic interaction and culture—both the cultural foundations that underlie and shape our social interactions and the ways that meaning emerges in and from those interactions. They explore a range of social environments, groups, and communities while showing how symbolic interactionism provides important tools with which to study culture in particular contexts and with which to illuminate meaningful individual and group activities in everyday life.

First, Michael Ian Borer provides an overview of the general interactionist approach to culture, stressing that interactionists put great emphasis on the local and emergent practices that give life to cultural norms and patterns of meaning. That is, culture arises in the cooperative dialogue among human actors in their settings and situations as they translate deep and underlying cultural meaning systems into more tangible group norms. Thus, culture is "simultaneously mutable and durable." Next, William Ryan Force analyzes subcultural contexts as they relate to interaction and identity, exploring how subcultures serve as contexts and communities of meaning-making while also providing resources for people to manage various troubling issues and situations. Force examines how authenticity, hierarchy, and power relate to subcultures as well as how resistance is negotiated within subcultural contexts. E. Doyle McCarthy then roots the sociological study of emotions "in early social pragmatism and interactionism." These perspectives saw the "structuring of mind, self, and emotion as sociocultural processes," McCarthy argues, and these same principles still hold in the constructionist theories of emotions found in social psychology and cultural theory today. Demonstrating that our seemingly personal experiences are actually intersubjective—shaped via shared culture and sociocultural interaction—and that emotions are thus also socioculturally constructed, McCarthy highlights the contributions of interactionist thinking to our understanding of emotions.

Following McCarthy, Enrico Campo analyzes shopping malls as "spaces of consumption" and shopping as "processes of identity construction," highlighting how recent research has illuminated acts of shopping as situated and contextually rooted activities through which identity is negotiated via consumption as cultural practice. From Campo's perspective, shopping malls and other sites of consumption are not just functional spaces of economic exchange, they are also always "symbolic spaces" where meaning is constructed. Taking a similar perspective on a very different topic, Joseph A. Kotarba examines the developments and uses of symbolic interactionism to study music and music contexts and explores how people build communities and craft identities in music scenes. Thinking broadly about music with a flexible interactionist lens, Kotarba emphasizes how the sensitizing concepts of "subculture, self, identity, community, scene, sense of place, idioculture, interaction, organization, and authenticity" can illuminate music's role in social life for all generations.

Julie B. Wiest then explores how symbolic interactionism provides an invaluable perspective for interpreting and illuminating "the sociocultural influences of mass media and new media, as well as the relationship between new media and social change." Wiest focuses on the relationship between these media and processes of interpretation, reality construction, self-presentation and identity, and community relations. She emphasizes the ways in which the meanings of media arise in social interaction and, in turn, influence our relationships and our understandings of the world. In the following chapter, Qian Li and Xiaoli Tian examine how new information and communication technologies (ICTs) are continually evolving to redefine our relationships and experiences. Developing and applying traditional tools of symbolic interactionism to study online venues, they explore the ways that new technologies have impacted "how users present themselves and how they construct collaborative meaning in social encounters." Complementing the chapters by Wiest and Gottschalk and Fuller, Li and Tian analyze what new and constantly evolving technologies mean for the construction of self and identity, the meaning of community, and for the foundations of "publics" and the civil sphere more generally.

Finally, Andrea Salvini and Irene Psaroudakis highlight the importance of symbolic interactionism as a perspective for understanding religion, especially insofar as we can and should view religion as processes and practices of everyday life. Salvini and Psaroudakis argue that symbolic interactionists should pay more attention to religion as an important lens through which we can understand broadly relevant social phenomena including identity and social change.

In Part III, contributors present analyses that locate power and inequality as integral parts of the symbolic interactionist project. Understanding the relationships between processes of cultural meaning-making, interaction and identity, and central sociological issues of power, privilege, discrimination, and inequality is important for many contemporary interactionists. Some contributors to this section develop general theories of power while others focus on more particular manifestations of inequality or modes of discrimination including issues pertaining to race, gender, and sexuality, as well as inequalities in criminal justice and healthcare systems.

First, Wayne Brekhus explores how cultural markedness and unmarkedness shape perception, communication, power, and performance in everyday life and the implications of this for symbolic interactionist theorizing about the production and reproduction of social inequalities. Brekhus highlights the shifting nature of the SI canon, tracing contemporary SI approaches interested in markedness and identity back to W. E. B. Du Bois and other scholars who linked theories of self and identity through a critical lens focused on inequalities. A more expansive SI, he argues, one that broadens the canon to make marked and unmarked identities a focal point, allows SI to integrate with critical standpoint theories, especially intersectional theories that look at multiple overlapping systems of oppression, to better illuminate dimensions of power in social life. Next, Carmelo Lombardo and Lorenzo Sabetta connect "two types of social nothingness" explored by Erving Goffman and Harold Garfinkel, respectively, and Herbert Blumer's three premises of symbolic interactionism with contemporary sociologies of nothingness and the unmarked to analyze "concealed strategic actions." In the process, they illuminate dimensions of power underlying default options in social interaction. They advance the blending of SI, sociologies of the default, and nudge theory to further develop a sociological approach to illuminating the ways that actors can conceal their actions behind the appearance of nothingness, cloaking them with the social force of uneventful routines and circumstances.

Developing an important framework with broad implications, Michael Schwalbe and Kelsey Mischke argue that "symbolic interactionism can illuminate the ontological roots of power as it operates on larger, structural scales." They develop a Meadian understanding of power as "the *capacity* to modify an environment [. . .] to satisfy needs and desires" and argue that this understanding of power has broad macro implications. Thus, Schwalbe and Mischke show us that it is not only the traditions of Marx, Weber, and other structural and political sociologists that are important to our understanding of power, but the tradition and potential of symbolic interactionism as well.

Following these three broad and general frameworks, Margaret A. Hagerman analyzes the power of racial socialization, demonstrating how interactionist principles have informed a great deal of sociological scholarship on the production and meanings of race. Furthermore, Hagerman shows us how SI can continue to be a valuable tool with which we can grasp the social foundations of the racial order. S. L. Crawley and Ashley Green then analyze gender and gendered embodiment as a function of negotiated relations, specifically focusing on how gendered meanings about bodies and identities emerge in social interactions, and how gendered stories and practices contribute to a matrix of social experience imbued with power and privilege. Crawley and Green synthesize feminist theory, ethnomethodology, and queer theory with traditional interactionist work to provide a critical look at gender as "a constant and emergent production enveloping all of social life." In the following chapter, Cirus Rinaldi examines and considers sex and sexuality as a diverse set of social practices, identities, and cultural forms. Arguing that interactionist understandings emphasize "how sexualities are *produced*, organized, and negotiated," Rinaldi explores how we perform modern notions of sexuality and our sexual selves as we define the world around us.

Thaddeus Müller then presents us with a framework for analyzing "deviant selves, transgressive acts, and moral narratives," illuminating how SI provides a foundation for an understanding of crime as a social and political concept. Müller details the implications of symbolic interactionism for the broader field of criminology, and the implications of crime and justice studies for symbolic interactionism. Next, Giuseppina Cersosimo highlights the contributions and potential of symbolic interactionism for studying healthcare. She traces the beginnings of an SI approach to medicine and health in studies of disease as a social construction, patient negotiation studies, and in methods focused on grounded theory, sensitizing concepts, and a "holistic approach" that prioritizes "the everyday life of patients." Cersosimo argues that symbolic interactionism gives us important tools with which to make sense of new practices and technologies in the healthcare field, and to understand the nature of various problems as well.

In Part IV, contributors provide illustrative examples of how symbolic interactionism can shed light on important issues pertaining to the environment, disasters, and risk. With the salience of climate crisis as an existential problem of the twenty-first century, showing how interactionist research can contribute to an understanding of these issues is one way of demonstrating the adaptability and utility of SI as a framework for addressing social problems in a changing world.

First, Braden Leap examines interactionist tools for studying community resilience in the face of environmental change, focusing on how changing environmental conditions affect meaning, patterns of interaction, and relationships among community residents. Leap shows how SI can help us to understand the ways that communities can adapt in the face of environmental threat and transformation. Daina Cheyenne Harvey then analyzes eco-uncertainty as a frame and an ongoing characteristic of social life. Focused on New Orleans's Lower Ninth Ward in the post-Hurricane Katrina era, Harvey explores how environmental risk is understood in an interactional context and how inequalities affect communication and interaction to shape understandings of the causes and consequences of environmental harm, along with the potential to affect change and mitigate risk. Consistent with new research that emphasizes power and inequality in contemporary symbolic interactionism, Harvey focuses on how interaction structured by uncertainty contributes to environmental suffering and the exacerbation of social inequalities. Finally, Margarethe Kusenbach and Gabriela Christmann focus on how disasters affect the lived experiences of people who go through them, with attention to how they influence community, decision-making, and identity. Kusenbach and Christmann provide a road map for an interactionist sociology of disasters that merges disaster and environmental studies, emphasizes the impact of new technologically mediated modes of social interaction, addresses the "global interdependence of people, places, and systems" in our world, and takes seriously different cultural perspectives with regard to addressing and understanding disasters in different contexts.

Notes

1. Our argument in this section builds on several points first raised by Gary Alan Fine (1993).
2. While many ethnographers refer to their methodological and theoretical approach as grounded theory construction (based on the cooperative work of Barney Glaser, who studied at Columbia with Paul Lazarsfeld and Robert Merton, and Anselm L. Strauss, an interactionist who studied with Blumer and Burgess at the University of Chicago), the analytic basis of this approach often involves the interpretive lens of symbolic interactionism. Today, the core influence of pragmatism on ethnographic analysis is especially evident in Iddo Tavory and Stefan Timmermans's (2014) *Abductive Analysis*.

3. The notion of habit or habitual action found in the work of C. S. Peirce and John Dewey can also be interpreted as an early pragmatist vision of culture in the form of routine patterns of action and interaction. See Emirbayer and Mische (1998:977) and Tavory and Timmermans (2014:28) for contemporary applications.

4. See Schwalbe (2008/2015) and Athens (2015) for two important statements on power and inequality.

REFERENCES

Alexander, Jeffrey C. 2004. "Cultural Pragmatics: Social Performance Between Ritual and Strategy." *Sociological Theory* 22(4):527–73.

Alexander, Jeffrey C. 2017. *The Drama of Social Life*. Cambridge, UK: Polity Press.

Athens, Lonnie. 1994. "The Self as a Soliloquy." *Sociological Quarterly* 35(3):521–32.

Athens, Lonnie. 2015. *Domination and Subjugation in Everyday Life*. New Brunswick, NJ, and London: Transaction Publishers.

Becker, Howard. S. 1963. *Outsiders: Studies in the Sociology of Deviance*. New York: Free Press.

Benzecry, Claudio. E., and Daniel Winchester. 2017. "Varieties of Microsociology." Pp. 42–74 in *Social Theory Now*, edited by C. E. Benzecry, M. Krause, and I. A. Reed. Chicago: University of Chicago Press.

Berger, Peter. L., and Thomas Luckmann. 1966. *The Social Construction of Reality: A Treatise in the Sociology of Knowledge*. New York: Doubleday.

Best, Joel. 1987. "Rhetoric in Claims-Making: Constructing the Missing Children Problem." *Social Problems* 34(2):101–21.

Best, Joel. 1997. "Victimization and the Victim Industry." *Society* 34(May/June):9–17.

Best, Joel, and Kathleen A. Bogle. 2014. *Kids Gone Wild: From Rainbow Parties to Sexting, Understanding the Hype Over Teen Sex*. New York: NYU Press.

Blumer, Herbert. 1969. *Symbolic Interactionism: Perspective and Method*. Berkeley, CA: University of California Press.

Brekhus, Wayne H. 1998. "A Sociology of the Unmarked: Redirecting Our Focus." *Sociological Theory* 16:34–51.

Brekhus, Wayne H. 2003. *Peacocks, Chameleons, Centaurs: Gay Suburbia and the Grammar of Social Identity*. Chicago: University of Chicago Press.

Brekhus, Wayne H. 2008. "Trends in the Qualitative Study of Social Identities." *Sociology Compass* 2(3):1059–78.

Brekhus, Wayne H. 2020. *The Sociology of Identity*. Cambridge, UK: Polity Press.

Butler, Judith. 1990. *Gender Trouble: Feminism and the Subversion of Identity*. New York: Routledge.

Butler, Judith. 1991. "Imitation and Gender Insubordination." Pp. 13–31 in *Inside/Out: Lesbian Theories, Gay Theories*, edited by Diana Fuss. New York: Routledge.

Cohen, Albert. 1955. *Delinquent Boys: The Culture of the Gang*. Glencoe, IL: Free Press.

Collins, Patricia Hill. 1990/2000. *Black Feminist Thought: Knowledge, Consciousness, and the Politics of Empowerment*. London and New York: Routledge.

Collins, Patricia Hill. 2019. *Intersectionality as Critical Social Theory*. Durham and London: Duke University Press.

Cressey, Paul G. 1932. *The Taxi-Dance Hall*. NYC: Greenwood Press.

DeGloma, Thomas. 2014. *Seeing the Light: The Social Logic of Personal Discovery*. Chicago: University of Chicago Press.

DeGloma, Thomas. 2019. "The Expanding Interactionist Community: On the Remarkable Breadth and Depth of Symbolic Interactionism." *Italian Sociological Review* 9(2):165–69.

DeGloma, Thomas, and Erin. F. Johnston. 2019. "Cognitive Migrations: A Cultural and Cognitive Sociology of Personal Transformation." Pp. 623–42 in *The Oxford Handbook of Cognitive Sociology*, edited by Wayne H. Brekhus and Gabe Ignatow. Oxford and New York: Oxford University Press.

DeGloma, Thomas, and Max Papadatonakis. 2020. "The Thematic Lens: A Formal and Cultural Framework for Comparative Ethnographic Analysis." Pp. 88–110 in *Beyond the Case: The Logics and Practices of Comparative Ethnography*, edited by Corey M. Abramson and Neil Gong. New York: Oxford University Press.

Dewey, John. 1922. *Human Nature and Conduct*. New York: Modern Library.

Dingwall, Robert. 2001. "Notes Toward an Intellectual History of Symbolic Interactionism." *Symbolic Interaction* 24(2):237–42.

Dingwall, Robert, Thomas DeGloma, and Staci Newmahr. 2012. "Editors' Introduction: Symbolic Interaction – Serving the Whole Interactionist Family." *Symbolic Interaction* 35(1):1–5.

Edgley, Charles, ed. 2013. *The Drama of Social Life: A Dramaturgical Handbook*. London and New York: Routledge.

Eliasoph, Nina, and Paul Lichterman. 2003. "Culture in Interaction." *American Journal of Sociology* 108(4):735–94.

Emirbayer, Mustafa, and Ann Mische. 1998. "What Is Agency?" *American Journal of Sociology* 103(4):962–1023.

Ezzy, Douglas. 1998. "Theorizing Narrative Identity: Symbolic Interactionism and Hermeneutics." *Sociological Quarterly* 39(2):239–52.

Fine, Gary Alan. 1979. "Small Groups and Culture Creation: The Idioculture of Little League Baseball Teams." *American Sociological Review* 44(5):733–45.

Fine, Gary Alan. 1993. "The Sad Demise, Mysterious Disappearance, and Glorious Triumph of Symbolic Interactionism." *Annual Review of Sociology* 19:61–87.

Fine, Gary Alan. 2003. "Towards a Peopled Ethnography: Developing Theory from Group Life." *Ethnography* 4(1):41–60.

Fine, Gary Alan. 2021. *The Hinge: Civil Society, Group Cultures, and the Power of Local Communities*. Chicago: University of Chicago Press.

Fine, Gary Alan, and Iddo Tavory. 2019. "Interactionism in the Twenty-First Century: a Letter on Being-in-a-Meaningful-World." *Symbolic Interaction* 42(3):457–67.

Giddens, Anthony. 1991. *Modernity and Self-Identity: Self and Society in the Late Modern Age*. Stanford, CA: Stanford University Press.

Go, Julian. 2020. "Race, Empire, and Epistemic Exclusion: Or the Structures of Sociological Thought." *Sociological Theory* 38(2):79–100.

Goffman, Erving. 1959. *The Presentation of Self in Everyday Life*. New York: Anchor Books, Doubleday.

Goffman, Erving. 1961. *Asylums: Essays on the Social Situation of Mental Patients and Other Inmates*. New York and Toronto: Anchor Books.

Goffman, Erving. 1963. *Stigma: Notes on the Management of a Spoiled Identity*. New York: Simon and Schuster.

Goffman, Erving. 1974/1986. *Frame Analysis: An Essay on the Organization of Experience*. Boston, Massachusetts: Northeastern University Press.

Goffman, Erving. 1979. *Gender Advertisements*. New York: Harper and Row.

Gross, Neil. 2009. "The Pragmatist Theory of Social Mechanisms." *American Sociological Review* 74(3):358–79.

Gross, Neil. 2018. "Pragmatism and the Study of Large-scale Social Phenomena." *Theory and Society* 47:87–111.

Gubrium, Jaber F., and James A. Holstein. 2000. "The Self in a World of Going Concerns." *Symbolic Interaction* 23(2):95–115.

Habermas, Jurgen. 1987. *The Theory of Communicative Action, Volume Two: Lifeworld and System: A Critique of Functionalist Reason*. Boston, MA: Beacon Press.

hooks, bell 1984. *Feminist Theory; From Margin to Center*. Boston, MA: South End Press.

Huebner, Daniel R. 2014. *Becoming Mead: The Social Process of Academic Knowledge*. Chicago: University of Chicago Press.

Huebner, Daniel R. 2016. "History and Social Progress: Reflections on Mead's Approach to History." *European Journal of Pragmatism and American Philosophy* 8(2):120–42.

Joas, Hans. 1996. *The Creativity of Action*. Chicago: University of Chicago Press.

Lofland, John. 1995. "Analytic Ethnography: Features, Failings, and Futures." *Journal of Contemporary Ethnography* 24(1):30–67.

Loseke, Donileen R. 1992. *The Battered Women and Shelters: The Social Construction of Wife Abuse*. Albany: State University of New York Press.

Loseke, Donileen R. 1999. *Thinking About Social Problems: An Introduction to Constructionist Perspectives*. New York: Aldine deGruyter.

Loseke, Donileen R. 2019. *Narrative Productions of Meaning*. Lanham, Maryland: Lexington Books.

McCarthy, E. Doyle. 2017. *Emotional Lives: Dramas of Identity in an Age of Mass Media*. Cambridge, UK: Cambridge University Press.

McGinty, Patrick J. W. 2014. "Divided and Drifting: Interactionism and the Neglect of Social Organizational Analyses in Organization Studies." *Symbolic Interaction* 37(2):155–86.

Mead, George Herbert. 1934/2015. *Mind, Self, and Society*. Chicago: University of Chicago Press.

Mills, C. Wright. 1966. *Sociology and Pragmatism: The Higher Learning in America*. New York: Oxford University Press.

Morris, Aldon D. 2015. *The Scholar Denied: W. E. B. Du Bois and the Birth of Modern Sociology*. Oakland: University of California Press.

Owens, B. Robert. 2015. "New Directions in Pragmatism." *Perspectives*, December 23, 2015. Retrieved April 2022, http://www.asatheory.org/current-newsletter-online/new-directions-in-pragmatism.

Parsons. Talcott. 1937. *The Structure of Social Action*. New York: The Free Press.

Parsons, Talcott. 1951/1991. *The Social System*. New York: Routledge.

Prus, Robert. 1987. "Generic Social Processes: Maximizing Conceptual Development in Ethnographic Research." *Journal of Contemporary Ethnography* 16(3):250–93.

Ricoeur, Paul. 1988. *Time and Narrative*, Vol. 3. Chicago: University of Chicago Press.

Ricoeur, Paul. 1991. "Narrative Identity." *Philosophy Today* 35(1):73–81.

Ruiz-Junco, Natalia. 2017. "Advancing the Sociology of Empathy: A Proposal." *Symbolic Interaction* 40(3):414–35.

Ruiz-Junco, Natalia, and Baptiste Brossard, eds. 2019. *Updating Charles H. Cooley: Contemporary Perspectives on a Sociological Classic*. London and New York: Routledge.

Schwalbe, Michael. 2008/2015. *Rigging the Game: How Inequality Is Reproduced in Everyday Life*. New York: Oxford University Press.

Sutherland, Edwin H. 1939. *Principles of Criminology*. Philadelphia, PA: J.B. Lippincott Company.

Tavory, Iddo, and Nina Eliasoph. 2013. "Coordinating Futures: Toward a Theory of Anticipation." *American Journal of Sociology* 118(4):908–42.

Tavory, Iddo, and Stefan Timmermans. 2014. *Abductive Analysis: Theorizing Qualitative Research*. Chicago: University of Chicago Press.

Thomas, William Isaac, and Dorothy Swaine Thomas. 1928. *The Child in America: Behavior Problems and Programs*. New York: Alfred A. Knopf.

Thrasher, Frederick Milton. 1927. *The Gang: A Study of 1,313 Gangs in Chicago*. Chicago: University of Chicago Press.

West, Candace, and Don. H. Zimmerman. 1987. "Doing Gender." *Gender and Society* 1(2):125–51.

West, Candace, and Sarah Fenstermaker. 1995. "Doing Difference." *Gender and Society* 9(1):8–37.

Wiley, Norbert. 1994. *The Semiotic Self*. Chicago: University of Chicago Press.

Wiley, Norbert. 2006. "Pragmatism and the Dialogical Self." *International Journal for Dialogical Science* 1(1):5–21.

Wiley, Norbert. 2016. *Inner Speech and the Dialogical Self*. Philadelphia, PA: Temple University Press.

Zerubavel, Eviatar. 1980. "If Simmel Were a Fieldworker: On Formal Sociological Theory and Analytic Field Research." *Symbolic Interaction* 3(2):25–34.

Zerubavel, Eviatar. 2021. *Generally Speaking: An Invitation to Concept-Driven Sociology*. New York: Oxford University Press.

PART I

THEORETICAL AND METHODOLOGICAL ORIENTATIONS

CHAPTER 2

THE HISTORICAL FOUNDATIONS OF SYMBOLIC INTERACTIONISM

ROBERT DINGWALL

CONVENTIONALLY, chapters of this kind begin from some iconic founder of a lineage that has proceeded in unbroken succession to the present day. The present is legitimized through its ancestry and its connections to the great symbols of the tribe. Elvi Whittaker and Virginia Olesen (1964) demonstrate this process in their interactionist analysis of the references to Florence Nightingale in different accounts of the origins of modern nursing. The problem with this approach is that it is not particularly sociological, in that it tends to tell a story of historical inevitability, of a march of progress that leads ineluctably to the present rather than seeing the present as shaped by a great deal of chance and contingency. As we shall see, such an approach would be particularly ill-suited to a style of doing sociology where the uncertainty of the world is taken for granted and the sociologist's task is to understand how this is made sufficiently orderly for actions in the here and now to be possible. The chapter will, then, begin by discussing what kinds of sociological work the label "symbolic interactionism" might be applied to. It will then travel backward to investigate the elements that have contributed to this *bricolage*—the word comes via the French anthropologist Claude Lévi-Strauss (1966) to describe an assembly of ideas from whatever happens to be lying around and useful at the time.

THE INVENTION OF SYMBOLIC INTERACTIONISM

The label "symbolic interactionism" seems to have a clear and definite history. In an introductory essay to a selection of his published work, under the general title *Symbolic*

Interactionism: Perspective and Method, Herbert Blumer (1969:1) describes how the term "has come into use as a label for a relatively distinctive approach to the study of human group life and human conduct." He links this to a footnote that describes the term as "a somewhat barbaric neologism that I coined in an offhand way in an article written in MAN AND SOCIETY (Emerson P. Schmidt, ed. New York: Prentice Hall, 1937). The term somehow caught on and is now in general use." The essay associates a range of scholars with the program—George Herbert Mead, John Dewey, W. I. Thomas, Robert E. Park, William James, Charles Horton Cooley, Florian Znaniecki, James Mark Baldwin, Robert Redfield, and Louis Wirth. We shall meet several of these figures again, but it is worth noting that the essay itself is largely an exposition and commentary on the translation of Mead's philosophical analysis of human minds, actions, and society into a program for sociology.

If we go back to the original formulation, however, it clearly refers to a program for social psychology—indeed, Blumer is contributing a chapter with that title to a volume compiled as an introductory text for a general course in social sciences taken by first-year students at the University of Minnesota. The chapters on "Sociology and Culture" and on "Social Institutions" are written by other authors, Elio D. Monachesi from Minnesota and Joyce O. Hertzler from Nebraska. There is also a separate chapter on "Psychology and Some of its Applications" by Howard P. Longstaff, from Minnesota. Longstaff's chapter is positioned squarely within the behaviorist tradition that represented the mainstream of the discipline at that time.

Blumer's chapter begins by noting that social psychology was originally conceived as the study of "group minds," the idea that human groups, such as crowds, mobs, panics, and the like, might be driven by a consciousness above and beyond that of the individuals involved. As he notes, by the 1930s this had come to be regarded as a metaphysical idea that could not be verified empirically and had been discarded. These phenomena were now the topic of the field of "collective behavior," which did not assume that joint actions required supra-individual mental states.

> Today, the interest of social psychology is focused largely on the *social development of the individual*. It is now generally agreed that every human being grows up inside of some form of group life, that in this development he is subject to the stimulation and influence of his associates, and that his conduct, his character, his personality, and his mental organization are formed inside of this association with his fellows. The central task is that of studying how the individual develops socially as a result of participating in group life.
>
> (Blumer 1937:146)

Blumer emphasizes both the distinctive identity of social psychology and the porousness of its boundaries with both psychology and sociology.

> Social psychology is particularly subject to the importation of theories and points of view from surrounding sciences and disciplines. The very nature of its central

THE HISTORICAL FOUNDATIONS OF SYMBOLIC INTERACTIONISM   29

problem has placed it between the older and more recognized fields of psychology and sociology, and has invited the borrowing of the theories of both. Any general theory that gains any vogue in these two fields is rather certain to be applied to the field of social psychology. This means that the general theoretical disputes in psychology and sociology are transferred to social psychology, where, furthermore, are to be found the theoretical contentions as they exist between psychology and sociology.

(Blumer 1937:146–47)

The chapter then proceeds to review the field and to develop a position in the terms of "social behaviorism," as formulated by G. H. Mead (1962, 2015).

Briefly, Blumer rejects the idea of an innate human nature characterized by a set of instincts, derived from some readings of Charles Darwin's work. His argument reflects earlier writings by Chicago sociologists (Bernard 1921; Faris 1921; Dingwall, Nerlich, and Hillyard 2003). This idea of an innate human nature is vaguely specified and inconsistent with empirical observation of the diversity and complexity of actions and cultures. He then introduces the stimulus-response model, where an innate set of reflexes are organized into a capacity for complex action by processes of conditioning and reinforcement. The chapter contrasts this with the symbolic interactionist understanding of humans as being born only with a capacity to engage actively with the social world. Through this interaction, the essentially plastic nature of the infant is shaped into membership of a society in ways that are not fully determined. The shape of the chapter broadly follows Meltzer's (1967) respecification of Mead's (2015) classic trinity as Society → Self → Mind. Group life establishes a symbolic context within which individuals learn to interact while coordinating actions or pursuing projects. Through these interactions, a sense of self is created, as an individual distinct from others but capable of cooperating with them through shared "definitions of the situation"—a term that Blumer uses but does not acknowledge by citation. The process of cooperation is taken from Cooley's (1912:28) discussion of sympathy: ". . . Cooley thinks of 'sympathy' not in the sense of pity or compassion, but instead as the unique human ability to project oneself imaginatively into the position of another and to experience vicariously his feelings and state of mind." Blumer elaborates the account through more specific discussion of standard psychological topics like personality, motivation, and attitudes, where he seeks to define the differences between Mead's social behaviorism and the radical behaviorism of his Chicago contemporary, J.B. Watson (Dingwall 2001).

One version of the origin myth of symbolic interactionism would, then, represent it as quite a narrow story, focused very much on the legacy of Mead and Cooley. In his chapter, Blumer rarely cites other Chicago colleagues. There is an approving mention of Ellsworth Faris and a rather dismissive reference to Thomas's (1917) Four Wishes—fundamental human interests or desires that were proposed as drivers for action. Conceived as social psychology, Blumer's legacy is rather limited. It can be seen in the work of Shibutani (1961) and, to some extent, in Strauss's (1959) *Mirrors and Masks*. In the introduction to the 1977 UK edition of this book, however, Strauss notes that it was intended to reconcile Mead's social psychology with the structural interactionism of Thomas, Park, and Everett Hughes: "These are still not at ease with each other—some interactionists moving almost totally toward Mead, others paying rather little attention to social psychological issues" (Strauss 1977:4). These comments remind us that Blumer was quite a divisive figure within the Sociology Department at Chicago, which was generally less harmonious than legend suggests (Abbott 1999; Lacaze 2017). His colorful life history, with a career in professional football and connections to the Chicago Mob and the brutal world of industrial labor, was very different from the more genteel experiences of some of his colleagues (Wiley 2014). There were also considerable political differences (Lyman and Vidich 1988; Abbott 1999). Blumer's contempt for Everett Hughes, for example, seems to have been a factor in his departure for Berkeley in 1952, when Hughes was installed as department chair in Chicago.

On the other hand, symbolic interactionist research tends to lay claim to a wider body of work derived from the supposed general heritage of Chicago sociology. If we look at what people who call themselves "symbolic interactionists" actually *do*, the specific debts to Blumer or Mead are quite limited, although they are often invoked as tribal ancestors, much as Whittaker and Olesen noted for Florence Nightingale. What is the legacy from sociology rather than social psychology?

Sociology and Social Ecology

While Blumer may have given symbolic interactionism its name, its practical legacy owes at least as much to the work of Ernest Burgess, Robert Park, and their students in urban studies during the 1920s and 1930s, and to the extension of this approach into studies of work and occupations, particularly by Everett Hughes and his students, immediately before and after World War II. Although this body of research and writing draws in a rather general fashion on the ideas of Mead and other pragmatist philosophers, its intellectual heritage is quite different. In particular, it borrows extensively from evolutionary and ecological ideas in biology (Dingwall 2016) in ways that give it a distinctive understanding of the nature of social order and its construction. These are not inconsistent with Blumer's social psychology, but they may partially explain how Blumer's department at Berkeley was able to assimilate more radical political traditions in the 1950s and 1960s in ways that still have an impact on symbolic interactionism.

When thinking about borrowings from biology, it is important to distinguish between the ecological metaphor and the organismic metaphor. The latter identifies human societies with the processes that go on *within* an organism, while the former examines the interactions *between* organisms. Ecological thinking tends to see social order as the spontaneous outcome of undirected social processes, where organismic thinking tends to see the processes as directed toward the functional requirements of the observable order. In practice, most sociologists use elements of both approaches in their work, but it is helpful to distinguish them for the purposes of analysis. The rise of ecological thinking

THE HISTORICAL FOUNDATIONS OF SYMBOLIC INTERACTIONISM   31

in Chicago sociology has been examined by Marlene Shore (1987). Park's (1915) first statement on a research program for studies of the city drew on biological thinking. The Park and Burgess (1969) textbook, first published in 1921, which defined the department curriculum for at least two generations, reproduced an extract from *Plant Succession*, published in 1916 by the influential plant ecologist Frederic Clements. Park regularly attended seminars in ecology with biologists from both the University of Chicago and Northwestern University, together with two prominent anthropologists, Robert Redfield, his son-in-law, and Alfred Kroeber. He also encouraged his younger son to take courses in plant and insect ecology during his own college studies (Raushenbush 1979).

The fundamental principles of ecology derive from Darwin's analysis of natural selection, where competition between species generates an equilibrium of mutual accommodation and adaptation. It is important to understand the dynamism of this account. Many popular versions tend to assume that the environment is fixed and that competition is a zero-sum game. As Darwin saw it, each species forms part of the environment for others so that changes in any one species that lead to an advantage change the context for others in ways that may select them for different characteristics. Order is local, temporary, and inherently unstable. By studying how plants colonize bare ground, botanists were able to show how the initial colonizers created conditions that favored their displacement by other species, a process that might be repeated over many generations. This approach is reflected in the work of one of Darwin's major popularizers, the sociologist Herbert Spencer.

Spencer's influence on early American sociology is well documented (Hinkle 1980). However, Chicago sociology tends to be seen in opposition to his influence on the conservative doctrines of Social Darwinism (Hofstadter 1955; Bannister 1979; Dickens 2000), a precursor of modern neoliberal skepticism about the possibility of collective action to ameliorate poverty or other social ills. Because most of those involved did not share this political analysis, Spencer's influence on interwar Chicago thought is often overlooked. Spencer and Darwin are, though, two of the ten most frequently cited authors in the Park and Burgess textbook (Raushenbush 1979). What excited the Chicago reading of Spencer was his extension of Darwin's dismantling of the idea of a Divine and immutable natural order to consider social institutions. These, too, survived and prospered only as long as they maintained their fitness in an environment of other institutions seeking to change and adapt (Dingwall and King 1995). The city of Chicago was an ideal case study. The Great Fire of 1871 had razed most of the city center to the ground, so the processes of recolonization could be observed in action, or at least within living memory. The language of ecology—zones, succession, transition—was taken directly into sociological analysis (Park, Burgess, and McKenzie 1925). The same thinking informed Everett Hughes's sociology of occupations. His first published paper (Hughes 1928) specifically links the division of labor to human ecology. However, he was already beginning to invert the relationship and to see social organization as prior to spatial organization with the same dynamic character:

New occupations are created every day, and the concatenations of functions of old ones are subject to change. The industrial revolutions of every day mean to the individual that he is not sure of his job; or, at least, that one is not sure of one's son's job.... Occupational selection... becomes a fierce process which begins anew each day, atomizing families and tearing them loose from their soil.

(Hughes 1928:757)

In the same paper, he begins the Linnean task of producing a classificatory scheme for occupations, a challenge picked up again many years later by one of his most distinguished students, Eliot Freidson (1978). The emphasis on the social construction of occupational worlds is central to all those influenced by Hughes's work, notably Howard Becker (1970, 1982) and Anselm Strauss (1975) and into later generations, like Andrew Abbott (1988) and Gary Alan Fine (1995), or, more recently, to Sida Liu (2013, 2015; Liu and Emirbayer 2016).

The legacy of Darwin and Spencer is also important for understanding the politics of this element of the symbolic interactionist tradition. From the start, the Chicago department was defined by a commitment to scholarship rather than activism.

We have attempted to make students suspicious of all apparently easy solutions to the problems of society... we once more propose the scholarly ideal—not investigation as a substitute for civic service but investigation as both promise and performance of civic duty... Scientific students of society ought to oppose with all their power the many mischievous tendencies to construct mountainous social philosophies out of molehills of social knowledge... This is not to urge that sociologists should be reactionaries. There is little likelihood that men who personally observe actual social conditions, according to the method which we propose, instead of speculating about them in the study, will want to fold their hands and let social evil work out its own salvation. In the interest of larger and truer knowledge, and better social cooperation in the future, it is, nevertheless, necessary to distinguish very clearly between provisional action prompted by sympathy, and the discovery of social principles attested by science.

(Small and Vincent 1894:373–74)

This commitment has often been seen through the lens of those critical of the interactionist tradition, particularly in the increasing distance between the sociology faculty and Jane Addams's work at the Hull House settlement as a community organizer (Deegan 1988, 2006). Some sociologists have difficulty in dealing with liberal or moderate conservative thought, which is represented as an undefined other in relation to more radical approaches. How should we, for example, assess the award to women of 10 percent of PhDs between the department's foundation in 1893 and 1935 (Faris 1979)? Do we castigate the department for not doing more or celebrate its achievement relative to the general environment for women in higher education? Do we focus on the appointment of Annie Marion Maclean (PhD 1900) to the extension faculty in 1903 or regret the contingencies that limited her impact (Deegan 2014)? Similarly, do we recognize the handful of dissertations on Black groups and institutions, including that of E. Franklin Frazier (PhD 1931), who became the first Black president of the American Sociological

THE HISTORICAL FOUNDATIONS OF SYMBOLIC INTERACTIONISM 33

Association in 1948, or ask why there were so few? Differing views of the history of symbolic interactionism stem from different political orientations. However, the part of symbolic interactionist thought distinguishing scholarship from activism sits squarely within a tradition known as "spontaneous order" (Polanyi 1941). Order is not created by planned and conscious acts but by local and contingent interactions. In this respect, it presents a problem for many of the claims for sociology as a science of society, although it does not necessarily exclude empirical generalizations that provide a foundation for practical actions, much as Small and Vincent imply. The point has, perhaps, been better understood by the French advocates of the Chicago School, who have used this as a means of challenging the Marxist orthodoxies that dominated their discipline in the postwar period, culminating in the long hegemony of Pierre Bourdieu (Peneff 2018).

The notion of "spontaneous order" may not quite capture the Chicago position, which could better be described as "improvised order" created from joint and purposive human actions, as Blumer and Mead proposed, but located within a context of structural and material conditions, as recognized by the ecological metaphor. Polanyi's label does, however, provide a basis for digging deeper into the genealogy of the Chicago tradition. Before doing so, though, we should look briefly at three other contemporary bodies of work that sometimes invoke, or are assigned to, the tradition of symbolic interactionism. Each is important in its own domain, and the brevity of the treatment here is mainly a reflection of the limited space available.

Fellow Travelers

The three strands that make up this section have very little in common apart from their problematic affiliation with symbolic interactionism: the postmodern strand identified particularly with Norman Denzin and his associates; the legacy of Erving Goffman; and the contribution of Harold Garfinkel, Harvey Sacks, and Emanuel Schegloff in the form of ethnomethodology and conversation analysis. They are only grouped here as a matter of convenience.

Postmodern Interactionism

Denzin began his career as an orthodox symbolic interactionist, trained at Iowa in the early 1960s, when it was a major center for this type of work. From the mid-1980s onward, however, his work increasingly turned toward postmodernism and cultural studies with a more explicitly political thrust toward social justice movement activism. While this work has continued to have an influence on symbolic interactionism, and to be recognized as part of the family, it has tended to move into different journals, conferences, and other publication outlets. It has also adopted a variety of representational strategies as alternatives to conventional academic forms of journal papers and monographs, including experimental forms of narrative writing, performance texts, and poetry, intended to evoke emotions in the audience response rather than scientific rationalism. Audiences are encouraged to share the author's moral response to the problems being described rather than to remain detached observers of the injustices of the world.

In these terms, the tensions with many of the traditions of symbolic interactionism should be apparent. While the anticipated mobilization may fall within that heritage, the basis in emotion rather than reason does not (Deegan 2006). There is also a division on the extent to which sociology is a vehicle for activism or a foundation for understanding problems. Is it better to be right or right-on (Strong 1988)? Postmodernism certainly adopts the same vision of a world that is socially constructed rather than given, a spectacle rather than a necessary reality. While this may free the imagination to envisage alternatives, it may also overlook the real physical and material constraints, from the structures and processes of human bodies and cognition to the environments within which we live and work—we may imagine walking on water but we are likely to get our feet wet. Postmodern social constructionism emphasizes the freedom to make the world any way we choose—and our moral responsibility for that—while symbolic interactionism has generally acknowledged the importance of context, reflecting the ecological principles that influenced early writers.

Postmodernism and symbolic interactionism are, though, clearly cousins in terms of genealogy, beyond the specific track of Denzin's own career. Although postmodernism had little direct influence on French sociology, it can be traced back to the existentialist writings of Jean-Paul Sartre and Simone de Beauvoir, which, in turn, are shaped by phenomenological philosophers, mainly German, whose influence is felt elsewhere in symbolic interactionism and related work. The attempt by Jurgen Habermas (1984b, 1984a) to incorporate symbolic interactionism into his version of critical theory draws on the same traditions and runs into many similar problems (Rochberg-Halton 1989). Nevertheless, German philosophical work has had an important part in shaping symbolic interactionism and will be discussed further later in this chapter.

Erving Goffman

It may seem odd to relegate such an iconic figure as Erving Goffman to a relatively small note within this chapter. Certainly, his work is widely identified with symbolic interactionism. There have, though, also been constant questions about how canonical it really is (Trevino 2003). Although Goffman is widely cited within symbolic interactionism, his approach owes much more to currents in anthropology and linguistics that run in parallel to the sources drawn on by Blumer, Hughes, and their students than directly connecting with them. As Jaworski (2000) points out, Goffman's relationship with Hughes was decidedly ambiguous, although his thinking on total institutions owed a good deal to Hughes's work. His principal mentor seems to have been Lloyd Warner, an anthropologist, and his 1953 PhD dissertation, "Communication Conduct in an Island

Community," is a classic piece of fieldwork in the British tradition. British social anthropology is a neglected influence on Chicago social science—A. R. Radcliffe Brown visited and worked there during the 1930s, although this was after anthropology and sociology split into separate departments in 1929. Even so, important ties of kinship and friendship remained through to the 1950s.

The big difference between Goffman and the main symbolic interactionist position was his emphasis on the structures within which interactions were framed. This is very characteristic of British social anthropology, with its agenda of structural functionalism, although Goffman seems to have been less concerned with the second element. Where the influence of Blumer fell on the scope for freedom in the creation of order, Goffman was more focused on the restraints. As Goffman (1967, 1988) himself put it, he was engaged in the study of "moments and their men" rather than "men and their moments." The structures surrounded the actors and defined the spaces within which they could improvise. This may, for example, help to explain Goffman's (1969) sympathetic treatment of Parsons's (1951; Parsons and Fox 1952) concept of the sick role as a constraint on interactions between patients on respirators and the health professionals attending them. When reading Goffman, it is important to recognize the extent to which he used a changing vocabulary to express relatively constant ideas over the course of his career. His disagreement with the ethnomethodologists, for example, is couched in terms of "frames" rather than "structures" but comes to essentially the same thing (Goffman 1981). Even in his very last paper, "Felicity's Condition" (Goffman 1983), he is looking to the pressure of the audience: what can we say in this situation and not disconfirm their assumptions about our sanity and competence?

Ethnomethodology

Ethnomethodology and symbolic interactionism have often had the relationship of feuding cousins on adjacent plots of land. Looking back to the 1960s, leading symbolic interactionists had a definite interest in ethnomethodology: Strauss and his collaborators (1964) refer approvingly to Garfinkel's (1967) work on the indeterminacy and localized interpretation of rules, for example. Denzin contributed to the collection *Understanding Everyday Life*, edited by Jack Douglas (1971), which was something of a manifesto for the development of ethnomethodology beyond Garfinkel's original work.

While there are important differences of topic and substance between these two bodies of work, many of these reflect differences in the philosophical traditions that they have drawn on. At various points, these gaps have not appeared to be unbridgeable. Berger and Luckmann (1966), for example, proposed an explicit synthesis between the legacies of Mead and of Alfred Schutz (Barber 2004), a social phenomenologist whose work was an early influence on ethnomethodology. Schutz's work had a clear impact on Olesen and Whittaker's (1968) classic study of the professional socialization of student nurses, which also recognizes their debts to many of Hughes's students. Although Garfinkel's work is in many ways *sui generis* (vom Lehn 2014), it does look back to the philosophical circles of 1930s Vienna and to conversations between scholars that have been prised apart by subsequent disciplinary claims on precursors. Garfinkel once acknowledged to me the influence of Aron Gurwitsch, and others in his circle have clearly taken inspiration from Wittgenstein (Wootton 1975). If we were to look for a macro theory to accompany ethnomethodology, it would be probably be found in the work of Friedrich Hayek and Ludwig Von Mises and their more radical approach to spontaneous order (Hayek 1945; Gamble 1996).

Ethnomethodology and its sibling, conversation analysis, are however indifferent to the traditional concerns of sociology with larger-scale structures. While they share symbolic interaction's interest in the here and now, they do not generally see it as an enactment of anything else. It is what it is. Perhaps the most important difference lies in the role of the analyst. Symbolic interactionism is a *verstehende* sociology, which assumes that observers can, in some sense, enter into or replicate the minds of those who are being studied. This is an extension of the notion of sympathy, which Blumer took from Cooley. Ethnomethodology takes a much stricter approach. Since humans are not known to be a telepathic species, we must create orderliness in interaction through public acts, particularly language. These acts are equally visible to the participants and to the observer. To the extent that there is an agreed program, it rests on the detailed examination of actions and responses to understand how alignments, or misalignments, occur. Moral or ethical critiques of the outcomes of this process belong in a different realm to an understanding of their production.

These three consorts of symbolic interactionism each emphasize different aspects of a shared heritage and look to sources beyond that. It is, though, now time to consider where the ideas embedded in the classic tradition of symbolic interactionism have their origins. As we do this, we may be able to recognize how and where branchings or parallel developments have taken off. This journey takes us across the Atlantic, first to Germany and then to Scotland.

THE GERMAN IMPRINT

The transient prejudices of two world wars and the mythology of American exceptionalism have obscured the extent to which science and scholarship in the United States were influenced by the intellectual dynamism of nineteenth-century Germany. This is, perhaps, best recognized by historians of science: Bonner (1963), for example, documented the interplay between American medicine and German science in the years before World War I. This exchange fundamentally shaped the approach of US doctors to the 1918 influenza pandemic (Barry 2009). Similarly, German developments in biblical criticism had a wide impact across the humanities (Reventlow 1984; Baird 1992). Like many of the other pragmatist philosophers, Mead studied in Germany (1888–90) (Joas 1985), as did Albion Small (1879–81) (Dibble 1975) and Robert Park (1899–1903) (Raushenbush 1979). Small went on to publish a book on German social thought (Small

1909) and to include many translations of German work in early issues of the *American Journal of Sociology*. Park attended lectures given by Georg Simmel, which included the only formal course in sociology that he ever took. This is likely to have introduced him to Spencer's work, which featured strongly in the original version of Simmel's doctoral dissertation, although he was required to delete it from the published text (Levine 1997).

Max and Marianne Weber spent a week in Chicago in 1904, en route to the Congress of Arts and Sciences in St Louis, but there is no record of them visiting the university—although they did go to Northwestern University on the other side of the city. Weber was involved in events organized by Albion Small, and they are likely to have met, especially given Small's networks and family connections in Germany—but Small clearly did not leave an impression (Scaff 2011). The leading pragmatist philosophers largely boycotted the St Louis Congress over its attempt to formulate a unified view of science, including social science, rather than respecting a diversity of methods appropriate to problems. Weber spoke about his work on rural communities but otherwise mostly seems to have talked to the economists—and gone to the receptions (Scaff 2011).

The German influences on symbolic interactionism have been explored in some depth by Paul Rock (1979). He focuses on the pivotal role of Immanuel Kant in responding to the work of the Scottish philosopher David Hume (1975). Before Hume, philosophers had tended to assume that nature and society could both be understood by the systematic exercise of reason alone. There was a broad consensus that true knowledge was a direct copy of reality. Hume, and his Scottish contemporaries, pulled this apart. Nature, and society, were only understood through the conceptual schemes that were applied to them. Humans could not expose the hidden workings of the world, whether by induction or deduction, because they had no access to them other than through their perceptions. The world we see is a world we have constructed from our own prior framing. We cannot discover laws in nature, merely empirical generalizations: the sun will rise tomorrow because it always has done—so we might reasonably expect this to happen again—not because it is required to.

Given this radical skepticism, it is hard to see how there would be space for any kind of science, and, indeed, few of Hume's contemporaries followed him completely. Kant, however, explicitly modified Hume's account by arguing that it did not deal adequately with the nature of our lived experience. There were different ways of understanding the world, which were complementary rather than competitive or mutually exclusive. One type of knowledge was formal and logical, producing ideas independently of observation. It would be evaluated in terms of its coherence and rigor rather than its empirical content. Another type was based on our immersion in the world. However, it is simply the knowledge derived from our own senses in a raw and unmediated form. Kant introduced a third type of knowledge, which occupied an intermediate position. We could, he suggested, never know things as they *are*, independent of our perceptions. Without a prior organization to our perceptions, however, we could not know what to see. We act in the world through the categories that we bring to it, what a later generation would call "culture." The results may allow us a dim view of the world itself and the opportunity to derive modest generalizations about it, which may, in turn, allow the categories of perception to evolve. Turning to biology and its treatment of forms, Mead (1938:629–30) responded to these proposals by urging a view where the concepts through which we observed the world were subject to correction by the materiality of the world itself.

As Rock notes, Kant cast a long shadow over German social science, provoking three main responses. Weber, he suggests, worked within the Kantian framework to produce a sociology that made no claims to general truths, rather than limited classifications from closely specified areas, like his taxonomies of religion or bureaucracy. The neo-Kantians, including Windelband, who supervised Park's doctoral dissertation (Raushenbush 1979), developed an approach that was closer to positivism. This abandoned inquiries into the "true nature" of reality in favor of a stress on the development of logical structures of knowledge, based on law-like processes, which could be tested and corrected by targeted empirical inquiries. This model did not, though, necessarily apply to the humanities and human sciences, which they saw as idiographic, understanding unique cases, rather than nomothetic, seeking universal laws. The phenomenologists, later exemplified by Schutz and others in the networks based in Vienna, focused on systematic introspection. If the world was unknowable, perhaps the self and its conditions of knowing might be. While some of these classifications are debatable in the light of more recent scholarship, they do provide a broad indication of the impact of Kant's work on the development of the sources that inspired Mead, Park, and others.

For Rock, the most direct influence on symbolic interactionism was, though, the work of Georg Simmel, another of the highly cited authors in the Park and Burgess (1969) textbook. Simmel took up the Kantian program to ask how it was possible to understand society as a human construction from experience. It was an order produced through collaborative work to impose structure on events in the world that were otherwise inherently meaningless. Rock (1979:37–38) notes that Simmel even tended to avoid the word "society" and to prefer "sociation," emphasizing the act of creation. This process of construction drew on a shared grammar of forms, which could constitute the topic for sociological inquiry, moving beyond the purely idiographic model proposed by the neo-Kantians.

A full explication would go well beyond the bounds of this chapter, but we should be able to recognize the ways in which this argument reappears in the work of Schutz and of Wittgenstein. Schutz (Schutz and Luckmann 1974) argues for the practical impossibility of reconstructing the world anew on each occasion that it is experienced and for the study of the shortcuts offered by common-sense knowledge of typifications and recipes for action, how "people like me" generally define and act in specific kinds of situations. Wittgenstein's (1961, 1972) view of language offers a similar approach. Language cannot be private: it is essentially a socially shared system for coding our experience of the world. We can only describe the world to each other through this system so that the relationship between our knowledge and our experience is inevitably social. Although Wittgenstein does not extend the argument in this way, he has created a space for sociology as the study of that knowledge and the ways in which it is used to create order—or, perhaps better, orderliness—in the world that we experience (Winch 1963).

THE HISTORICAL FOUNDATIONS OF SYMBOLIC INTERACTIONISM   39

If we bring these arguments back to the core position of symbolic interactionism, the continuities are not difficult to see. The Kantian heritage is one where the relationship between humans and the world is continuously uncertain, which is something that Blumer took over from Mead. The world is a social construction, and the program for sociology is to understand how that construction is accomplished. At the same time, the accomplishment is not random and unconstrained. There is a logic and an order to the process of ordering social relations, and the interactions between humans and their environments, that creates a degree of stability and certainty, even if only temporarily. Whether or not we accept the specific formulation of the zones of the city in Chicago urban studies, the zones are, in effect, Simmelian forms. The same might be said of Hughes's classification of occupations. Sociologists are creating second-order accounts of the practices of ordinary people that produce society. Symbolic interactionism does, however, have two key differences. The first is a recognition of the importance of materiality. Where the Kantian tradition can be uncertain about whether there is a world "out there" beyond our perceptions of it, most symbolic interactionists accept that there is something that can push back against human attempts to organize it. We may not be able to have direct knowledge of this world, and we may only be able to act on it within the frames that we bring to it, but it nevertheless exists. The second is that symbolic interactionism has not, on the whole, pursued the questions of language as fully as, say, ethnomethodology or conversation analysis. Although symbolic interactionists are concerned to learn the language of a setting, and to characterize the referents of specific vocabulary, they have been more interested in the substantive content than in the use of the language. When Becker (1993) describes his discovery of the term "crock" in the argot of medical students, for example, he is more concerned with developing a definition applicable across contexts than with the how and when of its usage, and the ways in which this might serve to identify membership of a group. These tasks are not mutually exclusive, of course, but they do mark out different genealogies.

At the beginning of this section, we noted Kant's debt to Hume. This flags the other line of descent to leave its mark on symbolic interactionism. For this we need to turn to Scotland in the eighteenth century.

THE ATHENS OF THE NORTH

The stamp of the Scottish Enlightenment may be less immediately visible in symbolic interactionism, but it is real enough. Albion Small's (1972) other major study, alongside his work on the German Cameralists, was a book on Adam Smith, where he concluded that:

> If logic and a deliberate methodology ruled the world, or even the supposedly intellectual part of it, Adam Smith would have been as immediately, if not as intensely, influential upon concrete moral philosophy, or sociology, as he was upon economics.... It is therefore not fanciful to repeat in substance the proposition with

which this inquiry began, viz.: Modern sociology is virtually an attempt to take up the larger program of social analysis and interpretation which was implicit in Adam Smith's moral philosophy, but which was suppressed for a century by prevailing interest in the technique of the production of wealth.

(Small 1972:96–97)

The influential *Heritage of Sociology* series, published by the University of Chicago Press, included a volume on "The Scottish Moralists," edited by Louis Schneider (1967), intended to provide students with an overview of their contribution. Interestingly, Schneider acknowledges the prompting of Hayek as an inspiration for his own reading in the area, underlining the links to the Viennese theorists of spontaneous order introduced earlier in this chapter.

The Scottish Enlightenment is a label for a group of scholars working mainly in Glasgow and Edinburgh over a period stretching from the appointment of Frances Hutcheson to a chair at the University of Glasgow in 1729 to the retirement of Dugald Stewart from a chair at the University of Edinburgh in 1810 (Berry 1997). The focal point was the years 1760–1790, when most of the key figures lived in what is now known as the Old Town district of Edinburgh. This was an overcrowded neighborhood of tenements where they would meet one another in the street and frequent the same drinking and dining clubs—hence the comparison with Classical Athens (Buchan 2003). Their work was widely read in Europe and influential in North America (Himmelfarb 2004). John Witherspoon, sixth president of Princeton, and a major influence on US higher education, was strongly influenced by Hutcheson and by Thomas Reid, from Aberdeen, who wrote on common-sense reasoning. Witherspoon, in turn, taught both James Madison and Aaron Burr and was admired by Alexander Hamilton, as well as being a member of the Continental Congress in his own right (Morrison 2003).

In the eighteenth century, Lowland Scotland also had something in common with late nineteenth-century Chicago as a last outpost of civilization before bandit country. The Scottish Highlands had risen in revolt twice against the English Crown, in 1715 and 1745, and these men had been caught in crises of identity as the rebel armies marched through their cities. Mostly, they actually identified as North Britons and tried to model their language and culture on that of London and Europe rather than on the feudal society of the Highlands. Like Chicago, Glasgow was also rapidly industrializing. When Adam Smith wrote about practical examples of factory work and the division of labor, this was from personal observation. The profits of trade in slaves, sugar, and cotton, and the benefits of the single market with England established in 1707, were being plowed into scientific and technological innovation, national infrastructure, and economic development. Just as in 1890s Chicago, questions about the nature of social and economic organization were not theoretical but intensely practical.

The legacy of David Hume has already been mentioned. His questioning of causal explanations still has a powerful legacy in the reluctance of symbolic interactionists to use causal language or to consider law-like or necessary connections between events. Interactionists will reason from observations of constant conjunctions to propose frames or principles that provide for the regular linkage of certain events but not determine that connection. Their approach operates more in terms of probability than necessity: If A, then B is more likely than C—but C cannot be ruled out if some contextual element is present or absent. In practice, this skepticism has been reined in by attention to the later attempt by John Stuart Mill to discipline the process for reasoning: grounded theory is essentially a restatement of Mill's methodological principles (Murphy et al. 1999).

Two other examples can be taken from the work of Adam Smith, whose impact on Albion Small has been noted. Smith is best known today for *Wealth of Nations* (Smith 1976a) but he made his name with his earlier book, *Theory of Moral Sentiments* (Smith 1976b). I commented earlier on the way in which Blumer took over the notion of "sympathy" from Cooley. Symbolic interactionism is strongly influenced by the idea of the "looking glass self" (Cooley 1902). Cooley argued that we developed a sense of self from the responses of others to our actions, which, in turn, led us to imagine those reactions in formulating further actions. The meaning of an act did not, then, lie wholly in the intentions of its author but in its reception by others. Mead (2015:154–59) extended this with his idea of the "generalized other," the imagined response of a disinterested observer as a constraint on actions that went beyond specific situations. This, for Mead, was an important glue between otherwise disconnected acts that purely reflected the local contingencies of context and actors.

This model, however, is clearly derived from Adam Smith, who uses very much the same imagery, although neither Cooley nor Mead acknowledges the debt. In *Theory of Moral Sentiments*, for example, Smith (1976b:112) discusses the emergence of a moral sense and our efforts to judge ourselves by imagining the response of others to our acts:

> We suppose ourselves to be the spectators of our own behaviour, and endeavour to imagine what effect it would, in this light, produce upon us. *This is the only looking-glass* by which we can, in some measure, with the eyes of other people, scrutinize the propriety of our own conduct. (emphasis added)

Our own judgment may, however, be overruled by that of the "impartial spectator" conceived of as a "man within" who judges the praiseworthiness or blameworthiness of our actions, both in anticipation and in retrospect. Smith's language is somewhat difficult here because he is trying to avoid identifying the impartial spectator with God, but without actually sliding into explicit atheism, which had led Hume, his great friend, into serious trouble with the Scottish church.

While *Theory of Moral Sentiments* and *Wealth of Nations* are often thought of as discontinuous projects, Smith did not see them that way. The market society he described in *Wealth of Nations* rested on a moral foundation that it did not itself generate, a theme echoed in Durkheim's (1964) work. *Moral Sentiments* is the basis of the self-restraint that checks tendencies toward monopoly and capitalist abuses. In this sense, we can see the echoes of Smith in the passage from Small and Vincent quoted earlier, the aspiration of Chicago sociology to develop capitalism with a conscience rather than the radical alternatives associated with Jane Addams. *Wealth of Nations* is, however, also important for its understanding of the division of labor and for its vision of a dynamic economy and society, which has a legacy in almost all later social science. Remember that Adam Smith was directly observing a society that was undergoing change at least as drastic and rapid as that of Chicago from the 1890s to the 1930s. The replacement of craft by factory processes of manufacture was bringing about huge increases in productivity and making many goods more affordable for the mass of the population. At the same time, it was rewriting the division of labor and social mobility (Dingwall 2016). People were no longer born into their parents' station in life and to the crafts or trades open to that class or locality. Occupational structures are not fixed but constantly in process. Changes in technology, market demand, or means of transport divide some occupations and combine others in processes of fission and fusion. This is precisely Hughes's (1928) starting point. We might also note that Darwin was familiar with Smith's work: there is an argument that this observation provided a basis for his shift away from the idea that species were fixed at a moment of creation to seeing them as moments of organization in a changing environment (Schweber 1980).

If we can show that symbolic interactionism, at least as articulated through the networks around the University of Chicago, had a strong foundation in the writings of the Scottish Enlightenment, can we take the story any further back? Whose shoulders were the Scots standing on?

THE CLASSICAL HERITAGE

In an earlier generation, the links to ancient Greece and Rome would probably have come at the beginning of the chapter, as a way of linking symbolic interactionism to the icons of the white tribes of Europe. However, there is more than a symbolic function in tracing the roots of interactionist ideas back to the years around 300 BCE. Many of the theoretical issues confronting interactionism today have, in fact, been present for a very long time and are probably not capable of being definitely resolved. This does not mean that they are not important or that we should not try to produce workable approximations to a solution—but we may not want to let them stand in the way of a mission to produce empirical knowledge of our contemporary world and the actors that create it. In the space available, we cannot go into the rediscovery of Latin and Greek learning in sixteenth-century Europe and the ways in which this reached Scotland, particularly through its contacts with the Netherlands. A shared version of Protestantism and a similar legal system meant that there were extensive scientific and scholarly interchanges, particularly in the seventeenth century (Emerson 2004). The writings of Justus Lipsius, Hugo Grotius—both Dutch—and Samuel von Pufendorf, from Germany, on law, nature, and social order circulated widely and were referenced by Adam Smith in his *Lectures on Jurisprudence* (Bastable 1898; Smith 1978). This body of work speaks

THE HISTORICAL FOUNDATIONS OF SYMBOLIC INTERACTIONISM   43

to the strength of the influence from Greek and Roman Stoicism on European thinking and the ways in which this was used to displace the Aristotelian doctrines that had held sway throughout much of the medieval period.

Although Robert Prus (2004; Puddephatt and Prus 2007) has made a case for the influence of Aristotle on symbolic interactionism, there is much more evidence in Adam Smith's *Theory of Moral Sentiments* for Stoic influence. Stoicism was founded as a school of philosophy around 312 BCE by Zeno, who came from Cyprus. He was succeeded by Cleanthes and Chrysippus, both from Turkey, and, in the next generation by Diogenes from Iraq and Antipater from Syria (Inwood 2003). The Stoics were outsiders to the genteel world of Athenian philosophy, expressed both in their criticisms of its institutions like gender roles and slavery and in their everyday life (Erskine 1990). Stoic thought was taken up by leading Roman thinkers like Cicero and its influence is generally considered to have ended with the death of Emperor Marcus Aurelius in 180 CE.

The Stoic vision of the world emphasized its indeterminacy. Change and movement were its natural states, which could only be temporarily stabilized. This was achieved by a process of human cognition. According to Zeno, this involved four steps. The human mind was constantly exposed to a stream of *impressions*. But these impressions were only absorbed and became a basis for action as the result of a deliberate act of selection or *assent*. This, in turn, was subject to the exercise of reason in determining whether it should become a matter of *conviction*. Finally, by comparing the present conviction with past experiences and the evidence of others, it might become a matter of *knowledge*. This is not a purely constructionist account, but it does shift the emphasis away from Aristotle's insistence that structures or forms were inherent in nature. In this account, the goal for human perception was to grasp these forms. The Stoics, in contrast, saw forms as tools used by humans to organize the world perceived by their sense, in a way that would be familiar to symbolic interactionists.

Similarly, human cognition was founded on a developmental process that would be recognizable in the work of Mead and Blumer. Aetius (ca. 100CE) summarized it in this fashion: "When a man is born, the Stoics say, he has the commanding part of his soul like a sheet of paper ready for writing upon" (Long and Sedley 1987:238). This is not a blank-slate theory—the sheet of paper has an affordance that prompts the user to write upon it. The Stoic child differs from the models of other ancient writers. She does not have innate knowledge of the world and its properties or have her development shaped purely by external stimuli of pain or pleasure (Becker 1998). The child was, rather, primed for the process of appropriating the world and creating a sense of self through interaction with society.

Early Stoic thought is hard to reconstruct from fragmentary evidence—Zeno's book on society and political order has not survived, for example. However, another way to write this chapter would be to see it as the beginnings of a golden thread that links two thousand years of social thought, of which symbolic interactionism is one modern version. As such it presents not just an epistemological but also an ethical challenge to many other contemporary approaches in sociology (Strong and Dingwall 1989).

Conclusion

Symbolic interactionism is often presented as if it sprang fully formed from the waters of Lake Michigan sometime between 1890 and 1940. This chapter has argued that it is not a fringe novelty in social science but heir to discussions about the nature of human beings and their relations to one another that go back to the earliest written arguments in societies that had sufficient economic surplus to support people to engage in them. As a group, symbolic interactionists have generally been more interested in acquiring knowledge about the world than in creating theoretical genealogies. Howard Becker's response to an uppity graduate student who asked how to choose a theoretical perspective—"just go out there and do it"—is deservedly famous. On the other hand, such family trees do matter a lot to other sociologists, and it is as well to recognize this. In the case of symbolic interaction, though, the family tree is more like that recognized by modern evolutionary biology: a straggly bush, full of false starts, dead ends, and competing branches, rather than an ineluctable, linear march toward the present.

References

Abbott, A. 1988. *The System of Professions: An Essay on the Division of Expert Labor.* Chicago: University of Chicago Press.

Abbott, A. 1999. *Department and Discipline: Chicago Sociology at One Hundred.* Chicago: University of Chicago Press.

Baird, W. 1992. *History of New Testament Research: From Deism to Tübingen.* Fortress Press.

Bannister, R. C. 1979. *Social Darwinism: Science and Myth in Anglo-American Social Thought.* Philadelphia: Temple University Press.

Barber, M. D. 2004. *The Participating Citizen: A Biography of Alfred Schutz.* Albany: State University of New York Press.

Barry, J. M. 2009. *The Great Influenza.* London: Penguin Books.

Bastable, C. F. 1898. "Adam Smith's Lectures on 'Jurisprudence.'" *Hermathena* 10(24):200–11.

Becker, H. S. 1970. "The Nature of a Profession." Pp. 87–104 in *Sociological Work: Method and Substance,* edited by H. S. Becker. Chicago: Aldine.

Becker, H. S. 1982. *Art Worlds.* Berkeley: University of California Press.

Becker, H. S. 1993. "How I Learned What a Crock Was." *Journal of Contemporary Ethnography* 22(1):28–35. doi: 10.1177/089124193022001003.

Becker, L. C. 1998. "Stoic Children." Pp. 45–61 in *The Philosopher's Child: Critical Essays in the Western Tradition,* edited by S. M. Turner and G. B. Matthews. Rochester, NY: University of Rochester Press.

Berger, P., and T. Luckmann. 1966. *The Social Construction of Reality.* Harmondsworth: Penguin.

Bernard, L. L. 1921. "The Misuse of Instinct in the Social Sciences." *Psychological Review* 28(2): 96–119.

Berry, C. J. 1997. *Social Theory of the Scottish Enlightenment.* Edinburgh: Edinburgh University Press.

THE HISTORICAL FOUNDATIONS OF SYMBOLIC INTERACTIONISM   45

Blumer, H. 1937. "Social Psychology." Pp. 144–98 in *Man and Society: A Substantive Introduction to the Social Sciences*, edited by E. P. Schmidt. New York: Prentice Hall.

Blumer, H. 1969. *Symbolic Interactionism: Perspective and Method*. Berkeley: University of California Press.

Bonner, T. N. 1963. *American Doctors and German Universities: A Chapter in International Intellectual Relations, 1870–1914*. Lincoln: University of Nebraska Press.

Buchan, J. 2003. *Crowded with Genius—The Scottish Enlightenment: Edinburgh's Moment of the Mind*. New York: HarperCollins.

Cooley, C. H. 1902. *Human Nature and the Social Order*. New York: Charles Scribner's Sons.

Cooley, C. H. 1912. *Social Organization: A Study of the Larger Mind*. New York: Charles Scribner's Sons.

Deegan, M. J. 1988. *Jane Addams and the Men of the Chicago School, 1892–1918*. New Brunswick, NJ: Transaction Publishers.

Deegan, M. J. 2006. "The Human Drama Behind the Study of People as Potato Bugs." *Journal of Classical Sociology* 6(1): 101–22. doi: 10.1177/1468795X06061288.

Deegan, M. J. 2014. *Annie Marion Maclean and the Chicago Schools of Sociology 1894–1934*. New Brunswick, NJ: Transaction Publishers.

Dibble, V. K. 1975. *The Legacy of Albion Small*. Edited by M. Janowitz. Chicago: University of Chicago Press (The Heritage of Sociology).

Dickens, P. 2000. *Social Darwinism*. Buckingham: Open University Press.

Dingwall, Robert. 2001. "Notes Toward an Intellectual History of Symbolic Interactionism." *Symbolic Interaction* 24(2): 237–42.

Dingwall, Robert. 2016. "The Ecological Metaphor in the Sociology of Occupations and Professions." Pp. 31–48 in *Professions and Metaphors: Understanding Professions in Society*, edited by A. Liljegren and M. Saks. London: Routledge.

Dingwall, R., and M. D. King. 1995. "Herbert Spencer and the Professions: Occupational Ecology Reconsidered." *Sociological Theory* 13(1): 14–24.

Dingwall, R., B. Nerlich, and S. Hillyard. 2003. "Biological Determinism and Symbolic Interaction: Hereditary Streams and Cultural Roads." *Symbolic Interaction* 26(4):631–44. doi: 10.1525/si.2003.26.4.631.

Douglas, J. D., ed. 1971. *Understanding Everyday Life: Toward the Reconstruction of Sociological Knowledge*. London: Routledge & Kegan Paul.

Durkheim, E. 1964. *The Division of Labor in Society*. New York: Free Press.

Emerson, R. L. 2004. "The Founding of the Edinburgh Medical School." *Journal of the History of Medicine and Allied Sciences* 59(2): 183–218. doi: 10.1093/jhmas/jrh066.

Erskine, A. 1990. *The Hellenistic Stoa: Political Thought and Action*. London: Duckworth.

Faris, E. 1921. "Are Instincts Data or Hypotheses?" *American Journal of Sociology* 27(2): 184–96.

Faris, R. E. L. 1979. *Chicago Sociology 1920–1932*. Chicago: University of Chicago Press.

Fine, G. A. 1995. *Kitchens: The Culture of Restaurant Work*. Berkeley: University of California Press.

Freidson, E. 1978. "The Official Construction of Occupations: An Essay on the Practical Epistemology of Work." In *9th World Congress of Sociology*. Uppsala.

Gamble, A. 1996. *Hayek: The Iron Cage of Liberty*. Cambridge: Polity Press.

Garfinkel, H. 1967. *Studies in Ethnomethodology*. Englewood Cliffs, NJ: Prentice Hall.

Goffman, E. 1967. *Interaction Ritual: Essays on Face-to-Face Behavior*. New York: Doubleday.

Goffman, E. 1969. "The Insanity of Place." *Psychiatry* 32(4): 357–87.

Goffman, E. 1981. *Forms of Talk*. Oxford: Basil Blackwell.

Goffman, E. 1983. "Felicity's Condition." *American Journal of Sociology* 89(1): 1–53.

Goffman, E. 1988. *Les moments et leurs hommes*. Edited by Y. Winkin. Paris: Seuil/Minuit.

Habermas, J. 1984a. *The Theory of Communicative Action*. Beacon Press.

Habermas, J. 1984b. *The Theory of Communicative Action: Reason and the Rationalization of Society*. Boston: Beacon Press.

Hayek, F. A. 1945. "The Use of Knowledge in Society." *The American Economic Review* 35(4): 519–30.

Himmelfarb, G. 2004. *The Roads to Modernity: The British, French, and American Enlightenments*. New York: Alfred A. Knopf.

Hinkle, R. C. 1980. *Founding Theory of American Sociology 1881–1915*. London: Routledge and Kegan Paul.

Hofstadter, R. 1955. *Social Darwinism in American Thought*. Boston: Beacon Press.

Hughes, E. C. 1928. "Personality Types and the Division of Labor." *American Journal of Sociology* 33(5): 754–68. doi: 10.1086/214539.

Hume, D. 1975. *Enquiries Concerning Human Understanding and Concerning the Principles of Morals*. Third Edition. Edited by L. A. Selby-Bigge and P. H. Nidditch. Oxford: Oxford University Press.

Inwood, B. 2003. *The Cambridge Companion to The Stoics*. Cambridge: Cambridge University Press (Cambridge Companions).

Jaworski, G. D. 2000. "Erving Goffman: The Reluctant Apprentice." *Symbolic Interaction* 23(3): 299–308.

Joas, H. 1985. *G. H. Mead: A Contemporary Re-Examination of his Thought*. Cambridge: Polity.

Lacaze, L. 2017. "Ellsworth Faris: An Outsider of the Chicago School?" retrieved November 5, 2020 (https://www.academia.edu/33855036/ELLSWORTH_FARIS_AN_OUTSIDER_OF_THE_CHICAGO_SCHOOL_FROM_WACO_TO_CHICAGO_VIA_BOLENGE_1).

vom Lehn, D. 2014. *Harold Garfinkel: The Creation and Development of Ethnomethodology*. Walnut Creek, CA: Left Coast Press.

Levine, D. N. 1997. "Simmel Reappraised: Old Images: New Scholarship." Pp. 173–207 in *Reclaiming the Sociological Classics: The State of the Scholarship*, edited by C. Camic. Oxford: Blackwell.

Lévi-Strauss, C. 1966. *The Savage Mind*. London: Weidenfield and Nicolson.

Liu, S. 2013. "The Legal Profession as a Social Process: A Theory on Lawyers and Globalization." *Law and Social Inquiry* 38(3):670–93. doi: 10.1111/lsi.12007.

Liu, S. 2015. "Boundary Work and Exchange: The Formation of a Professional Service Market." *Symbolic Interaction* 38(1):1–21. doi: https://doi.org/10.1002/symb.137.

Liu, S., and M. Emirbayer. 2016. "Field and Ecology." *Sociological Theory* 34(1):62–79. doi: 10.1177/0735275116632556.

Long, A. A., and D. N. Sedley. 1987. *The Hellenistic Philosophers*. Cambridge: Cambridge University Press.

Lyman, S. M., and A. J. Vidich. 1988. *Social Order and the Public Philosophy: An Analysis and Interpretation of the Work of Herbert Blumer*. Lafayette: University of Arkansas Press.

Mead, G. H. 1938. *The Philosophy of the Act*. Edited by C. W. Morris. Chicago: University of Chicago Press.

Mead, G. H. 1962. *Mind, Self and Society from the Standpoint of a Social Behaviorist*. Edited by C. W. Morris. Chicago: University of Chicago Press.

Mead, G. H. 2015. *Mind, Self and Society: The Definitive Edition*. Edited by C. W. Morris, D. R. Huebner, and H. Joas. Chicago: University of Chicago Press.

Meltzer, B. N. 1967. "Mead's Social Psychology." Pp. 5–24 in *Symbolic Interaction: A Reader in Social Psychology*, edited by J. G. Manis and B. N. Meltzer. Boston: Allyn and Bacon.

Morrison, J. H. 2003. *John Witherspoon and the Founding of the American Republic*. Notre Dame, IN: Notre Dame Press. Retrieved November 30, 2020. https://undpress.nd.edu/9780268035082/john-witherspoon-and-the-founding-of-the-american-republic.

Murphy, E., et al. 1999. "Qualitative Research Methods in Health Technology Assessment: A Review of the Literature." *Health Technology Assessment* 2(16):1–276. doi: https://doi.org/10.3310/hta2160.

Olesen, V. L., and E. W. Whittaker. 1968. *The Silent Dialogue: A Study in the Social Psychology of Professional Socialization*. San Francisco: Jossey-Bass.

Park, R. E. 1915. "The City: Suggestions for the Investigation of Human Behavior in the City Environment." *American Journal of Sociology* 20(5):577–612.

Park, R. E., and E. W. Burgess. 1969. *Introduction to the Science of Sociology*. Chicago: University of Chicago Press.

Park, R. E., E. W. Burgess, and R. D. McKenzie. 1925. *The City: Suggestions for Investigation of Human Behaviour in the Urban Environment*. Chicago: University of Chicago Press.

Parsons, T. 1951. *The Social System*. London: Routledge and Kegan Paul.

Parsons, T., and R. Fox. 1952. "Illness, Therapy and the Modern Urban American Family." *Journal of Social Issues* 8(4):31–44. doi: 10.1111/j.1540-4560.1952.tb01861.x.

Peneff, J. 2018. *Howard S Becker: Sociology and Music in the Chicago School*. Translated by R. Dingwall. New York: Routledge.

Polanyi, M. 1941. "The Growth of Thought in Society." *Economica* 8(32):428–56.

Prus, R. 2004. "Symbolic Interaction and Classical Greek Scholarship: Conceptual Foundations, Historical Continuities, and Transcontextual Relevancies." *The American Sociologist* 35(1):5–33.

Puddephatt, A. J., and R. Prus. 2007. "Causality, Agency, and Reality: Plato and Aristotle Meet George Herbert Mead and Herbert Blumer." *Sociological Focus* 40(3):265–86.

Raushenbush, W. 1979. *Robert E. Park: Biography of a Sociologist*. Durham, NC: Duke University Press.

Reventlow, G. H. 1984. *The Authority of the Bible and the Rise of the Modern World*. London: SCM Press.

Rochberg-Halton, E. 1989. "Jürgen Habermas's Theory of Communicative Etherealization." *Symbolic Interaction* 12(2):333–60. doi: https://doi.org/10.1525/si.1989.12.2.333.

Rock, P. 1979. *The Making of Symbolic Interactionism*. London: Macmillan.

Scaff, L. A. 2011. *Max Weber in America*. Princeton: Princeton University Press.

Schneider, L. 1967. *The Scottish Moralists on Human Nature and Society*. Chicago: University of Chicago Press (The Heritage of Sociology).

Schutz, A., and T. Luckmann. 1974. *The Structures of the Life-World*. London: Heinemann.

Schweber, S. S. 1980. "Darwin and the Political Economists: Divergence of Character." *Journal of the History of Biology* 13(2):195–289. doi: 10.1007/BF00125744.

Shibutani, T. 1961. *Society and Personality: An Interactionist Approach to Social Psychology*. Englewood Cliffs, NJ: Prentice Hall.

Shore, M. 1987. *The Science of Social Redemption: McGill, the Chicago School and the Origins of Social Research in Canada*. Toronto: University of Toronto Press.

Small, A. W. 1972. *Adam Smith and Modern Sociology*. Clifton, NJ: Augustus M. Kelley (Reprints of Economic Classics).

Small, A. W. 1909. *The Cameralists: The Pioneers of German Social Polity*. New York: Burt Franklin (Burt Franklin Research and Source Works Series No. 43).

Small, A. W., and G. E. Vincent. 1894. *An Introduction to the Study of Society*. New York: American Book Company.

Smith, A. 1976a. *An Inquiry into the Nature and Causes of the Wealth of Nations*. Edited by E. Cannan. Chicago: University of Chicago Press.

Smith, A. 1976b. *The Theory of Moral Sentiments*. Edited by D. D. Raphael and A. L. Macfie. Oxford: Clarendon Press.

Smith, A. 1978. *Lectures on Jurisprudence*. Edited by R. L. Meek, D. D. Raphael, and P. G. Stein. Oxford: Clarendon Press.

Strauss, A. L. 1959. *Mirrors and Masks: The Search for Identity*. Glencoe, IL: Free Press.

Strauss, A. 1975. *Professions, Work and Careers*. New Brunswick, NJ: Transaction Books.

Strauss, A. L. 1977. *Mirrors and Masks: The Search for Identity*. London: Martin Robertson.

Strauss, A. L., et al. 1964. *Psychiatric Ideologies and Institutions*. New York: Free Press.

Strong, P. M. 1988. "Qualitative Sociology in the UK." *Qualitative Sociology* 11(1–2):13–28. doi: 10.1007/BF00988686.

Strong, P. M., and R. Dingwall. 1989. "Romantics and Stoics." Pp. 49–69 in *The Politics of Field Research: Sociology Beyond Enlightenment*, edited by J. F. Gubrium and D. Silverman. London: SAGE.

Thomas, W. I. 1917. "The Persistence of Primary Group Norms in Present-Day Society and Their Influence in Our Educational System." Pp. 159–97 in *Suggestions of Modern Science Concerning Education*, edited by H. S. Jennings et al. New York: The Macmillan Company.

Trevino, A. J., ed. 2003. *Goffman's Legacy*. Lanham, MD: Rowman and Littlefield.

Whittaker, E. W., and V. L. Olesen. 1964. "The Faces of Florence Nightingale; Functions of the Heroine Legend in an Occupational Sub-culture." *Human Organization* 23(Summer) 123–30.

Wiley, N. 2014. "Interviewing Herbert Blumer." *Symbolic Interaction* 37(2):300–8. doi: 10.1002/symb.98.

Winch, P. 1963. *The Idea of a Social Science and Its Relation to Philosophy*. London: Routledge and Kegan Paul.

Wittgenstein, L. 1961. *Tractatus Logico-Philosophicus*. London: Routledge & Kegan Paul.

Wittgenstein, L. 1972. *Philosophical Investigations*. Oxford: Basil Blackwell.

Wootton, A. J. 1975. *Dilemmas of Discourse: Controversies about the Sociological Interpretation of Language*. London: George Allen & Unwin.

CHAPTER 3

....

SYMBOLIC INTERACTIONISM AND SOCIAL RESEARCH

....

ANDREA SALVINI

INTRODUCTION

....

RESEARCH methodology is a central and much debated aspect in developing the inter-actionist perspective. Exploring the enormous amount of contributions on the methodological question risks being incomplete in a few pages. Bearing this limitation in mind, this chapter is articulated into three parts. The first illustrates the central elements of the methodological orientation of symbolic interactionism, starting from the contribution offered by Herbert Blumer. Moreover, the main criticisms that have been made of this orientation over time will be discussed. The second part has a more strictly methodological character since it presents the essential elements of the empirical research process inspired by symbolic interactionism. Finally, the third part focuses on the influence that symbolic interactionism has exerted on three main methodological perspectives, namely, ethnography, grounded theory, and the postmodernist approach to social research.

The temporal boundaries that have been adopted in this chapter privilege the tendencies that have emerged in the last two decades. This does not mean underestimating the historical roots in which the described tendencies are embedded. There is a vast literature that can be drawn on to grasp their intimate interconnection with the methodological tradition that has developed over time within the perspective (Reynolds and Meltzer 1973; Benzies and Allen 2001; Hermann-Kinney and Verschaeve 2003; Atkinson and Housley 2003; Denzin 2004; Berg 2007; Morrissette, Guignon, and Demazière 2011; Carter and Montes Alvarado 2018). The only exception to this choice is the discussion of the "methodological position" expressed by Herbert Blumer in his most famous essay. Without reducing the importance of other perspectives that emerged in the second half of the last century, such as those known as "Iowa School" and "Indiana School," Blumer's methodological proposal, although not without considerable limits, constitutes an inescapable point of reference for those who are engaged in empirical research on a daily basis—as evidenced by the critical examinations that are frequently published on Blumer's work (see, e.g., Schwalbe 2019). Finally, it is important to note that, in recent years, the interactionist perspective has attracted a significant number of scholars beyond the established geographical and intellectual boundaries in which it was born (Engdhal and Müller 2015). If symbolic interactionism is to propose itself as a truly international perspective, it will have to emphasize its pivotal elements on a theoretical and methodological level, so that they can be combined with the empirical experiences and intellectual atmospheres of other national contexts. Blumer's thought constitutes, in this slow but effective process of "globalization," an inescapable as well as controversial departure.

The Methodological Position of Symbolic Interactionism

This paragraph recalls the famous chapter introducing Herbert Blumer's best-known text, *Symbolic Interactionism: Perspective and Method*. Beginning with this text does not imply an underestimation of the enormous contribution made by the interactionist authors before 1969; on the contrary, here we want to argue how the contents of that chapter summarize the main tenets of the research experiences carried out in previous decades, and specifically by the Chicago School of Sociology. In "The Methodological Position of Symbolic Interactionism," Blumer reconstructs the epistemological and conceptual frameworks of the perspective and comes up with consistent indications on the methodological level. The preeminent methodological perspectives, in the social-historical context in which Blumer wrote, were based on the belief that the properties of the social phenomena could be quantitatively measured through the mechanism of operationalization, which involves the transformation of abstract concepts into measurable variables—a procedure still central to survey research today. The problems that this approach poses to the interactionist scholar are at least two: on the one hand, the measurement process requires the researcher to turn his attention to the construction of the variables. This circumstance is only possible by considering the concepts as abstract entities that cannot be modified during the research process. On the other hand, the centrality assumed by quantitative indicators replaces the relevance of social actors who are excluded or "forgotten" by empirical analysis. These characteristics violate the fundamental assumptions of interactionist epistemology, which instead place social actors, their interactions, how they construct and assign meaning to their conduct and the contexts in which it occurs, at the center of the scholar's interest (Grills and Prus 2008).

According to Blumer, the "survey research" approach has considerable shortcomings in terms of actual knowledge of reality: sociologists often do not have a precise knowledge of what they study because they lack first-hand experience—that is, direct and personal—of the analyzed phenomena. This "distance" between the scholar and empirical reality does not just concern the lack of personal and direct involvement in the social life of one's subjects, but is also relies on an argumentative logic that uses overly abstract and "closed" concepts, which are translated into quantitative indicators whose causal connections are the scholar's main concern.

Contrasting these positions, Blumer offers "alternative" methodological guidelines that can be summarized as follows:

a) the study of the empirical world must be directed towards the concrete social actors that participate in the construction of social processes being studied;
b) this direct study allows the researcher to acquire *first-hand knowledge* of the phenomenon and to reach an *intimate familiarity* with it; this is possible only through the presence of the researcher within the studied context;
c) with the *exploration*, which is the direct observation of the empirical world using the most diverse sources and techniques, sociologists collect data in an organized way;
d) with *inspection*, data analysis is carried out connecting and comparing data and their properties through a process of interpretation;
e) the analysis is finalized to formulate propositions about those connections and to place those propositions in coherent theoretical frameworks;
f) finally, these theoretical frameworks are "validated" through a new analysis of the empirical world; there is a return "to the field"—from which the scholar actually never strays—to compare his theoretical acquisitions with the research participants' points of view.

These guidelines constitute the methodological consequence of the need to "respect the nature of the empirical world," since reality is, to use Blumer's language again, "obdurate." It is "resistant" in the sense that the empirical world can "talk back" to our representations or statements about it (Blumer 1969:23). This image of a "resistant" reality has provoked many criticisms of Blumer. First of all are those according to which he has not entirely emancipated himself from a substantially "essentialistic" vision of social reality and the way of studying it—if it is conceived as "resistant," reality would have autonomous and distinct characteristics (McPhail and Rexroat 1979; Blumer 1980). Moreover, this orientation does not seem to substantially question the relevance of the hypothetical-deductive approach, which is consolidated in the social sciences (Hammersley 1989). Blumer argues the need for the researcher to continually negotiate his conceptual acquisitions during the investigation, which is provisional by nature. Even when the scholar has reached a level of theoretical elaboration that he considers satisfactory, he will need to compare these acquisitions with the empirical world, which, as we know, is composed of people's lives. Theories and sociological concepts must be generated in the empirical dimension and must find their roots in that dimension. Some scholars have observed that the orientation expressed by Blumer is so incredibly ambitious and difficult to achieve in its radicality, that it risks confusing young researchers who find themselves having to negotiate these assumptions with the most consolidated methodological standards in science and with the concrete situations in which they make their methodological choices (Becker 1988; Weller 2000). Blumer himself does not seem to have succeeded, in the rare research experiences he has carried out, in putting into practice the principles he has given (Best 2006).

Despite these limitations, the characteristics of the Blumerian methodological orientation can be understood as a relevant reference that researchers should try to follow, within the limits of the concrete conditions in which they carry out their research (Schwalbe 2019).

THE PROCESS OF EMPIRICAL RESEARCH IN SYMBOLIC INTERACTIONISM: AN OVERALL LOOK AT ITS MAIN FEATURES

Symbolic interactionism is a multifaceted perspective that inspires a vast plurality of methodological choices that researchers can make within their research processes: "interactionist's current methods are diverse, as diverse as the society they attempt to study" (Hermann-Kinney and Verschaeve 2003:242; see also Benzies and Allen 2001). However, it is not difficult to see a pronounced predisposition of the interactionist researchers in adopting qualitative methods, which show greater consistency with the epistemological and methodological assumptions of the perspective. This does not mean that quantitative methods have not been used and cannot be used within the perspective (Reynolds and Metzer 1973; Ulmer and Wilson 2003; Hanzel 2011). However, I agree with those who state that "the future of research methods within interactionism may best be predicted from recent trends" (Hermann-Kinney and Verschaevehe 2003:241); if we look at the articles published in recent years in the main interactionist journals, as well as the papers presented at international conferences held by the Society for the Study of Symbolic Interaction, we will notice a significant prevalence of empirical experiences using qualitative methods over those using quantitative methods. This chapter focuses on some of the main perspectives that employ qualitative methods as research strategies, trying to detect their main tenets, and to understand why they are so diffused in the interactionist community, especially among young scholars and practitioners. Drawing on these wide empirical traditions, what follows is a tentative synthesis of the main characteristics of an interactionist's inspired research process, pointing at:

a) the aims of the research (discover, describe, explain),
b) the researcher's position in the research process,
c) data and their "collection," and
d) data analysis and theorization.

The Aims of the Research: Discover, Describe, and Explain

According to a commonplace view, as widespread as it is incorrect, interactionist researchers aim to "discover," "describe," or "interpret" phenomena under study, but they are precluded from "explaining." "Explaining," in the methodological field, conventionally refers to the possibility of identifying empirical regularity in the observed phenomena. In the essentialist epistemological framework, the explanation is the result of a path that starts from hypotheses to be verified through the collection of data, and ends with the statistical treatment of quantitative variables between which it is possible to identify cause-effect relationships. In the interactionist perspective, "explaining" means bringing to evidence processes and mechanisms that characterize events and situations generated by social actors' conduct based on the interpretation of the context in which they act (Puddephatt and Prus 2007). Patterns and regularity in the behavior of individuals can be brought to the fore because they share meanings, within specific contexts, and adopt common strategies of action, or are committed to "negotiate" shared forms of action. Such meaning-making processes are not the "projection" of some "natural" event or some "social law," but are the emerging effect of the interaction between individuals (Lincoln and Guba 2013:52).

"Explaining," consequently, constitutes an analytical purpose closely connected with the other two general purposes of interactionist research, that is, "discover" and "describe." Discovery is a process through which the scholar is committed to representing the characteristics of contexts, interactions, and events that are considered significant to the thematic framework of the investigation and to research questions—here "representing" means taking on the research participants' point of view. The discovery has to do, therefore, with an exploratory strategy that practically translates into the collection of data from a plurality of sources and the constant comparison between the available data; the resulting interpretations remain as "anchored" as possible to the life of the empirical world being studied (Blumer 1969:73). Discovery does not mean that there is something to "take out" from the data, as if they "contain" some "hidden resource" and as if the task of the scholar should be to adopt the most appropriate tools to "find" this treasure, "bringing it to light" from within the data—these are metaphors and images commonly used also in the educational field. This way of conceiving "data" and "discovery" is in logical contradiction with the interactionist epistemology, according to which data and analysis are generated (co-constructed) in social interaction. Description is an analytical process in which linguistic expressions and concepts are used to illustrate an event's characteristics (a situation, an interaction) to convey its constitutive elements, properties, and dynamics. Descriptions may appear as objective "statements," but they are not, since every description, even the simplest, implies a purpose, at least a "public" for which the description is intended (see Corbin and Strauss 2008:54). Therefore, the description does not generate "objective" accounts of the observed reality, but statements that are the result of the "selective eye" of the scholar about "what is happening here"; these statements form the basis, along with other materials, for more abstract interpretations of the data. Discovery, description, and explanation are processes that always imply a process of interpretation, meaning-making, and understanding. Meanings do not "stand" in the data, of course, but are the result of the scholars' interpretative work (Oliver 2012).

What (and How) Do You "Observe" in the Research Process? The Researcher's Position

Interactionist research is a process through which the researcher approaches the studied social worlds by assuming their inhabitants' perspective, learning, through a continuous exercise of role-taking, from their attitudes and behaviors. The researcher is interested in the research participants not only as "social actors," but also as individuals who share—with the other participants—the ability to "say" something relevant about the studied phenomenon. To varying degrees and intensities, they "share" with each other some biographical and identity aspects according to which they "participate" in the research: these "points of intersection" between stories and life experiences constitute the "social placement" of the participants (Kleinmann, Stenross, and McMahon 1994) and represent an essential analytical focus for the researcher. The research process will therefore be oriented to the reconstruction of these "social placements" and to interpret the participants' point of view on their "placements."

The researcher is sensitive to the aspects that express the inner conversation processes of the participants, how they indicate to themselves their courses of action, how those courses of action intertwine with those of others (joint action), and how they are renegotiated and possibly modified. These aspects are "collected" through a communicative process (for example, the interview), in which the researcher "puts into play" their own biographical, cultural, cognitive characteristics; they are therefore engaged in the process of inner dialogue aimed at "giving meaning" to the data.

In engaging in this interpretative dialogue, the researcher is aware that they have previous knowledge and develop their point of view on the topics they are studying and familiarity with the existing literature on those topics. They do not assume a "naive attitude" concerning this knowledge, "pretending" to be a tabula rasa or ignoring the effects of this knowledge on how they relate communicatively with the research participants. On the contrary, they consider their knowledge as a significant reference framework for identifying guiding concepts, conceptual anchors through which they can orient in empirical practice of exploration of the participants' social worlds. The continuous clarification of those sensitizing concepts is rooted in the empirical dimension, in the data, which, as they are collected, requires being constantly compared with each other and with the "provisional" theoretical constructions elaborated by the researcher.

Connecting conceptualizations to data means considering similarities and differences and identifying common elements. The researcher accesses new sources, meets different people, and learns new points of view: they do not only "describe" those points

Data and Their "Collection"

Data are pieces of information to which the research participants and the researcher assign a linguistic form through which the former make statements about their own life and about events concerning it, and express opinions and emotions (Flick 2014). Through qualitative and quantitative data, scholars generate interpretations on those statements and expressions and, above all, on the ways and conditions in which those statements and expressions are reconstructed (Charmaz and Belgrave 2019). The "natural" linguistic forms are constitutively "qualitative data" because through them, people, in their daily interactions, implicitly and explicitly express meanings that become the focus of the analysis.

One of the most common expressions used in social research is "data collection," which designates a particular chronologically distinct "phase" in the research process in which data are elicited through the use of specific protocols such as the interview— more or less structured. Data collection would therefore be a process of "recording" the "given" information, and the latter would be an objective reflection of the studied reality, relatively impermeable to the influences derived from the communicative dynamics in which it is "elicited." Such a concept of "collection" is not appropriate in the context of interactionist research, according to which the idea that data are generated in the interaction between the subjects participating in the research prevails; that is, more appropriately, it is co-constructed in that interaction (Charmaz 2014; Fontana and Prokos 2007).

Data Analysis and Construction of Theoretical Propositions

Data analysis means "systematizing" or, again, "orderly organizing" the information generated and "collected" in the fieldwork. There is no single "ordering principle" through which data would be organized, but there can be many. In grounded theory, for example, the empirical basis is "ordered," in codes that can be considered semantic "containers" to which bunches of text are assigned. The distinctive aspect of the "grounded" analysis is that every single "piece" of text can be "contained" in one or more "conceptual classes" (codes and categories) by the interpretative process conducted by the scholar. Therefore, the "ordering principle" is not based on the properties of the phenomenon being observed but concerns the process of meaning-making by the analyst, according to which the same property (a sentence pronounced by a respondent) can be "treated" by assigning to it different meanings. In this regard, Corbin and Strauss use the expression "conceptual ordering": this order refers to the organization of data within discrete categories, consistent with their properties and dimensions. Properties are "characteristics" or "qualities" of concepts that assign specificity and "differentiate" a concept (category) from others, while dimensions refer to the margins of oscillation within which a property can vary (Corbin and Strauss 2008:53, 46). The analysis must be seen, therefore, from a twofold point of view: on the one hand, as an ordered systematization of the data (for example, based on the period of collection, the characteristics of the interviewees, the content of the interviews), and on the other hand, as a process through which that order is continuously modified through the comparison between the collected data and the analyst's interpretation.

The analytical path gradually leads the scholar to make continuous steps from a level of "raw" analysis to one of more "refined" analysis where the difference lies in the character of analytical detail achieved. The more nuanced analyses are characterized by an increasing degree of abstraction and are constituted by the theoretical propositions related to the studied phenomenon. This set of theoretical propositions can be considered, to all effects, as a theory. According to Strauss and Corbin, a theory "denotes a set of well-developed categories (themes, concepts) that are systematically interrelated through statements of relationship to form a theoretical framework that explains some phenomenon" (Corbin and Strauss 2008:55). Interactionist research aims to construct a system of conceptual interconnections that constitute interpretations of phenomena observed at a higher level of abstraction than that of the collected data but closely related to them, adopting a mix of inductive, deductive, and abductive logic (Timmermans and Tavory 2012).

POST-BLUMERIAN INTERACTIONIST RESEARCH

The wider legitimization and diffusion of qualitative methods, especially among young researchers, has been favored since overcoming the conflict between epistemological frameworks in the 1980s. In the new century, favorable conditions have been created not only for mutual recognition of the richness that different methods can bring to an adequate knowledge of empirical reality, but also to develop forms of methodological combination, as shown by the development of mixed methods in the social sciences.

Post-Blumerian symbolic interactionism presents itself as a composite community of scholars, differentiated on the criterion of "adherence" to its fundamental premises (Maines 2001); scholars engage in an extreme multiplicity of fields, developing theoretical and methodological innovations that have been gradually combined with the more "classical" elaborations. Despite this vast multiplicity of methodological perspectives generated in the framework of symbolic interactionism, it is possible to observe a convergence of researchers' interests around three main areas: ethnography, grounded theory, and the postmodern approach. This trend does not reduce the importance of other methodological approaches, such as the use of life stories (Plummer 2000) or the dramaturgical approach (Smith 2013). However, this section will consider the three major methodological fields that have been assuming an essential role in the interactionist community, namely ethnography, grounded theory, and the postmodern approach. Our intention is not to reduce the richness of empirical experiences and the plurality of methods used by scholars in the field. However, these three are configured more than others as "theory-method packages" that coherently connect the interactionist epistemological premises with a consistent methodological structure.

Ethnography

Ethnography is a methodological approach that is entirely consistent with symbolic interactionism's epistemological framework (Rock, 2001). Indeed, it is a preferred choice for many scholars inspired by it. There is a pervasive and very significant literature that discusses the intimate connection between ethnographic research and symbolic interactionism (e.g., Prus 1996; Grills 1998; Atkinson et al. 2001; Lofland et al. 2005). Some of the earliest ethnographic researchers were affiliated with the Chicago School. They introduced innovative research strategies in social sciences, particularly the researcher's involvement in the direct observation of the social contexts being studied. The essential character of this method is that the researcher is completely immersed in the settings that constitute their research interest; in a certain sense, as we will see, this aspect constitutes both the strength and the weakness of the approach. The objective of ethnographic research is to draw in-depth overviews of "social worlds" endowed with their own cultural and social specificity. The investigation gives an accurate and in-depth description of the interactions, practices, and processes that occur in those contexts, caught in a diachronic temporal perspective. To achieve this goal, the researcher directly enters those worlds, choosing to share their daily life for prolonged periods and producing data through total involvement in observational contexts.

The ethnographic approach involves a remarkably consistent and involving fieldwork, based on participant observation, the continuous writing of notes, the elaboration of hypotheses, and their direct validation with the research participants. This allows the scholar to make precise descriptions of contexts and behaviors and proceed through cumulative interpretations of the observed situations, providing their possible modifications over time, as the scholar's awareness is refined and increased. Ethnographic research is, therefore, an endeavor that requires a twofold condition: on the one hand, a particular vocation for research in the field, accompanied by a high level of interest in knowing different existential spheres, and on the other, the ability to exercise self-reflexivity concerning methodological and procedural problems that the scholar must face in the field. For the researcher, the constant need to position themselves in the observed situations implies a constant exercise of hypothesis and problem-solving, aimed at a deeper understanding of the behaviors and meanings connected to them.

Ethnographic research design provides a very general definition of the aspects that will characterize the work in the field:

a) The researcher must define the object of investigation (and preliminary research questions). Here, the researcher will commit to identifying the "social world" that they want to explore—specifying its relational, cultural, and, eventually, structural/geographical boundaries. In a few words, ethnographic research is based on an in-depth "case study" investigated from a temporal perspective.

b) Getting close to the field involves the definition of two primary and strategic elements at the operational level. The first step is the creation of conditions that allow the researcher to "enter" the context in which they intend to carry out the research. This process often occurs through the support of "gatekeepers" as "mediators." The second step is the definition of "agreement" between the social-world members and the scholar, aimed at building conditions for collaboration between the research participants and making explicit the researcher's role and position in that context. In terms of data-collection methods, the researcher generally uses a plural approach that revolves around two essential strategies: participant observation and interviews (Adler and Adler 1994).

c) Data analysis is also conducted in a relatively open and plural way. The researcher will have to identify the most appropriate ways to systematize the empirical evidence. The analysis is aimed at the detailed description of the observed context, identifying interpretative hypotheses regarding the behaviors, interactions, meanings, and events that occur in the context. These hypotheses will guide the subsequent exploratory steps in the field. The analytical process does not follow preestablished procedural "standards" (unlike data coding in grounded theory). However, analysis will be oriented to identifying relevant themes and areas through the support of descriptive and interpretative grids.

d) The investigation's conclusion involves adopting a strategy of "detachment" from the field and elaborating a report based on a narrative account of the research experience.

Ethnography is a research method that has been attracting many interactionist scholars because of its congruence with the epistemological premises of the perspective and the characteristics that make this method unique in the qualitative landscape. At the same time, there are several challenges and problems that the scholar faces during the research process, the overcoming of which is essential to assign validity to the empirical findings.

Firstly, the method's openness and plurality do not imply that the researcher can "improvise" the methodological process. On the contrary, the method involves self-discipline, especially regarding the analytical data collection and systematization. The scholar's position about "membership" in the group and context is a controversial topic, frequently discussed in literature. The researcher brings to the field their personal and professional qualities, which are continuously interpreted and negotiated with the research participants. This "intense reputational dynamic" (Grills 1998) is one of the most involved aspects in the research process; the degree of "acceptance" of the researcher in the group ultimately influences the effectiveness of the investigation and the validity of the data collected. The familiarity the researcher builds over time with the members of the studied group implies the construction of obligations and the adoption of social and cultural practices that may conflict with the ethical and professional frameworks of the researcher and sometimes requires crucial choices that may be relevant to the continuation of the research itself. Another problematic aspect is related to how the researcher accounts for the experience to a broader audience through the research report. The scholar, adopting a narrative approach, moves from the experiential dimension of the field setting to the narrative reconstruction of that experience to enable the reader to understand the studied contexts precisely through that personal experience. In this framework, the scholar has to mediate between the research participants' accounts and a theoretical analysis that is based on those accounts, which involves linguistic and conceptual abstractions more consistent with academic language.

Ethnographic research is a demanding method because it implies the researcher's total involvement in the observed context. Consequently, it is a "selective approach" since not all researchers are in the most favorable conditions to appropriately adopt it. The need to live in the contexts studied for longer periods may conflict with researchers' professional and existential tasks, making it necessary to eventually formulate compromises that influence the process and the research results (Kleinmann, Stenross, and McMahon 1994).

Although the ethnographic investigation poses several methodological, procedural, and ethical questions to the researcher, it provides the ability to cope with the uncertainty and difficulties arising from exploring new and often challenging social and cultural assets. It constitutes a methodological perspective that, more than others, allows one to acquire in-depth knowledge about the contexts observed through getting close to those contexts via direct involvement of the scholar. The assessment of the investigation's quality is not based on the criterion of reliability, nor is it expected that the generalization of theoretical dimensions will go beyond the observed case studies. However, these limitations are offset by a consistent level of validity of the proposed accounts, especially if the researcher can analytically discuss and document the procedures they followed and the conclusions they reached.

Grounded Theory

At the end of the 1960s, grounded theory was "discovered" as a reaction to the excess of abstraction in theories built within predefined and preordained conceptual frameworks, considered "universally" valid and applicable (Glaser and Strauss 1967). The grounded theory perspective overturned the way of considering the role of concepts in sociological work and introduced the idea that theory should be an outcome rather than an antecedent of empirical work. Therefore, the theory must be essentially referred to the contexts in which the research was carried out. Through the constant comparison of "small amounts of data," grounded theory is an analytical process that proceeds toward the definition of increasingly high and refined conceptual levels, whose interconnection allows one to outline a theory related to the studied phenomena.

Grounded theory presents itself today as a plural proposal, articulated in "versions" according to the different accentuation assigned to some characteristics present in Glaser and Strauss's original formulation (Bryant 2019). In this regard, it is possible to identify three different GT formulations: the first two derive from the "divorce" between the two founders. Next to the "classical" perspective, which is advanced and still supported by Barney Glaser, the version of Anselm Strauss and Juliet Corbin is obviously worth mentioning. In the latter, the theoretical and empirical dimensions are combined in analytical and procedural schemes that present a high level of procedural formalization (Corbin and Strauss 1990; Corbin and Strauss 2008). The third perspective, constructivist grounded theory, is a product of the tireless work of Kathy Charmaz and represents a groundbreaking reference for many interactionist scholars and qualitative researchers. Through a significant number of empirical studies and theoretical systematizations, Charmaz has contributed to translating the methodological position of symbolic interactionism within grounded theory, formulating guidelines and analytical procedures consistent with the constructionist epistemological perspective (Charmaz 2014).

Grounded theory further developments come from the work of Adele Clarke, who promoted the so-called situational analysis (Clarke 2005; Clarke, Friese, and Washburn 2015), which is a revision of Anselm Strauss's methodological proposal through the lens of a postmodernist framework.

The iterative character of the investigation process and the constant comparison of data are two peculiar characteristics of grounded theory. The analyst moves "back and forth" between the data they collect and from the data to the concepts and interpretations they generate to understand processes, events, and situations related to the studied phenomena. There is, therefore, a movement between the "empirical basis" (the data) and the set of interpretations that are progressively elaborated in conceptual frameworks (Ralph, Birks, and Chapman 2015). As the analysis proceeds, the analyst plays a very relevant role. This movement is necessary because it guarantees that the process of interpretation and conceptualization is generated through continuous reference to data while, as Blumer says, "reality exists in the empirical world and not in the methods used to study that world" (Blumer 1969:27).

The main steps in grounded theory research can be described as follows:

a) The research design. Once the research questions have been defined, the scholar identifies a first set of "sensitizing" concepts as guidelines for collecting and analyzing data through which they will be further developed and specified (Van den Hoonaard 1996; Bowen 2006; Charmaz 2014). Considering every possible interpretation line concerning the data, the scholar identifies thematic areas to refer to and people who are believed to provide useful indications, information, and insights about those interpretation lines. The choice of the areas to study and the people to interview depends on the salient interpretative hypotheses that the researcher gradually constructed, that is, it depends on theoretical refinement rather than statistical representativeness (Mills, Bonner, and Francis 2006). This process is called *theoretical sampling*.

b) Fieldwork is guided by theoretical sampling and is essentially based on observation and, above all, on conducting interviews. The latter constitute the privileged, although not exclusive, way through which the grounded researcher builds their communicative relationship with the research participants. Unlike other methods of investigation, data collection and analysis, as we have seen, are closely related processes and depend on each other. In this way, it is possible to ensure a constant comparison of data at different research stages. The interview is a dynamic of interaction between subjects who, beyond the formal roles (who asks the questions and who answers them), can generate unexpected lines of communication. In the interview, the knowledge generated is an outcome of the interaction, and at the same time, it is itself a source for further investigation.

c) Data analysis, consequently, takes on a double aspect. On the one hand, it "reconstructs" how knowledge has been generated in the communication dynamics and highlights its "punctuation," or the paths that have been taken (and eventually interrupted) in the interaction. On the other hand, it detects and enhances that same generated knowledge, deepening its details, identifying the recurring reasons, and pointing out elements that are useful for further interpretative development. The coding of data allows us to proceed toward an analytical level in which that knowledge is developed, gradually assuming a more abstract character. Ultimately, the assignment of a code to empirical data (an interview piece, a detail of an image) involves making a communicative, hermeneutical leap toward greater abstraction in the interpretative process that is finalized in the categorization and theorization phase. In grounded theory's peculiar vocabulary, coding, categorization, and memoing assume an essential role throughout the entire investigation process (Charmaz and Belgrave 2019).

d) The analytical-interpretative work that is carried out by the scholar is accomplished through the identification of "patterns" in the meanings expressed by the subjects in interviews or observed in the empirical work. On the other hand, these patterns are synthesized in categories, understood as conceptual keys in which groups of codes that share similar references of meaning are semantically clustered. This analytical activity aims to identify interpretative lines consistent with the analyzed data and therefore to proceed toward the construction of a more abstract and complex theoretical framework related to the research object. Beyond the technical and procedural aspects, "theorizing" means identifying paths that link concepts (categories) on a semantic level and building a set of propositions that will constitute the "grounded" theory of the studied phenomenon— grounded just because these propositions emerge from a work of gradual conceptual abstraction, which, however, is always connected to data (Charmaz 2008; Bryant 2017).

If we exclude the "classical" formulation, still "proudly" promoted by Glaser and his followers, the three main versions of grounded theory (that of Strauss-Corbin, Charmaz, and Clarke) are developed within the interactionist framework, although with different accentuation. All draw from the same intellectual atmospheres that characterize the symbolic interactionist's vast theoretical horizon and, therefore, can be considered the result of a fruitful line of continuity between theoretical frames and methodological positions. Among these three formulations of grounded theory, dialogue and convergence have increased in recent times. In other words, they tend to "align" and converge depending on the relevance assigned to the main tenets of the constructionist's and interactionist's epistemology (see Salvini 2019).

Postmodernism in Social Research

Interactionist scholars who are inspired by postmodernist intellectual frames in their research activity bring to the extreme consequences Blumer's invitation to acquire an "intimate familiarity" with the concrete situations under study through the researcher's direct involvement in the empirical reality. "Postmodernist" scholars strive to make their activity in a personal way, focusing on themselves as researchers and at the same time as research participants (Fontana and Prokos 2007). This "personalization" of the research processes is based on the conviction that it is impossible to build an "objective knowledge" of reality, which, on the contrary, is the result of the narrative accounts of the subjects who interact in the research processes. One of the most innovative and controversial aspects of this "personalization" is auto-ethnography. The researcher "analyzes himself" through forms of self-reporting and personal accounts while experiencing events, situations, and interactions with other subjects. The works of Carolyn Ellis and Laurel Richardson, for example (Ellis and Bochner 2000; Ellis and Flaherty 1992; Richardson 2001), are emblematic examples of this way of doing research. A milder version of auto-ethnography is given by the "impressionistic" approach, in which the scholar "returns" his "impressions," ideas, and emotions derived from the interactions she builds during the research process through stories or short prose (Van Maanen 1988).

Postmodern researchers encourage the "polyphony" of voices, making it possible for all the different subjects encountered during the research to express themselves and to talk about themselves, without any mediation by the researcher. Some authors highlight the needs of a narrative ethnography, that is, "the ethnographic study of narrativity" (Gubrium and Holstein 2008:250). The narrative approach has gained more and more visibility in the interactionist community, due to the centrality of the communicative features on which the research process and its outcomes are built. Narratives go well beyond the researcher descriptions and reflections of the research experience, but "comprise the interplay between experience, storying practices, descriptive resources, purposes at hand, audiences, and the environments that condition storytelling," considering the "myriad of layers of social contexts" that influence the flows of narratives from the side of research participants (Gubrium and Holstein 2008:250, 251; see also Gubrium and Holstein 2014).

At the basis of those kinds of investigations, there is a sort of "naive" but also "committed" epistemology, to give voice directly to those who live situations that make it difficult for them to express and "have a voice," due to processes of exclusion, marginalization, and stigmatization. Doing research means, first of all, "taking a position" for the benefit of those who are excluded from the most consolidated channels of communication, in support of those who suffer the effects of unbalanced power relations. Evoking Foucault's reflection, some authors have tried to highlight how consolidated forms of communication have the function of reproducing power relations between people and groups, and therefore to "show" social reality according to ideologically and culturally preestablished images. A final "provocation" that comes from postmodernist environments concerns the consideration that the sociological language that is generally used by scholars in publications and conferences is so specialized and abstract that it is too "distant" from empirical reality and the circumstances in which the data were collected and "constructed." This language risks being incomprehensible to most people, thus making knowledge accessible only to experienced professionals. Interactionist scholars inspired by the postmodernist perspective have adopted ways of returning the results of their research activities in the form of theatrical performances, using different modes of communication (prose, poetry, and dance). Both researchers and people who participated in the research are engaged as "actors" who "represent" themselves to an audience (Denzin 2014). These practices are not alternatives to the usual forms of publication in the scientific community, but they underline the importance of using different communication modalities to reach a wider audience and to allow a more direct relationship between the research dimension and the "real life" of people. These choices question the way sociological knowledge is conceived, its "production" and its "impact" in society itself, and more generally the consolidated concept of "science" as well as its "standards" and its specific language. These "provocations" have raised, even within symbolic interactionism, a significant number of objections (Prus 1996; Maines 1996) based primarily on the idea that sociological knowledge cannot in any way "conflate" with the individuals' points of view. The postmodern approach is pursued by a small and vibrant community of scholars and constitutes a distinctive field in the methodology of social research; its merit is to keep the attention high on how knowledge is generated and on the "public" effects of the knowledge itself.

Conclusion

Symbolic interactionism is a perspective that has developed through a close connection between theory and empirical research. Consistent with their roots in philosophical pragmatism, interactionists have questioned how knowledge is generated according to the principles of "classical" science (Shalin 1991) and have proposed new ways of doing empirical research.

Interactionists base their investigations on the methodological assumption that the scholar's task—if they want to develop an in-depth knowledge of social reality—is to acquire an "intimate familiarity" with people and social processes. Social research constitutes a "symbolic interaction" itself: it is a continuous learning process and gradual penetration into the research participants' social worlds. The research aims to capture how people define everyday life situations in which they act and how they orient their conduct to that definition. In this way, interactionist researchers are involved in a constant activity of observation and interaction in "natural settings" privileging the "inner" point of view of people under study. The research tools and methods privilege the communicative dimension in its different forms, from text, images, and sounds. Therefore, data are "co-constructed" in the interaction between the scholar, the research participants, and the observational context.

The different way of considering the relationship between the "observer" and the "object" under study and the process through which the empirical data is "constructed" have given rise to a vast horizon of methodological proposals, which in turn have allowed the gradual legitimization of qualitative methods in the scientific community. The scrutiny of empirical research handbooks disseminated in academia shows how the ethnographic perspective, grounded theory, and narrative approach have acquired full dignity and citizenship within the methodological landscape, a circumstance that only thirty years ago would have been unimaginable. Interactionist empirical research has contributed to the achievement of this result, together with the increasing relevance assumed by other perspectives, such as phenomenology and ethnomethodology, and critical thinking developed in Europe through authors such as Habermas, Foucault, Bourdieu, Giddens, and Joas—just to mention some of the main interpreters of contemporary philosophy and sociology.

This outcome was made possible thanks to the ability of symbolic interactionism to take on the theoretical and methodological implications of the deep cultural and social changes that have crossed societies in late modernity. The three premises formulated by Blumer, Goffman's dramaturgical approach, and the theories that constitute the conceptual legacy of the perspective have constituted an essential guide for scholars in the study of social phenomena. Many interactionists have wondered whether this heritage is still able to adequately meet the challenges posed by the profound transformations that contemporary societies are undergoing. These are challenges that take on a global dimension, and which have continuous impacts on the local dimension. The growing complexity of phenomena, the social and health emergencies resulting from the crisis of environmental sustainability, the economic imbalances and the dynamics of political domination, the advent of social networks, and changes in forms of communication are some of the processes that generate profound shifts in the lives of people and communities. These transformations require, according to many authors, a renewed commitment of symbolic interactionism to mature its capacity of analysis and interpretation.

Some authors have stressed the need to broaden the analytical view of the interactionist perspective by introducing new conceptual categories and integrating the established premises and frames. In particular, David Snow (2001) and Gary Alan Fine (Fine and Tavory 2019) have proposed a more substantial theoretical investment for the analytical understanding of the interconnections between the contexts of action, the processes of formation and consolidation of social structures, and their effects on the dynamics of interaction. Others have advanced the need to study in depth the dynamics of power and domination that occur in the interactions between individual and collective social actors (Athens 2013). Still others have advocated the relevance of studies on new communication processes, particularly in social networks and new media.

These areas of exploration are challenges on which symbolic interactionism depends to legitimize itself as a significant and useful theoretical perspective in current social sciences, to avoid the "sad demise" predicted years ago by Gary Alan Fine in a well-known essay (Fine 1993). These challenges have direct and evident implications also in the methodological dimension—given the close connection, repeatedly evoked in this chapter, between theory and empirical research.

The proposals for theoretical integration, which have only been briefly mentioned here, imply the need to broaden the analytical view from the micro level—on which most of the empirical interactionist experiences have focused—to the meso, and perhaps even "macro," level. In other words, it means taking seriously into account the analytical and causal circularity that is established between the micro-meso and macro dimensions, without considering extraneous to the epistemological interactionist orthodoxy the hypothesis that there are processes at the macro level that causally influence the processes of interaction, through the role assumed by the dynamics that take place in the meso dimension, that is, in the dynamics of interconnection of situations, groups, and contexts.

The complexity of the interconnections between analytical levels intervenes concretely in the way we construct the design of research, we identify the "sensitizing concepts," we adopt tools for data collection and analysis, and, finally, we construct theories.

The methodology of interactionist research must be able to dialogue not only with the "closest" perspectives in theoretical and epistemological terms, but also with the apparently more distant ones. For example, the invitation to adopt a "relational" perspective in the study of interaction contexts (Fine and Tavory 2019) cannot occur without starting a comparison with the theoretical and methodological perspectives that have made relationality the center of interest, such as the sciences of complexity and network science. Although this dialogue is difficult and uncertain in its outcomes (Salvini 2010), it represents an inescapable challenge for symbolic interactionism.

The methodological maturity of the perspective should ensure the adoption of a pragmatically more open approach to the combination of methods and the participation of interactionist scholars in multidisciplinary research teams (Kotarba 2014), since the complexity of phenomena implies the integration of different analytical insights. The commitment of interactionist researchers within the vast methodological area of mixed methods still seems to be limited, and deserves to be encouraged.

A further methodological area that requires more development is the exploration of new media and online social networks. The studies of David Altheide (Altheide and Schneider 2013) and those of Gottschalk (2010, 2013) point to a growing interest in these areas. "Net-ethnography" can also be a particularly useful field of application for interactionist researchers on both the theoretical and methodological side.

Many other fields of methodological application could be added to the short list above, and other topics are waiting to be further specified. But it is clear that symbolic interactionism requires the maturity to meet the challenges posed by social transformation, to dialogue with other theoretical perspectives, and to apply creativity and innovation by imagining new ways of doing empirical research.

References

Adler, Peter, and Patricia Adler. 1994. "Observational Technique," Pp. 377–92 in *Handbook of Qualitative Research*, edited by Norman K. Denzin and Yvonna S. Lincoln. Thousand Oaks, CA: SAGE.

Altheide, David L., and Christopher J Schneider. 2013. *Qualitative Media Analysis*. Thousand Oaks, CA: SAGE.

Athens, Lonnie. 2013. "Radical and Symbolic Interactionism: Demarcating Their Borders." *Studies in Symbolic Interaction* 41:1–24

Atkinson, Paul, Amanda Coffey, Sara Delmont, John Lofland, and Lyn Lofland, eds. 2001. *Handbook of Ethnography*. London: SAGE.

Atkinson, Paul, and William Housley. 2003. *Interactionism: An Essay in Sociological Amnesia*. London: SAGE.

Becker, Howard S. 1988. "Herbert Blumer's Conceptual Impact." *Symbolic Interaction* 11:13–21.

Benzies, Karen M., and Marion N. Allen. 2001. "Symbolic Interactionism as a Theoretical Perspective for Multiple Method Research." *Journal of Advanced Nursing* 33(4):541–47.

Berg, Bruce L. 2007. *Qualitative Research Methods for the Social Sciences*, 6th ed. Boston: Pearson.

Best, Joel. 2006. "Blumer's Dilemma: The Critic as a Tragic Figure." *The American Sociologist* 37(3, fall):5–14

Blumer, Herbert. 1969. *Symbolic Interactionism: Perspective and Method*. Englewood Cliffs: Prentice Hall.

Blumer, Herbert. 1980. "Mead and Blumer: The Convergent Methodological Perspectives of Social Behaviorism and Symbolic Interactionism." *American Sociological Review* 45(3):409–19.

Bowen, Glenn A. 2006. "Grounded Theory and Sensitizing Concepts." *International Journal of Qualitative Methods* 5(3):12–23.

Bryant, Anthony. 2017. *Grounded Theory and Grounded Theorizing: Pragmatism in Research Practice*. Oxford: Oxford University Press.

Bryant, Anthony. 2019. *The Varieties of Grounded Theory*. London: SAGE.

Carter, Michael J., and Andrea Montes Alvarado. 2018. "Symbolic Interactionism as a Methodological Framework." Pp. 169–87 in *Handbook of Research Methods in Health Social Sciences*, edited by P. Liamputtong. Singapore: Springer.

Charmaz, Kathy. 2008. "Grounded Theory as an Emergent Method." Pp. 155–70, in *Handbook of Emergent Methods*, edited by Hesse-Biber, Sharlene Nagy, and Patricia Leavy. New York: The Guilford Press.

Charmaz, Kathy, and Linda L. Belgrave. 2019. "Thinking about Data with Grounded Theory." *Qualitative Inquiry* 25(8):743–53.

Charmaz, Kathy. 2014. *Constructing Grounded Theory*, 2nd ed. London: SAGE.

Clarke, Adele. 2005. *Situational Analysis: Grounded Theory After the Postmodern Turn*. Thousand Oaks, CA: SAGE.

Clarke, Adele E., Carrie Friese, and Rachel Washburn, eds. 2015. *Situational Analysis in Practice: Mapping Research with Grounded Theory*. London: Routledge.

Corbin, Juliet, and Anselm Strauss. 1990. "Grounded Theory Research: Procedures, Canons, and Evaluative Criteria." *Qualitative Sociology* 13(1):3–21.

Corbin, Juliet, and Anselm Strauss, 2008. *Basics of Qualitative Research: Grounded Theory Procedures and Techniques for Developing Grounded Theory*. Thousand Oaks, CA: SAGE.

Denzin, Norman K. 2014. "Writing and/as Analysis or Performing the World." Pp. 569–84 in *The SAGE Handbook of Qualitative Data Analysis*, edited by Uwe Flick. London: SAGE.

Denzin, Norman K. 2004. "Symbolic Interactionism." Pp. 81–87 in *A Companion to Qualitative Research*, edited by Uwe Flick, Ernst von Kardorff, and Ines Steinke. London: SAGE.

Ellis, Carolyn, and Art P. Bochner. 2000. "Autoethnography, Personal Narrative, and Reflexivity: Researcher as Subject." Pp. 733–68 in *Handbook of Qualitative Research*, edited by Norman K. Denzin and Yvonna S. Lincoln. Thousand Oaks: SAGE.

Ellis, Carolyn, and Michael Flaherty, eds. 1992. *Investigating Subjectivity: Research on Lived Experience*. Newbury Park: SAGE.

Engdhal, Emma, and Thaddeus Müller. 2015. "The European Contribution to Symbolic Interactionism." *Symbolic Interaction* 38(3):431–41.

Fine, Gary A. 1993. "The Sad Demise, Mysterious Disappearance, and Glorious Triumph of Symbolic Interactionism." *Annual Review of Sociology* 19:61–87.

Fine, Gary A., and Iddo Tavory. 2019. "Interactionism in the Twenty-First Century: A Letter on Being-in-a-Meaningful-World." *Symbolic Interaction* 42(3):457–67.

Flick, Uwe. 2014. "Mapping the Field." Pp. 3–18 in *The SAGE Handbook of Qualitative Data Analysis*, edited by Uwe Flick. London: SAGE.

Fontana, Andrea, and Anastasia H. Prokos. 2007. *The Interview: From Formal to Postmodern*. Walnut Creek: Left Coast Press.

Glaser, Barney, and Anselm Strauss. 1967. *The Discovery of Grounded Theory*. Chicago: Aldine.

Gottschalk, Simon. 2010. "The Presentation of Avatars in Second Life: Self and Interactions in Social Virtual Spaces." *Symbolic Interaction* 33(4):504–25.

Gottschalk, Simon, and Jennifer Whitmer. 2013. "Hypermodern Dramaturgy in Online Encounters." Pp. 309–34 in *The Drama of Social Life: A Dramaturgical Handbook*, edited by Charles Edgley. Farnham: Ashgate.

Grills, Scott. 1998. "An Invitation to the Field: Fieldwork and the Pragmatists' Lesson." Pp. 1–18 in *Doing Ethnographic Research: Fieldwork Settings*, edited by Scott Grills. Newbury Park: SAGE.

Grills, Scott, and Robert Prus. 2008. "The Myth of the Independent Variable: Reconceptualizing Class, Gender, Race, and Age as Subcultural Processes." *The American Sociologist* 39(1):19–37.

Gubrium, Jaber F., and James A. Holstein. 2014. "Analytic Inspiration in Ethnographic Fieldwork." Pp. 35–48 in *The SAGE Handbook of Qualitative Data Analysis*, edited by Uwe Flick. London: SAGE.

Gubrium, Jaber F., and James A. Holstein. 2008. "Narrative Ethnography." Pp. 241–264 in *Handbook of Emergent Methods*, edited by Sharlene Nagy, Hesse-Biber, and Patricia Leavy. New York: The Guilford Press.

Hammersley, Martin. 1989. *The Dilemma of Qualitative Method: Herbert Blumer and the Chicago Tradition*. London: Routledge.

Hanzel, Igor. 2011. "Beyond Blumer and Symbolic Interactionism: The Qualitative-Quantitative Issue in Social Theory and Methodology." *Philosophy of the Social Sciences* 41(3):303–26.

Herman-Kinney, Nancy, and Joseph M. Vershaeve. 2003. "Methods of Symbolic Interactionism." Pp. 213–252 in *Handbook of Symbolic Interactionism*, edited by Larry T. Reynolds and Nacy J. Herman-Kinney. Walnut Creek: AltaMira Press.

Kleinmann, Sherryl, Barbara Stenross, and Martha McMahon. 1994. "Privileging Fieldwork Over Interviews: Consequences for Identity and Practice." *Symbolic Interaction* 17(1):37–50.

Kotarba, Joseph A. 2014. "Symbolic Interaction and Applied Social Research: A Focus on Translational Science." *Symbolic Interaction* 37(3):412–25.

Lincoln, Yvonna S. and Egon G. Guba. 2013. *The Constructivist Credo*. Walnut Creek: Left Coast Press.

Lofland, John, David Snow, Leon Anderson, and Lyn Lofland. 2005. *Analyzing Social Settings: A Guide to Qualitative Observation and Analysis*. Belmont: Wadsworth Publishing.

Maines, David R. 1996. "On Postmodernism, Pragmatism, and Plasterers: Some Interactionist Thoughts and Queries." *Symbolic Interaction* 19(4):323–40.

Maines, David R. 2001. *The Faultline of Consciousness: A View of Interactionism in Sociology*. New York: Aldyne de Gruyter.

McPhail, Clark, and Cynthia Rexroat. 1979. "Mead vs. Blumer: The Divergent Methodological Perspectives of Social Behaviorism and Symbolic Interactionism." *American Sociological Review* 44:449–67.

Mills, Jane, Ann Bonner, and Karen Francis. 2006. "Adopting a Constructivist Approach to Grounded Theory: Implications for Research Design." *International Journal of Nursing Practice* 12:8–13.

Morrissette, Joëlle, Sylvie Guignon, and Didier Demazière. 2011. "De l'usage des perspectives interactionnistes en recherche." *Recherches Qualitatives* 30(1):1–9.

Oliver, Carolyn. 2012. "The Relationship Between Symbolic Interactionism and Interpretive Description" *Qualitative Health Research* 22(3):409–15.

Plummer, Ken. 2000. *Documents of Life 2: An Invitation to a Critical Humanism*. London: SAGE.

Prus, Robert. 1996. *Symbolic Interaction and Ethnographic Research*. Albany: University of New York Press.

Puddephatt, Antony J., and Robert Prus. 2007. "Causality, Agency, and Reality: Plato and Aristotle Meet George Herbert Mead and Herbert Blumer." *Sociological Focus* 40(3):265–86.

Ralph, Nicholas, Melanie Birks, and Ysanne Chapman. 2015. "The Methodological Dynamism of Grounded Theory." *International Journal of Qualitative Methods* (November):1–6.

Reynolds, Larry T., and Bernard N. Metzer. 1973. "The Origins of Divergent Methodological Stances in Symbolic Interactionism." *Sociological Quarterly* 14(2):189–99.

Richardson, Laurel. 2001. "Poetic Representation of Interviews." Pp. 877–92 in *Handbook of Interview Research*, edited by Jaber F. Gubrium and James A. Holstein. Thousand Oaks, CA: SAGE.

Rock, Paul. 2001. "Symbolic Interactionism and Ethnography." Pp. 26–38 in *Handbook of Ethnography*, edited by Paul Atkinson, Amanda Coffey, Sara Delamont, John Lofland, and Lyn Lofland. London: SAGE.

Salvini, Andrea. 2010. "Symbolic Interactionism and Social Network Analysis: An Uncertain Encounter." *Symbolic Interaction* 33(3):364–88.

Salvini, Andrea. 2019. "The Methodological Convergencies between Symbolic Interactionism and Constructivist Grounded Theory." *Przegląd Socjologii Jakościowej* 15(3):10–29.

Schwalbe, Michael. 2019. "The Spirit of Blumer's Method as a Guide to Sociological Discovery." *Symbolic Interaction* 43(4):597–614.

Shalin, Dmitri N. 1991. "The Pragmatic Origins of Symbolic Interactionism and the Crisis of Classical Science." *Studies in Symbolic Interaction* 12:223–251.

Smith, Greg. 2013. "The Dramaturgical Legacy of Erving Goffman." Pp. 57–72 in *The Drama of Social Life: A Dramaturgical Handbook*, edited by Charles Edgley. Farnham: Ashgate.

Snow, David. 2001. "Extending and Broadening Blumer's Conceptualization of Symbolic Interactionism." *Symbolic Interaction* 24(3):367–77.

Timmermans, Stefan, and Iddo Tavory. 2012. "Theory Construction in Qualitative Research: From Grounded Theory to Abductive Analysis." *Sociological Theory* 30(3):167–86.

Ulmer, Jeffrey T., and Mindy S. Wilson. 2003. "The Potential Contributions of Quantitative Research to Symbolic Interactionism." *Symbolic Interaction* 23(4):531–52.

Van den Hoonaard, Will C. 1996. *Working with Sensitizing Concepts: Analytical Field Research.* Thousand Oaks, CA: SAGE.

Van Maanen, John. 1988. *Tales of the Field: On Writing Ethnography.* Chicago: University of Chicago Press.

Weller, Jack. 2000. "Tests of Concepts in Herbert Blumer's Method." *Social Thought & Research* 23(1/2):65–86.

CHAPTER 4

TOWARD A CONCEPT-DRIVEN SOCIOLOGY

Sensitizing Concepts and the Prepared Mind

EVIATAR ZERUBAVEL

SOCIOLOGISTS often exaggerate the conventional distinction between "theory" and "methodology," as is so pronouncedly embodied in the artificial curricular split between "theory" and "research methods" courses in many sociology programs. Following in the footsteps of Emile Durkheim, who masterfully integrates the two in *The Rules of Sociological Method* (Durkheim 1895/1982), I nevertheless consider it a false distinction (Zerubavel 1980:32), using the composite term *theoretico-methodological* to convey the actual inseparability of "theory" and "methodology" from each other.

There are two effectively antithetical ideal-typical ways of conducting sociological research. On the one hand, there is a *data-driven* style of scholarship in which projects begin with the researcher identifying a particular body of data associated with a particular social group (family, movement, organization), setting (school, factory, neighborhood), or event (political demonstration, economic crisis, natural disaster). On the other hand, there is a *theory-driven* style of scholarship, in which projects begin with the researcher's particular theoretical concerns. As the founder of symbolic interactionism, Herbert Blumer, wrote in a paper explicitly titled "The Methodological Position of Symbolic Interactionism,"

> [t]he possession and use of a prior picture or scheme of the empirical world under study . . . is an unavoidable prerequisite for any study of the empirical world. *One can see the empirical world only through some scheme or image of it.* The entire act of scientific study is oriented and shaped by the underlying picture of the empirical world that is used. This picture sets the selection and formulation of problems, the determination of what are data, the means to be used in getting data, the kinds of relations sought between data, and the forms in which propositions are cast.
>
> (Blumer 1969:24–25, emphasis added)

The distinction between those two ideal-typical approaches to research is often articulated in terms of the difference between inductive ("bottom-up") and deductive ("top-down") modes of reasoning that, in their extreme form, respectively promote strictly empiricist projects and "pure" theory. The very notion of those two ideal-typical modes of reasoning underscores the two effectively antithetical kinds of theoretico-methodological "pull" that those two styles of conducting research present to scholars, a far more significant "pull" than the one conventionally presented by so-called quantitative and qualitative epistemologies.

Although I have never been attracted to data-driven, fact-gathering scholarship (Zerubavel 1979:xv), nor have I ever accepted the premise that it necessarily follows that I should therefore be testing existing theories. Defying such a supposedly binary choice between inductive empiricism and deductive positivism, I have thus come to identify a third style of social inquiry that is *theoretically—yet not necessarily "Theory—driven.* And I have come to characterize such an approach to scholarship, one that I have been using for the past forty-five years in both my research and teaching, as *concept driven* (see also Zerubavel 1980:28–29).

Concept-driven research defies the seemingly binary choice conventionally made between the acts of "describing" (as in inductive empiricism) and "explaining" (as in deductive positivism), instead highlighting the acts of *identifying patterns* and *analyzing*, which are neither descriptive nor explanatory but, rather, *analytical*. When conducting such research, one's goal is indeed identifying and analyzing socially patterned phenomena in an effort to reveal their fundamental features. I therefore call such an intellectual endeavor *social pattern analysis* (Zerubavel 2007).

SENSITIZING CONCEPTS

As one might expect, in concept-driven scholarship, *concepts* constitute the metaphorical "lenses" through which researchers access the empirical world, their role defined primarily in terms of *attentional sensitization*. Effectively "sensitizing" researchers' attention (Zerubavel 1980:31), they thus help give them a general sense of what they might find relevant to attend to by suggesting "where" to look. *Sensitizing concepts*, as Blumer so aptly dubbed them, thus provide researchers with "a general sense of reference and guidance in approaching empirical instances . . . . [They] suggest directions along which to look . . . . [T]hey rest on a general sense of what is relevant" (Blumer 1954:7; see also Blumer 1931:518, 526–28; Van den Hoonaard 1996). Like magnets attached to their minds, they figuratively "attract" empirical data to their awareness, thereby helping them collect many they would have probably overlooked otherwise.

Over the years I have indeed managed to study many phenomena that had traditionally been relatively neglected in sociology (distinctions, social rhythms, conspiracies of silence, default assumptions, historical narratives, visions of genealogical "relatedness"), such academic "invisibility" being only a function of traditional conventions of sociological relevance. As Marcel Proust put it quite bluntly, "[t]he only true voyage of discovery" may very well be "not to visit strange lands but to possess other eyes" (Proust 1923/2006:657)! Indeed, like eating the fruits of the proverbial tree of knowledge for Adam and Eve, it is the figurative *eye-opening* (Zerubavel 2015:84) function of the sensitizing concepts I use that has allowed me to access those otherwise academically invisible fruits. "[A] new perspective opens up, *allowing things formerly not perceived to come into view* (Meyer et al. 2010:ix, emphasis added).

Such *conceptual magnets* were very helpful, for example, when I was writing *The Fine Line* (Zerubavel 1991/1993), to which for many years I was referring in my mind as "my boundaries book." By using the concept "boundary," I thus developed a heightened sensitivity to the numerous mental distinctions we make. Having essentially primed myself to notice any form of boundary, from the time I started thinking about writing the book and the time I completed it ten years later, I in fact generated hundreds of distinctions-related observations. And the meager number of such observations I have generated in comparison since then—a thirty-year period during which my "boundary" magnet has effectively been deactivated—only further attests to the formidable role of attentional sensitization in concept-driven research.

FOCUS

Although every researcher faces the fundamental epistemic dilemma regarding what s/he should attend to and what s/he can effectively ignore, concept-driven sociologists are exceptionally conscious of the *selective* manner in which they attend to social reality, essentially directing their attention to only a few selected aspects of the groups, situations, or events they study (Simmel 1917/1950:11; Zerubavel 1979:xvi), which also implies an equally conscious effort to purposely "disattend" (Zerubavel 2015:60) others. That is made possible, of course, by the mental act of *focusing* (Zerubavel 2015:2). After all, even in the "hard" sciences, "[t]he operations and measurements that a scientist undertakes in the laboratory . . . are not what the scientist sees—at least *not before . . . his attention [is] focused*" (Kuhn 1962/1970:126, emphasis added; see also Fleck 1935/1979). The conscious effort to approach the groups, situations, or events one studies selectively is therefore a necessary precondition for staying "focused."

Given concept-driven sociologists' fundamentally theoretical orientation, the focus of their attention, of course, is pronouncedly *thematic* (see also DeGloma and Papadantonakis 2020). After all, even if their study happens to be situated *in* a specific setting, it is not necessarily a study *of* that setting. Although my doctoral dissertation study, for example, "took place *in* a hospital, it was never intended as a study *of* the hospital, since its . . . focus was clearly the temporal structure of social organization rather than hospital life" (Zerubavel 1979:xvii; see also Zerubavel 1981/1985:x–xi):

> I knew before I entered the hospital that my intention would not be to produce an exhaustive ethnography of hospital life, but, rather, to isolate its temporal aspects only,

in order to study the temporal structure of social organization. If I presumed to in-
novate in any way, it was certainly not in my selection of the setting to be observed,
but, rather, in my choice of the *analytical perspective* from which to observe it . . . .
I [thus] focused my observations on only one aspect of hospital life, namely, its temporal structure, deliberately ignoring . . . the history of the hospital, its national reputation, the quality of its patient care, its architectural design and spatial organization,
its finances, the religious and ethnic makeup of its staff, and so on. I was interested in
learning about the social organization of the hospital and the social interaction within
it only insofar as it contributed to further my understanding of its temporal structure.

> (Zerubavel 1979:xvi–xvii, emphasis added)

Concept-driven sociology, in short, implies a *thematically focused* kind of inquiry. It is
particular theoretical "themes," therefore, that guide researchers' attention as they look
for "theoretically relevant" (Glaser and Strauss 1971:183) data.

Although effectively promoting a theoretically driven kind of inquiry, however,
I am by no means advocating here the notion of "pure" theory, devoid of any empirical
"meat." But in sharp contrast to grounded theory, for example, which initially proceeds
from the empirical to the theoretical, concept-driven research initially proceeds from
the theoretical to the empirical. Unlike grounded-theory practitioners, concept-driven
sociologists establish their theoretical concerns (but not conclusions) *before* they even
start collecting their data. It is their pronouncedly thematic focus, in other words, that
drives the empirical part of their research.

In short, concept-driven researchers start collecting their data *only after having committed themselves to a particular thematic focus* (Zerubavel 1979:xvi; 1980:30–31) in the
form of a concept-related *topic*. After all, they "are in the business of *studying sociological
topics, not people* . . . . Their job is to make a set of integrated observations on a given topic
and place them in an analytical framework" (Schwartz and Jacobs 1979:289, emphasis
added). As such, they study whiteness rather than whites, liberalism rather than liberals,
poverty rather than the poor. Establishing such *focal commitment* thus constitutes the
very first step in their inquiry.

Choosing that topic is the most critically consequential part of a concept-driven
research project, as it provides researchers a general sense of attentional "direction"
(Zerubavel 1979:xvi), thereby helping them notice patterns that might have never
emerged as the result of mere perception (Zerubavel 1980:31). I could not have collected the data I later used in *The Fine Line, The Elephant in the Room, Taken for Granted,
Time Maps*, and *Ancestors and Relatives*, for example, had I not first committed myself
to focusing my attention "thematically" on distinctions, conspiracies of silence, default
assumptions, historical narratives, and visions of genealogical "relatedness."

THE PREPARED MIND

John Locke notwithstanding, the researcher's mind is not a tabula rasa, and even what
might seem like a chance observation can in fact "enter" it only if s/he is actually mentally

prepared for it (Kantorovich 1993:113; see also Fleck 1935/1979:92, 99). As Louis Pasteur famously put it, "[i]n the fields of observation chance favors only the mind which is prepared" (Pearce 1912:941). It is their *epistemic readiness*, in other words, "the mind prepared to utilize scientific imagination," that actually allows researchers to "grasp the opportunity offered by 'chance' observation" (Pearce 1912:944).

Consider, for example, the discovery of the asteroids in the early nineteenth century. Strictly perceptually, after all, given the state of eighteenth-century telescopy, they could have definitely been spotted much earlier. Yet it was the surprise discovery of Uranus in the 1780s, the first "new" planet to be discovered in several millennia, that epistemically prepared an entire generation of astronomers to the very possibility of spotting additional ones (Kuhn 1962/1970:116). Only their new attentional sensitivity, indeed, can account for the rather rapid discovery of some of the largest asteroids by three different astronomers between 1801 and 1807 (Zerubavel 1997:45–46).

By the same token, although it was the socially naive question "Daddy, what's Thursday?" posed to me by my then-three-year-old daughter that was the actual spark that inspired me to write *The Seven-Day Circle* (Zerubavel 1985/1989:1), I might not have even noticed it had I not been epistemically prepared prior to that, having read *The Social Construction of Reality* (Berger and Luckmann 1966), not to take culturally reified social conventions for granted (Zerubavel 1985/1989:138–41; Zerubavel 2016). By the same token, although it was watching a double-bassist play the typically inattended bass lines of a Bach Brandenburg Concerto that sparked my decision to write *Hidden in Plain Sight* (Zerubavel 2015:ix–x), I might not have paid any special attention to them had I not been epistemically prepared for almost thirty years prior to that, having read Harold Garfinkel's (1967) *Studies in Ethnomethodology*, to think sociologically about "the background" we typically take for granted and thereby inattend (Zerubavel 1981/1985:19–30).

As one examines the actual process by which a mentally "unprepared" mind is transformed into an epistemically "ready" one, it becomes quite clear that in the initial stages of the project, the researcher's focus of attention is often still defined in terms of vaguely formulated, "hazy" mental constructs respectively characterized by Ludwik Fleck (1935/1979:23–27) and Robert Merton (1984:267) as mere *proto-ideas* or *proto-concepts*. Far from being fully formed, such "pre-ideas" (Fleck 1935/1979:23–27) are effectively inarticulable, yet even at that early stage of the study they already guide researchers' attention in terms of "where" to look for empirical manifestations of the social patterns they conceptually identify.

As the project proceeds, however, through a process of conceptual "incubation," such early pre-ideas gradually become mentally crisper, as the initial sensitizing proto-concepts become increasingly sharper and thus more explicitly articulable. Such *epistemic "fine tuning"* occurs, for example, as the researcher keeps reading (preferably widely rather than confining oneself to a prefabricated, almost formulaically lumped cluster of texts conventionally canonized as "the literature") and thinking as well as begins writing. And it also occurs, of course, as s/he begins to collect data. Although in concept-driven research the process of theorizing begins before researchers start to collect their data, by no means does it stop there.

Thus, for example, when I was collecting the data for *Patterns of Time in Hospital Life*, it was my early theoretical interest in the still only vaguely defined "social organization of time" (Zerubavel 1976) that nevertheless tacitly guided my decision what to consider relevant to my study and therefore attend to, thereby sensitizing me to many time-related social patterns I would have most likely missed without it. Thus, for example, it was my initially vague proto-concept "temporal coordination" that helped sensitize me to the way doctors and nurses organized their lunch breaks, vacations, and days off (Zerubavel 1979:61–62, 72–73), and my equally vague early theoretical interest in the moral aspect of punctuality that helped me notice the way they responded to latecomers (Zerubavel 1979:27–28, 56, 130). I would have most likely also failed to note in which kinds of situations they referred to their watches and in which ones to the hospital wall clocks, had I not already been theoretically sensitized to the different functions of timepieces (Zerubavel 1979:95–96, 108–09).

By the same token, it was my early theoretical interest in continuity that sensitized me to various institutional efforts to ensure the continuous coverage of hospitalized patients such as doctors' morning rounds and nurses' change-of-shift reports (Zerubavel 1979:27, 54–55), and my still-vague interest in the temporal delineation of professional responsibility that likewise sensitized me to otherwise-trivial events such as calling an off-duty nurse at home (Zerubavel 1979:53). And I would have probably never paid attention to doctors' and nurses' actual time-measurement and time-reckoning vocabularies (and thereby also to disputes between nurses and patients over whether "There are still three persons ahead of you" is a proper answer to the question "When will the doctor see me?" [Zerubavel 1979:90–91]), had I not already been proto-conceptually sensitized to what I only later came to explicitly refer to as "temporal reference frameworks" (Zerubavel 1979:88–94).

Equally revealing, in this regard, was my heightened attentional sensitivity to doctors' and nurses' response to situations that deviated from the hospital's typically regular and therefore socially expected temporal order. Consider, for example, the case of an in-patient unit whose attending physician would routinely arrive at 10:00 for his daily conference with his medical team following their routine morning round, which was usually completed by 9:30. One morning the round was still not over a few minutes past 10:00, when the resident and intern suddenly saw the attending arriving at the unit. Both of them immediately glanced at their watches, evidently trying to "make sense" of the cognitively incongruous coincidence of their morning round and the attending's arrival, two events that were normally segregated in time (Zerubavel 1981/1985:25). I would have probably never even noticed, much less paid special attention to, such an otherwise trivial incident had I not already been sensitized to the initially vague proto-conceptual notion of "temporal regularity" (Zerubavel 1981/1985:12–30).

The same epistemic dynamic seems to operate even when the data one collects are only quasi-experimentally "observable." Thus, for example, when writing *The Elephant in the Room* (Zerubavel 2006), I found the concept "open secret" particularly helpful in heightening my attentional sensitivity to (thereby allowing me to almost "hear") virtually inaudible conspiracies of silence. I likewise found "the background" an extremely useful sensitizing concept when exploring in *Hidden in Plain Sight* (Zerubavel 2015) what we habitually disregard as irrelevant. That was also true of the concepts "historical continuity" and "historical discontinuity" when I was analyzing in *Time Maps* the social construction of historical narratives (Zerubavel 2003:37–54, 82–100), as well as of the "bloodline," "roots," and "side branch" metaphors when analyzing visions of genealogical "relatedness" in *Ancestors and Relatives* (Zerubavel 2011:20, 55–56, 66, 80, 83–84, 86, 95–97, 103, 120, 126–30).

In fact, such an epistemic dynamic operates even when what one collects is the conspicuous *absence* of certain data! Thus, for example, when I was writing *Taken for Granted*, using the concept "unmarked" helped sensitize me to our otherwise elusive conventional notions of ordinariness and normality, which we habitually take for granted and thereby assume by default. That explains my heightened attentional sensitivity to our tacit *non*-use of culturally redundant and therefore semiotically superfluous terms such as *working dad*, *female nurse*, and *openly straight*, in sharp contrast to our common use of their pronouncedly "marked" counterparts *working mom*, *male nurse*, and *openly gay* (Zerubavel 2018:1, 4–6, 9, 15, 19). It also explains my heightened sensitivity to the added qualifiers in "*marital* rape," "*reverse* discrimination," and "*white-collar* crime" (Zerubavel 2018:96, 28), as well as to the way we conventionally distinguish "alternative" medical practices from those we consider simply "medicine" (Zerubavel 2018:59).

Furthermore, sensitizing concepts are in fact very helpful even in strictly conceptual projects that involve no actual data. Thus, for example, when trying in *Social Mindscapes* to call attention to the suprapersonal dimension of the way we think in an effort to lay the foundations for a sociology of thinking (Zerubavel 1997), it was Durkheim's notion of the "impersonal" aspect of human cognition (Durkheim 1914/1973) and Fleck's notion of "thought communities" (Fleck 1935/1979:45, 103) that sensitized me to our indisputably social norms and traditions of perceiving, attending, classifying, and remembering (see also Zerubavel 2019). At the same time, however, it was Pitirim Sorokin's (1943) notion of the "sociocultural" sensibility separating the social from the natural sciences that heightened my attentional sensitivity to cognitive conventions that, while definitely suprapersonal, are nevertheless by no means universal (see, for example, Zerubavel 1997:9–10, 54–55, 73–79, 105–08). Those three sensitizing concepts, along with Alfred Schutz's notion of "intersubjectivity" (Berger and Luckmann 1966; Schutz and Luckmann 1973), thus played a critical role in my coming to appreciate the way we think not only as individuals and as human beings but also as social beings.

ATTENTIONAL SOCIALIZATION

Needless to say, the concept-driven manner of collecting data is very different from the way sociologists are conventionally trained in social-research-methods courses to approach their objects of study. And while it definitely requires considerable rigor, it is *focal rigor*, effectively requiring researchers to commit themselves to a particular conceptual focus (rather than a particular statistical sampling procedure, as in survey research, or "field," as in ethnographic research) and thereby stay thematically *focused*.

In cultivating a *focused mind*, so to speak, concept-driven sociologists very much resemble birders, mushroomers, pearl divers, deminers, and security baggage screeners. After all, as part of their professional socialization, they all cultivate the mental skill of *spotting* figure-like "targets" by differentiating them from their background-like surroundings in which they are embedded (Zerubavel 2015:24–27). Only by undergoing a process of professional *attentional socialization* (Zerubavel 2015:63–69) and thereby acquiring a "sociological imagination," indeed, do sociologists come to develop the distinctly sociological attentional sensitivities that allow them to envision social movements, labor markets, power structures, and influence networks. And as I have demonstrated elsewhere (Zerubavel 1997:49–50), such socialization also takes place at the level of particular "schools" or "paradigms" within sociology.

In fact, in the graduate courses I teach, I include in my syllabi every week not only a list of the actual readings for that particular class but also a list of major concepts I want the students to specifically attend to in those readings, not unlike the way students in special "appreciation" courses are instructed by expert *attentional mentors* (Zerubavel 2015:64) what they should specifically attend to when looking at a painting, listening to a piece of music, watching a film, or tasting a glass of wine. Thus, for example, for one of the "Classical Theory" classes where we discuss the work of Georg Simmel, the list of readings for that week is preceded by the following list of concepts: "social interaction, forms of sociation, social circles and social networks, multiple affiliations, divided and undivided commitment, social mobility, and social marginality." By the same token, for my "Cognitive Sociology" class on the social organization of attention, the list of readings for that week is preceded by the following list of concepts: "the social organization of relevance and noteworthiness, attentional communities, attentional traditions, norms of attending and disattending, attentional socialization, attentional deviance, attentional battles, joint attention, joint disattention, co-denial, conspiracies of silence, agenda-setting, and foregrounding." No wonder, indeed, that many of my students have in fact chosen to launch concept-driven doctoral dissertations revolving around concepts such as intercultural interpretation (Collins 1985), intellectual snobbery (Brodsky 1987), the social construction of kinship (Gricar 1991), beauty as a vocation (Wolfe 1994), integrated and segmented identities (Nippert-Eng 1996), the politics of ambiguity (Foster 2000), the social construction of parity (Purcell 2001), liminality (Isaacson 2001; Saeki 2017), sociomental "connectedness" (Chayko 2002), marked and unmarked identities (Brekhus 2003), cognitive design (Watson 2005), sociocognitive myopia and hyperopia (Simpson 2006), abstinence-based identities (Mullaney 2006), the temporal management of identity careers (Howard 2008), hyphenated identities (Germana 2012), "sexpectations" (Friedman 2013), cognitive "awakenings" (DeGloma 2014), mnemonic engineering (Yeh 2018), backhanded compliments (Malyk 2014), temporary selfhood (Stein 2019), "doing" identity (Campion 2019), and including and excluding (Peña-Alves 2021).

As exemplified by the above list, concept-driven sociology presupposes certain cognitive skills that anyone, I believe, can cultivate. In fact, it involves several such skills—namely *focusing, generalizing, "exampling,"* and *analogizing*—that have been tacitly utilized by various sociologists yet never explicitly analyzed from a strictly methodological standpoint.

In other words, although never comprehensively articulated yet (for some partial attempts, though, see Zerubavel 1980; Zerubavel 2007), concept-driven sociology nevertheless presupposes an implicit methodology that, if it can only be made explicit, can in fact also be taught to others. Making the mental processes underlying concept-driven scholarship more explicit is indeed the very reason why I wrote my most recent book, *Generally Speaking: An Invitation to Concept-Driven Sociology* (Zerubavel 2021).

REFERENCES

Berger, Peter L. and Thomas Luckmann. 1966. *The Social Construction of Reality: A Treatise in the Sociology of Knowledge*. Garden City, NY: Doubleday.

Blumer, Herbert. "Science without Concepts." 1931. *American Journal of Sociology* 36:513–33.

Blumer, Herbert. 1954. "What Is Wrong with Social Theory?" *American Sociological Review* 19:3–10.

Blumer, Herbert. 1969. *Symbolic Interactionism: Perspective and Method*. Englewood Cliffs, NJ: Prentice Hall.

Brekhus, Wayne H. 2003. *Peacocks, Chameleons, Centaurs: Gay Suburbia and the Grammar of Social Identity*. Chicago: University of Chicago Press, 2003.

Brodsky, Jodi E. 1987. "Intellectual Snobbery: A Socio-Historical Perspective." PhD dissertation, Columbia University.

Campion, Lisa. 2019. "Doing Identity: A Social Pattern Analysis Exploring the Process of Identity Construction and Maintenance." PhD dissertation, Rutgers University.

Chayko, Mary. 2002. *Connecting: How We Form Social Bonds and Communities in the Internet Age*. Albany, NY: State University of New York Press.

Collins, Lynn E. 1985. "Intercultural Interpretation of Experience: A Phenomenological Approach." PhD dissertation, Columbia University.

DeGloma, Thomas. 2014. *Seeing the Light: The Social Logic of Personal Discovery*. Chicago: University of Chicago Press.

DeGloma, Thomas and Max Papadantonakis. 2020. "The Thematic Lens: A Formal and Cultural Framework for Comparative Ethnographic Analysis." Pp. 84–106 in *Beyond the Case: Competing Logics and Approaches to Comparative Ethnography*, edited by Corey M. Abramson and Neil Gong. New York: Oxford University Press.

Durkheim, Emile. 1895/1982. *The Rules of Sociological Method*. New York: Free Press.

Durkheim, Emile. 1914/1973. "The Dualism of Human Nature and Its Social Conditions." Pp. 149–63 in *Emile Durkheim: On Morality and Society*, edited by Robert N. Bellah. Chicago: University of Chicago Press.

Fleck, Ludwik. 1935/1979. *Genesis and Development of a Scientific Fact*. Chicago: University of Chicago Press.

Foster, Johanna. 2000. "Feminist Theory and the Politics of Ambiguity: A Comparative Analysis of the Multiracial Movement, the Intersex Movement and the Disability Rights

Movement as Contemporary Struggles Over Social Classification in the United States." PhD dissertation, Rutgers University.

Friedman, Asia. 2013. *Blind to Sameness: Sexpectations and the Social Construction of Male and Female Bodies*. Chicago: University of Chicago Press.

Garfinkel, Harold. 1967. *Studies in Ethnomethodology*. Englewood Cliffs, NJ: Prentice Hall.

Germana, Rachelle. 2012. "Hyphenation and Its Discontents: Hyphenators, Hyphen-Haters, and the Cultural Politics of Ambiguity." PhD dissertation, Rutgers University.

Glaser, Barney G. and Anselm L. Strauss. 1971. *Status Passage: A Formal Theory*. Chicago: Aldine and Atherton.

Gricar, Julie M. 1991. "How Thick Is Blood?: The Social Construction and Cultural Configuration of Kinship." PhD dissertation, Columbia University, 1991.

Howard, Jenna. 2008. "Recovering from Recovery: The Temporal Management of Disorder Identity Careers." PhD dissertation, Rutgers University.

Isaacson, Nicole. 2001. "'The Unfinished Infant': An Analysis of the Cultural Representations and Practices to Finish The Premature Baby." PhD dissertation, Rutgers University.

Kantorovich, Aharon. 1993. *Scientific Discovery: Logic and Tinkering*. Albany: State University of New York Press.

Kuhn, Thomas S. 1962/1970. *The Structure of Scientific Revolutions*, 2nd ed. Chicago: University of Chicago Press.

Malyk, Maria V. 2014. "Sincere Backhanded Compliments: Exploring Social, Semiotic, and Cognitive Dimensions of Cryptosemic Interaction." PhD dissertation, Rutgers University.

Merton, Robert K. 1984. "Socially Expected Durations: A Case Study of Concept Formation in Sociology." Pp. 262–83 in *Conflict and Consensus: A Festschrift in Honor of Lewis A. Coser*, edited by Walter Powell and Richard Robbins. New York: Free Press.

Meyer, Jan H. F. et al., eds. 2010. *Threshold Concepts and Transformational Learning*. Rotterdam, The Netherlands: Sense Publishers.

Mullaney, Jamie L. 2006. *Everyone Is NOT Doing It: Abstinence and Personal Identity*. Chicago: University of Chicago Press.

Nippert-Eng, Christena. 1996. *Home and Work: Negotiating Boundaries through Everyday Life*. Chicago: University of Chicago Press.

Pearce, Richard M. 1912. "Chance and the Prepared Mind." *Science* New Series 35.912 (June 21):941–56.

Peña-Alves, Stephanie. 2021. "Inclusion, Exclusion, and the Formal Politics of Access." PhD dissertation, Rutgers University.

Proust, Marcel. 1923/2006. *Remembrance of Things Past*, Vol. 2. Hertfordshire, UK: Wordsworth Editions.

Purcell, Kristen. 2001. "Leveling the Playing Field: Constructing Parity in the Modern World." PhD dissertation, Rutgers University.

Saeki, Eiko. 2017. "Contested Boundaries of Personhood: The Moral Status of the Fetus and the Infant in Japan, 1750–1886." PhD dissertation, Rutgers University.

Schutz, Alfred, and Thomas Luckmann. 1973. *The Structures of the Life-World*. Evanston, IL: Northwestern University Press.

Schwartz, Howard and Jerry Jacobs. 1979. *Qualitative Sociology: A Method to the Madness*. New York: Free Press.

Simmel, Georg. 1917/1950. "The Field of Sociology." Pp. 3–25 in *The Sociology of Georg Simmel*, edited by Kurt H. Wolff. New York: Free Press.

Simpson, Ruth. 2006. "The Germ Culture: Modernity, Metaphor, and Epidemic Disease." PhD dissertation, Rutgers University.

Sorokin, Pitirim A. 1943. *Sociocultural Causality, Space, Time: A Study of Referential Principles of Sociology and Social Science*. Durham, NC: Duke University Press.

Stein, Karen. 2019. *Getting Away from It All: Vacations and Identity*. Philadelphia, PA: Temple University Press.

Van den Hoonaard, Will C. 1996. *Working with Sensitizing Concepts: Analytical Field Research*. Thousand Oaks, CA: SAGE.

Watson, Ian. 2005. "Cognitive Design: Creating the Sets of Categories and Labels that Structure Our Shared Experience." PhD dissertation, Rutgers University.

Wolfe, Deborah. 1994. "Beauty as a Vocation: Women and Beauty Contests in America." PhD dissertation, Columbia University.

Yeh, Hsin-Yi. 2018. "The Construction of Identification with Mnemonic Engineering: Toward a Conceptual Framework of Identity-Remembering." *Identity* 18:218–31.

Zerubavel, Eviatar. 1976. "Timetables and Scheduling: On the Social Organization of Time." *Sociological Inquiry* 46:87–94.

Zerubavel, Eviatar. 1979. *Patterns of Time in Hospital Life: A Sociological Perspective*. Chicago: University of Chicago Press.

Zerubavel, Eviatar. 1980. "If Simmel Were a Fieldworker: On Formal Sociological Theory and Analytical Field Research." *Symbolic Interaction* 3(2):25–33.

Zerubavel, Eviatar. 1981/1985. *Hidden Rhythms: Schedules and Calendars in Social Life*. Berkeley, CA: University of California Press.

Zerubavel, Eviatar. 1985/1989. *The Seven-Day Circle: The History and Meaning of the Week*. Chicago: University of Chicago Press.

Zerubavel, Eviatar. 1991/1993. *The Fine Line: Making Distinctions in Everyday Life*. Chicago: University of Chicago Press.

Zerubavel, Eviatar. 1997. *Social Mindscapes: An Invitation to Cognitive Sociology*. Cambridge, MA: Harvard University Press.

Zerubavel, Eviatar. 2003. *Time Maps: Collective Memory and the Social Shape of the Past*. Chicago: University of Chicago Press.

Zerubavel, Eviatar. 2006. *The Elephant in the Room: Silence and Denial in Everyday Life*. New York: Oxford University Press.

Zerubavel, Eviatar. 2007. "Generally Speaking: The Logic and Mechanics of Social Pattern Analysis." *Sociological Forum* 22:31–45.

Zerubavel, Eviatar. 2011. *Ancestors and Relatives: Genealogy, Identity, and Community*. New York: Oxford University Press.

Zerubavel, Eviatar. 2015. *Hidden in Plain Sight: The Social Structure of Irrelevance*. New York: Oxford University Press.

Zerubavel, Eviatar. 2016. "The Five Pillars of Essentialism: Reification and the Social Construction of an Objective Reality." *Cultural Sociology* 10:69–76.

Zerubavel, Eviatar. 2018. *Taken for Granted: The Remarkable Power of the Unremarkable*. Princeton, NJ: Princeton University Press.

Zerubavel, Eviatar. 2019. "Cognitive Sociology: Between the Personal and the Universal Mind." Pp. 567–84 in *The Oxford Handbook of Cognitive Sociology*, edited by Wayne H. Brekhus and Gabe Ignatow. New York: Oxford: Oxford University Press.

Zerubavel, Eviatar. 2021. *Generally Speaking: An Invitation to Concept-Driven Sociology*. New York: Oxford University Press.

CHAPTER 5

DE-REALIZATION AND INFRA-HUMANIZATION
A Theory of Symbolic Interaction with Digital Technologies

SIMON GOTTSCHALK AND CELENE FULLER

SYMBOLIC interactionist theory posits that individuals develop a sense of self and reality by interacting with others. Throughout most of human history, those interactions took place in face-to-face encounters. In the contemporary moment, however, we increasingly interact with others through digital technologies, and those others are real humans but also nonhuman agents. Although they differ from one another on a wide number of criteria, digital technologies enable us to go online—a "space" we visit mainly to interact with others and to access, acquire, store, produce, edit, and transmit information. In light of their merging and rapid mutations, it is a bit difficult to advance statements that would be true for all of these technologies and for any length of time. In the pages that follow, therefore, some statements will be more relevant to some of those technologies and some of their functions.

The new and increasingly mandatory interaction with digital technologies requires users to adjust central aspects of their human experiences and capacities in ways we do not yet fully grasp, and will continue to do so in ways we cannot yet fathom. In this chapter, we propose that, among their many effects, our adjustments to those interactions induce the experiences of de-realization and infra-humanization. *De-realization* includes distortions in one's relation to time, space, objects, the senses, social reality, and the self. *Infra-humanization* refers to distortions in one's relations to others. Of course, both are interrelated, and the following sections will contain some overlap. We have separated them for purposes of organization and (hopefully) clarity. It also goes without saying that interactions with digital technologies impose many more adjustments than the ones we discuss here, and that these adjustments include more distortions than de-realization and infra-humanization.

By emphasizing the idea of adjustments, we want to avoid the potential charge of technological determinism. However, if we agree that—generally—technologies do not "force" users to act in predetermined directions, they still shape them in multiple and subtle ways. Whether it's a microscope or Microsoft, technologies have "preferred encodings;" they are designed to be used in prescribed ways, and they have "manipulated probabilities" (Bauman and Lyon 2013:79). To operate them efficiently and safely, users must develop certain skeletal, muscular, sensory, cognitive, or neural habits. Those then become routine, taken for granted, and incorporated in their physical, perceptual and sensory orientations, mental processes, and social arrangements, among others (Gillespie 2003). Those adjustments are especially significant when the technologies in question are mental ones, as they are "genuine social indicators of what a society thinks of itself, how it represents itself, and hence realizes itself" (Dubey 2001:275). Such technologies embody "an intellectual ethic, a set of assumptions about how the human mind works or should work," which they systematically transmit into the minds and culture of its users (Carr 2011:45). For Baym (2010), technologies "do not make history by themselves. But some kinds of machines help make different kinds of histories and different kinds of people than others." Colonizing the landscape and re-wiring the mindscape, digital technologies become

> the windows through which we are experiencing, organizing, and interpreting the world in which we live . . .They are the interfaces through which we express who we are and what we believe to everyone else . . . They are fast becoming the boundaries of our perceptual and conceptual apparatus; the edge between our nervous systems and everyone else's, our understanding of the world and the world itself.
>
> (Rushkoff 2011:138–39)

Although there are notable exceptions, the introduction of a new technology in a society unleashes neither Armageddon nor Nirvana. Its effects tend to be gradual, uneven, differently experienced in various social groups, and often unintended. Digital technologies, however, are different. Their speed of global colonization is unmatched by any other technology. In addition, they evolve rapidly and take on a life of their own; they become smarter, faster, and increasingly intrusive. They can scan eyes, sense movements, obey vocal commands, track people down, and prevent them from accessing important resources. Increasingly autonomous, they can gather, store, share, and analyze information, which they use to make quick decisions and to execute them. They are—to quote Dator et al. (2015:109)—"mutative technologies" that are "once again redefining what it means to be humans living on a planet mutating faster than ever . . . "

Hypermodernism: Excess and Acceleration

Our adjustments to online interaction are taking place in a historical moment that a number of scholars designate as "hypermodern." Interdisciplinary and inspired by critical humanism, the hypermodern project seeks to understand the contemporary moment by analyzing four interrelated areas of everyday life: (1) the impact of digital technologies on individuals' behaviors and lifestyles; (2) the individual manifestations and consequences of a new relation to time, to others, and to the self; (3) the consequences of the society of hyperconsumption and the integration of the commercial mindset in individuals' everyday life; and (4) the effects of new technologies on working styles and their consequences on individual and collective life (Gottschalk 2018).

Two interrelated social forces are especially important in the hypermodern approach: excess and acceleration. For Nicole Aubert, hypermodern society is one where:

> everything (consumption, competition, profit, the search for pleasure, violence, terrorism, capitalism) is exaggerated, pushed to the limit and to an outrageous level. It results from the globalization of the economy, the generalized flexibility that it produces, the ever-increasing levels of performance, adaptability and reactivity that it requires, and the profound modification in our behaviors that it induces. . . It is also a society captured by the triumphant mercantile logic and shattered by the explosion of all the limits that had until now structured the construction of individual identities. (2006a)

For Cournut (2005:64) also, the hypermodern era is characterized by a disorienting "collusion between the temptation toward excess and the means to achieve it." Meeting neither resistance nor alternatives, the logic of excess is noticeable in the arts, in religious fundamentalism, in the spheres of production, of administration, and of the management of cultural activities (Tapia 2012:19).

Hypermodern scholars also integrate Hartmut Rosa's theory of acceleration in their approaches to social phenomena. Tracing its beginning with the industrial revolution, Rosa examines the destabilizing effects of this exponential force in technological innovations, the pace of change in social institutions, and in subjective experience. Assessing the importance of acceleration, a number of social scientists debate whether they should not also accelerate their theoretical models so as to be better attuned to the present, or on the contrary, whether they should slow them down (Gane 2006). In any case, writes Rosa, "a critical analysis of the temporal structures of society, of its accelerators, and of the alienation it creates is the only rationally valid option in a world that has become too fast and unstable to allow an in-depth analysis of its characteristics" (2013:99). Like other forms of totalitarian power, acceleration exerts pressure on the wills and actions of subjects, is inescapable, is all pervasive, and is almost impossible to criticize and resist. Accordingly, argues Rosa (2012:61), it must be confronted in the same way as every other form of totalitarianism.

As sites of irrational excess and as the "technological means of speed" (Hassan 2009:120), digital technologies are not only devices that perform a near-infinite number of functions; they are also useful tools to think with. For example, notes Ebert (2011:130),

> Only in an age in which the private microsphere of the individual has become the basic elementary socio-cosmological unit, could cell phone technology exist. Indeed,

the technology itself actually makes the hidden ontology visible. We have cell phones because each of us is now a world-island, a cosmos-in-miniature, unto himself and the cell phone, correspondingly, is a technological outgrowth made possible by this basic ontological fact of the status of the human individual who now exists "outside" of any protective macropshere.

Accordingly, one first and hopefully useful step in resisting the irrational forces of excess and acceleration consists in becoming aware of the adjustments imposed on users of digital technologies and the social and psychological consequences of these adjustments. Before attempting to address these questions, however, it is useful to reflect on the increasing colonization of everyday life and consciousness by digital technologies and our growing dependance on them.

Digital Dependence

In order to participate competently in contemporary society, we *must* interact with digital technologies; there is no escape and no relief. We are, to quote Hassan (2012:90), "increasingly becoming victims of digital slavery" because "we *need* to be connected to live and work and to be part of the 'normal' mainstream of networked life" (Hassan 2009:134). Thus, the 2017 Pew report found that nearly nine in ten Americans today are online, roughly three-quarters of Americans (77 percent) own a smartphone, and 92 percent of young adults own one. A third of a sample of American adults report that their mobile devices are "something they can't imagine living without," with almost half deeming their attachment to these devices "an addiction" (Bodford et al. 2017:320; see also Rainie and Anderson 2017; Smith 2017). It is useful to remember that pre-digital technologies such as televisions, telephones, or typewriters were neither necessary for participation in everyday life nor pervasive. Individuals could function quite effectively for long periods of time without using them, some lived without them altogether and were not perceived to suffer from social exclusion, boredom, boorishness, or deprivation as a result.

We confront our near-organic dependance on digital technologies in those instances when we find ourselves paralyzed because there is no internet connection, because "computers are slow," batteries are empty, the wi-fi signal is weak, or "the system is down." These moments of paralysis remind us that "our ability to perform the everyday competently is now contingent on the widest range of obscure factors" about which we understand very little (Greenfield 2017) and over which we have no control. We also experience this dependence more routinely, when we daily realize our inability to master the enormous capacities these technologies contain, the power they bestow, and the risks they present. As a result, the smarter our digital technologies become, the stupider we feel (Rosa 2012:87). And this subjective experience already lays the ground for our mode of interaction with them.

De-realization

In *Simulation and Its Discontent*, Turkle (2009:8) remarked that, in the advanced sciences, the technological reliance on virtual simulation and immersion "can tempt its users into a lack a fealty to the real." As research suggests, however, this effect is not limited to complex scientific endeavors or sophisticated minds, as adjusting to interactions with digital technologies induces, normalizes, and rewards "symptoms" that the *Diagnostic and Statistical Manual of Mental Disorders* (American Psychiatric Association 2004) classifies as de-realization. Those include: temporal disorganization; visual, auditory, olfactory, and gustatory alteration; perception of unreality of surroundings; detachment from physical body or parts, mind, thoughts, feelings behaviors, and actions; experiencing the self as absent; and emotional and physical numbing.

Temporal Disorganization

One of the two main reasons individuals use digital technologies is to go online, where they can transmit any passing thought, emotion, or desire whenever, wherever, and to whomever. Although taken for granted, this ability is unique in human history and psychology, to say nothing of politics. Syncing to our digital devices, we adjust to a completely destructured temporal order, which is enabled by our 24/7 ability to access the internet, and to an exhausting regime of immediacy and urgency (see Aubert 2018; Hassan 2009, 2012) that is well aligned to the acceleration operating at the institutional and macro-societal levels.

At an implicit and quasi-visceral level, we adjust to this sense of immediacy by simply operating our digital devices. When we turn them on, tap on their screens, move our cursor, or click, they immediately respond and prompt us to respond. Concretely, they ask us to make decisions, perform certain gestures, and enter information, and as soon as we do, they react instantly. This rapid pace naturally invites us to follow suit and to accelerate our own response time. While inherently rewarding, this dialogue is not conducive to the deep analysis and comprehensive assessment that are often required when making important decisions online. To complicate matters, our digital devices can increasingly guess what we are looking for, complete our sentences, and anticipate our next move, thereby implicitly reducing the importance of our informed input in the digital dialogue.

As these devices become faster and more responsive, this new norm of immediacy increasingly organizes both our online and offline behaviors and shapes our expectations that those with whom we interact will conform to it as well. We both adjust to—and impose on others—a sense of urgency because of the implicit and explicit pressures to respond quickly to the messages that appear on the screens of our digital devices. For example, Derks, Daantje, and Bakker (2010) find that "inherent in e-mail communication is the expectation that people can be reached easily and quickly," and Turkle (2011) notes that this expectation is even more compelling when individuals communicate via text messages. As the number of messages multiply, and as many require a prompt answer, we find ourselves having to accelerate the process by which we attend to, classify, and respond to these competing and simultaneous demands for attention. To complicate matters, those demands are articulated in different registers (personal, professional, serious, desperate, funny, sad), and require appropriate and often immediate responses. In his research on cell phone use in France, Jauréguiberry (2014:32) found that these multiplying solicitations "produce a deterioration, an erosion and a tiredness that is manifested in bursts of exasperation, of mood swings, in a sentiment of saturation, and of overflowing." Others adjust by developing the "connectivity syndrome" whose symptoms include:

> the anxiety of wasted time, the stress of the last minute, the constantly frustrated desire to be here and elsewhere at the same time, the fear of missing out on something important, the dissatisfaction of hasty decisions, the fear of not being connected at the right time on the right network, and the confusion resulting from an ephemeral information saturation.
>
> (Jauréguiberry 2005:91)

Baym also finds that "autonomy is increasingly constrained by the expectation that we can be reached for communication anytime, anywhere, and we will owe an appropriate and timely response" (2010:4). Decisions about when to respond, how, to whom, etc. can be stress-inducing, and so does the decision not to answer at all. On the other hand, not receiving an answer can also be quite stressful. In face-to-face interaction we expect that *when* we interact with another, s/he at the very least acknowledges *that* we have communicated and have been heard. As Goffman (1955:227) put it,

> By saying something, the speaker opens himself up to the possibility that the intended recipients will affront him by not listening . . . And should he meet with such a reception, he will find himself committed to the necessity of taking face-saving action against them.

Thwarting the "fundamental needs of belonging, self-esteem, control, and meaningful existence" (Wesselmann and Williams 2011:128–29), being ignored in digital interaction activates "the part of the brain involved in experiencing physical pain" (see also O'Reilly et al. 2015).

As early as 1964, Joseph Weizenbaum—the creator of the crude ELIZA language-processing software—was dismayed to find that "extremely short exposures to a relatively simple computer program could induce powerful delusional thinking in quite normal adults" (Carr 2011:205). These reactions seem to have persisted among individuals using more sophisticated software as well. For example, individuals report discomfort and anxiety when they do not receive instant online feedback (Roberts 2014), and other research reports significant decrease in self-esteem among subjects who experience "cyber-ostracism" (Giumetti et al. 2012), even when the perpetrator is but a computer program (Williams, Cheung, and Choi 2000). Importantly also, these effects do not disappear once digital devices are turned off. An individual who has felt the pain of cyber-ostracism is likely to manifest its emotional correlates in offline encounters as well. Yet, such incidents are frequent in online interactions, and, in sharp contrast to the solemn promises aired on commercial ads for digital devices, their causes are often merely technological.

We must also adjust to a more explicit sense of urgency when our digital devices order us to act quickly if we want to secure resources or avoid undesirable outcomes. Trying to reserve hotel rooms, plane seats, train tickets, concert tickets, merchandise, and other commodities or services, we are repeatedly warned that we need to decide quickly and "click now" in order to secure whatever resources are now available *only* online.

Interactions with digital technologies distort our relation to time in other ways. For cultural critic Rushkoff,

> It's not just the line between public and private activity that has vanished, but the distance between now and then. The past is wound up into the present and no longer at an appropriate or even predictable scale . . . Nothing, no matter how temporally remote is off-limits. A forgotten incident can resurface into the present like an explosion, threatening one's reputation, job, or marriage. (2013:157)

Sundials, calendars, clocks, timetables, and other technologies transformed individuals' relation to time by structuring it differently and by reorganizing their relation to it. In contrast, digital interactivity completely disintegrates time as the distinctions among past, present, and future have all but collapsed. Such an adjustment inevitably destabilizes our orientation to time, erodes our sense of agency, confuses our experience of reality, and compromises our ability to root our life-project in a recognizable past, to adjust it to a solid present, and to orient it toward a desired future (Aubert 2008, 2006).

Ephemerality

The temporal disorientation prompted by our adjustment to digital interactivity is aggravated by the routine experiences of ephemerality. If Jean Piaget's theory of cognitive development posits that a successful sensorimotor stage culminates in the embodied realization of object permanence, adjusting to the repeated experiences of ephemerality shatters the permanence of this realization. We experience this ephemerality on at least two levels.

On a first level, digital devices are of course material objects, but in contrast to pre-digital ones that individuals often preserved during their lifetime and passed on to the next generation, digital ones have a life expectancy of about five years. Because every new generation of digital devices performs better and faster than the previous one, ignoring the constant prods to replace those we own with newer models results in decreased performativity, malfunctioning, inability to use particular applications, software, accessories, and so on. In other words, the seemingly exciting acquisition of a new digital device is in fact coercive. And even if we do decide to keep our rapidly obsolete devices in spite of the risk of decreasing performativity, we must also constantly adjust to the successive waves of "bug fixes," upgrades, changing webpage designs, graphics, architectures, versions, and so on that are remotely and autonomously activated on them. Thus, while users of pre-digital technologies have to adjust to their predetermined and fixed properties, users of digital devices must adjust to their accelerating and unpredictable transformations. This experience of ephemerality naturally extends to our sense of ownership of those technologies (see Belk 2013; Ebert 2011). We might own our devices and might invest quite a bit of money and time personalizing, protecting, and accessorizing them, but we mainly use them to access a constantly growing array of immaterial *digital* resources that we neither really own, nor control, nor understand (Rainie and Wellman 2012; Rosa 2012).

On a second and more distressing level, we experience this ephemerality when we confront the random and often catastrophic disappearance of content. Inexplicably, once-reliable bookmarked links lead to extinct pages, downloaded digital books magically disappear, datasets do not "transfer," hard drives crash, e-mails vanish, music playlists are wiped out, songs cannot be played, photo albums are emptied, files are purged, and "corrupted" documents cannot be opened (see also Belk 2013). In such conditions, the real time and labor we have invested in creating those vanished documents have lost all meaning. One downloaded song disappears as quickly as a thousand, and a one-page draft I wrote in an hour ago disappears as quickly as a book chapter it took me months to complete. Similarly, the real time and labor it would normally take to physically destroy or erase hundreds of documents have shrunk to milliseconds and a click. To complicate matters, we must adjust to disorienting rules whereby some digital artifacts can disappear unpredictably, others replicate uncontrollably, and still others appear unexepectedly.

Spatial Detachment

The distorted relation to time and the destabilized sense of permanence are aggravated by a weakened relation to space, as the increasing separation of "social relevance" from "spatial proximity" (Rosa 2012:84) significantly alters how one engages the immediate physical and social environment. As Gauchet (2005:298) reminds us:

> Sensing a firm location in space is generative of a certain wisdom that asks individuals to compose with their environment and those who populate it. Immersed in digital space, you can perceive those who surround you as negligible variables. You do not really see them as part of your real world.

For neuroscientist Damasio, intelligence can be understood as an organism's ability to represent the external environment to itself, to represent itself in its environment, and to represent itself to itself. As he notes, "the organism must *sense* the environment (smell, taste, touch, hear, see), so that appropriate actions can be taken in response to what is sensed" (1994:225). Spending an increasing amount of time in digital spaces weakens the grounding forces of physical contexts, reduces their gravity and solidness, blurs their distinctive features, and encourages the dematerialization of everyday life (Belk 2013; Greenfield 2017). As a result, the representations we attend to, create, and transmit in digital spaces are likely to become literally groundless and senseless.

The GPS is an interesting example of this digitally induced degradation in the ability to orient oneself and navigate intelligently in space. Like the fate of so many other skills, geolocation has shrunk from a mode of embodied attention that mobilizes memory, the senses, "gut feelings," and common sense to an effortless, passive, and decontextualized "following of directions." If I want to reach a certain place, I no longer have to activate my memory, consult a map, imagine myself in it, chart a trajectory, find shortcuts, calculate my estimated time of arrival, and so on. If I miss a turn, I no longer have to quickly activate my mental maps, locate my position, and quickly plan a series of moves that will bring me back onto the right path. The GPS will autonomously relieve me of all this mental work and "re-route" me. For Carr, "the automation of wayfaring distances us from the environment that shaped us. It encourages us to observe and manipulate symbols on screens rather than attend to things in real places" (2015:137). And as wayfaring is our most fundamental way of being in the world (p. 132), one can reasonably suspect that this degradation is not limited to navigation in physical environments but spreads to social ones as well. Thus, hypermodern citizens find it increasingly difficult to commit to long-term (professional, personal, romantic, and other) objectives, unsure about how to reach them, find their journey suddenly rerouted, are urged to accelerate, and are constantly distracted along the way (Hassan 2012; Jackson 2009).

Sensory Incongruity

We also experience de-realization when we adjust to a radical disconnect between manual gestures on our digital devices and their consequences. As a simple example, the same mouse click can translate into an on-screen outcome as trivial as inserting a comma, in this sentence, or as moving my queen in a virtual chess game. But the very same gesture can also translate into outcomes as serious and real as clicking "submit payment" on a digital invoice, as accidentally sending a private e-mail to hundreds of recipients, or as deleting years of accumulated data from my hard drive. That the same simple pressure of the index finger can instantly trigger widely different and often irreversibly *real* outcomes completely disrupts the commonsensical and embodied understanding that—in the physical world—gestures (their types, motions, angles, forces, frequencies, etc.) materialize in corresponding and typically concrete effects. Challenging our sense of agency and competence, this disconnect makes it increasingly difficult to literally grasp what we are doing and what are the enduring and sometimes irreversible consequences of the deceptively simple gestures we type on the keyboard or tap on the screen. If Franks remarked that "the shared experience of the way the physical world responds to our manipulative actions on it remains an important source of intersubjectivity" (2003:625), adjusting to these kinetic disconnects can be particularly unsettling because we experience those alone, on our personalized and individual devices.

We also experience these disconnects when we try to adjust to the incomprehensible communicative power at our fingertips and must resolve the paradoxes it presents. For example, we must reconcile the contradictions between (a) our spontaneous communicative acts and the permanent records they leave in digital memories, (b) the specific context of our communicative acts and their decontextualized reception, and (c) the seemingly private nature of our communicative acts and the always-present risk of mass dissemination.

The Software Mindset

Adjusting our cognitive functions to the logic of digital interaction also compromises our ability to correctly manage information. For example, although reading a text on a digital device has been shown to induce less engagement, focusing, and retention than reading it on paper, an increasing number of texts are now available only in digital format. On a different level, as more and more scholars cite fewer and fewer articles, what they cite is predicated by algorithms that "give precedence to popularity and recency over diversity of opinion, rigor of argument or quality of expression" (Carr 2011). How scholars read the articles they cite is also significant. As a study conducted by the British Library finds, 60 percent of serious scholars do not read more than three pages of an e-journal, and 65 percent of them never come back for a second look (Carr 2011:134–35). Instead, readers are more likely to scan a text in order locate and extract those bits of information that seem immediately relevant for the task at hand. While expeditious, this type of reading has been shown to inhibit deep understanding, critical thinking, and creative association. It decreases randomness and serendipity, decontextualizes information, promotes passive learning, and yields incomplete knowledge. Reducing our capacity to understand phenomena (Lynch 2016) and encouraging a "new way *not* to think" (Turkle 2011:240), "Google-knowing" may also create changes in brain architecture, which complicates the performance of future complex cognitive endeavors (Hayles 2012). We are unlikely to notice this degradation because—among other reasons—we have fewer alternative models with which to gauge our cognitive decline.

In addition, as the information we access online is increasingly personalized and as we lack solid epistemic principles with which to evaluate it, we can also lose the capacity to share it, reach a consensus about it, and act collectively on it. Thus, Domonoske's research at Stanford University (2016) finds that students have a dismaying inability to distinguish between fake and real news, and this affliction is not limited to students. Adult Facebook users are more likely to share fake (but dramatic) news than real ones, a finding that is especially worrisome when one considers that 62 percent of adult American users get their news from social media (Rainie, Anderson, and Albright 2017), that 44 percent of them get their news from Facebook, and that those who do so are less engaged and knowledgeable than those who do not (Mitchell et al. 2020). Paradoxically, therefore, while the sheer volume of information and analytic power unleashed by our digital technologies should enhance our capacity to understand a wide range of topics at a most sophisticated level, the opposite obtains. The analysis of big data "yields correlations and predictions but rarely explanations" (Andrejevic 2013). We may have access to more information and faster than at any other time in the history of our species, but, "blinded by the proliferation of information" (Jauréguiberry 2014:48), we are decreasingly capable of evaluating it. More worrisome, our ability to authenticate the information we need is increasingly and fatally compromised by recent innovations such as "deep fakes"—audiovisual depictions of people and events that never happened but that look compellingly authentic (Knight 2018; *New York Times* Editorial Board 2016; Toews 2020).

Personalization

Although our coercive dependence on digital devices should prompt a spirited resistance, it does not. On the contrary, we seem to joyfully adjust to it. One explanation for this adjustment is the *personalization* affordance, which scholars of the internet describe as the game changer that launched Web 3.0—the third internet revolution. Enhancing the experience of de-realization, personalization occurs on at least three levels: appearance, content, and functioning.

On the level of appearance, we can personalize our digital devices by deciding on the number, types, location, and animations of the icons that populate our screen. We can also adjust the screen's brightness, the color intensity, and its haptic sensitivity. We select the screensavers, the background images, and the windows sizes. We calibrate the speed of the mouse clicking, scrolling, and tracking. We choose the fonts, assign the shortcuts, and set the toolbars. We schedule back-up functions and decide on our "security" and "privacy" parameters. In addition, we can alter those very settings to match our moods and needs whenever we desire.

Personalization also occurs at the level of content. Tripped by enigmatic algorithms, our digital devices record the kind of information we are more likely to attend to and daily recommend newspapers we'd probably like to read, music we'd probably like to hear, movies we'd probably like to watch, food we'd probably like to eat, places we'd probably like to visit, people we'd probably like to "friend," and political causes we'd probably support (see Karakayali, Kotsem, and Galip 2018). In addition, if we are offended, irritated, or bored by any type of content, we can easily delete it, report it, and avoid all future similar ones. As we increasingly personalize the content of our digital devices and as they continuously fine tune it, we come to inhabit a "filter bubble." As Pariser notes (2012:12, 125),

> Ultimately, the proponents of personalization offer a vision of a custom-tailored world, every facet of which fits us perfectly. It's a cozy place, populated by our favorite people and things and ideas . . . If we never click on the articles about cooking, or gadgets, or

the world outside our country's borders, they simply fade away. . . We're never bored. We're never annoyed. Our media is a perfect reflection of our interests and desires.

These "fun" adjustments compromise not solely our perceptions of reality and our relation to it but, inevitably, our relations to the others who populate it. Discussing our personalized Google maps, Greenfield (2017) concludes that "we can no longer even pretend that what we see on the screen is a shared, consistent representation of the same, relatively stable underlying reality. A map that interpellates us in this way ensures, in a strikingly literal sense, that we can only ever occupy and move through our own separate lifeworlds."

Personalization also occurs on the level of functioning, as interactions with our digital devices normalize the regressive expectation of constant, instant, and nonjudgmental gratification. Whether we want to access the GPS, listen to music, play a videogame, or message a friend, we expect that our digital devices will respond to, and even anticipate, our every impulse. For example, Gilbertson (2012) finds that adult users expect a webpage to load at—literally—the blink of an eye, and delays in ability to connect or download that were routine a mere fifteen years ago have now become intolerable. Accordingly, while we are attached to our devices because we depend on them and because we inscribe our identity in them, this attachment might be more invested in the personalized *experiences* they offer than in the devices themselves.

This adjustment to what, at first glance, feels like a most welcoming environment might prompt a radical change in our expectations of how the world should operate— online and offline (Bauman 2005:87). As Paul Watzlawick (1977) famously remarked, believing that one's view of reality is the only reality is the most dangerous of all delusions. However, our personalized "mental theme park" promotes precisely this delusion. It endorses our narcissistic fantasies, flatters us at every click, and confirms that our perception of reality is indeed sound and sufficient. In so doing, digital technologies usher in the "society of denial" where "everything becomes organized so as to be able to ignore what one does not want to know. . . The role of the virtual sphere will be to normalize this refusal" (Tisseron 2008:224–25).

In sum, interactions with digital technologies require users to adjust how they experience time, space, objects permanence, and sensory activities. These adjustments compromise their capacities to process and evaluate information, to experience intersubjective reality, and to appropriately locate the self in a now personalized narcissistic environment. Remarkably similar to the symptoms of de-realization, these adjustments inevitably also compromise how users perceive and treat those they encounter. Online and, one suspects, offline as well.

Infra-humanization

Dehumanization—perceiving others as less than human—has been the topic of a recent and dynamic scholarship. While early contributors approached dehumanization within the framework of group conflicts and violence, Leyens and his team opened up an important new line of inquiry by introducing the concept of infra-humanization (Haslam 2006). As they define it, infra-humanization is a subtle process that can occur outside of awareness and requires neither group conflicts nor strong negative emotions (Leyens et al. 2003). This definition partly derives from Leyens et al.'s approach to *humanness*, which refers to qualities such as language, intelligence, and those *sentiments* that are considered both central to human nature and distinguishing humans from animals. Developing this concept, Haslam and Loughnan (2014) distinguish between qualities classified as "human uniqueness" and those classified as "human nature." Human uniqueness distinguishes humans from animals and includes qualities such as cognitive capacity, civility, and refinement. Human nature distinguishes us from inanimate objects and includes qualities such as emotionality, vitality, depth, and warmth (Haslam and Loughnan 2014:403). To those two aspects of humanness correspond two types of dehumanization. Individuals who deny others *human uniqueness* perceive those others as lacking unique human traits such as civility, refinement, moral sensibility, rationality/logic, and maturity. They are more likely to commit *animalistic* dehumanization. Individuals who deny others *human nature* perceive those others as lacking qualities that are inherent to being human such as emotional responsiveness, interpersonal warmth, agency, cognitive openness, and depth. They are more likely to commit *mechanistic* dehumanization.

Animalistic infra-humanization is accompanied by disgust and contempt, but because mechanistic infra-humanization is not necessarily motivated by strong emotions or group conflict, it can take the form of "an indifferent, instrumental, distancing, and objectifying orientation" toward the target (Haslam 2006:261). It may not necessarily motivate actors to physical aggression, but rather to *indifference* when it is visited upon the infra-humanized other. Three aspects of digital interactivity are likely to facilitate mechanistic infra-humanization. The first pertains to several unique characteristics of the digital environment, the second concerns its regime of constant surveillance, and the third refers to its invasion by nonhuman agents.

Digital Interactions

When we interact with human others on text-based platforms such as texting, posting comments on social-media websites, or emailing, we can neither convey nor perceive the kind of information we typically depend on when we interact face to face. Here, we are mute, invisible, and literally out of touch. And although we may know—offline—those with whom we interact, we are blind to their proxemics, kinesics, and facial gestures; deaf to their paralanguage and sounds; and unaware of the contexts where they happen to be (Rhoads 2010). Impairing focused attention (Rettie 2009), mutual communication (Orcutt and Anderson 1977), the delicate dance of "facework" (Gottschalk and Whitmer 2013), and the demarcation between front stage and back stage (Marwick and boyd 2010), these conditions facilitate mechanistic infra-humanization in a number of ways.

If Levinas suggested that the ethical dimension of interaction stems from "the sentiment present in the visual perception of a human face" (Honneth 2007:119), replacing the human face with faceless messages de-faces interactants, diminishes their full humanness, and obscures the ethical implications inherent to interpersonal encounters. That interactants cannot speak to or hear each other is also significant. Turkle notes that "detaching words from the person uttering them can encourage a certain coarsening. . . . Online, we can ignore people's feelings and choose not to hear how hurt or angry they sound in their voice" (2011:236, 184). Thus, for example, Schroeder and her colleagues (2017) found that experimental subjects were less likely to dehumanize others with whom they disagreed when they could hear these others' voices than when they could only read these others' words.

The very communication styles of text-based online interactions also normalize mechanistic infra-humanization in other ways. As Rushkoff (2011:35–36) puts it,

> we reduce the length and complexity of our responses . . . making almost everything we transmit sound like orders barked over a walkie-talkie in a war zone . . . But those commands are coming at us now in increasingly rapid bursts, stimulating us to respond at rates incompatible with human thought and emotion—and in ways that are not terribly enjoyable.

In concert, the absence of face and voice and the communication styles of text-based online interaction make it especially difficult to convey and perceive interpersonal qualities such as emotional responsiveness, interpersonal warmth, cognitive openness, agency-individuality, depth, and those other qualities identified by Haslam as constituting "human nature."

Mechanistic infra-humanization in text-based online interactions is complemented by animalistic dehumanization as well. For example, Aboujaoude (2011:21) notes that communicating online "often gives voice to some less mature and antisocial impulses, aspects of ourselves that have historically been kept in check by culture, expectation, religion, and what one might call the social contract" (2011:21; see also Baruch 2005). As research conducted at the Pew Research Center finds, 66 percent of adult internet users have seen someone be harassed in some way online, 40 percent have personally experienced online harassment, and 62 percent consider that it is a problem (Duggan 2017).

As importantly, the negative emotions triggered by exposure to an "everyday viciousness" (Aboujaoude 2011) persist beyond the immediate context of communication. After the immediate "chilling effect" (Duggan 2017), "reading and writing online rants are associated with negative shifts in mood for the vast majority of people," and those can persist when the device is turned off (Martin et al. 2013:121–22). To wit, Facebook has just agreed to pay $52 million to moderators who have developed PTSD as a result of their exposure to toxic online content (Osborne 2020).

Social psychologists of various stripes have long established that a person's ability to role-take and self-reflect from the perspective of another is key to mental-moral evolution, to emotional and social intelligence, and to sanity. Yet, while digital interactivity has multiplied the number of people with whom we could potentially role-take and self-reflect, Turkle's research (2011) suggests that today's youth are decreasingly capable of role-taking and of finding much value in the ability to do so.

As early as 1977, Orcutt and Anderson's research on human-computer interaction found that subjects who had interacted with computers in a virtual Prisoner's Dilemma experiment tended to dehumanize others. Defining dehumanization as the failure to "switch back" from a digital mode of interaction to a human one, they found that this failure resulted "in a behavior which is reminiscent of impersonal exploitation and control in the technocratic society" (1977:394). In the same vein, Turkle warns against "a real risk that we come to see others as objects to be accessed—and only for the parts we find useful, comforting, or amusing" (2011:154–55). As we spend an increasing amount of time interacting with digital devices and with others through digital devices, it does not seem unreasonable to anticipate that this inability to switch back will worsen.

Surveillance

"We know where you are. We know where you have been. We can more or less know what you're thinking about," Google CEO Eric Schmidt once famously claimed (Rainie and Wellman 2012:18). "Google knows more about us than we can remember ourselves," writes Mayer-Schönberger (2011:7). "It knows us so well that it finishes our sentences," remarks Lynch (2016:155). If digital technologies differ in the type of information they enable users to exchange, the synchronicity of interactions (see Hogan 2010; Litt 2012; Rettie 2009; Zhao 2005), their portability, functions, and many other variables, they all surveil us. It bears remembering that, up until quite recently, everyday activities such as buying anything, reading a newspaper, listening to music, looking at pictures, watching a movie, searching for a phone number, locating an address on a map, or playing a videogame were dispersed, anonymous, and unrecorded. In other words, the pre-digital era allowed individuals quite a wide latitude in what Goffman called "information control"—the ability to control the information others have about oneself (Feaster 2010). Today, most of these activities take place on digital technologies that generate, collect, store, analyze, share, and manipulate information about us. More worrisome, it has now become cliché to remark that even when our devices are turned off, they are still constantly collecting and transmitting information about our private activities. In the hypermodern moment, "intense scrutiny—even in unexpected situations—is a realistic possibility," "transparency is a new requirement" (Rainie and Wellman 2012), and conditions of total surveillance that were once confined to dystopian novels or paranoid delusions have become normalized.

Perhaps one reason explaining our adjustment to this regime of constant surveillance is that it does not feel concrete or coercive. On the contrary, hypermodern surveillance is "soft" (Marx 2007), "remote and silent" (Ball 2009), "intrusive and invisible, more invasive but perceived as normal" (Ragnedda 2011:187). A second reason explaining why we adjust to the new regime of total surveillance is because, as we saw above, it informs and fine tunes the personalization of our online experience, which is inherently rewarding.

By normalizing the routine violation of privacy, interaction with digital devices forces users to adjust to conditions of visibility typically enforced on children, incarcerated populations, and other social groups deemed dangerous or suspect. As a form of psychological intimidation that targets everyone, this constant "electronic stalking" (Christl 2017) extends mechanistic infra-humanization from the interpersonal domain to the intrapersonal one. Thus, researchers report that individuals who discover they have been unwillingly and unknowingly surveilled experience "emotional, psychoanalytic and corporeal responses which are sometimes stultifyingly profound" (Ball 2009:650). Others react to the onslaught on privacy with "despair, hopelessness, anxiety, or plain denial" (Turkle 2011), "psychological distortion" (Acquisiti 2011), effective "exile from their own behavior" (Zuboff 2015:75), and "a relationship to authority that blends culpability, panic, a feeling of inferiority, and eventually, of submission" (Dubey 2001). When we cannot control access to our private information, our autonomy and dignity as free individuals are severely undermined. This is partly why Pieter Omtzigt, the Dutch deputy at the parliamentary assembly of the Council of Europe, considers that mass-surveillance is a fundamental threat to human rights (2015). On their end, individuals who collect and analyze this private information are more likely to infrahumanize their targets as well. Displaying "formal indifference" (Zuboff 2015), they perceive those they surveil "not as persons but as objects to be understood and controlled" (Lynch 2016:107). More alarmingly, those agents of surveillance will soon be replaced by nonhuman agents or bots.

Interactions with Non-human Agents

"Are you human?" a sign-in computer screen asks. "Please confirm you're not a robot," requires another. Tragically, human users now have to increasingly prove their humanity by entering an alphanumeric string of characters on the screens of digital devices or indicate they recognize information, such as images. If they cannot (or refuse to) do so, intelligent computer programs will prevent them from proceeding and will probably record their noncompliance as well. "You've been disconnected." In other instances, users find themselves summarily expelled from a "secure" website because they've been "inactive" for too long. Nonhuman agents are not only becoming more efficient at recording, storing, sharing, and updating torrential flows of information about human behavior, they are also significantly improving their abilities to analyze it, to use it to make their own decisions, and to act on them—in real time.

If, as we saw above, users of digital technologies are increasingly unable to grasp the full humanity of those with whom they interact or surveil, or to distinguish real news from fake ones, they might also become increasingly unable to tell real people from bots. Thus, Ferrara et al. (2016:99–100) report that intelligent bots can engage users in conversations, comment on their posts, and answer questions. Some can search a social network to locate influential people and capture their attention. They can infiltrate popular discussions, zero in on topics, and participate in them. Others can "'clone' the behavior of legitimate users, by interacting with their friends and posting topically coherent content with similar temporal patterns." Programmed by "drone vision" (Greene 2015), bots are increasingly deployed by key social organizations to make decisions about "who to deal with and how to deal with them" (Beer 2009:990), and to "allocate different levels of service to different users on an increasing automated basis" (Christl 2017). Treating humans as pure information, bots (inter)act accordingly. They "brain-hack" users (Cooper 2017) and manipulate their behaviors (Donnath 2017). To complicate matters, rapid mutations in artificial intelligence are driving nonhuman agents to reach *un*programmed autonomy, potentially bringing about what social psychologist Zuboff calls a *coup des gens* (2015:83). Unlike the *coup d'état*, it does not overthrow political regimes but human beings. As Dator, Sweeney, and Yee (2015:109) warn:

> humans may in many ways, no longer be primarily in the driver's seat. As a result we may see the technologies themselves taking on a much more profound role in the shaping of society in the futures beyond the capacity of human agency, which has already been shaped by the tools that make and remake us as humans.

Digital media designer Jaron Lanier argued that "when developers of digital technologies design a program that requires you to interact with a computer as if it were a person, they ask you to accept in some corner of your brain that you might also be a conceived of as a program" (2010:4–5). As the algorithms that encode digital interactions infra-humanize humans, they simultaneously humanize nonhumans. The accelerating synergy between those two forces will soon escape our ability to understand their consequences, let alone resist them.

CONCLUSION

We use digital technologies mainly to find information and interact, and it goes without saying that these technologies have extended our ability to do both at levels that are difficult to understand or manage. In order to use this ability with a modicum of success, we must adjust important aspects of our human experience to the digital logic that encodes these technologies. Significantly degrading our experiences of reality, self, and others, these distortions can be categorized as de-realization and infra-humanization. Those are certainly not the only consequences of our adjustments to interactivity with digital devices, but we believe that they deserve our critical interactionist attention.

In order to interact efficiently with digital technologies, users must adjust— increasingly quickly—to an environment where taken-for-granted correspondences among time, space, gestures, materiality, selfhood, and a sense of reality have been torn asunder and reassembled according to digital rather than human rules. Lacking

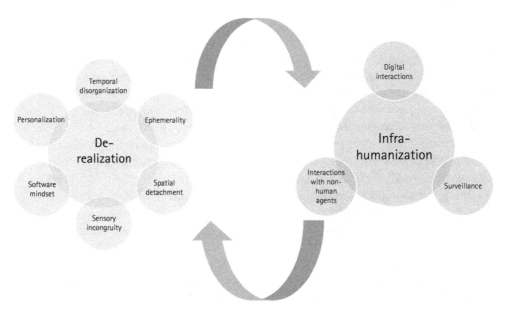

FIGURE 5.1. De-realization and Mechanistic Infra-humanization

a stable orientation in time and space, users find it increasingly difficult to keep their bearings and balance. Incongruities between manual gestures and their effects induce confusion in one's embodied experiences. Repeated encounters with radical ephemerality erodes their faith in object permanence. Immersion in personalized and endless "you-loops" compromises their ability to distinguish between self-centered delusional thinking and intersubjective reality. Randomly pushed around by the forces of immediacy and urgency, users find it increasingly challenging to analyze and intelligently respond to the fusillade of events that relentlessly appear on the screens of their digital devices.

Interacting on text-based platforms and under conditions of constant surveillance, users also lack the ability to fully attune to each other and are decreasingly able to tell whether those with whom they interact are human or not. Unable to achieve the mutual perceptiveness and empathy needed to role-take, they find it increasingly difficult to engage the other's full humanity, and perhaps their own as well. In so doing, de-realization invites infra-humanization and vice versa (see Figure 5.1).

The aptitude for empathic symbolic interaction has always been considered the hallmark of humanness, the fundamental process that enables complex sociality and a sense of self. Digital technologies increase the opportunities to interact and the reach of these opportunities, but they also degrade the quality of interaction and thwart two of its main objectives: agreement on the nature of reality and self-validation. As the artificial intelligence that powers our devices is quickly developing interaction capacities that will soon surpass our own, it is becoming a "fundamental existential risk for human civilization and the scariest problem humanity faces" (Elon Musk, quoted in Dowd 2017).

A twenty-first-century symbolic interactionist project should seek to understand not only how we adjust to online interactions but also, and especially, how we adjust to the increasing *interpenetration* between face-to-face and digital interactions. Informed by this understanding, we should be better able to resist the de-realization and infra-humanization unleashed by the digital revolution.

REFERENCES

Aboujaoude, Elias. 2011. *Virtually You: The Dangerous Powers of the E-Personality*. New York: W. W. Norton.

Acquisiti, Alessandro. 2011. "Les Comportements de Vie Privée Face au Commerce Électronique." *Réseaux* 167:107–30.

American Psychiatric Association. 2004. *Diagnostic and Statistical Manual of Mental Disorders DSM-IV-TR*. Washington DC.

Andrejevic, Mark. 2013. *Infoglut: How Too Much Information Is Changing the Way We Think and Know*. New York: Routledge.

Aubert Nicole. 2006. "Sur L'hypermodernité et de la Société Hypermoderne." *Next Modernity* 10:30.

Aubert, Nicole. 2008. "Violence du Temps et Pathologies Hypermodernes." *Cliniques Méditerranéennes* 78:23–38.

Aubert, Nicole. Ed. 2018. @ *La Recherche du Temps: Individus Hyperconnectés, Société Accélérée*. Toulouse: Érès.

Ball, Kirstie. 2009. "Exposure: Exploring the Subject of Surveillance." *Information, Communication and Society* 12(5):639–57.

Baruch, Yehuda. 2005. "Bullying on the Net: Adverse Behavior on E-mail and Its Impact." *Information and Management* 42:361–71.

Bauman, Zygmunt. 2005. *Liquid Life*. Cambridge: Polity.

Bauman, Zygmunt and David Lyon. 2013. *Liquid Surveillance*. Cambridge: Polity.

Baym, Nancy K. 2010. *Personal Connections in the Digital Age*. Cambridge: Polity.

Beer, David. 2009. "Power through the Algorithm? Participatory Web Cultures and the Technological Unconscious." *New Media & Society* 11(6):985–1002.

Belk, Russel W. 2013. "Extended Self in a Digital World." *Journal of Consumer Research* 40(3):477–500.

Bodford, Jessica E., Virginia S. Y. Kwan, and David S. Sobota. 2017. "Fatal Attractions: Attachment to Smartphones Predicts Anthropomorphic Beliefs and Dangerous Behaviors." *Cyberpsychology, Behavior, and Social Networking* 20(5):320–26.

Carr, Nicholas. 2011. *The Shallows: What the Internet is Doing to Our Brains*. New York: W. W. Norton.

Carr, Nicholas. 2015. *The Glass Cage: Where Automation Is Taking Us*. London: The Bodley Head.

Christl, Wolfe. 2017. "Corporate Surveillance in Everyday Life." *Institute for Critical Digital Culture*. https://crackedlabs.org/en/corporate-surveillance.

Cooper, Anderson. 2017. "What Is Brain Hacking? Tech Insiders on Why You Should Care." 60 Minutes. CBS. April 9. https://www.cbsnews.com/news/what-is-brain-hacking-tech-insiders-on-why-you-should-care/.

Cournut, Jean. 2005. "Les Défoncés." Pp. 61–71 in *L'Individu Hypermoderne*, edited by Nicole Aubert. Toulouse: Érès.

Damasio, Antonio. 1994. *Descartes' Error: Emotion, Reason, and the Human Brain*. New York: Penguin.

Dator, James A., John A. Sweeney, and Aubrey M. Yee. 2015. *Mutative Media: Communication Technologies and Power Relations in the Past, Present, and Futures*. Lecture Notes in Social Networks. Springer: Switzerland International Publishing.

Derks, Daantje, and Arnold B. Bakker. 2010. "The Impact of E-Mail Communication on Organizational Life." *Cyberpsychology: Journal of Psychosocial Research on Cyberspace* 4(1). Retrieved December 12, 2013 (http/::cyberpsychology.eu:view.php%3Fcisloclanku=2010052 401&article=1).

Domonoske, Camilia. 2016. "Students Have 'Dismaying' Inability To Tell Fake News From Real, Study Finds." KNPR. Retrieved November 23, 2016 (https://www.npr.org/secti ons/thetwo-way/2016/11/23/503129818/study-finds-students-have-dismaying-inabil ity-to-tell-fake-news-from-real).

Donnath, Judith. 2017. "The Robot Dog Fetches for Whom?" *Medium*. Retrieved June 15, 2017 (https://medium.com/berkman-klein-center/the-robot-dog-fetches-for-whom-a9c1d d0a458a).

Dowd, Maureen. 2017. "Elon Musk's Billion-Dollar Crusade to Stop the A.I. Apocalypse." *Vanity Fair* March, 26. Retrieved July 18, 2017 (https://www.vanityfair.com/news/2017/03/ elon-musk-billion-dollar-crusade-to-stop-ai-space-x).

Dubey, Gérard. 2001. *Le Lien Social à l'Ère du Virtuel*. Paris: Presses Universitaires de France.

Duggan, Maeve. 2017. "2017 Online Harassment." Pew Research Center. https://www.pewresea rch.org/internet/2017/07/11/online-harassment-2017/.

Ebert, John David. 2011. *The New Media Invasion: Digital Technologies and the World They Unmake*. North Carolina: McFarlane.

Feaster, John. 2010. "Expanding the Impression Management Model of Communication Channels: An Information Control Scale." *Journal of Computer-Mediated Communication* 16:115–38.

Ferrara, Emilio, Onur Varol, Clayton Davis, Filippo Menczer, and Alessandro Flammini. 2016. "The Rise of Social Bots." *Communications of the Association for Computer Machinery* 59(7). doi:10.1145/2818717.

Franks, David. 2003. "Mutual Interests, Different Lenses: Current Neuroscience and Symbolic Interaction." *Symbolic Interaction* 26(4):613–30.

Gane, Nicholas. 2006. "Speed Up or Slow Down? Social Theory in the Information Age." *Information, Communication & Society* 9(1):20–238.

Gauchet, Marcel. 2005."Vers une Mutation Anthropologique?" Pp. 290–301 in *L'Individu Hypermoderne*, edited by Nicole Aubert. Toulouse: Érès.

Gilbertson, Scott. 2012. "Users Expect Websites to Load in the Blink of an Eye." *Wired* March 2, 2012. Available at https://www.wired.com/2012/03/users-expect-websites-to-load-in-the- blink-of-an-eye/.

Gillespie, Tarleton. 2003. "The Stories Digital Tools Tell." Pp. 2–21 in *New Media: Theses on Convergence Media and Digital Reproduction*, edited by John Caldwell and Anna Everett. London: Routledge.

Giumetti, Gary W., Eric S. McKibben, Andrea L Hatfield, Amber N. Schroeder, and Robin M. Kowalski. 2012. "Cyberincivility @ Work: The New Age of Interpersonal Deviance." *Cyberpsychology, Behavior and Social Networking* 15(3):148–54.

Goffman, Erving. 1955. "On Face-Work: An Analysis of Ritual Elements in Social Interaction." *Psychiatry* 18(3):213–31.

Gottschalk, Simon. 2018. *The Terminal Self: Everyday Life in Hypermodern Times*. London: Routledge.

Gottschalk, Simon, and Jennifer Whitmer. 2013. "Hypermodern Dramaturgy in Online Encounters." Pp. 309–34 in *The Drama of Social Life: A Dramaturgical Handbook*, edited by Charles Edgley. Ashgate.

Greene, Daniel. 2015. "Drone Vision." *Surveillance & Society* 13(2):233–49.

Greenfield. Adam. 2017. *Radical Technologies: The Design of Everyday Life*. Verso. Available at: https://longreads.com/2017/06/13/a-sociology-of-the-smartphone/.

Haslam, Nick. 2006. "De-humanization: An Integrative Review." *Personality and Social Psychology* 10(3):252–64.

Haslam, Nick, and Steve Loughnan. 2014. "Dehumanization and Infra-humanization." *Annual Review of Psychology* 65:339–423.

Hassan, Robert. 2009. *Empires of Speed: Time and the Acceleration of Politics and Society*. Leiden: Brill.

Hassan, Robert. 2012. *The Age of Distraction*. New Brunswick: Transactions

Hayles, N. Katherine. 2012. *How We Think: Digital Media and Contemporary Technogenesis*. University of Chicago Press.

Hogan, Bernie. 2010. "The Presentation of Self in the Age of Social Media: Distinguishing Performances and Exhibitions Online." *Bulletin of Science, Technology & Society* 30(6):377–86.

Honneth, Axel. 2007. *Disrespect: The Normative Foundations of Critical Theory*. Cambridge: Polity.

Jackson, Maggie. 2009. *Distracted: The Erosion of Attention and the Coming Dark Age*. New York: Prometheus.

Jauréguiberry, Francis. 2005. "L'Immédiaté Télécommunicationnelle." Pp. 85–98 in *Nouvelles Technologies et Modes de Vie: Aliénation ou Hypermodernité ?*, edited by Philippe Moati. Paris: Éditions de l'Aube.

Jauréguiberry, Francis. 2014. "La Déconnection aux Technologies de Communication." *La Découverte-Réseaux* 186(4):15–49.

Karakayali, Nedim, Kostem, Burc, and Galip, Idil. 2018. "Recommendation Systems as Technologies of the Self: Algorithmic Control and the Formation of Music Taste." *Theory, Culture & Society* 35(2):3–24.

Knight, Will. 2018. "Fake America Great Again." *MIT Technology Review* 121(5):36–41.

Lanier, Jaron. 2010. *You are Not a Gadget: A Manifesto*. New York: Vintage.

Leyens, Jacques-Philippe, Brezo Cortes, Stephanie Demoulin, John F. Dovido, Susan T. Fiske, Ruth Gant, Maria-Paola Paladino, Armando Rodriguez-Perez, Ramon Rodriguez-Torres, and Jeroen Vaes. 2003. "Emotional Prejudice, Essentialism, and Nationalism: The 2002 Tajfel Lecture." *European Journal of Social Psychology* 33:703–17.

Litt, Eden. 2012. "Knock, Knock. Who's There? The Imagined Audience." *Journal of Broadcasting & Electronic Media* 56(3):330–45.

Lynch, Michael Patrick. 2016. *The Internet of Us: Knowing More and Understanding Less in the Age of Big Data*. New York: Liveright.

Martin, Ryan. C., Kelsey Ryan Coyier, Leah M. VanSistine, and Kelly L. Schroeder. 2013. "Anger on the Internet: The Perceived Value of Rant-Sites." *Cyberpsychology, Behavior, and Social Networking* 16(2):118–22.

Marx, Gary. 2007. "Soft Surveillance: The Growth of Mandatory Volunteerism in Collecting Personal Information." Pp. 37–56 in *Surveillance and Security: Technological Politics and Power in Everyday Life*, edited by T. Monahan. London: Routledge.

Marwick, Alice, and Danah Boyd. 2010. "I Tweet Honestly, I Tweet Passionately: Twitter Users, Context Collapse, and the Imagined Audience." *New Media & Society* 13(1):114–33.

Mayer-Schönberger, Viktor. 2011. *Delete: The Virtue of Forgetting in the Digital Age*. Princeton, NJ: Princeton University Press.

Mitchell, Amy, Mark Jurkowitz, J. Baxter Oliphant, and Elisa Sharer. 2020. "Americans Who Mainly Get Their News on Social Media Are Less Engaged, Less Knowledgeable." Pew Research Center, July 2020. Available at: https://www.journalism.org/2020/07/30/americ ans-who-mainly-get-their-news-on-social-media-are-less-engaged-less-knowledgeable/.

New York Times Editorial Board. 2016. "Facebook and the Digital Virus Called Fake News" November 19. Retrieved November 20, 2016 (https://www.nytimes.com/2016/11/20/opin ion/sunday/facebook-and-the-digital-virus-called-fake-news.html).

O'Reilly, Jane, Sandra L. Robinson, Jennifer L. Berdahl, and Sara Banki. 2015. "Is Negative Attention Better Than No Attention? The Comparative Effects of Ostracism and Harassment at Work." *Organization Science* 26(3):774–93.

Omtzigt, Pieter. 2015. "Mass Surveillance." Parliamentary Assembly, Council of Europe, January 26, 2015. https://assembly.coe.int/nw/xml/XRef/Xref-XML2HTML-en.asp?fileid= 21583&lang=en.

Orcutt, James D., and Ronald E. Anderson. 1977. "Social Interaction, Dehumanization and the 'Computerized Other.'" *Sociology and Social Research* 61(3):380–97.

Osborne, Charlie. 2020. "Facebook o Pay $52 million to Former Content Moderators Who Suffered Mental Trauma." *ZDNet* May 13, 2020. https://www.zdnet.com/article/facebook-to-pay-52-million-to-former-content-moderators-who-developed-ptsd/.

Pariser, Eli. 2012. *The Filter Bubble: How the New Personalized Web Is Changing What We Read and How We Think*. New York: Penguin.

Ragnedda, Massimo. 2011. "Social Control and Surveillance in the Society of Consumers." *International Journal of Sociology and Anthropology* 3(6):8–18.

Rainie, Lee and Barry Wellman. 2012. *Networked: The New Social Operating System*. Cambridge: MIT Press.

Rainie, Lee, Janna Anderson, and Jonathan Albright. 2017. "The Future of Free Speech, Trolls, Anonymity, and Fake News Online." Pew Research Center, March 2017. Available at: http://www.pewinternet.org/2017/03/29/the-future-of-free-speech-trolls-anonymity-and-fake-news-online/Downloaded 6/9/2017.

Rainie, Lee, and Janna Anderson. 2017. "Code-Dependent: Pros and Cons of the Algorithm Age." Pew Research Center, February 2017. Available at: http://www.pewinternet.org/2017/02/08/code-dependent-pros-and-cons-of-the-algorithm-age.

Rettie, Ruth. 2009. "Mobile Phone Communication: Extending Goffman to Mediated Interaction." *Sociology* 43(3):421–38.

Rhoads, Mohja. 2010. "Face-to-Face and Computer-Mediated Communication: What Does Theory Tell Us and What Have We Learned So Far?" *Journal of Planning Literature* 25(2):111–22.

Roberts, Paul. 2014. *The Impulse Society: America in the Age of Instant Gratification*. New York: Bloomsbury.

Rosa, Hartmut. 2012. *Alienation and Acceleration: Towards a Critical Theory of Late Modernity*. Helsingforth: NSU Press.

Rushkoff, Douglas. 2011. *Program or be Programmed: Ten Commands for a Digital Age*. Berkeley, CA: Soft Skull Press.

Rushkoff, Douglas. 2013. *Present Shock: When Everything Happens Now*. New York: Penguin.

Schroeder, Julianna, Michael Kardas, and Nicholas Epley. 2017. "The Humanizing Voice: Speech Reveals, and Text Conceals, more Thoughtful Mind in the Midst of Disagreement." *Psychological Science* 28(12):1745–62.

Smith, Aaron. 2017. "Record Shares of Americans Now Own Smartphones, Have Home Broadband." http://www.pewresearch.org/.

Tapia, Claude. 2012. "Modernité, Postmodernité, Hypermodernité" *Connexions* 1:15–25.

Tisseron, Serge. 2008. *Virtuel, Mon Amour: Penser, Aimer, Souffrir à l'Ère des Nouvelles Technologies*. Paris: Albin Michel.

Toews, Rob. 2020. "Deepfakes Are Going To Wreak Havoc On Society. We Are Not Prepared." *Forbes* May 25, 2020. https://www.forbes.com/sites/robtoews/2020/05/25/deepfakes-are-going-to-wreak-havoc-on-society-we-are-not-prepared/?sh=bca266974940.

Turkle, Sherry. 2009. *Simulation and Its Discontents*. Cambridge: MIT Press.

Turkle, Sherry. 2011. *Alone Together: Why We Demand More of Technology and Less of Each Other*. New York: Basic Books.

Watzlawick, Paul. 1977. *How Real Is Real? Confusion, Disinformation, Communication* New York: Vintage.

Wesselmann, Eric D., and Kipling D. Williams. 2011. "Being Ignored and Excluded in Electronic-Based Interactions." Pp. 127–44 in *Strategic Uses of Social Technology: An Interactive Perspective of Social Psychology*, edited by Zachary Birchmeier, Beth Dietz-Uhler, and Garold Stasser. Cambridge: Cambridge University Press.

Williams, Kipling D., Christopher K. T. Cheung, and Wilma Choi. 2000. "Cyberostracism: Effects of Being Ignored over the Internet." *Journal of Personality and Social Psychology* 79(5):748–62.

Zhao, Shanyang. 2005. "The Digital Self: Through the Looking-Glass of Telecoprent Others." *Symbolic Interaction* 28(3):387–405.

Zuboff, Shoshana. 2015. "Big Other: Surveillance Capitalism and the Prospects of an Information Civilization." *Journal of Information Technology* 30(1):75–89.

CHAPTER 6

QUANTITATIVE MEASUREMENT AND THE PRODUCTION OF MEANING

HÉCTOR VERA

INTRODUCTION

IN this chapter, I apply insights from symbolic interactionism and cognitive sociology to interrogate underlying assumptions of quantitative measurement, to show how researchers work to assign meaning to measures, and to depict measurement as an intersubjective—cooperative and social—accomplishment. I develop three main ideas on the social nature of quantitative measurement: 1) measurement is a socio-cognitive operation, 2) measurement is the result of meaningful interactions, and 3) measurement is a cooperative effort. This chapter is *not* a new installment on the *methodenstreit* between qualitative and quantitative approaches in social sciences; neither is a compilation of the symbolic interactionists' critiques on statistics (Znaniecki 1934:307–19; Blumer 1969:124–39; Wiley 2011). I analyze how social scientists employ quantification and statistics, but I do not make any explicit *epistemological* argument on statistics or any other research method.

The first section of the chapter interrogates underlying assumptions and premises of quantitative measurement. After presenting a definition of measurement and quantification as *socio*-cognitive processes, I show how measurement is a radical form of *single-mindedness*, a mental attitude that focuses on one aspect of a multiform reality at the expense of anything else; it is a form of attention fixed on only one dimension shared by different objects. Then, I argue that measurement produces quantitative differences among qualitatively fluid realities, and in particular occasions those quantitative differences are used to demarcate and segregate entities in the qualitative continuum of reality. This *splitting by measuring* is a social process in which measurement is used to draw lines of demarcation that create (mentally) discrete entities.

The second section highlights how researchers work to assign meaning to quantitative methods and measures. It shows how measurements function as instruments that define situations and construct realities. Social scientists are social actors themselves, and as such they actively construct a meaningful world; as part of their work they collaborate—and wrestle—to produce units and methods of measurement, and to define what is a measurable object. Statistics are both meaning-making instruments and objects infused with meaning. The relationship between statistics and the production of meaning is thus twofold. First, a statistical datum is only understandable within a framework of meaning; numbers are constructed, and they only acquire meaning when they are seen through that frame of reference that renders them meaningful. Secondly, statistics are used to create—or reify—meaningful entities.

The third and final section shows that quantitative measurement is a collective and cooperative accomplishment. Sociology is a "world," a network of people that act cooperatively and that is organized through a shared knowledge of traditions and conventional means of doing things. Quantitative research methods are an important part of the bank of knowledge that helps members of the sociology world to act cooperatively; it aids in the coordination of large numbers of people interrelated but working separately at great social distances. Since sociology does not work under a common vocabulary or theoretical model, statistics has become a common ground that is shared by the majority of its practitioners. Vocabulary and theoretical models are fractured across an abundance of subfields; statistics is an inter-group language that transcends those distinctions. Finally, statistics is useful for coordination because it is a standard procedure of acquiring, processing, and interpreting data that also fit harmoniously with the standard formats of how science is communicated nowadays (in forms such as conference papers and scientific articles).

MEASUREMENT AS A SOCIO-COGNITIVE PROCESS: THE PREMISES OF QUANTITATIVE MEASUREMENT

Technically speaking, measurement "is the quantitative characteristic of a set, object, or entity of any description which is subject to correlation with some subset of the set of real numbers" (Wren 1973:335); but there is much more to it than that. Measurement is a mental operation that implies quantification, calculation, and comparison. It consists in associating numbers with physical quantities and phenomena. More specifically, measurement involves comparing a quantity with its corresponding unit to know how many times the latter is contained in the former. Through measurement it is possible to calculate sizes, magnitudes, dimensions, extent, degrees, values, and so on.

Quantification is "an attempt to reduce statements about the world to statements about quantities and relations among them" (Rapoport 1953:192), or more loosely is "the production and communication of numbers" (Espeland and Stevens 2008:402). One of the essential characteristics of quantification is to see reality—which is fluid and heterogeneous—as an aggregate of uniform units, as *quanta* (Crosby 1997:10). These quanta may be created to measure and quantify physical entities—like distance in meters, volume in liters, weight in grams, time in seconds, electricity in watts, temperature in Fahrenheit degrees—or social phenomena, such as life expectancy, fertility rate, unemployment rate, inflation, educational attainment, school enrollment, cultural capital, political participation, voter enthusiasm, status of occupations, intelligence quotient, subjective well-being, self-expression values, and so on.

Measurement and quantification are *socio*-cognitive processes. The act of measuring is never a mere individual action. People measure as members of specific thought communities. Forms of quantitative measurements present significant differences among various cultures, social groups, and historical periods. Measurement is intersubjective and follows conventional traditions (Zerubavel 1997). Moreover, measuring is not an action that all human beings perform in the same way; methods, instruments, and practices of measurement are socially and historically contingent. Measurement implies certain manners of perceiving and analyzing that facilitate the coordination of a human community.

Numbers, quantification, and measurement, like any other type of language, are social institutions (Fauconnet and Mauss 1901/2005:6–7). By practice and study, we learn to use numbers whose names, symbols, and internal relations are many centuries old. We receive them completely fashioned, and we are expected to accept and to use them without much variation. It would be useless for a single individual to attempt to create an original number system; such a system would only be a clumsy imitation of some other existing system. Furthermore, parting from rules and traditional usages of numbers would encounter energetic resistance. Measuring is an activity collectively shaped. It is previous and exterior to individuals, and it is organized through collective instruments and conventions. And like any other social fact, measuring implies a logic that a collectivity imposes over its members.

We measure different objects to determine what is similar among them and what makes them comparable. This process requires reducing them to one dimension and ignoring their many other potentially meaningful characteristics. Changes in what is attended and what is ignored in the mental apprehension of things will determine how to measure them. Witold Kula (1986:87) described this cognitive process:

> Of the many features exhibited by every object in a variety of contexts, we abstract one, and consequently, objects qualitatively as diverse as, say, a man's pace, a suit of clothing, a stretch of road, or the height of a tree, acquire a commensurability in our eyes, for we view them from but a single perspective, that of their length. The perfect divisibility and cumulativeness of [measurement systems] enables us to "compare" very great magnitudes, such as the length of terrestrial meridian, with very small ones, such as the thickness of a sheet of paper.

Measurement is, thus, a radical form of *single-mindedness*, a form of attention that is fixed on only one dimension or characteristic shared by different and comparable objects or phenomena, a mental attitude focused on one aspect of a multiform reality at the expense of all other existing aspects. As Kristen Purcell (1996) has argued, measurement involves comparison across highly varying objects that is only possible when some similarity is perceived and mentally heightened among those disparate objects; such comparability derives from a process of "mental leveling."

One of the most important effects of measurement and quantification is their effectiveness to separate entities, draw divisions, and set boundaries. Measurement produces quantitative differences that are regularly used to demarcate and segregate entities in the qualitative continuum of reality. This is a process of *splitting by measuring* through which quantities are used to draw lines among classificatory categories and create mentally discrete entities. Splitting by measuring contributes greatly to the way in which social groups classify the world. Numerical thresholds mark the boundaries that signal the beginning and ending of the classificatory category (Eco 1976:77). By setting quantitative thresholds, the different categories used in a system of classification became clearer and more easily distinguishable—that is, they became more meaningful. We then tend to reify these entities as if they were naturally set apart from others.

A few examples can illustrate this idea. Think about the way people are classified. Often, persons are classified and categorized according to specific *qualities*: gender, religion, ethnicity, nationality, and so forth. But there are frequent occasions when categories or kinds of people are differentiated from one another first by *quantifying* one of their multiple attributes, and second by lumping or splitting them in groups or classes that are differentiated by such quantities. Thus, people could be classified by age (i.e., by measuring the time elapsed since the moment when they were born). Age is used to determine voting rights, legal autonomy for sexual consent, draft eligibility, access to "senior citizen" privileges, and plenty other things. Income places people in different tax brackets. Grade point averages (GPA) are used to separate students who will make Dean's List recognizing their high level of scholarship and those who will not. The intelligence quotient (IQ) is used to determine eligibility for the Paralympics Summer Games. The body mass index (BMI), derived from the weight and height of a person, is employed to discriminate the "normal" from the "obese," the "overweight," and the "underweight."

Let us now explore an example in greater detail. Poverty is a category that is amply used in common discourse and social sciences. To determine what is "poverty" and who is "poor" is something that many persons think cannot be done with exactitude, that there is not a clear line between the poor and the not poor. Someone could argue that poverty is not a dimension with measurable magnitudes, but a condition. That is why most definitions of poverty point to a particular quality or situation. In medieval France, for example, "poor" referred to people "who beg for bread" or a person "who drinks sour milk, whose rye bread is full of straw and lives in the countryside with no roof" (Batany 1978:66). In current English poor means "having little money or few possessions," "lacking adequate supply of something." These definitions may capture something of the way we understand the experience of being poor, but they also fail to set clear and distinct criteria for determining who exactly we are talking about when we try to analyze poverty.

To achieve specificity—to think clearly and distinctly as Descartes mandated—social scientists quantify phenomena like poverty. Through quantification it is possible to establish clear and stable categories of people, and build classifications that draw lines among categories based on quantitative measurements. Governments and international agencies, like the World Bank, classify poverty based on the percentage of the population eating less food than is required to sustain the human body, approximately 2,000–2,500 calories per day. Others define poverty as living on 1.2 USD or less per day. Sharp numerical boundaries are constructed to categorize reality through measurement. The multiple and qualitative characteristics of poverty are abstracted to privilege a numerical index that determines on what side of the poverty line people should be located. Then, this determinant has consequences for our perceptions and social judgments, but also for the allocation of resources and moral valuations. We give the line that separates one side from the other a strong and meaningful social weight.

To be clear, measurement itself does not create the categories in which we classify reality, but it is often used to transform ambiguous categories into insular compartments. Language is certainly the main social instrument to create categories and to segment the world into meaningful chunks of reality (Zerubavel 1991:78). Naming categories is also a way of creating such categories; language constructs what social groups consider to be real. But numbers and quantities—not just words—are crucial to solidify and reify categories. Quantitative measurements segregate entities in an impersonal and inflexible way, promoting *rigid-mindedness* (Zerubavel 1991:35). The rigid mind rejects fluid thinking and intermediate entities, and using numbers is an effective way to mentally eliminate the intermediates between entities. Measures are, thus, an important ally of rigid-mindedness and its forms of classification; by eliminating ambiguity and helping rigid classifications to appear "objective," "impersonal," and "universal," quantification plays a decisive role in the process of "making up people" (Hacking 1986) and, more generally, in the process of making up the world.

Becoming a Statistics User: Measurement as a Meaningful, Collective Action

Symbolic interactionism puts the role of meaning in the formation of human behavior at the center of sociological inquiry (Blumer 1969:3). As an analytical approach, it is concerned with how individuals' meanings are created and negotiated through interaction with other individuals and how those meanings are embodied in symbols and discourse

(Brekhus 2015:11). Social worlds are an emergent and evolving space of meaning formed and negotiated through cycles of interaction, symbol generation, and interpretation and definition (Benzecry and Winchester 2017:45).

How could these principles be used to study the social life of measures? Paraphrasing Blumer's (1969:2) premises of symbolic interactionism, we can say that individuals act toward quantitative measures on the basis of the meanings that quantitative measures have for them; the meaning of quantitative measures is derived from, or arises out of, the social interaction that an individual has with her fellows; these meanings are handled in, and modified through, an interpretative process used by the person in dealing with the things she encounters.

One of the most famous studies on how people interacting in social groups produce and modify meanings is Howard Becker's "Becoming a Marihuana User" (1963:41–58). Becker described how marihuana consumers need to learn—with others and from others—to view pot smoking as something that can give them pleasure. In this process they learn the adequate smoking techniques, the way to perceive the effects, and how to enjoy those effects. They participate in a socially shaped appreciation of physical experience and in the collective interpretation of what kind of substances are pleasurable. To define—or redefine—the sensations they experience from getting high as pleasant ones, first-time smokers need to interact with more experienced users who "teach the novice to find pleasure in this experience which is at first so frightening" (1963:54–55). If beginners find that smoking weed is something enjoyable, they will continue with this practice. They will gradually grow a stable set of categories for experiencing the drug effects and become connoisseurs (1963:52).

Statistics users are not that different from marihuana users. They need to learn with others and from others that statistics, numbers, and tables are meaningful. When they feel that they are not consuming statistics in the right—enjoyable—way, they ask more experienced users for advice. Interaction with other users of statistics has an important role in acquiring the necessary concepts and abilities to find meaning and pleasure in quantitative measurements. Only then the novices become able to *get high* on statistics and continue its consumption and production. They have then obtained the necessary tools to express to others the meaning that numbers have for them. However, if they do not learn the proper techniques to read and make quantitative measurements, the full meaning of those numbers will not emerge, and they will not continue consuming that intellectual stimulant. If those techniques are not (adequately) learned by aspiring social scientists, statistics will become a meaningless object, and this will stop its consumption.

Let us take this analogy between pot practitioners and quantification stoners one step further to show how a social group uses quantification to produce meaning.

The communities of marihuana consumers, sellers, and producers develop conventions to participate and communicate with one another. Instruments and techniques are invented, codified, and shared to improve the experience of using marihuana. Part of this process of social distribution of marihuana-related knowledge is the standardization of labels and categories to describe and classify different types of marihuana, which are key to obtaining the desired experience from smoking.

Users frequently ask if they are buying the marihuana strain that is more relaxing or the one that is more psychoactive. In other words, they want to know if they will consume *sativa* ("day-time pot") or *indica* ("night-time pot"). But the multiplicity of strains on the market makes it difficult for consumers to know exactly what they are consuming (Posner 2018). And the abundance of street names—such as Durban, Poison, Sour Diesel, Jack Flash, and Jillybean—are not sufficiently shared among the community of users to solve this conundrum. These names, in other words, are not standardized and are not reliable. This is very different from the nomenclature of wines: a Malbec is recognized as a Malbec by the people involved in the world of wine and is distinct from other varieties, such as Pinot Noir.

Since marihuana was legalized in some states of the United States, producers have tried to create a market with commodities that are more stable, standardized, and reliable, and which can be more easily understandable by consumers. Cannabis entrepreneurs label strains like "70 percent sativa" or "60:40 sativa/indica ratio." These labels, even if they present percentages that look pretty exact, are actually intuitively assigned. They are done by people smoking that strain and deciding whether they get an indica or sativa effect from that joint. So, percentages of indica and sativa are subjectively established; or more precisely, they are intersubjectively established, as people smoking and estimating the sativa/indica ratio are following shared understandings of what kind of feelings one can get from the consumption of different types of marihuana. Even if the percentages are not exact, they are not meaningless.

The community of marihuana users transforms subjective appreciations into alleged quantities to facilitate communication and coordinated action. It matters little that those quantities are not actually determined with great accuracy or by following sound procedures. The label "70 percent sativa" conveys—for the people immersed in the world of marihuana consumption—a clear enough message about what that particular strain of weed would do to them if they smoked it. Here quantification is not used as a strict measurement. Rather, it is *employed to communicate in a meaningful way* to consumers the sensation produced by a drug. To smokers these intersubjectively assigned measurements are more meaningful to understand what they will feel than the strain names given in the street, like Cherry Star or Black Rhino.

Scientific communities—including sociologists—act collectively in a somewhat similar way. Of course, in science the methodology of measurement is more rigorous and follows stricter intersubjective principles, but the objective of producing meaningful numbers to communicate and coordinate better is crucial for both sociologists and marihuana users. That is why communities *construct* meaning through the use of numbers. *Quantification is used, by experts and lay people alike, to define the situations with which they are presented and to attach meaning to objects and events.*

Measurements and statistics are cultural products. They are produced by human communities that share meanings. Social scientists that employ measurement and statistics are like comic book readers, songs writers, or tattoo artists. Social scientists are social actors themselves, and as such they actively construct a meaningful world.

Quantitative social scientists measure and quantify to convey more effectively their discoveries and to find better ways to communicate their shared—and shifting—understanding of what they are talking about when they talk about society.

How are the numbers they use rendered meaningful? As with any other type of information, statistical numbers only became significant when read through the eyes of a certain worldview. Numbers do not have an intrinsic or transcending meaning, but there is no such thing as "mindless numbers" either. Rather, numbers can be interpreted in many different ways (Darnton 1999:258); pure, uninterpreted numbers do not exist. In the telling words of Lisa Gitelman (2013), "raw data is an oxymoron." A framework of meaning is indispensable to transform a number into a comprehensible and significant piece of information (Berger 1963:11). This framework of meaning also gives shape to the methods of measurement a community uses to create numbers.

The relationship between statistics and the production of meaning is, thus, twofold. First, a statistical datum is only understandable within a frame of meaning. Second, statistics are used to create or reify meaningful entities within that framework. Let us illustrate this double move with Emile Durkheim's *Suicide*, a pioneer quantitative work and probably the most famous sociological book based on statistical analysis.

The production of "moral statistics" in nineteenth-century Europe allowed Durkheim to resignify suicide as something more than an individual act caused by psychological factors like insanity, nervous disorder, alcoholism, or imitation. Durkheim rejected the emphasis put on the intentions of the individuals who committed suicide and stressed instead the importance of *suicide rates*. These rates could be compared among different groups and populations and showed definite patterns. Suicide *rates* allowed Durkheim to see suicide as a collective phenomenon and characterize it as a "social fact," instead of a purely psychological phenomenon. As Durkheim put it:

> The suicide-rate is therefore a factual order, unified and definite, as is shown by both its permanence and its variability. For this permanence would be inexplicable if it were not the result of a group of distinct characteristics, solidary one with another, and simultaneously effective in spite of different attendant circumstances; and this variability proves the concrete and individual quality of these same characteristics, since they vary with the individual character of society itself. In short, these statistical data express the suicidal tendency with which each society is collectively afflicted. (1897/2002:L)

Conversely, the conceptual framework built by Durkheim gave new meanings to the numbers collected by statisticians. The theoretical ideas of social integration and moral regulation, along with the typology of different kinds of suicide (altruistic, egoistic, and anomic) reconfigured the meaning attributed to the suicide rates "discovered" by the scholars and state agencies that collected and analyzed the data in the first instance. Seen through Durkheim's eyes, the difference in suicide rates—among nations, religious denominations, professions, marital status, and rural and urban areas—became something that made sense in an unexpected way. So, first statistics created a new and meaningful phenomenon (suicide as a *sui generis* social fact); then a novel framework of interpretation transformed the numbers into entities with a completely new meaning.

This twofold process of meaning production is also present in other scientific domains. This is what Peter Caws said about measurement in physics: "measurement presupposes something to be measured, and unless we know what that something is, no measurement can have any significance"; at the same time, there is a general feeling that "no physical property can really qualify as such unless we know how to measure it, i.e., unless we know how to describe situations involving it in mathematical terms" (1959:3).

Quantification and measurement give meaning to things. In doing that they are *instruments that define situations and construct realities.* They also *create* new social entities in both social and medical sciences. As Ian Hacking puts it, "quantification has an intrinsic tendency to generate new classifications of people" and to make new kinds of people (2007:308). Quantification has created new kinds of "normal" people and normal practices. For instance, sexual mores were (re)made after Alfred Kinsey surveyed the sexual behavior of Americans in the 1940s and 1950s. Individuals who considered themselves "lost" or "queer" found reassurance in the statistical data Kinsey presented to the public. What previously was an adult male's "abnormal attraction for men" or an adolescent propensity to masturbate became something "normal" when people compared their practices with the anonymous numbers of tables and percentages (Igo 2008:266). Quantification, on the other hand, also creates ill persons. When quantitative thresholds used to diagnose persons are changed, individuals considered "normal" suddenly became something else. That happened in 1998 when the National Institutes of Health changed their guidelines to define "overweight" and "obese." By lowering the threshold to be medically considered "fat," 25 million Americans entered suddenly into that category. Similarly, in 2017, when the American Heart Association changed the definition of "high blood pressure" from a cutoff of 140 over 90 to a one of 130 over 80, the percentage of Americans with "high blood pressure" jumped from 32 percent to 46 percent from one day to the next.

One of the tricky aspects of measures is that they are frequently based on other measures. Even some of the "simplest" forms of measurement present that characteristic. The *liter*, for example, is used to measure volume and is based on the meter (its official definition is 0.001 cubic meters). The *meter*, which measures length, is based on a unit of time, the *second* (the official definition of the meter is "the length of the path travelled by light in a vacuum during a time interval of 1/299 792 458 of a second"). The same goes for measures of social reality. The definition of economic recession depends on the measurement of the gross domestic product (GDP). And the GDP itself comprises a lot of agreements and assumptions about economic life. As Philipp Lepenies puts it:

> GDP is not a self-explanatory figure like the temperature in Fahrenheit, last year's CO_2 emissions in tons, or the total calories of your breakfast. Instead, it is a calculation method that includes certain aspects but excludes others. It relies on a

well-established convention, on one interpretation of what we understand output and the economy to be.

(Lepenies 2016:ix)

Lepenies is right, the GDP is not a self-explanatory figure, but neither are Fahrenheit degrees, tons, and calories. He fails to notice that the measurements of temperature, mass, and energy are achieved by human communities that work with *mental forms of exclusions and inclusion*, follow *conventions*, and develop changing forms *interpretation* and understating. Behind every unit, method, and interpretation of measurement there is a history of cooperation, dispute, and compromise.

Measurements in social sciences—as measurement in every activity—are not "snapshots" of processes; they do not "capture" reality, they do not "seize" the essence of a phenomenon. Rather, measurements are meaningful and collective constructs. They are conventional ways of seeing objects through radically reductionist lenses with hopes that by doing so they can make those objects comparable and comprehensible.

COOPERATION, CONVENTIONS, AND INERTIA: MEASUREMENT AS AN INTERSUBJECTIVE ACCOMPLISHMENT

Quantitative measurements are a collective and cooperative accomplishment. They require the coordinated and long-lasting action of small professional cliques or massive national—and even global—organizations and networks (Vera 2016, 2017). Some measures are only relevant for esoteric specialists; others have repercussions on whole countries (like a population census) or the entire planet (like standard time zones and the decimal metric system).

In sociology, statistics has been for a long time the most common form of measurement and quantification. It is completely intertwined with the discipline. Sociologists are not united by a common theoretical framework—in their vocabulary almost every key concept is polysemic and an object of dispute—but they have found in statistics a common ground that is assumed that the majority of practitioners share. This distinctive feature has not always been there, but since the first half of the twentieth century it has become ingrained in the profession. This is due to the influence of what Howard Becker (1995, 2008) called of *inertia* and the *conventions* of a social world.

Sociology could be seen as a "world." Paraphrasing Becker's (2008:xxiv) characterization of the art world, the *sociology world* is the network of people whose cooperative activity, organized via their joint knowledge of conventional means of doing things, produces the kind of sociological works that the sociology world is noted for.[1]

Statistics is an important part of that joint knowledge of the conventional means of doing sociological things.

The sociology world keeps using statistics (and a particular kind of statistics) due to a series of interconnected practices, relationships, and instruments that form a "package." Each piece in the package presupposes the existence of the others; pieces are connected in such a way that by choosing one of them it is very easy to take everything that comes with that choice, and enormously difficult to make substitutions (Becker 1995:304). What could be called the *package of statistical practices* ("statistics package") is an intertwined bundle. The most common and better-known software used to train new sociologists already presupposes a particular way of collecting, storing, processing, and presenting numerical data. Many of the middle and advanced statistical software and applications replicate several formats, functions, and commands of the basic software that many people now learn to use in high school, like Microsoft Excel. People are accustomed to using those tools and can work (individually and cooperatively) with them. Using Excel to teach introductory courses in statistics reduces the educational transaction costs. It is quicker and more effective to teach that way, because instructors can build on previous knowledge shared by a large number of students.

Other elements of this package of practices include the interaction between sociologists and people outside their inner professional circle. Sociologists need—intermittently—to communicate with a wider audience, an audience that expects certain kinds of information that they not only would consider as solid and reliable, but they also want it presented in a way that is understandable. Lay people can grasp percentages and can read basic graphs and charts (like pie and column graphs), but they do not want to see (or simply cannot comprehend) regressions or sophisticated probabilistic vocabulary.

Likewise, sociologists need to present their work in a comprehensible manner to the people who finance their work. Administrators in universities, foundations, and state agencies who evaluate projects tend to reward projects that they consider methodologically sound from the standpoint of quantitative techniques (since the 1950s scholars like William Foote Whyte [1955] have complained that is nearly impossible to get funding to do exploratory fieldwork, which is indispensable for adequate ethnographic research). On the other hand, people who finance research projects expect to receive proposals that they can grasp—too much innovation could go unrewarded. As Peter Berger (1963:11) noted, "The prominence of statistical techniques in American sociology today has [. . .] certain ritual functions that are readily understandable in view of the power system within which most sociologists have to make a career."

Support personnel also constrain the range of intellectual possibilities available. Cooperation all around is mediated by the use of conventions, which make the production of work easier but innovation more difficult (Becker 2008:63–66). The interdependence that links experts and laypeople imposes limitations to any plan to radically transform existing forms of measurement and suggests specific ways to legitimize and maintain the existing methods of measurement (Vera 2015:176).

Conversely, the outer circles of the sociology world are what in most cases make possible the existence of quantitative inquiry in sociology. Let us go back to our Durkheim example. The notable difference between Durkheim and previous social thinkers in terms of how they used numbers is not a product of their personal inclinations or intellectual skills. The rudimentary use of statistics among savants of the eighteenth and early nineteenth centuries in their observations of demography or economics, for example, is the result of a world where the production of numbers on social matters was virtually inexistent. Durkheim, on the other hand, took advantage of a world where official statistics were rapidly growing. Durkheim did not participate in the making of suicide statistics; he just made an innovative use of material that his world created.

In the 1950s, Pitirim Sorokin lashed into common practices among sociologists that he labeled as "fads and foibles." While talking about "quantophrenia"—a term he coined—Sorokin described some peculiar "rites" among researchers:

> everyone can be a "researcher" and a "scientific investigator," because everyone can take a few sheets of paper, fill them with all sorts of questions, mail the questionnaires to all possible respondents, received the answered copies, classify them in this or that way, process them through a tabulating machine, arrange the results into several tables (with all the mechanically computed percentages, coefficients of correlation, Chi-Square indices, standard deviations and probable errors), and then write a paper or a book filled with the most impressive array of tables, formulae, indices, and other evidence of an "objective, thorough, precise, quantitative" research. These are the typical "rites" in "contemporary quantitative research." (1956:172–73)

Even though this was written more than six decades ago, it feels pretty similar to our present experience. It only shows its age for the reference to *mechanical* computing, which is telling of the nature of how sociologists have operated since those years. The basic principles of quantitative training have been mostly static for decades, but the artifacts used to put those principles in practice have changed continuously. From the point of view of its material tools, statistics may look like a constantly changing field. The dates of inventions of some of the most popular statistical gadgets demonstrate this: slide rule (1859), adding machine (1902), calculator (1921), electronic calculator (1957), scientific calculator (1968), personal computers (1977), and then the statistics software— Statistical Package for the Social Sciences (SPSS) (1968), Microsoft Excel (1985), Stata (1985), R (1995), and so on. However, despite the constant improvement in computational capabilities, the basic training in statistics has remained remarkably stable.

Furthermore, one can take five different textbooks on criminology, culture, or race, and almost certainly one will find five different takes on the main arguments; but if you compare five textbooks on statistics for social scientists, you will find that they are interchangeable. For more than half a century, methodology textbooks and statistics manuals for social science majors have used the same rhetorical formulas and have encouraged the teaching of the same substantive topics. No matter if these textbooks are from the 1960s or the 2010s, from Germany (Kellerer 1967), France (Duverger 1964), or the United States (Blalock 1960; Frankfort-Nachmias, Nachmias, and DeWaard 2015), the elementary features on the basics of statistics have remained unchanged. The themes taught are identical in those texts: mean/median/mode, probability, correlation, representativeness, regressions, sample size, and so forth.

The overall justification of the importance to learn and use statistics has also been the same everywhere. Authoritative texts present statistics as the surest way to reach more precise information, certainty, scientificity, objectivity, rigor, pertinent knowledge for decision making, faster and stronger analysis of data, and so on. French sociologist Maurice Duverger presented this idea eloquently in his introductory textbook to social science methods:

> In striving to introduce 'quantification' and mathematics into their disciplines as far as possible, specialists in the social sciences, contrary to what many laymen think, are not merely deferring to a fashion, but are recognizing that mathematics provides analytical tools incomparably more effective than classical comparative methods. The results obtained by methods described in previous chapters [content analysis, interviews, participant observation] are as different from those which mathematics can achieve as walking is from travel by jet aircraft (1964:277).

Even what methodologists and statisticians perceive as the main obstacles to teaching quantitative methods have remained pretty much the same: students are intimidated by a subject that seems too complicated, lack of basic mathematical training, misconceptions among students and the general public about why numbers and measurements are important, unwillingness to learn a new way to see the world, previous teachers were unable to transmit the exciting possibilities of statistics, and so on. Sixty years ago Blalock put it this way in his *Social Statistics*: "One of the most difficult problems encountered in the teaching of applied statistics is that of motivating students, both in enabling them to overcome their fears of mathematics and in learning to apply statistics to their own field of interest" (1960:vii). At the beginning of the twenty-first century, Ferris Ritchey's *Statistical Imagination* reproduced the same idea: "Unfortunately, students do not always appreciate how much fun a statistics course can be" (2000:xvii).

This continuity and homogeneity—in both the research techniques taught and the justifications to use them—show the power of inertia. Statistics is a package of practices and relationships that help to make up a sociological world. It is always convenient to use the already present elements of the package as it is to justify the purpose of the actions related to the package. It is the package that contains the inertial force (Becker 1995:304). In the midst of inertia, innovations are still possible, but they meet considerable resistance from the status quo.

The power of inertia can be witnessed in the fact that the present form of statistics in sociology has prevailed despite repeated criticisms about its limitations that came from within the quantitative camp in sociology and from professional statisticians. A decade after Sorokin made his critique of "quantophrenia," "metrophrenia," and "testomania," Skipper, Guenther, and Nass published in *The American Sociologist* a piece on "the sacredness of.05" to condemn sociologists' use of statistical levels of significance. "Casual examination of the literature," they said, "discloses that the common, arbitrary and virtually sacred levels of. 05, .01, and .001 are almost universally selected regardless of the nature and type of problem. Of these three, .05 is perhaps most sacred" (1967:16). They stressed how using that convention demands little "psychic energy" on the part of researchers and that "blind adherence to the .05 level denies any consideration of alternative strategies, and it is a serious impediment to the interpretation of data" (1967:17). Calls to leave behind this kind of uncritical reproduction of statistical commonplaces have been continuous. Scientists from several disciplines have made calls in journals like *Nature* (Amrhein et al. 2019) and *The American Statistician* (McShane et al. 2019) to change how statistical significance ought to be used. However, this piece of the interconnected package of statistical practices apparently will not crumble any time soon. How can the durability of these practices be explained? They persist for sociological reasons, and they are part of operative conventions within a professional community.

Finally, we should take another idea from Becker to analyze how statistics facilitate coordination and cooperation among social scientists: the production of standardized representations of society. In other words, statistics are a conventional form of representing the social world. They are a standard language that consists of recognizable symbols and well-known formats that facilitate understanding and coordination among the members of a community. Furthermore, quantitative methods are conventional forms of inquiry that fit harmoniously with the main formats and codes of communications among scientific communities. Representations are the products of these communities. Social scientists produce representations of society in a standard form that everyone understands and knows how to make and use. These standards are taken for granted. Data in social science sciences are frequently presented in numeric tables, organized in a standard form. The producers and readers of these tables take them as unproblematic, and as such they are an effective means of communication. People also develop standard ways of reading those tables. Standardized formats allow readers to find the information they want in an article more quickly and choose what articles to read according to their level of statistical knowledge (Becker 2007:71–73).

Likewise, many forms previously used to represent society today are simply deemed "unscientific." Fictional narrations, dialogs, and poems, for example, were amply used in previous centuries, but nowadays no professional journal—no matter how mainstream or unconventional—would publish a representation of society that follows those specific forms. Actually, fiction and poetry would not be acceptable for any of the common vehicles of scientific communication: dissertations, conference papers, journal articles, lectures, and so on. However, poetry and literature—as statistics—are communicative modes with which to make arguments and advance ideas about the nature of society. The narrowing of acceptable forms is not about the adequacy of old forms of scientific communication. Dialogues—that venerable genre cultivated by Plato, Galileo, and Hume—could be far more effective for presenting opposite views on an intellectual issue than our dry and dull literature reviews. However, dialogues have been abandoned for more than a century.

Poetry was another literary device amply used to create representations of society—like Voltaire's *The Henriade* (1723/1797), a fifty-thousand-word poem that celebrates the life of Henry IV of France, which reflects on topics like religious radicalism and civil discord, and evaluates the political situation of France prior to the seventeenth century. Later poetry was reduced to pedagogical purposes. Poems that use meter and rhyme are useful to remember important things (e.g., Townsend 1852). Nowadays it is unimaginable that a sociology textbook would be written in verse, despite its possible usefulness. Verse is not only easier to remember than plain prose; people can even add a melody to the verses to make them even easier to memorize. Regardless, poems and songs are not acceptable conventions of scientific communication.

Representations of society through the creation of fictional characters and situations have also been expelled from the sociology world, despite some great examples of its fruitfulness. Think, for instance, on Montesquieu's *Persian Letters* (1721/2008). The book consists of the correspondence of two Persian noblemen who travel to Paris and reflect on French morals, customs, and institutions. It was a representation of France from the point of view of an outsider. *Persian Letters* was a pioneer in defamiliarization, by presenting to the French public their own society in an unfamiliar way. Creating a story with fictional characters was an effective and powerful representation of French society. However, today fiction can only be used as a vignette and maybe as counterfactuals. Not even narratives that aim to describe social relations in a naturalistic style or novels that required years of documental research would be acceptable as valid representations of society, as Montesquieu's work was in his time.

Contrary to our current compulsion to quantify reality, Montesquieu did not feel the urge to express his ideas in a mathematically sophisticated way; not even when he wrote about demographic issues, like his chapter "on laws and their relation to the number of inhabitants" in *The Spirit of the Laws* (1748/1989:427). For him, Lord Kelvin's famous dictum—"When you can measure what you are speaking about, and express it in numbers, you know something about it, when you cannot express it in numbers, your knowledge is of a meager and unsatisfactory kind" (Thompson 1891:80)—would have been an alien idea. And more importantly, for Montesquieu's intellectual world it was unnecessary to use a fully developed language of quantification. They met in salons and *cafés* to discuss philosophical ideas about society and were able to communicate effectively in an almost innumerate way. That world operated with different conventions of truth and communicability than ours.

Vis-à-vis Montesquieu's world, ours is more attuned to Kelvin's idea of reliable knowledge, and it operates under new group understandings of what is good, effective, and believable communication. Even more recent thinkers like Simmel could still write in the 1900s dozens of pages about the "quantitative conditioning of the group" (Simmel

1908/2009) without using graphs, tables, or curves. It is symptomatic of our time that contemporary scholars felt the urge to translate the ideas of classical sociologists in a formalized, mathematized way, presenting their interpretation of thinkers like Simmel (Caplow 1969) or Tocqueville (Elster 2009) using graphics and equations.

Measurements and statistics function today as shorthand to share our work with others. In professional meetings a 60-minute roundtable can easily hold three papers. In 15 minutes or less presenters pose a research question, pass around handouts with a couple of tables, point out the "statically significant" results they got, and finally present a brief conclusion. Eloquence, elegance, and the art of conversation were imperative in Montesquieu's world. In our current sociology world simplicity and succinctness are a premium. One could fly coast to coast to present a paper in 12 minutes and listen to 40 colleagues do the same—and being honest, many of us think that the majority of those presentations could have been better if they lasted just 10 or 8 minutes long. Montesquieu and Voltaire would have been shocked to learn that in the twenty-first century scientists considered that a conference poster, showing a table and a couple of graphs, would be an acceptable form of intellectual communication. Statistics has become crucial to achieve brevity in the communication of scientific ideas; it is a great time-saving device when it comes to conveying sociological ideas.

Conclusion

The topics addressed in this chapter could be useful to refine our understanding of measurement. Quantification and measurement are crucial in modern societies. However, we ought to develop a clearer understanding of how scholars use them (or, perhaps are used by them) to make and shift their meanings. A symbolic interactionist approach to the production of measurement could be a welcome addition to the burgeoning field of the sociology of quantification and measurement. It is already well known that measurement is intertwined with social life, that it is influenced by social activity and, at the same time, influences society. By bringing the analytical focus to cognition, meanings, interactions, and cooperative worlds, this field can gain a finer understanding of the significance and endurance of our current compulsion to translate all areas of human endeavor into numbers.

Note

1. Even though Becker's concept of "world" underplays the dimensions of power, domination, and inequality that permeate cooperative networks of people, here we would take the concept at face value. It should just be said briefly that different groups may enter in power disputes to define which methods of measurement are better (Vera 2018).

References

Amrhein, Valentin, Sander Greenland, and Blake McShane. 2019. "Scientists Rise Up Against Statistical Significance." *Nature* 567:305–7.

Batany, J. 1978. "El vocabulario de la categorías sociales en algunos moralistas franceses hacia 1200." Pp. 63–82 in *Ordenes, estamentos y clases*, edited by D. Roche. Madrid: Siglo Veintiuno.

Becker, Howard S. 1963. *Outsiders: Studies in the Sociology of Deviance*. New York: The Free Press.

Becker, Howard S. 1995. "The Power of Inertia." *Qualitative Sociology* 18:301–9.

Becker, Howard S. 2007. *Telling About Society*. Chicago: University of Chicago Press.

Becker, Howard S. 2008. *Art Worlds*. Berkeley: University of California Press.

Benzecry, Claudio, and Daniel Winchester. 2017. "Varieties of Microsociology." Pp. 42–74 in *Social Theory Now*, edited by Claudio Benzecry, Monika Krause, and Isaac Reed. Chicago: University of Chicago Press.

Berger, Peter. 1963. *Invitation to Sociology: A Humanistic Perspective*. Garden City: Doubleday.

Blalock, Hubert M. 1960. *Social Statistics*. New York: McGraw Hill.

Blumer, Hebert. 1969. *Symbolic Interactionism: Perspectives and Method*. Englewood Cliffs, NJ: Prentice Hall.

Brekhus, Wayne H. 2015. *Culture and Cognition: Patterns in the Social Construction of Reality*. London: Polity.

Caplow, Theodore. 1969. *Two against One: Coalitions in Triads*. Englewood Cliffs, NJ: Prentice Hall.

Caws, Peter. 1959. "Definition and Measurement in Physics." Pp. 3–17 in *Measurement, Definitions and Theories*, edited by West Churchman and Philburn Ratoosh. New York: John Wiley.

Crosby, Alfred W. 1997. *The Measure of Reality: Quantification in Western Europe, 1250–1600*. Cambridge: Cambridge University Press.

Darnton, Robert. 1999. *The Great Cat Massacre and Other Episodes in French Cultural History*. New York: Basic Books.

Durkheim, Emile. 1897/2002. *Suicide: A Study in Sociology*. London: Routledge.

Duverger, Maurice. 1964. *Introduction to the Social Sciences; with Special Reference to Their Methods*. London: G. Allen & Unwin.

Eco, Umberto. 1976. *A Theory of Semiotics*. Bloomington: Indiana University Press.

Elster, Jon. 2009. *Alexis de Tocqueville, the First Social Scientist*. Cambridge: Cambridge University Press.

Espeland, Wendy Nelson, and Mitchell Stevens. 2008. "A Sociology of Quantification." *European Journal of Sociology* 49:401–36.

Fauconnet, Paul, and Marcel Mauss. 1901/2005. "Sociology." Pp. 1–31 in *The Nature of Sociology*, edited by Marcel Mauss. New York: Berghahn Books.

Frankfort-Nachmias, Chava, David Nachmias, and Jack DeWaard. 2015. *Research Methods in the Social Sciences*. New York: Worth Publishers.

Gitelman, Lisa, ed. 2013. *"Raw Data" Is an Oxymoron*. Cambridge: MIT Press.

Hacking, Ian. 2007. "Making Up People." Pp. 222–36 in *Reconstructing Individualism*, edited by T. C. Heller et al. Stanford: Stanford University Press.

Hacking, Ian. 1986. "Kinds of People, Moving Target." *Proceedings of the British Academy* 151:285–318.

Igo, Sarah. 2008. *The Averaged American: Surveys, Citizens, and the Making of a Mass Public*. Cambridge: Harvard University Press.

Kellerer, Hans. 1967. *La estadística en la vida económica y social.* Madrid: Alianza.

Kula, Witold. 1986. *Measures and Men.* Princeton: Princeton University Press.

Lepenies, Philipp. 2016. *The Power of a Single Number: A Political History of GDP.* New York: Columbia University Press.

McShane, Blakeley et al. 2019. "Abandon Statistical Significance." *The American Statistician* 73:235–45.

Montesquieu. 1721/2008. *Persian Letters.* New York: Oxford University Press.

Montesquieu. 1748/1989. *The Spirit of the Laws.* Cambridge: Cambridge University Press.

Posner, Joe (producer and writer). 2018. *Weed Explained.* Video file. Retrieved from https://www.netflix.com/mx-en/title/80216752.

Purcell, Kristen. 1996. "In a League of Their Own: Mental Leveling and the Creation of Social Comparability." *Social Forum* 11:435–56.

Rapoport, Anatol. 1953. *Operational Philosophy Integrating Knowledge and Action.* New York: Harper & Brothers.

Ritchey, Ferris. 2000. *The Statistical Imagination.* London: McGraw Hill.

Simmel, Georg. 1908/2009. *Sociology: Inquiries into the Construction of Social Forms.* Leiden: Brill.

Skipper, James, Antony Guenther, and Gilbert Nass. 1967. "The Sacredness of.05: A Note Concerning the Uses of Statistical Levels of Significance in Social Science." *The American Sociologist* 2:16–18.

Sorokin, Pitirim. 1956. *Fads and Foibles in Modern Sociology.* Chicago: Henry Regnery Company.

Thompson, William. 1891. *Popular Lectures and Addresses.* London: Macmillan.

Townsend, Hannah. 1852. *History of England, in Verse, from the Invasion of Julius Cæsar to the Present Time.* Philadelphia: Lindsay & Blackiston.

Vera, Hector. 2015. "The Social Construction of Units of Measurement: Institutionalization, Legitimation and Maintenance in Metrology." Pp. 173–87 in *Standardization in Measurement: Philosophical, Historical and Sociological Issues,* edited by Lara Huber and Oliver Schlaudt. London: Pickering and Chatto.

Vera, Hector. 2016. "Weights and Measures." Pp. 459– 471 in *Blackwell Companion to the History of Science,* edited by Bernard Lightman. Oxford: Blackwell Publishers.

Vera, Hector. 2017. "Counting Measures: The Decimal Metric System, Metrological Census, and State Formation in Revolutionary Mexico, 1895–1940." *Histoire & Mesure* 32:121–40.

Vera, Hector. 2018. "Breaking Global Standards: The Anti-Metric Crusade of American Engineers." Pp. 189–215 in *Technology and Globalisation: Networks of Experts in World History,* edited by David Pretel and Lino Camprubí. New York: Palgrave.

Voltaire. 1723/1797. *The Henriade: An Epic Poem in Ten Cantos.* London: Burton and Co.

Whyte, William Foote. 1955. *Street Corner Society: The Social Structure of an Italian Slum.* Chicago: Chicago University Press.

Wiley, Norbert. 2011. "The Chicago School: A Political Interpretation." Pp. 39–74 in *Interactionism: The Emerging Landscape,* edited by Lonnie Athens and Ted Faust. Bongley: Emerald.

Wren, F. Lynwood. 1973. *Basic Mathematical Concepts.* New York: McGraw Hill.

Zerubavel, Eviatar. 1991. *The Fine Line: Making Distinctions in Everyday Life.* New York: The Free Press.

Zerubavel, Eviatar. 1997. *Social Mindscapes: An Invitation to Cognitive Sociology.* Cambridge: Harvard University Press.

Znaniecki, Florian. 1934. *The Method of Sociology.* New York: Rinehart & Company.

CHAPTER 7

SOCIAL ORGANIZATION, MACRO PHENOMENA, AND SYMBOLIC INTERACTIONISM

PATRICK J. W. MCGINTY

THE interactionist study of social organization is at a crossroads, and the concept—as the interactionist approach to social structure—remains largely problematic within the larger discipline of sociology. This current situation is the result of numerous conditioning influences that have been exacerbated over time, including: the disciplinary dichotomization of micro- and macro-phenomena; the reification process through which symbolic interactionism has been crafted into a micro-oriented perspective; and a unique disciplinary false consciousness about the relationship between interactionism and the larger discipline. As a result, while the interactionist analysis of social structural and macro phenomena is believed to be a rarity, the use of broadly interactionist theoretical insights throughout the discipline is a fundamental disciplinary standard. Furthermore, interactionist insights are playing a more noticeable role in sociological theorizing as the discipline continues to call for more relational forms of sociological analysis. This chapter explores the historically conditioned and consequential nature of these developments while identifying a set of concerns interactionist scholars will need to address in attending to a call for increasing interactionist attention to the study of social organization and macro phenomena.

SYMBOLIC INTERACTIONISM'S CONCEPT OF SOCIAL ORGANIZATION

While a history of symbolic interactionism's understanding and conceptualization of social organization is necessary to contextualize the remaining argument, an initial caveat is required: symbolic interactionism is not a monolithic entity—there is no one single symbolic interactionism. This grossly pragmatic assertion is a necessary preface to all that follows, simply because the social-organization concept—while generally consistent in application—does vary by the interactionism being practiced by the concept user. This is so much the case that even the origin, history, and development of the concept is worthy of a brief conversation.

When Charles H. Cooley wrote *Human Nature and the Social Order* (1902/1922), *Social Organization* (1909), and later *Social Process* (1918/1966), it was not necessarily with an eye toward unpacking anything more than his own sociological perspective on the social condition. Each work demonstrates—albeit in different ways—sets of concerns similar to those that would eventually be taken up by followers of George H. Mead, the Chicago School of Sociology, and eventually those scholars that would self-identify as "symbolic interactionists." For Cooley, social unity is found through the social mind—the historically linked, interactional, unified, and cooperative nature of mental acts. Furthermore, said unity is found "not in agreement, but in organization . . . by virtue of which everything that takes place in it is connected with everything else, and so is an outcome of the whole" (Cooley 1909:4). Cooley continues, "this differentiated unity of mental or social life, present in the simplest intercourse but capable of infinite growth and adaptation, is what I mean in this work by social organization" (Cooley 1909:4). For Cooley, this condition—the social organization of social life—was such that we need "only to open our eyes to *see* organization; and if we cannot do that no definition will help us" (Cooley 1909:4, emphasis in original). In his early work, Cooley considered "social organization" to be the historically linked organization of social life and interaction as an empirically verifiable reality. From its earliest association with what would eventually come to be identified as "symbolic interactionism," it is clear that the social-organization concept was rooted in social intercourse (interaction) relative to empirically verifiable social conditions that are historically and conditionally linked.

Similarly, George Herbert Mead's ([1934] 2017) most general use of the social-organization concept in the context of his expression of society is based on the interrelationship of social units. Mead writes:

> The interlocking interdependence of human individuals upon one another within the given organized social life-process in which they are all involved is becoming more and more intricate and closely knit and more highly organized as human social evolution proceeds on its course. The wide difference, for example, between the feudal civilization of medieval times, with its relatively loose and disintegrated social organization, and the national civilization of modern times, with its tight and integrated social organization (together with its trend of development toward some form of international civilization), exhibits the constant evolution of human social organization in the direction of greater and greater relational unity and complexity, more and more closely knit interlocking and integrated unifying of all the social relations of interdependence which constitute it and which hold among the individuals involved in it.

> (Mead 1934/2017:310–11)

Evolutionary assumptions about society aside, Mead's insights into modern social organization as interlocking, integrated, and social relational with involved human actors cannot be overlooked.

Following Mead, albeit in an interpretation all his own, Herbert Blumer's (1969) expression of the society concept provides evidence of a maturing set of focal concerns for the concept of social organization. In taking up the idea of society as symbolic interaction, Blumer places the fragmentary interactionist expression of the society concept at the feet of "Charles Horton Cooley, W. I. Thomas, Robert E. Parks [sic], E. W. Burgess, Florian Znaniecki, Ellsworth Faris, and James Mickel Williams" along with "William James, John Dewey, and George Herbert Mead" (Blumer 1969:78). Using the concept of "situations" to move his analysis, Blumer provides an analysis of the key distinction between the mainstream sociological approach to social structures—which he identifies as being devoid of human interpretation—and the interactionist conception in which human actors do not act toward social structures, but rather act toward situations (Blumer 1969:89). Coalescing around the idea of situations Blumer provides a distinctly interactionist social organizational approach, he writes:

> First, from the standpoint of symbolic interaction the organization of human society is the framework inside of which social action takes place and is not the determinant of that action. Second, such organization and changes in it are the product of the activity of acting units and not of "forces" which leave such acting units out of account.
>
> (Blumer 1969:87)

Just as Blumer's explanation clearly identifies how the interactionist conceptualization of social organization differs from the mainstream sociological concern for social structure, his comments also define the origin of social organization through social action.

In furthering the interactionist analysis of social organization, David R. Maines highlights Blumer's expression of the concept and identifies three important concerns. First, the coalescing of the concept around an explicit set of concerns is difficult to identify—suggesting that the early contemporary concept may have its roots in the "synthesis of Mead and Park, initially through the work of Hughes, and later through scholars such as Becker, Habenstein, Roy, and Stone" (Maines 1982:267). Second, it is clear to Maines that the work of Anselm Strauss (1959, 1978) is central to the development of the contemporary concept and that the concept is grounded in "Strauss' publication Mirrors and Masks (1959), in which he advocated the merging of social organization and social psychology" (Maines 1982:267). Third, Maines argues that the negotiated order perspective (Strauss 1978; Strauss et al. 1963) provides the initial framework for the contemporary interactionist study of social organization.

By this historical telling, what do we know about symbolic interactionism's social-organization concept? We know it is not a unitary monolithic concern—there is not just one social-organization concept. Following the above point, we do know that the responsibility for the development of the concept is shared by some combination of scholars including Becker, Blumer, Burgess, Cooley, Dewey, Faris, Habenstein, Hughes, James, Mead, Park, Roy, Stone, Strauss, Thomas, Williams, and Znaniecki. We also know that the core symbolic interactionist understanding of the social-organization concept is that it is a mechanism that provides the basis for the viewing of the conditioning, consequential, and emergent nature of activity that occurs in social situations. Subsequently, social organization is not simply a social force that exists outside human activity that compels limited ranges of action. Finally, following the above, we know that the social-organization concept is not simply the symbolic-interactionist approach to social structure. In a generic way it is that, but at the same time, such a view would be extremely limiting. To that end, the contemporary understanding of the social-organization concept is a conditioned response to a series of academic conversations about symbolic interactionism, the relationship of the interactionist perspective to the larger discipline of sociology, the sociological definition and study of social structure, and the capacity of the interactionist perspective to attend to macro phenomena.

THE EMERGENCE OF THE CONTEMPORARY SOCIAL-ORGANIZATION CONCEPT

While Blumer's publication of *Symbolic Interactionism: Perspective and Method* (1969) definitely provided institutional legitimacy for the symbolic-interactionist perspective in the form of a shared set of foundational concerns, it also served as a basis for the coalescing of criticism from both inside and outside the perspective regarding interactionism's capacity to attend to particular social forms, most notably, social structure and macro phenomena.

There is no question that the bulk of the criticisms noting interactionism's presumed micro-level, astructural biases develop after Blumer's (1969) polemical treatise. Additionally, while there are undoubtedly other still unidentified conditioning factors, the disciplinary critique of symbolic interactionism as having an inherent micro-level, astructural bias must be seen as a response to the growth and development of a symbolic-interactionist perspective that was increasingly attentive to Blumer's (1969) three premises of the perspective.

Given the nature of the disciplinary critiques of symbolic interactionism as maintaining micro and astructural biases, the study of social organization within the interactionist perspective quickly became the academic arena in which the debate about interactionism's presumed biases played out. The result was the development of a sophisticated body of literature that explored how symbolic interactionism approaches macro phenomena and social structures. At the same time, the responses of interactionist scholars to said disciplinary critiques provided new depth, breadth, and sophistication of the social-organization concept within interactionism.

There is a certain degree of irony—as well as messiness and inconsistency—in these developments. On the one hand, consider the wide-ranging criticisms of interactionism as being ahistorical (Block 1973; Smith 1973; Ropers 1973), acritical (Kanter 1972), and astructural (Gouldner 1970; Wagner 1964). In general, each of the scholars offering up said critiques are responding to the interactionist perspective from standpoints that are grounded in theoretical traditions in sociology that assumes social structure to be a phenomenon apart from, and acting upon, human activity through social forces. On the other hand, consider the insight that prior to Blumer's (1969) identification of symbolic interaction, the work of the scholars associated with the Chicago School of Sociology whose work—albeit in different ways is generally recognized as contributing to the interactionist concept of social organization—was simply considered "good sociology." Before Blumer (1969), the undefined interactionism of the Chicago School of Sociology was to be lauded. However, after Blumer (1969) the perspective that is now "named" (symbolic interactionism) is apparently incapable of attending to the very concerns it had already been attending to.

Andrew Abbott (2009) alludes to this discrepancy as the source of the disciplinary divide. Abbott's point is that the critiques of interactionism are rooted not in the inability of interactionist scholars to actually attend to structural concerns, but rather in their rejection of the dominant disciplinary language surrounding social structural phenomena.

While the responses of interactionist scholars to the external critiques varied, the social-organization concept and the interactionist study of social organization became the primary means of addressing the external critiques. In the responses to the external critiques, the work of David Maines (1977, 1982, 1988; Maines and Morrione 1990) serves up an initial orienting narrative about the historical conditioning of the social-organization concept and sets the stage for the contemporary shaping of the concept. In turn, the body of work from Peter M. Hall (1987, 1995, 1997; Hall and Spencer-Hall 1982; Hall and McGinty 1997) further specifies the social-organization concept by outlining a set of sensitizing concerns that can be used to drive the interactionist study of social organization.

Maines's orienting narrative centers on two key considerations, and he uses both considerations together to concretize the foundational basis for the contemporary analysis of social organization. First, Maines develops the idea that a "social organizational approach in symbolic interactionism . . . is much better developed than commonly believed by sociologists" (Maines 1977:235). Furthermore, Maines (1977) organizes attention to the presentation of evidence in favor of the assertion that "symbolic interactionism can maintain its conceptual integrity and at the same time embrace a social structural position" (1977:243). In support of this assertion, Maines highlights the negotiated-order perspective (Strauss et al. 1963) and how negotiated orders are evident in both small-scale negotiations (such as situated interactions) as well as large-scale ones (such as institutions, organizations, and markets).

Second, building on the idea of the negotiated order, Maines (1982:268) advances the notion that the "mesostructure" is "the realm of social life" to which the study of social organization is best applied. Maines uses the mesostructure concept in an effort to reduce the disciplinary divide between interactionist and larger disciplinary concerns regarding the micro-macro divide (1982:277). To that end, Maines concludes that mesostructures are:

> realms of human conduct through which social structures are processed and social processes become structured . . . It is not just that new processes lead to new

structural arrangements, or that structural change leads to associated processual change as Strauss (1978:257) notes, but that structural arrangements exist in and through processes that render those structures operative. It is in this sense of the *interpenetration* of structure and process that negotiated orders specify a macrostructural realm of reality.

(Maines 1982:277–78, original emphasis)

That is, the mesostructure concept is designed to explore the dialectical relationship of micro and macro structures and processes.

In addition to orienting interactionists to contemporary social organization using the concept of "mesostructures," Maines (1988) and Maines and Morrione (1990) would come to apply the general contours of their concern for social organization to the exposition and analysis of Blumer's sociological attention to institutional and structural phenomena. Their primary assertions included two interrelated ideas. First, that Blumer's sociology was not, despite accusations otherwise, inherently microsociological. Second, that the real issues behind the disciplinary myth(s) and assumptions about Blumer's microsociological bias are rooted in: (1) the symbolic interactionist inattention to a mythical construction of Blumer, and (2) the inattention to the evidence of Blumer's attention to macrostructural concerns, by both interactionist and non-interactionist scholars. As a form of critical analysis, Maines easily demonstrates how the very disciplinary concepts of micro and macro are uniquely situated negotiated orders.

Building from Maines' concern for the mesostructure concept as the mechanism to explore social organization, Peter M. Hall identifies a number of sensitizing concerns that form a sophisticated framework for the interactionist study of social organization. In its fullest formulation, Hall's approach to the study of social organization—mesodomain analysis—is understood in terms of a handful of core concepts: conditions, action context, network of collective activity, tasks, interests/intentions, conventions/practices, contingencies/opportunities, consequences, and linkages. However, Hall explains the general mesodomain framework in these terms:

> Mesodomain analysis explores social organization as recurring patterns of collective activity, linked contexts, and social conditions across space and time. It examines the intersection of historical, structural, and action contexts, showing how history and "structure" shape action and how actions (re)produce history and "structure." Its conceptual framework includes collective activity, networks, power, conventions, intentions, processibility, and temporality.

(Hall 2003:37)

The results of the use of these sensitizing concepts employed by mesodomain analysis are three-fold. First, mesodomain analysis is able to attend to issues of temporality and location as well as the associated concerns of trajectory and history. That is, the social-organization concept becomes linked to temporal, contextual/structural, and action contexts. Second, mesodomain analysis serves to highlight the processual ordering of the transformation of actors' intentions (Hall and McGinty 1997). The significance of this contribution is explained in this way, "transforming intentions . . . is a consequence of human agency. The transformation of intentions is a generic social process" (Hall and McGinty 1997:465). Cast in this way, mesodomain analysis is not only a framework for the study of social organization: it is also a framework that outlines the constituent components of generic social processes and links them into a theoretically consistent whole.

Lastly, mesodomain analysis explains the relationship between power and the study of social organization. In effect, the emphasis here is one of turning the study of social organization back on itself by emphasizing the influences that shape social organization (Hall 1997). Here Hall focuses on the single conceptual concern of power and offers as a corrective to traditional forms of interactionist discussions of power, the idea of meta-power—a power relationship occupying a position in an organizational or inter-organizational field that includes multiple processes and practices including strategic agency, rules and conventions, structuring contexts, organizational culture and socialization processes, and delegation (Hall 1997).

In addition to the work of Maines and Hall and their respective collaborators, prior to the end of the 1990s, a number of additional contributions to the study of social organization had also developed. Among the most significant is Adele Clarke's (1991) often overlooked concern for "social worlds" as organization theory. Clarke's analysis outlines a set of concerns that develops how the social worlds/social arenas theory—a product of the thinking of Anselm Strauss, modified by Clarke—can be used to theorize the structure, networks, and processes of organizations. Or, in more explicitly interactionist terms: social worlds/social arenas theory is a theory of social organization.

In sum, prior to the turn of the century, there had emerged a readily identifiable set of concerns and expressions regarding the interactionist study of social organization. The social-organization concept had reached a level of sophistication and depth that made it seem as if the next decade would offer continued development in the interactionist analysis of social organization. To that end, at the turn of the century it was a common argument that such insights would allow the interactionist exploration and understanding of social organization and macro phenomena to attend to increasingly critical areas of concern within the discipline. However, as it would happen, little of that would come to fruition.

The Study of Social Organization Since the Turn of the Century

While there was significant conceptual development through the 1970s and 1980s, those developments also saw continuing sophistication through the 1990s and into the early 2000s. By the time the early 2000s rolled around, the handful of interactionists actively working on, writing about, and studying social organization were beginning to set new research agendas for the first decade of the new century.

Kent Sandstrom and Gary Fine (2003) addressed the future of symbolic interactionism relative to micro/macro orders and the agency/structure dichotomy. Regarding the implications for the former, Sandstrom and Fine note that

> one of the unique contributions of the SI perspective is its recognition that the analyses of mesostructure will allow sociologists to examine the social dynamics that permit institutions, organizations, economies, and state regimes to compel commitment or obedience from individual actors. (2003:1044)

For Sandstrom and Fine, the very core of the effort to demonstrate the linkage of micro and macro concerns is the manner in which interactionism can explore how "institutions influence individuals' outlooks and actions and in how the life of institutions is ultimately grounded in the actions of their participants" (2003:1044). Regarding the related concern of the agency/structure divide, Sandstrom and Fine (2003:1045) follow Fine's (1993) assessment that maintains that symbolic interactionism "recognizes that both agency and structure are important, and that insightful analyses should reveal how these forces dually influence people's thoughts, feelings, and actions." Together, the research agenda Sandstrom and Fine outline include a very real concern for the contemporary analysis of the classical debates within symbolic interactionism as well as the manner in which the interactionist agenda connects to similar concerns within the larger sociological discipline.

Gideon Sjoberg, Elizabeth Gill, and Joo Ean Tan (2003) identify five primary areas of development within the study of social organization, including: (1) the work of Herbert Blumer, (2) the body of work of Erving Goffman, (3) negotiated order and the associated work by Anselm Strauss, (4) the market and industry writings of Harvey Farberman (1975) and Norman Denzin (1977), and (5) the mesoanalytic work of Peter Hall and colleagues. Drawing from each of these five traditions in the interactionist literature on social organization, Sjoberg et al. (2003) suggest that future avenues of interactionist research in the study of social organization should include a number of new core concerns. Included among those essential concerns for Sjoberg et al. (2003) are the joint simultaneous constraints on behavior and expressions of agency in formal organizational arrangements—such as through hierarchical structures or divisions of labor; the ways in which collective activity directs or inhibits organizational change; and the manner through which human actors both draw on organizational power arrangements as well as find their efforts are constrained by them.

Peter Hall's (2003) consideration for the future of social organizational analyses includes the need to further specify and explore four areas that are more typically thought to be "structural" concerns, but that also have an identifiable past and an emergent present within interactionism. The four emergent agendas needing further attention within interactionism include the analysis and explication of "inequality orders, institutional analysis, collective action across time and space, and the specification of spatiotemporal orders" (Hall 2003:40). With respect to the social organization of inequality, Hall intentionally draws on the idea of inequality orders in order to demonstrate how said orders involve,

> those conditions, organizational arrangements, processes, and actors that shape categories and patterns of inequality and their intersections. Like other social orders, they have a foundation in action, are always in process, and are dynamic. . . Nevertheless, the issues hold such critical sociological and social importance that they require sustained attention.
>
> (Hall 2003:43)

Similarly, the idea of interactionism paying greater attention to institutional analysis means that symbolic interactionism must come to terms with its own understanding of and appreciation for the relationship between empirically accessible sites of action and meaning construction—such as a health clinic, a family, a school, a church—and the "institutional" contexts that condition the collective activities in said locales. On the one hand, while Hall identifies a number of ways in which such analyses might proceed, it is also essential that such endeavors are linked to interactionism's longstanding (but commonly overlooked) history of institutional analysis as well as the changing perceptions in the discipline's expression of institutions as social forms.

Today, it is almost cliché to want to talk about social phenomena "across space and time." The discipline of sociology, as well as the interactionist perspective within the discipline, has seen a significant increase of interest in temporality, place, and space as conditioning influences on collective activity over the last two decades. However, the agenda proposed by Hall—highlighting collective activity across space and time— remains underdeveloped. As a result, the pursuit of explanations of purposive collective activity remains underdeveloped as well. On this point, Hall's suggestion is for greater attention to spatiotemporal orders.

To that end, the goals of such social organizational analyses of spatiotemporal orders would be

> to determine the social production of that order by those with authority to organize time and space and timings and spacings, to note what cultural logic(s) support this order, and to observe how it is accomplished, maintained, or changed. It would be useful to determine contexts and social conditions that support or contradict the produced order and the extent to which that order offers opportunities for variation, flexibility, and agency.
>
> (Hall 2003:48)

That is, the foremost goal of social-organizational analyses is to explore the intertwined processes of human activity and interaction and the emergence of social orders across sites of activity over time. Associated with the above, "a second and related intention would be exploration of the processes of social construction of spacings and timings and their impact" (Hall 2003:48). Together these pursuits represent significant opportunities for the study of social organization—and symbolic interactionism more generally—to develop insights that build upon and enhance the interactionist social organizational perspective, but also the capacity with which interactionism attends to macro phenomena.

Despite rampant growth in the waning decade(s) of the twentieth century—with a generally shared, well-defined, and well-articulated agenda for future research also appearing in the first years of the twenty-first century—very little formal work has developed through the first two decades of the twenty-first century. I have explored this phenomenon elsewhere (McGinty 2014), but to gain a sense of just how little social organizational macro-oriented research is currently being produced within interactionism, consider the following. If one were to execute a quick search of abstracts in ProQuest using the terms "social organization" and "interactionism" while returning only those materials published since 2000, one would likely receive a list with fewer than twenty published materials. In fact, searching these very terms yielded a list of nineteen published works, six of which were duplicate entries. Of the remaining thirteen entries: two were my own articles (McGinty 2014, 2016), three were written in honor of the work of David Maines (Hall 2001; Gronbeck 2001; Maines 2001), three were written in honor of Peter M. Hall (Katovich 2003; Neitz 2003; Hall 2003), one is the chapter from the former *Handbook of Symbolic Interactionism* on the topic of social organization (Sjoberg, Gill, and Tan 2003), and one is the introduction to a special issue on the state of symbolic interactionism (Vannini 2008); only the remaining three articles represented new academic contributions to the field (Dennis and Martin 2005; Adler and Adler 2008; Best 2018). If one conducts the same search with the terms "social organization" and "symbolic interaction," the result is a list including eight pieces of work. Of those eight pieces, two are duplicate entries in the list. Regarding the remaining six pieces of work: one is already represented in the list from the previous search results (Hall 2003), three are dissertations (Wright 2013; Currie 2010; Nowacek 2006), one spotlights the work of David Maines in communication studies (Chen and Bochner 2001), and one is an application of social organizational thinking to the analysis of crime (Matsueda 2006). Together, this means that roughly eighteen noticeably interactionist-grounded social-organizational articles or book chapters have been published since the agenda-setting statements of the early 2000s were produced. For a sense of the travesty in the making, during that same period of time (2000–19), the journal *Symbolic Interaction* alone published roughly 400 articles. However, since it is not only *Symbolic Interaction* potentially publishing such work, it is likely that the total population of interactionist articles reaches well into the thousands, if not the tens of thousands. Maybe, at best, the eighteen identifiable social-organizational analyses represent no more than one in every 100–200 articles published—or roughly .5 percent to 1 percent of all published interactionist work. I think this estimate is extremely generous to the share of the interactionist literature that the study of social organization occupies. Nonetheless, it is illustrative of the point being made—the interactionist study of social organization is a dying agenda if it is not immediately reclaimed and reinvigorated.

As the interactionist social-organizational agenda was looking forward to the next few decades of development on the front-end of a new century, I do not think that many would have predicted the current silence of social organizational analyses. While this issue will be revisited later in the chapter, the real travesty associated with the waning lack of interest in the study of social organization is that the social-organizational realm of the interactionist perspective has been—as was previously noted—the arena in which interactionism clearly demonstrated its orientation toward and capacity to attend to macro phenomena. Quite simply, as interest in the study of social organization has gone by the wayside, so too in many respects has the interactionist study of macro phenomena—save perhaps those that emphasize culture and are reflective of the cultural turn in symbolic interactionism and the discipline more generally.

Symbolic Interactionism and the Study of Macro Phenomena

Broadly speaking, both historical and contemporary interactionist analyses of macro phenomena are related to the interactionist study of social organization. While those analyses that predate the growth of the contemporary social-organization concept did not use the concept to further their analyses, the work was nonetheless impacted by the perspective in general ways. Furthermore, the work of interactionist scholars in this arena helped to condition the emergence and development of the contemporary concept. Similarly, the more recent interactionist analyses of macro phenomena are inextricably linked to the social-organization concept as a result of the central role of the concept in addressing the disciplinary critique of interactionism's presumed astructural bias. Accordingly, eight notable areas of interactionist interest in macro phenomena developed prior to, during, or after the concretization of the social-organization concept in symbolic interaction. Those areas of research interest include organizations, institutions, networks, power, inequality, social change, markets, and social policy.[1]

Each of the eight areas of study involving macro-oriented interactionist analyses includes both classical as well as contemporary exemplars. In some areas, the classical analyses are more temporally distal, having been developed in the 1950s and 1960s. In other areas, the organizing/original statements are less distal, having developed in the 1970s and 1980s. At the same time, the more contemporary contributions to each area may or may not necessarily represent an unbroken connection from the classical statements. While many do identify how they relate to or draw on the older research, some of the more contemporary contributions also represent emergent agendas and concerns that share an affinity with the more classical work but are not directly connected to that literature. As a result, each area of research interest represents a broad arena for ongoing development in the interactionist analysis of macro phenomena.

As already alluded to, the best-documented arena of social-organizational analysis is that of organizations and institutions. Historically, the interactionist approach to organizations has been institutional in scope—even if it was never read in that way. Accordingly, the interactionist study of institutions is not new or unique, but it has been commonly overlooked by both interactionist and non-interactionist scholars alike. Consider the many ways in which organizations have been attended to in the interactionist literature, including: the organization of labor relations and large organizations (Blumer 1954); the institutional analyses associated with the work of Erving Goffman (1959, 1961), Howard S. Becker (1963, 1982), and Everett Hughes (1971); and the study of organizational culture and professional socialization (Becker et al. 1961/1977); the explication of negotiated order analyses of organizations (Dingwall and Strong 1985); the mesodomain analysis of the family (Pestello and Voydanoff 1991); personnel performance evaluations and career ladders in organizations (Henson and Hall 1993); the temporal ordering of organizational negotiations (Mellinger 1994); the theorization of ecologies of communication (Altheide 1995); the critique of new institutionalism's understanding of isomorphism (Glazier and Hall 1996); the analysis of religious organization and practice (McCallion, Maines and Wolfel 1996; McCallion and Maines 2002); the social organization of collective responses to criminal behavior (Matsueda 2006); the explication of the variety of interactionist approaches to organizations and institutions (Gibson and Vom Lehn 2018); the analysis of schools and professional educational socialization (Everitt 2012, 2013, 2017); and the theorization of organizational settings as human "inhabited institutions" (Hallett 2003; Hallett and Ventresca 2006a, 2006b; Hallett 2007; Hallett 2010; Gougherty and Hallett 2013; Hallett and Meanwell 2016).

While it is clear that organizational and institutional analyses are present in past and contemporary interactionism, approaching both from a social-organizational perspective solidifies the claim not only that there is a clearly discernable form of interactionist institutionalism, but also that it is also possible to further expand the field of study to be more attentive to "institutions as relatively bounded domains characterized by social organization, culture, social actors, constituencies, history, temporality, social geography, and demography" (Hall 2003:44). To this point, consider Fine and Hallett's (2014) argument regarding the manner in which mesoanalyses can be attentive to organizational culture, institutional logics, and institutional work. One very real consideration is the manner in which analyses of "institutional work" might be explored from using an interactionist lens in which "work" is simply cast as mesoprocessual forms of human activity.

Although less attended to than the organizations and institutions concepts, the interactionist analysis of networks is not a new concern either. Howard S. Becker's *Art Worlds* (1982) identifies the collective network of actors that play roles in the definition and production of art. Becker's analysis demonstrates how the definition, production, and distribution of art is based on established (organizational/institutional) conventions for action, the mobilization of resources, and the networked relationships among actors within art worlds. In many ways, Becker's work lays the groundwork for future interactionist analyses of networked relationships. Drawing on the groundwork laid by Becker,

Andrea Salvini's (2010) work teases out the tenuous relationship between interactionism and social-network analysis. At the same time, Nick Crossley's (2010) contribution to the analysis of networks pushes interactionists to consider the relational nature of the perspective—both in historical context as well as in contemporary analyses. The effective outcome of these statements on networks suggests numerous opportunities to develop the concept in interactionist terms as well as using the concept to bridge the relational analyses of interactionism and those of the larger discipline.

While Arnold Rose (1967) wrote about the power structure in the context of political processes, he did so with little direct connection to the concerns and orientations of symbolic interactionism. By contrast, it was David Luckenbill (1979) who made a formal effort to provide an interactionist conceptualization of power—primarily as a collective transaction. Accordingly Luckenbill's work served to inspire and condition the contemporary interactionist analyses of power. Peter M. Hall (1985) draws on Luckenbill's analysis in his exploration and explication of the power as processual emergent asymmetrical relationship. Later, building on his conceptualization of power and in an expansion of the study of social organization, Hall (1997) draws on the meta-power concept from Thomas Baumgartner, Walter F. Buckley, and Tom R. Burns (1975) and argues for a broader and more critical interactionist analysis of power. Following Hall's interactionist gaze toward the study of power, Alex Dennis and Peter Martin (2005) develop a statement on the state of the interactionist perspective on power by highlighting Hall's developing meta-power analysis alongside that of Robert Prus's statement on power as intersubjective accomplishment (Prus 1999). However, it was soon thereafter that Burns and Hall began to coordinate their efforts in a formal way in the definition and application of the meta-power concept. As a coordinated effort, the collaboration of Burns and Hall (and associated scholars) would eventually solidify Burns and Hall (2012) and collaborators as leading interpreters of the meta-power concept (McGinty, Burns and Hall 2016; Burns, Hall and McGinty 2012). Additionally, Russell, Dirsmith, and Samuel (2004) and Dirsmith et al. (2009) formally apply the interactionist conceptualizations of power and meta-power in their analysis of worker and management relations and entrepreneurial professions. Finally, in the most recent statements on the matter, Natalia Ruiz-Junco (2016) offers the interactionist expression and conceptualization of power as a significant entry point in understanding interactionism's longstanding interest in macro phenomena; and Jean-François Côté (2019) takes the interactionist analysis of power to its next phase of development by working through an interactionist approach to the dialectical relationship of domination and emancipation. Even then, the conclusions of each of these authors over time has been consistent: more work on the interactionist analysis of power is needed.

Regarding the study of social inequalities, Ruth Horowitz (2001) provides an analysis that highlights how the ethnographies of the Chicago School—located in impoverished, predominately minority communities—emphasized the ways in which structural inequalities limited access to varying forms of public, democratic, participatory processes. To that end the analysis of racial inequalities (Shibutani and Kwan 1965) and racial prejudice (Blumer 1958) have figured prominently in the interactionist analysis inequalities.

Still, the interactionist analysis of inequality has not always been limited to racial inequalities. For example, Johannes Chang (2000) unpacks the Chinese class structure, and Michael Sauder (2005) provides an argument for the interactionist study of social status. Horowitz (1997) identifies the ways in which ethnographies unpack class mobility and stratification, and Covaleski, Dirsmith, and Weiss (2012) develop a social-organizational approach to welfare reform in an analysis of orders of economic inequality. Plus, the body of work from Scott Harris (1997, 2001, 2003, 2004) explores the different dynamics of inequality within the institution of the family from an interactionist perspective. From status inequality to the dynamics of inequality in marriage, Harris's research demonstrates how the shared arena of institutional analysis and the study of inequality from an interactionist perspective can produce insightful institutionally relevant results.

Finally, Schwalbe et al. (2000) couple a negotiated order/social-organizational framework with the pursuit of generic social processes in order to explore unique opportunities for the interactionist understanding of inequality. In highlighting the broad history of interactionism's attentiveness to inequality and in identifying prospective concerns for future research, the authors conclude:

> For decades, interactionist and other qualitative research has looked at how inequalities are created and linked, how actors simultaneously resist inequality and recreate it, and how relations of domination and subordination depend on complex and problematic negotiation. It makes sense to build on this work if we want to achieve deeper sociological insights into the processes through which people create and sustain the arrangements that benefit some and hurt others.
>
> (Schwalbe et al. 2000:444)

Truer words might never have been written.

There is a certain level of irony in the interactionist analysis of social change. On the one hand, the concept of change is central—even if unexpressed—to the interactionist perspective. On the other hand, the definition of the concept of social change has been shown to be one of the factors that distinguishes different varieties of interactionism from one another (Vaughan and Reynolds 1968). So, while the concept is omnipresent in interactionist analyses, it is often a background or assumed concern, not a focal one. Two excellent examples in which the concept of social change can be shown to be both an intentional concern as well as an omnipresent background concern are Herbert Blumer's (1990) *Industrialization as an Agent of Social Change* and Carl Couch's (1984) *Constructing Civilizations*. Both works demonstrate different ways in which the concept of social change might be attended to in interactionist analyses of macro phenomena. The key to moving the interactionist perspective forward on this front is simply to ensure that such macro analyses of social change continue to be developed.

Despite contemporary society's obsession with economic activity and constructions of the health of modern society as connected to the health of economic markets, two of the most commonly cited foundational pieces of research in the emergence of the social organizational and mesoanalyses both highlighted criminogenic market structures. Harvey Farberman (1975) develops a critical, class-aware, power-sensitive analysis of the automobile industry across networked sites of activity that demonstrates how car dealerships engaged in legitimated but illegal activity, in the pursuit of profit. Norman Denzin (1977) takes up a past-conditioned analysis of the post-Prohibition liquor industry and the manner in which different linked sites of activity produce both intended and unintended forms of legal and illegal acts. More recently, minus the criminogenic focus, Michael Haedicke (2016) brings many of these same concerns to the forefront in his analysis of the emergence of the organic food market. Haedicke's analysis draws on issues of organizational culture, institutional logics, and the conditioning influence of sites of activity across space and time, and he develops a power-sensitive and interactionist-aware analysis of the social processual construction of organizational and institutional forms. To date, the market, and the construction and emergence of markets as macro phenomena, remains underdeveloped in the interactionist literature, even though markets are ripe for analysis using any number of social-organizational sensitizing concepts.

Just as the preceding arenas of development have been jointly influential in the development of social-organizational analyses while remaining in need of further development as conceptual sites for research, this is no less the case for analyses of politics, political processes, and social policy. Early forays into this arena included definitive statements on the interactionist analysis of politics (Hall 1972) and the presidency and impression management (Hall 1979). Soon thereafter, Carroll L. Estes and Beverly C. Edmonds (1981) took up the interactionist analysis of social policy, noting that *"the process becomes the policy outcome*—that is, the outcome is generated in the process, so that the policy is the process" (p. 81, original emphasis). In turn, Hall and McGinty (1997) borrow the insight from Estes and Edmonds and build a social-organizational model of policy, redefining policy as the "transformation of intentions where policy content, practices, and consequences are generated in the dynamics across time and space" (p. 441). In turn, this social-organizational analysis of the policy process was subsequently developed to demonstrate the transformation of intentions as "generic social process" (Hall and McGinty 2002). While this area of interactionist analysis and research developed in direct response to the claims of an interactionist astructural and acritical bias, the resulting insights and generic principles associated with this work have not yet been fully explored.

The Problem: Dichotomies of Attention and Interpretation

The evidence is clear—despite the ongoing disciplinary labeling of the symbolic-interactionist perspective a "micro" perspective, it is not limited to such an orientation.

The interactionist perspective maintains the capacity for the analysis of macro phenomena just as much as it does for the explication of micro phenomena.

However, there remains a very real tension between the larger discipline of sociology and the interactionist approach to social phenomena. First, there continues to be the issue of the conceptual language on structures and processes. Broadly, the discipline of sociology continues to prefer a general understanding of social structures as phenomena external to the human experience that produce social forces as conditioning influences on social behavior, experience, and the outcomes of human activity. On the other hand, the interactionist perspective highlights the processual construction of conditioning influences that serve to organize action (and as a result limit and/or condition action, experience, and outcomes). In promoting a nonstandard view of social structure as "social organization," symbolic interactionism rejects the standard disciplinary conception of social structures. This disjuncture remains the source of the longstanding and woefully inaccurate disciplinary critique of interactionism's astructural bias (McGinty 2016).

Second, there is the issue of contemporary interactionism as a conditioned, consequential pursuit. While this matter has been referred to as a ruinous reification for the interactionist perspective (McGinty 2016), Maines (1988) first addressed it in terms of interactionist complicity and the lack of interactionist attention to Blumer's macro sociology. Clearly, this is not a new problem, and as generations of interactionists have remained complicit in their lack of attention to macro phenomena, the perspective has produced a rather concretized set of consequential conditions that impact the practice and application of the perspective. As a result, the lack of social-organizational macro analyses by interactionists has created a condition in which there are few guideposts for current and emergent scholars to follow as they shuck off the complicity of their forebearers. From a social-organizational vantage point, this problem is what makes the historical introduction to the issue at the front end of this chapter so important—it provides the context for emergent action.

Given the above concerns, the final concern is that how we interpret the problem matters. For example, as the symbolic-interactionist perspective solidified around Blumer's three premises, and the Society for the Study of Symbolic Interaction (SSSI) took shape in response to the disciplinary critiques of the perspective, symbolic interactionists came to be labeled "the loyal opposition to structural functionalism" (Mullins 1973:98). However, over time, the idea of interactionists as "the loyal opposition" has come to be interpreted as an orientation to the larger discipline of sociology as a whole, not just structural functionalism. Gary Alan Fine and Iddo Tavory (2019) recently offered an analysis of the state of the perspective and proposed the need to jettison its position as "the loyal opposition." Their suggestion is simply that the future of interactionism's relevance to the discipline of sociology is in more fully embracing the language and concerns of the discipline. Fine and Tavory are not wrong, but they are not necessarily correct either. To the extent that the interactionist analysis of social organization is rooted in a set of assertions that provide real alternatives to common disciplinary assumptions about agency and action, structure and process, micro and macro phenomena, and the limits and value of the interactionist perspective itself, it is important that practitioners of the interactionist perspective maintain a form of critical/oppositional loyalty to the discipline (McGinty 2019).[2]

While the first and second concerns are matters of attention, the latter point is really a matter of interpretation, and just like the concerns that preceded it, it too is both conditional and consequential for the future of interactionism's attention to social organization and macro phenomena. The real value and currency of symbolic interactionism relative to the study of social organization and macro phenomena moving forward is not in dichotomizing our attention to macro or micro phenomena, or in driving sharp wedges through either/or interpretations of the social. Instead, the study of social organization within the interactionist perspective must embrace its pragmatist roots, recognize the validity of alternative solutions to our shared problems of attention and interpretation, and seek to resolve our conceptual dichotomies whenever and wherever they are encountered.

CONCLUSION AND CALL TO ACTION

Pragmatically speaking, there is not simply one best way forward in revitalizing the interactionist study of social organization. Following the sensitizing concepts of mesodomain analysis is one way forward. Pursuing the explication of generic social processes is a different, but related, project. Organizing attention to the transformation of intentions, or empirically demonstrating the relationship between the conditioning influences of the past and collective activity in the present are both equally important pursuits. Contributing to the analysis of institutional work as an interactional phenomena would also be valuable. Nonetheless, as the study of social organization gains new life in the second quarter of this new century, we will better understand the conditioned, consequential, and collective endeavors that we find ourselves contributing to as well as those we remain bound up in.[3]

The focal concern of this entry has been explicating the current state of the symbolic interactionist analysis of social organization and macro phenomena. In order to accomplish that task, it has been necessary to point out the issues and conditioning influences that have limited the study of social organization within symbolic interactionism. To that end, it has been argued that contemporary interactionists have not fully addressed, and have left to languish, both the past calls for future research as addressed at the turn of the century, as well as the explication of the sensitizing concepts associated with the study of social organization. As a result, if contemporary interactionists are willing to take up the pursuit of social organizational analyses, the impacts of their work have the potential to: (1) address the continued relevance of the perspective within the discipline; (2) address the disciplinary divide in attention; (3) enhance the understanding of the processual, action-oriented pragmatic roots of interactionism; and (4) address the sensitizing concepts of the study of social organization as well as the broadly macro arenas in which human actors interact with objects. The possibility of these insights having positive impacts on the field is significantly increased as the study of social organization addresses the still incomplete attention to: gaps in the micro/macro debate; the relationship of agency and "structure"; the connection of the interactionist perspective to the larger discipline; the manner in which the perspective can address inequalities, institutional analysis, and networked collective activity across space and time; and the nature of spatio-temporal orders. Additionally, specific concerns or research sites for exploring said ideas will undoubtedly prove to be fruitful as they include the interactionist analyses of organizations, institutional settings, networks and networked relationships, power and meta-power, social change, policy processes, and the emergence of markets and industries. In the end, the realization must be this: there is still much to be done and plenty of opportunities to engage in the work.

NOTES

1. To date the study of culture and macro-cultural phenomena has not been included in the list of concerns given active consideration within the social organizational framework. Why this is the case is undoubtedly varied. However, it is likely that the disassociation of "culture" from "social organization" is bound up in conditioning and consequential disciplinary processes. For example, Hall (1987) looks to culture as one of the sensitizing concepts of the framework being proposed for the study of social organization, thus making culture an aspect of social organization. While this does not minimize culture in any way, it does seemingly symbolically diminish it. Additionally, the cultural turn in sociology was taking shape simultaneous to the downturn in interest in social-organizational analyses. As a result, it seems plausible to suggest that while scholars pursuing social-organizational analyses were downplaying culture as macro phenomena, those scholars pursuing the study of macro-cultural phenomena were doing so without the benefit and guidance of the social organizational literature.

2. This also is not the first time that Gary Fine has attempted some form of prognostication, and both times he notes the dangers of engaging in such work. Previously, Fine suggested that 2001 would have found interactionism fully "addressing the standard issues of sociology: agency, structure, contingencies, status mobility, resources, political economy, and the like" (Fine 1990:146). Simultaneously, by that same point in time, the issues of interactionism will have become the mainstream issues of the discipline. While the former is far from reality, the latter has come to pass to some degree. However, it is clear that both sets of issues can still be addressed as soon as scholars are ready to attend to them.

3. Even now, as I think about the current state of affairs—with the clear majority of global citizens experiencing some form of restriction on daily movement and/or public gathering—I cannot avoid considering how a social-organizational analysis of the COVID-19 phenomena would demonstrate the capacity of the interactionist perspective to attend to macro phenomena. Whether we talk about it in terms of interaction orders (Goffman 1983), the conditional matrix (Strauss and Corbin 1990), in the context of situational analysis (Clarke 2005), or using any of the sensitizing concepts of mesodomain analysis (Hall and McGinty 2002), the opportunity to engage in a sustained conversation about the relationship between

interactionism and macro phenomena is global in scope. On the other hand, it should not take a pandemic to demonstrate what should already be clear to each of us: the common as well as disparate experiences we are having—in this case, as the world responds to COVID-19—are socially organized.

REFERENCES

Abbott, Andrew. 2009. "Organizations and The Chicago School." Pp. 399–420 in *Oxford Handbook of Sociology and Organization Studies: Classical Foundations*, edited by P. Adler. New York: Oxford University Press.

Adler, Patricia A., and Peter Adler. 2008. "The Cyber Worlds of Self-Injurers: Deviant Communities, Relationships, and Selves." *Symbolic Interaction* 31:33–56.

Altheide, David. 1995. *An Ecology of Communication*. New York: Aldine de Gruyter.

Baumgartner, Thomas, Walter F. Buckley, and Tom R. Burns. 1975. "Meta power and Relational Control in Social Life." *Social Science Information* 14:49–78.

Becker, Howard S. 1963. *Outsiders: Studies in the Sociology of Deviance*. New York: Free Press.

Becker, Howard S. 1982. *Art Worlds*. Berkeley: University of California Press.

Becker, Howard S., Blanche Geer, Everett C. Hughes, and Anselm Strauss. 1961/1977. *Boys in White: Student Culture in Medical School*. Chicago: University of Chicago Press.

Best, Joel. 2018. "Outside the Interactionist Mainstream: The Contributions of Orrin E. Klapp." *Symbolic Interaction* 41:533–46.

Block, Fred. 1973. "Alternative Sociological Perspectives." *Catalyst* 7:29–41.

Blumer, Herbert. 1954. "Social Structure and Power Conflict?" Pp. 232–39 in *Industrial Conflict*, edited by A. Kornhauser, R. Dubin, and A. M. Ross. New York: McGraw Hill.

Blumer, Herbert. 1958. "Race Prejudice as a Sense of Group Position." *Pacific Sociological Review* 1:3–7.

Blumer, Herbert. 1969. *Symbolic Interactionism: Perspective and Method*. Berkeley: University of California.

Blumer, Herbert. 1990. *Industrialization as an Agent of Social Change*, edited by D. R. Maines and T. J. Morrione. New York: Aldine De Gruyter.

Burns, Tom R., and Peter M. Hall. 2012. *The Meta-power Paradigm: Impacts and Transformations of Agents, Institutions, and Social Systems*. New York: Peter Lang.

Burns, Tom R., Peter M. Hall, and Patrick J. W. McGinty. 2012. "Conceptualizing Power and Meta-Power: Causalities, Mechanisms and Constructions." Pp. 19–82 in *The Meta-power Paradigm: Impacts and Transformations of Agents, Institutions, and Social Systems*, edited by T. R. Burns and P. M. Hall. New York: Peter Lang.

Chang, Johannes H. 2000. "Symbolic Interaction and the Transformation of Class Structure: The Case of China." *Symbolic Interaction* 23:223–51.

Chen, Shing-Ling S., and Arthur P. Bochner. 2001. "Symbolic Interaction and Communication: NCA Spotlight on the Contribution of David R. Maines." *Studies in Symbolic Interaction* 24:3–6.

Clarke, Adele. 1991. "Social Worlds/Arenas Theory as Organizational Theory." Pp. 119–58 in *Social Organization and Social Process: Essays in Honor of Anselm Strauss*, edited by D. R. Maines. Hawthorne, NY: Aldine de Gruyter.

Clarke, Adele. 2005. *Situational Analysis: Grounded Theory After the Postmodern Turn*. Thousand Oaks, CA: SAGE.

Cooley, Charles H. 1902/1922. *Human Nature and the Social Order*. New York: Scribner.

Cooley, Charles H. 1909. *Social Organization: A Study of the Larger Mind*. New York: Scribner.

Cooley, Charles H. 1918/1966. *Social Process*. Carbondale: Southern Illinois University Press.

Côté, Jean-François. 2019. "The Past, Present, and Future of G. H. Mead in Symbolic Interactionism: A Dialectical Encounter Around the Issue of Feminism, Power, and Society." Pp. 117–40 in *The Interaction Order: Studies in Symbolic Interaction*, vol. 50, edited by N. Denzin. Corydon, UK: Emerald.

Couch, Carl. 1984. *Constructing Civilizations*. Greenwich, CT: JAI Press.

Covaleski, Mark A., Mark Dirsmith, and Jane Weiss. 2012. "The Mesodomain of Welfare Reform: Renegotiating the order of Economic Inequality." *Studies in Symbolic Interaction* 39:3–49.

Crossley, Nick. 2010. *Towards Relational Sociology*. London: Routledge.

Currie, A. Scott. 2010. *Sound Visions: An Ethnographic Study of Avant-garde Jazz in New York City*. Unpublished thesis or dissertation available from Sociological Abstracts (758131621; 201062522).

Dennis, Alex, and Peter J. Martin. 2005. "Symbolic Interactionism and the Concept of Power. *British Journal of Sociology* 56:191–213.

Denzin, Norman K. 1977. "Notes on the Criminogenic Hypothesis: A Case Study of the American Liquor Industry." *American Sociological Review* 42:905–20.

Dingwall, Robert, and Phil M. Strong. 1985. "The Interactional Study of Organizations: A Critique and Reformulation." *Urban Life* 14:205–31.

Dirsmith, Mark W., Sajay Samuel, Mark Covaleski, and James Heian. 2009. "The Inter-play of Power and Meta-power in the Social Construction of 'Entrepreneurial' Professional Services Firms: A Processual Ordering Perspective." *Studies in Symbolic Interaction* 33:347–87.

Estes, Carroll L., and Beverly C. Edmonds. 1981. "Symbolic Interaction and Social Policy Analysis." *Symbolic Interaction* 4:75–86.

Everitt, Judson G. 2012. "Teacher Careers and Inhabited Institutions: Sense-Making and Arsenals of Teaching Practice in Educational Institutions." *Symbolic Interaction* 35:203–20.

Everitt, Judson G. 2013. "Teacher Careers and Inhabited Institutions: Sense-Making and Arsenals of Teaching Practice in Educational Institutions." *Symbolic Interaction* 36:177–96.

Everitt, Judson G. 2017. *Lesson Plans: The Institutional Demands of Becoming a Teacher*. New Brunswick, NJ: Rutgers University Press.

Farberman, Harvey A. 1975. "A Criminogenic Market Structure: The Automobile Industry." *The Sociological Quarterly* 16:438–57.

Fine, Gary A. 1990. "Symbolic Interactionism in the Post-Blumerian Age." Pp. 117–57 in *Frontiers of Social Theory: The New Syntheses*, edited by G. Ritzer. New York: Columbia University Press.

Fine, Gary A. 1993. "The Sad Demise, Mysterious Disappearance, and Glorious Triumph of Symbolic Interactionism." *Annual Review of Sociology* 19:61–87.

Fine, Gary A., and Tim Hallett. 2014. "Group Cultures and the Everyday Life of Organizations: Interaction Orders and Meso-Analysis." *Organization Studies* 35:1773–92.

Fine, Gary A., and Iddo Tavory 2019. "Interactionism in the Twenty-First Century: A Letter on Being-in-a-Meaningful-World." *Symbolic Interaction* 42:457–67.

Gibson, Will, and Dirk vom Lehn. 2018. *Institutions, Interaction, and Social Theory*. London: Palgrave.

Glazier, Jack D., and Peter M. Hall. 1996. "Constructing Isomorphism in an Interorganizational Network." *Humboldt Journal of Social Relations* 22(2):47–62.

Goffman, Erving. 1959. *The Presentation of Self in Everyday Life*. Garden City, NY: Doubleday/Anchor Books.

Goffman, Erving. 1961. *Encounters: Two Studies in the Sociology of Interaction*. Indianapolis, IN: Bobbs-Merrill.

Goffman, Erving. 1983. "The Interaction Order." *American Sociological Review* 48:1–17.

Gougherty, Matthew, and Tim Hallett. 2013. "Revisiting Learning to Labor: Interaction, Domination, Resistance and the 'Grind.'" *Studies in Symbolic Interaction* 41:123–59.

Gouldner, Alvin W. 1970. *The Coming Crisis in Western Sociology*. New York: Basic Books.

Gronbeck, Bruce E. 2001. "The Idea of Structure and Communication in David Maines' Work." *Studies in Symbolic Interaction* 24:7–14.

Haedicke, Michael A. 2016. *Organizing Organic: Conflict and Compromise in an Emerging Market*. Stanford, CA: Stanford University Press.

Hall, Peter M. 1972. "A Symbolic Interactionist Analysis of Politics." *Sociological Inquiry* 42:35–75.

Hall, Peter M. 1979. "The Presidency and Impression Management." *Studies in Symbolic Interaction* 2:283–305.

Hall, Peter M. 1985. "Asymmetric Relationships and Processes of Power." Pp. 304–44 in *Foundations of Interpretive Sociology: Original Essays in Symbolic Interaction*, edited by H. A. Farberman and R. Perinbanayagam. Greenwich, CT: JAI Press.

Hall, Peter M. 1987. "Interactionism and the Study of Social Organization." *The Sociological Quarterly* 28:1–22.

Hall, Peter M. 1995. "The Consequences of Qualitative Analysis for Sociological Theory: Beyond the Microlevel." *The Sociological Quarterly* 36:397–415.

Hall, Peter M. 1997. "Meta-Power, Social Organization, and the Shaping of Social Action." *Symbolic Interaction* 20:397–418.

Hall, Peter M. 2001. "The Maines Stream: A Pragmatist Perspective on Social Organization and Policy Production." *Studies in Symbolic Interaction* 24:15–31.

Hall, Peter M. 2003. "Interactionism, Social Organization, and Social Processes: Looking Back and Moving Ahead." *Symbolic Interaction* 26:33–55.

Hall, Peter M., and Dee Ann Spencer-Hall. 1982. "The Social Conditions of the Negotiated Order." *Urban Life* 11:328–49.

Hall, Peter M., and Patrick J. W. McGinty. 1997. "Policy as the Transformation of Intentions: Producing Program from Statute." *The Sociological Quarterly* 38:439–67.

Hall, Peter M., and Patrick J. W. McGinty. 2002. "Social Organization Across Space and Time: The Policy Process, Mesodomain Analysis, and Breadth of Perspective." Pp. 303–22 in *Structure, Culture, and History: Recent Issues in Social Theory*, edited by S. C. Chew and D. Knottnerus. Lanham, MD: Rowman and Littlefield.

Hallett, Tim. 2003. "Symbolic Power and Organizational Culture." *Sociological Theory* 21:128–49.

Hallett, Tim. 2007. "Between Deference and Distinction: Interaction Ritual through Symbolic Power in an Educational Institution." *Social Psychology Quarterly* 70:148–71.

Hallett, Tim. 2010. "The Myth Incarnate: Recoupling Processes, Turmoil, and Inhabited Institutions in an Urban Elementary School." *American Sociological Review* 75:52–74.

Hallett, Tim, and Marc Ventresca. 2006a. "Inhabited Institutions: Social Interactions and Organizational Forms in Gouldner's Patterns of Industrial Bureaucracy." *Theory and Society* 35:213–36.

Hallett, Tim, and Marc Ventresca. 2006b. "How Institutions Form: Loose Coupling as a Mechanism in Gouldner's Patterns of Industrial Bureaucracy." *American Behavioral Scientist* 49:908–24.

Hallett, Tim, and Emily Meanwell. 2016. "Accountability as an Inhabited Institution: Contested Meanings and the Symbolic Politics of Reform." *Symbolic Interaction* 39:374–96.

Harris, Scott R. 1997. "Status Inequality and Close Relationships: An Integrative Typology of Bond-Saving Strategies." *Symbolic Interaction* 20:1–20.

Harris, Scott R. 2001. "What can Interactionism Contribute to the Study of Inequality? the Case of Marriage and Beyond." *Symbolic Interaction* 24:455–80.

Harris, Scott R. 2003. "Studying Equality/Inequality: Naturalist and Constructionist Approaches to Equality in Marriage." *Journal of Contemporary Ethnography* 32:200–32.

Harris, Scott R. 2004. "Challenging the Conventional Wisdom: Recent Proposals for the Interpretive Study of Inequality." *Human Studies* 27:113–36.

Henson, Bruce E., and Peter M. Hall. 1993. "Linking Performance Evaluations and Career Ladder Programs in One School District." *Elementary School Journal* 93:323–53.

Horowitz, Ruth. 1997. "Barriers and Bridges to Class Mobility: Ethnographies of Stratification." *Sociological Methods and Research* 25:495–538.

Horowitz, Ruth. 2001. "Inequalities, Democracy, and Fieldwork in the Chicago Schools of Yesterday and Today." *Symbolic Interaction* 24:481–504.

Hughes, Everett C. 1971. *The Sociological Eye: Selected Papers*. Chicago: Aldine-Atherton.

Kanter, Rosabeth M. 1972. "Symbolic Interactionism and Politics in Systemic Perspective." *Sociological Inquiry* 42:77–92.

Katovich, Michael A. 2003. "Hall's Hope and the Focus Next Time: Let Us Now Study Social Structure." *Symbolic Interaction* 26:57–66.

Luckenbill, David F. 1979. "Power: A Conceptual Framework." *Symbolic Interaction* 2:97–114.

Maines, David R. 1977. "Social Organization and Social Structure in Symbolic Interactionist Thought." *Annual Review of Sociology* 3:235–59.

Maines, David R. 1982. "In Search of Mesostructure: Studies in the Negotiated Order." *Urban Life* 11:267–79.

Maines, David R. 1988. "Myth, Text, and Interactionist Complicity in the Neglect of Blumer's Macrosociology." *Symbolic Interaction* 11:43–57.

Maines, David R. 2001. *The Faultline of Consciousness: A View of Interactionism in Sociology*. New York: Aldine de Gruyter.

Maines, David R., and Thomas J. Morrione. 1990. "On the Breadth and Relevance of Blumer's Perspective: Introduction to his Analysis of Industrialization." Pp. xi–xxiv in *Industrialization as an Agent of Social Change*, edited by D. R. Maines and T. J. Morrione. New York: Aldine De Gruyter.

Matsueda, Ross L. 2006. "Differential Social Organization, Collective Action, and Crime." *Crime Law and Social Change* 46:3–33.

McCallion, Michael J., and David R. Maines. 2002. "Spiritual Gatekeepers: Time and the Rite of Christian Initiation of Adults." *Symbolic Interaction* 25:289–302.

McCallion, Michael J., David R. Maines, and Steven E. Wolfel. 1996. "Policy as Practice: First Holy Communion as a Contested Situation." *Journal of Contemporary Ethnography* 25:300–26.

McGinty, Patrick J. W. 2014. "Divided and Drifting: Interactionism and the Neglect of Social Organizational Analyses in Organization Studies." *Symbolic Interaction* 37:155–86.

McGinty, Patrick J. W. 2016. "The Astructural Bias in Symbolic Interactionism." Pp. 19–56 in *The Astructural Bias Charge: Myth or Reality?*, edited by G. R. Musolf. Bingley, UK: Emerald.

McGinty, Patrick J. W. 2019. "Stop Micro-waving Me: Ending the Reification of Symbolic Interactionism in Introductory Textbooks and the Discipline." Paper presented at the Annual Meeting of the Midwest Sociological Society, Chicago, IL.

McGinty, Patrick J. W., Tom R. Burns, and Peter M. Hall. 2016. "Meta-power," in *The Blackwell Encyclopedia of Sociology (Online)*, 2nd edn., edited by G. Ritzer. Oxford: Blackwell Publishing.

Mead, George H. 1934/2017. *Mind, Self, and Society: The Definitive Edition*. Edited by Charles W. Morris. Annotated edition by Daniel R. Huebner and Hans Joas. Chicago: University of Chicago Press.

Mellinger, Wayne W. 1994. "Negotiated Orders: The Negotiation of Directives in Paramedic-Nurse Interaction." *Symbolic Interaction* 17:165–85.

Mullins, Nicholas C. 1973. *Theories and Theory Groups in Contemporary American Sociology*. New York: Harper and Row.

Neitz, Mary Jo. 2003. "Conversations and Engagements: Contributions to Theory in the Work of Peter M. Hall." *Studies in Symbolic Interaction* 26:7–12.

Nowacek, David M. 2006. *Pragmatism in American Jurisprudence and Social Organization: Reconstructing the Discursive Background of the Judicial 'Revolution' of the 1930s*. Unpublished thesis or dissertation available from Sociological Abstracts (61592930; 200701799).

Pestello, Frances G., and Patricia Voydanoff. 1991. "In Search of Mesostructure in the Family: An Interactionist Approach to Division of Labor." *Symbolic Interaction* 14:105–28.

Prus, Robert. 1999. *Beyond the Power Mystique: Power as Intersubjective Accomplishment*. Albany, NY: SUNY Press.

Ropers, Richard. 1973. "Mead, Marx and Social Psychology." *Catalyst* 7:42–61.

Rose, Arnold M. 1967. *The Power Structure: Political Processes in American Society*. New York: Oxford University Press.

Ruiz-Junco, Natalia. 2016. "The Persistence of the Power Deficit? Advancing Power Premises in Contemporary Interactionist Theory." Pp. 145–65 in *The Astructural Bias Charge: Myth or Reality? Studies in Symbolic Interaction*, vol. 46, edited by G. R. Musolf. Corydon, UK: Emerald.

Russell, John D., Mark Dirsmith, and Sajay Samuel. 2004. "Stained Steel: ESOPs, Meta-Power, and the Ironies of Corporate Democracy." *Symbolic Interaction* 27:383–403.

Salvini, Andrea. 2010. "Symbolic Interactionism and Social Network Analysis: An Uncertain Encounter." *Symbolic Interaction* 33:364–88.

Sandstrom, Kent L., and Gary A. Fine. 2003. "Triumphs, Emerging Voices, and the Future." Pp. 1041–57 in *Handbook of Symbolic Interactionism*, edited by L. T. Reynolds and N. Herman-Kinney. Lanham, MA: AltaMira.

Sauder, Michael. 2005. "Symbols and Contexts: An Interactionist Approach to the Study of Social Status." *The Sociological Quarterly* 46:279–98.

Schwalbe, Michael, Sandra Godwin, Daphne Holden, Douglas Schrock, Shealy Thompson, and Michele Wolkomir. 2000. "Generic Processes in the Reproduction of Inequality: An Interactionist Analysis." *Social Forces* 79:419–52.

Shibutani, Tomatsu, and Kian Kwan. 1965. *Ethnic Stratification*. New York: Macmillan.

Sjoberg, Gideon, Elizabeth Gill, and Joo Ean Tan. 2003. "Social Organization." Pp. 411–32 in *Handbook of Symbolic Interactionism*, edited by L. T. Reynolds and N. Herman-Kinney. Lanham, MA: AltaMira.

SOCIAL ORGANIZATION, MACRO PHENOMENA   145

Smith, Dusky L. 1973. "Symbolic Interactionism: Definitions of the Situation from Howard Beckers and John Lofland." *Catalyst* 7:62–75.

Strauss, Anselm. 1959. *Mirrors and Masks*. New York: Free Press.

Strauss, Anselm. 1978. *Negotiations*. San Francisco: Jossey-Bass.

Strauss, Anselm, and Juliet Corbin. 1990. *Basics of Qualitative Research: Grounded Theory Procedures and Techniques*. Thousand Oaks, CA: SAGE.

Strauss, Anselm, Leonard Schatzman, Danuta Ehrlich, Rue Bucher, and Melvin Sabshin. 1963. "The Hospital and its Negotiated Order." Pp. 147–69 in *The Hospital in Modern Society*, edited by E. Friedson. New York: Free Press.

Vannini, Phillip. 2008. "The Geography of Disciplinary Amnesia: Eleven Scholars Reflect on the International State of Symbolic Interactionism." *Studies in Symbolic Interaction* 32:5–18.

Vaughan, Ted R., and Larry T. Reynolds. 1968. "The Sociology of Symbolic Interactionism." *The American Sociologist* 3:208–14.

Wagner, Helmut R. 1964. "Displacement of Scope: A Problem of the Relationship Between Small-Scale and Large-Scale Sociological Theories." *American Journal of Sociology* 69:571–84.

Wright, Benjamin A. 2013. *Sound From Start to Finish: Professional Style and Practice in Modern Hollywood Sound Production*. Unpublished thesis or dissertation available from Sociological Abstracts. (1322727444; 201317677).

CHAPTER 8

DRAMATURGICAL TRADITIONS

Performance and Interaction

SUSIE SCOTT

INTRODUCTION

SYMBOLIC Interactionism is always concerned with the "how" of social process: the micro-level mechanisms and techniques through which order is achieved. Performance is a key dimension of this and refers to how the *appearance* of harmonious cooperation is constructed and displayed. Regardless of what is going on beneath the surface—conflict, confusion, challenge, competition—all that matters is that social life keeps running smoothly and the view seems convincingly real. Performances are given both by individuals, who present their self-identities, and by groups, whose ritual practices symbolize their common values. Social situations therefore have a performative dimension insofar as people carefully assemble them to make recognizable scenes.

The most important figure in this theoretical tradition is Erving Goffman, whose dramaturgical perspective uses the theatre as a metaphor for social life. Individuals are actors, performing characters to audiences in frontstage, situated encounters. These presented versions of the self may be more or less convincing, depending on the actor's technical skills of impression management, their teammates' cooperative support, and the audience's willingness to provide tactful acceptance. Symbolic interactionism more broadly shares an interest in social performance, identifying broader patterns of identity work, role-making, communicative gestures, and public behavior. Social scenes are managed collectively as well as individually, to define and uphold normative displays of interaction order. This chapter will review the main ideas about performance in dramaturgical theory, discuss some key concepts, and demonstrate their relevance to contemporary social life.

Performing Reality: Theatre and Social Drama

Performance can be defined as the deliberate enactment of a representational front that is directed at an audience to communicate a meaning. This can apply to portraying a character, demonstrating a skill, or presenting an artistic creation. Although performance often involves movement, gesture, and embodied action, it is the way these techniques are used that is important, rather than their intrinsic content. Performances are motivated and intentional, designed and rehearsed; they tell us what actors are aiming to do and why—how they want scenes to appear and be interpretively read.

The idea of performance implies something contrived and artificial, rather than authentic and directly given. Schechner (2002:2) describes it as *"any action that is framed, presented, highlighted or displayed"* and suggests that it involves *"twice behaved behaviours."* By this he means that the performative process operates simultaneously on two levels: there is not only the manifest scene that is shown, but also the productive action of showing it, through careful timing, rehearsal, and effort. The latter particularly intrigues symbolic interactionists because it reveals the mechanics of social life—the "dirty work" (Hughes 1962) that is always going on behind the scenes in private, "backstage" (Goffman 1959) regions.

Theatre studies examine the techniques, skills, and devices that professional actors use to create versions of unreality. Cultural anthropologists argue that many of these principles apply equally to social life, where everyday dramas mirror the aesthetic of the stage (Turner 1997). Historically, the theatre has served various social functions, including entertainment, education, persuasion, and community building (Hinton 1987). In social life, we see the same pattern, as cultural identity performances allow groups to tell convincing stories that are dialogic and relational (Jackson 2002). Performance helps to transmit social myths—versions and accounts that are presented and usually believed (Scheff 1968). It is a curious paradox that, although we may suspect that scenes are not as they appear, suspending disbelief helps us to maintain a reassuring sense of order. Audiences are performing too, immersed in their own show of observing attentively and giving supportive reactions (Goffman 1959). This implies an optimistic view of calm cooperation toward a common goal. As Berger and Luckmann (1966) argued, "paramount reality" is a precarious social construction, and we are all conspiratorial impostors.

Stripping away the layers of setting, scenery, costume, and props, the essence of theatre is the communicative relationship between player and audience (Southern 1962). It is through this direct, immediate encounter that ideas are suggested and versions of reality presented for interpretation and response. Acts of designation (Hinton 1987) can turn any space into a performative arena: just as a gallery turns material objects into exhibits, so too can social spaces be symbolically "framed" as settings for a drama. However, what makes or breaks the success of a performance is the interactional dynamic between the two parties. Actors must be skilled and ready to perform, while audiences must be willing to suspend their disbelief. Alexander's (2004) notion of "fusion" describes a harmonious sense of mutual understanding that arises when actors convey a set of deep, authentic meanings with which the audience can identify.

Characterization can be naturalistic or contrived. In professional theatre, this is taught through the respective techniques of the Stanislavskian method or Brechtian distance. That is, actors may attempt to draw their audiences into a shared, make-believe world, which appears to everyone as if it were real, or they may wish more subversively to challenge the audience's assumptions and invite critical thought. In social life, the same principle applies to the way people present themselves as having certain kinds of characters. As we shall see below, this corresponds to Goffman's (1959) dramaturgical ideas about sincere versus cynical role performance, and occasional slips out of character.

The skill of improvisation is also important to making social situations flow smoothly. Hodgson and Richards (1966) describe how theatrical actors must react to the unexpected by finding practical, creative solutions and maintaining a flexible repertoire. Social actors also remain constantly alert and prepared to respond, using what Goffman (1959) called "dramaturgical discipline." Audiences, in their turn, improvise appropriate responses to unpredictable scenes, for example by tactfully ignoring embarrassing mistakes (Goffman 1956, Gross and Stone 1964).

Social performances often take a ritualistic form, at both the micro and macro levels of analysis. Durkheim's (1912) functionalist theory of religious worship, as a collective practice by which societies symbolically represent to themselves common values and shared morality, influenced two major contemporary perspectives. Firstly, Collins's (2005) interaction ritual theory examined how interpersonal exchanges perform the same function, by displaying observance of normative values. Interaction rituals unfold in a standardized way, through sequential chains, which generate emotional energy (Collins 2005). One dramaturgical example is the apology ritual, discussed more below, which serves as a reparative device (Goffman 1967). Secondly, Alexander's (2004, 2006) theory of cultural pragmatics shows how groups and societies perform scripted stories about their history, politics, or collective identity. This can be important when telling about trauma, suffering, and victimhood, particularly when a group's voice has been silenced and struggles to be heard (Plummer 2019). It can also help to build shared understandings of events in the past, through popular or social memory (Halbwachs 1925/1992). In this respect, Alexander (2006) argues that social performances are more structurally embedded than Goffman argued and the interactionists acknowledged. Actors draw upon a deeper background repertoire of shared cultural codes, symbolic representations, values, and sentiments that make them feel intuitively resonant and widely understandable.

Cultural scripts are communicated through symbolic forms and interactional processes, such as the discourses of news journalism and social media platforms (Potter 1996). They tend to reproduce dominant myths, but these may be critically subverted (Jackson 2002). For example, Tyler (2013) critically discusses the British mass media's stigmatizing representations of certain social groups, such as young working-class single mothers, Gypsy travelers, and asylum seekers. In the wider cultural context of neoliberalism and austerity measures, this serves the political purpose of scapegoating the structurally oppressed and legitimizing social inequality. However, Tyler suggests that these populations may subversively "revolt" against their abject subjectification, if supported by a more collectivist left-wing agenda of social justice.

PERFORMING SELVES: CHARACTERS
AND ACTORS

At the heart of social performance is the actor. Symbolic interactionism works with the idea, common to modern Western social theory, of the individual self as a separate and contained, boundaried unit with an essential core (Elliott 2007). Acting requires agency, and so there is a thinking, rational, reflexive actor-self working behind the scenes to design and execute their performance. There is little room for emotions, irrationality, or spontaneous surprises. While this one-dimensional view of selfhood has been criticized for lacking nuance and complexity (Smith 2006), it does resonate intuitively with common-sense ideas about personal selfhood, making the concept of social identity performance easier to understand.

By contrast, the post-structuralist notion of "performativity" describes a feature of the exhibited display rather than of the person who gives it. Butler's (1990) theory of gender performativity, for example, referred to the repertoire of stylized expressions through which ideas of gender are shown. Gender can be "done" in many different ways by every kind of person, and it is not tied to biological sex (West and Zimmerman 1987). Dramaturgy and symbolic interactionism diverge from this anti-essentialist view, by focusing on the motivations of the individual actor. Subjectivity means subjecthood, a coherent sense of oneself as a conscious being. However, this does not mean that social identity is fixed and stable; far from it. Identity is an ongoing, flexible process, which is negotiated with others and shaped by interaction (Scott 2015).

Social actors are self-consciously aware of and responsive to the others they encounter in everyday life through the symbolic conversation of gestures (Blumer 1969). The dramaturgical performer epitomizes Mead's (1934) concept of the reflexive social self, as an internal dialogue between two perspectival phases. "I" am the thinking subject, who acts to present a version of myself, while "Me" is formed through how I think the audience view and appraise my performance. Similarly, Cooley's (1909) concept of the "looking glass self" explains why we care so much about how we appear (or imagine we appear) in other people's eyes: social "face" (Goffman 1967) is contingent upon external judgments of appropriateness, or situational propriety (Goffman 1963a).

Here again, we see the contrast behind what appears on the surface and what goes on behind the scenes. Despite giving a carefully orchestrated front and keeping the show running, actors are always aware of the risk of making an embarrassing blunder that will bring down the whole façade. Just like theatrical performers on the stage, social actors can feel shy, doubtful, and nervous when they reflect upon their skills (Scott 2007, 2017). Thus, although dramaturgy presumes a shrewd and rationally calculating self (Smith 2006), this does not mean that individuals lack emotion or responsibility toward the wider social scene.

PRESENTING SOCIAL SCENES

Symbolic interactionism regards everyday life as a sequence of scenes that actors move between, just like in a film or a play. Each scene, or social situation, is carefully designed and presented to appear familiar, orderly, and easy to navigate. Often this involves aspects of visual display—the architectural design of buildings, furniture, and material objects—and the coordination of movement around social space. For example, imagine a railway station, complete with trains, platforms, ticket office, and waiting room, through which masses of people move calmly around. However, from a symbolic interactionist perspective, what is most important for making scenes work are the unspoken rules of social behavior that help to produce orderly conduct.

Goffman (1983) defined "the interaction order" as a moral and institutional domain, encompassing all forms of socially patterned behavior. He mapped out a wide realm, ranging from the causal, fleeting exchanges of strangers in mere co-presence to close and familiar teammates engaged in focused encounters (Goffman 1967). Embodied individuals move like vehicles around social space, navigating paths in relation to others (Goffman 1971). This is particularly noticeable in public places that bring strangers together, such as the city street, parks, shopping malls, and waiting areas. Self-conscious actors try to avoid direct acknowledgment of each other by preventing bodily contact and presenting a facial expression of "civil inattention" (Goffman 1963a). Each type of scene within the interaction order has its own set of rules, norms, and expectations for governing contextually appropriate social behavior. Tacitly learned through the process of socialization, these patterned arrangements create an overall structure of normative consensus (Goffman 1983).

This raises the question of *how* exactly such orderliness emerges—how people learn the right ways to behave. Beneath the polished surface of "normal appearances" (Goffman 1969), what are the mechanical processes by which rules are produced, observed, and cooperatively enacted? The "definition of the situation" (Thomas and Thomas 1928) is determined during a stage of examination and deliberation that occurs when actors enter a scene and try to work out what is going on. Actors are generally pragmatic and want to get on with the business at hand; they share a motivation to decide how to interpret the situation and what to expect from each other. Thus they tacitly agree to "frame" (Goffman 1974) the scene as a recognizable type, such as a lecture, party, bus queue, or meeting, and to coordinate their lines of action.

The definition of the situation provides the cast with a template set of roles to perform and scripts to follow. In social phenomenology, Schütz (1972) described these resources as "typifications," which offer "recipe knowledge" for building a scene. However, given that actors have the capacity to improvise, adapt, and sometimes make mistakes, the appearance of cooperation is precarious and easily disturbed. Strauss (1978) described a process of *negotiated* order, whereby actors rather messily and clumsily assemble working scenes, attending to the faults and glitches that threaten to undermine the show.

A further complication is that situations may not really be as they appear. Actors may collude to present different versions of reality, both to their audiences and to one another. Goffman (1969) warned that it was risky to take performances at face value and trust in characters' authenticity. The concept of "awareness contexts" (Glaser and Strauss 1964) describes the variable amounts of information that actors hold about one another's true identities and the meaning of the situation. Glaser and Strauss devised a typology of four awareness contexts, which they demonstrated with the example of terminally ill patients in a hospital. In an open-awareness context, both doctors and patients knew the latter's fate and could talk about it honestly. Closed awareness occurred when patients did not know that they were dying but the medical staff did, which leant itself to secrecy and deliberate concealment. Suspicion awareness involved the patient guessing what was happening but not being able to prove it. Finally, pretense awareness emerged when everybody knew the hidden truth but nobody acknowledged it.

The last of these offers a refreshing insight into one form of interaction order. It explains why sometimes there is a discrepancy between "believed" and "presented" realities (Scheff 1968) that goes unchallenged, even when the truth seems blindingly obvious. When all actors share an interest in maintaining a false definition of the situation, they collude to ignore the elephant in the room. Burns (1992) called these "polite fictions," and we find them particularly in scenes involving the threat of embarrassment. For example, studies of nudity in naturist camps (Weinberg 1965) and swimming pools (Scott 2009) reveal how people make a show of decency by ignoring each other's bodies and pretending that "nothing unusual is happening" (Emerson 1970).

Goffman's Dramaturgy: Individual Performances

The dramaturgical perspective is Goffman's most famous metaphor for understanding interaction order. It was inspired by Kenneth Burke's (1945) dramatism, which suggested that social situations mirrored the same pentad structure (what, where, when, why, how) as mystery detective stories. Goffman began as a student of social anthropology at the University of Chicago and was always reluctant to call himself a sociologist. His works catalog the minutiae of human behavior, using taxonomies, typologies, and classification systems (Lofland 1980). Goffman wanted to explain how the orderliness observed in everyday situations was practically accomplished through the rituals and routines of social interaction.

Dramaturgy draws a comparison between social life and the theatre, using striking visual imagery and precise terminology to highlight their common elements. A key concept is *self-presentation*: individuals are social actors who perform versions of themselves in a similar way to professional actors (Goffman 1959). These role performances are tailored to each situation and audience, giving social interaction a live, unpredictable format. Self-presentation is accomplished using the techniques of *impression management*: actors try to project distinctive images or create particular impressions by carefully designing their appearance, lines, and moves. This is a way of making identity claims, or "announcements" (Stone 1962), about the type of person whom one is. Usually, it involves self-enhancing qualities that create positive impressions of competence, reliability, and "normalness," but sometimes we try to appear different or subversive. Goffman (1959:32) thus defines performance as *"all of the activity of an individual which occurs during a period marked by his continuous presence before a particular set of observers and which has some influence on the observers."*

Goffman (1959) suggested that the performative self has two theatrical "regions": the frontstage and backstage. These may be physical, geographically separated spaces, or more symbolic distinctions between the public and the private. Frontstage is where performances are shown deliberately to audiences—where we present stylized, contrived versions of ourselves. The material design of this region is important: it combines the "setting" (furniture, decoration, layout, and space) and the "personal front" (items of expressive equipment carried around by the actors, including costume, prop objects, posture, and demeanor). The personal front signals to the audience how a character should be read: their situational role, status, or condition and the manner in which they convey this. Riggins (1990) suggests a taxonomy of prop objects, which serve different self-presentational functions. As well as Goffman's status and esteem symbols, there may be "occupational objects" confirming one's credentials (e.g., a certificate on the wall of a doctor's office), "exotic objects" that display experience and ambition (e.g., souvenirs from traveling), and "collective objects" that signify belonging and social group membership (e.g., flags, tattoos, and fan memorabilia).

Backstage is a different matter. This is the region in which actors relax out of role, dropping their face and reverting to being their "real," true selves. *"Behind many masks and many characters, each performer tends to wear a single look, a naked unsocialised look"* (Goffman 1959:235). Backstage regions are private and usually concealed from audience view, for example bedrooms and bathrooms, or work areas marked "staff only." When safely backstage, actors review and rehearse their performances to make them more convincing next time. This may involve chastising oneself for making embarrassing mistakes, reflecting on the audience's reactions, or preparing a conversational script to counteract feelings of shyness (Scott 2007). We will return to the backstage region later in this chapter, in the discussion of hidden and negative aspects of drama. But first, let us consider the ways in which frontstage performances are intentionally given.

Self-presentation is crucial for maintaining "face": the sense of dignity and respectability that comes from playing a role appropriately and meeting public approval. Goffman (1967) argued that an actor's face was only "on loan from society," as personal reputation is contingent upon maintaining external esteem. Actors are concerned with the processes of *keeping* face, avoiding discrediting *losses* of face, and *saving* face if such inopportune incidents occur. The "facework" that individuals perform for themselves is therefore mainly "defensive," although it can serve to positively enhance one's social image.

Goffman (1959) described various "arts" or techniques of impression management that individuals perform to this end. *Dramaturgical circumspection* refers to prudent and careful preparation for a role, by setting up the scene in a favorable way. For example, a schoolteacher arranges for their most obedient pupils to be present when the inspector is visiting (Goffman 1959:220). *Dramaturgical discipline* involves the vigilant management of one's conduct during a performance, while at the same time appearing casual and nonchalant. For example, swimmers waiting for a vacant shower pretend to be immersed in a daydream, but are actually keeping a close eye on the queue (Scott 2009). *Dramatic realization* is the exaggeration of a role performance, highlighting its most salient aspects to ensure that the audience grasps the right meaning. Goffman (1959) describes a nurse almost caricaturing her part by taking a patient's temperature and checking his blood pressure chart. *Idealization* is similar but involves emphasizing how a role performance fits with socially desirable values: for example, a student in the library pores over their books.

Actors can have different levels of belief in the parts they are playing (Goffman 1959). A *sincere* performance occurs when an actor is so fully immersed in their role that they do not feel they are acting. They see their role as an extension of their real self and give themselves over to it completely. A *cynical* performance is the opposite, when actors are self-consciously aware of presenting a character and feel quite detached from their contrived display. This corresponds to Hochschild's (1983) distinction between deep and surface acting, respectively, as two ways of performing emotion work. Actors may shift from one attitude to the other as they become used to their role. This happens particularly in the workplace, where new employees eagerly remain in character (sincere/deep acting), but over time become jaded and start breaking the rules (cynical/surface acting).

When performing to a critically evaluative audience, actors try to present themselves in socially normative ways. Rather than boosting their individual status, they seek to align themselves with the values of the group. This demonstrates that they are good team players, who can be trusted to uphold the scene. Aligning actions (Stokes and Hewitt 1976) are particularly important in response to deviance: when an actor realizes that they have broken or are about to break a rule, they perform certain symbolic actions that attempt to correct it or minimize the damage. *Disclaimers* (Hewitt and Stokes 1975) are made prospectively, as verbal prefaces to an utterance that might otherwise be heard as offensive. They reassure the audience that any deviant views are not the individual's own, placing him or her on the same side of moral judgment as those who might be critical. For example, hedging involves asserting that one feels uncertain about what one is going to say, in case the audience rejects it: "*I'm not entirely sure, but I think . . .*" *Accounts* are statements people make retrospectively, to explain why they did something wrong. They draw upon the group's shared vocabulary of motive (Mills 1940), which provides a stock of culturally sanctioned, acceptable reasons for behavior. For example, Scott and Lyman (1968) distinguished between excuses (which acknowledge a rule-breaking act but deny responsibility for it) and justifications (which claim responsibility but deny the act was wrong).

GOFFMAN'S DRAMATURGY: TEAMWORK

Performances can be collective as well as individual. Goffman suggested that, in many situations, actors cooperate like the members of a theatrical cast to give a convincing show. Their shared interest in making the scene flow smoothly is greater than any individual's motives for self-presentation, and so everyone plays their part in a supportive, facilitative manner. The performance team (Goffman 1959:85) is defined as "*any set of individuals who co-operate in staging a single routine.*" The aim is to create an "*emergent team impression*" (Goffman 1959:85), which may be a definition of the situation or a claim to group identity. Throughout everyday life, people move around between different scenes, and so the same individual may switch from being on one team to another, acting alone in response to a team, or being an audience member observing the whole drama.

Teams employ their own collective arts of impression management. The most important principle is *dramaturgical loyalty*—one must be able to trust and rely upon one's teammates—and this leads to carefully selective practices of recruitment. For example, Van Maanen (1990) showed how Disneyland employees had to look a certain way (young, tall, slim, blonde, tanned) and follow a spoken script in order to uphold the company image. Even when members of a team privately disagree about the content of a show, they pull together to present it as a united front, toeing a "*thin party line*" (Goffman 1959:91). We see this in contemporary politics, where leaders rely upon the solidarity of party members to boost their credibility. However, this puts teammates in a vulnerable position: every member knows the backstage secrets that they share and sees the risk of being betrayed if anyone stops playing along. Goffman (1959:88) referred to the "bonds" of reciprocal dependence and familiarity that hold teammates together, implying that it may be fear rather than altruism that keeps a lid on their dissent.

Teammates display their collective identity with prop objects and items of expressive equipment, as well as through ritualized forms of exchange. Clothing and dress can be signifiers of membership, for example when staff wear a company uniform, sports players wear their team's kit (Green and Jones 2005), and fans of a subculture consume distinctive merchandise (Sandvoss 2005). *Tie signs* (Goffman 1971) are symbolic relationship markers, which tell the audience that two or more actors are bound in an intimate team: these include wedding rings, holding hands, or pushing someone else's wheelchair. Conversational rituals similarly allow teammates to perform to each other a display of their mutual regard and continued loyalty. For example, greetings and farewells usually involve some form of pleasantry that suggests either the desire to meet up again or regret that it has taken so long (Scott 2015). Goffman (1971) calls these *supportive interchanges* as they show sympathy, care, and concern. However, just as with individual performances, these displays may be sincere or cynical, genuine or fake.

The facework that teammates provide for one another is generous, aimed at maintaining a harmonious front. *Protective facework* is performed by one individual for another to save their personal face: for example, pretending not to notice someone tripping over on the street, so as to reduce the acuteness of embarrassment and help them restore poise (Goffman 1956). *Collective facework* defends the shared front of a group (Rossing and Scott 2014), for example, laughing along at an offensive joke with a gathering of friends. *Tact* describes this whole set of generous practices that "*help the performers save their own show*" (Goffman 1959:222). Tact can be given retroactively, when teammates politely disattend to faux pas that have actually occurred, but also proactively, in anticipation that they might. For example, we knock on doors before entering to allow performers time to compose themselves and get "in face" (Goffman 1959:223). Audiences also show tact toward performance teams that they perceive to be in trouble, for example, when restaurant guests pretend to ignore the argument going on between a family on a nearby table.

Ethnomethodology has shown how conversational exchanges are structured and follow ritualized formats (Garfinkel 1967; Sacks 1992; Drew and Heritage 1992). Utterances are patterned, paired, or arranged in sequential order to ensure that each correct move is made and the overall effect is accomplished (Schegloff 1968). For example, standard turn-taking sequences occur in rituals of greeting, questioning, apologizing, and asking for help (Whalen and Zimmerman 1987; Zimmerman 1992). Action sequences are performed by teams of museum and gallery visitors to display their practical engagement with interactive exhibits (Heath and vom Lehn 2008). Goffman (1981) was interested in how these "forms of talk" are managed between teammates and contribute toward interaction order. *Remedial interchanges* (Goffman 1971) serve as a form of corrective repair work for deviant conduct, addressing the face needs of virtual offenders and claimants. These interaction rituals have four stages: challenge, offering, acceptance, and thanks (Goffman 1971).

Apart from the apology sequence, the *request* is an interesting remedial interchange. Goffman explains how, when one actor needs to impose on another for dramaturgical assistance, they acknowledge the intrusiveness in their opening line. Hence, requests are phrased as polite forms of address (Goffman 1981), such as, "*Excuse me, would you mind if I sit here?*" Fascinatingly, Goffman points out that this considerate formatting induces the potential claimant to collude with the offender, by inviting and offering willingly: "*Oh yes, of course, that's fine!*"—even if they privately feel the opposite way. This avoids any conflict, discomfort, or threat of disruption, smoothing over the cracks in the collective face. Remedial interchanges are therefore a cooperative aligning action (Stokes and Hewitt 1976), whereby teammates demonstrate their shared awareness of normative conventions and commitment to appropriate conduct. As always, what matters most is not the convenience of individual actors, but that the overall show can go on.

HIDDEN PERFORMANCES

So far, we have seen how social actors can manage their performances skillfully to give a convincing display. This paints a persuasive picture of dramaturgical competence and explains why most situations in everyday life appear to run smoothly. But symbolic interactionists also have plenty to say about the other side of the social theatre. Despite a common criticism that the perspective neglects conflict, "radical" theorists within it recognize the micro-politics of power (Athens 2007; Katovich 2013). This raises some important questions: what happens when performances go wrong, need rehearsing, are sabotaged from within, or break down completely?

Goffman's (1959) backstage region is a symbolic space designed to deal with precisely these contingencies. It serves as a container of all the mess, faults, mistakes, and undignified "dirty work" (Hughes 1962) that are necessary to uphold our front, and without it, performances could not run. Goffman depicts the backstage as a source of relief—a chance to drop guard, rest, and retreat from the exhausting labor of presenting ourselves. He suggests that without it, actors would quickly burn out and be unable to continue the show. So, the backstage is vital, but insofar as it undermines what is presented out front, its very existence must be kept hidden and secret. One of the most important arts of impression management, therefore, is *mystification*: putting a barrier between the front and back regions and preventing the audience from seeing into the latter (Goffman 1959).

Even when frontstage, actors can give less-than-convincing performances. Apart from the cynical attitude, described above, when parts are played without sincere belief, actors may also show *role distance* by standing aside from the part altogether (Goffman 1961a). Role distance occurs when we have to perform in ways that feel boring, demeaning, irrelevant, or surreal. There is a felt disconnection between the required character and one's real self, which makes it difficult to get immersed in the show. Actors deal with this by playing their parts with an attitude of ironic amusement and critical detachment: for example, by joking and messing around in the workplace. Goffman (1961a:95) suggests that role distance serves as a *"symbolic apology"* for the undignified impressions made by the currently presented front. It proudly tells the audience that "I am more than just this situational role" and pleads with them to look beyond it to the deeper, smarter self.

Actors may also engage in deliberate deception, or what Goffman (1959) calls the *misrepresentation* of their frontstage persona. Sometimes we are acutely aware of a "dark secret" about our true self that we do not want the audience to see; this may be something embarrassing or shameful that threatens a loss of face. Goffman (1963b) explored this in his discussion of *stigma*, a potential "blemish of character" caused by a discrepancy between one's virtual (presented or claimed) and actual (real) selves. The discrediting stigma are those that are immediately apparent, such as a physical disability, while discreditable stigma are those that are hidden but may be discovered. In the latter case, actors use dramaturgical techniques to manage the risk of exposure. These include information control (deciding carefully what and how much to tell different audiences) and passing (disguising oneself as a non-stigmatized person and hoping to remain undetected). For example, Schneider and Conrad (1981) found that people with epilepsy adopted strategies of disclosure that depended on how tactful and supportive they expected each audience to be. Over the long term, actors may develop a *moral career* (Goffman 1961b) as they manage the cumulative effects of living with a stigmatized attribute. The moral career is a sequence of stages through which an individual's conduct is morally judged against normative standards, resulting in a changed sense of status and social identity.

When identity performances are discredited, actors face social failure and a humiliating loss of status. *Cooling out* (Goffman 1952) is the process of adaptation to this, through which actors restore their place in the interaction order. Actors may cool themselves out to defend their pride, for example a suitor who is turned down when he asks for a date pretends that he did not like the woman so much anyway (Goffman 1952). Teammates may also cool out each other, for example a university sending polite rejection letters reassuring applicants that the competition was very tough. On a societal level, Goffman suggests that cooling out happens routinely and often, and so it must be structurally accommodated. Organizations and institutions exist to provide "resting places" for those who have been permanently cooled out, such as prisons, ghetto neighborhoods, and asylums (Goffman 1952, 1961b).

Teammates can perform deviously to outwit each other, despite maintaining a united front. Goffman (1969) argued that cooperation in teams is often pragmatic rather than altruistic and involves shrewd, rational calculation. Self-presentation is risky and dangerous, because we cannot always rely on our teammates to keep us in face—occasionally, friends become enemies and betray our trust. Aggressive facework (Goffman 1967) describes the sabotage of another's performance, by catching them out or deliberately humiliating them, for example through teasing and bullying. Uncovering moves (Goffman 1969) are gestures that shamefully expose another's discreditable status, instead of tactfully ignoring it. More subtle manipulation occurs with *response cries* (Goffman 1981), short utterances designed to invoke a response from the fellow actors in a scene. For example, the "floor cue" is a performance that seems self-absorbed and mysterious; it is designed to tantalize bystanders into requesting more detail. A husband reading the newspaper gives a sudden laugh, provoking his wife to ask, "*What's so funny?*" (Goffman 1981:105). Floor cues are useful when actors wish to appear modest but really want to be called onto the center stage.

Finally, actors may collude with (or against) the audience, to subvert the success of the show. *Communication out of character* (Goffman 1959) occurs when an actor momentarily slips out of role and acknowledges that they are giving a performance. This may happen spontaneously, when something unexpected and surprising happens that threatens poised composure: for example, losing one's balance and exclaiming with swear words. Teammates communicate out of character deliberately to change their relationship with the audience. In a pretense-awareness context, when everybody knows that things are not really as they appear, actors make coded gestures to each other to indicate their mutual knowledge of the truth. This serves as a meta-commentary on the performance, by effectively saying, "*Let's agree to play along, but we really mean something else.*" Teammates speak indirectly, using irony and innuendo to say one thing while contradicting it with another. At all times, actors sustain a surface, manifest definition of the situation to revert to if things go awry. This often happens in the context of salesperson bartering, veiled gestures between colleagues, and even the risky venture of romantic flirting (Tavory 2009). It mirrors the technique used in theatrical drama of "breaking the fourth wall," when actors turn to address the audience directly and invite them in to join the scene.

Conclusion

This chapter has explored the performative dimensions of social interaction, focusing particularly on Goffman's dramaturgical perspective. Symbolic interactionists are interested in how social situations get constructed through everyday rituals and practices, and how the resultant scenes are displayed for external view. Even though interaction can feel spontaneous and unpredictable, actors tacitly agree to uphold the appearance of order so that the show can go on. The definition of the situation may therefore be a polite fiction that belies the contingency of life behind the scenes.

Dramaturgy unpacks the mechanics of this process, by examining the minutiae of interpersonal encounters and highlighting the skills and techniques that are used. The theatre provides a helpful metaphor for social life, with actors presenting different versions of themselves like the characters in a play. They design and rehearse these performances backstage before going frontstage to impress situational audiences. The arts of impression management include dramaturgical circumspection, discipline and loyalty, idealization, dramatic realization, and mystification. Actors also work cooperatively in teams, like a theatrical cast. Bound by bonds of reciprocal dependence, they provide support and protection to keep each other safely in the face. Audiences are generally sympathetic and tactfully disattend to embarrassing mistakes that would otherwise disrupt the show.

However, sometimes performances do not run smoothly, and actors must work hard to cover the cracks. Identity claims get discredited, status is lost, and trust is betrayed by competitive teammates. Actors also enjoy playful moments of subtle subversion, through role distance, collusion, and slips out of character. Beneath the veneer of manifest appearances, interaction is a precarious drama, and we are all swept along for the ride. Actors, audience, and teammates are not separate groups but perspectives, alternate positions that fit neatly together through mutually sustained hard work. This complex and collective endeavor creates the magical theatre that we know as social life.

References

Alexander, Jeffrey C. 2004. "Cultural Pragmatics: Social Performance between Ritual and Strategy." *Sociological Theory* 22(4):527–73.

Alexander, Jeffrey C. 2006. "Cultural Pragmatics: Social Performance between Ritual and Strategy." Pp. 29–90 in *Social Performance: Symbolic Action, Cultural Pragmatics and Ritual*, edited by J. C. Alexander, B. Giesen, and J. L. Last. Cambridge: Cambridge University Press.

Athens, Lonnie. 2007. "Radical Interactionism: Going beyond Mead." *Journal for the Theory of Social Behavior* 37:137–65.

Berger, Peter L., and Thomas Luckmann. 1966. *The Social Construction of Reality*. New York: Anchor Books.

Blumer, Herbert. 1969. *Symbolic Interactionism: Perspective and Method*. Englewood Cliff, NJ: Prentice Hall.

Burke, Kenneth. 1945/1969. *A Grammar of Motives*. Berkeley: University of California Press.

Burns, Tom. 1992. *Erving Goffman*. London: Routledge.

Butler, Judith. 1990. *Gender Trouble: Feminism and the Subversion of Identity*. London: Routledge.

Collins, Randall. 2005. *Interaction Ritual Chains*. Princeton, NJ: Princeton University Press.

Cooley, Charles H. 1909/1983. *Social Organization*. New Brunswick, NJ: Transaction.

Drew, Paul, and John Heritage. 1992. *Talk at Work: Language Use in Institutional and Workplace Settings*. Cambridge: Cambridge University Press.

Durkheim, Emile. 1912. *The Elementary Forms of Religious Life*. Translated by J. W. Swain. London: Allen & Unwin.

Elliott, Anthony. 2007. *Concepts of the Self*. Cambridge: Polity.

Emerson, Joan P. 1970. "Nothing Unusual Is Happening." Pp. 208–22 in *Human Nature and Collective Behavior: Papers in Honor of Herbert Blumer*, edited by T. Shibutani. Englewood Cliffs, NJ: Prentice Hall.

Garfinkel, Harold. 1967. *Studies in Ethnomethodology*. Englewood Cliffs, NJ: Prentice Hall.

Glaser, Barney G., and Anselm L. Strauss. 1964. "Awareness Contexts and Social Interaction." *American Sociological Review* 29(5):669–79.

Goffman, Erving. 1952. "On Cooling the Mark Out: Some Aspects of Adaptation to Failure." *Psychiatry* 25:451–63.

Goffman, Erving. 1956. "Embarrassment and Social Organization." *American Journal of Sociology* 62(3):264–71.

Goffman, Erving. 1959. *The Presentation of Self in Everyday Life*. Harmondsworth: Penguin.

Goffman, Erving. 1961a. *Encounters: Two Studies in the Sociology of Interaction*. Indianapolis: Bobbs-Merill.

Goffman, Erving. 1961b. *Asylums*. New York: Anchor Books, Doubleday & Co.

Goffman, Erving. 1963a. *Behavior in Public Places*. New York: Free Press, Macmillan.

Goffman, Erving. 1963b. *Stigma: Notes on the Management of Spoiled Identity*. Harmondsworth: Penguin.

Goffman, Erving. 1967. *Interaction Ritual*. New York: Pantheon.

Goffman, Erving. 1969. *Strategic Interaction*. Philadelphia: University of Pennsylvania Press.

Goffman, Erving. 1971. *Relations in Public: Microstudies of the Public Order*. Harmondsworth: Penguin.

Goffman, Erving. 1974. *Frame Analysis: An Essay on the Organization of Experience*. New York: Northeastern Press.

Goffman, Erving. 1981. *Forms of Talk*. Philadelphia: University of Pennsylvania Press.

Goffman, Erving. 1983. "The Interaction Order." *American Sociological Review* 48:1–17.

Green, B. Christine, and Ian Jones. 2005. "Serious Leisure, Social Identity and Sport Tourism." *Sport in Society* 8(2):164–81.

Gross, Edward, and Gregory P. Stone. 1964. "Embarrassment and the Analysis of Role Requirements." *American Journal of Sociology* 70(1):1–15.

Halbwachs, Maurice. 1925/1992. *On Collective Memory*. Translated and edited by L.A. Coser. Chicago: University of Chicago Press.

Heath, Christian, and Dirk vom Lehn. 2008. "Configuring 'Interactivity': Enhancing Engagement in Science Centres and Museums." *Social Studies of Science* 38(1):63–91.

Hewitt, John P., and Randall Stokes. 1975. "Disclaimers." *American Sociological Review* 40:1–11.

Hinton, J. 1987. *Performance*. Basingstoke: Macmillan.

Hochschild, Arlie R. 1983. *The Managed Heart: Commercialisation of Human Feeling*. Berkeley: University of California Press.

Hodgson, John, and Ernest Richards. 1966. *Improvisation*. London: Eyre Methuen.

Hughes, Everett C. 1962. "Good People and Dirty Work." *Social Problems* 10(1):3–11.

Jackson, M. 2002. *The Politics of Storytelling: Violence, Transgression and Intersubjectivity*. Chicago: Museum Tusculanam Press.

Katovich, Michael. 2013. "Dominance, Deference, and Demeanor in *Mad Men*: Toward a Convergence of Radical Interactionism and Radical Dramaturgy." *Studies in Symbolic Interactionism* 41:161–89.

Lofland, John. 1980. "Early Goffman: Style, Structure, Substance, Soul." Pp. 24–51 in *The View From Goffman*, edited by J. Ditton. New York: St Martin's Press.

Mead, George. H. 1934. *Mind, Self and Society*. Chicago: University of Chicago Press.

Mills, C. Wright. 1940. "Situated Actions and Vocabularies of Motive." *American Sociological Review* 5:904–13.

Plummer, Kenneth. 2019. *Narrative Power: The Struggle for Human Value*. Cambridge: Polity.

Potter, Jonathan. 1996. *Representing Reality: Discourse, Rhetoric and Social Construction*. London: SAGE.

Riggins, Stephen H., ed. 1990/2010. *Beyond Goffman*. Hawthorne, NY: Aldine de Gruyter.

Rossing, Hilde, and Susie Scott. 2014. "Familiar Strangers: Facework Strategies in Pursuit of Non-binding Relations in a Workplace-based Exercise Group." *Studies in Symbolic Interaction* 42:161–84.

Sacks, Harvey. 1992. *Lectures on Conversation*. Oxford: Blackwell.

Sandvoss, Cornel. 2005. *Fans*. Cambridge: Polity.

Schechner, Richard. 2002. *Performance Studies: An Introduction*. London: Routledge.

Scheff, Thomas. J. 1968. "Negotiating reality." *Social Problems* 16:3–17.

Schegloff, Emanuel A. 1968. "Sequencing in Conversational Openings." *American Anthropologist* 70(6):1075–95.

Schneider, Joseph W., and Peter Conrad. 1981. "Medical and Sociological Typologies: The Case of Epilepsy." *Social Science and Medicine* 15A:211–19.

Schütz, Alfred. 1972. *The Phenomenology of the Social World*. London: Heinemann, London.

Scott, Marvin B., and Stanford M. Lyman. 1968. "Accounts." *American Sociological Review* 33:46–62.

Scott, Susie. 2007. *Shyness and Society*. Basingstoke: Palgrave.

Scott, Susie. 2009. "Re-clothing the Emperor: The Swimming Pool as a Negotiated Order." *Symbolic Interaction* 32(2):123–45.

Scott, Susie. 2015. *Negotiating Identity: Symbolic Interactionist Approaches to Social Identity*. Cambridge: Polity.

Scott, Susie. 2017. "Transitions and Transcendence of the Self: Stage Fright and the Paradox of Shy Performativity." *Sociology* 51(4):715–31.

Smith, Gregory. 2006. *Erving Goffman*. London: Routledge.

Southern, Richard. 1962. *The Seven Ages of the Theatre*. London: Faber & Faber.

Stokes, Randall, and John P. Hewitt. 1976. "Aligning Actions." *American Sociological Review* 41:838–49.

Stone, Gregory. 1962. "Appearance and the Self." Pp. 86–118 in *Human Behavior and Social Processes*, edited by A. Rose. Boston: Houghton-Mifflin.

Strauss, Anselm L. 1978. *Negotiations: Varieties, Contexts, Processes and Social Order*. San Francisco: Jossey-Bass.

Tavory, Iddo. 2009. "The Structure of Flirtation: On the Construction of Interactional Ambiguity." *Studies in Symbolic Interaction* 33:59–74.

Thomas, W.I., and Thomas, D.S. 1970 [1928]. "Situations Defined as Real Are Real in Their Consequences." Pp. 154–155 Reprinted in *Social Psychology Through Interaction*, edited by G. Stone and H. Farberman, Waltham: Ginn-Blasidell.

Turner, Victor T. 1997. "Are There Universals of Performance in Myth, Ritual and Dance?" Pp. 8–18 in *By Means of Performance*, edited by R. Schechner and W. Appel. Cambridge: Cambridge University Press.

Tyler, Imogen. 2013. *Revolting Subjects: Social Abjection and Resistance in Neoliberal Britain*. London: Zed Books.

Van Maanen, John. 1990. "The Smile Factory: Work at Disneyland." Pp. 58–76 in *Reframing Organisational Culture*, edited by P. J. Frost et al. London: SAGE.

Weinberg, Martin S. 1965. "Sexual Modesty, Social Meanings, and the Nudist Camp." *Social Problems* 12(3):311–18.

West, Candace, and Don Zimmerman. 1987. "Doing Gender." *Gender and Society* 1(2):125–51.

Whalen, Marilyn, and Don H. Zimmerman. 1987. "Sequential and Institutional Contexts in Calls for Help." *Social Psychology Quarterly* 50:172–85.

Zimmerman, Don H. 1992. "The Interactional Organization of Calls for Emergency Assistance." Pp. 418–69 in *Talk at Work: Social Interaction in Institutional Settings*, edited by P. Drew and J. Heritage. Cambridge: Cambridge University Press.

CHAPTER 9

SOCIAL CONSTRUCTIONISM IN THE SYMBOLIC INTERACTIONIST TRADITION

ARA A. FRANCIS

SOCIAL constructionism became part of the sociological lexicon in the 1970s following the publication of Peter Berger and Thomas Luckmann's (1966) *The Social Construction of Reality*. Now part of the discipline's canon and used widely by scholars from different traditions of thought, constructionism has long had special resonance with symbolic interactionism. In this chapter, I offer a symbolic interactionist's introduction to social constructionism, review the key tenets of Berger and Luckman's treatise with an eye toward the relationship of their work to the interactionist tradition, give a brief history of constructionist debates in symbolic interactionist scholarship, and consider how recent critiques of constructionism in academic and public discourse might inform future interactionist scholarship.

AN INTERACTIONIST INTRODUCTION TO SOCIAL CONSTRUCTIONISM

The social constructionist perspective proposes that reality and knowledge are born of social processes. In other words, everything we perceive as existing beyond our own imaginations and all of the information we possess about those realities is produced, in an ongoing fashion, by human beings in interaction with one another. This framework defines symbolic interactionists' orientation to the study of topics ranging from social problems (e.g., Spector and Kitsuse 1977; Best 1990; Altheide 2006) to roles and identities (e.g., Laws and Schwartz 1977; Frankenberg 1993; Schrock et al. 2018) to science and the natural world (e.g., Greider and Garkovich 1994; Dingwall et al. 2003; McKee 2013).

Consider Joel Best's (1990) work on children and risk perception. In the 1970s and 1980s, there emerged a wave of public concern about threats to children's safety. While anxieties about rebellious, deprived, and sick children had surfaced in previous eras, people's attention had now turned to what Best calls "the child victim" (pp. 5–6). News coverage during that period was rife with stories about deviant adults who preyed upon children: kidnappers, pedophiles, drug dealers, and Satan worshippers. Rather than taking for granted the nature of children's victimization and asking questions about its causes or consequences, Best asks how and why child victims had emerged as a major public concern when it did. He finds that interest groups deployed savvy rhetorical strategies to frame missing children and child abuse as pressing social problems. Other claimants took advantage of that momentum, linking their causes to the quickly expanding domain of child abuse. Playing upon a sentimentalized image of childhood— an image born of anxieties about the family, the economy, and modernity itself—claims about child victims were readily taken up by newsmakers who reached broad public audiences. Best's work exemplifies how symbolic interactionists take social problems to be social constructions, the products of collaborative action that lead the public to view conditions in a particular way. In Best's analysis, the problem of the child victim did not stem naturally or inevitably from a particular set of circumstances but rather emerged when particular groups of people brought those circumstances to the public's attention and framed them as a social problem. As demonstrated here, a constructionist orientation also draws our attention to how taken-for-granted realities, such as children's vulnerability, are embedded in particular historical, cultural, and situational contexts.

This perspective hints at the social nature of human perception, a topic that Asia Friedman (2013) explores more directly in her study of cognition and the sexed body. When compared to other species, human beings are only weakly dimorphic. While sex differences do exist (e.g., breasts, genitalia), most of our body parts (e.g., ears, shins, ankles, knees) are not sex-specific. Conceiving of bodies as male or female, then, is an act of perception that requires us to focus on a small proportion of the body to the exclusion of a majority of its features. Friedman thus explores the role of perception in the social construction of sex, illustrating how we apprehend bodies through a mental filter that primes us to see sex difference, rather than sex sameness. This filter is a social one, acquired through socialization, and we use it to actively sort bodies into binary categories that distort the biological information available to our senses.

Friedman's analysis captures the relationship of social constructionism to the physical world. Our knowledge of material reality is always and inextricably bound to social life, if for no other reason that we use language to codify it. To know a word for a something is to know its shared meaning and the position of that meaning within a larger system. The meanings themselves are not inherent to particular objects, situations, or experiences but are the variable, mutable projects of ongoing human interaction. It can be said, then, that symbols, whether they are words, gestures, or objects, do more than signify reality. They also inevitably produce and organize it. The constructionist approach does not deny or dismiss physicality but rather highlights how sensation and perception are social endeavors that filter our apprehension of it. In this case, the mere existence of sex differences does not provide a full accounting of the realities of sex. Rather, human perception, a social activity produced in and by particular cultures and histories, is a key component in the generation of what we know about maleness and femaleness.

Friedman's work also underscores how distinctions that we take to be natural or essential are, instead, products of social convention. As Eviatar Zerubavel (1981) demonstrated in his work on schedules and calendars, even something as fundamental and seemingly immutable as time is socially constructed. Our experience of time, he argues, is organized according to four major dimensions: things happen in a particular order, last for particular durations, occur at particular times, and recur at particular frequencies. It is true that some of what we experience is governed by what Zerubavel calls the physiotemporal and biotemporal orders (p. 2); lightning comes before thunder, human gestation occurs within a relatively fixed window, puberty begins at a particular time in the life span, and the earth rotates around the sun at regular intervals. Yet much of human experience is structured by the sociotemporal order, which, unlike the physiotemporal and biotemporal orders, is more normative than imperative. That we sing happy birthday before cutting the cake, a workday is eight hours long, people can legally consume alcohol when they turn twenty-one years old, and we celebrate Christmas on the 25th of December each year are matters of convention and tradition. We nonetheless experience the rhythms of social life as natural and inevitable, and, in turn, they regulate our thoughts, feelings, and behaviors.

These interactionist studies illustrate the basic proposition of social constructionism: reality as we understand it is not inherent to particular objects, experiences, or situations. Rather, truths are social phenomena, collectively produced by human beings, even as they organize, enable, and constrain our thoughts, feelings, and actions. Social constructionism dovetails somewhat naturally with a symbolic interactionist understanding of social life, and, indeed, Peter Berger and Thomas Luckmann (1966) drew from foundational interactionist writers in their seminal text, *The Social Construction of Reality*. Even so, at the time Berger and Luckmann were writing, constructionism afforded a more structural orientation to the study of the human condition than did symbolic interactionism, which had been critiqued for its overemphasis on human agency and the emergent, contingent nature of social life.

INTERACTIONISM AND BERGER AND LUCKMANN'S *THE SOCIAL CONSTRUCTION OF REALITY*

Berger and Luckmann characterized the social construction of reality as a threefold process involving externalization, objectivation, and internalization. Externalization refers, simply, to the ongoing human activities that generate culture. The satisfaction of even the most basic human needs is organized through systems of our own, collective design. These systems begin, Berger and Luckmann argue, with the constant "outpouring" of human beings into the world; we say things, we do things, and, over time, particular ways of saying and doing things become patterned. Objectivation is the process by which those patterns come to be seen as existing outside human volition. Patterns of activity harden into institutions, and those institutions confront us with independent force. Indeed, we do not experience the systems that organize our conduct as human inventions, but rather we encounter them as objective facts, as *the way things are*. Internalization, in turn, captures how those social patterns, comprised of human activity yet experienced as independent of such activity, generate human beings, the processes of socialization yielding selves that are, in the most basic sense, made up of social and cultural materials.

Berger and Luckmann drew extensively from the interactionist canon when articulating the social psychological dimensions of these processes. In their discussion of society's objective dimension, for example, they built upon W. I. Thomas's and Florian Znaniecki's (1918) "definition of the situation" to capture how shared expectations organize human activity and form the bedrock of institutions (Berger and Luckmann 1966:53–54). Institutions, they argued, are rooted directly in social interaction, with patterns of action emerging reciprocally between people. Here Berger and Luckmann relied on Mead's (1934) language of role taking. We "play roles vis-à-vis each other," they explained, formulating our own lines of action in relationship to those of others (p. 56). In this way, the habitual conduct of other people becomes integral to our own.

Berger and Luckmann's discussion of internalization and the subjective dimension of social life also reveals interactionist influences. People are born, they point out, into a social world that is already underway (p. 129). That world is an ongoing human production. However, because it predates and exists apart from any particular individual, people encounter it as objective, as fact. To become a member of a society, then, is to align one's internal, subjective reality with external, objective reality, a process that Berger and Luckmann articulate using Mead's scholarship. Through role taking and the acquisition of language, they explain, children come to see themselves as having an identity. That identity is simultaneously part of the child's own consciousness *and* part of the social world, externally derived from the attitudes and actions of significant others. Those subjective and objective realities develop symmetrically, though never perfectly so, as children learn to take the role of a generalized other and to understand themselves not only from the perspective of individual people but of people writ large. This means that the development of selfhood is fundamentally a process of internalization, the basic means by which society generates individuals who, in their turn, collaborate in the ongoing generation of society.

Berger and Luckmann's reliance on, and extension of, Mead's work meant that social constructionism as it was taken up in the social sciences had much in common with symbolic interactionism. Language resides at the center of both traditions. Both honor human agency, recognize the emergent and contingent nature of social life, and actively eschew essentialism. Nonetheless, the social constructionist perspective arguably lent itself to structural analyses more readily than symbolic interactionism did, at least at the time of Berger and Luckmann's publication. A side-by-side reading of *The Social Construction of Reality* with Herbert Blumer's (1969) *Symbolic Interaction*, published just three years later, highlights this difference. Both texts characterize institutions as the repetitive ways that people think about and behave toward particular situations. However, Blumer warns scholars against imbuing institutions with independent force, separate from the human actors whose patterns of conduct comprise them. He expresses concern, in particular, about the tendency among sociologists to frame society, culture, institutions, roles, norms, and the like as playing upon people and causing particular kinds of conduct. "Under the perspective of symbolic interaction," he explains, "social action is lodged in acting individuals who fit their respective lines of action to one another through a process of interpretation; group action is the collective action of such individuals. As opposed to this view, sociological conceptions generally lodge social action in the action of society or in some unit of society" (p. 84). Here Blumer critiques traditions such as functionalism for their inattention to the social psychological foundations of social life.

Berger and Luckmann are similarly attentive to selves, identities, and interactions, but they describe institutions as acting upon people with independent force. Objectivation hinges on "reification," or the apprehension of human-produced realities as though they are supra-human (p. 89). "Through reification," Berger and Luckmann write, "the world of institutions appears to merge with the world of nature. It becomes necessity and fate, and is lived through as such, happily or unhappily as the case may be" (p. 91). Roles, they argue, are particularly powerful when reified; when the expectations associated with our positions are experienced as given or natural, we are prone to assuming that we have no choice but to meet them.

Berger and Luckmann's framework for understanding the relationship of self and society is not oppositional to Blumer's, but their work is more attentive to the sway that social structures have on individuals. Symbolic interaction later came under fire for what some scholars argued was Blumer's neglect of social structure, a problem that David Snow (2001:368) notes in his re-articulation of the principles that underpin the perspective.

> [Blumer identified] meaning and interpretation as the central, orienting concerns of symbolic interactionism, thereby riveting empirical and analytic attention to these two interconnected concerns. Simultaneously, it deflects attention from other principles and topics relevant to both symbolic interactionism and sociology more generally, such as social structure and culture and variation in their levels and degrees of constraint.

In short, social constructionism might have found a home among symbolic interactionists not just because of the natural affinity between the perspectives, both building upon Meadian social psychology as they did, but because constructionism offered a clear vantage point from which to analyze social structures without undermining the key tenets of symbolic interactionism. Although Snow (2001) does not cite Berger and Luckmann or use the phrase "social constructionism," his discussion of the principle of "interactive determinism" nonetheless captures the dialectical relationship between self and society articulated by Berger and Luckmann. "Neither individual or society nor self or other are ontologically prior," Snow (2001) writes, "but exist only in relation to each other; thus one can fully understand them only through their interaction, whether actual, virtual, or imagined" (p. 369).

DEBATES AMONG SOCIAL CONSTRUCTIONISTS

In the decades immediately following the publication of Berger and Luckmann's work, scholars with symbolic interactionist leanings used the framework of social construction to explore topics ranging from news (Altheide and Rasmussen 1976; Tuchman 1978) to time (Zerubavel 1979, 1981, 1985). It was in the study of social problems, though, that a body of scholarship at the intersection of symbolic interactionism and social constructionism emerged most clearly. This area built upon interactionist studies of deviance, such as Howard Becker's (1963) seminal articulation of the reactivist perspective, that were constructionist in their orientation but not necessarily in dialogue with Berger and Luckmann's text. As Joel Best's work on child victims demonstrates, this new generation of social problems scholars sought to understand the processes by which people come to see particular conditions as problematic.

Key debates about the social constructionist perspective played out in the burgeoning social problems literature. Most notably, Steve Woolgar and Dorothy Pawluch (1985) challenged the constructionist enterprise on two fronts. First, they argued that most constructionist analyses hinge on a "selective relativism" (p. 214). By this they meant that constructionist scholars tend to assume the existence of independent or objective realities around which people attach fluid, socially constructed meanings. As Peter Ibarra (2008) explains, Howard Becker's (1963) *Outsiders* exemplified this tendency. Becker constructed his classic typology along two dimensions, rule breaking and social reaction, thereby allowing for the recognition of secret deviants (i.e., those who have broken the rules but escaped the deviant label) and falsely accused deviants (those who have been labeled as deviant but have not actually broken the rules). These categories are premised on the presence or absence of rule breaking as separate from social labeling. Although Becker gestured toward the constructed nature of rules themselves—noting, for example, that people labeled as deviant might not see the rules or understand their own conduct in the same way—his argument nonetheless relied on a selective, objective orientation to rule breaking.

In a second but related critique, Woolgar and Pawluch (1985) argued that social constructionist scholars endow their own knowledge claims with a privileged ontological status, even as they seek to demonstrate how all such claims are socially constructed. In other words, despite their professed commitment to the notion that all truths are social and provisional, constructionist writing implies that scholars' own assertions are somehow exceptional, perhaps even more "truthful," than lay assertions. Woolgar and Pawluch referred to this particular kind of selective relativism as "ontological gerrymandering" (p. 214), a practice that is common in social problems scholarship. Scholars who utilize a constructionist framework to study crack cocaine (Reinarman and Levine 1997), road rage (Best and Furedi 2001), and sex trafficking (Weitzer 2007), for example, underscore the how newsmakers and moral entrepreneurs make inaccurate claims about the nature and magnitude of their respective problems. In doing so, these scholars make claims of their own but usually fail to recognize or analyze their own claims as socially constructed.

Constructionist scholars acknowledged the validity of these critiques, but they disagreed about their ramifications for empirical scholarship. Some argued that selective relativism should be avoided through vigilant writing; they suggested that scholars remain consistent with the constructionist position by refraining from making assertions about objective conditions (Schneider 1985). In a similar vein, others encouraged constructionist scholars to abandon questions that might tempt them into selective relativism, focusing instead on questions related to language and the rhetorical strategies that people use in claims-making campaigns (Ibarra and Kitsuse 1993). Contrary to these positions, others asserted that selective relativism is an inevitable and tolerable part of any research endeavor. Even when scholars refrain from making explicit statements about objective conditions, they argued, their assumptions about the empirical world shape their inquiries. As Joel Best (1993) points out, scholars who studied the satanism scare in the 1980s were more likely to ask, "Who believes this stuff, and why?" than "Why haven't the authorities done more about this?" (p. 137). The opposite was true of those studying the AIDS crisis. Indeed, the very questions we ask reveal our assumptions about a social problem's legitimacy. Best worried, too, that if they avoided assertions about objective reality, social constructionists would make their scholarship irrelevant to other scholars and the broader public, whose concerns are quite distant from the abstract theoretical concerns raised by selective relativism.

These debates led to a split within social constructionist scholarship, a strict constructionism emerging, on the one hand, and a contextual constructionism emerging, on the other (Best 1989). Strict constructionists turned away from empirical case studies and toward analyzing the nature of sociological inquiry itself, while contextual constructionists accepted selective relativism as a necessary evil and plunged ahead with questions about when, where, how, and why particular phenomena emerge as problems in the public imagination. There is widespread agreement that the latter approach was more successful than the former. Few scholars were willing to adhere to the tenets of strict constructionism, and the challenges raised by Woolgar and Pawluch eventually became moot (Best 2008; Ibarra 2008).

The practice of analytic bracketing, as articulated by Jaber Gubrium and James Holstein (1997), offers one possibility for navigating between the two poles of strict and contextual constructionism. Taking this approach, a scholar oscillates between seeing realities as fluid, emergent products of social interaction, on the one hand, and solid sets of resources that enable and constrain social interaction, on the other. Analytic bracketing thus acknowledges the duality of socially constructed realities—process and structure, subjectivity and objectivity, how and what—and requires the scholar to place one dimension temporarily out of focus while exploring the other. In the words of Peter Ibarra (2008), perhaps "constructionists need not make an ontological choice" (p. 368).

Debates about selective relativism and ontological gerrymandering unfolded among constructionist scholars, but the perspective has been subject to outside challenges as well, both from other areas of academe and in public discourse. Some of those challenges have resurfaced in the past few years, raising concerns about the implications of constructionism at a time when identity politics are salient and alternative facts are widely understood to be a social problem.

THE CONTEMPORARY POLITICS OF SOCIAL CONSTRUCTIONISM

The social constructionist perspective often has been met with skepticism, if not outright disdain, from scholars beyond disciplines such as sociology and anthropology, where its relevance and value are largely taken for granted. Most critiques stem from a particular understanding (or what some argue is a misunderstanding) of the perspective itself. Some people take "socially constructed" to mean "false," as though socially constructed realities are separate from, or oppositional to, objective realities. This understanding is what Joel Best (1995) refers to as "vulgar constructionism" (p. 345), an orientation that social constructionists inadvertently fuel when they analyze empirically dubious claims. As Best points out, social constructionists have tended to advance their perspective by choosing cases that offer maximum analytical leverage. It is easy to demonstrate the value of social constructionism when examining the fallibility of science, for example, or the inaccuracy of inflated social-problems claims. Even though constructionism holds that all knowledge—even knowledge that captures the world accurately—is an ongoing social endeavor, scholars have been far more likely to use the perspective to analyze bogus ideas. To call something "socially constructed," then, is sometimes read as a denial of the thing's truth, salience, or consequences.

The assertion that social constructionism is a dangerous form of antirealism garnered public attention in the mid-1990s when the cultural studies journal *Social Text* published a tongue-in-cheek article submitted by the physicist Alan Sokal. In the piece titled "Transgressing the Boundaries: Toward a Transformative Hermeneutics of Quantum Gravity," Sokal (1996a) used the jargon of literary criticism to make a number of preposterous claims about the natural world. He then revealed his hoax, arguing that his parody had been accepted for publication mostly because it aligned with the editors' intellectual and political assumptions (Sokal 1996b). Sokal granted that social constructionism could be useful in the analysis of some phenomena, such as how science is influenced by its sources of funding, but he contended that, at its worse, the perspective downplays and even denies the existence of objective realities. Social constructionism, he concluded, will not help us solve problems such as AIDS or global warming, and if we reject the distinction between truth and falsity, we will have no point of departure for critiquing fallacious claims.

This critique is especially relevant in our current political era, when right-wing populism challenges not just the legitimacy of particular facts but the existence of facts altogether. What is the place of social constructionism at a moment when scholars must defend the very notion of truth? This question was salient even before the election of leaders such as Donald Trump and Boris Johnson. In 2004, Bruno Latour suggested that the social constructionist orientation to science used by critical theorists had outlived its utility. Having spent much of his own academic career engaged in the critical analysis of scientific authority, Latour worried that the logic of constructionism was now being used by extremists to deny, for example, climate change. He called upon scholars to retool the constructionist approach—to revise it from scratch, if necessary (p. 231)—to better address the challenges of our age. In recent discussions framed by post-truth politics, some scholars in science and technology studies have taken up this project of renovation. Joanna Kempner (2020) and David Hess (2020) advocate for the study of scientific ignorance. Such a sociology would focus, in Kempner's words, on how "political and economic elites produce, manufacture, and sustain ignorance" (p. 239). Latour himself (Latour and Porter 2019) has turned his attention to how and under what conditions people receive or accept scientific knowledge, rather than focusing solely on its production. Still others, such as Joan Fujimura and Christopher Holmes (2019), urge scholars not to be distracted by the din of post-truth politics. Constructionist analyses do not undermine science, they contend, but contribute to it by offering expert knowledge that helps citizen-consumers navigate the current political landscape.

Another recent controversy, this time steeped in the politics of gender and race, emerged in the summer of 2015 following coverage of Caitlyn Jenner's gender transition in *Vanity Fair* (Bissinger 2015) and the high-profile controversy surrounding Rachel Dolezal's racial identity. Caitlyn Jenner is a pop-culture personality who went public about her life as transgender woman and experience of transitioning from man to woman. Her story seemed to mark a turning point in the public discourse on transgender identity; in some quarters, at least, there seemed to be growing recognition and validation of transgender identities. Just as Jenner's story was garnering attention, news broke of Rachel Dolezal (Johnson et al. 2015). Living as a black woman, Dolezal had been occupying a leadership position at the NAACP when she was discovered to have grown up white, the biological child of two white parents. Publicly condemned for deceptively misappropriating black identity, Dolezal insisted on the legitimacy of her blackness, claiming that her identity is "transracial."

Social constructionism became implicated in the Dolezal affair when, in a 2017 article published in *Hypatia*, the white feminist philosopher Rebecca Tuvel used the language of social constructionism to defend the logic of transracialism. Staging the piece with Jenner's and Dolezal's stories specifically, Tuvel contends that arguments in support of

SOCIAL CONSTRUCTIONISM IN THE SYMBOLIC INTERACTIONIST TRADITION   171

transgenderism are applicable to transracialism. Central to her proposition is the assertion that both gender and race are socially constructed and, thus, malleable. Tuvel was quickly and roundly rebuked by critical scholars of gender and race, as well as social-media commentators, who rushed to point out that the ostensibly fluid nature of Dolezal's racial identity hinges on her whiteness and privilege. Indeed, blackness is not a choice for people who are born black. "Please spare me your 'Race is a social construct' tears," wrote Yesha Callahan (2017) for the online magazine *The Root*,

> Yeah, this same "social construct" seemingly allows black people to be discriminated against when they apply for mortgages and car loans. Also, *hello,* police brutality. And do I need to mention "White" and "Colored" water fountains from back in the day? Or did we all forget about the civil rights movement?

Further underscoring Tuvel's lack of engagement with scholarship by queer authors and authors of color, an anonymous group of academics sent an open letter, signed by approximately 800 of their colleagues, to *Hypatia*'s editorial board, requesting the article's retraction.

Although the Tuvel controversy played out in the discipline of philosophy, it nonetheless highlights potential challenges and pitfalls in contemporary symbolic interactionist scholarship. Given how pervasive and taken for granted the social constructionist approach is among interactionists, there is a tendency to use the language of constructionism without fully explaining what it means (Hacking 1999:35) or doing the analytical work of demonstrating *how* the phenomena under consideration are socially constructed (Hollander and Gordon 2006:184). A careful constructionist analysis pays close attention to the historically and culturally entrenched nature of taken-for-granted meanings, recognizing that realities are durable *precisely because* of their relationship to particular histories and cultures. To merely state that something is socially constructed does not have much analytical value and, in the absence of elaboration, can serve to obscure rather than illuminate the topic at hand. Consider Tina Fernandes Botts's (2018) rebuttal of Rebecca Tuvel's argument about the equivalency of gender and race. Botts concedes that, yes, race and gender are both socially constructed; what Tuvel does not consider is how they are socially constructed in different ways. The construct of race, Botts argues, is linked to ancestry, a condition that is externally derived and resides, for the most part, beyond a person's subjective experience. The construct of gender, on the other hand, has an internally derived dimension, making it less fixed. Perhaps more importantly, the constructs of race and gender are *experienced* differently, something that Tuvel does not consider in her analogy. As Botts's critique suggests, the framework of social constructionism can be rendered meaningless when it does not address the specific content, processes, or lived experiences of particular constructions.

The Tuvel affair also illustrates how the social constructionist perspective can do symbolic violence. Constructionist work often seeks to reveal how meanings are arbitrary, normative, or historically contingent, opposed to natural or essential. By focusing on a meaning's social origins, it is possible to neglect the brute force of that meaning's consequences. Rebecca Tuvel's defense of transracialism on the grounds that race is socially constructed baldly violated many commentators' lived experiences of being black. By failing to recognize the significance of her own social location or take seriously accounts of race that emphasize the obdurate, material dimensions of discrimination and racialized violence, Tuvel's deployment of social constructionism contributed to the longstanding pattern of white feminists' complicity with the marginalization of black experience. The tensions and discrepancies between how meanings are constructed and how they are experienced—particularly when those meanings are bound up in identities and hierarchies—warrants careful attention, as does the broader political implications of any particular social constructionist analysis.

What these debates mean for symbolic interactionists engaged in social constructionist analyses is an open question. What seems clear, at the very least, is that we must write with increased political attunement and reflexivity, remaining attentive, always, to the lived experiences of social constructions. Given its political history, we might resist the temptation to use the phrase "socially constructed" in an offhanded way and take greater care to explain what we mean by it when we do deploy it in our work. Beyond writing in ways that acknowledge contemporary challenges and debates, we might also answer the call to continue extending and revising the social constructionist perspective to meet the exigencies of our times.

REFERENCES

Altheide, David L., and Paul K. Rasmussen. 1976. "Becoming News: A Study of Two Newsrooms." *Sociology of Work & Occupations* 3(2):223–46.

Altheide, David L. 2006. *Terrorism and the Politics of Fear*. Lanham, MD: AltaMira Press.

Becker, Howard S. 1963. *Outsiders: Studies in Sociology of Deviance*. New York: Free Press.

Berger, Peter L., and Thomas Luckmann. 1966. *The Social Construction of Reality: A Treatise in the Sociology of Knowledge*. New York: Doubleday.

Best, Joel. 1989. "Afterword." Pp. 243–53 in *Images of Issues*, edited by Joel Best. Hawthorne, NY: Aldine de Gruyter.

Best, Joel. 1990. *Threatened Children: Rhetoric and Concern about Child-victims*. Chicago: University of Chicago Press.

Best, Joel. 1993. "But Seriously Folks: The Limitations of the Strict Constructionist Interpretation of Social Problems." Pp. 129–47 in *Reconsidering Social Constructionism: Debates in Social Problems Theory*, edited by James A. Holstein and Gale Miller. Hawthorne, NY: Aldine de Gruyter.

Best, Joel. 1995. "Constructionism in Context." Pp. 337–54 in *Images of Issues*, 2nd ed., edited by Joel Best. Hawthorne, NY: Aldine de Gruyter.

Best, Joel. 2008. "Historical Development and Defining Issues of Constructionist Inquiry." Pp. 41–64 in *Handbook of Constructionist Research*, edited by James A. Holstein and Jaber F. Gubrium. New York: The Guilford Press.

Best, Joel, and Frank Furedi. 2001. "The Evolution of Road Rage in Britain and the United States." Pp. 107–28 in *How Claims Spread: Cross-National Diffusion of Social Problems*, edited by Joel Best. Hawthorne, NY: Aldine de Gruyter.

Bissinger, Buzz. 2015. "Caitlyn Jenner: The Full Story." *Vanity Fair*. https://www.vanityfair.com/hollywood/2015/06/caitlyn-jenner-bruce-cover-annie-leibovitz.

Blumer, Herbert. 1969. *Symbolic Interactionism: Perspective and Method*. Englewood Cliffs, NJ: Prentice Hall.

Botts, Tina Ferdinand. 2018. "Race and Method: The Tuvel affair." *Philosophy Today* 62(1):51–72.

Callahan, Yesha. 2017. "No, You Can't Just Wake Up and Decide to Be Black." *The Root*. https://thegrapevine.theroot.com/no-you-can-t-just-wake-up-and-decide-to-be-black-179 1801464.

Dingwall, Robert, Brigitte Nerlich, and Samantha Hillyard. 2003. "Biological Determinism and Symbolic Interaction: Hereditary Streams and Cultural Roads." *Symbolic Interaction* 26(4):631–44.

Frankenberg, Ruth. 1993. *White Women, Race Matters: The Social Construction of Whiteness*. Minneapolis: University of Minnesota Press.

Friedman, Asia. 2013. *Blind to Sameness: Sexpectations and the Social Construction of Male and Female Bodies*. Chicago: University of Chicago Press.

Fujimura, Joan H., and Christopher J. Holmes. 2019. "Staying the Course: On the Value of Social Studies of Science in Resistance to the 'Post-Truth' Movement." *Sociological Forum* 34(December):1251–63.

Greider, Thomas, and Lorraine Garkovich. 1994. "Landscapes: The Social Construction of Nature and the Environment." *Rural Sociology* 59(1):1–24.

Gubrium, Jaber F., and James A. Holstein. 1997. *The New Language of Qualitative Method*. New York: Oxford University Press.

Hacking, Ian. 1999. *The social construction of what?* Harvard: Harvard University Press.

Hess, David J. 2020. "The Sociology of Ignorance and Post-Truth Politics." *Sociological Forum* 35(1):241–49.

Hollander, Jocelyn A., and Hava R. Gordon. 2006. "The Processes of Social Construction in Talk." *Symbolic Interaction* 29(2):183–212.

Ibarra, Peter. 2008. "Strict and Contextual Constructionism in the Sociology of Deviance and Social Problems." Pp. 255–69 in *Handbook of Constructionist Research*, edited by James A. Holstein and Jaber F. Gubrium. New York: The Guilford Press.

Ibarra, Peter R., and John Kitsuse. 1993. "Vernacular Constituents of Moral Discourse: An Interactionist Proposal for the Study of Social Problems." Pp. 25–58 in *Reconsidering Social Constructionism: Debates in Social Problems Theory*, edited by James A. Holstein and Gale Miller. Hawthorne, NY: Aldine de Gruyter.

Johnson, Kirk, Richard Pérez-Peña, and John Eligon. 2015. "Rachel Dolezal, in Center of Storm, Is Defiant: 'I Identify as Black.'" *New York Times*. https://www.nytimes.com/2015/06/17/us/rachel-dolezal-nbc-today-show.html.

Kempner, Joanna. 2020. "Post-Truth and the Production of Ignorance." *Sociological Forum* 35(1):234–40.

Latour, Bruno. 2004. "Why Has Critique Run out of Steam? From Matters of Fact to Matters of Concern." *Critical Inquiry* 30(2):225–48.

Latour, Bruno, and Catherine Porter. 2019. *Down to Earth: Politics in the New Climatic Regime*. Cambridge: Polity.

Laws, Judith Long, and Pepper Schwartz. 1977. *Sexual Scripts the Social Construction of Female Sexuality*. Hinsdale, IL: Dryden Press.

McKee, Robert J. 2013. "The Symbolic Meanings of Physical Boundaries: The F Street Wall." *Space & Culture* 16(1):4–15.

Mead, George Herbert. 1934. *Mind, Self and Society: From the Standpoint of a Social Behaviorist.* Chicago: University of Chicago Press.

Reinarman, C., and H. G. Levine. 1997. "Crack Attack: Politics and Media in the Crack Scare." Pp. 18–51 in *Crack in America: Demon Drugs and Social Justice*, edited by Craig Reinarman and Harry G Levine. Berkeley: University of California Press.

Schneider, Joseph W. 1985. "Defining the Definitional Perspective on Social Problems." *Social Problems* 32(3):232.

Schrock, Douglas, Janice McCabe, and Christian Vaccaro. 2018. "Narrative Manhood Acts: Batterer Intervention Program Graduates' Tragic Relationships." *Symbolic Interaction* 41(3):384–410.

Snow, David A. 2001. "Extending and Broadening Blumer's Conceptualization of Symbolic Interactionism." *Symbolic Interaction* 24(3):367–77.

Sokal, Alan. 1996a. "Transgressing the Boundaries: Towards a Transformative Hermeneutics of Quantum Gravity." *Social Text* 46/47(1):217–52.

Sokal, Alan. 1996b. "A Physicist Experiments With Cultural Studies." *Lingua franca* 6(4):62–64.

Spector, Malcolm, and John I. Kitsuse. 1977. *Constructing Social Problems.* Menlo Park, CA: Cummings.

Thomas, William Isaac, and Florian Znaniecki. 1918. *The Polish Peasant in Europe and America.* New York: Octagon Books.

Tuchman, Gaye. 1978. *Making News: A Study in the Construction of Reality.* New York: The Free Press.

Tuvel, Rebecca. 2017. "In Defense of Transracialism." *Hypatia* 32(2):263–78.

Weitzer, Ronald. 2007. "The Social Construction of Sex Trafficking: Ideology and Institutionalization of a Moral Crusade." *Politics & Society* 35(3):447–75.

Woolgar, Steve, and Dorothy Pawluch. 1985. "Ontological Gerrymandering: The Anatomy of Social Problems Explanations." *Social Problems* 32(3):214.

Zerubavel, Eviatar. 1979. *Patterns of Time in Hospital Life: A Sociological Perspective.* Chicago: University of Chicago Press.

Zerubavel, Eviatar. 1981. *Hidden Rhythms: Schedules and Calendars in Social Life.* Berkeley: University of California Press.

Zerubavel, Eviatar. 1985. *The Seven Day Circle: The History and Meaning of the Week.* Chicago: University of Chicago Press.

CHAPTER 10

THE NARRATIVE STUDY OF SELF AND SOCIETY

AMIR B. MARVASTI AND JABER F. GUBRIUM

VARIETY and popularity are narrative bywords. The concept of narrative varies broadly in meaning. Some approach it formally, analyzing key components such as themes, emplotment, syntax or complexity, and characterization. Others adopt a substantive view, as in this statement by narrative sociologist Ken Plummer: "Stories exude from past myths, epics, legends, folklore, fairy tales and the grand millennia-old religious tracts, but they can also be found today in the contemporary banalities of mundane scribbles on bathroom walls, Post-it labels, and everyday tweets" (2019:4).

Stories and storytelling are immensely popular. Everything seems to have or can be assigned a story, and everyone can engage in, or be ascribed, storytelling (for the latter, see Pollner and McDonald-Wikler 1985, for instance). Virtually anything can be viewed as having a timeline or be communicatively "diachronic" (Strawson 2004) with a beginning, a middle, and an ending. The personal computer used to write this chapter has a story that ostensibly starts with technological innovation and progresses with incremental improvements. The authors of this chapter have intellectual histories. And the discipline informing the writing, sociology, has conceptual lineage.

FORMS AND AIMS OF NARRATIVE ANALYSIS

The same bywords apply to the narrative analysis of self and society. Studies vary in their forms of analysis and differ in their research aims and substantive interests (Holstein and Gubrium 2012). Applied to lived experience, the forms fall roughly into three groups—ethnographic, strategic, and conversational. Each is popular and flourishing in having major proponents and large audiences, and generating significant research findings. The forms move in different directions in their emphases on the place of stories as opposed to storytelling in constructing self and society. The grouping is rough because specific contributions may fall into, or touch upon, more than one group.

The aim of ethnographic studies is bidirectional, depending on who or what is in view (Atkinson et al. 2001; Reynolds and Herman-Kinney 2003). When personal experience is in view, such as the everyday life of those who are chronically ill, the aim is to "give voice" through compelling personal accounts to experiences otherwise publicly unheard (for example, Charmaz 1991; Gubrium 1993; Karp 1996). When an aspect of society is in view, such as the lives of a marginalized group or community, the aim is to "make visible" through eye-opening accounts conditions that are publicly invisible (for example, Whyte 1943; Anderson 1999; Brekhus 2003; Grazian 2008; Sandberg and Pedersen 2011). Except for the qualities of being compelling and true to life, the organization of the storytelling process itself is a relatively minor concern.

The aim of strategic studies overlaps with the ethnographic form, but centers more on interactional stakes, tactics, and narrative risks especially in the context of social problems and social movements (Emerson 1969; Kitsuse and Spector 1987; Miller and Holstein 1993; Loseke and Best 2003; Holstein and Gubrium 2008). We place strategic studies in a group of its own because the aim is not just to provide stories of unheard or invisible experience, but especially to feature adjustments to, or attempts to resist or alter, ways of life in society under problematic conditions such as incarceration or suffering from disease, disadvantage, and marginalization (for example, Gubrium and Holstein 2009: parts 2 and 4; Spencer 1994; Marvasti 2003; Mason-Schrock 1996; Rosenfeld 2003; Weinberg 2005; Åkerström, Wästerfors, and Jacobsson 2016; Wästerfors 2019). Stake-centered stories and strategic storytelling are showcased in these studies.

Conversation analysis focuses on tellings in social interaction regardless of whether they are storied in the conventional sense of having points, and beginnings, middles, and endings (Heritage 1984; Silverman 1998; Heritage and Clayman 2010). This lessens interest in their content and the stakes or risks, foregrounding instead what have been called their operating "devices" or "mechanisms" within "turns" at, and "sequences" of, talk. Mindful of the conversational "space" required for conveying a story (Silverman 1998:8–9), storytelling is defined accordingly by conversation analysts as an "extended turn" at talk. This *ipso facto* transforms interest in narrative contents into an interactional problem. The resulting aim is to identify the communicative devices applied to open, maintain, and close conversational space. With concerted analytic adjustment, however, substantive concerns such as story contents and their various purposes can be discerned in the everyday activity of various circumstances and organizations (for example, Dingwall 1977; Buckholdt and Gubrium 1979; Gubrium and Buckholdt 1982; Riessman 1990; Holstein 1993; Chase 1995; Presser 2008; Mik-Meyer and Silverman 2019).

AN INTERACTIONIST RESEARCH TRADITION

Before comparing the way these forms of narrative study work (or don't work) empirically to produce results, consider the tradition of interactionist research out of which they emerged. The tradition begins in the 1920s with studies of everyday life within the so-called Chicago school of sociology. Pragmatist in orientation, this eventually centers on Erving Goffman's preeminent research program, which begins in the 1950s, reviving the tradition after a fallow period. For decades, Goffman's research has been at the cusp of all three forms of narrative research, linking them in empirically fruitful ways.

Life stories were viewed as uniquely informative of lived experience and thus focal in classic texts such as *The Jack Roller* (Shaw [1930] 1966) and *The Polish Peasant in Europe and America* (Thomas and Znaniecki [1918–1920] 1984). Studies dealt with the accounts and related identities and interactions of ordinary people in the context of their everyday lives, the one in crime and the other in immigration.

Using written correspondence between Polish immigrants in America and relatives in Poland, *The Polish Peasant* explores a wide range of topics, with special attention given to the shifting relationships and identities of immigrants over time. In particular, some of the analysis portends contemporary conceptual interest in the formulation of narrative types. The section on "The Peasant Letter," for example, begins this way:

> All the peasant letters can be considered as variations of one fundamental type, whose form results from its function and remains always essentially the same, even if it eventually degenerates. We call this type the "bowing letter" [as in respectfully leaning forward].
>
> (Thomas and Znaniecki [1918–1920] 1984:98)

The authors identify the basic structure of a bowing letter this way: (1) "it begins with a religious greeting," (2) "there follows the information that the writer, with God's help, is in good health and is succeeding," and (3) "finally come greetings, 'bows' for all the members of the family" (Thomas and Znaniecki [1918–1920] 1984:99). As such, the analysis deals with the substance, organization, and function of the *ordinary* stories characteristic of strategic research.

Erving Goffman's Contribution

"Scorned by scholars aspiring to scientific authority, narrative analysis was largely abandoned in the 1930's and 1940's" (Ewick and Silbey 1995:197–98), until, that is, Goffman's and other substantial contributions began to appear in the 1950s. We focus on Goffman's studies more than others, as they were exceptional in working in tandem with all three forms of analysis distinguished earlier. The publication of his 1959 book *The Presentation of Self in Everyday Life* fueled an expanding appreciation for narrative structures and functions in lived experience, suggesting how in life generally, not only in the context of social problems, stories are not just more or less authentic. Rather, authenticity is performatively managed as an integral feature of daily life (cf. Gubrium and Holstein 2009:part iv). All stories are "recipient-designed," in other words, constructed with the audience in view, as conversation analysts would have it (Hootkoop-Steenstra 2000:chap. 4). By extension, so are selves and identities.

Combining ethnographic and strategic forms of analysis, Goffman's (1961) *Asylums: Essays on the Social Situation of Mental Patients and Other Inmates* presages a growing interest in how institutional environments narratively inform "self-stories" (see Gubrium and Holstein 2001). In the essay titled "Characteristics of Total Institutions," Goffman writes:

> I would like to consider some dominant themes of the inmate culture. First in many total institutions a peculiar kind and level of self-concern is engendered. The low position of the inmates relative to their station on the outside, established initially through stripping processes, creates a milieu of personal failure in which one's fall from grace is continuously pressed home. In response, the inmate tends to develop a story, a line, a sad tale—a kind of lamentation and apologia—which he constantly tells to his fellows as a means of accounting for his present low estate. (1961:66–67)

Later in the book, in another essay titled "The Moral Career of the Mental Patient," Goffman offers excerpts from such preferred patient identity stories:

> The others here are sick mentally but I'm suffering from a bad nervous system and that is what is giving me these phobias.
> I got here by mistake because of a diabetes diagnosis, and I'll leave in a couple of days. [Goffman adds parenthetically, "The patient had been in seven weeks."] (1961:153)

Similarly, in *Stigma: Notes on the Management of Spoiled Identity*, Goffman (1963) writes of how "those with a particular stigma" try to manage their marginalized selves (read: societal identity) through stories, as we will exemplify later in the context of the start of a violent sex offender's narrative:

> Often those with a particular stigma sponsor a publication of some kind which gives voice to shared feelings. . . . Here the ideology of the member group is formulated— their complaints, their aspirations, their politics. . . . Success stories are printed, tales of heroes of assimilation who have penetrated new areas of normal acceptance. Atrocity tales are recorded, recent and historic, of extreme mistreatment by normal. Exemplary moral tales are provided in biographical and autobiographical form illustrating a desirable code of conduct for the stigmatized. (p. 25)

Greg Smith (2006) indicates that Goffman evinced a keen interest in the "sociology of storytelling" (pp. 44 and 62), the activities of which run through the everyday terrain of selves in relation to what is told, what is not told, and how all that is realized in sites of interaction. Similarly, Ann Rawls (2003) explains that

> Goffman suggested a focus on narrative accounts as a clue to how individuals interpret and manage not only situations but also institutional orders. In doing so, he built on [C. Wright] Mills' (1940) argument that the key to institutional orders lay

in accounts produced in institutional settings. After the publication of [Goffman's] *Frame Analysis*, sociologists took up the cause of accounts in earnest. The idea of a sociology of narrative, rumor, and account—an interpretive sociology—came into being. (p. 231)

In *Frame Analysis*, Goffman's (1974) interest in self-presentation is superimposed on stories, apparent in this statement: "Often what the individual presents is not himself but [is framed by] a story containing a protagonist who may happen also to be himself" (p. 541). Here, Goffman is working at the cusp of the strategic form of narrative analysis. As Goffman puts it elsewhere in the book: "What a speaker does usually is to present to his listeners a version of what happened to him . . . . He runs off a tape of a past experience" (1974:503–4). Goffman adds that these accounts of the past, or "replayings" of experience, as he words it, are not just informational, but rather are purposeful—strategic, in a word—and facilitate preferred selves and identities. Goffman explains that "what the individual spends most of his spoken moments doing is providing evidence for the fairness or unfairness of his current situation and other grounds for sympathy, approval, exoneration, understanding, or amusement" (1974:503).

In his subsequent book, *Forms of Talk*, Goffman (1981) identified and analyzed the typical roles and related selves associated with storytelling in everyday encounters, bringing the sensibilities of a conversation analyst into play:

A full-scale story requires that the speaker remove himself for the telling's duration from the alignment he would maintain in ordinary conversational give and take, and for this period of narration maintain another footing, that of a narrator whose extended pauses and utterance completions are not to be understood as signals that he is now ready to give up the floor. (p. 152)

As a whole, Goffman's body of work gave voice to the stories of the marginalized and at the same time showed how their stories were constructed strategically for a variety of purposes.

THE SOCIAL CONSTRUCTION OF SELVES

Expanding on the interactionist tradition's empirical legacy, consider examples of how the three forms of narrative study (ethnographic, strategic, and conversational) have been applied in the social construction of selves. Here we consider two areas of emphasis: (1) narrative representations of individual selves and societal identities and (2) analyses of self-construction in social interaction. It is not unusual for these to be combined, and it is important to note that selves in this tradition are construed as inescapably operating in the narrative spaces of society. They are not viewed as insular psychodynamic entities.

Stories of Selves and Group Identities

A compelling aspect of the relationship between interaction and narratives is the way stories can incorporate personal experience and social context within a single testament. As Norman Denzin (1992) puts it:

> Self-stories make sense, through the process of telling, of the self and its experiences. Personal experience stories frame self-stories within larger narratives that connect the self to the oral tradition of a group, family, or relationship. (p. 84)

A subgenre of ethnographic narrative analysis called "autoethnography" is an especially personalized and compelling kind of self-presentation (Rambo et al. 2010). While there are different models of the subgenre (Anderson 2006; Ellis, Adams, and Bochner 2011), what they have in common is an emphasis on the author's vivid sharing of a significant life experience, often articulated through innovative writing:

> When researchers write *autoethnographies*, they seek to produce aesthetic and evocative thick descriptions of personal and interpersonal experience. They accomplish this by first discerning patterns of cultural experience evidenced by field notes, interviews, and/ or artifacts, and then describing these patterns using facets of storytelling (e.g., character and plot development), showing and telling, and alterations of authorial voice.
>
> (Ellis, Adams, and Bochner 2011:para. 15)

In her moving autoethnography titled *Final Negotiations: A Story of Love, Loss, and Chronic Illness*, Carolyn Ellis (1995) narrates the experience associated with her partner's growing illness and eventual death. The emotional depth of the story and its intimate portrayal of loss are painfully apparent in this passage, where Ellis describes the moment of her partner's passing in a hospital:

> His breathing stops again. This time for a longer period. It doesn't return. I watch for a while. I hold the hand that is now lifeless. Nothing has arrived. There is no clear demarcation between life and death. It looks like there is still spirit in the body. I think I feel it, I want to feel it. But I am not sure. I don't see it leave. (p. 295)

In such accounts, the researcher bears witness to and is ensnared in the suffering. The storytelling itself is thought to be therapeutic for both author and readers alike: "As witnesses, autoethnographers not only work with others to validate the meaning of their pain, but also allow participants and readers to feel validated and/or better able to cope with or want to change their circumstances" (Ellis, Adams, and Bochner 2011:para. 27). In the telling, the story effectively becomes the story of *us*, of the way individual life experience can be deeply shared as a felt presence by all.

Many accounts emphasize the "auto" parts that led to the "ethnographic" parts of their stories, describing the significant personal experiences that eventually caused

THE NARRATIVE STUDY OF SELF AND SOCIETY   181

the authors to write both specifically and generally about something they share with readers. For example, Barbara J. Jago (2002) tells the story of depression by sharing her own struggle with mental illness, self and other combining into a single narrative.

> Coming to school, an activity that was once mundane now feels monumental, a place that was once a haven now feels dangerous. I take half the morning to get here, a pot of tea, a hot shower, the right costume, a stack of books to prop me up. One step at a time. That's the way through depression, one foot in front of the other, or at least that's what Sibylle my therapist says. After a year, I am not so sure. (p. 730)

In his own "auto" initiated narrative, Arthur Frank (2013) begins the second edition of *The Wounded Storyteller: Body, Illness, and Ethics* with these words:

> I wrote the outline of *The Wounded Storyteller* in early spring 1994, while I still had stitches from the biopsy that determined I was not having a recurrence of cancer.... Writing *The Wounded Storyteller* was as much a work of self-healing as of scholarship. (p. xi)

Frank goes on to connect his story with those of his research participants and his readers: "The wounded storyteller is anyone who has suffered and lived to tell the tale" (2003:xi).

David Karp (1996) begins his book *Speaking of Sadness: Depression, Disconnection, and the Meanings of Illness* with this self-disclosure: "In greater or lesser degree I have grappled with depression for almost 20 years. I suppose that even as a child my experience of life was as much characterized by anxiety as by joy and pleasure" (p. 3). Karp then fuses his narrative with the experiences of his respondents and others with the same condition: "People who have lived with depression can often vividly remember the situations that forced them to have a new consciousness as a troubled person" (Karp 1996:3).

The persuasive eloquence of these accounts is palpable. Whether the writer introduces his or her own story first and then turns to others, or initially tells the story of others' lives and then weaves in or shares his or her own related experience, the powerful impact of these stories on readers derives from recognizable accounts of selves and lived experiences that are shared. These are eminently social accounts, extended narratives of lives or living that any of us, but for the grace of destiny, could have or endure.

Not all stories of the self in social life are person centered, but rather are stories of group identities. These are identities commonly invisible in the public sphere. Stories of inequality, the vulnerable, and the oppressed have long been part of narrative research on lived experience. Denzin (1992) describes this form of narrative study:

> Interactionist narratives often convey pathos, sentimentalism, and a romantic identification with the persons being written about.... Interactionists study the marked, deviant, stigmatized, lonely, unhappy, alienated, powerful, and powerless people in everyday life. (p. 25)

The group's eventually public story is evident in studies such as that presented in Elliot Liebow's (1993) book titled *Tell Them Who I Am*. Its publicizing intent is longstanding in social science and can be traced back to Henry Mayhew's (1861–1862/1968) four-volume nineteenth-century observational survey of London's "humbler classes" titled *Life and Labour of the London Poor*. In his own book, Liebow vividly relays the unheard stories of homeless persons, filtered through the researcher's lens and his or her personal assessment of the stories' credibility. He offers this sympathetic, yet judgmental, observation:

> At first sight, one wonders why more homeless people do not kill themselves. How do they manage to slog through day after day, with no end in sight? How in the world of unremitting grimness, do they manage to laugh, love, enjoy friends, even dance and play the fool? How in short do they stay fully human while body and soul are under continuous and grievous assault? (p. 25)

Self-Construction in Society

In discussing studies of self-construction in which social life is foregrounded, it is useful to distinguish what Jaber Gubrium and James Holstein (1998; 2009) describe as the *whats* and *hows* of the construction process. The *whats* refer to the substantive elements of the process, such as the personal or societal conditions under consideration, the institutional context, local understandings, the interactional stakes and risks, and applicable public discourses. The *hows* refer to the actions taken to construct particular selves and group identities, bring them into play, or manage them interactionally in the context of various *whats*. The *hows* are more or less tactical depending on the form of analysis. The *hows* in strategically oriented studies are substantively deliberative and considered in relation to narrative stakes and risks. The *hows* in conversation analysis are inclined to be less so and treated as mechanically driven with the flow of talk in interaction.

Plummer (2019) suggests that the difference between an interest in the substance of stories (the *whats*) versus the process of their construction (the *hows*) can be delineated by reserving the word "story" for the substantive focus and the word "narrative" for the constructive process: "most commonly, stories direct us to what is told, while narratives tell us how stories are told" (p. 4). While this might seem arbitrary, the larger point is that stories or narratives (used interchangeably in this chapter) can be approached in terms of what they are about (stories of) or in terms of their process of unfolding (storytelling) without designating which has priority.

The reflexive relationship between the *whats* and *hows* of narrative construction is evident in studies that examine how identities are interactionally accomplished in particular settings. For example, Douglas Mason-Schrock (1996) showed how the substance of transsexual identities is achieved in support groups wherein "established members" molded the self stories of "new members" using strategies that included "modeling, guiding, affirming, and tactful blindness" (p. 189). Mason-Schrock notes that: "In learning to tell different stories about themselves, transsexuals learned to be different

THE NARRATIVE STUDY OF SELF AND SOCIETY   183

people. This happened only because they encountered the transgender community and learned to use its storytelling tools" (p. 178). In essence, the support groups provided a suitable narrative environment for the construction of transsexual selves.

Another example of how selves are narratively constructed in social interaction can be found in a brief interview exchange excerpted from Lois Presser's (2004) article titled "Violent Offenders, Moral Selves: Constructing Identities and Accounts in the Research Interview." In the larger study from which the article's material derives, Presser (2008) deftly incorporates the analytic sensibilities of all three forms of narrative study in her interpretations. The interpretations not only deal with talk and interaction, but are thickly descriptive of related risks and extended narrative spaces within which interaction transpires.

The analysis of the short strip of conversation from one of Presser's interviews that follows is our own, presented for the purpose of showing how limiting analysis to the mechanics of talk-in-interaction without incorporating contextualizing information can pose serious interpretive problems. Making a point about the conjoined identities at play in interviews with violent offenders, in this case a violent sex offender named Ralph, Presser comments on the safety and comfort of the occasion for her at the start and the related credibility and comfort of the occasion for Ralph. While Presser was aware of, and had to contend with, both personal and institutional issues going into the interview, the related talk in the interaction was worked out *in vivo*. As she explains and we will illustrate, the respondent, Ralph, like her other interviewees, used the occasion to set the stage for a particular moral order, one that Ralph hoped would be construed as rational and comfortable, not "nuts" and threatening. Narrative stakes and related identity work were evident on both sides of the engagement.

In the excerpt that follows, the turns of which have been numbered for convenience (see Clift 2016; Sidnell 2010), notice the way the constructed *whats* (the situated working identities of the participants ostensibly in focus) emerge and develop with turns of the sequential *hows* of the exchange. The point is that the operating identities are not just there, but are an outcome of the related constructive work of the participants. Conversation analysts view the combination as "collaboratively accomplished," not tactically realized, which distinguishes their approach from that of the strategic form of narrative study.

1. Ralph: Now, I don't know—based on me having this interview, or—How do you feel? Do you feel comfortable? Do you feel like you're in here with some nut (chuckle)?
2. Lo: (Shake head).
3. Ralph: Huh, okay (laughing). You know wha' I mean. I'm—people have a sense of understandin' and feelin' comfortable with people. . . . (Presser 2004:94)

In turn 1, Ralph hesitantly asks interviewer Lo (Lois Presser) if she could feel comfortable taking him to be speaking rationally and not as "some nut." In her commentary in the article from which the excerpt is taken, Presser (2004) takes this to mean that Ralph was asking her (Lo) to "confirm that he was not, in fact, [just?] a rapist" (p. 94), which is not evident in the excerpt, but which is nonetheless something that all respondents tried to establish in one way or another, according to Presser. Regarding turn 2, identified as "shake head," Presser explains further that she thereby "politely allowed Ralph to conclude that she (Lo) "did feel comfortable with him" speaking other than as a rapist (Presser 2004:94). This again is not evident in the excerpt, but is a conclusion drawn from the larger corpus of findings in tow. In turn 3, Ralph awkwardly confirms that he takes Lo's headshake as a positive response to the request presumably articulated in turn 1. And so on and so forth with Presser's commentary on the one hand, and the flow of the conversational mechanics in place on the other. There are two points to this. One, noted earlier, is that a seemingly trivial interactional exchange is not just an incidental formality, but in communicative practice establishes a working moral environment with locally discerned identities. The other point is that it is the broader social context of the exchange that makes the first point interactionally compelling.

Society as a Complex Narrative Environment

Given the contextual knowledge presented in both the article and the larger study, what else could be made of what is transpiring in the interview? Does narrative pertinence end at the borders of the foregoing exchange between Ralph and Lo? Does it not reach into the substantive and moral complexity of what Gubrium (2005) calls the attendant "narrative environment" at stake in the encounter? Isn't Presser's excerpt, her associated comments, and our brief sequential analysis surrounded by a whorl of unarticulated *whats* of possible interest to both participants but silently present in the exchange? Aren't the two preceding points, in effect, inextricably related?

Presser's ethnographic material provides compelling empirical warrant for suggesting as much. She and Ralph are not just any two members of just any course of talk-and-interaction, but also members of a diverse self-interested narrative environment, which, while unarticulated in the encounter, effectively shouts issues of stakes and risks ethnographically for both participants. There is warrantable risk for Presser's safety because Ralph has been convicted as a violent sex offender, and there is risk for Ralph's physical well-being because of his possible perceived treachery by fellow inmates for violating a well-known and long-documented "convict code" against "snitching" to outsiders (see Wieder 1974; Copes, Brookman, and Brown 2013; Mitchell, Fahmy et al. 2016).

Such possibilities turn us to the narrative study of society, which is, or should be, a vital concern to all three forms of narrative study. Early on, Lawrence Wieder (1974) brought the concern to his fieldwork in a halfway house for ex-convicts. He argued that the ex-cons didn't just converse and interact with him and one another, but deliberatively used the convict code for a variety of purposes. This transforms the code—a shared moral entity—into an interest-ridden and risk-laden social commodity that is neither just latently cultural nor just mechanical, but strategically managed in relation to the situated stakes, risks, and possible consequences of usage (see Sykes 1958 in conjunction with Jimerson, and Oware 2006).

The attendant narrative environment of talk and interaction in Presser's interviews of offenders is elaborately evident in her (2008, 2016) ethnographic descriptions. The institutional context in play, including incarcerated life's official and unofficial roles, its everyday understandings, its groups and networks, its rules of conduct, and its organizational tensions resonate loudly in remarks that broach on both narrativity and safety:

> In the criminal justice system offenders face demonstrable institutional incentives for portraying themselves in particular, not-necessarily-true ways. Offenders' stories are taken as devices meant for manipulation. A perspective tied too closely to their stories would likely seem suspect.
>
> (Presser 2016:146)

> The concerns of advisors, friends, and my institutional review board convinced me to act with my safety foremost in mind—specifically, that I hold interviews where security personnel were close by. The premises of correctional agencies readily qualified in that way. Later, connection through the agencies gave me a feeling of safety: the men were accountable to formal agents even when an interview was held off-site, such as at a coffee shop . . . .
>
> (Presser 2004:85)

But there is even more to the unarticulated knowledge problem. Just as pertinent are distant forms of silences evident in contrasting institutional knowledge, such as the rather common knowledge about the comparative moral and performative contours, if not the safety, of noncorrectional facilities. While a correctional facility is a place of confinement and reform, it is generally well known that it is not the same interactionally and morally as other places of confinement such as a locked unit for dementia patients or a cloistered monastery for avowedly silent monks. Their respective institutional selves and "codes" of silence are enormously different.

For these reasons, narrative studies of self-construction necessarily must be fully part of the study of society. A great deal—we don't know how much—of what is articulated in social interaction is understood by and through what is unarticulated, by what Harold Garfinkel (1967) called its "background expectancies." Analytically, the related silences can be deafening. And that is the rub for purely conversational forms of narrative analysis (see Gubrium and Holstein 2009; Holstein and Gubrium 2012). Reflexively combining analytic attention to both the *whats* and the various *hows* brings into focus the elaborately social selves we are, continually mediated in practice by meanings and structures unapparent in the equally essential constructive activities of social interaction.

Plummer (2019) goes a step further by expanding the narrative horizons of self-construction to the *whats* of the public sphere, to what some refer to as applicable cultures, both small and large (see Fine 2012; Chase 1995; Loseke 2019:chap. 2). In writing about coming to terms with his gay identity as a young man in 1960s England, Plummer tersely comments about how coming-out narratives of the time worked to construct his own self story: "Everywhere I turned, I heard stories and saw images that suggested my being was a problem and I was doomed for a tragic experience. My life became a dialogue with queer stories" (p. xi). Simultaneously, both following and moving beyond Goffman (1959), Plummer (1995) approaches the self as an expansively shaped and strategic narrative performance, the relevancies of which, let alone the risks, are both nearby and far removed from the ordinary exchanges of life.

Indeed, the pertinent *whats* of contemporary living increasingly come out of rampantly growing imaginings of the selves we could be. The strong institutional focus of many studies of self-construction tends to sideline the substantively distinct yet important influence of social movements (for example, see Loseke 2019, especially chaps. 4 and 5). Valorizing future selves, the goal of social movements ostensibly is to question and change social life and existing identities. In contrast, the goal of institutions ostensibly is to manage and sustain social life and existing identities, including identities in need of repair. One would hardly know the difference for self-construction this would make if the mechanical *hows* of talk-in-interaction were exclusively in focus.

This has led narrative researchers to distinguish between narratives that affirm, as opposed to narratives that challenge everyday life and its accountabilities. The difference is captured by the distinction between so-called master narratives and counter-narratives. Both are sources of narrative pertinence (Bamberg and Andrews 2004; Plummer 1995), but the consequences of their mediations of everyday life differ. The different goal-specific *whats* at stake—to change or to manage—would appear to present strikingly contrasting stakes and risks for individual selves and for group identities. As Donileen Loseke (2019:122) points out, "Studies focusing tightly on the processes of meaning creation often do not continue exploring the *consequences* of this meaning."

Narrative psychologists Michael Bamberg and Molly Andrews (2004) explain that counter-narratives become meaningful in relation to a "master narrative" that is being challenged, which is a substantive contrast: "Counter-narratives only make sense in relation to something else, that which they are countering. The very name identifies it as a positional category, in tension with another category" (p. x). As Bamberg and Andrews put it, "what is dominant and what is resistant are not, of course, a static question, but rather are forever shifting placements" (2004:x). Thusly they make a case for organizing the narrative study of self and society in the purview of both institutional processing and the forces of institutional change (see Wodak 2013).

Narrative Power and Practice

Harkening the socially activating capacity of stories in his latest book *Narrative Power*, Plummer (2019) encourages us to attend not only to the content of self and identity

THE NARRATIVE STUDY OF SELF AND SOCIETY   187

stories, but equally important to expand our analytic horizons by raising the question of how self-construction achieves what it does. This is decidedly not a plea to revert to the mechanical *hows* of self-construction in the mold exemplified earlier. Rather the expansion would come from critical attention to the diverse strategic *hows* at hand in social interaction, extending narrative pertinence to issues of power and influence (see Heiner 2016; Fairclough 1995; Wodak 2013):

> Simply: ask not what a narrative says, but ask what people do with it. Ask how people listen to stories. Ask how people bring the full richness of their embodied, emotional senses to them. And ask how people interact with others through them. (p. 25)

As the title of his book suggests, Plummer urges us to focus on the extended forces of stories. Leading questions on this front are who has the ability to tell stories and using what resources, especially in "asymmetrical" situations, and what goals do stories achieve? While Plummer does not dispense with the notion of truth (p. 4), his emphasis on activation is key to resolving the truth–fiction tension in understanding narratives. Whether or not narratives have an intrinsic truth value is a legitimate philosophical concern; however, for the purpose of sociological analysis, what matters in everyday life is what people do with narratives, what they draw upon in constructing them, and what they accomplish by storytelling, all of which are facets of narrative practice.

This realization brings us full circle to what was suggested long ago by social phenomenologist Alfred Schutz (1945), who urged us to direct analytic attention to the narrative reflexivity of the lifeworld:

> Thus, we work and operate not only within but upon the world. . . . On the other hand, these objects offer resistance to our acts which we have either to overcome or to which we have to yield. In this sense it may be correctly said that a pragmatic motive governs our natural attitude toward the world of daily life. World, in this sense, is something that we have to modify by our actions or that modifies our actions. (p. 534)

To paraphrase Schutz, stories and storytelling are real enough for us in practice, never mind what "in reality" might mean epistemologically (Gubrium 2003). As Gubrium and Holstein (1998; also Holstein and Gubrium 2000) write, narrative practice—not exclusively either what we do or how we do it—offers a broad analytical mandate for attending to the working conditions, risks, and the consequences of everyday life.

> We use the term "narrative practice" to characterize simultaneously the activities of storytelling, the sources used to tell stories, and the auspices under which stories are told. Considering personal stories and their coherence as matters of practice centers attention on the relation between these *hows* and *whats* of narration. . . . Orienting to practice allows us to see the storytelling process as both actively constructive and locally constrained. (p. 164)

Cautionary Concern

As stories, storytelling, and the narrative study of self and society flourish, they understandably generate cautionary concern. Some are procedural, about research design, conceptualization, and applicable methods. For example, Paul Atkinson (1997) argues that "the ubiquity of the narrative and its centrality . . . are not license simply to privilege those forms" (p. 341). Atkinson is an ethnographer and refers to the risk of overshadowing the societal contexts of narrativity. On another front, Plummer (2019) reminds us that narrative form and narrative content are not inherently good or moral, especially in the digital age:

> Here we find rafts of new digital stories posing new risks. All bring the possibility of people being harmed or functioning less well in the world. Quite centrally, there has been the proliferation of new forms of *cruel stories*—tales calculated to bring hurt. (p. 93)

Others express caution on existential grounds, such as the extent to which narratives are at all suited for capturing the sense of what the self "really" is. In his essay "Against Narrativity," Galen Strawson, for example, challenges the underlying assumptions of statements such as: "each of us constructs and lives a 'narrative' . . . this narrative is us, our identities" (Sacks 1987:110; cited in Strawson 2004:435). Casting doubt on the idea that storytelling is universal and that stories can uniquely represent self-understanding, Strawson explains,

> Self-understanding does not have to take a narrative form, even implicitly. I'm a product of my past, including my very early past, in many profoundly important respects. But it simply does not follow that self-understanding, or the best kind of self-understanding, must take a narrative form, or indeed a historical form. (pp. 448–49)

Strawson critiques the idea of a self fully capable of restorying itself, the socially reflexive self conceptualized by George Herbert Mead (1959) and others, for example. It was a self ongoingly infused with the stories we presently tell about ourselves and diversely share with others in varied contexts of everyday life. Strawson's self, in contrast, is profoundly if not essentially shaped by the past, especially early life, and to that extent relentlessly independent of the present. Such a self, without defining stories constructed and construed in time and place and in relation to others, was not envisioned by early interactionists. Nor has it been adopted by interactionists since then, except perhaps discovered in the rhetorical assertions of participants found in empirical material such as Presser's (2004).

Personal life history aside, it is difficult to imagine concretely what Strawson portrays as "the best kind" of self-understanding. Imagination itself is narratively situated in the vicissitudes of practice. As one of Strawson's critics asserts, "It's all very well to attack 'narrativity,' but it's much harder to escape it in self-presentation. We're part of a narrative identity system whether we like it or not" (Eakin 2006:186).

REFERENCES

Åkerström, Malin, David Wästerfors, and Katrina Jacobsson. 2016. "Struggling for One's Name: Defense Mechanisms by Those Accused of Small-Time Corruption." *Sociological Focus* 49(2):148–62.

Anderson, Elijah. 1999. *Code of the Street: Decency, Violence, and the Moral Life of the Inner City.* New York: Norton.

Anderson, Leon. 2006. "Analytic Autoethnography." *Journal of Contemporary Ethnography* 35(4):373–95.

Atkinson, Paul. 1997. "Narrative Turn or Blind Alley?" *Qualitative Health Research* 7(3):325–44. doi: 10.1177/104973239700700302.

Atkinson, Paul, Amanda Coffey, Sara Delamont, John Lofland, and Lyn Lofland, eds. 2001. *Handbook of Ethnography.* London: SAGE.

Bamberg, Michael G. W., and Molly Andrews. 2004. *Considering Counter Narratives: Narrating, Resisting, Making Sense.* Philadelphia: J. Benjamins.

Brekhus, Wayne. 2003. *Peacocks, Chameleons, Centaurs: Gay Suburbia and the Grammar of Social Identity.* Chicago: University of Chicago Press.

Buckholdt, David, and Jaber Gubrium. 1979. *Caretakers: Treating Emotionally-Disturbed Children.* Thousand Oaks, CA: SAGE.

Chase, Susan. 1995. *Ambiguous Empowerment: The Work Narratives of Women School Superintendents.* Amherst: University of Massachusetts Press.

Charmaz, Kathy. 1991. *Good Days, Bad Days: The Self in Chronic Illness and Time.* New Brunswick, NJ: Rutgers University Press.

Clift, Rebecca. 2016. *Conversation Analysis.* Cambridge, UK: Cambridge University Press.

Copes, Heith, Fiona Brookman, and Anastatia Brown. 2013. "Accounting for Violations of the Convict Code." *Deviant Behavior* 34(10):8841–58.

Denzin, Norman K. 1992. *Symbolic Interactionism and Cultural Studies: The Politics of Interpretation.* Oxford, UK: Blackwell Publishing.

Dingwall, Robert. 1977. *The Social Organization of Health Visitor Training.* London: Croom Helm.

Eakin, Paul J. 2006. "Narrative Identity and Narrative Imperialism: A Response to Galen Strawson and James Phelan." *Narrative* 14(2):180–87. doi:10.1353/nar.2006.0001.

Ellis, Carolyn. 1995. *Final Negotiations: A Story of Love, Loss, and Chronic Illness.* Philadelphia: Temple University Press.

Ellis, Carolyn, Tony E. Adams, and Arthur P. Bochner. 2011. "Autoethnography: An Overview." *Forum Qualitative Sozialforschung/Forum: Qualitative Social Research*, Institute for Qualitative Research 12(1):art. 10. www.qualitativeresearch.net/index.php/fqs/article/view/1589.

Emerson, Robert M. 1969. *Judging Delinquents: Context and Process in Juvenile Court.* Chicago: Aldine.

Ewick, Patricia and Susan Silbey. 1995. "Subversive Stories and Hegemonic Tales: Toward a Sociology of Narrative." *Law and Society Review* 29:197–226.

Fairclough, Norman. 1995. *Critical Discourse Analysis.* London: Routledge.

Fine, Gary A. 2012. *Tiny Publics: A Theory of Group Action and Culture*. New York: Russell Sage Foundation.

Frank, Arthur W. 2013. *The Wounded Storyteller: Body, Illness, and Ethics*. 2nd ed. Chicago: University of Chicago Press.

Garfinkel, Harold. 1967. *Studies in Ethnomethodology*. Englewood Cliffs, NJ: Prentice Hall.

Goffman, Erving. 1959. *The Presentation of Self in Everyday Life*. New York: Anchor Books.

Goffman, Erving. 1961. *Asylums: Essays on the Social Situation of Mental Patients and Other Inmates*. New York: Anchor Books.

Goffman, Erving. 1963. *Stigma: Notes on the Management of Spoiled Identity*. New York: Simon & Schuster.

Goffman, Erving. 1974. *Frame Analysis: An Essay on the Organization of Experience*. Boston: Northeastern University Press.

Goffman, Erving. 1981. *Forms of Talk*. Philadelphia: University of Pennsylvania Press.

Grazian, David. 2008. *On the Make: The Hustle of Urban Nightlife*. Chicago: University of Chicago Press.

Gubrium, Jaber F. 1993. *Speaking of Life: Horizons of Meaning for Nursing Home Residents*. New York: Aldine de Gruyter.

Gubrium, Jaber F. 2003. "What Is a Good Story?" *Generations* 27(3):21–24.

Gubrium, Jaber F. 2005. "Narrative Environments and Social Problems." *Social Problems* 52(4):525–28.

Gubrium, Jaber F., and David Buckholdt. 1982. *Describing Care: Image and Practice in Rehabilitation*. Cambridge, MA: Oelgeschlager, Gunn & Hain.

Gubrium, Jaber F., and James A. Holstein. 1998. "Narrative Practice and the Coherence of Personal Stories." *The Sociological Quarterly* 39(1):163–87.

Gubrium, Jaber F., and James A. Holstein, eds. 2001. *Institutional Selves: Troubled Identities in a Postmodern World*. New York: Oxford University Press.

Gubrium, Jaber F., and James A. Holstein. 2009. *Analyzing Narrative Reality*. Thousand Oaks, CA: SAGE.

Heiner, Robert. 2016. *Social Problems: An Introduction to Critical Constructionism*. New York: Oxford University Press.

Heritage, John. 1984. *Garfinkel and Ethnomethodology*. Cambridge, UK: Polity.

Heritage, John, and Steven Clayman. 2010. *Talk in Action: Interactions, Identities, and Institutions*. Malden, MA: Wiley-Black well.

Holstein. James A. 1993. *Court-Ordered Insanity: Interpretive Practice and Involuntary Commitment*. New York: Aldine de Gruyter.

Holstein, James A., and Jaber. F. Gubrium. 2000. *The Self We Live By: Narrative Identity in a Postmodern World*. New York: Oxford University Press.

Holstein, James A., and Jaber. F. Gubrium, eds. 2008. *Handbook of Constructionist Research*. New York: Guilford.

Holstein, James A., and Jaber. F. Gubrium. 2012. *Varieties of Narrative Analysis*. Thousand Oaks, CA: SAGE.

Hootkoop-Steenstra, Hanneke. 2000. *Interaction and the Standardized Survey Interview*. Cambridge, UK: Cambridge University Press.

Jago, Barbara J. 2002. "Chronicling an Academic Depression." *Journal of Contemporary Ethnography* 31(6):729–57. doi: 10.1177/089124102237823.

Jimerson, Jason, and Matthew Oware. 2006. "Telling the Code of the Street: An Ethnomethodological Ethnography." *Journal of Contemporary Ethnography* 23:24–50.

Karp, David A. 1996. *Speaking of Sadness: Depression, Disconnection, and the Meanings of Illness*. New York: Oxford University Press.

Kitsuse, John and Michael Spector. 1987. *Constructing Social Problems*. New York: Taylor & Francis.

Liebow, Elliot. 1993. *Tell Them Who I Am: The Lives of Homeless Women*. New York: Free Press.

Loseke, Donileen R., and Joel Best, eds. 2003. *Social Problems: Constructionist Readings*. New York: Taylor & Francis.

Loseke, Donileen R. 2019. *Narrative Productions of Meanings: Exploring the Work of Stories in Social Life*. Lanham, MD: Lexington.

Marvasti, Amir B. 2003. *Being Homeless: Textual and Narrative Constructions*. New York: Lexington Books.

Mason-Schrock, Douglas. 1996. "Transsexuals' Narrative Construction of the 'True Self.'" *Social Psychology Quarterly* 59(3):176–92.

Mayhew, Henry. 1861–1862/1968. *London Labour and the London Poor*. New York: Dover.

Mead, George H. 1959. *The Philosophy of the Present*. Lasalle, IL: Open Court.

Mik-Meyer, Nanna, and David Silverman. 2019. "Agency and Clientship in Public Encounters: Co-constructing 'Neediness' and 'Worthiness' in Shelter Placement Meetings." *British Journal of Sociology* 70(4):1–21.

Miller, Gale, and James A. Holstein, eds. 1993. *Constructionist Controversies: Issues in Social Problems Theory*. New York: Routledge.

Mills, Charles W. 1940. "Situated Action and the Vocabularies of Motive." *American Sociological Review* 5(6):904–13.

Mitchell, M. Meghan, Chantal Fahmy, David C. Pyrooz, and Scott H. Decker. 2016. "Criminal Crews, Codes, and Contexts: Differences and Similarities across the Code of the Street, Convict Code, Street Gangs, and Prison Gangs." *Deviant Behavior* 38(10):1197–222. doi: 10.1080/01639625.2016.1246028

Plummer, Kenneth. 1995. *Telling Sexual Stories: Power, Change, and Social Worlds*. London: Routledge.

Plummer, Kenneth. 2019. *Narrative Power: The Struggle for Human Value*. Cambridge, UK: Polity Press.

Pollner, Melvin, and Lynn McDonald-Wikler. 1985. "The Social Construction of Unreality: A Case Study of a Family's Attribution of Competence to a Severely Retarded Child." *Family Process* 24:241–54.

Presser, Lois. 2004. "Violent Offenders, Moral Selves: Constructing Identities and Accounts in the Research Interview." *Social Problems* 51(1):82–101. doi:10.1525/sp.2004.51.1.82

Presser, Lois. 2008. *Been a Heavy Life: Stories of Violent Men*. Urbana: University of Illinois Press.

Presser, Lois. 2016. "Criminology and the Narrative Turn." *Crime Media Culture* 12(2):137–51.

Rambo, Carol, Brittany Presson, Victoria Gaines, and Brandi Barnes. 2010. "Autoethnography as a Methodology for Researching Social Problems." Pp. 122–38 in *Researching Social Problems*, edited by A. Marvasti and J. Trevino. London: Routledge.

Rawls, Anne W. 2003. "Orders of Interaction and Intelligibility: Intersections Between Goffman and Garfinkel by Way of Durkheim." Pp. 216–53 in *Goffman's Legacy*, edited by J. Trevino. Lanham, MD: Rowman and Littlefield.

Reynolds, Larry T., and Nancy J. Herman-Kinney, eds. 2003. *Handbook of Symbolic Interactionism*. Walnut Creek, CA: AltaMira.

Riessman, Catherine K. 1990. *Divorce Talk: Women and Men Make Sense of Personal Relationships*. New Brunswick, NJ: Rutgers University Press.

Rosenfeld, Dana. 2003. *The Changing of the Guard: Lesbian and Gay Elders, Identity, and Social Change*. Philadelphia: Temple University Press.

Sacks, Oliver. 1987. *The Man Who Mistook His Wife for a Hat and Other Clinical Tales*. New York: Harper.

Sandberg, Sveinung, and Willy Pedersen. 2011. *Street Capital: Black Cannabis Dealers in a White Welfare State*. Bristol, UK: Policy Press.

Schutz, Alfred. 1945. "On Multiple Realities." *Philosophy and Phenomenological Research* 5(4):533–76

Shaw, Clifford. 1966. *The Jack-Roller: A Delinquent Boy's Own Story*. Chicago: University of Chicago Press.

Sidnell, Jack. 2010. *Conversation Analysis*. Malden, MA: John Wiley & Sons.

Silverman, David. 1998. *Harvey Sacks: Social Science and Conversation Analysis*. New York: Oxford University Press.

Smith, Greg. 2006. *Erving Goffman*. New York: Routledge.

Spencer, J. William. 1994. "Homeless in River City: Client Work in Human Service Encounters." Pp. 29–46 in *Perspectives on Social Problems*. Vol 6, edited by James A. Holstein and Gale Miller. Greenwich, CT: JAI Press.

Strawson, Galen. 2004. "Against Narrativity." *Ratio* 17(4):428–52. doi:10.1111/j.1467-9329.2004.00264.x

Sykes, Gresham. 1958. *The Society of Captives*. Princeton, NJ: Princeton University Press.

Thomas, William I., and Florian Znaniecki. 1984. *The Polish Peasant in Europe and America*. Urbana: University of Illinois Press.

Wästerfors, David. 2019. "Things Left Unwritten: Interview Accounts Versus Institutional Texts in a Case of Detention Home Violence." *Social Inclusion* 7(1):248–58.

Weinberg, Darin. 2005. *Of Others Inside: Insanity, Addiction, and Belonging in America*. Philadelphia: Temple University Press.

Whyte, William F. 1943. *Street Corner Society*. Chicago: University of Chicago Press.

Wieder, D. Lawrence. 1974. *Language and Social Reality*. The Hague, NL: Mouton.

Wodak, Ruth, ed. 2013. *Critical Discourse Analysis*. Four volumes. London: SAGE.

PART II

CULTURE, CONTEXT, AND SYMBOLIC INTERACTION

CHAPTER 11

CULTURE, OR THE MEANING OF MEANING MAKING

MICHAEL IAN BORER

INTRODUCTION

IT has become customary at the end of each year for various publications, as well as individuals with a social media account, to look back upon the last twelve months and list their favorite movies, albums, books, and so on. The dictionary industry—a sort of gatekeeper and promoter of language's lasting stability and consistent emergence—gets in on the game too by naming the "word of the year." In 2014, the Oxford English Dictionary chose "vape," catching the early buzz of the rising use of e-cigarettes, while Dictionary.com chose "exposure" to connect to other social health issues like the Ebola virus. Merriam-Webster took a more staid approach by declaring CULTURE the word of the year. What they meant by "culture" had a lot to do with various generic collectivities.

"Culture is a word that we seem to be relying on more and more. It allows us to identify and isolate an idea, issue, or group with seriousness," Peter Sokolowski, editor-at-large for Merriam-Webster, said in a statement. "And it's efficient: we talk about the 'culture' of a group rather than saying 'the typical habits, attitudes, and behaviors' of that group." The types of "groups"—in quotes because these are more like aggregates than people working together or convening face-to-face—they have in mind are: pop culture, celebrity culture, consumer culture, military culture, culture wars, cultural clashes, company culture, startup culture, cultures of violence, cultures of silence, drug culture, Western culture, surf culture, high culture, teenage culture, culture shocks, police culture, the NFL's culture, media culture, and hookup culture. Can such a broad term as culture retain any analytic meaning if it can encompass so many things? Perhaps the fact that culture holds these things together in ways that we can then separate and explore them as different entities means it does have analytic, and presumably vernacular, value and fortitude.

I will not attempt to define culture here beyond some purposely vague notion of collectivities and their meaningful practices and expressions. A useful starting point for our discussion of symbolic interactionism (SI) and cultural sociology (CS) is Raymond Williams's seminal work *Keywords* (1985:87), where he notes that culture is one of the most complicated words in the language. Once connected to agriculture, it was a "noun of process" synonymous with tending to or cultivating something. We will address the paradox of culture as noun and verb further below, but we have already seen the differences. Clearly, the term can be defined from a single disciplinary view. Merriam-Webster seemed to ride the familiar anthropological definition of culture as "[that] complex whole which includes knowledge, belief, art, morals, law, custom, and any other capabilities and habits acquired by [humans] as a member of society" (Eagleton 2000:34). Despite its breadth, Terry Eagleton (2000:35) notes that this definition presumes that "[c]ulture is just everything which is not genetically transmissible". As something that is transmittable, it is something that moves whereby the various cultures listed above should be recognized as flexible and emergent rather than simply as static or hermetically sealed entities. And this is precisely where SI comes into play: to focus on the practices and performances of meaning making that make a "meso level" structure like culture connect the macro and the micro as a simultaneously mutable and durable entity.

From Code to Context

Whether we are exploring and investigating groups (Fine and Hallet 2014), communities (Fine and Van den Scott 2011; Gardner 2020), organizations (McGinty 2014), subcultures (Williams 2011), or scenes (Irwin 1977; Kotarba, Fackler, and Nowotny 2009; Borer 2019)—or the actions of individuals within those designated collectivities—the focus for both SI and CS is on meaning and meaning making. David Maines (2000:578) tells us, with a nod to Herbert Blumer (1969), that meaning "is at best a sensitizing concept . . . [whereby] most sociologists draw from a general social behavioristic framework to direct attention to shared or common responses, significations, intentions, and goals, and, in general, the interpretive and representational process that underlie human conduct." We should qualify that "most sociologists" in Maines's statement might be more accurate if he specified which kinds of sociologists, since some have altogether failed to put culture at the forefront of their analyses. In fact, even those whose work exists under the umbrella of SofC are only interested in culture and meaning as epiphenomenal, as dependent upon the supposedly more powerful and influential social forces of politics and economics (see Borer 2006; Grindstaff 2008).

The focus on meaning, then, is arguably the main difference between CS and SofC. The latter often reduces culture to a "dependent variable" with society as the "independent variable," as if culture were merely reactionary in predictable ways. We can see this most often in the "production of culture" culture perspective ushered by "neo-institutionalists" like Paul DiMaggio and Richard Peterson.[1] Though they share similar interests and subjects of inquiry (e.g., the arts) with the mid-twentieth century neo-Marxian Frankfurt School, the production-of-culture folks are less politically aligned or motivated (Peterson and Anand 2004). Still, both perspectives start from elsewhere to show the effects of other forces, like the market, on culture in its limited forms. For example, typical SofC studies examine the "gate-keeping" of elites and their "sacred" museums (DiMaggio 1982; 1996; Glynn et al. 1996), music industries (Peterson 1994; Lena and Peterson, 2008), or publishing houses (Childress 2017). These are the studies of Culture with a big "C" or *Kultur* with a capital "K" as their German forebears would have it: dependent and determined.

Those who embrace the relatively newer "school" of CS, instead, view society as already and unrelentingly cultural. Indeed, the social is in very significant ways culturally constituted to the point that Christian Smith (2003:66) argues that what most sociological theories "badly miss is the necessity for any good sociology to be a deeply and thoroughly *cultural* sociology—despite all the messiness and indeterminacy that entails." Such recognition of "messiness and indeterminacy" aligns perfectly with seminal interactionist George Herbert Mead's idea about the processes of emerging meanings and their corresponding actions. "The doctrine of emergence," writes Mead, "asks us to believe that the present is always in some sense novel, abrupt, something which is not completely determined by the past out of which it arose" (1932:16). The past does not determine the present, or the future, because of individuals' relative amounts of agency. That is, humans have the ability to makes choices that affect their present and future lives, though, to paraphrase Karl Marx, they do so under conditions they have not chosen themselves. We have to play the cards we are given regardless of how good or bad the hand may be. How we choose to play those cards is another matter.

Card games, like other organized leisure activities, have rules that must be followed. Social life is similar in many respects. Cultural sociologists are interested in the meanings of those rules and how they affect the actions of both rule followers and rule breakers. We can liken such rules to "shared meaning structures" and thereby focus on the ways they foster expectations and conventions for everyday communication and behavior (see Karp et al. 2016:21–22). For Jeffrey Alexander (2003) and his fellow supporters of the "Strong Program in Cultural Sociology," the goal of cultural analysis is to provide the best map of the meaning structures that social actors rely on to navigate through their social worlds. The Strong Program approaches culture as an "independent variable" capable of "shaping actions and institutions, providing inputs every bit as vital as more material or instrumental forces" (Alexander and Smith 2003:12). By arguing for culture's relative autonomy, the Strong Program recognizes that culture is not defined by social life, but rather that culture itself takes part in, and is ever responsible for, defining it.

If we take seriously the idea that the world does not come pre-interpreted, then we cannot decide in advance which features of social life will be meaningful to individuals, groups, and populations. The key categories of sociological analysis (e.g., race, ethnicity, class, gender, sexuality, religion) are important and meaningful, but we cannot decide in advance how they will be meaningful, or how they will be combined with other categories of meaningfulness. Alexander and others (see Eyerman 2004; Reed 2011) engage in a "structural hermeneutics" to explore specific meaning structures in order to understand how the different elements of meaning fit together. As such, they tend to take a relatively macro perspective to investigate the overarching symbolic system under which people live while simultaneously recognizing the influence of cultural codes on action.

When exploring the dynamics of American civil society, for example, Alexander and Philip Smith (1993) turned toward the "internal symbolic logic" of that particular meaning structure. Drawing liberally from Emile Durkheim, Claude Levi-Strauss, and Roland Barthes among others across multiple disciplines, they identify a binary code of sacred and profane ideals that cut civil discourse into two camps: democratic and counter-democratic. They address how each side of the code affects actors, social relationships, and institutions in the ways they operate through a seemingly secular version of the sacred and profane or, put differently, the not-so-rational discourse of politics in social life. Alexander and Smith (Smith 1993:196) write:

> We argue that culture should be conceived as a system of symbolic codes which specify the good and the evil. Conceptualizing culture in this way allows it causal autonomy—by virtue of its internal semio-logics—and also affords the possibility for generalizing from and between specific localities and historical contexts. Yet, at the same time, our formulation allows for individual action and social-structural factors to be included in the analytical frame.

From their point of view, both macro and micro considerations are influenced by the presumed relative autonomy of culture. Again, to use the game metaphor, players can make their own moves but only within the confines of what is allowed by the game. As such, the game's meaning structures take precedent over the ways individuals uphold, or seek to upend, such structures.

Though the Strong Program purports to attend to "individual action" and agency, studies under its umbrella often remain at a high level of abstraction. With too much emphasis on structure, social actors themselves can get lost in the analysis. Perhaps that is why an ethnographic void exists within the Strong Program. And maybe that is why symbolic interactionists have not fully engaged with their work. And perhaps that is why Gary Alan Fine announced and has promulgated a version of SI-friendly cultural sociology that gets closer to the inner workings of small groups and individuals without getting caught in the reified quagmire of so-called overarching social structures.

With tongue playfully planted in cheek yet with "vital purpose," Fine's "Puny Program of Cultural Sociology" is defined by a move toward a "sociology of the local" that honors the legacy and continued persistence of grounded and peopled ethnographic studies (2010:359). As a means for avoiding too much theoretical abstraction, the local context of any specific study becomes a key "variable" for understanding meaning-making processes. This involves a conceptual move from studying symbolic codes to studying emergent practices as they take place within and adhere to local cultural norms. The emphasis, then, is less on the product of cultural actions within particular codes than with the "processual how" of codes, which themselves are constructed and then maintained or deconstructed.

The emphasis on process is a cornerstone of SI, as depicted by Herbert Blumer's claim that "Human social interaction is more like a cauldron than a stamping machine, more in the nature of a dynamic, ongoing development than a static repetition. It represents human life in process" (Blumer 2004:38). And the newer realm of cultural sociology—Strong, Puny, or otherwise—is primarily concerned with, as Lyn Spillman (2002:5) notes, "the processes of meaning-making." Explicitly paying attention to process allows us to move from the local to make more generalizable statements about human behavior and meaning making. Meanings of situations and scenes are not created anew through each interaction. They are based on shared histories that foster expected behaviors and actions from participants' roles. Fine writes:

> Since every act constitutes and is constituted by a local context, particularity is universal. If everything is situated, that situated quality becomes a feature of social organization. However, simultaneously a situated context shapes the evaluation and interpretation of action. Put another way, the local provides a *stage* for action and creates a *lens* by which participants typify groups or gatherings, establishing boundaries. As a result, the local is both a material reality and a form of collective representation. Action is always generated in response to other actions within a local scene as well as to the local meaning of that scene. (2010:356)

Though local contexts are affected by external forces and, in effect, other local contexts (see Borer 2019), everyday life is lived through the local as a stage for individual and collective action and participation. Such practices emerge within the context of interaction between participants and are often based on a "group style" that, as Nina Eliasoph and Paul Lichterman note, *both* depends on *and* creates rules for group membership, responsibilities, and speech norms (2003:739). In their comparative study of suburban environmental activists and rural bar patrons, they conclude that "one cannot fully understand a group's shared culture in an everyday setting without understanding the group's style" (Eliasoph and Lichterman 2003:737).

Taking the local context seriously makes the "generalized other" more tangible and empirical and, in effect, grounds studies of culture in real spaces and places with real people interacting with others. For example, in Jooyoung Lee's (2016) study of an improvisational freestyle hip-hop collective, he observes the ways that young Black males in a particular setting in South Central Los Angeles created music as a way to get away from the stress and distress of their daily lives. Here, the local urban context is especially important because "in areas like South Central LA . . . young people grow up in neighborhoods that constrain the scope of their peer groups. The specter of gang violence and restrictive gang injunctions makes it difficult for young people to move freely and make friends across neighborhoods" (Lee 2016:4). The specific context, then, of the Project Blowed—where members can participate in the playful wordplay and dance moves of hip-hop—becomes the case to explore where and how culture is learned, created, and practiced. But Lee's analysis does not just stay within the geographical context of his study. He extends his analysis beyond the group to address a more universalized experience of angst that drives many of the youth he studied who were trying to turn their hobby into a career. He calls this "existential urgency," a condition felt as "a person's diminishing time to achieve life and career goals" (Lee 2016:7). Such a condition is likely not unique to these particular persons and thereby extends beyond the group Lee studied to be generalized across settings.

To respect both the unique particularities of group and the universal human process are the crux of SI-friendly culture studies. Comparative ethnographic studies are rare, but possible. And they help solidify those practices that span across specific local culture. Richard Ocejo (2017) achieves this by staying in one geographic location— New York City—but looks at four different occupations. These jobs, which were once mainstays of the working class, now don the honorific labels of "craft" or "artisanal" in the so-called new service economy: bartenders, booze makers, barbers, and butchers. Ocejo finds that, for the sake of meeting the ideal of authenticity, "the art of doing these jobs means learning how to follow, bend, and sometimes break a set of rules that their occupational community follows and enforces" (Ocejo 2017:180). Through these emergent practices, participants in these occupations have given new and updated meaning to their jobs for themselves but also for their respective clientele. They all engage in acts of "service teaching" to provide the visceral knowledge for their consumers to appreciate the crafted cocktails, whiskeys, hairdos, and unknown strips of meat offered to them.

In his study of music festivals, Jonathan Wynn (2015) conducted a comparative ethnography that brought him to three different cities: Austin, TX; Nashville, TN; and Newport, RI. This allowed him to focus on how various groups in particular settings engaged in "festivalization" as a means for creating and promoting their respective local cultures. Instead of taking a view from above, Wynn analyzes the festivals and their ancillary events as "occasions" and provides a nuanced reading of Goffman's seminal work on interaction orders. Here, Wynn follows Fine's lead in addressing the meso level of social life by recognizing it as the key link between the smaller occasions of interaction—within festivals and the occasions (like the festivals themselves)—that depend on the ways that groups "varyingly consume, distribute, and take advantage of resources through heightened moments of sociality" (Wynn 2015:258). This builds upon Anselm Strauss's central argument that all social orders are in some respects negotiated orders (1978). The negotiation process happens at the meso level within and between groups and organizations. According to David Maines (1982:267), focusing on the negotiated order of the meso structure provides "important insights into how social orders are maintained, how they change, and how structural limitations interact with the capacity of humans to reconstruct their worlds creatively." As such, we might do well to say that, for symbolic interactionists, the study of culture is essentially the study meso-level negotiated orders. At its root, SI concerned with "how people do things together" (Becker 1986). Culture— as a process of meaning making—is that thing that they are doing together.

CULTURE IN AND OF EVERYDAY LIFE

As matter of inquiry, "everyday life" is at the heart of symbolic interactionist studies. In fact, examining what we do on a daily basis—from the time we wake up to the time we go to bed and even while we sleep—provides us with an awfully large amount of situations that are negotiated by individuals within particular settings. In the introduction to their edited volume *Popular Culture in Everyday Life*, Dennis Waskul and Phillip Vannini (2016:9) write:

> The study of everyday life, both within sociology and cultural studies, is a strong, dynamic, and captivating research field with long and rich theoretical traditions. From its outset symbolic interaction has played a central role in the development of this field by allowing researchers to examine ordinary and mundane topics, aby allowing them to take a unique methodological and theoretical approach to the pragmatics of day-to-day life.

Waskul and Vannini collected almost thirty essays that encompass a whole spectrum of practices, though, of course, not exhaustive due to the almost infinite possibility of everyday cultural acts. "From play and hobbies to texting and exercising, from enjoying food and drink to dressing oneself in the morning, rom going to the bathroom to interacting with ones pets, from watching a TV show to updating one's Facebook profile" (Vannini 2016:8), we see everyday life in action. Of note, each of the essays begins with a verb (e.g., watching, sharing, playing, consuming) rather than a noun, once again showing how culture moves, shifts, sways, and bends through everyday interactions.

In their review of critical works on the sociology of everyday life, Peter Adler, Patricia Adler, and Andrea Fontana (1987:219) comment: "Naturally occurring interaction is the foundation of all understanding of society. Describing and analyzing the character and implications of everyday life interaction should thus serve as both the beginning and end point of sociology". This is not to suggest that sociologists should give up the study of social structure in favor of the study of human interaction. In fact, this is where culture—as a binding mechanism—comes into play because social structures are created and sustained through everyday interactions. Writing well before the advent of either SI or CS, German social philosopher Georg Simmel concluded one of his essays on human interaction with the following mandate:

> One will no longer be able to consider as unworthy of attention the delicate, invisible threads that are spun from one person to another if one wishes to understand the web of society according to its productive, form-giving forces—this web of which sociology hitherto was largely concerned with describing the final finished pattern of its uppermost phenomenal stratum. (1907/1997:120)

These "delicate, invisible threads" are precisely the objects of inquiry that sociologists who recognize the foundational aspects of everyday life attempt to make visible. We can detect these threads by focusing on the "form-giving forces" that individuals enact and rely upon to makes sense of their interactions, encounters, and experiences with others.

Though so much of everyday life is constituted by mundane behavior that might fall under the realm of the involuntary and habitual, the unexpected can shock us by revealing the "delicate, invisible threads" of our taken-for-granted connectedness. In her study of celebrity sightings, Kerry Ferris (2004) addresses what happens when the ordinary and the extraordinary collide. The paradox of celebrity encounters is that fans know way more about the celebrities than celebrities know about them, making this an unusual type of "stranger interaction" (Lofland 1998). Even though they are serendipitous and unexpected, Ferris found that public celebrity sightings adhere to a relatively stable moral order. She notes that the "the intersection of fame and mundanity . . . generates its own values [and shows] that the moral order of celebrity sightings appears informal, spontaneous, and naturally occurring, but it is clearly patterned, and its patterns are visible in participants' accounts" (Ferris 2004:242).

Interaction patterns of celebrity sighting are established by two main cultural practices: "recognition work" and "response work." When someone sees a celebrity, they first need to verify if that person is who they think they are. "Recognition work" is necessary because the extraordinary (i.e., the celebrity) has thrown the expected routine out of whack for the mundane observer. They work to identify the celebrity, primarily based on information they have learned or gained from popular media sources like a sense of familiarity or a signature smirk. Once they have confirmed that the celebrity is who they think they are, the observer enters the phase of "response work" when debating about what to do next. The key tactics include "staying cool" (i.e., acting as if the famous person is just like anyone else), approaching the celebrity as their "biggest fan," and, if the celebrity looks as if they want the attention of others, disregarding the celebrity's presence because they are in violation of the taken-for-granted moral order.

Both extraordinary and ordinary physical objects and other nonhumans can play roles in shaping the culture and moral order of everyday life. According to Colin Jerolmack and Iddo Tavory, these things influence expectations and interactions as mediators of meaning. Relying on their own respective works, they highlight Jerolmack's (2009, 2013) study of "pigeon flyers" to show how the totemic quality of pigeons provided a sense of identity and an interactional sphere for men who breed domestic pigeons in New York City. Participants in this culture enact their distinct social world with one another and with their birds. Jerolmack shows how each flyer's interactions with his pigeons aroused an awareness of himself as part of the collective by eliciting both real and imagined social ties through interactions. Shared customs dictated certain acts, like breeding, whereby each participant internalized the attitudes of the group and aimed to foster pigeons that aligned with the standards of his peers. Moreover, the men campaigned for status at "the pet shop" based on their birds' abilities to "look good" and "fly nice." The personal feeling of satisfaction that each man had from their birds' respective appearances and performances resulted from invoking membership in a group of "pigeon flyers" who valued these aesthetics and imbued respect on those who achieved them (Jerolmack 2013:107). The pigeons were not simply emblems of pre-given social arrangements or meanings. Instead, they helped shape the patterns of belonging, identity, and membership onto the culture of pigeon breeders, flyers, and those who judged both pigeons and their owners.

Nonhuman objects can also *mold* everyday interactions. Expanding on Goffman's idea of "interactional hooks," Tavory (2010) found that Orthodox Jewish men who wore yarmulkes (skullcaps) were often "called upon" as Jews as they walked through their neighborhood. That is, random anonymous people in the bus station, for example, asked them on an almost daily basis about their religious beliefs. Other Orthodox Jews often nodded to them, and, on a rare occasion, someone would shout an anti-Semitic slur. They told Tavory that they often forgot that they were wearing the yarmulke. Orthodox men constantly wore it as a habitual, nonreflexive aspect of their daily appearance. Instead of just signifying their group memberships, the yarmulke provided strangers with a stable social identification for interaction and constrained the Jewish men's abilities to enact other parts of their person identities.

Sticking to the realm of religion, Nancy Ammerman (2014) argues for the study of religion in everyday life under the guise of "lived religion." Combatting sociology's Protestant legacy of confounding religion with belief as well as the religious studies that focus solely on "sacred texts," Ammerman and others (McGuire 2008; Bender 2010) have established an SI-informed paradigm where they "look for the material, embodied aspects of religion as they occur in everyday life, in addition to listening for how people explain themselves. It includes both the experiences of the body and the mind" (Ammerman 2014:190). Such practices and narratives can be found within both marginal and institutionalized "spiritual tribes," so that scholars can see how religion and spirituality merge, like celebrity encounters, the extraordinary and mundane. A key sight for such insights is the everyday workplace. At first glance work is the place of rational mundanity. But, as Ammerman tells us from the stories people told her, there are ways that some sacralize their occupations. "Listening to stories about work made very clear that there is a great deal more going on everyday than merely an economic exchange of labor for monetary reward" (Ammerman 2014:197). This line of thinking can help solidify the roles that culture—religion here being an explicit manifestation—plays in everyday lives.

CONCLUSION

The notion that people assign meaning to the things around them and act accordingly is a basic tenet of SI. The same can be said about the sociological study of culture and cultures, especially CS. What CS helps us focus on are the wider contexts of everyday interactions and practices including the shared histories of inhabited institutions. It reminds us that meanings are not created anew in and through every situation. People, places, and things often come pre-labeled, so to speak, by someone else. It also helps us move from studying the meanings of things to the study of things that are meaningful. This distinction is akin to the one that anthropologist Clifford Geertz makes about blinks and winks (see Geertz 1973). A blink is involuntary action, so much so that we hardly recognize how many times we blink while talking to someone or reading this chapter for that matter. Winks, on the other, are voluntary and intentional. They convey a meaning between the winker and their intended audience.

We can push Geertz's argument further by saying that some intentional acts are more meaningful than others. And those based on the actions and interactions of collectivities beyond and into, as Geertz says, the web of meaning. As such, culturally oriented scholars find themselves looking at the expressive side of humanity and the processes by which a person, place, or thing becomes meaningful, sometime to the point of consecration. Where do we find the meaningful, one might ask. The perhaps too glib answer is everywhere. The less glib answer points us to the people, places, and things that people hold dear and hope to be near. SI and CS provide scholars with the tools to seek out what others seek out; that is, we care what other people care about, the good, the bad, the ugly, and all that fall in between.

NOTE

1. It is interesting to note that, early in his career, DiMaggio was interested in the ways institutions work but then became one of the leading scholars of cognitive sociology and its relationship to culture.

REFERENCES

Adler, Patricia A., Peter Adler, and Andrea Fontana. 1987. "Everyday Life Sociology." *Annual Review of Sociology* 13(1):217–35.

Alexander, Jeffrey C., and Philip Smith. 1993. "The Discourse of American Civil Society: New Proposal for Cultural Studies." *Theory and Society* 22(2):151–207.

Alexander, Jeffrey C. 2003. *The Meanings of Social Life: A Cultural Sociology*. Oxford: Oxford University Press.

Ammerman, Nancy T. 2014. "Finding Religion in Everyday Life." *Sociology of Religion* 75(2):189–207.

Becker, Howard S. 1986. *Doing Things Together*. Evanston, IL: Northwestern University Press.

Bender, Courtney. 2010. *The New Metaphysicals: Spirituality and the American Religious Imagination*. Chicago: University of Chicago Press.

Blumer, Herbert. 1969. *Symbolic Interactionism*. Englewood Cliffs, NJ: Prentice Hall.

Blumer, Herbert. 2004. *George Herbert Mead and Human Conduct*. Lanham, MD: Rowman Altamira.

Borer, Michael Ian. 2006. "The Location of Culture: The Urban Culturalist Perspective." *City & Community* 5(2):173–97.

Borer, Michael Ian. 2019. *Vegas Brews: Craft Beer and the Birth of a Local Scene*. New York: New York University Press.

Childress, Clayton. 2017. *Under the Cover: The Creation, Production, and Reception of a Novel*. Princeton, NJ: Princeton University Press.

DiMaggio, Paul. 1982. "Cultural Entrepreneurship in Nineteenth-Century Boston: The Creation of an Organizational Base for High Culture in America." *Media, Culture & Society* 4(1):33–50.

DiMaggio, Paul. 1996. "Are Art-Museum Visitors Different from Other People? The Relationship between Attendance and Social and Political Attitudes in the United States." *Poetics* 24(2–4):161–80.

Eagleton, Terry. 2000. *The Idea of Culture*. Oxford: Blackwell.

Eliasoph, Nina, and Paul Lichterman. 2003. "Culture in Interaction." *American Journal of Sociology* 108(4):735–94.

Eyerman, Ron. 2004. "Jeffrey Alexander and the Cultural Turn in Social Theory." *Thesis Eleven* 79(1):25–30.

Ferris, Kerry O. 2004. "Seeing and Being Seen: The Moral Order of Celebrity Sightings." *Journal of Contemporary Ethnography* 33(3):236–64.

Fine, Gary Alan. 2010. "The Sociology of the Local: Action and its Publics." *Sociological Theory* 28(4):355–76.

Fine, Gary Alan, and Tim Hallett. 2014. "Group Cultures and the Everyday Life of Organizations: Interaction Orders and Meso-Analysis." *Organization Studies* 35(12):1773–92.

Fine, Gary Alan, and Lisa-Jo Van den Scott. 2011. "Wispy Communities: Transient Gatherings and Imagined Micro-Communities." *American Behavioral Scientist* 55(1):1319–35.

Gardner Robert Owen. 2020. *The Portable Community: Place and Displacement in Bluegrass Festival Life*. New York: Routledge.

Geertz, Clifford. 1973. *The Interpretation of Culture*. New York: Basic Books.

Glynn, Mary Ann, C. B. Bhattacharya, and Hayagreeva Rao. 1996. "Art Museum Membership and Cultural Distinction: Relating Members' Perceptions of Prestige to Benefit Usage." *Poetics* 24(2–4):259–74.

Grindstaff, Laura. 2008. "Culture and Popular Culture: A Case for Sociology." *The ANNALS of the American Academy of Political and Social Science* 619(1):206–22.

Irwin, John. 1977. *Scenes*. Beverly Hills, CA: SAGE.

Jerolmack, Colin. 2009. "Primary Groups and Cosmopolitan Ties: The Rooftop Pigeon Flyers of New York." *Ethnography* 10:435–57.

Jerolmack, Colin. 2013. *The Global Pigeon*. Chicago: University of Chicago Press.

Karp, David A., William C. Yoels, Barbara H. Vann, and Michael Ian Borer. 2016. *Sociology in Everyday Life*. New York: Waveland Press.

Kotarba, Joseph A., Jennifer L. Fackler, and Kathryn M. Nowotny. 2009. "An Ethnography of Emerging Latino Music Scenes." *Symbolic Interaction* 32(4):310–33.

Lee, Jooyoung. 2016. *Blowin' Up: Rap Dreams in South Central*. Chicago: University of Chicago Press.

Lena, Jennifer C., and Richard A. Peterson. 2008. "Classification as Culture: Types and Trajectories of Music Genres." *American Sociological Review* 73(5):697–718.

Lofland, Lyn H. 1998. *The Public Realm: Exploring the City's Quintessential Social Territory*. New York: Aldine de Gruyter.

Maines, David. 1982. "In Search of Mesostructure: Studies in the Negotiated Order." *Urban Life* 11:267–79.

Maines, David R. 2000. "The Social Construction of Meaning." *Contemporary Sociology* 29(4):577–84.

McGinty, Patrick J. W. 2014. "Divided and Drifting: Interactionism and the Neglect of Social Organizational Analyses in Organization Studies." *Symbolic Interaction* 37(2):155–86.

McGuire, Meredith B. 2008. *Lived Religion: Faith and Practice in Everyday Life*. New York: Oxford University Press.

Mead, George Herbert. 1932. *The Philosophy of the Present*. Chicago: University of Chicago Press.

Ocejo, Richard E. 2017. *Masters of Craft: Old Jobs in the New Urban Economy*. Princeton, NJ: Princeton University Press.

Peterson, Richard A. 1994. "Culture Studies through the Production Perspective: Progress and Prospects." Pp. 163–90 in *The Sociology of Culture: Emerging Theoretical Perspectives*, edited by Diana Crane. Oxford: Blackwell.

Peterson, Richard A., and Narasimhan Anand. 2004. "The Production of Culture Perspective." *Annual Review of Sociology* 30:311–34.

Reed, Isaac Ariail. 2011. *Interpretation and Social Knowledge: On the Use of Theory in the Human Sciences*. Chicago: University of Chicago Press.

Smith, Christian. 2003. *Moral, Believing Animals: Human Personhood and Culture*. Oxford: Oxford University Press.

Simmel, Georg. 1907/1997. "Sociology of the Senses." Pp. 109–20 in *Simmel on Culture*, edited by D. Frisby and M. Featherstone. London: SAGE.

Spillman, Lyn, ed. 2002. *Cultural Sociology*. Oxford: Blackwell.

Strauss, Anselm. 1978. *Negotiations: Varieties, Contexts, Processes and Social Order*. San Francisco: Jossey-Bass.

Tavory, Iddo. 2010. "Of Yarmulkes and Categories: Delegating Boundaries and the Phenomenology of Interactional Expectation." *Theory and Society* 39:49–68.

Waskul, Dennis D., and Phillip Vannini, eds. 2016. *Popular Culture as Everyday Life*. New York: Routledge.

Williams, J. Patrick. 2011. *Subcultural Theory: Traditions and Concepts*. Malden, MA: Polity.

Williams, Raymond. 1985. *Keywords: A Vocabulary of Culture and Society*. Oxford: Oxford University Press.

Wynn, Jonathan R. 2015. *Music/City: American Festivals and Placemaking in Austin, Nashville, and Newport*. Chicago: University of Chicago Press.

CHAPTER 12

....

SUBCULTURES

....

WILLIAM RYAN FORCE

THIS chapter provides an overview of subculture in symbolic interactionist sociology. This includes a description of the social and historical origins of subculture (and its scholarship) in the United States and United Kingdom, as well as the relationship between these conditions and its earliest theorization. In the United States, this is first undertaken by the social reform-minded urban ecologists and strain theorists of the Chicago School. Meanwhile in the United Kingdom, the Centre for Contemporary Cultural Studies (sometimes called "the Birmingham School") forges a Marxist analysis of subculture centered on class struggle and the spectacle of aesthetic style. After summarizing these traditions and their internal debates, this chapter provides a survey of the subsequent literature that charts out the landscape of subcultural practices.

This review touches upon conceptual themes that emerge from the literature on various subcultures. The role of power, and specifically the idea of *resistance*, is something of a conceptual bugaboo that has beleaguered sociological attempts to distinguish subculture from other forms of cultural difference. Scholarly accounts of how (mostly youth) use subculture as a site for meaning-making are also outlined below. In many cases, subculture can be understood as a set of resources for managing interactional troubles and institutional problems that include class, race, gender, and sexual dynamics. Of fundamental importance in all interactionist treatments of subculture is the question of how people who participate in subculture do so in ways that influence their identities, experiences, and social realities—all of which are power-laden. Various examples are used to illustrate the major debates and issues within the sociology of subculture. In closing, the impact of commodification, mass media, and the rise of the internet is detailed. This leads to the inevitable question of subculture's demise.

THE CHICAGO SCHOOL(S)

....

Most scholars trace the provenance of subculture as a concept to two traditions: the Chicago School and the Birmingham School (properly known as the Centre for

Contemporary Cultural Studies). It is the latter who typically receive credit for coining the term and employing it regularly in their own analyses. Nonetheless, Chicago School sociologists like Robert Park, Everett Hughes, William Whyte, Paul Cressey, William I. Thomas, and Florian Znaniecki are often cited for their contribution to the emerging field. While through a contemporary lens much of the Chicago tradition falls more neatly into criminology or delinquency studies, it is the distinctly ethnographic approach to the subject matter that shaped what would go on to become the earliest attempts at mapping out what became known as subculture. These pioneering ethnographies include Thomas and Znaniecki's (1996) exploration of the Polish immigrant's social milieu in the United States, Cressey's (1932) work on the deviant occupation of "taxi dancers," and Whyte's (1943) analysis of the lives of impoverished Italian-Americans. Each of these case studies considers the social situation of cities' inhabitants as fundamental to their experiences.

Collectively, the work of the early Chicago School is described under the rubric of human or urban ecology: in each instance the deviance associated with a particular group is re-framed as the consequence of maladjustment to modern society. In a conceptual move that was radical at the time, the Chicago scholars argue that it is not the innate or essential capacities of these groups that best explain their behavior but the unequally distributed opportunities for navigating and succeeding within urban life. Rather than attributable to one's ethnicity itself, it is the ethnic cleavages that characterize political and social life in the United States that lies behind these folks' "poor adjustment." Instead of the alleged cultural backwardness that so many at the time would scapegoat for these groups' inability to assimilate into a new social situation, it is social disorganization—the technological shifts (especially in regard to capitalist production), political skullduggery, and lack of social support—of the modern metropolis that deserve the blame.

This position is further developed by the second wave of Chicago scholars like Robert Merton (1938) who would come to characterize this as a matter of *strain*. Put simply, Merton suggests that the mismatch between culturally prescribed goals and the sanctioned means for pursuing those goals result in what we consider rule-breaking behavior. Worded differently, what is perceived by those in power as the erratic actions or dysfunctional lifestyle of the less privileged are better thought of as innovative attempts to make sense of a broken social world. The hapless circumstances one finds themselves caught up in, and the sometimes delinquent or criminal maneuvers undertaken by those who wish to escape these dire circumstances, are structural in origin.

While some scholars like Frances Fox Piven moved this in a more policy-oriented direction, others like Erving Goffman and Howard Becker merged the strain and urban ecology models with the then-budding field of symbolic interaction to explore in further detail the social situations of inveterate rule-breakers. Goffman (1963), for instance, is primarily concerned with how one's commitment to a deviant identity is curbed by the sometimes-nefarious forces of social control. Goffman (1963:143), however, was minimally interested in what he called "social deviants" who rejected conventional society's imperative to obliterate or conceal deviant behavior. On the other hand, Becker (1963) focuses primarily on these exact characters—such as avid marijuana users and jazz musicians—to develop his notion of *outsiders*. In using this term, Becker underscores the relational quality of deviance and honors the symbolic reality of so-called deviant lifestyles. This is a significant move from the original Chicago School's (perhaps inadvertent) tendency to lend a sense of semantic primacy to the conventional society's norm system as seen, for instance, in differential association theory (Sutherland and Cressy 1992). Through this interactionist intervention in the urban ecologists' theoretical approach, it became possible to consider the subcultural realm as one of equal legitimacy to the mainstream it resists. The critical potential of the symbolic interactionist orientation is laid bare through Becker's shift toward the sociological consideration of rule-breaking as a purely relative, amoral phenomenon. Chicago sociologists increasingly approached the possibility of subculture from a perspective that considered the latent power of the social order as a moral order (Goffman 1963). It is this second Chicago School that begins to tread the same ground of the Marxists from Birmingham.

THE BIRMINGHAM SCHOOL

While the tumult of the postwar United States began to reverberate in the microsociology of the Chicago Schools, parallel troubles beset the social fabric of the United Kingdom. In both the United States and Britain, one's mode of consumption increasingly replaces a relationship to the means of production as the primary source of identity. The social climate of the United States was lurching away from the radicalism and permissiveness of the 1960s, toward a horizon in which Reaganite economic policies and a shift toward cultural conservativism awaited. Likewise, similar pressures were building as the United Kingdom entered the postwar era. The advent of mass media in the occidental world, the United Kingdom's weakening class structure, successive waves of immigration stemming from the loosened grasp of British colonialism, and technological changes that resulted in increased leisure time—each provided the threats and opportunities that would be exploited over the next decades by the political class. As did the United States under Reagan, a new reactionary current would eventually find fruition in the neoliberal Thatcher premiership. The Centre for Contemporary Cultural Studies (CCCS) responded in turn to the British situation.

Rooted in the neo-Marxism of Antonio Gramsci (1947/1989), and his notion of *hegemony* in particular, the founders of the CCCS (more commonly known by the less syllabically daunting moniker "The Birmingham School") forged a new approach to the study of cultural difference in response to these sociological upheavals. The youth subcultures that exploded onto the streets of postwar England were understood by the Birmingham scholars through the lens of a Marxist base-superstructure model in which subcultural formations represented a pointed critique of mainstream institutions in late capitalism. This is evident in the work of the cultural studies tradition as it developed in the thinking of Stuart Hall, Tony Jefferson, Richard Hoggart, and Raymond Williams.

Hall (1973/2007), arguably the theoretical mastermind behind the CCCS's unique approach, synthesized Gramsci's critical theory and Althusser's psychoanalytic Marxism with feminism and semiotics to produce the centre's guiding framework in the form of his encoding/decoding model. This argument centers on the idea that signs gain their meaning only through social linkages, and that different social groups (more notably in the form of socio-economic classes) can assign various different values to the same referents. Following Gramsci's (1947/1989) argument that overt political domination has given way to the subtle hegemonic manipulation of popular culture, Hall (1973/2007) argues that the encoding and decoding of signs is generally governed by an interpretive framework enforced by the political and economic elite and thus (coercively) shared among people with different material interests. The multiplicity of meanings engendered by signs—called *polysemousness*—is often foreclosed upon by the power of *myth*. Myth, in the sense used here by Roland Barthes (1957/1972), implies a level of meaning that has become so pervasive as to achieve taken-for-grantedness. Combining multiple strands of social theory, Hall (1973/2007) arguably salvages the somewhat problematic Marxist notion of "false consciousness" through an analytic approach that emphasizes the cultural terrain as the primary site of contemporary class struggle.

With this conceptual tool at their disposal, the Birmingham School produced powerful inquiries into the way that social critique is accomplished in youth revolt. Whereas the Chicago School sympathetically implied that the various subaltern cultural formations they studied were the logical consequence of dis-equilibrium in a social system, the Birmingham approach characterizes these new subcultures as heroic confrontations with the economic and political order. Crucial to the Birmingham view is the idea that subcultures are engaged in a meaningful form of *resistance*. This resistance, much to the chagrin of the Old Left, is not necessarily or even primarily expressed through explicitly political action or social movements (Willis 1977; see also Haenfler 2004). Instead, it is the cultural and symbolic levels of stylistic refusal that preoccupy the Birmingham School. This is perhaps most clearly explained by Dick Hebdige (1979:105), who uses the admittedly melodramatic phrase "semiotic guerilla warfare" (by way of Umberto Eco) to describe this precise mode of resistance used by subculturalists. Hebdige concludes that the meaning of subculture is best sussed out by an exploration of subcultural *style*: the expressive dimensions of clothing, musical aesthetics, hygiene standards, and use of artifacts that mark their bearer as waging semiotic war on conventional society.

This position is clarified by the generation of academics who use the CCCS model as a lens for exploring the youth subcultures that emerge in the 1960s and 1970s. Although these studies focus on British iterations of subculture like the mods, original skinheads, and rudeboys (Hall and Jefferson 1976; Hebdige 1979), their approach would go on to become an influential template for looking elsewhere. Furthermore, the steadily-growing power of mass media resulted in cross-pollination: the greasers of the United States morphed into the Teds in the United Kingdom, for example, while punk seemingly evolves almost simultaneously from different sources in the two countries (the rudeboys and the rockers in the United Kingdom; the glam and garage scenes in the

United States). The Birmingham approach balanced out the micro-structural, technical proclivities of the Chicago tradition by underscoring the visceral subversive power of spectacle.

Symbolic Interactionist Studies of Subculture

Taken together, the dual traditions of semiotic Marxism and interactionist ethnography proved to be fertile ground for the sociological analysis of subculture. This happy marriage is facilitated in part by the shared conceptual ground between Hall's (1973/2007) theory of culture and the work of Harold Garfinkel (1967), who claims that meaning is *indexical*: dependent on the particulars of social interactions. Garfinkel's (1967) influence can be seen in the SI that emerges from the second wave of Chicago School sociologists. Similarly, Goffman's (1959) analysis of everyday life as a dramaturgical performance guided by social scripts contributes to the language of *doing* developed by West and Zimmerman (1987; see also: West and Fenstermaker 1995). These sociologies of everyday life collectively treat meaning as a contingent product of social intercourse among actors who are both guided by shared cultural knowledge(s) and (re)make it in turn. Another contribution to what was still a budding field of subcultural studies, Gary Alan Fine and Sherryl Kleinman (1979) offered a distinctly symbolic interactionist definition of the subject. They suggest a circumvention of the structural bias in other definitions where subculture is reduced to a "subset" of society defined by shared institutional position or dis-location (Fine and Kleinman 1979).

These strands weave together a working definition of subculture: the diffuse social network of social actors who employ an oppositional framework for meaning that crystallizes in shared behaviors, rituals, sartorial codes, and (ultimately) identities. In response to the Birmingham tradition, symbolic interactionists are asked to entertain the self-understandings of group members as a key consideration. Part of Fine and Kleinman's (1979) rethinking of subculture underscores how actors are informed by an existing subculture while building one through their collaborative meaning-making. The grounded, mundane subcultural activity documented by folks working through an SI perspective would by most accounts be said to occur at the level of *scene*. John Irwin (1977) explains that the idea of localized subcultural spaces, which he calls "scenes," turn us to the particulars of grounded cultural activity in which any number of cultural and subcultural influences converge. By re-centering "the local as a central point of reference" (Bennett 2000:197), SI scholars of subculture tend to frame their studies as ethnographies of individual scenes and thus avoid grand proclamations about any subculture as a whole while still acknowledging the heuristic value of the concept (Bennett and Peterson 2004; DuPont 2019; Force 2009; Glass 2012; Haenfler 2004).

Subsequent to the Chicago and Birmingham traditions, the field of subcultural studies exploded with a dizzying array of colorful and conceptually varied work. Myriad groups have been subjected to the ethnographic treatment. Listed here alphabetically so as to avoid the impression of authorial bias, a non-exhaustive list includes: bodybuilding (Klein 1993; Wellman 2020), gay subcultures (like the clones [Levine 1998], radical faeries, bears, and leathermen [Hennen 2008]), goth (Hodkinson 2002; Wilkins 2008), heavy metal (Kahn-Harris 2007; Weinstein 2000), hip-hop (Clay 2003; Lee 2016; Rose 1994), mod (Cohen 1972; Hebdige 1979), outlaw motorcycle clubs (Hopper and Moore 1990; Schmid 2021), punk (Fox 1987; Force 2009; Leblanc 1999) and its various cousins (like alternative rock [Schippers 2002], riot grrrl [Pavlidis 2012], and straight edge [Haenfler 2004; Williams and Copes 2005]), raves/dance clubs (Thornton 1995), skateboarding (Dupont 2019), tabletop gaming (Williams 2006), tattooing and body modification (Irwin 2003; Sanders 1989; Thompson 2015; Force 2020), tearooms (Humphreys 1970), vaping (Tokle and Pedersen 2019), and virginity pledging (Wilkins 2008). While not all of these examples are explicitly interactionist, each contributes to an understanding of subcultures that builds upon the conceptual assumptions of interpretivist, micro-sociology. Rather than detail each of these in turn, this section will address some theoretical and conceptual threads that run through these studies.

Hegemony and Resistance

As Ross Haenfler (2010) has suggested, it is the combination of social marginalization and cultural resistance that distinguishes subcultures from other sociological formations (like subgroups, gangs, and idiocultures). This resistance, often characterized as aesthetic or expressive (Hall and Jefferson 1976; Hebdige 1979), is marked by a lifestyle politics rather than vanguardist political activity (Haenfler 2004). There is the additional question, however, of whom is being resisted. While subculture is often conflated with "youth," adult culture is an amorphous target. Many subcultures, in fact, have primarily adult participation (e.g., outlaw bikers, gamers, and bodybuilders). Likewise, the idea that subculturalists inevitably "age out" has been challenged by studies that explore the shifting meanings of cultural practice in the life-course (Andes 1998). Following the lead of the CCCS and its Gramscian proclivities, many studies highlight opposition to the cultural mainstream and hegemonic social norms. This can be witnessed not only in the rejection of conventional society but also in intra-subcultural skirmishes. Some work considers the way a subculture necessary involves a dialectic tension of internal critique, as in Lauraine Leblanc's (1999) description of young women's rejection of gender oppression within punk. Other work investigates even more pronounced conflicts over what counts as resistance in a given subculture, such as the "Revolution Summer" of 1985 in the DC hardcore punk scene (Moore and Roberts 2009) and the entire subgenre of riot grrrl (Pavlidis 2012).

The counter-hegemonic potential of subcultures is best unpacked by symbolic interactionism and other sociologies of everyday life, alive to micro-political forms of resistance. Subculture can be conceptualized as a toolkit for managing interactional troubles and institutional problems. This approach, thinking of subcultures as identity projects (Wilkins 2008), brings in to relief the relationship between culture and power found in Goffman's (1959, 1963) diagnosis of the interactive order as a moral one. From its inception, the Birmingham School made a Marxian class analysis the core of their interpretive tradition (Hall and Jefferson 1976; Hebdige 1979), analyzing the degree to which the symbolic refusal of working-class youth was efficacious (Willis 1977). The class struggle expressed by youth subcultures in aesthetic and moral terms may not meet vanguardist criteria. However, it merges effortlessly with the interpretivist work of symbolic interactionism. J. Patrick Williams (2009) catalogues additional nuance in the ways SI can document resistance as it plays out along passive/active, micro/macro, and overt/covert dimensions in different subcultures. These axes also help illuminate the potential for subcultural identity to be used as a tool for mapping and manipulating the interactive domains of sexuality, gender, race, and class without conscious intent (Wilkins 2008).

Subculture often facilitates a contemplation *on* and critical response *to* normative racial, gendered, and sexual imperatives in mainstream society. Whereas hip-hop is often (and correctly) analyzed as a subcultural dialogue on race (Clay 2003; Lee 2016; Rose 1994), it is worth keeping in mind that hip-hop simply wrestles with racial meaning in the most overt and active fashion. In ways that prefigured later discussions of race, ethnic cultural difference (itself often cross-coded and intertwined with socio-economic status) preoccupied early Chicago School forays into the subcultural (Thomas and Znaniecki 1996; Whyte 1943). Additionally, Hebdige (1979) viewed punk as moving the Teds' or skinheads' class critique into ethnic territory. This is evidenced in the early punk anthem "White Riot," in which The Clash (1977) lament the failure of white working-class youth to be radicalized by the intersectional oppressions that motivate black youth's political violence. Hebdige (1979) would go on to suggest punk hairstyles as a covert Anglo analogue to the overtly racialized refusal of Rastafarian dreadlocks. Heavy metal is not usually mined for its racial philosophy, but (like punk) it can be treated as a response to the mis-representation of whiteness as a monolithic, economically privileged category in social discourse. Early studies anticipated the SI model that enables sociologists to see subculture in just such a way: as micro-level identity projects with which young people test the strength of the social order and negotiate their place within it (Wilkins 2008).

While the sociology of subculture definitely appears preoccupied with boys and men, this may have more to do with sociological realities than disciplinary myopia. The field's concentration during a time when gender heavily influenced structural and interpersonal barriers to public life, as well as a tendency in the West to discourage girls and women from cultural production, offer a partial explanation. Many scholars have addressed the relative absence of feminine subjectivities in the scholarship (Hopper and Moore 1990; Leblanc 1999; McRobbie 2000; Pavlidis 2012; Schippers 2002; Thompson 2015; Wilkins 2008). Still others analyze the way in which men rethink and recreate masculinity by way of subcultural practice, very often through the lives of gay subcultural groups (Hennen 2008; Levine 1998) although not exclusively (Humphreys 1970; Klein 1993). Insofar as the majority of documented subcultural activity is undertaken by masculine people, much of that work suggests that hegemonic masculinity is passively highlighted and covertly prodded by subculturalists (Force 2009; Haenfler 2004; Rose 1994; Schippers 2002). Subcultural norms, rituals, and meanings are patterned to demonstrate aversion to square or "normie" ways of doing things even if these rebellions may not be as righteous or pure as scholars might wish. Covert resistance is not meant to be fully grasped by outsiders, after all.

Authenticity and Hierarchy

Subcultures can be identified by their own indigenous practices, artifacts, and knowledges, but just as readily by the way in which they reject conventional cultural meanings. These two elements—who's in and who's out—are often patterned within a subculture in the shape of *authenticity* debates. While some work has tended to view the matter of insider-ship in the form of a stable typology (Fox 1987), internal forms of differentiation have been more commonly represented as processual in nature. Sarah Thornton's work notably applied Pierre Bourdieu's (1984) theory of cultural distinction to the subcultural level in her studies of rave and club cultures, with studies of hip-hop youth (Clay 2003) and tabletop card gamers (Williams 2006) similarly approaching the matter of authenticity as the result of a subcultural schematic for hierarchically ranking actors' relationship to commodities and practices. Understanding subcultures as internally stratified illuminates how anti-conventionality can still be conventionalized, at least to the extent necessary for the existence of a coherent (alternative) social order.

Subcultures can in this way be considered Bourdieusian "taste cultures" built around commodity hierarchies, patterns of consumption, ritualized displays of knowledge, and commitment to aesthetic style. Subcultural authenticity takes on the appearance of an ontological condition within the lived reality of the subculture, but it is best understood analytically as an epistemological product (Force 2009; Widdicombe and Wooffitt 1990). Utilizing the ethnomethodological language of "doing" (West and Zimmerman 1987; West and Fenstermaker 1995), authenticity amounts to a socially coherent performance, which requires adhering to the criteria formed within the particulars of a scene in interaction with other members. In subcultures, authenticity is a matter of fluency in the "codes" used to translate the oppositional language of subcultural style (Hall 1973/ 2007). In short, "being" authentic is a matter of "doing" the subculture consistently and, according to the appraisal of one's audience, correctly (Clay 2003; Dupont 2019; Force 2009; Thornton 1995; Widdicombe and Wooffitt 1990; Williams 2006; Williams and Copes 2005). The exact subcultural capital (Thornton 1995) used in this fluid process of assigning subcultural meaning to the grounded particulars of individual and group experience is, of course, unstable within the larger subculture, which is fundamentally diffuse and decentralized. This returns the attention of interactionists to the idea of the scene as a place or space where subculture manifests in the everyday interactions of participants.

SUBCULTURES: UNDERGROUND OR SIX FEET DEEP?

Since the earliest moments of subculture's conceptual existence hands have wrung over the same's demise. When Hall (1973/2007) laid out the map for resistant meaning, he made it clear that neither the hegemonic nor oppositional reading of any text is as likely as the *negotiated* position where shades of discourse and counter-discourse blend and dull their ideological edges. Hebdige (1979) warned that culture is found in both material objects and the ideas they embody, and that it is the artifacts or *commodities* that have talismanic value for both consumer capitalism and subcultural practice. Commodities also lend themselves most easily to recuperation, that is to say, incorporation into normative culture (Hebdige 1979:94). Anybody with the time, money, or inclination might obtain a hairstyle or a record collection, but this can be distinguished from possession of the knowledge, moral structure, and social codes embedded in those physical traces. Analyses of subculture in the twenty-first century reveal that the marketization of a subculture does not obliterate it but only reshapes the conditions under which actors artfully manage their own identity and practice (Force 2009; Hennen 2008; Hodkinson 2002; Muggleton 2000; Thompson 2015). Part of this is a turn toward recognizing the fuzzy boundaries of individual subculture in a time of media saturation and open access to information.

Mass media and other shifts create what can be described as a *cultic milieu* (Haenfler 2010): subcultures are now used as a palette of colors that actors blend into countless individual hues, tints, shades, and tones. This appears from one perspective to be a breaking down of subculture as a concept, but is perhaps more usefully treated as an illustration of the dialectic between subculture and scene. While subculture can be envisioned as a somewhat coherent set of practices and meanings that manifest in the form of localized scene, it is more pragmatic to think of subculture as a heuristic distillation of the activities of various scenes. In other words, subcultures are the abstraction that we can pull from the myriad empirically observable and (typically geographically bound) collectives of social actors who make culture together in subversive and resistant ways. Scenes at once generate unique styles and syncretize with others, spreading through interactions with other cultural traditions to form what can be identified from a long view as an interrelated system called subculture. The cultic milieu and its supermarket of weird style could be understood as a stage or phase in a complex cultural interchange rather than the decline of subculture as a concept.

Online scenes offer a useful example. The internet has influenced the movement of scene from a geographically bounded place to a more flexible theorization as non-physical space. Online scenes, historically limited to particular groups like goths, have increased in number and significance in the last twenty years (Bennett and Peterson 2004; Dupont 2019; Force 2020; Hodkinson 2002; Wilkins 2008; Williams and Copes 2005; Wellman 2020). Through online modalities like forums or textboards and social media applications like Instagram, virtual interaction can forge an auxiliary to the grounded scene (Dupont 2019; Force 2020; Hodkinson 2002; Wellman 2020) and in some instances even serve as its primary site (Bennett and Peterson 2004; Williams and Copes 2005). Authenticity and credibility—core to subculture in many theorizations—are key to the success of an online influencer's stock in trade (Wellman 2020). Within skateboarding (Dupont 2019) and bodybuilding for example (Wellman 2020), this represents a shift in the way gender is negotiated by participants who must toggle between the norms of subcultures which are decidedly masculine and the demands of internet-based social interaction and self-marketization that are perceived as feminized forms of labor (Whitmer 2019). The "influencer" phenomenon on social media changes the shape of the broader subculture in significant ways. Online scenes also conform to many of the characteristics one anticipates in a "grounded scene," including shared meanings attached to particular cultural objects and practices, interlocking social networks, and other situational specifics upon which more diffuse sub/cultural configurations are mapped and mutually understood (Bennett 2000; Bennett and Peterson 2004; Glass 2012; Irwin 1977).

While scenes may exist online, they tend to be tied to a wider subculture that remains dependent upon places and bodies. In many instances, as with tattoos, those that participate in the scene in the "real world" appear to comprise its active and core membership without whom the internet scene's substantive existence would not be possible (Force 2020). In regard to the IG tattoo scene, this deepest level would be occupied by tattooists who make the tattoos and the individuals who collect tattoos (amass large bodily coverage) by patronizing these artists. In the straightedge subculture where the consumption of hardcore punk and related subgenres are historically central to one's membership, this has typically manifested in norms that connect authenticity to participation in a non-virtual space like "shows" (concerts performed in small, sometimes "underground" venues) or a geographically bound scene. As Williams and Copes (2005) observe, this requirement has been challenged by straightedgers who experience the internet as an alternative arena for developing authenticity criteria.

Individual scenes may furthermore maintain an attachment to the subcultural origins of a practice that has been otherwise diffused into mainstream practice. Heavy metal, for instance, is originally a subcultural style but its symbols (like the "devil horns" or "metal horns") and music (the riffs of Metallica) can now be found in football stadiums every autumn. Nonetheless, the black metal scene in Norway is designed to be virtually unassimilable (Kahn-Harris 2007). Hip-hop is now quoted on the floor of the US Senate, but the "pop culture" of Jay-Z exists in juxtaposition to the subcultural refusal of conscious rappers like Talib Kweli. The claim that subculture is dead, whether uttered from a place of jaded exasperation as an "old school" semiotic warrior or in the context of striking a conceptual pose, is by all accounts neither new nor entirely defensible. Subculture has certainly changed, but change is typically associated with the living and not the dead.

Within two years of its birth (in London during the summer of 1976, by many accounts) people in the punk subculture were already writing its eulogy. "Punk is Dead" is recorded by Crass in 1978, taking aim at The Clash's record deal with a major corporate media publisher (CBS Records), which had been signed just a year prior:

> *Movements are systems and systems kill.*
> *Movements are expressions of the public will.*
> *Punk became a movement 'cause we all felt lost,*
> *But the leaders sold out and now we all pay the cost.*
> *. . .*
> *I watch and understand that it don't mean a thing,*
> *The scorpions might attack, but the systems stole the sting.*
>
> *PUNK IS DEAD.*

Though presented in a distinctly punk subcultural argot, the core ideas expressed by Steve Ignorant and Penny Rimbaud of Crass resonate with the sociological analysis distilled above. Subcultures are generally theorized within symbolic interactionism as diffuse social groupings bound by a decentralized, oppositional meaning system. In a sense, naming a subculture as such begins the process of its conceptual taming and semiotic domestication.

Sociologists of everyday life have undertaken ethnographic analyses of subculture tempered by methodological reflexivity and girded by a theoretical sensitivity to the mundane reality of their participants. The key insights of the Chicago Schools (Becker 1963; Cressey 1932; Goffman 1963; Merton 1938; Sutherland and Cressy 1992; Thomas and Znaniecki 1996; Whyte 1943) and the Birmingham centre scholars (Hall 1973/2007; Hall and Jefferson 1976; Hebdige 1979; Willis 1977) were fine-tuned by the interpretivist sensitives of SI (Fine and Kleinman 1979; Garfinkel 1967; Goffman 1959; Irwin 1977) to generate a substantial body of work. These studies, as described in this chapter, seek to develop the sociological insights to be found in the life of subculturalists without reifying or over-determining a thing that is by definition resistant to square logic. Any attempt to fully systematize subculture, to incorporate it into the logic of conventional culture, betrays the analyst's failure to grasp the resistant power of its spectacle.

References

Andes, Linda. 1998. "Growing Up Punk: Meaning and Commitment in a Contemporary Youth Subculture." Pp. 212–31 in *Youth Culture: Identity in a Postmodern World*, edited by J. Epstein. Malden: Blackwell.

Barthes, Roland. 1957/1972. *Mythologies* (translated by Annette Lavers). London: Paladin.

Becker, Howard. 1963. *Outsiders: Studies in the Sociology of Deviance*. New York: Free Press.

Bennett, Andy. 2000. *Popular Music and Youth Culture*. New York: St. Martin's.

Bennett, Andy, and Richard A. Peterson, eds. 2004. *Music Scenes: Local, Translocal, and Virtual*. Nashville: Vanderbilt Press.

Bourdieu, Pierre. 1984. *Distinction: A Social Critique of the Judgment of Taste*. Cambridge: Harvard University Press.

The Clash. 1977. "White Riot." *The Clash*. CBS Records.

Clay, Adreana. 2003. "Keepin' It Real: Black Youth, Hip-Hop Culture, and Black Identity." *American Behavioral Scientist* 46(10): 1346–58.

Cohen, Stanley. 1972. *Folk Devils and Moral Panics: The Creation of the Mods and the Rockers*. London: Routledge.

Crass. 1978. "Punk Is Dead." *The Feeding of the 5000*. Crass Records.

Cressey, Paul G. 1932. *The Taxi-Dance Hall*. NYC: Greenwood Press.

Dupont, Tyler. 2019. "Authentic Subcultural Identities and Social Media: American Skateboarders and Instagram." *Deviant Behavior* 41(5):649–64.

Force, William Ryan. 2009. "Consumption Styles and the Fluid Complexity of Punk Authenticity." *Symbolic Interaction* 32(4):289–309.

Force, William Ryan. 2020. "Tattooing in the Age of Instagram." *Deviant Behavior*. https://doi.org/10.1080/01639625.2020.1801176

Fox, Kathryn Joan. 1987. "Real Punks and Pretenders: The Social Organization of a Counterculture." *Journal of Contemporary Ethnography* 16(3):344–70.

Fine, Gary Alan, and Sherryl Kleinman. 1979. "Rethinking Subculture: An Interactionist Analysis." *American Journal of Sociology* 85(1):1–20.

Garfinkel, Harold. 1967. *Studies in Ethnomethodology*. Malden: Blackwell.

Glass, Pepper. 2012. "Doing Scene: Identity, Space, and the Interactional Accomplishment of Youth Culture." *Journal of Contemporary Ethnography* 41(6):695–716.

Goffman, Erving. 1959. *The Presentation of Self in Everyday Life*. New York: Doubleday.

Goffman, Erving. 1963. *Stigma: Notes on the Management of Spoiled Identity*. New York: Simon & Shuster.

Gramsci, Antonio. 1947/1989. *Selections from the Prison Notebooks of Antonio* Gramsci (edited and translated by Quintin Hoare and Geoffrey Nowell Smith). New York: International Publishers.

Haenfler, Ross. 2004. "Rethinking Subcultural Resistance: Core Values of the Straight Edge Movement." *Journal of Contemporary Ethnography* 33(4):406–36.

Haenfler, Ross. 2010. *Goths, Gamers, and Grrrls: Deviance and Youth Subcultures*. New York: Oxford University Press.

Hall, Stuart. 1973/2007. "Encoding and Decoding in the Television Discourse." Pp. 386–98 in *CCCS Selected Working Papers*, Volume 2, edited by Ann Gray et al. London: Routledge.

Hall, Stuart, and Tony Jefferson, eds. 1976. *Resistance Through Rituals: Youth Subcultures in Post-War Britain*. London: Hutchinson.

Hebdige, Dick. 1979. *Subculture: The Meaning of Style*. New York: Routledge.

Hennen, Peter. 2008. *Faeries, Bears, and Leathermen: Men in Community Queering the Masculine*. Chicago: University of Chicago Press.

Hodkinson, Paul 2002. *Goth: Identity, Style and Subculture*. New York: Berg.

Hopper, Columbus B., and Johnny Moore. 1990. "Women In Outlaw Motorcycle Gangs." *Journal of Contemporary Ethnography* 18(4):363–87.

Humphreys, Laud. 1970. *Tearoom Trade: Impersonal Sex in Public Places*. New Brunswick: Transaction Publishers.

Irwin, John. 1977. *Scenes*. Thousand Oaks: SAGE.

Irwin, Katherine. 2003. "Saints and Sinners: Elite Tattoo Collectors and Tattooists as Positive and Negative Deviants." *Sociological Spectrum* 23:27–57.

Kahn-Harris, Keith 2007. *Extreme Metal: Music and Culture on the Edge*. New York: Berg Publishers.

Klein, Alan M. 1993. *Little Big Men: Bodybuilding Subculture and Gender Construction*. Albany: SUNY Press.

Leblanc, Lauraine. 1999. *Pretty in Punk: Girl's Gender Resistance in a Boy's Subculture*. New Brunswick: Rutgers University Press.

Lee, Joonyoung. 2016. *Blowin' Up: Rap Dreams in South Central*. Chicago: The University of Chicago Press.

Levine, Martin. 1998. *Gay Macho: The Life and Death of the Homosexual Clone*. New York: NYU Press.

McRobbie, Angela. 2000. *Feminism and Youth Culture*. London: Macmillan.

Merton, Robert. 1938. "Social Structure and Anomie." *American Sociological Review* 3(5):672–82.

Moore, Ryan, and Michael Roberts. 2009. "Do-It-Yourself Mobilization: Punk and Social Movements." *Mobilization: An International Quarterly* 14(3):273–91.

Muggleton, David. 2000. *Inside Subculture: The Postmodern Meaning of Style*. New York: Berg.

Pavlidis, Adele. 2012. "From Riot Grrrls to Roller Derby? Exploring the Relations Between Gender, Music and Sport." *Leisure Studies* 31(2):165–76.

Rose, Tricia. 1994. *Black Noise: Rap Music and Black Culture in Contemporary America*. Middletown: Wesleyan University Press.

Sanders, Clinton. 1989. *Customizing the Body*. Philadelphia: Temple University Press.

Schippers, Mimi. 2002. *Rockin' Out of the Box: Gender Maneuvering in Alternative Hard Rock*. New Brunswick: Rutgers University Press.

Schmid, Christian Johann. 2021. "Ethnographic Gameness: Theorizing Extra-methodological Fieldwork Practices in a Study of Outlaw Motorcycle Clubs." *Journal of Contemporary Ethnography* 50(1):33–56.

Sutherland, Edwin H., and Donald Cressey. 1992. *Principles of Criminology*, 11th ed. Lanham: AltaMira Press.

Thomas, William I., and Florian Znaniecki. 1996. *The Polish Peasant in Europe and America*. Chicago: University of Illinois Press.

Thompson, Beverly Yuen. 2015. *Covered in Ink*. New York: NYU Press.

Thornton, Sarah. 1995. *Club Cultures: Music, Media, and Subcultural Capital*. Middletown: Wesleyan University Press.

Tokle, Rikke, and Willy Pedersen. 2019. "Cloud Chasers" and "Substitutes": E-cigarettes, Vaping Subcultures and Vaper Identities. *Sociology of Health & Illness* 41(5):917–32.

Weinstein, Deena. 2000. *Heavy Metal: The Music and Its Culture*. Boston: Da Capo Press.

Wellman, Mariah L. 2020. "What It Means To Be a Bodybuilder: Social Media Influencer Labor and the Construction of Identity in the Bodybuilding Subculture." *The Communication Review* 23(4):273–89.

West, Candace, and Sarah Fenstermaker. 1995. "Doing Difference." *Gender & Society* 9(1):8–37.

West, Candace, and Don Zimmerman. 1987. "Doing Gender." *Gender & Society* 1(2):125–51.

Whitmer, Jennifer M. 2019. "You are Your Brand: Self-branding and the Marketization of Self." *Sociology Compass* 13(3). https://doi.org/10.1111/soc4.12662

Whyte, William F. 1943. *Street Corner Society: The Social Structure of an Italian Slum*. Chicago: University of Chicago Press.

Widdicombe, Sue, and Robin Wooffitt. 1990. "'Being' versus 'Doing' Punk: On Achieving Authenticity as a Member." *Journal of Language and Social Psychology* 9(4):257–77.

Wilkins, Amy. 2008. *Wannabes, Goths, and Christians: The Boundaries of Sex, Style, and Status.* Chicago: University of Chicago Press.

Williams, J. Patrick. 2006. "Consumption and Authenticity in Collectible Strategy Games Subculture." Pp. 77–99 in *Gaming as Culture: Social Reality, Identity, and Experience in Fantasy Games*, edited by J. P. Williams, S. Q. Hendricks, and W. K. Winkler. Jefferson: McFarland.

Williams, J. Patrick. 2009. "The Multidimensionality of Resistance in Youth-Subcultures." *The Resistance Studies Magazine* 1:20–33.

Williams, J. Patrick, and Heith Copes. 2005. "'How Edge Are You? Constructing Authentic Identities and Subcultural Boundaries in a Straightedge Internet Forum." *Symbolic Interaction* 28(1):67–89.

Willis, Paul. 1977. *Learning to Labour: How Working Class Youth Get Working Class Jobs.* New York: Columbia University Press.

CHAPTER 13

INTERACTIONIST THEORIES
OF EMOTION
From G. H. Mead to Culture Theory

E. DOYLE MCCARTHY

> ... it is the continuity of thought that systematizes our emotional reactions into attitudes with distinct feeling tones, and sets a certain scope for the individual's passions ... by virtue of our thought and imagination we have not only feelings, but a *life of feeling.*
>
> (Suzanne K. Langer 1953:372)

> Not only ideas, but emotions too, are cultural artifacts ....
>
> (Clifford Geertz 1973:81)

IN two interrelated fields—(1) interactionist social psychology including its early roots in American pragmatism and (2) contemporary cultural sociology—one finds a theory and a set of presuppositions for studying human emotions within the domain of "culture." Summarily stated, *emotions are best grasped as objects of investigation within the domain of cultural forms and meanings.*

In works from sociology's classical period (1890–1930) by the sociologists Max Weber (1949) and Georg Simmel (1950), we find the first arguments of a cultural sociology. These arguments address the relationship of social-scientific concepts and their interpretations (*Verstehen*) to the ideas and interpretations of ordinary social actors in everyday life, what we call today the *cultural meanings that shape people's everyday lives.* These were followed in the mid-twentieth century by Alfred Schutz's body of work in "phenomenological sociology" (1962–66a, b, c). Schutz elaborated the necessary and important relationship of (a) everyday "pre-theoretical" or "quasi" concepts of social actors to (b) those "second-order" concepts and interpretations developed and used by social scientists. Briefly stated, *the concepts and interpretations of scientific categories in emotion studies cannot be imposed from outside; rather, they must be grounded in the ideas and beliefs about emotions that social actors themselves hold about emotions and their (pre-theoretical or everyday) meanings.*

This line of thinking offers fertile suggestions for a theory and method to investigate the everyday beliefs of social actors about emotions and the cultures they draw from in their understanding of what emotions are and what they mean. Everyday beliefs typically include people's ideas about what emotions are and what they signify—whether or not the meanings of emotions, for example, are indicators of "health" or "illness," of "sincerity" or "authenticity," and so forth. In Max Weber's term, such social-scientific concepts must be "meaning-adequate" (*sinnadaequat*; for a commentary on this concept, see Berger and Kellner 1981): that is, these social-scientific concepts must be tied to the cultural meanings that actors in everyday life bring to those situations that are "emotional," for themselves and for others.

Among the many meanings of this "adequacy" is that social actors will recognize themselves and their interpretations in social-scientific studies of the beliefs of everyday social actors. In the final analysis, it is up to scientists to present and to defend their studies in two ways (using emotion studies as an example): first, by engaging with several different but related bodies of work on emotions, thereby enlarging the scope of their own interpretations (using, *inter alia*, histories of emotion, works by emotion scholars on "emotional cultures," and studies of the modern social self—itself a social construct); and second, by linking their work to current studies of the everyday beliefs of social actors, beliefs grounded in these actors' particular lifeworlds (Husserl's *Lebenswelt*).

Today's concept of "culture" in social and psychological science has its roots in arguments like those of Alfred Schutz and, before him, Max Weber and Georg Simmel, about the important place of "culture" in understanding the entire realm of human psychology and experience: how language and symbol both express and shape everything that human beings perceive about themselves, and thus how their lifeworlds are culturally shaped or "constructed" (Husserl (1936/1954; cf. Schutz and Luckmann 1973:Vol. 2).

That said, the enterprise of studying emotions today, as others have pointed out, is an important topic to explore from many disciplinary perspectives in the sciences and humanities (e.g., Weigand 2004a, 2004b; Rorty 1980). David Franks's interdisciplinary work (2003, 2010, 2013; Franks and Turner 2013) is particularly important for studying the interface of interactionism and neuroscience on the topic of emotions.

As I have argued before (McCarthy 1989b, 1994), interdisciplinary studies follow only after each discipline has argued for its own distinct perspective and set of assumptions. On the topic of emotions, a sociologist outlines *how emotions can be examined within an autonomous sociological perspective and set of assumptions*; the one I outline here is drawn from works in interactionism and cultural sociology, since both of these theories contain arguments that offer a thoroughly social view of mind, self, and emotions. Only when this perspective has been elaborated can multiple disciplinary perspectives be brought together as an effective *interdisciplinary project*, one where no single discipline, such as psychology or biology, carries the principal weight and authority of defining what emotions are and how they can be studied.

In the review that follows, I will focus first on the foundational concepts and theories of Meadian social pragmatism, what is now called "social interactionism." G. H. Mead's legacy for the study of interactionist human psychology is well known. I will then update these theories, comparing them to current developments in theories of culture, from social constructionism to contemporary culture theory.

THE CULTURAL ARGUMENTS

Meadian Social Psychology

The work of George Herbert Mead and the Meadian tradition of symbolic or social interactionism may be the most important *theoretical* contribution to social science in America. A centerpiece of his work was its criticism of Western philosophy's strict epistemological division of subjective versus objective domains. Mead relieved mentality and experience of its "subjectivity," anticipating those contemporary movements for whom subject/object terms and methods no longer make sense (for an important example, see Rorty 1979). Mead described his own philosophical task as one of returning to the world its stolen goods (1934:4, 1938:658), of freeing psychology from a concern with mental states by locating mind and its objects "in the world," of explaining immediate experience in terms of objects whose existence is outside of immediate experience. In other words, what we call reality is neither to be found in so-called subjectivity nor is it to be found in objects that stand on their own. For social psychology, in particular, the significance and the originality of Mead's work is found in its emphasis on the primacy of society in the understanding of human psychology and behavior. More precisely, social situations are the preconditions of selves, self-consciousness, mind, thought, and meanings.

Mead was part of the movement known as American Pragmatism, a movement that embodied one of the earliest attempts to describe the domain of "subjectivity" in new terms. The Pragmatists included the jurist Oliver Wendell Holmes; the philosopher C. S. Peirce; the philosopher, educator, and psychologist John Dewey; and the philosopher and psychologist William James (Menand 2001). As part of this movement, the social philosopher George Herbert Mead (1934) developed theories of the "social genesis" of mind, self, and consciousness, ideas in important respects that are compatible with the sociology of knowledge (McCarthy 1993, 1996). Both pragmatism and the sociology of knowledge give primacy to the universe of shared social meanings in the understanding of all things psychical and experiential.

Investigations of subjectivity and consciousness, Mead argued, must be made the concern of both the social and biological sciences because all psychical phenomena—everything experienced—*is neither principally individual nor subjective*, as we normally use these words, as belonging to or possessed by a single autonomous individual. For

Mead, everything conceptualized and spoken involves language and a social or common "universe of discourse." These assumptions brought Mead to investigate the social foundations of thinking and consciousness. In Mead's words (1910/1964:102–3), we are

> beholden to social science to present and analyze the social group with its objects, its interrelations, its selves, as a precondition of our reflective and self-consciousness.

Arguably, the most important implication of Mead's theory of the social genesis of mind and self is that *mind and meaning originate in the social act*; mind unfolds as the social process—involving shared words, attitudes, and gestures—enters into the experiences of individuals (Mead 1922/1964:247; 1934:133, 329, 332; 1938:372). In the 1927 course Social Psychology (Mead 1934), we read of the importance of language (a system of shared symbols): "Out of language"—out of the symbolic universes that form and fashion mind—"emerges the field of mind" (Mead 1934:133). It is a social emergent (Mead 1934:132–34, 329–34). As the metaphor of the field suggests, mind has its existence in and through what he called universals—the languages, images, meanings held in common by this or that social universe or human community (1938:388–92). Mead also argued that the objects of the human mind are social: social objects are anything that humans can indicate to themselves (Mead 1934:Section 18).

Mead's concept of the "social object" (Blumer 1966; McCarthy 1989a) offers to social science one of his most fertile theories for studying topics that are psychological, whether identity, an attitude, a type of mental illness, or emotion(s). For each of these exist, like mind, in a field, meaning that each is inseparable from social relations and the forms of language and speech within which they are communicated (Mead 1917/1982:163, 184–85, 1932:169–70). Mead's theory of the "social genesis of mind" looks at everything produced by human beings as *social objects*; these exist relative to a social world. For their meaning exists objectively within the fields of social relations and language.

The prominent mid-twentieth-century American sociologist C. Wright Mills (1939/1963: 424–26) advanced Mead's social psychology claiming that a term connecting mind and other collective processes was *reflection*. Drawing from Mead's work, Mills argued that reflection is a process in which beliefs are doubted, discarded, reformulated. In short, as people reflect, they enter into their own activities, break them up, and attend to one thing over another. Reflective intelligence always implies language and is essential for the development of mind. Reflection is conversational. By acquiring the categories of language, we acquire the structured "ways" of a group and the "value-implications" of those ways (Mills 1939/1963:433).

To recapitulate, social pragmatism has advanced foundational arguments for the study of the everyday beliefs of social actors, arguing for new ways to conceptualize human subjectivity, thereby giving greater salience to subjective experience itself, arguing that all subjective experience is socially grounded in systems or structures of language and culture. *Most important here is the argument that "subjectivity"—the collection of a person's perceptions and experiences—is best understood as deeply "cultural," that is, inescapably related to shared ideas, attitudes, meanings, beliefs, and language itself.*

In other words, subjectivity is more than we think it is; for it has the quality of something "objective," meaning it is something we can scrutinize as integral to "culture" itself. As something collective, *subjectivity's formation and development take place in society in interaction with others.* Accordingly, language categories and cultural meanings are no longer viewed "subjectively," as if standing on their own within the domain of individual experience. They share, in Richard Harland's (1987:68) words, "a kind of objectivity which is not the objectivity of things, [they share] a kind of idea which is not the idea of a subjective mind".

Social Constructionism

In contemporary emotion studies, many today work within the cultural approach called "social constructionism," a movement in social science that began in the mid-1960s and continues today (Galbin 2014; Gergen 1985, 1991, 2009; Gergen and Davis 1985; Harré 1986). Briefly stated, social constructionism is rooted in the fields of social or symbolic interactionism and phenomenology and, particularly, in the influential statement of Berger and Luckmann's *The Social Construction of Reality* published in 1966. The argument advanced here was an early semiotic one: namely, the social construction of meaning. *Meaning(s) is something communicated through a society's or group's signifying systems (languages, knowledges, icons, symbols, etc.); culture and knowledge are the means through which a people establishes the reality of things and themselves.*

Despite the relatively wide range of perspectives and working assumptions that the term *social constructionism* encompasses, early social constructionists typically took their lead from both the Berger and Luckmann text (1966) and, later, a diversity of studies from the 1990s in the humanities and social sciences that focused on the interpretation of culture and its operation (e.g., Alexander 1990; Denzin 1992; Munch and Smelser 1992).

In emotion studies, constructionism's emphasis, one that varied considerably from study to study (Thoits 1989), has been on the cognitive and cultural aspects of emotion, an emphasis shared with those identified with the early social constructionist movement in several disciplines: for example, in psychology (Averill 1980, 1982, 1986; Gergen 1985; Gergen and Davis 1985; Harré 1986), in cultural anthropology (Lutz 1988; Shweder and LeVine 1984), and in philosophy (De Sousa 1987; Rorty 1980; Solomon 1984). Works on emotions by self-identified interactionists of the same period included those of Norman Denzin (1989/2017), Harvey Farberman (1989), and David Franks and Doyle McCarthy (1989).

In emotion studies, constructionist arguments may be summarized this way: *emotions are best grasped as objects of investigation within the domain of cultural forms and meanings; emotions cannot be divorced from a whole host of cultural and social phenomena.* For example, emotion scientists have used the analogies of language and speech to frame emotions. Accordingly, emotions can operate as signifiers or as "speech acts" (Austin 1962); or emotions are examined using what Hildred Geertz (1959) famously called "vocabularies of emotion," pointing to the culturally specific categories used in people's everyday lives. Other related frameworks include studying (a) the various rules governing expression and feeling (rules called "emotional culture" or "emotionology") or (b) the idioms (both "everyday" idioms and theoretical or scientific ones) within which emotions are experienced and expressed, or studying (c) the cultural patterns and interactional processes within which they emerge and are sustained (Gordon 1990). Emotions have also been described as (d) cognitive and evaluative phenomena, as "language forms" (Perinbanayagam 1991, 2011, 2016), for they *communicate* and signal things about self and society in the larger sense of these terms or in the immediate situational sense of, for example, Goffman's (1983) face-to-face interactions.

Other examples can be taken from early constructionist works in US social psychology, such as Gordon's (1981:562; see also 1989) "socially emergent properties of emotion that transcend psychological or physiological explanation". These emergent dimensions *are explicable only in relation to other social phenomena.* Accordingly, emotions combine features of body, gesture, and cultural meaning. In a range of leading studies, emotions are seen as inextricably social or cultural, precisely because, as Gordon first argued, they are emergent properties of social relations and sociocultural processes (Harré 1991; Harré and Parrott 1986; Illouz 2007, 2008; Williams 2001:607). Statements like the ones cited here gave us early theories of emotion as preeminently cultural. These statements were compatible with the early and classic statement of Clifford Geertz (in the opening epigraph to this chapter): "not only ideas, but emotions too, are cultural artifacts" (1973:81).

Despite this cultural emphasis, others took the lead in emotion studies from the prominent sociologist Arlie Hochschild, whose well-known early work (e.g. Hochschild 1983:201–22), for example, is explicitly critical of any and all cognitive reductionisms, which would subsume emotion under other categories of human experience, including cognition (see an early discussion of this by social psychologists Gergen and Gergen 1988:43).

Constructionist approaches to emotion also drew (unwittingly or not) from classical pragmatist theories, like those discussed here, emphasizing *action, the act*, or *social action* or *practice* (Blumer 1966; Mead 1938), thereby rejecting a view of emotions, for example, *as* physiological states or as *natural objects*, arguing that emotions or emotional processes *are best construed as acts or as kinds of symbolic actions, or as social performances.* In the works of the prominent social psychologist James Averill (1986:100), emotions are "cultural performances" or "socially constituted syndromes," response elements that involve both cognitive and physical processes. Averill intentionally employed these terms to provide alternative views of emotion as principally subjective, bodily, experiential, or irrational phenomena.

To summarize, debates on the role of "culture" in the study of human psychology, including the emotions, have been varied, as this brief and selective review has shown. And despite their claims of offering theories unique or distinctive to the social sciences and humanities, the constructionists, like the early pragmatists, shared an interest in framing studies of subjectivity or the social self as *social emergents within acts*; more specifically, emotions were seen as social emergents from "situations" or *social situations*, a concept central to interactionism from G. H. Mead (1934:200–9), W. I. Thomas (1923), and W. I. Thomas and Dorothy Thomas (1928:571–72), to Howard Becker (1963:chapter 1; Plummer 2003), Herbert Blumer (1969/1986, 2004), and Erving Goffman, who referred to situations in a number of ways, including that of a "situated activity system" (Goffman 1961/2013:preface).

The *situation* (the concept) typically referred to the social context of interactants who "negotiate" the meaning(s) of situations; it is also the site where social actors confront "society" and/or its structures. As these ideas developed over time in sociology, the focus of the situation—becoming more explicit and systematic in its understanding of "meaning" and its emergence in interaction—opened up social and psychological studies to a variety of culture theories, however undertheorized or implicit the concept of culture was.

For example, in an early paper by Carr (1945) on "Situational Sociology," published when sociology was still defining its terms and its methods, situations are defined as "emergent patterns or configurations" that included culture traits, meanings, and relations (1945:138). Decades later, in Perinbanayagam's widely cited paper "Definition of the Situation" (1974), "culture" has become more explicitly integral to the "situation." For the situation, as is the case for all social facts, is something *communicated* (1974:537) in a field of interaction where social meanings are displayed, enacted, and exchanged by those present.

As this brief summary has shown, interactionist sociology, with its roots in early pragmatism, was—over a period of decades—working to maintain its pragmatist premises (about the genesis of the mind and self, or the field of mind) while developing cultural theories of meaning and meaning-making and their emergence in various forms of interaction. In this process, the concept of the *situation* proved to be a particularly rich one for updating this decades-old history of interactionist theories. This can be seen in more recent works by leading symbolic interactionists like R. S. Perinbanayagam (1985:xiii–xv; 2011, 2018), Adele Clark (2005), and Donileen Loseke (2019), important works that drew directly from different contemporary theories of "culture," theories like semiotics, structuralism and poststructuralism, dramatism, and narrative studies. In short, tracing a central concept in social theory over time—like the social situation—can show us how varied and multiple are the influences on our discipline's theories and methods as they develop (Diehl and McFarland 2010). This also shows us how theories like social constructionism that represented such a major change in sociology's foundational ideas will, in time, find a place in other bodies of work in sociology like interactionism. Put differently, a discipline or subdiscipline (like interactionism) is always changing its leading theories—changes that occur through our "conversations" with the ideas and knowledges operating both in our societies (Loseke 2019:chapter 6) and in our scholarly communities. Furthermore, it seems from the arguments I made here about changes in the meaning of the *situation* that sometimes it is not an easy matter to distinguish one body of work from another (pragmatism, interactionism, constructionism). However, it seems a worthwhile effort to try to make these distinctions, since, in doing so, we are trying to understand changes in our discipline's leading ideas and the assumptions on which they are drawn. In fact, this chapter can be read as one such attempt to scrutinize how ideas about emotions have undergone changes over time, marked by shifting ideas in the social sciences and humanities about "culture" and its operations and their relevance for emotion studies today.

Contemporary Culture Theory

Today, leading ideas on the importance of a cultural approach to social science have come from sociologist Jeffrey C. Alexander's "strong program in cultural sociology," distinguished by a rethinking of what culture is, how it is construed, and how its operations are studied (Alexander and Smith 2004; Alexander 2017). These cultural sociologists share with their contemporaries a view of "culture" that has been influenced by several disciplines inside and outside of social science: literary studies, studies and theories of drama and performance, linguistics, cultural anthropology, structuralism, and semiotics. These newer ventures have moved many of us in social science (including interactionism) to examine the conceptual implications of using theories like structuralism and semiotics or newer studies of drama and performance. In fact, these fields are principally responsible for giving greater attention to social studies of the many *forms of signifying* in social life and interaction—such as the signifying features of social institutions in texts, images, and ideologies. What this means is that institutions, for example, are not just there to be scrutinized for how they operate and for whom; institutions also operate as signs, signifying and transmitting social meanings. So the Boy Scouts of America or the NAACP serve as *cultural representations about abstract principles* like civic virtue and decorum, boyhood, race, equity, and so forth.

To summarize, today's social scientific theory of culture has been undergoing some of the changes described here—changes that signify changes in the foundational assumptions and presuppositions that have distinguished social science since its classics were written in the era 1890–1930 (Hughes 1958). Both to generalize and to state this in formulaic terms: yesterday's "attitude of analysis" (Ricoeur 1986:255–56) was causal and explanatory, and its privileged model was natural science. Today's attitude and its methods of research are increasingly interpretive and conversational, seeking to enlarge the universe of human discourse, "an aim to which a semiotic concept of culture is peculiarly well adapted" (Geertz 1973:14, 1983). *The semiotic study of culture is directed toward the study of symbolic and signifying systems through which a society, group, or community is communicated and reproduced.*

Accordingly, when culture is viewed *as a semiotic process* (and this returns us to the 1964 Berger and Luckmann text and its argument), *culture is no longer seen solely or principally as a product or effect of "social structure" or social organization or material life.* (For another early formulation of these ideas, see Sahlins 1976:206–7.) Rather, all social realities are *themselves* embedded with signs and social meanings that call out for interpretations.

Culture and Emotion Today

Using these newer theories to study emotions is to reason this way: *emotions are cultural objects that have meaning within a system of relations. They "unfold in a world already symbolized" and are constructed as what they are "by the concept" we have of them* (to borrow and reapply Marshall Sahlins's terms, 1976:123). Or, as "discursive objects," emotions emerge within a discourse, an organization of written and spoken forms, areas of language use identified by particular historical groups and institutions—the discourses of professions like psychology, psychiatry, and medicine, but also academic and theoretical discourses such as philosophy and literary studies, or meta-theoretical discourses such as liberal humanism. The "truths" about emotions, the self, and so forth are contained within the operations of these discourses and are, in turn, experienced by the subjects who live them as truths, socially constructed truths.

Culture theory and Jeffrey Alexander's "strong program" have redirected studies from emotions themselves—that marked early works in the sociology of emotions—to the *discursive operations that constitute our "emotional lives" and to the cultural systems and practices through which emotions are known, controlled, released, cultivated, and worked on.* The emphasis on psychological phenomena as *forms of discourse* has already directed some of the early work in the social study of emotions, during the 1980s and 1990s, in both social psychology and the social sciences (Franks and McCarthy 1989; Perinbanayagam 1989, 2011; Shotter and Gergen 1989). But studies of "emotionology" (Stearns and Stearns 1986), of "ethnopsychology" (Lutz 1988), and of "emotional culture(s)" (Gordon 1989; McCarthy 2017:32–40; Thoits 2004), terms identified with both pioneering and contemporary works in our field, are being given even greater emphasis and elaboration in emotion studies today. To cite one current example, Sarah Ahmed's (2004) work on emotions, bodies, and politics studies emotions within the frame, *inter alia*, of culture theory: *emotions are conceptualized as cultural practices, not psychological states.*

As I have argued here, these ideas have their roots in early pragmatist theories of Mead and others where the human mind was best grasped as an *activity or practice*: the activities of mind are one facet of an active, developing relationship between organisms and their environments, rather than between knowing subjects and known objects (Mead 1938; Menand 2001; Rorty 1979).

Subjectivity and Culture

Four Propositions

Returning to a central theme in this discussion—*the importance of people's everyday beliefs about emotions*—how do classical and contemporary theories of culture integrate *the study of everyday beliefs into today's theories of culture and its operations?* The following is offered as a summary of four propositions that, as I have argued, are highly compatible with classical and contemporary arguments in interactionist sociology.

1   Culture theory has given greater emphasis to the study of everyday beliefs of social actors, arguing that the entire domain of "subjectivity" is not (as commonly understood) devoid of social and cultural influence; rather, subjectivity itself is "socially constructed" (Berger 1966/1970; Berger and Luckmann 1966:part 3; Gergen 2009; Mahoney and Yngvesson 1992; Reed 2011:chapter 1,VI). The implications of this understanding for interactionists is vitally important, since we belong to a tradition whose emphasis has often been on the relatively autonomous "self-reflexive subject" (Blumer 1969/1986; Hewitt 2002; Williams 2019:606), a subject without cultural moorings.
2   Culture theory has enlarged and changed the idea of "subjectivity" from something isolated and unique and purely individual to something "objective" and observable. This is because subjectivity's continual formation and development take place in society in interaction with others.
3   Culture theory provides a set of arguments about how ordinary social actors understand feelings and emotions, their own and the emotions of others. Its emphasis has been on particular social or group cultures—*emotional cultures*—that we draw from in everyday life studies (Gordon 1989; McCarthy 2017; Solomon 1984; Stearns 1994, 2004).
4   Culture theory—from Max Weber and Alfred Schutz to Michel de Certeau (1984)— has argued that *everyday life in the modern world* provides a special lens on the larger culture of the modern and late modern world, a theme of the now-classic work by Henri Lefebvre (1971/1984) and taken up today in the work of Ben Highmore (2002). Everyday life studies today closely overlap with the field of cultural studies. For both emphasize the importance of the taken-for-granted (Schutz) and habit (the deeply ingrained things we do and feel), such as in the influential work of Pierre Bourdieu beginning with *Distinction* (1979/1984). His concepts of *habitus* and *practice* can be used as ways to study the world of the quotidian and to study how deeply and habitually the structures of modernity and capitalism are lived out in our lives and practices. For our purposes here, everyday-life studies have as their central assumption the importance of theorizing *culture-as-habitual practice*.

These four propositions admittedly point to some important and unresolved tensions of culture theory and its view of subjectivity, including the emotions. For it opens up the problem intensified by modern and late modern culture itself—of the role of human "agency" in the construction and production of culture. In short, an emphasis on the operations of "culture" seems to lead to a diminishment in the role of the free human agent as a producer of culture. This problem is one addressed in several commentaries on culture and agency (Alexander 1988; Emirbeyer and Mische 1998; Mahoney and Yngvesson 1992; Reed 2011:chapters 1 and 2; Reddy 1997). In an effort to address the tensions of culture theory, especially its emphasis on subjectivity *versus* culture, I offer the following tentative and analytic resolution, one that is compatible with contemporary culture theory itself. In this, I use the study of emotions as an example.

The study of everyday beliefs about emotions can teach emotion scientists how and what ordinary people think about emotions, thereby giving greater value and emphasis to the study of people's knowledges and experiences. In doing so, emotion scientists are also engaged in a firsthand examination of the languages, beliefs, and ideas that people draw from in their own understandings of and in their own responses to what emotions are, what emotions mean, and how they operate in our own everyday life experiences.

In this sense, everyday beliefs open up to me, the investigator, the beliefs and other aspects of a common culture that shape these so-called subjective and personal understandings of emotion. To do this is also to open up a conversation with others about *what people's emotions signify or mean to them*, bringing culture and meaning back into the topic of interpreting people's everyday beliefs. Following this logic then, *subjective understandings can both disclose the cultural sources of people's understandings of emotions as well as show us how these understandings are used in people's own responses and actions ("agency") that follow upon these cultural understandings.* For emotions are deeply cultural (socially constructed) signs, telling us things about ourselves and others. Emotions are emergents from our lives with others in the world.

But emotions are even more than this, for they also reveal the ways in which social actors confront the power of their own agency in the face of the constraints of culture. Put differently, emotions today are also vital resources for selves engaged in the world. As a modern history of emotions has shown us (McCarthy 2002, 2017; Reddy 2001; Stearns 2018; Taylor 1989), *emotions today* have a special reality and vitality for selves in the modern and contemporary world. In fact, early works in the social study of emotions also described the special nature of emotions for modern and contemporary selves (Barbalet 1998; Illouz 2007, 2008; Lupton 1998; Pribram and Harding 2002; Williams 2001).

Another related theme concerns the distinctly modern task of identity; related to this is the theme of *making up one's identity* (Baumeister 1986; Calhoun 1994:chapter 1). To extrapolate these arguments: to be a self today involves persons in the pursuit and acquisition of self-knowledge, a knowledge not for its own sake but for the purpose of controlling and for "fashioning" one's identity, for making up oneself, for articulating one's own presence in the world. "Self-fashioning," as Stephen Greenblatt (1980) calls it, is not an invention of modernity; there were selves and "a sense that they could be fashioned" before this era. But what *was* born in the early modern era of the sixteenth century was both an "increased self-consciousness about the fashioning of human identity as a manipulable, artful process" and a newfound sense of autonomy: "the power to impose a shape upon oneself is an aspect of the more general power to control identity—that of others at least as often as one's own" (Greenblatt 1980:1; cf. Elias 1939/2000:85–109).

So what I mean to say here is that *for us today* (not for everyone at every historical moment), "human agency" operates along with our emotions as special tools and skills, even as forms of "cultural capital" as we navigate our worlds and ourselves. Emotions as we experience them today are social objects that we use, assert, and enlist as our helpers in our exchanges with self and others, just as emotions are instruments for changing who we are and what we do. Emotions are "articulatory and evident" (Perinbanayagam 1989:73). Emotions today show us our own freedom (agency) to act on ourselves and on our lifeworlds, to *navigate* (Reddy 2001) with some degrees of freedom the cultural worlds in which we are embedded. In fact, the very use of *theories of the social construction of emotions* opens up to us as investigators the *constructed character of emotions* and of all social things (Gergen 1985, 2009): emotions are not ready-made states as much as they are social objects made and remade by ourselves as social actors. I speak collectively here (i.e., everything human is produced by us humans), but as I speak the language of "social constructionism," I also speak of each of us making our way in the world and using emotions to navigate its dilemmas, constraints, and ambiguities. We are the agents and the makers of everything we deem "constructions," so we can remake them too.

A case in point: in the classroom and in my own research, I have heard others describe to me how important emotions are to them. They have even told me that emotions are the "most real" and "natural" and "authentic" things about them as individuals. As I tell my interlocutors, "These ideas of yours are *beliefs*!" Then we go on to argue about the status of emotions as this-or-that.

Beliefs like these have opened up to me-as-investigator the study of contemporary "emotional cultures," a term in current emotion studies discussed here. These inquiries, then, of everyday beliefs have led me-the-investigator directly to other sources (histories of emotion, studies of people's digital practices, studies of contemporary emotional cultures, to name some of these sources) to enlarge my understanding of what my interlocutors tell me about emotions and the various meanings they give to their emotions and to others' emotions. These academic pursuits are not, then, purely academic. For I pursue them so that I can broaden my own understanding of the beliefs of my interlocutors and myself and, in that way, understand more adequately their beliefs as well as my own beliefs about emotions and the emotional culture(s) we both draw from as we make our way through everyday life. For example, I have heard my interlocutors tell me about how they reflect upon, use, and change their feelings and emotions in their everyday-life encounters. This also gives me some entrance into the domain of "agency" or the ways that my subjects attempt to maneuver and even to resolve the many dilemmas and choices that they confront in their everyday lives where we see, among other things, our mundane attempts "to rescue the everyday from conformity" and to make it our own (Highmore 2002:174).

Concluding Thoughts: Culture and Subjectivity

I conclude by returning to this chapter's central theme: *the importance of grounding cultural studies in people's everyday-life experiences*. I have used this proposition to study the *emotional cultures* that we draw from in everyday-life studies. For *personal statements of people's beliefs are* today viewed as vital to what culture is and how it operates. Studies of statements like these can serve as markers of some of the central elements of today's "structure of feeling," as Raymond Williams (1961) referred to it—or, what amounts to the same thing, the term "emotional culture(s)," which I use here.

In each of the accounts that follow here, we read of the salience and vitality of emotions for the self today, emotions as vital and signifying experiences, as the keys for finding and unlocking our authenticity. These five examples point to only some of the elements of today's emotional culture: including the salience of people's emotional experiences, people's pursuits of emotions in public with others, the joy and pleasure at our own and/or others' spontaneous and intense emotional expressions, the standard of emotional intensity in those we admire and follow (in sports, entertainment, politics), the belief that authenticity is found in our spontaneous emotional experiences and those of others (Vannini and Williams 2009; Williams 2019).

1. A report of a participant at the Women's March on Washington, January 19, 2019:

   "I came two years ago. It's definitely smaller, but the spirit is very much alive," said an educator from Salem, Oregon. She added: "The experience I had two years ago was indescribable. I wanted to feel that way again"

   (Wines and Stockman 2019).

2. **A story that "went viral" as an online source of enjoyment and entertainment for those present and those of us at-a-distance:** a nine-year-old boy, at the conclusion of a classical concert, loudly exclaims, "Wow!" The incident was reported in a Boston musical society's newsletter, which stated:

   "As the solemn and harmonic music of Mozart's Masonic Funeral Music came to an end, there was silence in Boston's Symphony Hall. And then, from somewhere in the audience, a young child's voice pierced the silence: 'Wow!'" (*Boston, Handel and Haydn Society* 2019).

   According to one of the witnesses reported here in the newsletter, "The awe in his [the boy child's] voice made the whole audience and ensemble erupt into laughter and applause, which the orchestra's CEO David Snead described as "one of the most wonderful moments I've experienced in the concert hall."

3. *Soccer Madness* **by Janet Lever (1983/1995) was an early and prescient account of the emotional intensity of sports competitions, documenting the intensity of Brazilian soccer games for fans. "Fastforward" to 2019 to the US Women's World Cup competition.** In a full-page color ad by Nike, Inc., in *The New York Times* (July 2019), the team's captain, Megan (Maggie) Rapinoe, is shown with an open-mouth scream while holding tightly to her sister players; the photo caption, in large letters and a red background. reads: "I believe we will win."

   The caption, paraphrased here, reads: "I believe we will be champions and keep winning . . . we are the best female soccer team and the best soccer team in the world . . . we will keep fighting and make history and change it forever." In print at the bottom of the ad, we read: **Nike Swoosh** [and] **Just do it!** [Nike's current online slogan].

4. An account of the need to mourn publicly after a mass killing:

A woman interviewed on the CNN news said to the anchor Poppy Harlow, "All day, families, friends, and community people have come to honor the victims . . . Families need to come here to grieve and to process this tragic event" (Field Notes, December 13, 2015).

5. **A grief counselor writes online about the need for people to grieve publicly**: A grief counselor, Dave Kessler (an interpreter of the meanings of memorializing for participants), writes this (Pawlowski 2019, emphasis in original):

. . . memorials become very important. We want our *grief* to be seen. We want people to know what has been lost. When we go to these community gatherings, it helps families know we get what has happened, we see the enormity of their loss. Gathering at a candlelight vigil or a funeral—it's how we let them know their loss matters to us too.

These cases also suggest to me something central to today's emotional culture: that *personal experiences*—recounted ("narrated") in words and gestures—are a primary element of emotional culture today and, perhaps, of all of US culture today. I refer to the central value of *experience itself* as the mark of what matters today in one's personal life, in friendships, intimacy, schooling, politics, work, and so forth (Pine and Gilmore 1998; Wadhere 2016). As designers and business gurus already tell us, ours is an "experience-culture" (Thomas 2010). In the realm of emotions, intense experiences are what matters, and what we ordinary social actors pursue or want to pursue, whether at a march, a sports event, a memorial or, vicariously, at a concert.

I close by pointing out what I have underscored in this chapter. Namely, these statements each points us to the location of "culture" in the domain of subjective beliefs about emotions and feelings and their expression. Our challenge as investigators is to offer interpretations of the meanings of these statements, as argued in this introduction, so that the subjects who speak to us will recognize themselves in our scientific treatises in emotion science. If we meet this challenge, we will have brought culture and interaction closer together.

References

Ahmed, Sarah. 2004. *The Cultural Politics of Emotion*, 2nd ed. New York and London: Routledge.

Alexander, Jeffrey C. 1988. *Action and Its Environments: Toward a New Synthesis*. New York: Columbia University Press.

Alexander, Jeffrey C. 1990. "Analytic Debates: Understanding the Relative Autonomy of Culture." Pp. 1–27 in *Culture and Society*, edited by J. C. Alexander and S. Seidman. New York: Cambridge.

Alexander, Jeffrey C. 2017. *The Drama of Social Life*. Cambridge, UK: Polity Press.

Alexander, Jeffrey C., and Philip Smith. 2004. "The Strong Program in Cultural Sociology: Elements in a Structural Hermeneutics." Pp. 11–26 in Jeffrey C. Alexander, *The Meanings of Social Life*. New York: Oxford University Press.

Austin, J. L. 1962. *How to Do Things with Words*, 2nd ed. Cambridge: Harvard University Press.

Averill, James R. 1980. "A Constructionist View of Emotion." Pp. 305–39 in *Theories of Emotion*, edited by R. Plutchik and H. Kellerman New York: Blackwell.

Averill, James R. 1982. *Anger and Aggression*. New York: Springer-Verlag.

Averill, James R. 1986. "The Acquisition of Emotions During Adulthood." Pp. 98–119 in *The Social Construction of Emotions*, edited by R. Harré. New York: Basil Blackwell.

Barbalet, J. M. 1998. *Emotion, Social Theory, and Structure*. Cambridge, UK: Cambridge University Press.

Baumeister, Roy F. 1986. *Identity: Cultural Change and the Struggle for Self*. New York: Oxford University Press.

Becker, Howard S. 1963. *Outsiders: Studies in the Sociology of Deviance*. New York: Free Press Glencoe.

Berger, Peter L. 1966/1970. "Identity as a Problem in the Sociology of Knowledge." Pp. 373–84 in *The Sociology of Knowledge: A Reader*, edited by J. E. Curtis and J. W. Petras. New York: Praeger.

Berger, Peter L., and Hansfried Kellner. 1981. *Sociology Reinterpreted: An Essay on Method and Vocation*. New York: Penguin Books.

Berger, Peter L., and Thomas Luckmann. 1966. *The Social Construction of Reality: A Treatise in the Sociology of Knowledge*. Garden City, NY: Doubleday/Anchor Books.

Blumer, Herbert. 1966. "Sociological Implications of the Thought of George Herbert Mead." *American Journal of Sociology* 71(5):535–44.

Blumer, Herbert. 1969/1986. *Symbolic Interactionism: Perspective and Method*. Berkeley: University of California Press.

Blumer, Herbert. 2004. *George Herbert Mead and Human Conduct*, edited with introduction by Thomas J. Morrione. Walnut Creek, CA: AltaMira Press.

Boston Handel and Haydn Society. 2019. *Boston Alive* (May 9). https://www.masslive.com/boston/2019/05/child-yells-wow-at-end-of-moving-mozart-concert-in-symphony-hall-and-now-the-orchestra-wants-to-know-who-he-is.html

Bourdieu, Pierre. 1979/1984. *Distinction: A Social Critique of the Judgment of Taste*. English Translated by R. Nice. Cambridge, MA: Harvard University Press.

Calhoun, Craig. 1994. *Social Theory and the Politics of Identity*. Cambridge, MA: Blackwell.

Carr, Lowell J. 1945. "Situational Sociology." *American Journal of Sociology* 51(2):136–41.

Clark, Adele E. 2005. *Situational Analysis: Grounded Theory After the Postmodern Turn*. Thousand Oaks, CA: SAGE.

de Certeau, Michel. 1984. *The Practice of Everyday Life*. Translated by S. Randall. Berkeley: University of California Press.

De Sousa, Ronald. 1987. *The Rationality of Emotion*. Cambridge, MA: MIT Press.

Denzin, Norman K. 1989/2017. *On Understanding Emotion*. New York and London: Routledge.

Denzin, Norman K. 1992. *Symbolic Interaction and Cultural Studies*. Cambridge, MA: Blackwell.

Diehl, David, and Daniel McFarland. 2010. "Toward a Historical Sociology of Social Situations." *American Journal of Sociology* 115(6):1713–52.

Elias, Norbert. 1939/2000. *The Civilizing Process: Sociogenic and Psychogenetic Investigations*. Revised edition, edited by E. Dunning, J. Goudsblom, S. Mennell. Translated by E. Jephcott, with some notes and corrections by the author. Oxford: Blackwell.

Emirbeyer, Mustafa, and Ann Mische. 1998. "What Is Agency?" *American Journal of Sociology* 103 (4):962–1023.

Farberman, Harvey A. 1989. "The Sociology of Emotions: Feedback on the Cognitive and A-Structural Biases of Symbolic Interaction." Pp. 271–88 in *The Sociology of Emotions: Original Essays and Research Papers*, edited by D. D. Franks and E. D. McCarthy. Greenwich, CT: JAI Press.

Franks, David D. 2003. "Mutual Interests, Different Lenses: Current Neuroscience and Symbolic Interaction." *Symbolic Interaction* 26(4):613–30.

Franks, David D. 2010. *Neurosociology: The Nexus Between Neuroscience and Social Psychology*. New York: Springer Press.

Franks, David D. 2013. "Introduction." Pp. 1–5 in *The Handbook of Neurosociology*, edited by David D. Franks and Jonathan H. Turner. New York: Springer Publishers.

Franks, David D., and E. Doyle McCarthy, eds. 1989. *The Sociology of Emotions: Original Essays and Research Papers*. Greenwich, CT: JAI Press.

Franks, David D., and Jonathan H. Turner, eds. 2013. *The Handbook of Neurosociology*. New York: Springer Publishers.

Galbin, Alexandra. 2014. "An Introduction to Social Constructionism." *Social Research Reports* 26(November):82–92.

Geertz, Clifford. 1973. *The Interpretation of Cultures*. New York: Basic Books.

Geertz, Clifford. 1983. *Local Knowledge*. New York: Basic Books.

Geertz, Hildred. 1959. "The Vocabulary of Emotion." *Psychiatry* 22:225–37.

Gergen, Kenneth J. 1985. "The Social Constructionist Movement in Modern Psychology." *The American Psychologist* 40(3):266–75.

Gergen, Kenneth J. 1991. *The Saturated Self*. New York: Basic Books.

Gergen, Kenneth J. 2009. *An Invitation to Social Constructionism*. London: SAGE.

Gergen, Kenneth J., and K. E. Davis, eds. 1985. *The Social Construction of the Person*. New York: Springer.

Gergen, Kenneth J., and Mary M. Gergen. 1988. "Narrative and Self as Relationship." *Advances in Experimental Social Psychology* 21:17–56.

Goffman, Erving. 1961/2013. *Encounters*. Mansfield Centre, CT: Martino Publishing.

Goffman, Erving. 1983. "The Interaction Order." American Sociological Association, 1982 Presidential Address. *American Sociological* Review 48 (1): 1–17.

Gordon, Steven L. 1981. "The Sociology of Sentiments and Emotions." Pp. 261–78 in *Social Psychology*, edited by M. Rosenberg and R. H. Turner. New York: Basic Books.

Gordon, Steven L. 1989. "Institutional and Impulsive Orientations in Selectively Appropriating Emotions to Self." Pp. 115–135 in *The Sociology of Emotions*, edited by D. D. Franks and E. D. McCarthy. Greenwich, CT: JAI Press.

Gordon, Steven L. 1990. "Social Structural Effects on Emotions." Pp. 145–79 in *Research Agendas in the Sociology of Emotions*, edited by T. D. Kemper. Albany, NY: SUNY Press.

Greenblatt, Stephen. 1980. *Renaissance Self-Fashioning. From More to Shakespeare*. Chicago: University of Chicago Press.

Harland, Richard. 1987. *Superstructuralism: The Philosophy of Structuralism and Post-structuralism*. London: Methuen.

Harré, Rom, ed. 1986. *The Social Construction of Emotions*. London: Basil Blackwell.

Harré, Rom. 1991. *Physical Being: A Theory for a Corporeal Psychology*. Oxford: Basil Blackwell.

Harré, Rom, and W. Gerrod Parrott, eds. 1986. *The Emotions: Social, Cultural, and Biological Dimension*. Thousand Oaks, CA: SAGE Publications.

Hewitt, John. 2002. *Self and Society: A Symbolic Interactionist Social Psychology*. 9th ed. Boston: Allyn and Bacon.

Highmore, Ben. 2002. *Everyday Life and Cultural Theory*. New York and London: Routledge.

Hochschild. Arlie R. 1983. *The Managed Heart: The Commercialization of Human Feeling*. Berkeley: University of California Press.

Hughes, H. Stuart. 1958. *Consciousness and Society: The Reorientation of Social Thought, 1890–1930*. New York: Knopf.

Husserl, Edmund. 1936/1954. *The Crisis of European Sciences and Transcendental Phenomenology*, vol. 6, edited by W. Biemel. The Hague: Martinus Nijhoff Publishers.

Illouz, Eva. 2007. *Cold Intimacies: The Making of Emotional Capitalism*. Cambridge, UK: Polity.

Illouz, Eva. 2008. *Saving the Modern Soul: Therapy, Emotions, and the Culture of Self-Help*. Berkeley: University of California Press.

Langer, Suzanne K. 1953. *Feeling and Form*. New York: Charles Scribner's Sons.

Lefebvre, Henri 1971/1984. *Everyday Life in the Modern World*. Translated by S. Rabinovich. New Brunswick, NJ: Transaction.

Lever, Janet. 1983/1995. *Soccer Madness: Brazil's Passion for the World's Most Popular Sport*. Long Grove, IL: Waveland Press.

Loseke, Donileen R. 2019. *Narrative Productions of Meanings*. Lanham, MD: Lexington Books.

Lupton, Deborah. 1998. *The Emotional Self*. London: SAGE.

Lutz, Catherine A. 1988. *Unnatural Emotions*. Chicago: University of Chicago Press.

Mahoney, Maureen A., and Barbara Yngvesson 1992. "The Construction of Subjectivity and the Paradox of Resistance." *Signs: Journal of Women in Culture & Society* 18(1):44–73.

McCarthy, E. Doyle. 1989a. "The Interactionist Theory of Mind." *Studies in Symbolic Interaction* 10:79–86.

McCarthy, E. Doyle. 1989b. "Emotions Are Social Things: An Essay in the Sociology of Emotions." Pp. 51–72 in *The Sociology of Emotions*, edited by D. D. Franks and E. D. McCarthy. Greenwich, CT: JAI Press.

McCarthy, E. Doyle. 1993. "George Herbert Mead and *Wissenssoziologie*: A Reexamination." Pp. 97–115 in *Search of Community: Essay in Memory of Werner Stark*, edited by E. Leonard, H. Strasser, and K. Westhues. New York: Fordham University Press.

McCarthy, E. Doyle. 1994. "The Social Construction of Emotions: New Directions from Culture Theory." *Social Perspectives on Emotions: A Research Annual* 2:267–79.

McCarthy, E. Doyle. 1996. *Knowledge as Culture: The New Sociology of Knowledge*. New York and London: Routledge.

McCarthy, E. Doyle. 2002. "Emotions: Senses of the Modern Self." *Österreichische Zeitschrift Für Soziologie* 27(2):30–49.

McCarthy, E. Doyle. 2017. *Emotional Lives: Dramas of Identity in an Age of Mass Media*. Cambridge, UK: Cambridge University Press.

Mead, George Herbert. 1910/1964. "What Social Objects Must Psychology Presuppose?" Pp. 105–13 in *Selected Writings: George Herbert Mead*, edited by A. J. Reck. New York: Bobbs-Merrill Co. Inc.

Mead, George Herbert. 1917/1982. "Consciousness, Mind, the Self, and Scientific Objects." Pp. 176–96 in *The Individual and the Social Self*, edited by David L. Miller. Chicago: University of Chicago Press.

Mead, George Herbert. 1922/1964. "A Behavioristic Account of the Significant Symbol." Pp. 240–47 in *Selected Writings: George Herbert Mead*, edited by A. J. Reck. New York: Bobbs-Merrill Co. Inc.

Mead, George Herbert. 1932. *The Philosophy of the Present*. Lasalle, IL: Open Court Publishing Company.

Mead, George Herbert Mead. 1934. *Mind, Self, and Soci*ety. Chicago: University of Chicago Press.

Mead, George Herbert. 1938. *The Philosophy of the Act*. Chicago: University of Chicago Press.

Menand, Louis. 2001. *The Metaphysical Club*. New York: Ferrar Straus and Giroux.

Mills, C. Wright 1939/1963. "Language, Logic, and Culture." Pp. 423–38 in *Power, Politics and People*, edited by Irving Louis Horowitz. New York: Oxford.

Munch, Richard, and Neil J. Smelser, eds. 1992. *Theory of Culture*. Berkeley: University of California Press.

The New York Times. 2019. July 8: page B6. Full-page advertisement by Nike, Inc.

Pawlowski, A. 2019. "How to Deal with Grief, Pain and Anxiety after the Mass Shootings." https://www.today.com/health/how-deal-grief-pain-anxiety-after-mass-shootings-t160209

Perinbanayagam, Robert S. 1974. "The Definition of the Situation: An Analysis of the Ethnomethodological and Dramaturgical View." *The Sociological Quarterly* 15 (4):521–41.

Perinbanayagam, Robert S. 1985. *Signifying Acts*. Carbondale: Southern Illinois University Press.

Perinbanayagam, Robert S. 1989. "Signifying Emotions." Pp. 73–92 in *The Sociology of Emotions: Original Essays and Research Papers*, edited by D. D. Franks and E. D. McCarthy. Greenwich, CT: JAI Press.

Perinbanayagam, Robert S. 1991. *Discursive Acts*. New York: Aldine de Gruyter.

Perinbanayagam, Robert S. 2011. "Emotions in Discourse." Pp. 167–97 in R. S. Perinbanayagam, *Discursive Acts*. New Brunswick, NJ: Transaction.

Perinbanayagam, Robert S. 2016. *The Rhetoric of Emotions*. New Brunswick, NJ: Transaction.

Perinbanayagam, Robert S. 2018. "Theaters of Emotions." Pp. 91–126 in R.S. Perinbanayagam, *The Rhetoric of Signs*. Bloomington, IN: Archway Publishing.

Pine II, B. Joseph, and James H. Gilmore. 1998. "Welcome to the Experience Economy." *Harvard Business Review* (July–August). https://hbr.org/1998/07/welcome-to-the-experience-economy

Plummer, Ken 2003. "Continuity and Change in Howard S. Becker's Work: An Interview with Howard S. Becker." *Sociological Perspectives* 46(1):21–39.

Pribram, E. Deidre, and Jennifer Harding. 2002. "The Power of Feeling: Locating Emotions in Culture." *Faculty Works: Communications*, vol. 8. https://digitalcommons.molloy.edu/com_fac

Reddy, William M. 1997. "Against Constructionism: The Historical Ethnography of Emotions." *Cultural Anthropology* 38:327–51.

Reddy, William M. 2001. *The Navigation of Feeling*. New York: Cambridge University Press.

Reed, Isaac Ariail. 2011. *Interpretation and Social Knowledge: On the Use of Theory in the Human Sciences*. Chicago: University of Chicago Press.

Ricoeur, Paul. 1986. *Lectures on Ideology and Utopia*. New York: Columbia University Press.

Rorty, A. O., ed. 1980. *Explaining Emotions*. Berkeley: University of California Press.

Rorty, Richard. 1979. *Philosophy and the Mirror of Nature*. Princeton, NJ: Princeton University Press.

Sahlins, Marshall. 1976. *Culture and Practical Reason*. Chicago: University of Chicago Press.

Schutz, Alfred. 1962–1966a. *Collected Papers*, vol. 1: *The Problem of Social Reality*, edited by M. A. Natanson and H. L. van Breda. Dordrecht, NL: Martinus Nijhoff Publishers.

Schutz, Alfred. 1962–1966b. *Collected Papers*, vol. 2: *Studies in Social Theory*, edited by A Brodersen. Dordrecht, NL: Martinus Nijhoff Publishers.

Schutz, Alfred. 1962–1966c. *Collected Papers*, vol. 3: *Studies in Phenomenological Philosophy*, edited by I. Schutz and A. Gurwitsch. Dordrecht, NL: Martinus Nijhoff Publishers.

Schutz, Alfred, and Thomas Luckmann. 1973. *The Structures of the Life-World* (*Strukturen der Lebenswelt*), vols. 1–2. Translated by R. M. Zaner and H. T. Engelhardt, Jr. Evanston, IL: Northwestern University Press.

Shotter, J., and K. Gergen, eds. 1989. *Texts of Identity*. Newbury Park, CA: SAGE.

Shweder, Richard A., and Robert A. LeVine, eds. 1984. *Culture Theory: Essays on Mind, Self, and Emotion*. New York: Cambridge University Press.

Simmel, Georg. 1950. *The Sociology of Georg Simmel*. Translated by K. H. Wolff. Glencoe, IL: Free Press.

Solomon, Robert C. 1984. "Getting Angry." Pp. 238–56 in *Culture Theory: Essays on Mind, Self, and Emotion*, edited by Richard A. Shweder and Robert A. LeVine. London: Cambridge University Press.

Stearns, Peter N. 1994. *American Cool: Constructing a Twentieth Century Emotional Style*. New York: NYU Press.

Stearns, Peter N. 2004. *Anxious Parents: A History of Modern Childrearing*. New York: NYU Press.

Stearns, Peter N. 2018. "An Emotional America." *The American Interest* (January 8). https://www.the-american-interest.com/2018/01/08/an-emotional-america/

Stearns, Carol Z., and Peter N. Stearns. 1986. *Anger: The Struggle for Emotional Control in American History*. Chicago, IL: The University of Chicago Press.

Taylor, Charles. 1989. *Sources of the Self: The Making of the Modern Identity*. Cambridge, MA: Harvard University Press.

Thoits, Peggy. 1989. "The Sociology of Emotions." *Annual Review in Sociology* 15:317–42.

Thoits, Peggy. 2004. "Emotion Norms, Emotion Work, and Social Order." Pp. 359–78 in *Feelings and Emotions*, edited by A. S. Manstead, N. Freda, and A. Fischer. New York: Cambridge University Press.

Thomas, Cynthia. 2010. "The Importance of Designing an Experience Culture." GAP online article 596. https://uxmag.com/articles/the-importance-of-designing-an-experience-culture

Thomas, W. I. 1923. *The Unadjusted Girl*. Boston: Little-Brown.

Thomas, W. I., and D. S. Thomas. 1928. *The Child in America*. New York: Knopf.

Vannini, Phillip, and J. Patrick Williams, eds. 2009. *Authenticity in Culture, Self, and Society*. London: Ashgate Publishing.

Wadhere, Mark. 2016. "The Information Age Is Over: Welcome to the Age of Experience." https://techcrunch.com/2016/05/09/the-information-age-is-over-welcome-to-the-experience-age/

Weber, Max. 1949. *Max Weber on the Methodology of the Social Sciences*. Translated and edited by E. A. Shils and H. A. Finch. Glencoe, IL: Free Press.

Weigand, Edda. 2004a. "Emotions: The Simple and the Complex." Pp. 3–29 in *Emotion in Dialogic Interaction: Advances in the Complex*, edited by E. Weigand. Amsterdam: John Benjamins.

Weigand, Edda, ed. 2004b. *Emotion in Dialogic Interaction: Advances in the Complex.* Amsterdam: John Benjamins.

Williams, J. Patrick. 2019. "Perceiving and Enacting Authentic Identities." Pp. 604–20 (chapter 32) in *The Oxford Handbook of Cognitive Sociology*, edited by W. H. Brekhus and G. Ignatow. New York: Oxford University Press.

Williams, Raymond. 1961. *The Long Revolution.* New York: Harper Torchbooks.

Williams, Simon. 2001. *Emotion and Social Theory.* London: Routledge.

Wines, Michael, and Farah Stockman. 2019. "Smaller Crowds Turn out for Third Annual Women's March." *The New York Times* (January 19). https://www.nytimes.com/2019/01/19/us/womens-march-2019.html

CHAPTER 14

SHOPPING, IDENTITY, AND PLACE

ENRICO CAMPO

Introduction

THE importance and centrality of commodity production and consumption processes is difficult to underestimate today. The (almost) universal extension of capitalist production and distribution processes has spread the "culture of consumption" to virtually every corner of the globe. Consumption is a fundamental research topic for sociology precisely because of its symbolic function. Yet, it has been a neglected object of study for a long while, and consumer studies have always been a multidisciplinary undertaking. This chapter will address the relationship between shopping malls and the processes of identity construction. In the next section, some initial analyses of consumer culture will be briefly discussed, while in the following section those related to shopping malls will be reviewed. In the fourth section, the way in which these same theoretical perspectives understand the processes of the constitution of subjectivity in consumer spaces will be analyzed. Finally, in the fifth section, perspectives that refer to symbolic interactionism more directly will be discussed as well as those that put the processes of identity negotiation and the practice of shopping as an ordinary, contextual, and situated activity at the center of analysis.

Consumption as an Object of Investigation

Although studies of consumption have grown enormously over the last thirty years, for a long time the world of consumption was neglected as an object of study by sociological analysis. There were numerous reasons for this lack of interest (Zukin and Smith Maguire 2004), but generally the autonomy of the consumer world was substantially denied for a long period due to its interpretation as the simple and automatic consequence of the development of capitalist production processes. Though some "classical," yet relatively marginal, authors like Georg Simmel [1858–1918] (1971), Thorstein Veblen [1857–1929] (1994), and Werner Sombart [1863–1941] (1967) assigned certain importance to it, it is really only since the 1970s and 1980s that consumption has become a legitimate focus of research in the social sciences. During this period, several studies were published that would later be recognized as canonical to the field (Bourdieu 1984; Douglas and Isherwood 1979; Appadurai 1986). This newfound interest in consumption was stimulated by the publication of a series of sociohistorical investigations into the origins of mass consumption, along with its typical sites and new codes of advertising (Ewen 1976; R. H. Williams 1982).

As a result, consumption began to be seen not simply as a counterbalance to the production of goods, but as a world with its own autonomy whose importance could not be overlooked. For example, consumer desires were interpreted as a simple consequence of the supply of goods in the market for a long time; instead, many subsequent studies have shown that the relationship between the world of supply and demand is much more articulated than was previously assumed and that consumer desires can play a decisive role in the development of modern economic and political processes (Schivelbusch 1992).

In this new context, which is essentially multidisciplinary, what emerges in the foreground is the intrinsically symbolic nature of both the processes of consumption and those involved in the construction of subjectivity. Since the 1980s and 1990s, therefore, the modern culture of consumption has been returned to the bedrock of the long-term historical processes of Western individualization and industrialization. It was particularly in the 1990s that consumption came to be used as a favored area of reference for characterizing the changes that occurred during the processes of construction of postmodern subjectivity. Consumption lent itself well to an interpretation of individuality as a self-reflexive path that was also expressed through choices of consumption, which in turn influenced identity in a circular fashion. The latter then was no longer seen as deriving solely from the work environment or from certain characteristics ascribed at birth, but as the result of a set of consumption choices that were the expression of one or more lifestyles (Featherstone 1995; Chaney 1996; Slater 1997; Bauman 2000). Such changes have often been associated with the spread of "postmodern consumption culture" and tend to re-propose a purely hedonist and individualist vision of the consumer who, at the price of their own safety, can freely choose through consumption and performance the self he or she prefers.

It was in this context that researchers began to take an interest in the spaces of consumption, no longer viewed as neutral backgrounds in which the distribution of goods took place, but rather as physical and symbolic spaces that better express the culture of consumption than others. The vast majority of the research investigated a specific form of space, the shopping mall—for reasons both practical (the ease of studying a single place that collected more than one consumption space) and theoretical (it represented the consumer space par excellence of contemporary Western societies).

The interpretation of these spaces was thus strongly influenced by the way in which the more general culture of consumption was understood, hence it followed the same interpretative oscillations. In the first phase, they were primarily ignored by researchers, while they were later read as the phenomenal expression of the almost universal diffusion of capitalist commodification and alienation. One of the first examples of this approach, often referred to as "apocalyptic," was represented by Jean Baudrillard's [1929–2007] *The Consumer Society* (1970). The book represented what was then an innovative attempt to criticize the capitalist system starting from the world of consumption (and not the world of production): the object of consumption was seen to be the expression of a system of signs and was therefore subject to semiotic analysis. The great merit of Baudrillard's work consists in its clarification that the meaning of the single consumer object depends on the broader ("global, arbitrary, coherent") symbolic system of which it is a part: a system that, in Baudrillard's view, "substitutes [the] social order of values and classification" (Baudrillard 1998:79).

Although his primary interest was in this "immaterial" system of signs, the French philosopher was also interested in the spaces of consumption, not only as spaces where the act of consumption takes place, but as structures that condition the practice of consumption and its interpretation. In Baudrillard's view (1998:29), shopping centers propose themselves as total spaces that, through the attraction of leisure, are based on the construction of a self-sufficient environment and thus structure time, family relationships, and identities so that they are consistent with the cultural form of capitalism (Lunt and Livingstone 1992).

This type of analysis that sees in the spread of shopping malls the expansion of the seductive logic of consumption to all spheres of life has then returned cyclically in consumer literature (Bauman 1993; Goss 1993). The films of George Andrew Romero [1940–2017], in which even zombies continue to frequent shopping malls as if driven by an urge to consume that extends beyond life, are an expression of the same cultural climate that sees these spaces as "islands of the living dead" (Ritzer 2003; Muzzio and Muzzio-Rentas 2008).

These interpretations are essentially founded on an overly deterministic role of objects and spaces with respect to the meaning attributed to consumption. As a result, the more general social relations tend to disappear, and the capacity of social actors to assign meaning to things or events is overwhelmed. One of the most extreme and well-known formulations of this reduction of shopping malls and their users to their consumptive dimension is probably that of the French anthropologist Marc Augé: shopping malls are deemed to be non-places, spaces that foster neither relationships nor identities nor a sense of the past (Augé 1995). The concept of non-place—defined in opposition to place—emphasizes the dissemination of spaces that are characterized by the non-possession of traits of identity, relationship, and history (Augé 1995). Non-places are thus spaces of circulation, consumption, and communication, conceived as ephemeral and passing. According to Augé, the user's basic need for non-places is freedom, and people go there to remain anonymous: the only possible identity seems to be its absence, as "identity is reduced solely to that of tourist, customer, passenger, visitor, or—more flattering—guest" (Gottschalk and Salvaggio 2015:7).

THE FALL OF THE PUBLIC MAN: SHOPPING MALLS AS DREAMLANDS OF EXCLUSION?

The debate of the 1980s and 1990s was driven by a strong concern about the progressive privatization of traditional public spaces and about the diffusion—first in the United States and then in the rest of the world—of apparently uniform spaces with the same characteristics, regardless of the specificity of the context (Kowinski 1985; Agier 2003; Sennett 1976). The concept of non-place clearly responds to this concern and is to be placed within this cultural climate. More generally, however, the studies discussed in the previous section were not based on research carried out on specific individual shopping malls; their meaning and significance were instead deduced based on their author's own personal interpretation of consumer culture. The research discussed below began to empirically study shopping malls primarily in the United States.

Precisely because it was believed that they were replacing traditional public spaces, shopping malls were also thought to be assuming the symbolic functions traditionally associated with them. They thus responded to an urban need, a desire for public space, but were stripped of elements perceived as being unpleasant. Several studies have highlighted the ideological character of these structures, which were oriented toward transmitting an ideal, purified image of the urban community (Berman 1986; M. Gottdiener 1993; Mark Gottdiener 2001; Staeheli and Mitchell 2006). Shopping centers acted as a sort of "surrogate for the city," from which central elements were taken (squares, avenues, benches, fountains, etc.).

The diffusion of shopping centers is therefore considered part of the universalization of the American cultural model: their design incorporates the values that typically represent the culture of American consumerism. An apparent freedom of access and movement is combined with the construction of spaces where abundance reigns and where every desire can be realized (Shields 1992). As Kenneth Jackson famously stated,

> The Egyptians have Pyramids, the Chinese have a great wall, the British have immaculate lawns, the Germans have castles, the Dutch have canals, the Italians have grand churches. And Americans have shopping centers.
>
> (Jackson 1996:1111)

This expansive logic is accompanied by a further totalizing trend, highlighted by Margaret Crawford (1992:4): shopping malls want to enclose the whole world within themselves: "Yet this implausible, seemingly random, collection of images has been assembled with an explicit purpose: to support the mall's claim to contain the entire world within its walls."

Crawford's article "The World in a Shopping Mall" is based on an investigation of the intentions of mall builders and designers. According to her, the mall model, beyond the differences in individual shopping malls, was first refined and then gradually and systematically replicated in all contexts. The only possible variation concerns the type of clientele for which the mall was designed, and therefore the distinction between malls essentially follows that of social class (Cohen 1996). Even if the possible variations are endless, "whatever form the system adopts, the message conveyed is the same—a repeated imperative to consume" (Crawford 1992:11).

According to this interpretation, the consumer experiences a sort of split between his or her desires continuously and artificially stimulated by store managers and the limits of his or her purchasing power. The consumer experience they tend to promote is similar to the oneiric experience. Based on the enlightening considerations of Walter Benjamin [1892–1940] (1999; Buck-Morss 1989), Jon Goss believes that developers and designers manipulate shoppers' behavior through the construction of a "dreamland space" (Goss 1993, 1999). The daily work of store managers consists of maintaining this dream-like atmosphere, both through the careful arrangement of spaces and by the removal of unwanted elements that clash with this scenario and may not be functional to consumption: the removal of conflict and more generally of the "different" in the broad sense of the term (i.e., of anyone from a class or race that does not correspond with the manager's notion of an ideal consumer).

From the point of view of these authors, the only possible identity for the user engaged in the different recreational activities permitted by these spaces is that of the "seduced consumer." Other approaches, politically opposed to the studies previously mentioned, instead argued for the strong emancipatory force represented by shopping malls and were based on a very different idea from that of the "seduced consumer," that is, the "sovereign consumer." Although the choices of consumption are founded on a very complex and stratified social context, the idea of a sovereign consumer who autonomously exercises his or her own will acts somewhat as a normative framework (Sassatelli 2007:154).

More generally, this theme recalls the long and lively historical debate on the emancipatory function of the department stores of the nineteenth and early twentieth centuries, the first spaces of access to the bourgeois public sphere for women (Leach 1984; Benson 1986; Remus 2019). Other research, very close to cultural studies, saw in contemporary shopping malls a place to carry out activity that implied self-realization and emancipation from family and gender relations experienced as oppressive. Starting from the consideration that subjects were not necessarily obliged to accept the norms contemplated by management, these scholars deduced that malls could become spaces, for particular groups like women and unemployed youth, where it was possible "to trick 'the system'" (Fiske 1989:3).

Both these perspectives, whether critical or more enthusiastic, seem to take on a moralistic posture with respect to shopping centers and the consumer society they represent. Rather than understanding consumer society in a sociological sense, they tend to interpret it as the highest expression of either the vices or virtues of our age (Sassatelli 2007). The shopping center is seen as the symbolic place of this society, which represents in an extreme form the total alienation of contemporary people or, from the opposite perspective, the possibility for their full emancipation. Beyond disagreement on the emancipatory or manipulative nature of shopping centers, these models share some assumptions whose limits later became evident:

- The results of research carried out on individual shopping centers (often the largest and most spectacular) were implicitly or explicitly generalized to the entire United States or even the entire world. It was often implicitly assumed that the contextual specificities were completely marginal or irrelevant.
- Researchers focused almost exclusively on consumption as a recreational activity. Moreover, in the critical approaches especially, there was a reliance on an overly sharp contrast between induced and original needs. The main risk consists not only in underestimating the complexity of each act of consumption, but above all in failing to recognize other forms of exploitation (such as, for example, the division of domestic tasks by gender and shopping as unpaid labor upon which the family sphere is maintained/sustained (DeVault 1991)).
- A collective and undifferentiated subject is often assumed, as if all the differences in identity and social position collapse and give way to that of "consumer" or as if they could all be reduced to a question of lifestyle. The identity that is constructed in shopping centers often coincides with that proposed by advertising discourse and the management of shopping centers.
- From a methodological point of view, the research limited to marketing managers runs the risk of assuming their point of view is effective and concrete: it was in fact the same managers who identified American society as the standard normative model toward which other societies must comply on their path to progress and modernization. (Applbaum 2004)
- These critical perspectives, moreover, tend to propose a dichotomous vision between private and public space, which conceives of the former as a space whose only function is the creation of profit through the satisfaction of consumer desires, and the latter as a (mythological) place in which one can experience an authentic sense of community belonging. This is a clearly nostalgic approach that underestimates the constant mixing of the two types of space. (Bottomley 2007)

The most recent studies on consumption and the approaches that have been most influenced by symbolic interactionism have made an essential contribution to bringing these limits to the fore and in attempting to overcome them. Their interest in the practice and procedural nature of acting and in identity formation could only lead them to reject these assumptions.

The Contextual and Negotiated Practice of Shopping

Although the approaches mentioned in the previous section recognize the centrality of the consumer world, they tend to automatically lead its meaning back to the sphere of marketing and distribution. From this point of view, although the symbolic importance of consumption is recognized, its interpretation therefore refers, in the final instance, to production rather than the meaning attributed to it by consumers (Sassatelli 2007). Already in the 1980s, but especially during the 1990s, dissatisfaction with these conceptual approaches became increasingly evident, and research began to be published that questioned their foundations. By the end of the 1990s, it was clear that models based on a linear and opposite logic were not useful for understanding the poles of production and consumption, as they came to be viewed instead as "continually interacting processes in a 'cultural circuit,' where products both reflect and transform consumers' behavior" (Zukin and Smith Maguire 2004:178).

Symbolic interactionism, which was relatively marginal in consumer studies until then, played a significant role within this interdisciplinary movement that ended up catalyzing this change in perspective. Herbert Blumer [1900–1987] (1969b; 1969a) was one of the first postwar sociologists to take an interest in phenomena related to consumption, to critically resume Simmel's theory on fashion, and to invite sociologists to explore these themes in depth. More generally, many of the authors whose work can be traced back to the "constellation" of symbolic interactionism, the classics in particular but also contemporary authors, discussed the complex relationship among space, the designed environment, and processes of self-construction and self-expression. Simmel, William James [1842–1910] (1890), along with George Herbert Mead [1863–1931] (1932) and Erving Goffman [1922–1982] (1963), were interested in how the physical world interacts with the self, not as a neutral background, but as a constituent part of the self: "We attribute symbolic meanings to the space through the way we occupy and appropriate it, but space also guides how we interact with each other by physically or symbolically signaling the expected norms of our actions associated with it." (Kato 2011:244; Milligan 1998). That is, more generally, "the self's relation with the physical world is a social relation" (McCarthy 1984:118).

Interactionists look at space in a particular way: they are less interested in how space expresses and incorporates certain traits of the social structure and the inequality of power, and instead focus on how space is a "medium" through which people develop their identities (Kato 2011). Thus, from their point of view, perspectives that attribute a strong meaning to design and management risk falling into a particular form of determinism. Ultimately, for symbolic interaction theory, it is the people who frequent and interact in certain spaces that attribute meaning to them. Consumer spaces have no meaning in themselves, nor can their meaning be automatically identified with that of their managers or designers. Their meaning depends on complex negotiation processes that are subject to user interpretation and can go beyond the intentions of their designers: symbolic interactionists would see designed forms "as suggesting possibilities, channeling communication, and providing impressions of acceptable activities, networks, norms and values" (Smith and Bugni 2006:129). Social relationships require physical settings to be carried out in, and at the same time, spaces incorporate certain norms that allow, encourage, or inhibit some types of interactions rather than others (Måseide and Grøttland 2015).

Therefore, in order to understand how consumer spaces influence such practices, it is necessary to put the actor's point of view and their concrete daily practices at the center of research. Of course, this conceptual passage also implied a change in the prevailing methodological approach. Since the objective was to understand how ordinary people relate to one another in these spaces, greater reliance was made on the tradition of qualitative methods: ethnographic observation, focus groups, and in-depth interviews allowed for greater in situ investigation of identity construction through the daily visits to these spaces (which became less and less interesting for their extraordinary character and more and more ordinary). It was thus possible to question the model of seduction-manipulation through consumption and show that subjects—even those of a "marginal" nature—were able to negotiate, at least in part, the meanings proposed to them by the "culture of consumption." Instead, the research discussed in the section above adopted an abstract and speculative approach, or showed little or no interest in the concrete practice of shopping as an everyday activity and its meaning from the actors' point of view. The meaning of shopping was thus deduced from that which was planned by the managers and the advertising system. Researchers who instead tried to put the actor's point of view at the center of their studies demonstrated them to be an active part in the process of construction and negotiation of proposed meanings (Douglas and Isherwood 1979; De Certeau 1980). This step involved a change in the general interpretation of the act of consumption, in the practice of shopping, and of the consumer themselves: he or she is not only, and not to such a degree, the individual who carries out a purely hedonistic and individualistic action but also, and above all, a practice incorporated and based upon the wider social context, of work and family, which can be carried out both in groups and alone, and which can have a recreational function or can instead fall within those tasks of domestic work, which has the capacity of being experienced pleasantly as much as it has of being experienced as constricting or obligatory.

It is therefore no coincidence that a meaningful contribution to this discussion came from feminist perspectives: also "because it had long been assumed (rightly or wrongly) that most 'consumers' were women" (Campbell 1995:97; Nava 1987; Miller 1995). In fact, one of the first empirical works, though not widely circulated, that laid the foundations for a work plan that was at least partially followed by others was Maeghan Morris's article "Things to Do with Shopping Centres." Her starting point was exactly that of analyzing individual shopping centers with respect to the daily practices of habitual users (particularly female users), rather than dedicating herself to deciphering the universal meaning of the "shopping center" category:

> I am more interested in a study that differentiates particular shopping centers. Differentiating shopping centres means, among other things, looking at how particular centres produce and maintain what the architectural writer Neville Quarry calls [. . .] 'a unique sense of place' – in other terms, a myth of identity. I see this as a 'feminist' project because it requires the predication of a more complex and localized affective relation to shopping spaces.
>
> (M. Morris 1988:194–95)

The image of shopping malls and the consumer experience that results from her study is rather distinct from the idea of places of consumption as dreamlands and places of constant seduction. In this way, Morris attempts to question the rhetoric portraying shopping malls as places of seduction as well as the "vision of shopping town as Eden" (1988:203). These are much more ambivalent places where such rhetoric also coexists with the experience of consumption as something unpleasant or as an activity that is part of domestic reproduction and, if possible, to be performed in a hurry/as quickly as possible (Stillerman and Salcedo 2012).

One of the first examples of research explicitly inspired by interactionism is that of Robert Prus and Lorne Dawson, who studied the different types of experiences related to shopping. According to them, shopping can be experienced as a recreational activity or as a laborious activity based on the perception of social obligations associated with it and thus based on how the self is incorporated within the specific shopping situation: "Notions of recreational and laborious activity are centrally linked to people's sense of self." Therefore, shopping tends to be seen as pleasant when, for example, "people approach these as 'games' or adventures in which the self is an active player," while conversely "shopping tends to be viewed as a more laborious activity when one experiences a confused, constrained, and irrelevant sense of self in shopping situations" (Prus and Dawson 1991:160).

The attention paid to regular visitors and to shopping as a practice of daily life— rather than as something extra-ordinary and exceptional—also served to question their supposed placelessness. To the contrary, precisely because they are ordinary, it is necessary to understand them as places, or spaces that have "been imbued with meaning through personal, group, and cultural processes." It is above all the average shopping malls, rather than the spectacular mega malls, that lend themselves to becoming significant places for their regular visitors. It is precisely frequent attendance itself that makes the development of place attachment to a particular shopping mall possible—that is, a "positive, affective bond people form with particular places where they feel comfortable and safe and desire to maintain their connection" (Cross 2015:494). As a consequence, it is quite possible that people also develop a place identity with respect to these places, which then becomes "a component of personal identity and the process through which people come to describe themselves as belonging to a particular place and adopting identifications which reflect places" (Cross 2015:494; Manzo and Devine-Wright 2014). It follows that a single space can correspond to multiple social places, in relation to different social groups that appropriate them symbolically (Gieryn 2000).

The title of one of the first studies to propose research on the practice of shopping in relation to specific malls and that significantly influenced the subsequent debate, *Shopping, Place, Identity* (Miller et al. 1998), refers to the inseparable connection between the practice and the processes of attribution of meaning to space. The researchers tried to investigate the mutual co-construction of the sense of place and identity of the consumers; the latter viewed not as preexisting fact, but as something constructed in interaction with others and with the material world:

> . . . consumers are involved in a creative reworking of gender, ethnicity, class and place. Whether shopping on their own or with others, they are making significant social investments in a relatively narrow set of family and domestic relationships as well as making economic choices about the utility of particular goods.
>
> (Miller et al. 1998, p. 185)

However, not all shopping malls respond to the same logic, and in some cases, such as those malls aimed at the working class in particular, do not share the ambition of representing a seductive or spectacular place. Moreover, the authors also invite us to look at these spaces from the point of view of the shop workers themselves—whose role was often overlooked. A notable exception to this was the study carried out by Christine L. Williams, *Inside Toyland: Working, Shopping, and Social Inequality*. At the center of her research are the "rituals of toy shopping" as an active and creative process of symbolic interaction, though the author is mainly interested in the interaction between clerks and customers in order to highlight how, even in an apparently playful context like a toy store, social inequalities are reproduced. She analyzes both the formal rules that govern interactions between customers and clerks, as well as the informal ones: the "ropes" "developed by workers to protect their dignity and self-respect" (C. L. Williams 2006:96–97). These informal rules are more flexible and are "shaped but not determined by the corporate cultures," while at the same time, "they more explicitly took into account the matrix of domination" (C. L. Williams 2006:105; Collins 2000):

> Actual interactions on the shopping floor strayed from these ideal rituals. Both clerks and customers drew on elaborate stereotypes in crafting their shopping practices, reflecting the existence of a "matrix of domination" that sorted individuals on the basis of race, gender, and class. Because of the matrix, white customers basically got whatever they wanted, and many developed a sense of shopping entitlement.
>
> (C. L. Williams 2006:133)

When these formal and informal rules are not followed, the interaction encounters difficulties and possibly produces conflict. Similarly, the very ability to repair these interactions depends on how the interactors interpret and negotiate the social inequalities that exist between worker and client.

Generally speaking, the progressive affirmation of a more multifaceted conception of the practice of consumption implied a consequent change in the basic questions asked, which were no longer oriented toward understanding the general category of the "shopping mall" as much as they were toward investigating the social context in which single shopping malls are placed and with which they interact. No act of consumption has a universal and unequivocal meaning; it has a determined sense only within a specific culture and at a specific historical and biographical moment. For example, Yuki Kato (2011) showed how the spatial metaphor of the "bubble" was used by middle-class teenagers of an American suburb as a symbolic boundary. The mall certainly played a central role in making this metaphor meaningful, but only within the broader context in which it was embedded. Beyond the moral posture of that which the idea of the "bubble" represents, the metaphor provided them "a concrete basis on which they could establish their identities" (Kato 2011:260).

The need of investigating the concrete contexts in which the situated practice of shopping takes place has become ever more pressing. As a result, a broad movement has developed to question the automatic universalization of results from studies conducted in the West, and in light of this, a lot of research has been directly conducted on the impact of specific shopping malls in some cities of the "Global South." Rather than assuming that globalization automatically implies the universal standardized adoption of Western models, it is important to bear in mind that the latter has always coexisted with heterogeneity and diversity (Appadurai 1996). The same is true for consumption models: Western models are not necessarily emulated (Wilk 1998). Rather than postulate the universal effects caused by the global spread of shopping malls, it is better to study their effects in each individual context. For example, with respect to the opposition between public and private spaces, it may well be that malls offer greater possibilities for encounters than traditional public spaces do, especially those of a romantic nature (Abaza 2001; Erkip 2003, 2005; Yan 2000). In this sense, and more generally, shopping malls can offer a space where traditional gender norms are, at least partially and temporarily, suspended and where men and women are treated equally (Yan 2000). Moreover, in contexts where domestic spaces are cramped, it is possible that some consumer spaces can be used to carry out activities that, in an overcrowded home environment, would be difficult. Ethnographic studies have shown, for example, that in Beijing and Singapore consumer spaces have been used to do homework (Beng-Huat 2000). Additionally, in certain contexts like Cape Town and Mumbai, designers and managers may have some difficulty in isolating shopping malls from the urban context in which they are situated (Cook 2008; Houssay-Holzschuch and Teppo 2009). Despite this, the effects of the segregation of urban space are even more evident, and the spread of shopping malls contributes to creating a highly stratified urban environment consistent with the imperatives of neoliberal capitalism (Abaza 2001).

Many Latin American cities have faced similar dynamics, also due to the fact that in some cases investments are concentrated above all on consumption rather than production. As a result, in some cities shopping malls have spread almost contemporaneously with those in the United States, albeit at a very different pace (Müller 1998; Bromley 1998). A rather widespread, though questionable, position is that represented by Joel Stillerman and Rodrigo Salcedo. Their research, conducted in two Chilean shopping centers, suggests that "consumers use malls as performance stages to enact meaningful relationships and engage in playful interactions" (Stillerman and Salcedo 2012:310). Building on Goffman's analysis, they claim that, from the users' point of view, the fact that the shopping center is privately owned or not is irrelevant for most of their activities: the rules of interaction and routines are identical to those from other public settings, as are the emotional and relational ties that are "imported" into the mall.

Very similar observations had already been made for other Latin American national shopping malls (Mexican, Colombian, Brazilian), whose success was attributed to the widespread climate of insecurity that has apparently helped to increase the attractiveness of monitored shopping malls as places for meeting and socializing. These researchers focused their attention on how mall-goers appropriate it symbolically into their daily lives and argued that, in recent years, these new public spaces have taken on an even greater symbolic importance than traditional public places (Müller 1998; Capron and Sabatier 2007; Lulle and Paquette 2007; Van Der Hammen, Lulle, and Palacio 2009; Cornejo Portugal 2006, 2007; Cornejo Portugal and Bellon Cárdenas 2001). The "historic" malls clearly have a great representative force, and in some cases, they are already used as a reference for certain macro areas of the city or are even already among the main symbols of the city (Silva Téllez 2003; Campo 2015). Despite these changes they are often presented with a certain enthusiasm; it is good to remember that even in this case there are still problems related to increased urban fragmentation as they are privately owned spaces whose access is limited by a marked social homogeneity.

CONCLUSION

The research discussed in the previous section provides a much more complex and articulated image of consumer practices and identity-formation processes than previous studies tended to. First of all, visitation of consumption spaces may also disregard consumption itself, and not only in the re-proposal of the figure of the *flâneur* /*flâneuse* in postmodern society sense, which has had so much success in consumer literature (Buck-Morss 1986; Wilson 1992; Bauman 1993). That is to say, shopping malls may be used by ordinary users as places to simply stroll, to socialize, for romantic meetings, to work or study, or just to spend time. That is not all, for there is more than one reason guiding the practice of shopping (multiple logics) that cannot so easily be reduced to a single unifying purpose. Even a single consumer action can (and usually is) guided by more than one form of logic.

As we have seen, approaches that focused on the daily practice of shopping were initially driven by a dissatisfaction with models that attributed a great amount of power to the designed environments themselves; in particular, the models of "seduction" or "manipulation" of the consumer were considered inadequate for understanding the complexity of consumer practices and the negotiations involved in them. Symbolic interactionist approaches helped understand the complexity of shopping as an ordinary and situated practice and have thus foregrounded the wide variety of meanings attributed to it as well as the need to investigate them contextually. On the other hand, the great merit of critical approaches was their placement of the political value of consumption in the foreground, even if, as subsequent empirical research clearly demonstrated, they were based on an overly passive model of the consumer. At the same time, research focusing on the daily practice of consumption suggested that users could in fact implement different strategies of resistance to the policies proposed by the management of consumer spaces, though they have often limited themselves to the transgression of a norm as proof of resistance. For example, to demonstrate a subject's maneuverability with respect to the intentions of managers, mall visits (typically by the young and the elderly) without any intention to purchase something are often indicated, although different management policies and architectural solutions—such as the removal of benches—tend to discourage such behavior.

The simple observation of the possibility of violating a rule obviously returns a very limited vision of conflict. More generally, such approaches, in order to restore dignity to the capacity of subjects to attribute meaning, have neglected the role of designed environments and managers and have focused mainly on how users interpret and influence shopping malls, overlooking the way in which physical environments tend to influence practices and orient their meaning to some extent. Yet, though interactionists have traditionally shown little interest in more specifically political issues, contemporary interactionists have instead taken up the challenge of considering broader social structures in their analyses. From this point of view, the fruitful dialogue between interactionist approaches and critical social theory is certainly capable of enriching studies. Therefore, to acknowledge that varied and complex actions are carried out in shopping malls and that these have a central symbolic and relational role cannot overshadow the fact that this is only possible so long as their raison d'être, that is, profit, is not questioned.[1] The problem is that shopping malls are, to quote Anne Bottompley's (2007) important considerations, a kind of hinge between private and public space: privately owned but with an important symbolic function. These have been alternatively understood as sites of "seduction, control, or self-expression" (Stillerman and Salcedo 2012:318); now perhaps it is the case to understand them as spaces of seduction, control, *and* self-expression.

Translated from the Italian by Ian Richard

NOTE

1. This is evident, for example, if we look at the complicated legal questions surrounding the conflict between the First Amendment of the United States Constitution (freedom of speech) and the private ownership of shopping malls.

REFERENCES

Abaza, Mona. 2001. "Shopping Malls, Consumer Culture and the Reshaping of Public Space in Egypt." *Theory, Culture & Society* 18(5):97–122 (https://doi.org/10/ddtsdk).

Agier, Michel. 2003. "La Ville Nue. Des Marges de l'Urbain Aux Terrains de l'Humanitaire." *Annales de la Recherche Urbaine* 93:57–66.

Appadurai, Arjun, ed. 1986. *The Social Life of Things. Commodities in Cultural Perspectives.* Cambridge: Cambridge University Press.

Appadurai, Arjun. 1996. *Modernity at Large:. Cultural Dimensions of Globalization.* Minneapolis: University of Minnesota Press.

Applbaum, Kalman. 2004. *The Marketing Era: From Professional Practice to Global Provisioning.* New York: Routledge.

Augé, Marc. 1995. *Non-places: Introduction to an Anthropology of Supermodernity.* London; New York: Verso.

Baudrillard, Jean. 1998. *The Consumer Society: Myths and Structures.* Reprinted. Theory, Culture & Society. Los Angeles: SAGE.

Bauman, Zygmunt. 1993. "From Pilgrim to Tourist—or a Short History of Identity." Pp. 18–36 in *Questions of Cultural Identity,* edited by Stuart Hall and Paul du Gay. London: SAGE.

Bauman, Zygmunt. 2000. *Liquid Modernity.* Cambridge: Polity Press.

Beng-Huat, Chua, ed. 2000. *Consumption in Asia: Lifestyles and Identities.* London: Routledge.

Benjamin, Walter. 1999. *The Arcades Project.* Edited by Rolf Tiedemann. Cambridge: Belknap Press.

Benson, Susan Porter. 1986. *Counter Cultures: Saleswoman, Managers, and Customers in American Department Stores, 1890–1940.* Chicago: University of Illinois Press.

Berman, Marshall. 1986. "Take It to the Streets. Conflict and Community in Public Space." *Dissent* 33(4):476–85.

Blumer, Herbert. 1969a. "Fashion: From Class Differentiation to Collective Selection." *The Sociological Quarterly* 10(3):275–91. https://doi.org/10/fwdhrs

Blumer, Herbert. 1969b. *Symbolic Interactionism: Perspective and Method.* Berkeley: University of California Press.

Bottomley, Anne. 2007. "A Trip to the Mall. Revisiting the Public/Private Divide." Pp. 65–94 in *Feminist Perspectives on Land Law,* edited by Hilary Lim and Anne Bottomley. Oxon; New York: Routledge-Cavendish.

Bourdieu, Pierre. 1984. *Distinction: A Social Critique of the Judgement of Taste.* Cambridge: Harvard University Press.

Bromley, Rosemary D. F. 1998. "Market-Place Trading and the Transformation of Retail Space in the Expanding Latin American City." *Urban Studies* 35(8):1311–33. https://doi.org/10/cq728w

Buck-Morss, Susan. 1986. "The Flaneur, the Sandwichman and the Whore: The Politics of Loitering." *New German Critique* no. 39:99–140. https://doi.org/10.2307/488122

Buck-Morss, Susan. 1989. *The Dialectics of Seeing: Walter Benjamin and the Arcades Project.* Cambridge: MIT Press.

Campbell, Colin. 1995. "The Sociology of Consumption." Pp. 95–124 in *Acknowledging Consumption. A Review of New Studies,* edited by Daniel Miller. London: Routledge. https://doi.org/10.4324/9780203975398

Campo, Enrico. 2015. "Consumption, Identity, Space: Shopping Malls in Bogotá." Pp. 258–87 in *Globalizing Cultures: Theories, Paradigms, Actions,* edited by Vincenzo Mele and Marina Vujnovic. Globalizing Cultures: Studies in Critical Social Sciences 82. Leiden: Brill.

SHOPPING, IDENTITY, AND PLACE   255

Capron, Guénola, and Bruno Sabatier. 2007. "Identidades Urbanas y Culturas Públicas En La Globalización: Centros Comerciales Paisajísticos En Río de Janeiro y México." *Alteridades* 17(33):87–97.

Chaney, David. 1996. *Lifestyles*. London: Routledge.

Cohen, Lizabeth. 1996. "From Town Center to Shopping Center: The Reconfiguration of Community Marketplaces in Postwar America." *The American Historical Review* 101(4):1050–81. https://doi.org/10/fdpbkf

Collins, Patricia Hill. 2000. *Black Feminist Thought*. New York: Routledge.

Cook, Daniel Thomas. 2008. *Lived Experiences of Public Consumption: Encounters with Value in Marketplaces on Five Continents*. Houndmills: Palgrave Macmillan. http://site.ebrary.com/id/10257712

Cornejo Portugal, Inés. 2006. "El Centro Comercial: Un Espacio Simbólico Urbano Más Allá Del Lugar Común." *UNIrevista* 1(3):1–30.

Cornejo Portugal, Inés. 2007. "En Centro Santa Fe: Vitrinear, Olisquear, Toquetear, Fisgonear." *Alteridades* 17(33):77–85.

Cornejo Portugal, Inés, and Elizabeth Bellon Cárdenas. 2001. "Prácticas Culturales de Apropiación Simbólica en el Centro Comercial Santa Fe." *Convergencia Revista de Ciencias Sociales* no. 24 (January):67–86.

Crawford, Margaret. 1992. "The World in a Shopping Mall." Pp. 3–30 in *Variations on a Theme Park: The New American City and the End of Public Space*, edited by Michael Sorkin. New York: Hill and Wang.

Cross, Jennifer Eileen. 2015. "Processes of Place Attachment: An Interactional Framework." *Symbolic Interaction* 38(4):493–520. https://doi.org/10.1002/symb.198

De Certeau, Michel. 1980. *The Practice of Everyday Life*. Berkeley: University of California Press.

DeVault, Marjorie. 1991. *Feeding the Family*. Chicago: University of Chicago Press.

Douglas, Mary, and Baron Isherwood. 1979. *The World of Goods. Towards an Anthropology of Consumption*. New York: Basic Books.

Erkip, Feyzan. 2003. "The Shopping Mall as an Emergent Public Space in Turkey." *Environment and Planning A* 35(6):1073–93. https://doi.org/10.1068/a35167

Erkip, Feyzan. 2005. "The Rise of the Shopping Mall in Turkey: The Use and Appeal of a Mall in Ankara." *Cities* 22(2):89–108. https://doi.org/10.1016/j.cities.2004.10.001.

Ewen, Stuart. 1976. *Captains of Consciousness. Advertising and the Social Root of Consumer Culture*. New York: McGraw Hill.

Featherstone, Mike. 1995. *Consumer Culture and Postmodernism*. London: SAGE.

Fiske, John. 1989. *Reading the Popular*. Hoboken: Taylor and Francis.

Gieryn, Thomas F. 2000. "A Space for Place in Sociology." *Annual Review of Sociology* 26:463.

Goffman, Erving. 1963. *Behavior in Public Places. Notes on the Social Organization of Gatherings*. New York: The Free Press.

Goss, Jon. 1993. "The 'Magic of the Mall': An Analysis of Form, Function, and Meaning in the Contemporary Retail Built Environment." *Annals of the Association of American Geographers* 83(1):18–47. https://doi.org/10/dqdhmr.

Goss, Jon. 1999. "Once-Upon-a-Time in the Commodity World: An Unofficial Guide to Mall of America." *Annals of the Association of American Geographers* 89(1):45–75.

Gottdiener, M. 1993. "A Marx for Our Time: Henri Lefebvre and the Production of Space." *Sociological Theory* 11(1):129–34. https://doi.org/10/fft23d.

Gottdiener, Mark. 2001. *The Theming of America: Dreams, Media Fantasies, and Themed Environments*, 2nd ed. Boulder: Westview Press.

Gottschalk, Simon, and Marko Salvaggio. 2015. "Stuck Inside of Mobile: Ethnography in Non-Places." *Journal of Contemporary Ethnography* 44(1):3–33. https://doi.org/10/ggmkch.

Houssay-Holzschuch, Myriam, and Annika Teppo. 2009. "A Mall for All? Race and Public Space in Post-Apartheid Cape Town:" *Cultural Geographies* 16(3):351–379. https://doi.org/10/fj99q2.

Jackson, Kenneth T. 1996. "All the World's a Mall: Reflections on the Social and Economic Consequences of the American Shopping Center." *The American Historical Review* 101(4):1111–21. https://doi.org/10/b6qhhf.

James, William. 1890. *The Principles of Psychology*, 2 vols. New York: Henry Holt and Company.

Kato, Yuki. 2011. "Coming of Age in the Bubble: Suburban Adolescents' Use of a Spatial Metaphor as a Symbolic Boundary." *Symbolic Interaction* 34(2):244–64. https://doi.org/10.1525/si.2011.34.2.244.

Kowinski, William Severini. 1985. *The Malling of America: An Inside Look at the Great Consumer Paradise*. New York: William Morrow & Co.

Leach, William R. 1984. "Transformations in a Culture of Consumption: Women and Department Stores, 1890–1925." *The Journal of American History* 71(2):319–42. https://doi.org/10/cwtgzj.

Lulle, Thierry, and Catherine Paquette. 2007. "Los Grandes Centros Comerciales y La Planificación Urbana." *Estudios Demograficos y Urbanos* 22(2):337–361.

Lunt, Peter, and Sonia Livingstone. 1992. *Mass Consumption and Personal Identity*. Buckingham: Open University Press.

Manzo, Lynne C., and Patrick Devine-Wright. 2014. *Place Attachment: Advances in Theory, Methods, and Applications*. New York: Routledge.

Måseide, Per, and Håvar Grøttland. 2015. "Enacting Blind Spaces and Spatialities: A Sociological Study of Blindness Related to Space, Environment and Interaction." *Symbolic Interaction* 38(4):594–610. https://doi.org/10.1002/symb.194.

McCarthy, E. Doyle. 1984. "Toward a Sociology of the Physical World: George Herber Mead on Physical Objects." *Studies in Symbolic Interaction* 5:105–21.

Mead, George Herbert. 1932. *Mind, Self, and Society*. Edited by Charles W. Morris. Chicago: University of Chicago Press.

Miller, Daniel, ed. 1995. *Acknowledging Consumption. A Review of New Studies*. London: Routledge.

Miller, Daniel, Peter Jackson, Nigel Thrift, Beverly Holbrook, and Michael Rowlands. 1998. *Shopping, Place and Identity*. New York: Routledge.

Milligan, Melinda J. 1998. "Interactional Past and Potential: The Social Construction of Place Attachment." *Symbolic Interaction* 21(1):1–33. https://doi.org/10.1525/si.1998.21.1.1.

Morris, Meaghan. 1988. "Things To Do With Shopping Centres." Pp. 193–225 in *Grafts: Feminist Cultural Criticism*, edited by Susan Sheridan. London; New York: Verso.

Müller, Jan Marco. 1998. "Grandes Centros Comerciales y Recreacionales En Santafé de Bogota." *Perspectiva Geográfica* 3: 48–87.

Muzzio, Douglas, and Jessica Muzzio-Rentas. 2008. "'A Kind of Instinct': The Cinematic Mall as Heterotopia." Pp. 137–49 in *Heterotopia and the City: Public Space in a Postcivil Society*, edited by Michiel Dehaene. London; New York: Routledge.

Nava, Mica. 1987. "Consumerism and Its Contradictions." *Cultural Studies* 1(2):204–10. https://doi.org/10/bh83th.

Prus, Robert, and Lorne Dawson. 1991. "Shop 'til You Drop: Shopping as Recreational and Laborious Activity." *The Canadian Journal of Sociology/Cahiers Canadiens de Sociologie* 16(2):145–64.

Remus, Emily. 2019. *A Shoppers' Paradise. How the Ladies of Chicago Claimed Power and Pleasure in the New Downtown*. Cambridge: Harvard University Press.

Ritzer, George. 2003. "Islands of the Living Dead: The Social Geography of McDonaldization." *American Behavioral Scientist* 47(2):119–36. https://doi.org/10/dgjwp7.

Sassatelli, Roberta. 2007. *Consumer Culture: History, Theory and Politics*. Los Angeles: SAGE.

Schivelbusch, Wolfgang. 1992. *Tastes of Paradise. A Social History of Spices, Stimulants, and Intoxicants*. New York: Pantheon Books.

Sennett, Richard. 1976. *The Fall of Public Man*. Cambridge: Cambridge University Press.

Shields, Rob. 1992. *Lifestyle Shopping: The Subject of Consumption*. London: Routledge.

Silva Téllez, Armando. 2003. *Bogotá imaginada*. Bogotá: Convenio Andrés Bello: Universidad Nacional de Colombia: Taurus.

Simmel, Georg. 1971. "Fashion." Pp. 294–323 in *From Value to Consumption: A Social-Theoretical Perspective on Simmel's Philosophie Des Geldes*. Chicago: Chicago University Press.

Slater, Don. 1997. *Consumer Culture and Modernity*. Cambridge: Polity Press.

Smith, Ronald W., and Valerie Bugni. 2006. "Symbolic Interaction Theory and Architecture." *Symbolic Interaction* 29(2):123–55. https://doi.org/10.1525/si.2006.29.2.123.

Sombart, Werner. 1967. *The Theory of the Leisure Class*. Ann Arbor: University of Michigan Press.

Staeheli, Lynn A., and Don Mitchell. 2006. "USA's Destiny? Regulating Space and Creating Community in American Shopping Malls." *Urban Studies* 43(5–6):977–92. https://doi.org/10/cbs776.

Stillerman, Joel, and Rodrigo Salcedo. 2012. "Transposing the Urban to the Mall: Routes, Relationships, and Resistance in Two Santiago, Chile, Shopping Centers." *Journal of Contemporary Ethnography* 41(3):309–36. https://doi.org/10/f32cv8.

Van Der Hammen, María Clara, Thierry Lulle, and Dolly Cristina Palacio. 2009. "La Construcción Del Patrimonio Como Lugar: Un Estudio de Caso En Bogotá." *Antipoda. Revista de Antropología y Arqueología* 8:61–85.

Veblen, Thorstein. 1994. *The Theory of the Leisure Class*. London: MacMillan.

Wilk, Richard. 1998. "Emulation, Imitation, and Global Consumerism." *Organization & Environment* 11(3):314–33. https://doi.org/10/bns7pk.

Williams, Christine L. 2006. *Inside Toyland: Working, Shopping, and Social Inequality*. Berkeley: University of California Press.

Williams, Rosalind Helen. 1982. *Dream Worlds: Mass Consumption in Late Nineteenth Century France*. Berkeley: University of California Press.

Wilson, Elizabeth. 1992. "The Invisible Flaneur." *New Left Review* 1(191) (February):90–110.

Yan, Yunxiang. 2000. "Of Hamburger and Social Space. Consuming McDonald's in Beijing." Pp. 201–25 in *The Consumer Revolution in Urban China*, edited by Deborah Davis. Berkeley: University of California Press.

Zukin, Sharon, and Jennifer Smith Maguire. 2004. "Consumers and Consumption." *Annual review of Sociology* 30:173.

CHAPTER 15

SYMBOLIC INTERACTION AND MUSIC

JOSEPH A. KOTARBA

Introduction: Conceptualizing Music

Symbolic interactionist research and writing on music have had a long and fruitful relationship. Symbolic interactionist researcher interests have ranged from classical music and jazz to the blues, to punk, and to hip-hop. Through their essentially qualitative research methods, symbolic interactionists have vividly described the everyday lives of fans, critics, musicians, promoters, producers, and others whose work creates the music that we love to experience.

In order to outline the symbolic interactionist (SI) approach to writing on music, we need a schema that is true to SI's theoretical and methodological agendas. The heart of SI's perspective on social life lies in the realm of concepts. Concepts are focused, summary, instructive, and illuminating portraits of particular aspects or components of social life. One of the major thinkers establishing the foundations of SI was Herbert Blumer (1969), who felt that concepts provide a practical mechanism for ordering and inspiring research on more complicated and broader features of social life. He argued through his notion of *sensitizing concepts* that concepts should be modest in scope and should serve most importantly as directions for further and more in-depth research into a topic.

Therefore, I will discuss SI's approach to understanding the social facets of music primarily in terms of the concepts used to flesh out research and the value of research for refining and developing SI concepts. Music is integral to social life, and thus studying music also contributes to our understanding of central sociological issues of culture, community, belonging, and identity. The major concepts used in SI writing on music are: *subculture, self, identity, community, scene, sense of place, idioculture, interaction, organization*, and *authenticity*. I will also discuss the relationship between standard variable analysis in mainstream sociology and the symbolic interactionist task of focusing on the ways people approach these variables in terms of making sense of everyday life. Sensitizing concepts shed analytic light on a topic area and allow us to better understand the topic as well as relate to ideas across different substantive areas. They also direct research toward specific directions of creative inquiry. They are at the core of how symbolic interactionists make sense of the world. In this chapter I will illuminate these concepts as they apply to interactionist work on music, beginning first with the concept of subculture.

SUBCULTURE

From its early days in the beginning of the twentieth century, SI was always interested in everyday life in the margins of urban society. Inner-city Chicago, with its great mix of ethnic and religious groups, its heavily working-class economy, and the fascinating musical phenomena that emerged from this cauldron provided a virtual social laboratory for social researchers. Howard Becker emerged from this milieu to become the originator and formulator of the spirit of interactionist study of music through what we have come to know as the concept of *subculture*. J. Patrick Williams (2011) defines *subculture* as "a culture that differs from the 'mainstream' through marginality or opposition". The members of a subculture, by definition, do not totally oppose the meanings and values of the dominant culture, but simply carve out a cognitive, and sometimes physical, space to address their particular wants and needs. Music subcultures can be assembled from any number of characteristics, ranging from ethnicity and gender to age and music style.

Becker (1951) conducted one of the foundational SI studies of music subcultures in examining the world of the professional dance musician and their audience. A regular practicing jazz pianist in the clubs of Chicago, himself, he conducted a participant-observation study of the scene. Jazz musicians, he argues, are members of a service occupation who must deal with interference from their clients at work. Dance musicians see themselves as different from their audiences, who are people who lack understanding of the music and the musicians, but who in fact exert great control. Control can come some from actually telling the musician how to do their work to withdrawing their patronage. Musicians feel isolated from society and increase this isolation through a process of self-segregation—creating their own subculture. A good deal of conflict and hostility arises as a result, and methods of defense against outside interference become a preoccupation of the members. The musicians feel that the only music worth playing is what they call "jazz," a term which can be defined only as that music which is produced without reference to the demands of outsiders. The most troublesome problem in the career of the average musician is the need to choose between conventional career success and their artistic standards. If a musician remains true to their standards, they are doomed to failure in their career. Musicians classify themselves according to the degree to which they give in to outsiders; the continuum ranges from the extreme "jazz" musician to the "commercial" musician. Becker continues his analysis by introducing and exploring terminology used by jazz musicians to establish boundaries between themselves and those not able, fit, or sufficiently talented to share the musicians' world, terms like "square," "be cool," "daddio," and "hip." Musicians maintain and reinforce a sense of subcultural distinctiveness and "coolness" in contrast to the mainstream through specific practices and meaning-making; among these practices the use of illicit drugs can establish identity and separate one from the square world.

Music Subcultures, Drugs, and Meaning

A common feature of music subcultures of special interest to interactionists is recreational and/or illegal drug use. Howard Becker extended his analysis of the jazz subculture by using the musicians' drug of choice, marijuana, as a tool to develop a theory of drug use that laid the ground for the very popular, powerful, and more general interactionist theory of deviance known as *labelling theory* (1963). Becker's theory is deceptively simple. After living with jazz musicians and as a jazz musician himself, he realized that the *meaning* of marijuana use is not inherent in the marijuana itself. Will Gibson and Dirk vom Lehn (2018) define meaning in interactionism as the message of communication either intended and/or received through interaction, in terms of the context within which communication takes place. Objects, behaviors, and ideas in one's mind do not by themselves have or transmit meaning. In this light, all smoking marijuana does is leave you with physical effects, such as dizziness, coughing, sleepiness, and disorientation. There is nothing inherently pleasurable about marijuana, so that the meaning of its use, like all aspects of everyday life experience, is subject to *situation* and *interpretation*.

Becker's study led him to conclude that jazz musicians were likely to obtain a definition of smoking marijuana that was pleasurable from fellow bandmates. Jazz ensembles tend to be closely knit groups that spend considerable time together rehearsing, performing, and just spending considerable leisure time with each other. The music itself is paradoxical. Although the style of jazz Becker performed was essentially improvisational, it requires extensive rehearsal time to acquire the skills needed to achieve improvisation. This arrangement develops the type of subculture that requires trust and a shared set of rules, language, and ethics. Scott Currie (2014) extended Becker's treatise by arguing that improvisational practice and performance allow jazz artists to create personae that they project to each other and the audience. These personae—or identities—consequently impact the direction of the musical improvisation.

The Internet and Music Subcultures

More recently, interactionist researchers have conducted studies of music subculture and drugs that have focused on internet platforms for communication among users. J. Patrick Williams (2011), for example, studied an internet forum dedicated to the straight-edge subculture, which is defined by its opposition to drug use. Emerging as a conservative reaction to punk's anarchic orientation, straight-edge participants adopted the label "straight edge" from a 1981 song title by the Washington, DC, band Minor Threat, and they eshew the drug use of their scene peers. Williams highlighted the fact that hard-rock music, such as heavy metal, was a valuable medium for a range of young people's values and desires and that the internet has become an important source for subcultural interaction. Williams has further developed his thinking on music and subcultures, within an interactionist framework, by focusing on rapidly changing media forms. The internet, in particular, communicates meanings that can either supplant or extend the music's meanings (e.g., lyrics) per se (Williams 2013).

Joseph A. Kotarba (2007) applied his *interactionist optic*, as Fred Davis (1991) once put it so elegantly, to a contrasting subcultural scene: music as a feature of the online discussion of illegal club drugs. Members of the world of popular music have developed many rich, functional, and complex discursive traditions through which they talk, disseminate information, and share experiences about drugs and music. The nature of this discourse has taken different forms over the years as styles of illegal drug use, the objectives of drug talk, and the media by which this talk takes place have all evolved.

One of the more recent forms of discourse on music and drugs is conducted on the internet. Kotarba (2007) conceptualized this specific form of insider (read: subcultural) discourse as *drugmusictalk*. A contemporary style of *drugmusictalk* is the communications taking place in the world of rave parties, techno dance clubs, and designer drugs—the focus of his study. Thus, the *drugmusictalk* that takes place in clubs provides us with a glimpse into the world of club or designer drugs, rave parties, dance, and high technology. As David Altheide (2016) notes, the logic and format that shapes the internet largely determine the structure and function of discourse that occurs on the internet. Contemporary media, especially the internet, empower speakers to create realities (Denzin 1997). Media is more than just the message: it is the world in which lives are lived and cultures are constructed. Kotarba (2002) maintains that the internet specifically allows people to re-create the self situationally and constantly. In sum, *drugmusictalk* serves as a medium to: facilitate aesthetic drug-music experiences, discuss the fit between particular drugs and styles of music, and share affective (e.g., sexual) aspects of sophisticated dance music.

The internet allows people to create and perform situational selfs and identities. As Simon Gottschalk (2018:56) explains the current situation through his concept of the *terminal self*:

> In its design, content, and functioning, the (computer) terminal provides us with an unusually intense personalized experience. In design, it promotes self-centeredness by inviting us to customize the terminal look and to materialize our unique personality in it.

The construction of self through subcultural style is further facilitated by the online world and its capacity for shaping identities.

The Self and Identity

As we have seen above in our discussion of subcultures, the *self* may be the most important concept for symbolic interactionism. The self is a reflexive object. George Herbert Mead (1934) reminds us that the self "is a constant process, a way of 'self-ing' ourselves into being as a result of our actions as a subject (the "I"), and as an object of our actions (the *"me"*)" (Kotarba 2018:67).

Song lyrics provide a useful avenue by which to see the Meadian view of the self in action. The self in the SI view is both simultaneously subject and object and thus the lyricist and the lyric, respectively. Songwriters may write about the self both as the I and as the generalized other, melding biography and assumptions about the preceptions of others.

Symbolic interactionists generally do not assume music is a somewhat unique experience in everyday life that emerges in certain groups under specific circumstances. Music is not simply the purview of subcultures. Music is a ubiquitous feature of everyday life. Often the sociological study of music has focused on the most intense and oppositional deviant music subcultures (e.g., heavy-metal, punk, and hip-hop fans), but music is central not only to the intense interests of these subcultures, but to people in all settings and at all times. Music is important to study because it is such a widespread, yet often taken-for-granted, source of meaning for self and situations. In this regard, symbolic interactionists take seriously a profound claim made by an earlier, honored scholar who was somewhat of a predecessor to the perspective: William James. James wrote about the idea—or concept—of *music-at-once*. This idea points to the complexity of the world that itself is packed with ideas, feelings, histories, events, and everything else scholars in the humanities and social sciences would ponder. As a recent scholar and skilled intellectual biographer of James, Bruce W. Wilshire (2016), put it: "The moreness of the world pummels, pokes, provokes, and pricks and feeds us from all directions." In interactionist terms, *moreness* is more or less synonymous with culture, and music is a great example of moreness.

Science, Music, and the Self

Joseph Kotarba (2013, 2019) has been studying the impact of the translational science movement on the work and self-identity of the contemporary bio-medical scientist (who scientists are to themselves and how they appear to and are defined by others). Kotarba found not only that scientists should integrate the arts into their self-identity, but also that they in fact do so. Music not only provides a charming accompaniment to thought but also serves as a particular sort of buffer between the scientist's self and the outside world. The concept of the *existential self* is a very useful framework for exploring the dynamics of this buffer. All paradigms in sociology posit essential relationships between the individual and society. In symbolic interaction this relationship is conceptualized in terms of the self and society, the self being the person's sense of and experience of individuality (Blumer 1969). A variation of the symbolic interactionist model of the self is the existential model, which posits a *confrontational* relationship between the self and society (Kotarba 1984). The existential self-concept regards the individual as an active agent in seeking meaning for problematic situations in everyday life (Melnikov and Kotarba 2017). Sources for meaning in our postmodern culture increase as the mass and electronic media continue to expand and access to the media becomes widely available in society. The point is that scientists already meld science and the arts into their self-identities. More specifically, a common strategy among translational scientists is to use music as a *buffer* against the stressors that the translational science movement both locally and in general places upon the security of their sense of self (Douglas 1970). For example, translational scientists use music to help achieve a sense of a *balanced self*, to reinforce the self-definition of intellectual, to serve as an escape from the over-rationalized culture of science, to provide another outlet for creativity, and to facilitate a rhythm for exploration. Younger, laboratory-based researchers often play rock music while working at the bench. They will play their music through noise-limiting headphones or buds for two purposes: to keep from disturbing other scientists in the lab, but also as an act of resistance, so to speak, to the seemingly endless meetings and discussions that accompany the growing team-science movement in every day biomedical research. In interviews, some foreign-born scientists take great pride in celebrating the music of their homeland, especially by contrasting the elegant "classical" styles they recall with the more common populist styles of popular music in the United States.

The Marginal Self

Thaddeus Muller (2016) designed a creative extension of the self-concept in music. The focus of his study was to locate the meaning that rock music has for fans of 1960s musician, Lou Reed. Muller conducted a content analysis of comments posted on the New York Times website following the report that Lou Reed had died. For some fans, the news of Reed's death resonated with their experience of an *aging self*. Reed's death caused them to reflect on youthful times. Others grieved for those who passed away and reflected on the pain of aging. Muller analyzes the deep transformative meaning attributed by some fans to Reed in the past. Fans would testify on how powerful Reed's persona was to help them cope with or even overcome their *marginal self*. The experience for them was escaping one's inauthentic self and accepting who one truly was. As Muller notes, existentially sublime stories like this dramatically highlight Tia DeNora's (1999) now famous observation that music *serves as "a technology of the self."*

Music is an important window to understanding the marginal self because there are numerous music styles that corrolate with numerous types of marginality in society. People who grew up with rock-and-roll and folk music in the 1960s and 1970s can feel very alienated from the current music styles marketed to and appreciated by young people such as rap and electronica. They can adhere to and rejuvenate their preferred syles of music by shairing these interests with others in the camping and environmentally oriented jam-festival scene. This geographically widespread community communicates and shares meanings by means of the internet (Gardner 2020).

COMMUNITY

Music is a shared activity that occurs in the presence of others. The self that is constructed through music, discussed in the previous section, is a social self constructed in communities. Communities provide a source of meaning and a sense of belonging to their participants (Ferris and Stein 2012). The concept of *community* orients us to attend to the ways that people come together, physically or virtually, around shared ideas, goals, and/or histories. Within interactionism there are particular aspects of community that fit our focus on music in everyday life. These are *scene*, *sense of place*, and *idioculture*.

Scene

The concept of the *social scene* has added the feature of physical location to symbolic interaction analysis. This concept in general has been applied to a wide range of cultural phenomena, including music. John Irwin (1977) posited the scene as an inclusive concept that involves all participants in a cultural phenomenon, such as artists, audiences, management, vendors, and critics; the ecological or geographical location of the phenomenon, such as districts, clubs, recording studios, and rehearsal rooms; and the products of the interactions among these participants, such as advertisements, concerts, recordings, and critical reviews. Scenes form the socio-cultural context for entertainment-oriented phenomena, such as music, theater, and dance. Music scenes acquire particular identities over time, as Barry Shank (1994) noted in his description of live music in Austin, Texas. He focused his analysis on the "6th Street" area, near to and nurtured by the University of Texas, in terms of its history, cultural roots, and economic context. His focus is on the effects the production of music scenes has on the identities of their participants. College towns are good examples of music scenes insofar as these scenes have identities, histories, and personalities, if you will, that transcend those of the particular artists that perform there, as Michael Ramirez (2018) writes about Athens, Georgia—home to the University of Georgia. Pete Peterson and Andy Bennett (2004) defined a music scene as the geosocial location that provides a stage on which all of the aesthetic, political, social, and cultural features of local music are played out. In terms of using music to forge a sense of community, participants use local music scenes to differentiate themselves from others.

These general definitions allow for the application of this concept of the scene to any number of musical styles and forms. Peterson and Bennett's (2004) list includes jazz, blues, rave, karaoke, Britney Spears, salsa, riot grrrls, goth, skatepunk, anarcho-punk, and alternative. Their focus, clearly, is on music scenes populated by young people. Examining a particular music scene known as Rock en Español illustrates some of the most important interactionist features of music scenes in general (Nowotny et al. 2010). Rock en Español is an international movement to create and perform original rock music in Spanish that incorporates themes relevant to the everyday lives of Latino artists and their audiences (Kotarba et al. 2009). A sociological approach to rock en Español sees the genre's relationship with other social processes, such as immigration: "it illustrates how third-generation Latinos acquire an identity that integrates their Latino heritage, love for the Spanish language, and awareness and concern for current Latino political issues; and it illustrates the postmodern process of globalization that affects culture in general and Latino culture specifically" (Kotarba and LaLone 2014). Rock en Español fans are typically upwardly mobile, young-adult (in their twenties), third-generation Mexican Americans who are proficiently and proudly bilingual. While on the surface, rock en Español's insistence on Spanish-language use may appear to block assimilation, this is not the case. For its overwhelmingly bilingual adherents, rock en Español provides a way for third-generation immigrants to share the world of their parents and grandparents within an integrated American identity. By creating a music that conforms to the sensibilities of both cultures, "the full integration of Spanish-language use, functions as an efficient resource for upwardly mobile, third-generation Latinos to become American in the 21st century" (Kotarba 2018:37).

Sense of Place

We engage in reflexive relationships with the spaces we occupy, creating a *sense of place*. Producers and others involved in creating music scenes construct a sense of place for musicians, fans, and critics. Thus, for example, in creating the Rock en Español scene, coffee houses meld the intellectual ambiance of the coffee-house environment with the bright and colorful aspects of Latino culture. As with other ethnic music styles, the Latino genre of Rock en Español creates realities and a sense of place that can include country of origin, America, or *La Raza* (Kotarba 2018:38). Artists and fans see a continuum ranging from musical centers like Monterey, Mexico, to production and marketing centers like Houston, Texas. The global dimension of the genre and its relation to the Latino experience of migration and movement is reflected in the ways that DJs sample from a wide array of musicians ranging from Central American folk musicians to South American pop bands. Central to the concept of sense of place is that we make places just as places make us and shape our selves and identities (Gruenewald 2003).

Idioculture

Gary Fine (1979) developed the concept of *idioculture* to emphasize that culture is lived in the small groups or local communities in which we interact. He defines idioculture as "a system of knowledge, beliefs, behaviors, and customs shared by members of an interacting group to which members can refer and employ as the basis of further interaction" (Fine 1979:734). This idea emphasizes the need to study culture in all its forms—including music—within the scenes and the everyday life interactions where it is lived.

The *becoming of self* is one of the most important and common processes that people experience using the scene for, and the idioculture that pervades it. The resources for assessing and shaping a sense of self ultimately come from cultural experiences. The process of the becoming of self is analytically noteworthy in Latino music scenes, in which many of the fans are faced with rapidly changing social, political, and cultural environments in which they experience the self (Kotarba 2018:39). Yet, the *becoming of self* can occur in any stage of life, with the possible and notable exceptions of early childhood and old age. In these two cases, the individual is not expected to search for meaning. The very young child is given meaning for self by parents, siblings, and others. The very old person does not ordinarily seek meaning for a new or reconstructed sense of self, being satisfied in recalling and enjoying the one they have acquired over the course of a lifetime (Kotarba 2023).

INTERACTION

Interaction is, of course, a key concept in the study of symbolic interaction. Interaction in everyday life consists of the communication people have, in various forms, through which they construct symbols—or meanings—they share, internalize, modify, and in many ways use to makes sense of everyday life (cf. Charmaz, Harris, and Irvine 2020:20–21). A major focus of research on interaction in music can be found in interaction among musicians. Music performance is one of the most obviously social of activities. Meaningful communication among musicians is necessary for all social forms in music, ranging from rock-music bands to symphonic orchestras.

Some of the most dramatic illustrations of interaction lie in the creation and production of jazz improvisation. William Gibson (2010) explores improvisation within jazz rhythm sections according to Howard Becker's (1982) concept of *conventions* in the arts. Drum-and-bass players make decisions during a song based upon their perceptions and understandings of their fit with the unfolding context and the (conventional) interactional roles of the other musicians (i.e., lead players or singers) in the setting. (See also Katz 1994).

Simon Gottschalk (2018) examined a very contemporary form of interaction involving music: music as a feature of video games. His analysis of improvisation in *Guitar Hero* points to the technological limitations placed upon the player's attempts to improvise—an action that we commonsensically assume is quite individualistic. For example, Guitar Hero has five uniform keys, strum bar, and whammy bar, in contrast to the six strings on a real guitar. These technological limitations mirror the social limitations prohibiting unrestrained improvisations in everyday-life interaction. Put simply, improvisation is always collaborative in music ensembles (Sawyer 2000).

ORGANIZATION

The symbolic interactionist approach to organizational life fits well in our discussion of music because there are in fact two complementary approaches. As Patrick McGinty (2014) notes, some interactionists focus on *organizational analysis*, whereas others focus on *organizational ethnography*. Organizational analysis refers to the assumption that "organizations" are specialized groups that are things apart from other forms of social life—much like the mainstream organizational sociologist would do. In contrast, organizational ethnography refers to the study of the actual work and meaning interpretation that takes place in locations referred to commonsensically as organizations (McGinty 2014:157–59). Although there have been attempts to integrate or resolve the two approaches (e.g., Hall 2011), symbolic interactionists in fact do both in regards to music. Rachel Skaggs and Jonathan R. Wynn (2018) describe Nashville, Tennessee, as an entity apart from the rest of the world of popular music. Nashville is at once a community and an organization commonly referred to as "Music City," but it is in sum what Howard Becker (1982:34) refers to as "*patterned cooperation,* the set of associations and practices that allow for the reproduction of a cultural good." The glue that holds everything together is the fact that Nashville is the center of the country music business. Another example of organizational analysis in interactionalism is the focus on music festivals as organizations. Robert Owen Gardner (2020) studied bluegrass jam-music festivals organizationally as *portable communities*. Although generally annual events, participants construct hubs of interaction—on the internet in particular—that persist well beyond the festival event to create a sense of belonging and place.

Organizational ethnography looks at how formal group processes actually occur, in contrast to a focus on any particular organization. Philip Vannini (2004) applied the logic of semiotics (i.e., the study of signs and symbols and their use or interpretation) to the analysis of music criticism, not as offered by professional journalists and critics, but as produced and disseminated by music fans themselves. The artist in question is Canadian singer Avril Lavigne, and her fans' aesthetic interpretations of her music serve as the material from which the mass media create their stories about her and her work.

Lori Holyfield et al. (2013) studied two country/bluegrass music festivals, "MusicFest" and the "Walnut Valley Festival," to examine the way attendees' narratives highlight the experienced emotionality that leads to the affective ties that bind these otherwise temporary communities. Their study illustrates the intricacies of producing, disseminating, and enacting stories that we come to know as nostalgia. The authors developed the concept of *affective heritage embracement* to signify this and related phenomena.

AUTHENTICITY

Authenticity is a very popular and powerful concept in symbolic interaction today. Whereas mainstream, structural sociology posits a social world where issues and data are either true or false, empirically supported or anecdotal, the presence of an idea like authenticity gives support to our claim that social life—as well as our interpretations of it—are problematic, subjective, slippery, questionable, and debatable. Authenticity, in sum, is an *idea* that the meaning of which, like art, is very much in the mind of the beholder. In their excellent collection of interactionist-inspired essays on authenticity, J. Patrick Williams and Phillip Vannini (2009) locate authenticity in several arenas: culture, self, and society. In one of the chapters, Joseph Kotarba takes a more in-depth, phenomenological approach by framing authenticity claims as tools by which the individual affects, modifies, justifies, excuses, or modifies the self, all of which takes place in particular concrete situations. Individuals will claim their expertise in discerning authentic popular music (e.g., in terms of artists' styles or talent) as a positive feature of their self-identity, whether or not the artist or performance in question is in any objective sense "authentic." William Force (2009:296) studied the punk music scene and found that authenticity among punks involves more than just music styles. Authenticity is also gauged by participants' consumption styles: "it was clear that rare or limited edition vinyl is more highly regarded than regular (black, nonnumbered, not limited) vinyl. Any color record has greater symbolic value than the CD format." Authenticity claims in music show the contested nature of scene credentials, subcultural tastes, and group identity. In Italy, an authenticity debate over what "counts" as Italian music and Italian identity occurred after Mahmood (Alessandro Mahmoud), born in Italy to a mother from Sardinia and a father from Egypt, won Italy's San Remo music festival and thus qualified to represent Italy in the 2019 Eurovision song competition; anti-immigrant political leaders in Italy complained, expressing anger that he beat out singers of "more Italian" songs (Brekhus 2020:2–3). Their nativist implication was that Mahmood's multiethnic background made his music (and his identity) "less Italian." Mahmood countered that his multifacted ethnic identity made him and his music just as authentically Italian as the other contenders, thus illustrating the dynamic nature of modern multidimensional ethnic identities (Brekhus 2020:3).

From Variables to Concepts

Mainstream—that is, structuralist or consensus sociology—approaches the study of society in terms of abstract variables. These variables reflect key features of society that allow for comparison and contrast across individuals and groups (e.g., DiMaggio 1991). Symbolic interactionists approach variables as abstractions that are socially constructed like any other meanings in social life. A number of writers have explored the way members deal with and make sense of the features of social life in everyday life highlighted by classic sociological variables.

Jonafa Banbury (2016) examined the relationship of race and religiosity in her field research on Christian hip-hop music. She described how members of the 51210 Movement in Austin, Texas, use Christian hip-hop music as a proselytizing and pedagogical tool to reach young adults of color. J. Patrick Williams and X. X. S. Ho (2016) explored the role national identity plays in the emergence of fan culture by examining how young Singaporeans consume Korean popular music, "K-Pop." Thaddeus Atzmon (2016) developed the concept of *musical pastiche* to assemble a case study of the ways a young Israeli rapper, Matisyahu, transitioned from membership in the very conservative Labuvitch movement to the Modern Orthodox Movement, and how this change in self-identity affected his music and his career.

Symbolic interactionist's interest in gender is reflected in recent studies such as Jeffrey E. and Dina C. Nash's (2016) discussion of the interactional dynamics of women increasingly participating in the traditional all-male barbershop quartet. The authors document the devices used to feminize the form, such as naming, song selection, and organizational style.

As has been the case with most paradigmatic approaches to music in sociology, symbolic interactionists have generally studied and written about music phenomena in terms of singular if not isolated periods of life. There are large literatures on music and childhood, adolescents and music, music in middle age, and music as an intervention for conditions such as dementia and cancer. The time has arrived for an integration of the many powerful concepts developed in symbolic Interaction in the form of a life course model. The *Music Across the Life Course Project*, housed at Texas State University, is working on this task now (Kotarba 2023). A *life course* is a patterned temporal trajectory of individual experiences. The life course model emphasizes the centrality of music across the human experience and reminds us again to analyze music as something integral to all age groups and not something to be studied only among the most intense youth subcultures. Some scholars, notably social psychologists and psychologists, like to identify objective and universal stages typical for all individuals. Interactionists and social constructionists are instead less interested in determining fixed stages and more in examining how individuals assign meanings to their progression through life. In the words of Clair, Karp, and Yoels (1993:vii), their focus is more precisely on "how persons occupying different locations in social space interpret and respond to repeated social messages about the meanings of age." Reflecting on the contribution of these authors, in an influential overview of the concept and research on the life course, interactionist sociologists Jaber Gubrium and James Holstein (1995) write that "(1) age and life stages, like any temporal categories, can carry multiple meanings; (2) those meanings emerge from social interaction; and (3) the meanings of age and the course of life are refined and reinterpreted in light of the prevailing social definitions of situations that bear on experience through time." In symbolic interactionist terms, the concept should be revised to read "course of life" in order to eliminate the sometimes rigid categories or stages in traditional life course models. The emphasis is increasingly instead on the various ways music can be used across demographic categories as a meaning resource in everyday life. For example, both very young children and very old adults are dependent on others to provide the music they love and enjoy (Kotarba 2023). The life course is therefore about the becoming of self: the fluid process through which we acquire new and diverse roles, social identities, and personal identities. Music provides a set of symbolic resources for the definition and reinterpretation of these identities; through music we continuously self ourselves into being.

CONCLUSION

I conclude this chapter by highlighting two analytic approaches to thinking about music from a symbolic interactionist perspective. The first approach proposed by Phillip Vannini and Dennis Waskul (2006) metaphorically posits *life-as-music*. The second approach, and one which I have further advanced in this chapter, celebrates the commitment that interactionist scholars of music share to more fully conceptualizing music (see also Kotarba 2010); and more broadly symbolic interactionist research on music employs sensitizing concepts to better understand not just music, but social life in general. Both of these approaches take seriously the analytic importance of music for unlocking conceptual development and meaning-making across the social world.

Vannini and Waskul (2006) argue that symbolic interaction functions very much as music does: both deal with esthetics, whereas interactionism discloses meaning and self in society much like music does. Analytical frameworks in SI such as dramaturgy and narrative analysis are grounded in metaphors that see life as theater and life as a story. In related fashion, Vannini and Waskul argue for the creation of another metaphor: life as music. Viewing selfhood and symbolic interaction as music sensitizes us to observe and understand an important but much too neglected dimension of social life: the esthetic. Drawing from the pragmatist philosophy of John Dewey, they say that the realm of the esthetic, of beauty, should not be confined to museums and art galleries. The perception of beauty constitutes the very foundation of individuals' embodied experiences of their life worlds. They argue that the metaphor of life as music can make us aware of the diverse rhythms, melodies, and harmonies that make social life alive and vibrant. Like Goffman's concept of seeing life as theater, or narrative analysts seeing life as story, seeing life metaphorically as music allows us to conceive of the social world as a patterned world with its changing tempos and varying esthetics.

What is symbolic interactionism's distinctive approach to the study of music? This major contribution may be in the power and intellectual mastery of conceptualizing social and cultural phenomena. Concepts are the magical names that interactionists apply to various phenomena in everyday life to illuminate their features: "Subculture. . . so, that's what we call the punks who hang out together, dress alike, play loud and obnoxious music, and wear earrings in their nose. . . now I get it."

"Now I get it." That's exactly what interactionism does. Conceptualizations range from the creation of sensitizing concepts that suggest questions to ask, as in the exploration of authenticity in popular music, to typological analysis by which we organize and make sense of otherwise complex and disparate phenomena, such as the designation of musical interaction into scenes, subcultures, and communities. Good concept work helps in two ways. First, it reveals sociological similarities among musical and nonmusical phenomena. There can be numerous types of communities based upon characteristics such as members' similarities, their survival needs, or their shared history. All communities need mechanisms to acquire meaning for the situations their members face, and music is one type of resource for acquiring meaning. Understanding the resources we use to acquire meaning in communities and our social interactions within communities is central to the SI perspective. Music as an integral feature of human lives is a meaningful site for this enterprise.

Second, and perhaps most importantly, good concept work provides a perceptual distance between the writer and the music. Kotarba notes that writing objectively—if not scientifically—and calmly about music is very difficult because:

> music is honey: we really love the music we study and share in its romance, wonder, imagination, and possibilities. Good concepts are analytical filters that let the magic of music through, but allow us to catch our breath long enough to think and write about what we just witnessed first hand. I do not think I could write much about Van Halen's "Jump" until I could *see* it as an example of children's music enjoyed by teenagers who were not quite ready to give up the joys of play.
>
> (Kotarba 2010:4)

It is this exercise of seeing the world through the analytic lens of concepts that allows us to appreciate music not just for its own sake but for the things music tells us about the social worlds we inhabit. Symbolic interactionism provides a unique perspective from which to appreciate the role of music in everyday life and the importance of music to interpreting social life.

REFERENCES

Altheide, David. 2016. *The Media Syndrome*. New York: Routledge.

Atzmon, Thaddeus. 2016. "Musical Pastiche: The Case of Matisyahu." Pp. 185–95 in *Symbolic Interactionist Takes on Music*, edited by Christopher J. Schneider and Joseph A. Kotarba. Studies in Symbolic Interaction 47. Bingley, UK: Emerald.

Banbury, Jonafa. 2016. "The Church and the Streets: An Ethnographic Study of the Christian Hip GHop Music in Central Texas." Pp. 151–68 in *Symbolic Interactionist Takes on Music*, edited by Christopher J. Schneider and Joseph A. Kotarba. Studies in Symbolic Interaction 47. Bingley, UK: Emerald.

Becker, Howard S. 1982. *Art Worlds*. Berkeley: University of California Press.

Becker, Howard S. 1963. *Outsiders*. New York: Free Press.

Becker, Howard S. 1951. "The Professional Dance Musician and his Audience." *American Journal of Sociology* 57(2):136–44.

Blumer, Herbert. 1969. *Symbolic Interactionism: Perspective and Method*. New York: Prentice Hall.

Brekhus, Wayne H. 2020. *The Sociology of Identity: Authenticity, Multidimensionality, and Mobility*. Cambridge: Polity.

Charmaz, Kathy, Scott R. Harris, and Leslie Irvine. 2020. *The Social Self and Everyday Life*. Hoboken, NJ: Wiley.

Clair, Jeffrey, David Karp, and William Yoels. 1993. *Experiencing the Life Cycle*. Springfield, IL: Charles Thomas.

Currie, Scott. 2014. "Scenes, Personae and Meaning: Symbolic Interactionist Semiotics of Jazz Improvisation." *Studies in Symbolic Interaction* 42:37–50.

Davis, Fred, 1991. *Passage Through Crisis*. New York: Transaction Publishers.

DeNora, Tia. 1999. "Music as a Technology of the Self." *Poetics* 27(1):21–56.

Denzin, Norman K. 1997. *Interpretive Ethnography*. Beverly Hills, CA: SAGE.

DiMaggio, Paul. 1991. "Social Structure, Institutions, and Cultural Goods: The Case of the United States." Pp. 133–55 in *Social Theory for a Changing Society*, edited by Pierre Bourdieu and James Coleman. Boulder, CO: Westview.

Douglas, Jack D., ed. 1970. *Understanding Everyday Life: Toward a Reconstruction of Sociological Knowledge*. Chicago: Aldine.

Ferris, Kerry, and Jill Stein. 2012. *The Real World: An Introduction to Sociology*. 3rd ed. New York: Norton.

Fine, Gary. 1979. "Idioculture: Small Groups and Culture Creation: The Idioculture of Little League Baseball Teams" *American Sociological Review* 4(5):733–45.

Force, William. 2009. "Consumption Styles and the Fluid Complexity of Punk Authenticity." *Symbolic Interaction* 32(4):289–309.

Gardner, Robert Owen. 2020. *The Portable Community: Place and Displacement in Bluegrass Festival Life*. London: Routledge.

Gibson, Will. 2010. "The group ethic in the improvising jazz ensemble: a symbolic interactionist analysis of music, identity, and social context." *Studies in Symbolic Interaction* 35: 11–28.

Gibson, Will, and Dirk vom Lehn. 2018. *Institutions, Interaction and Social Theory*. London: Palgrave.

Gottschalk, Simon. 2018. *The Terminal Self: Everyday Life in Hypermodern Times*. New York: Routledge.

Gruenewald, David A. 2003. "The Best of Both World: A Critical Pedagogy of Place." *Educational Researcher* 32(4):3–12.

Gubrium, Jaber F., and James A. Holstein. 1995. "Life Course Malleability: Biographical Work and Deprivatization." *Sociological Inquiry* 65(2):207–23.

Hall, Peter. 2011. "Interactionism, Social Organization, and Social Processes: Looking Back There, Reflecting Now Here, and Moving Ahead Then." *Symbolic Interaction*, Special Issue, edited by Kathy Charmaz and Lyn H. Lofland 26(1):33–55.

Holyfield, Lori, Maggie Cobb, Kimberley Murray, and Ashleigh McKinzie. 2013. "Musical Ties that Bind: Nostalgia, Affect and Heritage in Festival Narratives." *Symbolic Interaction* 36(4):457–77.

Irwin, John. 1977. *Scenes*. Beverly Hills, CA: SAGE.

Katz, Jack. 1994. "Jazz in Social Interaction: Personal Creativity, Collective Constraint, and Motivational Explanation in the Social Thought of Howard S. Becker." *Symbolic Interaction* 17(3):253–79.

Kotarba, Joseph A. 2023. *Music in the Course of Life*. New York: Routledge.

Kotarba, Joseph A. 2018. "Three Stages of Cultural Change in Translational Science." *Refereed abstract published in the Journal of Clinical and Translational Sciences* 1(1):44 (May).

Kotarba, Joseph A. 2019. "The Everyday Life Intersection of Translational Science and Music." *Qualitative Sociology Review* 15(2):44–55.

Kotarba, Joseph A. 2013. *Baby Boomer Rock 'n' Roll Fans: The Music Never Ends*. Lanham, MD: Rowman & Littlefield.

Kotarba, Joseph A. 2010. "Introduction: Interactionist Takes on Popular Music." Pp. 3–4 in *Studies in Symbolic Interaction* 35, edited by Christopher J. Schneider, Robert Owen Gardner and John Bryce Merrill. Bingley, UK: Emerald.

Kotarba, Joseph A. 2007. "Drugmusictalk On-Line: An Ethnographic Analysis." Pp. 161–179 in *Real Drugs in a Virtual World: Drug Discourse and Community Online*, edited by Edward Murguia. Boston: Lexington Press.

Kotarba, Joseph A. 2002. "Baby Boomer Rock and Roll Fans and the Becoming of Self." Pp. 103–126 in *Postmodern Existential Sociology*, edited by Joseph A. Kotarba and John M. Johnson. Walnut Creek, CA: Alta Mira.

Kotarba, Joseph A. 1984. "The Existential Self in Society: A Synthesis." Pp. 222–234 in *The Existential Self in Society*, edited by Joseph A. Kotarba and Andrea Fontana. Chicago: University of Chicago Press.

Kotarba, Joseph A., and Nicolas LaLone. 2014. "The *Scene*: A Conceptual Template for an Interactionist Approach to Contemporary Music." *Studies in Symbolic Interaction* 42:53–68.

Kotarba, Joseph A., Jennifer L. Fackler, and Kathryn M. Nowotny 2009. "An Ethnography of Emerging Latino Music Scenes." *Symbolic Interaction* 32(4):310–33.

McGinty, Patrick J. W. 2014. "Divided and Drifting: Interactionism and the Neglect of Social Organizational Analyses in Organization Studies." *Symbolic Interaction* 37(2):155–86.

Melnikov, Andrey, and Joseph A. Kotarba. 2017. "Jack Douglas and the Vision of Existential Sociology." Pp. 291–314 in *The Interactionist Imagination: Studying Meaning, Situation and Micro-Social Order*, edited by Michael Hviid Jacobsen. London: Palgrave Macmillan.

Muller, Thaddeus. 2016. "Saved by Rock 'n' Roll: Lou Reed, His Fans, and the Becoming of the (Marginal) Self." Pp. 1–20 in *Symbolic Interactionist Takes on Music*, edited by Christopher J. Schneider and Joseph A. Kotarba. Studies in Symbolic Interaction 47. Bingley, UK: Emerald.

Nash, Jeffrey E., and Dina C. Nash 2016. "Feminizing a Musical Form: Women's Participation as Barbershop Singers." Pp. 45–69 in *Symbolic Interactionist Takes on Music*, edited by Christopher J. Schneider and Joseph A. Kotarba. Studies in Symbolic Interaction 47. Bingley, UK: Emerald.

Nowotny, Kathryn M., Jennifer L. Fackler, Gianncarlo Muschi, Carol Vargas, Lindsey Wilson, and Joseph A. Kotarba. 2010. "Established Latino Music Scenes: Sense of Place and the Challenge of Authenticity." Studies in Symbolic Interaction 35:29–50.

Peterson, Richard A., and Andy Bennett. 2004. *Music Scenes*. Nashville, TN: Vanderbilt University Press.

Ramirez, Michael. 2018. *Destined for Greatness: Passions, Dreams, and Aspirations in a College Music Town*. New Brunswick, NJ: Rutgers.

Sawyer, Keith R. 2000. "Improvisational Cultures: Collaborative Emergence and Creativity in Improvisation." *Mind, Culture and Activity* 7(3):180–85.

Shank, Barry. 1994. *Dissonant Identities: The Rock'n'Roll Scene in Austin, Texas.* Middletown, CT: Wesleyan University Press.

Skaggs, Rachel, and Jonathan R. Wynn. 2018. "Business in the Music Community." Pp. 173–93 in *Understanding Society through Popular Music*, edited by Joseph A. Kotarba. New York: Routledge.

Vannini, Phillip. 2004. "The Meaning of a Star: Interpreting Music Fans' Reviews." *Symbolic Interaction* 27(1):47–69.

Vannini, Phillip, and Dennis Waskul. 2006. "Symbolic Interaction as Music: The Esthetic Constitution of Meaning, Self, and Society." *Symbolic Interaction* 29(1):5–18.

Williams, J. Patrick. 2013. "Music, the Internet and Deviant Subcultures" Pp. 96–100 in *Understanding Society through Popular Music*, edited by Joseph A. Kotarba et al. New York: Routledge.

Williams, J. Patrick. 2011. *Subcultural Theory: Traditions and Concepts.* Cambridge: Polity Press.

Williams, J. Patrick and Phillip Vannini. 2009. *Authenticity in Culture, Self and Society.* New York: Routledge.

Williams, J. Patrick, and X. X. S. Ho. 2016. "*Sasaengpaen* or K-Pop Fan: Singapore Youths, Authentic Identities, and Asian Media Fandom." *Deviant Behavior* 37(1):81–94.

Wilshire, Bruce W. Wilshire. 2016. *The Much-at Once: Music, Science, Ecstasy, the Body.* New York: Fordham University Press.

CHAPTER 16

SOCIOLOGY OF MASS AND NEW MEDIA THROUGH AN INTERACTIONIST LENS

JULIE B. WIEST

SYMBOLIC-INTERACTIONIST perspectives allow for better understanding of the soci-ocultural influences of mass media and new media, as well as the relationship between new media and social change. This chapter explores symbolic-interactionist insights and perspectives on both mass media and new media, with a focus on the ways in which different forms of media influence—and are influenced by—meaning making through social interaction. To this end, it examines the relations among various media and the construction and interpretation of social reality, the ways media shape the development and presentation of self, and the uses and interpretation of media within and between communities.

WHAT ARE MASS MEDIA AND NEW MEDIA?

In the broadest sense of the term, *mass media* include any messages that are constructed for and transmitted to a general audience for the purpose of informing and/or entertaining, as well as the various communication devices and applications commonly used for such construction and transmission. Traditional mass media include television programs, motion pictures, radio broadcasts, books, magazines, newspapers, and advertisements. Although mass-media messages traditionally have been constructed for one-way communication—from creators to receivers—there long have been opportunities for audience feedback (e.g., letters to the editor, fan mail sent to celebrities, and phone calls to local news stations). Yet, the two-way communication inherent to new media has substantially expanded those feedback opportunities.

The term *new media* generally describes communication transmitted using digital technology—most often via online or cellular networks—although this definition is debated among media scholars (see Golumbia 2011). Engagement with new media frequently is at least semi-personal, with messages constructed for and transmitted to a restricted (i.e., not general) audience. Examples include SMS (short-message service) communication such as texting, social-media interactions that are filtered through privacy settings, videoconferencing with applications like FaceTime and Skype, and so-called sharing activities that allow limited access to user accounts and/or information (e.g., via Google applications, Dropbox, or AirDrop).

Although mass media and new media are distinct concepts, they also are fundamentally intertwined. For instance, new media have increased opportunities for two-way engagement with mass media, as consumers can use new-media technologies to create and transmit messages about—and to—mass-media entities. And some types of new media can be rightfully considered mass media, including internet-based advertising, public-facing social media such as Twitter and YouTube, and websites maintained by corporations, government entities, traditional mass-media outlets, and celebrities. In addition, many new-media technologies allow individual users to engage with other users, who may be known or unknown to one another, in the spaces and contexts of mass media. This occurs in comment sections of news-media websites and YouTube videos, for example, as well as when individuals "share" mass-media content on their private social-media accounts or via interpersonal communication channels (e.g., texting or emailing a news story to friends).

It should be noted that scholarly definitions of mass media and new media are not universally understood or agreed upon by all who create, disseminate, and consume media. Shared meanings are influenced by social contexts and may be particularly unstable during times of social change. As for new media, the term itself suggests transformation, and iterations of new media are integrally tied to temporal circumstances (i.e., all media would be considered *new* at the point of inception). Further, the ongoing evolution of digital-communication practices and platforms poses challenges to the associated meanings. Many social-media users, for example, do not adequately understand the efficacy of privacy settings or the potential breadth of their online audiences (Madden 2012).

SYMBOLIC INTERACTIONIST PERSPECTIVES ON MASS MEDIA

Fundamental to the symbolic-interactionist perspective is that one's humanity is not innate to the nature of one's existence; rather, it must be *learned* through ongoing social interaction, wherein meaning is collectively created, exchanged, and maintained. Symbolic interactionists emphasize face-to-face interaction as the crucial site of the meaning-making process but also examine the influences of shifting social contexts and institutions, which shape the ways in which social meaning is recognized, interpreted, and employed to construct lines of action. All social institutions play an important role in cultural transmission, but mass media are particularly influential because of their enormous reach and the consistency with which they produce and reproduce dominant cultural messages (Gerbner 1998; Wiest 2016).

Sociocultural Influences on Uses of Mass Media

The cultural context is particularly influential, as culture constitutes a society's system of shared meaning. It makes both social interaction and society possible. Culture provides a framework for people to understand their lived experiences and to communicate that understanding with others in ways that make sense (Hall 1997). As such, it allows for the collective construction of history and shared visions for the future.

Cultural norms, practices, and beliefs help to guide interpretations of mass-media forms and content so that consumers may find them useful. The still-popular "uses and gratifications" theory has a long history in communication scholarship dating to the 1940s (Wimmer and Dominick 2011), and numerous scholars employing the approach over time have uncovered an array of sociocultural influences on consumers' reasons for selecting certain types of media (see Ruggiero 2000 for a thorough summary). Among the findings, engagement with media is used to promote sociability, to maintain relationships with friends and family, to encourage community solidarity, to enable sociopolitical participation, and to fulfill the needs of one's self (Katz, Gurevitch, and Haas 1973).

Katz and colleagues (1973:165) also argued that consumers' selections and uses of media content are "considerably influenced" by the expectations associated with their social role(s). For example, religious leaders are unlikely to conspicuously consume sexually explicit or violent media content, and parents with small children may feel obligated to stay current with parenting magazines and blogs. Likewise, individuals with high levels of education and/or occupational prestige may avoid media associated with so-called low culture (e.g., talk shows, blockbuster films, and top 40 radio), instead opting for documentaries, independent films, and public radio. Thus, social meanings provide a basis for evaluating appropriate engagement with mass media. Temporal meanings suggest what media should be consumed at what times and on what days, and these meanings also shift according to situational and social role expectations. Moreover, meanings associated with appropriate *amounts* of time to spend with mass media depend on the type of content being consumed, the social role(s) of the consumer, and other sociocultural expectations.

Sociocultural Influences on Interpretation of Mass-Media Messages

Media scholars have long debated the amount of freedom consumers have to interpret media messages (see McQuail 1985 for a thorough summary). Early models of media influence (e.g., Lasswell 1948; Shannon and Weaver 1949) assumed a seamless process by which creators "encoded" messages with meaning before transmitting them to passive audience members for "decoding," an interpretive process by which consumers received the intended meaning (Hall 1997). Conceptions of media influence evolved to allow for the possibility of a two-way process by which receivers could provide feedback to creators (e.g., Westley and Maclean 1957), but most continued to disregard the possibility for multiple interpretations during the "decoding" process. Later models suggested a less-direct media influence. The "two-step flow" model identified "opinion leaders" as intermediaries who interpret media messages for receptive audiences (Wartella and Reeves 1985), and "agenda-setting," which contended that media influence what receivers think *about* but not necessarily what they *think* (Shaw 1979).

The symbolic-interactionist perspective makes clear that sociocultural influences shape all interpretive processes (see Zerubavel 1997). Thus, media consumers' membership in particular communities and groups, along with their location in relevant social stratification systems, influence what they notice and acknowledge in and about social life, what rouses their emotional and cognitive processes, and what meanings they ultimately derive from environmental signals. Because meaning is not inherent or embedded in any object or message, humans must rely on shared social meanings, which vary across time, space, and other relevant social contexts. The meanings of mass media were constructed in dialogue with others—whether peers, family members, colleagues, or others—well before the advent of social media, as these interlocutors are fundamental to all processes of interpretation.

In an increasingly global media environment, mass messages are transmitted to a vast array of sociocultural environments wherein localized meaning systems provide the basis for interpretation. Language translation provides a good example. Comaneci (2014) examined the work of journalists tasked with translating Western news stories for Romanian audiences, noting that the process is fraught with potential pitfalls related to differences in language use, political and economic interests, historical and current international relations, and news-delivery standards. Language is full of complex cultural meaning, and converting the literal meaning of a word into another language rarely conveys the same sentiment. The likelihood of cross-cultural misunderstanding poses a problem for media companies that seek to distribute low-cost content internationally, as translation and editing take time and reduce profits. A common solution to this dilemma includes minimizing dialog while maximizing visual content that conveys near-universal meanings, and this may explain why much of the US entertainment media exported around the world includes enormous amounts of violent and sexual content (Gerbner, Gross, and Signorielli 1994). The moral and cultural implications of this, however, require more exploration.

Role of Mass Media in Constructing Social Reality

Mass media disseminate and reinforce sociocultural meaning, and media scholars are nearly unanimous in their agreement that media portrayals influence consumers' perceptions of social reality (e.g., Fox and Philliber 1978; Gamson et al. 1992; Hall 1975; Massoni 2004; McQuail 1979; O'Guinn and Shrum 1997; Samaniego and Pascual 2007;

Smythe 1954). Research uncovering media influence spans decades, continents, delivery formats, and wide-ranging topics related to consumer attitudes, beliefs, and behaviors (see Morgan and Shanahan 2010). Yet, most consumers underestimate the extent to which they are personally influenced by media exposure (Davison 1983; Kellner 1995).

Much of this scholarship is rooted in the decades-long Cultural Indicators Project, which began in the mid-1960s under the leadership of late media scholar George Gerbner to study the long-term effects of television consumption on the perceptions of viewers. Establishing the foundation for what later became known as cultivation analysis, the project aimed to uncover patterns in mainstream television content and to examine the potential impacts on viewers. Their findings uncovered a distinct media version of reality—a "television world"—in which the features and trends of social life are presented in a consistent and complementary manner across program types and modes (Gerbner 1998:179). Moreover, cultivation studies found that the cumulative amount of time spent engaged with television played a significant role in shaping viewers' perceptions, with "heavy viewers" expressing notions of the social world in closer alignment with media portrayals, compared to "light viewers" (Gerbner 1998; Gerbner et al. 1986). The distinction between heavy and light consumption has eroded over time, as people in many nations around the world have become immersed in mass-media messages. Gerbner (1998:176) marveled about this shift, writing:

> For the first time in human history, children are born into homes where mass-produced stories can reach them on the average of more than 7 hours a day. Most waking hours, and often dreams, are filled with these stories. The stories do not come from their families, schools, churches, neighborhoods, and often not even from their native countries.

By 2018, the average US adult spent more than eleven hours per day consuming mass media (The Nielsen Company 2019). The global daily average for the same year is estimated at eight hours (Zenith Media 2019), and the majority of that content is produced and distributed by US-based companies that operate transnationally (Mirrlees 2013; Winseck 2008). Cultivation analysis suggests that the inevitable result of immersion in a media-constructed reality over time—especially when that exposure begins at a young age—is what Gerbner (1998:181) called "the steady entrenchment of mainstream orientations for most viewers." An important consideration in media-effects scholarship, then, relates to *whose* version of reality is portrayed in an increasingly globalized media environment (Winseck 2008).

The symbolic-interactionist perspective makes clear that people come to understand the social world and their place in it by taking on the perspectives of others. Broad understandings of social reality are largely shaped by acquiring the perspective of the "generalized other" in the role-taking process (Mead 1934/2015), while influences from significant others and reference groups offer further nuance. As Mead explained it, the generalized other can be thought of as a proxy for the community at large, whose purpose is to provide a means for assessing oneself and others according to universally understood standards. Within most economically advanced nations, however, where people increasingly spend more time with media than engaged in social interaction, it seems worth considering whether mass media have indeed *become* the generalized other.

Mass Media Influences on Self and Identity

Media scholars have long argued that media representations not only influence perceptions of social reality and social groups, but also play a role in shaping the self-concept (e.g., Davison 1983; Jeffres et al. 2011; Kellner 1995; Sanders and Ramasubramanian 2012). Much of this research focuses on consumers' development of self-objectification and the self-surveillance of their physical bodies (Dittmar 2009; Vandenbosch and Eggermont 2016), with multiple scholars identifying differences in these processes based on respondents' gender (e.g., Knauss, Paxton, and Alsaker 2008; Manago et al. 2015; Slater and Tiggemann 2010). Yet, Milkie (1999) found that stereotypical media images of female beauty—which privilege the appearance of white women—harm white girls and women more than girls and women of color, who are less likely to identify with such images or believe that their peers are influenced by them. Milkie's analysis is rooted in classical symbolic-interactionist theorizing, particularly the concept of "reflected appraisals," as she demonstrates the process of learning to view oneself through the imagined viewpoint of significant others (peers, in this case). Put simply, girls who believed that their peers accepted the message were affected by it, and girls who believed that their peers rejected the message were relatively insulated from it.

Scholars have identified additional factors related to mass-media influences on consumers' self-concepts, particularly the notions of *identification* and *transportation* (see Sestir and Green 2010 for a thorough summary). *Identification* generally refers to circumstances in which consumers vicariously live the life of a media character, seeing themselves in the same situations and facing the same obstacles, with an amplified effect in cases when a consumer identifies with the character's behaviors and decisions. In contrast to the individual orientation of *identification*, the concept of *transportation* suggests an immersed media experience in which consumers express a sense of cognitive, emotional, and/or mental connection to a media narrative or experience. Regardless of potential individual effects, studies indicating the social influences of media-constructed versions of reality also suggest likely impacts on consumers' perceptions of their own social groups and even themselves.

SYMBOLIC INTERACTIONIST PERSPECTIVES ON NEW MEDIA

Although the term "new media" most often refers to communication via digital technology, as well as the technologies that enable such transmission, any mediated form of communication would have been considered new at one time. Theories such as Media

Evolution Theory (Stöber 2004) make clear that the widespread adoption of any innovation requires a meaning-making process that is rarely seamless. Indeed, every successive innovation in technologically mediated communication since the electric telegraph of the 1840s depended on established meaning for its adoption into social life. The telephone, for example, was originally known as a "speaking telegraph." Although the name stemmed mostly from the fact that both devices operated according to the same electromagnetic principles, it also enabled shared meaning about a known medium to be used for interpreting a new one. Likewise, established social meaning about the telephone aided understanding of the cellular phone, which is illustrated by smartphone apps for making calls that use images of landline phones, for example, and the continued use of terminology like "dialing" and "hanging up."

Sociocultural Influences on Uses and Interpretation of New Media

As technological advancement tends to occur at an exponential pace, the material potential of new media is immense. For any new-media technology to gain widespread social acceptance, however, it must make sense within the existing cultural environment. Fine (1987) has been especially clear in pointing out the influence of broader cultural content in all systems of shared meaning, including subcultures and "idiocultures" (i.e., well-defined, group-specific subcultures). Drawing on extensive data he collected about the idioculture of Little League teams, Fine (1987) made clear how even team-specific symbols are linked to broader cultural meanings that boys learn during the socialization process. An "inside joke" or unique hand signal within a Little League idioculture, then, is not only an example of private shared meaning among teammates; it is also a cultural object rooted both in the culture at large and in a pre-adolescent male subculture.

Fine's (1987) framework helps to explain the success or failure of any would-be cultural object, as well as reasons why some innovations see long lags between invention and cultural adoption. An apt example is video calling, which was not a widespread practice in the most technologically advanced nations until around 2010 (Rainie and Zickuhr 2010). The activity was technically possible as early as 1970, however, when Bell Labs' Picturephone was commercially available and being marketed for homes only to be discontinued three years later. The failure of the Picturephone, as well as that of other audiovisual telephone-based devices that followed, is at least partly explained by the device's incompatibility with larger cultural norms related to household privacy and social interaction (Laskow 2014). As cultural meanings and social conditions change over time, a new-media technology that was previously incompatible with the cultural environment may eventually gain entry into the culture. This appears to be the case for video calling, particularly when computer-based voice over internet protocol (VoIP) services experienced massive growth throughout the 2000s (Park 2010). In a study of the factors that influenced actual consumer use of VoIP services, Park (2010) found direct support for perceived usefulness, perceived cost-effectiveness, and motivation for instrumental use, but no direct support for perceived ease of use, internet self-efficacy, perceived quality, system functions, motivation for communication, or motivation for entertainment. In other words, Park's (2010) findings indicate that a large portion of the initial rise in VoIP service use was because of its practical utility. Indeed, millions of people worldwide found themselves newly displaced during the 2000s for reasons related to civil wars, social unrest, economic collapse, and environmental disasters, thus increasing the utility of cost-effective communication over long distances. More recently, many people separated from loved ones, colleagues, and neighbors because of the worldwide COVID-19 pandemic were able to maintain those connections via online technologies (Vogels 2020).

Cultural meaning also guides assessments about the utility, quality, and proper uses of new media. Cross-cultural studies of Facebook users, for example, have revealed group differences in preferred uses of the platform, such as whether it is primarily for collective communication or for the maintenance of personal relationships (Barry and Bouvier 2011), how much time is considered a reasonable amount to spend using the platform (Vasalou, Joinson, and Courvoisier 2010), and how selective users tend to be in compiling their friends list (Barker and Ota 2011). Other studies suggest a more nuanced influence of cultural meaning among multicultural users. For example, one study (Albarran 2009) that included Latinx respondents residing in the United States and in several Latin American countries found that respondents living in Latin America expressed a preference for face-to-face communication rather than using a cellphone to share social information with friends, while the US respondents preferred cellphones. Another study (Leonardi 2003) that included only US Latinx respondents found similar acceptance for socializing on cellphones but collective disapproval of using a computer for social purposes, with most saying the impersonal nature of computer-mediated communication would damage relationships.

Cultural boundaries that define appropriate uses of space (particularly the ways in which public space is distinguished from private space) have been used to explain differences among various groups in their assessments about where new media should be used. Shuter and Chattopadhyay (2010), for example, found that US cellphone users preferred texting in public settings and when accompanied by strangers and acquaintances, while Indian cellphone users preferred the opposite (i.e., texting in private settings and in the company of family and romantic partners). Campbell (2007) examined cross-cultural views about the acceptability of cellphone use in specific types of public spaces, uncovering several differences—but more similarities—among respondents from the United States, Japan, Taiwan, and Sweden. Respondents from the United States and Sweden appeared to draw the line at spaces that carried an expectation of collective attention and those that did not, expressing tolerance for cellphone use on a bus or sidewalk and in a grocery store but very little tolerance for such use in a classroom, a restaurant, or a movie theater. In contrast, Taiwanese participants expressed more tolerance for cellphone use in a classroom, a restaurant, or a movie theater than any other group, and Japanese participants expressed tolerance for cellphone use in a classroom but nowhere else (Campbell 2007).

Relationship Between New Media and Social Change

Change is a characteristic of every society, as social life is continually shaped by shifting cultural, political, legal, and economic conditions (Bouwman and Van Der Duin 2007; Fulk 1993). Yet, the sources and trajectory of social change are often complex and rarely linear. It is clear, however, that the relationship between new media and social change is a reciprocal one; that is, the introduction and availability of new media may lead to a variety of subtle *and* large-scale changes in a society, just as changing social conditions may foster an environment that is conducive to emerging types of new media. Scholars who focus on the latter field oftentimes (and understandably) apply a retrospective lens. For example, studies of the so-called (stranger-to-stranger) sharing economy that emerged in the United States after the Great Recession of 2007–2009 have largely focused on social and economic conditions that have restricted access to ownership (of homes, vehicles, and luxury goods) for certain groups, promoted environmental sustainability, and transformed the nature of work, among other (largely postindustrial) concerns (Frenken and Schor 2017; Sundararajan 2016).

Much of the scholarship in this area focuses on increasing opportunities that coincide with the spread of cellular and internet-based technologies around the world, particularly those that have expanded access to information and communication, educational and occupational prospects, and the means for building communities across long distances. Some scholars have focused on the ways that new media can empower people in nations where, for economic or political reasons, there traditionally has been little or no ability to participate in global discourse (Ali 2011). Studies of the widespread adoption of new media in the Middle East, for example, found that people commonly used the technologies in defiance of a long history of government control and censorship in that region. Some of these activities included searching for and sharing information about traditionally taboo subjects (e.g., sex, religion, substance use, and mental illness) and forbidden topics such as criticism of government operations and officials, support for democratic ideals, and pro-Israel sentiments (Beckerman 2007; Wiest and Eltantawy 2012). Other scholars who recognize these potential benefits of new-media technologies also emphasize the large-scale inequalities that prevent access for many (Hanson and Narula 1990; Chen and Wellman 2004).

New media—especially social media, blogs, and cellphones—have particularly been hailed as important resources for organizing and implementing collective action and social movements, especially for marginalized groups (e.g., Della Porta and Mosca 2005; Langman 2005; O'Lear 1999; Wasserman 2007). Indeed, so-called cyberactivism movements have effectively used new media for decades to raise awareness and support for anti-war, anti-globalization, and global-justice issues (Juris 2008; Kahn and Kellner 2005; Langman 2005; Lievrouw 2011). Perhaps there is no better example than the role of new media in the organization and implementation of the Arab Spring revolutions (i.e., the sociopolitical uprisings that occurred in 2010 and 2011 most prominently in Tunisia, Egypt, Libya, and Yemen). These technologies were widely deemed critical to the successes of those movements (e.g., Eltantawy and Wiest 2011; Khondker 2011), especially because they allowed for rapid and widespread dissemination of information, promoted a sense of camaraderie and collective identity among protesters, helped to establish connections with outside supporters and sympathizers, and allowed for the release of information and images to outside media outlets and global publics.

New and Old Interactions with New Media

Results from a 2019 survey conducted in thirty-four advanced and emerging nations (Schumacher and Kent 2020) found high rates of new-media use around the world, with majorities in all surveyed nations reporting that they own a mobile phone and in nearly all of the nations—thirty-two out of the thirty-four—reporting that they use the internet "at least occasionally" or own an internet-connected mobile device such as a smartphone. Moreover, the use of social media has increased dramatically in emerging and developing nations, with levels in recent years approaching those of more advanced economies (Poushter, Bishop, and Chwe 2018). Yet, increases in new media use have not been empirically linked to decreases in offline interaction. In fact, internet users worldwide tend to have larger social networks than non-users and spend similar amounts of time interacting with others in person (Pew Research Center 2006; Silver and Huang 2019). Furthermore, interactions via new media are also governed by shared social meanings and interaction norms, many of which draw on—or even simulate—those that function in physical interaction spaces (e.g., emoji use in the absence of visual cues, typographical indications like italics and all caps in place of vocal inflections, and socially scripted greetings and exits to frame a complete interaction).

Although increasing connectivity via new media allows communication across space and time with unprecedented speed and thrift, it is important not to overstate the novelty of these communications or the reasons for their use. Tamir and Ward (2015), for example, argue that there is nothing fundamentally new about the human desire to connect to others, to share personal experiences, to maintain relationships, or to seek communities that afford a sense of belonging. Instead, they attributed such desires to the human "social mind" and suggest that new media have merely simplified one's ability to fulfill "complex social needs" (Tamir and Ward 2015:432). Likewise, new media frequently fail to deliver anything that is materially innovative. In a study of "interactive television," which first emerged in the 1970s as digital technologies began replacing analog versions, Kim (2001) detailed the ways in which the supposedly new television medium had been designed, built, and implemented according to the "organizing ideology" of traditional television. Other scholars have identified similar discursive practices in online and offline interactions, especially on topics that relate to dominant cultural ideology (e.g., Cisneros and Nakayama 2015), as well as persistent interaction routines in the new media practices of traditional social institutions (e.g., Himelboim and McCreery 2012).

New-Media Influences on Self and Identity

Classical symbolic interactionist theorizing on the self emphasizes the importance of situational factors—such as meanings related to time, space, social roles, and social ties to proximate others—in influencing what identities an actor might draw on to guide their presentation of self. Yet, the notion of a *situated self* tends to assume the existence of boundaries around social interaction, and the associated shared meanings allow for near-seamless development of a working consensus among participants, each of whom performs one social role at a time. However, the dramatic rise in the adoption and use of new media technologies in recent decades appears to have chipped away at these boundaries such that the postmodern self is frequently compelled to play multiple social roles simultaneously. For example, studies have consistently found that integrating new-media technologies into home life and work life frequently blurs the distinction between the two spaces (Sarker et al. 2012; Schalow et al. 2013; Van Kessel 2020; Yun, Kettinger, and Lee 2012), which can lead to personal conflicts and feelings of work overload (Yun et al. 2012). This illustrates concepts such as *multiphrenia* (Gergen 1991) and *multiplication* (Zhao 2005), which suggest that increasing pressure to perform multiple social roles simultaneously—via new media technology—can conjure overwhelming feelings of insecurity and inadequacy, largely because actors must apply multiple (and sometimes contradictory) perspectives to evaluate these convoluted self performances.

At the dawn of the digital age, scholars identified apparent changes to the self that were largely attributed to the proliferation of new media technologies. There was far less agreement, however, on what the future would hold for the self. Some scholars bemoaned an impending demise of the self (e.g., Gergen 1991), while others suggested that the self is simply adapting to postmodern circumstances (Holstein and Gubrium 2000). Indeed, the ability to connect with other people without temporal and spatial constraints has expanded the number and types of possible influences on self development for many people around the world. Zhao (2005) deftly argued that the widespread adoption of internet-based technologies has created a new domain of social influence—disembodied strangers—for children and adolescents, who previously were socialized almost exclusively by tightknit groups of proximate others within the family, school, and neighborhood. The self developed in postmodern times, therefore, may be shaped by an infinitely larger number of possible significant others and reference groups compared to the past.

Attempting to reconcile both the corporeal and the mediated influences on the development of the postmodern self, some interactionist scholars have theorized new versions of the self, including the *virtual self* (Agger 2004), the *digital self* (Zhao 2005), and the *cyber self* (Robinson 2007). Others argue that it is becoming gradually more difficult to distinguish between online and offline spaces, especially within advanced nations where many people report using the internet "almost constantly" (Perrin and Kumar 2019). For example, Gottschalk (2018) developed the *terminal self* as a deliberate double entendre that predicts dire consequences for the self as integrations between people and technology proliferate.

New Media Influences on Mass Media

Prior to the digital age, the media landscape was more clearly delineated: Media professionals (e.g., journalists, screenwriters, editors) working for large companies (e.g., news organizations, motion picture studios, publishing houses) created content that was sold to consumers, either directly or through distribution companies. With few outlets for consumer feedback, this traditional model was primarily a one-way communication process. The increasing access to new-media technologies around the world, however, has fundamentally transformed the creation, distribution, and reception of mass-media content (Mitchell et al. 2018).

Changes to Gatekeeping Role and Media Production

The widespread adoption of new-media technologies has broadened the mediascape and upended classic claims-making processes. In traditional media models, only certain groups of people were granted the authority to make claims (e.g., members of law enforcement, government officials, eye witnesses, and relevant experts) to media professionals who controlled what claims would be disseminated—and how they would be framed—to receptive audiences (Hall 1997). Today anyone in the world with a smartphone or other internet-connected device has the ability to record and disseminate information widely, swiftly, and with little cost or expertise. Such was the case during the 2011 Egyptian revolution when the government eventually banned professional journalists, and the protesters themselves were able to broadcast written and audiovisual reports to the rest of the world (Eltantawy and Wiest 2011).

New media also have expanded opportunities for consumers to influence media creation and distribution. Internet-based platforms like Kickstarter and Indiegogo, for example, have been used to crowdfund the production of niche media content (Bennett, Chin, and Jones 2015), and there are plenty of examples of media superstars (e.g., pop singers Justin Bieber, Halsey, and Shawn Mendes) who used new media tools to gain exposure and a public following while bypassing industry gatekeepers. In addition, new media platforms have enabled changing consumption patterns, such as proclivities for time-shifted TV and so-called binge watching, which are intertwined with the emergence of a new category of media content creator-distributors, including Netflix, Amazon, and Hulu streaming services (Jenner 2017).

Changes to Agenda-Setting Role and Influencers

In a reversal of the traditional agenda-setting model—in which media influence what audience members *think about* but not necessarily what they *think* (Shaw 1979)—new media foster an environment in which audience members influence *what* media professionals attend to but not *how* they attend to it (Barnard 2018). Most news-media professionals pay a great deal of attention to conversations on social media and blogs (Farhi 2009), just as social-media users and bloggers continue to spend abundant time with mass media. As such, agenda setting in the digital age is complex, resembling a back-and-forth interaction between media professionals and so-called influencers, most of whom are social-media users and bloggers whose large followings create powerful platforms for shaping public conversations (Freberg et al. 2011; Neuman et al. 2014). Boynton and Richardson (2015) argue that new media play a unique role in agenda setting primarily because of characteristics such as wide reach, interactivity, flexibility, and broad scope of topics and ideas. Moreover, the constant evolution of these technologies has made contributing words, images, and even video to the public discourse relatively simple and inexpensive for the average member of a networked public (Neuman et al. 2014).

New media also have played a substantial role in transforming intermedia agenda setting. Prior to the widespread adoption of new-media technologies, economically and politically powerful news outlets enjoyed tight control over the public agenda. Internationally, that agenda has long centered on Western—and particularly US—interests, events, and conceptions of the world (Guo and Vargo 2017), just as US news outlets have long mirrored the coverage and framing of elite newspapers such as *The New York Times* and *The Washington Post* (Vargo and Guo 2017). Studies of both intranational and international intermedia agenda setting in the digital age, however, have uncovered a far more nuanced relationship between traditional news media and online-only publications, including niche media and blogs. In particular, the relationship is one of interdependence and reciprocity: Traditional news journalists follow bloggers and cover the issues they raise, just as bloggers pay attention to traditional news and may find inspiration in some of that coverage (Meraz 2011; Vargo and Guo 2017). Although powerful nations largely continue to set the media agenda for emerging nations, that influence appears to be diminishing, especially for online-only media (Guo and Vargo 2017).

Changes to Feedback Channels and Production of Media Culture

Traditional mass-media models tended to assume a one-way process, with media outlets primarily in control of creating and distributing content to audiences that could interpret it in a variety of ways but had few opportunities to provide feedback or shape future content. Traditional feedback consisted mostly of letters and/or phone calls to editors and producers that may or may not be acknowledged or answered. Online news brought new opportunities for public commentary, but most media outlets had absolute power to disable, delete, or edit such feedback (McElroy 2013). Social media helped to equalize the dialog between media professionals and consumers, as it introduced possibilities for consumer feedback in a public forum that could not be controlled by those professionals but still incentivized them to pay attention and respond. For example, the convergence of television and social media known as "social TV" has created a backchannel of public conversation during live broadcasts that media companies and marketers are eager to engage (Proulx and Shepatin 2012).

Scholars have long raised concerns about the pervasive dissemination of Western (particularly US) media content around the world and the potential destruction of local cultures (e.g., Katz 1977). The tendency toward cultural homogenization via the spread of new media is illustrated by concepts such as *apparatgeist* (Katz and Aakhus 2002), which suggests that new media tend to include taken-for-granted meanings about their adoption and use that remain consistent across cultures. For example, many new media users in the Arab world who speak Arabic in their everyday lives consistently use English in text messages (Haggan 2007; Salem and Mourtada 2012) and incorporate Western communication styles such as the use of emojis (Daoudi 2011). Yet, the rapid adoption of *digital* media technologies may further amplify that tendency because of their unparalleled connectivity, ease of use, and low cost (Cairncross 2001; United Nations 2020). Scholars are divided about the potential cultural consequences. Some have compared Western media exports via digital technologies to cultural imperialism (McQuail 2010), as well as suggested that non-Westerners "fear a future in which everybody speaks English and thinks like an American" (Cairncross 2001:266). Others, however, offer a more nuanced view. Wang (2008), for example, argued that the power of globalized media to influence local cultures is limited and that "imported media is never a sufficient condition to dominate local cultures."

Conclusion

All media include some type of communication process whereby meaning is exchanged between at least two parties. Although there are many procedural differences between mass-media and new-media communications—in terms of how messages are constructed and transmitted, for whom and for what purposes they are intended, and what opportunities and expectations exist for their use—the successful transmission of any message relies on the existence of shared social meanings. This fundamental fact about communication helps to explain the enduring utility of the symbolic-interactionist perspective in media studies. Symbolic interactionism's focus on meaning making is rooted in social interaction, to be sure, but communication that occurs via mass media or new media is understood using the same interpretive frameworks that aid in making sense of face-to-face communication. Thus, symbolic interactionism provides an ideal lens for scholars studying the evolving media landscape, especially at a time when digital technologies are shaping communication possibilities and cultural practices around the world.

REFERENCES

Agger, Ben. 2004. *The Virtual Self: A Contemporary Sociology*. Malden, MA: Blackwell Publishing.

Albarran, Alan B. 2009. "Young Latinos' Use of Mobile Phones: A Cross-Cultural Study." *Revista de Comunicacion* 8:95–108.

Ali, Amir Hatem. 2011. "The Power of Social Media in Developing Nations: New Tools for Closing the Global Digital Divide and Beyond." *Harvard Human Rights Journal* 24:185–219.

Barker, Valerie, and Hiroshi Ota. 2011. "Mixi Diary Versus Facebook Photos: Social Networking Site Use Among Japanese and Caucasian American Females." *Journal of Intercultural Communication Research* 40(1):39–63.

Barnard, Stephen R. 2018. *Citizens at the Gates: Twitter, Networked Publics, and the Transformation of American Journalism*. Cham, Switzerland: Springer International Publishing.

Barry, Wail Ismail A., and Gwen Bouvier. 2011. "Cross-Cultural Communication: Arab and Welsh Students' Use of Facebook." *Journal of Arab & Muslim Media Research* 4(2–3):165–84.

Beckerman, Gal. 2007. "The New Arab Conversation: Young Bloggers in the Middle East are Breaking Taboos, Reaching Out to the 'Other' and Possibly Sowing the Seeds of Reform." *Columbia Journalism Review* 45(5):17–23.

Bennett, Lucy, Bertha Chin, and Bethan Jones. 2015. "Crowdfunding: A *New Media & Society* Special Issue." *New Media & Society* 17(2):141–48.

Bouwman, Harry, and Patrick Van Der Duin. 2007. "Futures Research, Communication and the Use of Information and Communication Technology in Households in 2010: A Reassessment." *New Media & Society* 9(3):379–99.

Boynton, G. R., and Glenn W. Richardson Jr. 2015. "Agenda Setting in the Twenty-First Century." *New Media & Society* 18(9):1916–34.

Cairncross, Frances. 2001. *The Death of Distance 2.0: How the Communication Revolution Will Change Our Lives*. New York: Texere Publishing.

Campbell, Scott W. 2007. "Perceptions of Mobile Phone Use in Public Settings: A Cross-Cultural Comparison." *International Journal of Communication* 1:738–57.

Chen, Wenhong and Barry Wellman. 2004. "The Global Digital Divide—Within and Between Countries." *IT & Society* 1(7):18–25.

Cisneros, J. David, and Thomas K. Nakayama. 2015. "New Media, Old Racisms: Twitter, Miss America, and Cultural Logics of Race." *Journal of International and Intercultural Communication* 8(2):108–27.

Comaneci, Catalina. 2014. "Domesticating the Alien in Press Translation." *Linguistic and Philosophical Investigations* 13:721–32.

Daoudi, Anissa. 2011. "Globalisation and E-Arabic: The Emergence of a New Language at the Literal and Figurative Levels." Pp. 61–76 in *Language Contact in Times of Globalization*, edited by C. Hasselblatt, P. Houtzagers, and R. van Pareren. Amsterdam: Rodopi.

Davison, W. Phillips. 1983. "The Third-Person Effect in Communication." *Public Opinion Quarterly* 47(1):1–15.

Della Porta, Donatella, and Lorenzo Mosca. 2005. "Global Net for Global Movements? A Network of Networks for a Movement of Movements." *Journal of Public Policy* 25(1):165–90.

Dittmar, Helga. 2009. "How Do 'Body Perfect' Ideals in the Media Have a Negative Impact on Body Image and Behaviors? Factors and Processes Related to Self and Identity." *Journal of Social and Clinical Psychology* 28(1):1–8.

Eltantawy, Nahed, and Julie B. Wiest. 2011. "Social Media in the Egyptian Revolution: Reconsidering Resource Mobilization Theory." *International Journal of Communication* 5:1207–24.

Farhi, Paul. 2009. "The Twitter Explosion." *American Journalism Review* 31(3):27–31.

Fine, Gary Alan. 1987. *With the Boys: Little League Baseball and Preadolescent Culture.* Chicago: University of Chicago Press.

Fox, William S., and William W. Philliber. 1978. "Television Viewing and the Perception of Affluence." *The Sociological Quarterly* 19:103–12.

Freberg, Karen, Kristin Graham, Karen McGaughey, and Laura A. Freberg. 2011. "Who Are the Social Media Influencers? A Study of Public Perceptions of Personality." *Public Relations Review* 37(1):90–92.

Frenken, Koen, and Juliet Schor. 2017. "Putting the Sharing Economy into Perspective." *Environmental Innovation and Social Transitions* 23:3–10.

Fulk, Janet. 1993. "Social Construction of Communication Technology." *The Academy of Management Journal* 36(5):921–50.

Gamson, William A., David Croteau, William Hoynes, and Theodore Sasson. 1992. "Media Images and the Social Construction of Reality." *Annual Review of Sociology* 18:373–93.

Gerbner, George. 1998. "Cultivation Analysis: An Overview." *Mass Communication and Society* 1(3–4):175–94.

Gerbner, George, Larry Gross, Michael Morgan, and Nancy Signorielli. 1986. "Living with Television: The Dynamics of the Cultivation Process." Pp. 17–40 in *Perspectives on Media Effects*, edited by J. Bryant, and D. Zillman. Hillsdale, NJ: Lawrence Erlbaum Associates.

Gerbner, George, Larry Gross, and Nancy Signorielli. 1994. "Growing Up with Television: The Cultivation Perspective." Pp. 17–41 in *Media Effects: Advances in Theory and Research*, edited by J. Bryant and D. Zillmann. Mahwah, NJ: Lawrence Erlbaum Associates.

Gergen, Kenneth J. 1991. *The Saturated Self: Dilemmas of Identity in Contemporary Life.* New York: Basic Books.

Golumbia, David. 2011. "Cultural Studies and the Discourse of New Media." Pp. 83–92 in *The Renewal of Cultural Studies*, edited by P. Smith. Philadelphia: Temple University Press.

Gottschalk, Simon. 2018. *The Terminal Self: Everyday Life in Hypermodern Times.* New York: Routledge.

Guo, Lei, and Chris J. Vargo. 2017. "Global Intermedia Agenda Setting: A Big Data Analysis of International News Flow." *Journal of Communication* 67:499–520.

Haggan, Madeline. 2007. "Text Messaging in Kuwait: Is the Medium the Message?" *Multilingua* 26(4):427–49.

Hall, Stuart. 1975. "Introduction." Pp. 11–24 in *Paper Voices: The Popular Press and Social Change, 1935-1965*, edited by A. C. H. Smith. London: Chatto & Windus.

Hall, Stuart. 1997. "Introduction." Pp. 1–11 in *Representation: Cultural Representations and Signifying Practices*, edited by S. Hall. Thousand Oaks, CA: SAGE.

Hanson, Jarice, and Uma Narula. 1990. *New Communication Technologies in Developing Countries.* Hillsdale, NJ: Lawrence Erlbaum Associates.

Himelboim, Itai, and Steve McCreery. 2012. "New Technology, Old Practices: Examining News Websites from a Professional Perspective." *Convergence: The International Journal of Research into New Media Technologies* 18(4):427–44.

Holstein, James A., and Jaber F. Gubrium. 2000. *The Self We Live By: Narrative Identity in a Postmodern World*. New York: Oxford University Press.

Jeffres, Leo W., David J. Atkin, Jae-Won Lee, and Kimberly Neuendorf. 2011. "Media Influences on Public Perceptions of Ethnic Groups, Generations, and Individuals." *The Howard Journal of Communications* 22:101–21.

Jenner, Mareike. 2017. "Binge-Watching: Video-on-Demand, Quality TV, and Mainstreaming Fandom." *International Journal of Cultural Studies* 20(3):304–20.

Juris, Jeffrey S. 2008. *Networking Futures: The Movements Against Corporate Globalization*. Durham, NC: Duke University Press.

Kahn, Richard and Douglas Kellner. 2005. "Oppositional Politics and the Internet: A Critical/ Reconstructive Approach." *Cultural Politics* 1(1):75–100.

Katz, Elihu. 1977. "Can Authentic Cultures Survive New Media?" *Journal of Communication* 27(2):113–21.

Katz, Elihu, Michael Gurevitch, and Hadassah Haas. 1973. "On the Use of the Mass Media for Important Things." *American Sociological Review* 38(2):164–81.

Katz, James E., and Mark A. Aakhus. 2002. "Conclusion: Making Meaning of Mobiles—A Theory of *Apparatgeist*." Pp. 301–318 in *Perpetual Contact: Mobile Communication, Private Talk, Public Performance*, edited by J. E. Katz and M. A. Aakhus. Cambridge: Cambridge University Press.

Kellner, Douglas. 1995. *Media Culture: Cultural Studies, Identity and Politics Between the Modern and the Postmodern*. New York: Routledge.

Khondker, Habibul Haque. 2011. "Role of the New Media in the Arab Spring." *Globalizations* 8(5):675–79.

Kim, Pyungho. 2001. "New Media, Old Ideas: The Organizing Ideology of Interactive TV." *Journal of Communication Inquiry* 25(1):72–88.

Knauss, Christine, Susan J. Paxton, and Françoise D. Alsaker. 2008. "Body Dissatisfaction in Adolescent Boys and Girls: Objectified Body Consciousness, Internalization of the Media Body Ideal, and Perceived Pressure from Media." *Sex Roles* 59(9–10):633–43.

Langman, Lauren. 2005. "From Virtual Public Spheres to Global Justice: A Critical Theory of Interworked Social Movements." *Sociological Theory* 23(1):42–74.

Laskow, Sarah. 2014. "The First 'Picturephone' for Video Chatting was a Colossal Failure." *The Atlantic*. Retrieved January 10, 2020. https://www.theatlantic.com/technology/archive/2014/09/the-first-picturephone-for-video-chatting-was-a-colossal-failure/380093/.

Lasswell, Harold D. 1948. "The Structure and Function of Communication in Society." Pp. 37–51 in *The Communication of Ideas*, edited by L. Bryson. New York: Harper & Row.

Leonardi, Paul M. 2003. "Problematizing 'New Media': Culturally Based Perceptions of Cell Phones, Computers, and the Internet Among United States Latinos." *Critical Studies in Media Communication* 20(2):160–79.

Lievrouw, Leah A. 2011. *Alternative and Activist New Media*. Cambridge, MA: Polity Press.

Madden, Mary. 2012. "Privacy Management on Social Media Sites." Pew Research Center. Retrieved December 15, 2019. https://www.pewresearch.org/internet/2012/02/24/privacy-management-on-social-media-sites/.

Manago, Adriana M., L. Monique Ward, Kristi M. Lemm, Lauren Reed, and Rita Seabrook. 2015. "Facebook Involvement, Objectified Body Consciousness, Body Shame, and Sexual Assertiveness in College Women and Men." *Sex Roles* 72(1–2):1–14.

Massoni, Kelley. 2004. "Modeling Work: Occupational Messages in *Seventeen* Magazine." *Gender and Society* 18(1):47–65.

McElroy, Kathleen. 2013. "Where Old (Gatekeepers) Meets New (Media): Herding Reader Comments into Print." *Journalism Practice* 7(6):755–71.

McQuail, Denis. 2010. *McQuail's Mass Communication Theory*, 6th ed. Thousand Oaks, CA: SAGE.

McQuail, Denis. 1985. "Sociology of Mass Communication." *Annual Review of Sociology* 11:93–111.

McQuail, Denis. 1979. "The Influence and Effects of Mass Media." Pp. 7–23 in *Mass Communication and Society*, edited by J. Curran, M. Gurevitch, and J. Woolacott. Beverly Hills, CA: SAGE.

Mead, George Herbert. 2015. *Mind, Self and Society*, edited by C. W. Morris, D. R. Huebner, and H. Joas. Chicago: University of Chicago Press. (Original work published 1934).

Meraz, Sharon. 2011. "Using Time Series Analysis to Measure Intermedia Agenda-Setting Influence in Traditional Media and Political Blog Networks." *Journalism & Mass Communication Quarterly* 88(1):176–94.

Milkie, Melissa A. 1999. "Social Comparisons, Reflected Appraisals, and Mass Media: The Impact of Pervasive Beauty Images on Black and White Girls' Self-Concepts." *Social Psychology Quarterly* 62(2):190–210.

Mirrlees, Tanner. 2013. *Global Entertainment Media: Between Cultural Imperialism and Cultural Globalization*. New York: Routledge.

Mitchell, Amy, Katie Simmons, Katerina Eva Matsa, and Laura Silver. 2018. "Publics Globally Want Unbiased News Coverage, but Are Divided on Whether Their New Media Deliver." Pew Research Center. Retrieved December 15, 2019. https://www.pewresearch.org/global/2018/01/11/publics-globally-want-unbiased-news-coverage-but-are-divided-on-whether-their-news-media-deliver/.

Morgan, Michael, and James Shanahan. 2010. "The State of Cultivation." *Journal of Broadcasting & Electronic Media* 54(2):337–55.

Neuman, W. Russell, Lauren Guggenheim, S. Mo Jang, and Soo Young Bae. 2014. "The Dynamics of Public Attention: Agenda-Setting Theory Meets Big Data." *Journal of Communication* 64:193–214.

O'Guinn, Thomas C., and L. J. Shrum. 1997. "The Role of Television in the Construction of Consumer Reality." *Journal of Consumer Research* 23(4):278–94.

O'Lear, Shannon. 1999. "Networks of Engagement: Electronic Communication and Grassroots Environmental Activism in Kaliningrad." *Human Geography* 81(3):165–78.

Park, Namkee. 2010. "Adoption and Use of Computer-Based Voice Over Internet Protocol Phone Service: Toward an Integrated Model." *Journal of Communication* 60(1):40–72.

Perrin, Andrew and Madhu Kumar. 2019. "About Three-in-Ten U.S. Adults Say They are 'Almost Constantly' Online." Pew Research Center. Retrieved December 15, 2019. https://www.pewresearch.org/fact-tank/2019/07/25/americans-going-online-almost-constantly/.

Pew Research Center. 2006. "The Strength of Internet Ties." Retrieved August 31, 2018. https://www.pewresearch.org/internet/2006/01/25/the-strength-of-internet-ties/.

Poushter, Jacob, Caldwell Bishop, and Hanyu Chwe. 2018. "Social Media Use Continues to Rise in Developing Countries but Plateaus Across Developed Ones." Pew Research Center. Retrieved March 2, 2020. https://www.pewresearch.org/global/2018/06/19/social-media-use-continues-to-rise-in-developing-countries-but-plateaus-across-developed-ones/.

Proulx, Mike, and Stacey Shepatin. 2012. *Social TV: How Marketers Can Reach and Engage Audiences by Connecting Television to the Web, Social Media, and Mobile*. Hoboken, NJ: John Wiley & Sons.

Rainie, Lee, and Kathryn Zickuhr. 2010. "Video Calling and Video Chat." Pew Research Center. Retrieved January 10, 2020. https://www.pewresearch.org/internet/2010/10/13/video-calling-and-video-chat/.

Robinson, Laura. 2007. "The Cyberself: The Self-ing Project Goes Online, Symbolic Interaction in the Digital Age." *New Media & Society* 9(1):93–110.

Ruggiero, Thomas. 2000. "Uses and Gratifications Theory in the Twenty-first Century." *Mass Communication & Society* 3(1):3–37.

Salem, Fadi, and Racha Mourtada. 2012. "Social Media in the Arab World: Influencing Societal and Cultural Change?" *Arab Social Media Report* 2(1). Retrieved October 30, 2012. http://www.arabso cialmediareport.com/UserManagement/PDF/ASMR%204%20updated%2029%2008%2012.pdf.

Samaniego, Concepción Medrano, and Alejandra Cortés Pascual. 2007. "The Teaching and Learning of Values through Television." *International Review of Education* 53(1):5–21.

Sanders, Meghan S., and Srividya Ramasubramanian. 2012. "An Examination of African Americans' Stereotyped Perceptions of Fictional Media Characters." *The Howard Journal of Communications* 23:17–39.

Sarker, Suprateek, Xiao Xiao, Saonee Sarker, and Manju Ahuja. 2012. "Managing Employees' Use of Mobile Technologies to Minimize Work/Life Balance Impacts." *MIS Quarterly Executive* 11(4):1–15.

Schalow, Paul S. R., Till J. Winkler, Jonas Repschläger, and Ruediger Zarnekow. 2013. "The Blurring Boundaries of Work-Related and Personal Media Use: A Grounded Theory Study on the Employee's Perspective." *ECIS 2013 Completed Research* 212. Retrieved January 10, 2020. http://aisel.aisnet.org/ecis2013_cr/212.

Sestir, Marc, and Melanie C. Green. 2010. "You are Who You Watch: Identification and Transportation Effects on Temporary Self-Concept." *Social Influence* 5(4):272–88.

Shannon, Claude E., and Warren Weaver. 1949. *The Mathematical Theory of Communication.* Champaign: University of Illinois Press.

Shaw, Eugene F. 1979. "Agenda-setting and Mass Communication Theory." *International Communication Gazette* 25(2):96–105.

Schumacher, Shannon, and Nicholas Kent. 2020. "8 Charts on Internet Use Around the World as Countries Grapple with COVID-19." Pew Research Center. Retrieved April 3, 2020. https://www.pewresearch.org/fact-tank/2020/04/02/8-charts-on-internet-use-around-the-world-as-countries-grapple-with-covid-19/.

Shuter, Robert, and Sumana Chattopadhyay. 2010. "Emerging Interpersonal Norms of Text Messaging in India and the United States." *Journal of Intercultural Communication Research* 39(2):123–47.

Silver, Laura, and Christine Huang. 2019. "In Emerging Economies, Smartphone and Social Media Users Have Broader Social Networks." Pew Research Center. Retrieved January 10, 2020. https://www.pewresearch.org/internet/2019/08/22/in-emerging-economies-smartph one-and-social-media-users-have-broader-social-networks/.

Slater, Amy, and Marika Tiggemann. 2010. "Body Image and Disordered Eating in Adolescent Girls and Boys: A Test of Objectification Theory." *Sex Roles* 63(1–2):42–49.

Smythe, Dallas W. 1954. "Reality as Presented by Television." *The Public Opinion Quarterly* 18(2):143–56.

Stöber, Rudolf. 2004. "What Media Evolution Is: A Theoretical Approach to the History of New Media." *European Journal of Communication* 19(4):483–505.

Sundararajan, Arun. 2016. *The Sharing Economy: The End of Employment and the Rise of Crowd-Based Capitalism.* Cambridge, MA: MIT Press.

Tamir, Diana I., and Adrian F. Ward. 2015. "Old Desires, New Media." Pp. 432–55 in *The Psychology of Desire*, edited by W. Hofmann and L. F. Nordgren. New York: The Guilford Press.

The Nielsen Company. 2019. "The Nielsen Total Audience Report: September 2019." Retrieved January 2, 2021. https://www.nielsen.com/us/en/insights/report/2019/the-nielsen-total-audience-report-september-2019/.

United Nations. 2020. "The Impact of Digital Technologies." Retrieved September 15, 2020. https://www.un.org/en/un75/impact-digital-technologies.

Vandenbosch, Laura, and Steven Eggermont. 2016. "The Interrelated Roles of Mass Media and Social Media in Adolescents' Development of an Objectified Self-Concept: A Longitudinal Study." *Communication Research* 43(8):1116–40.

Van Kessel, Patrick. 2020. "How Americans Feel About the Satisfactions and Stresses of Modern Life." Pew Research Center. Retrieved February 10, 2020. https://www.pewresearch.org/fact-tank/2020/02/05/how-americans-feel-about-the-satisfactions-and-stresses-of-modern-life/.

Vargo, Chris J., and Lei Guo. 2017. "Networks, Big Data, and Intermedia Agenda Setting: An Analysis of Traditional, Partisan, and Emerging Online U.S. News." *Journalism & Mass Communication Quarterly* 94(4):1031–55.

Vasalou, Asimina, Adam N. Joinson, and Delphine Courvoisier. 2010. "Cultural Differences, Experiences with Social Networks and the Nature of 'True Commitment' in Facebook." *International Journal of Human-Computer Studies* 68(10):719–28.

Vogels, Emily A. 2020. "From Virtual Parties to Ordering Food, How Americans are Using the Internet During Covid-19." Pew Research Center. Retrieved May 2, 2020. https://www.pewresearch.org/fact-tank/2020/04/30/from-virtual-parties-to-ordering-food-how-americans-are-using-the-internet-during-covid-19/.

Wang, Dawei. 2008. "Globalization of the Media: Does It Undermine National Cultures?" *Intercultural Communication Studies* 17(2):203–11.

Wartella, Ellen, and Byron Reeves. 1985. "Historical Trends in Research on Children and the Media: 1900–1960." Pp. 53–72 in *The Wired Homestead: An MIT Press Sourcebook on the Internet and the Family*, edited by J. Turow and A. L. Kavanaugh. Cambridge, MA: MIT Press.

Wasserman, Herman. 2007. "Is a New Worldwide Web Possible? An Explorative Comparison of the Use of ICTs by Two South African Social Movements." *African Studies Review* 50(1):109–31.

Westley, Bruce H. and Malcolm S. Maclean, Jr. 1957. "A Conceptual Model for Communication Research." *Journalism Quarterly* 34:31–38.

Wiest, Julie B. 2016. "The Role of Mass Media in the Transmission of Culture." Pp. 203–19 in *Communication and Information Technologies Annual*. Studies in Media and Communications 11. Emerald Group Publishing Limited.

Wiest, Julie B. and Nahed Eltantawy. 2012. "Social Media Use Among UAE College Students One Year After the Arab Spring." *Journal of Arab & Muslim Media Research* 5(3):209–26.

Wimmer, Roger D., and Joseph R. Dominick. 2011. *Mass Media Research: An Introduction*, 9th ed. Boston, MA: Wadsworth.

Winseck, Dwayne. 2008. "The State of Media Ownership and Media Markets: Competition or Concentration and Why Should We Care?" *Sociology Compass* 2(1):34–47.

Yun, Haejung, William J. Kettinger, and Choong C. Lee. 2012. "A New Open Door: The Smartphone's Impact on Work-to-Life Conflict, Stress, and Resistance." *International Journal of Electronic Commerce* 16(4):121–51.

Zenith Media. 2019. "Consumers Will Spend 800 Hours Using Mobile Internet Devices This Year." Retrieved January 5, 2020. https://www.zenithmedia.com/consumers-will-spend-800-hours-using-mobile-internet-devices-this-year/.

Zerubavel, Eviatar. 1997. *Social Mindscapes: An Invitation to Cognitive Sociology*. Cambridge, MA: Harvard University Press.

Zhao, Shanyang. 2005. "The Digital Self: Through the Looking Glass of Telecopresent Others." *Symbolic Interaction* 28(3):387–405.

CHAPTER 17

THE PRESENCE, PERFORMANCE, AND PUBLICS OF ONLINE INTERACTIONS

QIAN LI AND XIAOLI TIAN

INTRODUCTION

SYMBOLIC interactionists have long focused on how the dynamics of interaction are influenced by context and settings (such as the presence of others, public versus private spaces, and number of participants in an interaction). In the past decade, new information and communication technologies (ICTs) have evolved at a rapid pace, thereby increasing social interaction online and reshaping interpersonal and social interactions. As a result, online venues have redefined how users present themselves and how they construct collaborative meaning in social encounters. This chapter presents research that addresses these and other related issues while showing how symbolic interactionism contributes to scholarship in new media and internet technologies.

Because different forms of digital media have different technical affordances, they facilitate interaction carried out by the use of information communication technology, that is, mediated interaction, in different ways. For example, some forms may empower certain social groups while disempowering others, and some users may have more control over the online interaction process while others are perplexed by unintended consequences. In many ways, social interaction today has been transformed in ways that classical symbolic interactionists like Goffman or Mead have never encountered. Thus, it has fallen to a new generation of symbolic interactionists to contribute to understanding social interaction in the digital era and advancing the theoretical boundaries of symbolic interactionism.

To be clear, we do not argue that technological developments drive interaction that is passively inhibited. Instead, users are active agents who continue to adapt to new technical features by innovating their own practices and shaping their own actions. Both technological features and users' agency shape the new dynamics of mediated interaction. In the following sections, we will see how symbolic interactionism can help us to elucidate three main aspects of mediated interaction: 1) perceptions of the presence of others, 2) online presentations of the self, and 3) uncertain publics and the subsequent unique intersubjectivities of online interactions.

Technical Affordances and Forms of Presence Online

From Mead to Cooley to Goffman, the presence of others is a core feature in social interaction. Goffman (1959:15) defined "interaction" as "the reciprocal influence of individuals upon one another's actions when in another's immediate physical presence." Also, others serve as the looking glass for ongoing modifications to the self that one wishes to present (Cooley 1902; Mead 1934).

In the classical literature on symbolic interactionism, face-to-face (FTF) communication is considered the prototype of social interaction through which all other cases derived (Berger and Luckmann 1966:43). On the one hand, individuals in FTF encounters engage with others who have a physical presence. This physical presence allows actors to know the recipient of their utterances, especially since the information is communicated through their "naked senses," including sight, hearing, and smells, that is, embodied information (Goffman 1963:15). On the other hand, the receivers are simultaneously "made naked" because they are exposed to others and thus become givers of information as well. In other words, FTF encounters demonstrate a richness of information flow and facilitation of feedback that prevails over mediated interactions (Goffman 1969:5). Consequently, the physical and immediate presence of others underlies the process of social interaction, through which one can determine how to best present themselves and then continuously make adjustments to their performance based on the expectations and responses of others (Cooley 1902; Goffman 1963; Mead 1934).

However, the development of ICT and the internet has created an environment where the presence of others can no longer be taken for granted. The "others" of a particular online interaction are no longer "within range" (Goffman 1963:17) and experienced by individuals' immediate senses due to the lack of physical copresence. It is through mutual acknowledgment of one another's presence in a certain space that people conduct interactions. Since ICT-mediated interaction venues have no physical boundaries, it is impossible to pinpoint who is present and if they are fully engaged in the interaction at a certain point of time. For example, when an instant message is sent to someone, we do not know if the recipient is available or has access to their phone to respond. Even if an app is being used at a particular moment, it is impossible to ascertain if the other party is fully engaged or is involved in something else concurrently. Except video-chatting, most mediated interaction provides ambiguous cues—that is, the cues to determine how others have responded to one's performances and utterances are vague. With no physical copresence, online interactants can only form their perceptions of others, including their understanding of who is actually present and the extent of their engagement, by relying on cues provided by the technical affordances of a platform. Therefore, the perception of the presence of others becomes a subjective quality of the medium (Short et al. 1976). This perception changes not only how individuals perceive "others," but also how they define a situation, their reciprocal responses, and the dynamics among the interactants, as we will elaborate below.

Media and Cue Richness

A typical FTF interaction begins the moment a person enters the presence of another. This is followed by their awareness of others and a subsequent performance based on the information that this person seeks and possesses. However, in mediated interactions, others no longer have a physical, immediate, and continuous presence. Therefore, the subsequent process of seeking information and acting accordingly is transformed.

One of the most important characteristics of early mediated interaction was the lack of non-textual cues (Baym 2010; Walther 2011; Zhao 2005). Researchers at that time argued that the inability to convey nonverbal cues creates difficulties in sensing the social presence of others. Defining social presence as "the degree of salience of the other person in the interaction and the consequent salience of interpersonal relationship," Short, Williams, and Christie (1976:65) compared different media by their degrees of social presence. They found that the lack of social cues conveyed through mediums, like embodied information, impedes people's perception of others as "present" and "real," especially when a higher degree of social presence is expected. A lack of social cues (i.e., lack of cue richness) further prevents interpersonal contact and feelings of warmth and involvement in communications.

While social presence theory emphasized the subjective quality of mediums, Daft and Lengel (1986) introduced a new term to evaluate the objective capacity of a communication medium to reproduce information: media richness. Media richness varies from "lean" to "rich," depending on the different cues and channels of communication used, capacity for immediacy of feedback, use of natural language, and degree of message personalization. Lean media is usually asynchronous with very little visual information available, and as a result, it is less effective at reducing uncertainty and ambiguity. Rich media provides many different cues and visual responses, which leaves little room for error when actors interpret feedback from others. To be more specific, Daft and Lengel classified media into four categories in descending order of richness: face to face, telephone, personal documents, and impersonal and numeric documents. Thereinto, computer-mediated communication, such as e-mail, was reckoned as relatively lean media and less efficient for complex tasks (Daft and Lengel 1986).

However, the concepts of media and cue richness were not adequate to capture future developments in digital media because such research was conducted decades ago when mediated interaction was mostly text based. Yet, the focus on cue richness was inherited by a history of research topics that fall under what is known as the cues-filtered-out model. Theories in the cues-filtered-out model imply that mediated interactions fail to convey important social cues and reduce the quality of communication, especially in comparison to FTF interaction, where people can see, hear, and feel the emotions of others, and thus better understand one another (Walther 2011). The cues-filtered-out model assumes that cues correspond to functions—namely, media's different capacities to carry cues leads to incomplete social functions, such as causing misunderstandings (Menchik and Tian 2008), reaching consensus less frequently in task-related discussion (Walther 1996), expressing more hostility, and making extreme decisions (Kiesler et al. 1984) in mediated interaction. This perspective still sees FTF as the prototype of social interaction and mediated interactions as a lesser form of interaction. However, more recently, the argument that mediated interaction is inferior to FTF interaction has been criticized.

Gleaning Information through Digital Media

With the development of ICT, growing familiarity with digital media use, and the different capabilities of digital media, there is a need to reconsider whether mediated interaction communicates less information than FTF interaction. While Goffman (1983:2) has stated that "the telephone and the mails provide reduced versions of the primordial real thing," some now believe that communication is not necessarily inhibited by fewer social cues. On the contrary, when cues are limited, the importance of each cue increases (Walther et al. 1994). For instance, studies of online dating suggested that without FTF interaction, small cues increase in prominence when gathering first impressions (Ellison et al. 2006; Gibbs et al. 2006). Moreover, digital media's increasing familiarity and evolving capabilities mean that even when there is limited information in dating profiles and other online interactions (Ellison et al. 2006; Goffman 1959), users rely on "expression given" (e.g., photographs and self-descriptions) and "expression given off" (e.g., grammar) to scrutinize others (Goffman 1959).

Additionally, individuals develop various strategies to compensate for the lack of social cues and even fill in the details during mediated interaction. To address the absence of paralinguistic cues such as gestures, individuals frequently use semiotic tactics, such as emojis and emoticons, during text-based online interaction to specify the tones of a particular utterance. Semiotic tactics reduce ambiguity or misinterpretation and also bring social context into text-based interactions to facilitate interactants' awareness of each other (Menchik and Tian 2008).

As such, it is possible to glean information from others and form a perception about them in mediated interaction; however, this perception still differs from the one obtained during FTF interaction because the way others were made perceptible has changed. Moreover, the development of interactive multimodal platforms has allowed for communication through multiple channels, including audio, video, and so on (Herring 2016).

The growing multimodality of digital media not only places more social cues into mediated interactions but also creates different types of presences. For example, emailing, which involves known recipients, differs from online posting, which engages with an undetectable audience. Aside from such asynchronous communication systems, there are also interactions through instant messaging tools, like WhatsApp and WeChat, where users can and are often expected to reply immediately. While text-based messages still account for most mediated interaction, images, audios, and even real-time videos are now available, which increase the informativeness of communications. There are also digital games, such as massive multiplayer online role-playing games (MMORPGs), where avatars interact with others in a virtual environment that is considered real and meaningful (Gottschalk 2010).

To compare different digital media types, their use, and their differences from FTF interaction, Baym (2010) used seven concepts: social cues, interactivity, temporal structure, storage, replicability, reach, and mobility. Different media vary in their availability of social cues, including contextual, verbal, and nonverbal information, which affects whether communication can be carried out smoothly and how messages are interpreted. Interactivity, or more specifically social interactivity, is "the ability of a medium to enable social interaction between groups or individuals" (Fornäs et al. 2002:23). The temporal structure of a medium determines whether communication is synchronous or asynchronous and the delay in time between messages. For example, real-time chatting, like phone calls, is synchronous with almost no time lag, while e-mail is asynchronous because it allows extended contemplation and editing prior to sending or responding. Storage and replicability are "the extent to which the messages endure" (Baym 2010:10), and mobility is the portability of the media. Lastly, the size of the audience that different media can reach also matters since the number of online interactants who are visible and invisible influences not only the composition of participants but also one's awareness of the audience.

These seven concepts allow us to thoroughly compare different media types, examine how the ever-evolving world of digital media affects mediated interaction, and understand the consequences that occur when changes in media influence how people interact. With the abovementioned developments, what individuals are facing in mediated interaction is no longer the "less" salient presence of others. Instead, as ICTs continue evolving, emerging questions need to be answered: how do individuals detect and perceive the growing variety of presences, and how will individuals' perception of each other's presence affect the dynamics of interaction?

Detecting Presence in Evolving Interactions

As suggested by Goffman (1961, 1963), mutual acknowledgment is the premise of so-cial interactions. Thus copresence, the condition that "renders people uniquely ac-cessible, available, and subject to one another" (Goffman 1963:22), is emphasized. In FTF situations, full copresence requires people be in physical proximity to each other. Although sensing that another is "within range" is influenced by many factors (Goffman 1963:17), such subjective feelings are usually based on the physical proximity of interactants. In mediated interaction, however, that is not the case. Moreover, the de-veloping ICTs are complicating the process of detecting others' presence in the evolving interactions.

Thus, Zhao (2003) differentiated two dimensions of copresence: its mode and sense. Mode of copresence refers to "a form of human colocation in space-time that allows for instantaneous and reciprocal human contact" (p. 446), while sense of copresence refers to one's perceptions and feelings of being together. Therein, six modes of copresence are defined based on physical distance and their corporeality in the colocation site: cor-poreal copresence, corporeal telecopresence, virtual copresence, virtual telecopresence, hypervirtual copresence, and hypervirtual telecopresence. Such cross-classification is divided according to two types of proximity (physical proximity—copresence; and electronic proximity—telecopresence) and three types of presence conditions (cor-poreal presence on both sides—corporeal; on one side—virtual; and on neither side—hypervirtual).

The sense of copresence varies among the different modes. Though not as vivid as in corporeal copresence mode (i.e., FTF interaction), Zhao suggested that the sense of copresence sustains in mediated interactions under the condition of colocation, either physical or electronic. Within different modes of colocation, the sense of copresence is affected by interface parameters, such as embodiment, immediacy, scale, and mo-bility. For instance, high embodiment always engenders a greater sense of copresence. To measure and evaluate the sense evoked, specific designs and interface arrangements should be examined (Zhao 2003).

Besides the technical affordances, the types of mediated interaction also influ-ence how we perceive others. In his research of social media use, Hall (2018) classified mediated interactions by their degrees of involvement and how they are presented in social media. He identified the following types: social attention, unfocused interaction, routine impersonal interaction, focused social interaction, and deep communication. For Hall, most social media use centers on browsing and broadcasting and fit more into the categories of social attention and unfocused interaction. As a result, social media use would not be considered social interaction because it lacks "mutual acknowledgment by both partners of a shared relationship," "conversation exchange," and "focused attention by both partners on that exchange" (Hall 2018). While the somewhat strict definition of social interaction raises further questions about the sociality of other behaviors outside the range of social interaction, like broadcasting and browsing, it also reminds us to place the perceptions of others' presence back into the dynamics of interaction. Zhao and Elesh (2008) also emphasized the willingness to engage as a key factor in the establishment of copresence for social contact. That is, detecting presence is not only about sensing others being there: it is also related to the perception of being interactive, which echoes Goffman's decades-old definition.

To that end, Sohn's (2011) syntactic model of interaction offers a framework to reconsider the presence of others. Sohn delineated three levels of perceived interactivity (sensory recognition, semantic interpretation, and behavioral response) and created criteria to compare different media and their effects. Besides the corporeal presence perceived by the naked senses, individuals in mediated interaction also experience others through recognizing relevant information, such as unique texts or symbols, and behavioral control, such as "likes" and "retweets." For example, immersive 3D virtual reality might be considered a vivid form of presence at the sensory level. An informative textual blog that enables a better understanding of the blogger can also serve as an acceptable form of semantic presence. So, too, can an accessible, "commentable," and sharable post. These three dimensions are indispensable, yet different media enable the perceptions of presence to different degrees.

It is important to note that the varying perceptions of others' presence are not only consequences of changing technical affordances and evolving mediated interactions; in the reciprocal dynamics of interaction, such variance also impacts how individuals respond, perform, and present themselves.

PERFORMANCE AND SELF-PRESENTATION ONLINE

In addition to the perceived presence of others, interaction is about performance and self-presentation, as well as conversational exchange. According to Goffman (1959), the actor's performance is intended to define a particular situation and is based on how that actor views the mutual expectations of that situation. When there are substantial changes in the presence of the others who serve as audience, performance and self-presentation in mediated interaction and the construction of the self through interaction also change. Moreover, through interaction with telecopresent others, individuals may construct and perform a digital self that corresponds to changed presences.

For example, Zhao (2005) noted that the disembodiment and anonymity in telecopresence altered the way people viewed themselves. The anonymity of the online environment created a safe domain in which people could reveal themselves because others do not know their real identity offline. As a result, individuals were inclined to perform a version of themselves that emphasized physical appearance less, and ideas and thoughts—or an inwardly oriented self—more. This process of self-description shaped the digital self and became narrative in nature. This narrative nature enabled individuals to craft their self-presentation more elaborately, such as creating avatars (Gottschalk

THE PRESENCE, PERFORMANCE, AND PUBLICS OF ONLINE INTERACTIONS 303

2010) and editing personal homepages (Davis 2010). Yet, with the help of ICTs, the digital self is not only editable but retractable. The freedom in the self-presentation, in conjunction with the abundant information on the internet, made it possible for individuals to cultivate a multiple and de-centered self (Zhao 2005).

Due to anonymity and disembodiment when compared to the offline world, earlier studies considered the internet an independent and separate field. It is believed that people can have a different self with the help of digital media. However, with the growing overlap between online and offline lives, the connection between the online and offline self has been emphasized. The current prevalence of social media and ICT's incursion into our everyday lives further blurs the boundaries between online and offline networks. As a result, people's offline encounters are affected by their online performances, and vice versa.

Idealization in a Separate Domain

Since online identities are separate from physical bodies and the nonverbal or paralinguistic cues we rely on in offline encounters are scant in online interaction, people can abandon the constraints of offline identities and construct a different self. Moreover, the temporal structure of digital media allows one to adopt several different roles at the same time (Zhao 2005). While not everyone would desire multiple identities, the temptation to present a more ideal self remains.

Selective self-presentation is supported on many online platforms because their interfaces allow plenty of time for people to edit and revise information. As a result, they can conceal less desirable information and present themselves in more desirable ways. Along with the physical separation of senders and receivers of information, digital interfaces are empowering because they allow actors to have more control over their performances (Davis 2010; Walther 1996, 2011).

Selective self-presentation is also found in real-name situations, such as online dating. While one would expect more self-disclosure because future FTF interactions are anticipated, people are still conflicted about the desire to present their ideal self over their authentic self. One strategy used to mediate this conflict is to present an enhanced or future version of the self, or positive self-disclosure (Ellison et al. 2006). When users attempt to do so, the interactive and interface design of digital media plays an important role. For example, profiles on online dating apps are structured by limited search parameters, such as age, career, and sexual orientation, which enable quick filters for preliminary matching. But people can circumvent search filters by creating more subtle and different profiles (e.g., lying about one's age). While such misrepresentation has become a tacit norm, those who shun this practice are disadvantaged (Ellison et al. 2006; Gibbs et al. 2006). Zhao et al. (2008) conducted a study on Facebook, which is also a space with familiar others, and suggested that there is a tendency to create and perform a "hoped-for possible self" with ideal qualities.

Re-approaching the Offline World: Authenticity and Self-disclosure

Because the interfaces of digital media allow us to construct a different self and more acutely manage our performance, mediated interactions can inevitably be plagued by problems of deception, resulting in a drama with deceitful actors. However, empirical research shows that aside from the potential for idealization and deception, individuals also present their truer selves in mediated interaction. In fact, many actors emphasize authenticity and accuracy in performance and self-disclosure online.

Rosenberg (1986) suggested two components of self-conception: the "social exterior" and "psychological interior." The psychological interior is the "real self" because it holds the innermost thoughts and feelings produced in the psyche. Sharing thoughts and feelings is felt to be safer in a disembodied and anonymous online presence because there is little risk of losing privacy. Thus, with few consequences for disclosure, the "real" self emerges in the online world, while it is concealed in offline identities by the "social exterior." High levels of spontaneous self-disclosure could therefore be said to be encouraged by visual anonymity (Joinson 2001; Tidwell and Walther 2002).

There are also expectations and sometimes obligations for honesty in mediated interaction. While anonymity creates a sense of security in revealing the true self, studies have shown that people prefer a more accurate self-presentation in more intimate spaces, such as online dating. To establish a future long-term relationship offline, the authenticity of the personal profile is important to prevent discrepancy between online and offline selves (Ellison et al. 2006; Ellison et al. 2012; Gibbs et al. 2006). That is also true of social network sites (SNSs) with familiar others, like Facebook. The overlap between online and offline social networks compels performative consistency in both online and offline interactions. Otherwise, "inauthentic" behaviors will be penalized to varying degrees by other interactants (Davis 2014; Marwick and boyd 2011). While not all SNSs switch from online to offline, participants who develop their social network and form a "chorus" on online platforms might also feel obliged to share more intimate information (Tian and Menchik 2016).

Collaborative Manipulation of Impression Management in Situations

If idealization and authenticity coexist in performances, how are these two seemingly contradictory selves balanced? How are impressions managed in mediated interaction? What kinds of strategies are used? And what is the role of digital media as it evolves in the process?

On the one hand, it would be naïve to believe that self-disclosure can eradicate deception in interactions. Even under the pressure of an anticipated FTF meeting or surveillance of offline acquaintances, online self-presentations still differ from the "real" self in varying degrees because of the "foggy mirror": the difference between one's self-perception and the assessment of others (Ellison et al. 2006). Sometimes individuals' self-knowledge will stray away from others' perception. As a result, their self-presentation, though sincere, may appear "unauthentic" to the others due to the "foggy" self-image. In mediated interaction, this difference is magnified since online profiles are mainly created based on self-perception (Ellison et al. 2006; Gibbs et al. 2006).

On the other hand, while people are able and willing to present a better self in mediated interaction, identities cannot be fabricated from imagination. Rutter and Smith (1999) examined an online newsgroup, which contained fewer social cues compared to most other digital media, and showed that fantasy selves that are entirely different from "real" selves were less prevalent than anticipated. Robinson (2007) also found that postmodern interpretations of such fabrications or "cyber-selfing," which emphasized the fluidity, disembodiment, and multiplicity of the self, were erroneously generalized based on early studies of multi-user domains. The diversity of the internet user population has dramatically increased, and the reasons for internet use have extended far beyond online role-playing.

These all suggest that the balance between idealization and authenticity cannot be achieved merely through individuals' wishful performance. Rather, the dynamics of interaction that exist in FTF interactions still underlie this process. Many researchers have used Goffman's analogies of "front region" (where performance of self takes place) and "back region" (where performance is being prepared), and "given" and "given off" in symbolic interactionism, to understand different performances online (Goffman 1959; Hogan 2010; Marwick and boyd 2011; Robinson 2007). Robinson (2007) argued that the cyber-selfing process is the same as the formation process of the offline self since both involve the "I/me" couplet and interaction with others. While the processes are similar, digital media is empowering people by increasing their control over the presentation of their selves in mediated interactions. Meanwhile, their audiences are checking their performances reciprocally.

The advent of social media and the overlap between online and offline domains further complicate this process. For people living in the networked era, their online and offline lives are intertwined so deeply that what happened in one sphere will have consequences on another. As a result, they are obliged to deal with the relationship between online and offline self together with the balance between ideal and authentic through a process called self-triangulation. According to Davis (2014), this process utilizes two degrees of self-triangulation called networked logic and preemptive action. In networked logic, one must manage this balance and maintain their performances coherently across different platforms and life spheres, including online and offline. In preemptive action, one engages in offline behaviors explicitly designed to enhance online presentation, and that online presentation ripples out into the offline world, affecting how one performs their offline identity in the future.

Moreover, actors can intentionally expose their "backstage" by using other's expectations about authenticity to manipulate their perception of closeness. For instance, in online dating, even though honesty is not necessarily the best policy (Gibbs et al. 2006), the level and quality of self-disclosure are positively associated with intimacy and attachment (Park et al. 2011). Marwick and boyd (2011) also suggested that celebrity practitioners on Twitter can cultivate intimacy with fans by sharing "authentic" performances. In fact, the interface design of Twitter allows for more intimate engagements because it facilitates the "illusion of first-person glimpses."

While authenticity is valued and manipulated, the storage and replicability of digital media means that past self-presentations also become online "artifacts." Because the majority of information disclosed by others is permanently recorded and searchable, online users tend to think that online artifacts are reliable indicators of how others have behaved over time and under different social occasions. As a result, online "artifacts" are considered more accurate and authentic than social cues in FTF interactions (Hogan 2010; Tian 2017).

Therefore, the boundaries between authenticity and idealization are themselves blurred. When people balance between them, they are actually adjusting how they define the interactional situation that contains expectations, obligations, and rules regarding impression management. For example, authenticity in mediated interaction is more about a collaborative perception of coherence among interactants. Based on varying situations, individuals' presentation of authenticity changes as well. Being "real" in online dating is different from in social networking sites. How one chooses to perform "self" depends on recognizing what their audience expects and the audience's awareness of those expectations. Although individuals in mediated interaction seem to have more time and space in mediated interaction, the self-presentations are still embedded in the reciprocal influence with one another. Relocating performance in the process of interaction reiterates that it is collaborative, and mutual agreement on situational definition is critical for fluent interactions.

Uncertain Publics: Challenges and Strategies

Thus far, we have discussed how evolving digital media affects the presence of others and how they are perceived, and how people present and construct their identities and selves. Since online interaction overcomes the limitations of temporal and spatial boundaries, the range and number of audiences encountered also change. During FTF interaction, publics are structured by their physical environment. However, online publics vary among the different internet-mediated interaction forms and digital media. As a result, online interaction affects the awareness of audiences involved and the audiences' expectations.

Online publics not only include undetectable others, but because of the recordability and searchability of online disclosures, others can also access past conversations. Therefore, online performances are subject to potentially higher degrees of spectatorship and an enduring potential for publicity. This fundamentally changes the spatial and temporal dynamics of online conversations, and consequently the intersubjectivity of online disclosures (Tian and Menchik 2016). Regardless, a corresponding performance is given based on how one perceives others in the interaction. However, as the audience size and technical affordances of digital media increase, the gap between imagined and actual audiences increases, which eventually leads to many unintended consequences that cause misunderstandings.

We are now living in an era characterized by fluid and fragmented networks with increasing connectivity between the online and offline worlds (Davis and Jurgenson 2014; Rainie and Wellman 2012). When Zhao (2005) discussed telecopresent others a decade ago, the main problem interactants faced was disembodied strangers with relatively clear boundaries. With time, the forms of presence and composition of audience continued to evolve. As a result, individuals faced new challenges brought about by the audience's responses: less freedom in their performances, increasing uncertainties about their audience, and difficulty reaching consensus on the definition of situations. These challenges reached a peak in the age of social media.

Characteristics of the different sites of interaction also played an important role in configuring the networked audience. For example, boyd (2010) summarized four SNS affordances: persistence, searchability, replicability, and scalability. While persistence and replicability are similar to storage and replicability in Baym's (2010) work, searchability signifies content that can be accessed through search, and scalability is the "possibility of tremendous visibility" of content. The aforementioned affordances elicit three dynamics that make for more uncertain publics and that cause some unintended consequences in mediated interaction: invisible audiences, collapsed contexts, and blurred public and private spaces (boyd 2010). But new opportunities are also made possible by digital media. For example, the lack of visible status symbols online makes customers feel more comfortable during online shopping (Tian 2018), and the easiness of publishing online makes it possible for amateur writers to find fame (Tian and Adorjan 2016).

Invisible Audiences

Online interaction involves an electronic screen, not corporeal people. While some websites provide features that visualize the presence of others, the audience is mostly invisible until interaction. This invisibility not only refers to the cueing systems and how the words of others are interpreted, but it also influences awareness of audience size and composition. That is, perceived others might not be the actual audience. There might be lurkers who search and view performances long after they have happened (boyd 2010). Virtual "curators" also add complexity as these algorithms filter, order, and distribute online artifacts based on site design rather than the intentions of the user (Hogan 2010).

If an audience is unknown, how then does one decide to behave? One strategy is to imagine an audience, then socially perform and navigate accordingly (boyd 2010). For example, personal homepages can be constructed in anticipation of virtual "generalized others" (Marwick and boyd 2011; Robinson 2007). However, the term "imagine" does not mean creating something out of nothing. Individuals' predictions are influenced by both structural and agent forces. Litt (2012) differentiated some factors under these two categories. Structural forces contain social norms in social roles and contexts, the active audience, and the features of online sites or services, while agent forces include one's sense of socially acceptable behaviors, social media motivations, and internet skills. Even though misalignment is inevitable, these forces help to construct a clearer conceptualization.

Collapsed Contexts

Besides uncertainty in who one is communicating with, the multiplicity of online audience results in another conundrum: context collapse. Interaction always occurs in a certain context. Based on situations, space settings, social networks, and relevant norms, corresponding identities are performed in defined contexts. The audience responds and evaluates the appropriateness of their performances based on their expectations. Since people have multiple identities and roles, sometimes there is the need to partition contexts. If boundaries are erased and different contexts collide, then there is the dilemma of simultaneously managing different identities, social norms, and audiences. Subsequently, context collapse occurs (boyd 2010; Davis and Jurgenson 2014).

As discussed, the reach of digital media and online platforms is extensive. Multiple audiences are amassed regardless of context. Since they are invisible, performances are received by many. Tian and Menchik (2016) defined this one-to-many structure as an n-adic organization. Online one-to-many interaction is n-adic because at a certain point the number of participants in the interaction is unknown compared to dyadic or triadic interaction as discussed by Simmel (1950). Tian and Menchik (2016) differentiated three types of audiences that bloggers encounter: an uncertain audience, the chorus, and influential others. With activity and content reciprocity, bloggers gradually establish relationships with regular interactants (the "chorus"). As reciprocity continues and other audiences mostly remain invisible, the bloggers interact with their chorus as if they were the only audience. However, there may be influential outsiders and even total strangers that are receiving their performances. When intimate and sometimes private information elicits a response, the collapse of context creates feelings of privacy invasion. Davis (2014) further extended the consequences of context collapse. Not only do unintended audiences seep into the context, but their contents also infiltrate that context. Aside from self-generated content, other-generated content also affects how observers judge a situation (Walther et al. 2009). Inappropriate other-generated content causes embarrassment and even a failed performance. Moreover, such collapses can blur the boundaries between online and offline realms and affect FTF interactions. For example, posted content can be viewed publicly even if it is not meant to be read by everyone. Coupled with the fact that online artifacts are considered more accurate and reliable than embodied cues in FTF interaction, others could notice mismatched information that misaligns their expectations in the FTF interaction and causes embarrassment (Tian 2017).

There are strategies to circumvent these issues. Many websites are equipped with technical affordances that give users control over access to posts, monitoring of posts, and even removal of inappropriate content (Davis 2014; Tian and Menchik 2016; Vitak et al. 2012). To address context collapse, Hogan (2010) proposed the "lowest denominator strategy," that is, information that is shared is appropriate for everyone—hence, it is the lowest denominator. At that point, the risk of inappropriate and offensive behavior is greatly reduced. Other strategies that are used to navigate the lowest denominator are self-censorship and balance. Self-censorship ensures that performances are safe even when there is a "nightmare reader." Balance is offsetting audience expectations with personal authenticity (Marwick and boyd 2011). Other researchers, such as Marder, Joinson, Shankar, and Thirlaway (2016), have also indicated that, rather than the lowest denominator, the strongest audience effect has a larger role in affecting online self-presentation. Their research about young Facebook users showed that, when facing audiences who score high in both standards and values, they were more cautious about communicating content and conducted self-cleansing more frequently.

Although people utilized these strategies to reconstruct the boundaries of context, either physically or subjectively, and align their performance accordingly, not all of them work ideally. For instance, self-censorship sacrifices depth and intimacy in sharing. And balance between audience expectation and personal authenticity sometimes makes revelation more like purposive strategies rather than sincere self-disclosure (Marwick and boyd 2011). When the misalignment between imagined audience and actual audience continues to exist, mutual agreement of definition about the situation cannot be achieved fluently and more problems will arise.

Blurred Public and Private Spaces

Finally, another unintended consequence of networked audiences in mediated interaction is the blurring of private and public spaces. In the networked era, most information is linkable, sharable, and accessible. As a result, personal information is made visible and publicly available in an uncontrollable way.

When mediated interaction contains networked audiences, privacy must be reconceptualized. As discussed earlier, oversharing can violate one's own privacy. However, such a blurred line is not caused by one's indifference about the sensitive information but by context collapse and n-adic audience. That is, individuals mistake the public venue as private due to the reciprocity with their chorus and unawareness of the actual audience (Tian and Menchik 2016; Vitak et al. 2015). Even with close attention to privacy and disclosure, a networked audience can still take the dissemination of information out of people's control. Considering that, Marwick and boyd (2014) suggested a networked privacy model, which indicated that information flow and norms are no longer constrained in certain groups and contexts, but are being negotiated constantly within the network in which individuals are embedded.

Other concepts to reconsider are the public and sociality. Given that situational and contextual perspectives are considered critical to our understanding of behaviors in public (Goffman 1963), how should we understand behavior when facing context collapse and blurred situations in mediated interaction? Take Twitter as an example. Murthy (2012) introduced "synthetic embedding" to describe interaction on Twitter. Through retweets, the utterance is continually re-embedded into the situated present of the retweeters and subsequent recipients. Moreover, the uncertain audience further complicates how the original utterance is synthetically embedded in different temporal and contextual frames. Therefore, what is situationally appropriate is under ongoing debate, and it threatens to decontextualize utterances and perplex actors in the public space.

In the age of social media, these three dynamics—the invisible audience, context collapse, and blurring private and public space—are continually shaping the uncertain audience and bringing about challenges to the mediated interaction. People have also developed strategies to recontextualize interaction. Yet more research is needed on the reciprocal influence of actors given their evolving presence, new types of collaborative performance, and the increasingly uncertain audience.

Conclusion

In this chapter, we summarized the major contributions of symbolic interactionists to mediated interaction. The development of new digital media has changed the settings and context as well as the modalities of interpersonal communication. Nonetheless, the key components of social interaction persist: perceptions of the presence of others, presentations of self, and publics. Many situations have changed with technology, and symbolic interactionism continues to inform how these changed contexts influence social interaction and its consequences and implications.

In summary, without physical colocation, the cues available during mediated interaction are determined by the platform of interaction. While mediated interaction has different levels of cue richness, "richer" is not always "better" because modes of copresence and levels of perceived interactivity also influence the structure of interaction and create various perceptions of the presence of others. Such varying perceptions further influence how users present themselves online. The lack of physical cues makes it possible for users to get rid of the constrictions of offline bodies and focus more on inner thoughts and ideas rather than appearances. The flexibility brought by asynchronous interaction and editable interface also allows for more control over self-presentation, hence an idealized self and "future" self is made possible. Meanwhile, the expectation of accuracy aroused from the interaction also shapes individuals' online performance. Subsequently,

THE PRESENCE, PERFORMANCE, AND PUBLICS OF ONLINE INTERACTIONS 311

people are obliged to balance between ideal and authentic. Since the authenticity and idealization in mediated interaction are determined by the mutual expectations of interactants in specific situated contexts, to achieve the balance is to coherently align the expectations. As such, people have gradually developed collaborative manipulation of impression management by negotiating situated contexts with the audience.

Nonetheless, new uncertainties have also emerged for digital media users. The most salient new uncertainty is interaction with an uncertain public. With the growing use of social media, every user is subjected to this type of interaction and needs to deal with the consequences of this new intersubjectivity. This is an avenue for further research as questions still have yet to be explored. For example, in what ways have expectations, behaviors, or online disclosures changed after past online disclosures brought about misunderstandings? Another direction for future research is examining how online interaction has influenced expectations, especially concerning the boundaries between the virtual and the real. For example, when users spend so much time in online role-playing games, would these virtual identities and interactions influence their offline identities and lives? Online interaction has infiltrated almost all facets of social life, but the repercussions are still not studied enough. Symbolic interactionism as an approach will continue to be relevant and important in the examination of such new phenomena.

REFERENCES

Baym, Nancy. 2010. *Personal Connections in the Digital Age*. Malden, MA: Polity Press.

Berger, Peter, and Thomas Luckmann. 1966. *The Social Construction of Reality: A Treatise in the Sociology of Knowledge*. Garden City, NY: Doubleday.

boyd, Danah. 2010. "Social Network Sites as Networked Publics: Affordances, Dynamics, and Implications." Pp. 39–58 in *A Networked Self: Identity, Community, and Culture on Social Network Sites*, edited by Zizi Papacharissi. New York: Routledge.

Cooley, Charles. 1902. *Human Nature and the Social Order*. New York: C. Scribner's Sons.

Daft, Richard, and Robert Lengel. 1986. "Organizational Information Requirements, Media Richness and Structural Design." *Management Science* 32(5):554–71.

Davis, Jenny. 2010. "Architecture of the Personal Interactive Homepage: Constructing the Self through MySpace." *New Media & Society* 12(7):1103–19.

Davis, Jenny. 2014. "Triangulating the Self: Identity Processes in a Connected Era." *Symbolic Interaction* 37(4):500–23.

Davis, Jenny, and Nathan Jurgenson. 2014. "Context Collapse: Theorizing Context Collusions and Collisions." *Information, Communication & Society* 17(4):476–85.

Ellison, Nicole, Rebecca Heino, and Jennifer Gibbs. 2006. "Managing Impressions Online: Self-presentation Processes in the Online Dating Environment." *Journal of Computer-mediated Communication* 11(2):415–41.

Ellison, Nicole, Jeffrey Hancock, and Catalina Toma. 2012. "Profile as Promise: A Framework for Conceptualizing Veracity in Online Dating Self-presentations." *New Media & Society* 14(1):45–62.

Fornäs, Johan, et al. 2002. *Into Digital Borderlands*. Edited by Fornäs Johan et al. Digital Borderlands: Cultural Studies of Identity and Interactivity on the Internet. New York: Peter Lang Publishing.

Gibbs, Jennifer, Nicole Ellison, and Rebecca Heino. 2006. "Self-presentation in Online Personals: The Role of Anticipated Future Interaction, Self-disclosure, and Perceived Success in Internet Dating." *Communication Research* 33(2):152–77.

Goffman, Erving. 1959. *The Presentation of Self in Everyday Life*. Harmondsworth: Penguin.

Goffman, Erving. 1961. *Encounters: Two Studies in the Sociology of Interaction*. Indianapolis: Bobbs-Merrill.

Goffman, Erving. 1963. *Behavior in Public Places: Notes on the Social Organization of Gatherings*. New York: Free Press.

Goffman, Erving. 1969. *Strategic Interaction*. Philadelphia: University of Pennsylvania Press.

Goffman, Erving. 1983. "The Interaction Order." *American Sociological Review* 48(1):1–17.

Gottschalk, Simon. 2010. "The Presentation of Avatars in Second Life: Self and Interaction in Social Virtual Spaces." *Symbolic Interaction* 33(4):501–25.

Hall, Jeffrey. 2018. "When Is Social Media Use Social Interaction? Defining Mediated Social Interaction." *New Media & Society* 20(1):162–79.

Herring, Susan. 2016. "New Frontiers in Interactive Multimodal Communication." Pp. 398–402 in *The Routledge handbook of language and digital communication*, edited by Alexandra Georgakopoulou and Tereza Spilioti. New York: Routledge.

Hogan, Bernie. 2010. "The Presentation of Self in the Age of Social Media: Distinguishing Performances and Exhibitions Online." *Bulletin of Science, Technology & Society* 30(6):377–86.

Joinson, Adam. 2001. "Self-disclosure in Computer-mediated Communication: The Role of Self-awareness and Visual Anonymity." *European Journal of Social Psychology* 31(2);177–92.

Kiesler, Sara, Jane Siegel, and Timothy McGuire. 1984. "Social Psychological Aspects of Computer-mediated Communication." *American Psychologist* 39(10):1123–34.

Litt, Eden. 2012. "Knock, Knock. Who's There? The Imagined Audience." *Journal of Broadcasting & Electronic Media* 56(3):330–45.

Marder, Ben, et al. 2016. "Strength Matters: Self-presentation to the Strongest Audience rather than Lowest Common Denominator when Faced with Multiple Audiences in Social Network Sites." *Computers in Human Behavior* 61:56–62.

Marwick, Alice, and danah boyd. 2011. "I Tweet Honestly, I Tweet Passionately: Twitter Users, Context Collapse, and the Imagined Audience." *New Media & Society* 13(1):114–33.

Marwick, Alice, and danah boyd. 2014. "Networked Privacy: How Teenagers Negotiate Context in Social Media." *New Media & Society* 16(7):1051–67.

Mead, George Herbert. 1934. *Mind, Self and Society*. Chicago: University of Chicago Press.

Menchik, Daniel, and Xiaoli Tian. 2008. "Putting Social Context into Text: The Semiotics of E-mail Interaction." *American Journal of Sociology* 114(2):332–70.

Murthy, Dhiraj. 2012. "Towards a Sociological Understanding of Social Media: Theorizing Twitter." *Sociology* 46(6):1059–73.

Park, Namkee, Borae Jin, and Seung- A. Annie Jin. 2011. "Effects of Self-disclosure on Relational Intimacy in Facebook." *Computers in Human Behavior* 27(5):1974–83.

Rainie, Lee, and Barry Wellman. 2012. *Networked: The New Social Operating System*. Cambridge, MA: MIT Press.

Robinson, Laura. 2007. "The Cyberself: the Self-ing Project Goes Online, Symbolic Interaction in the Digital Age." *New Media & Society* 9(1):93–110.

Rosenberg, Morris. 1986. *Conceiving the Self*. Malabar, FL: Robert E. Krieger.

Rutter, Jason, and Greg Smith. 1999. "Presenting the Offline Self in an Everyday, Online Environment." *Identities in Action Conference* (Gregynog).

Short, John, Ederyn Williams, and Bruce Christie. 1976. *The Social Psychology of Telecommunications.* London: John Wiley.

Simmel, Georg. 1950. *The Sociology of Georg Simmel.* New York: The Free Press.

Sohn, Dongyoung. 2011. "Anatomy of Interaction Experience: Distinguishing Sensory, Semantic, and Behavioral Dimensions of Interactivity." *New Media & Society* 13(8):1320–35.

Tian, Xiaoli. 2017. "Embodied versus Disembodied Information: How Online Artifacts Influence Offline Interpersonal Interactions." *Symbolic Interaction* 40(2):190–211.

Tian, Xiaoli. 2018. "Escaping the Interpersonal Power Game: Online Shopping in China." *Qualitative Sociology* 41(4):545–68.

Tian, Xiaoli, and Daniel Menchik. 2016. "On Violating One's Own Privacy: N-adic Utterances and Inadvertent Disclosures in Online Venues." Pp. 3–30 in *Communication and Information Technologies Annual 11*, edited by Laura Robinson, Jeremy Schulz, Shelia Cotton, Timothy Hale, Apryl Williams, and Joy Hightower. Bingley: Emerald Group Publishing Limited.

Tian, Xiaoli, and Michael Adorjan. 2016. "Fandom and Coercive Empowerment: the Commissioned Production of Chinese Online Literature." *Media, Culture & Society* 38(6):881–900.

Tidwell, Lisa Collins, and Joseph Walther. 2002. "Computer-mediated Communication Effects on Disclosure, Impressions, and Interpersonal Evaluations: Getting to Know One Another a Bit at a Time." *Human Communication Research* 28(3):317–48.

Vitak, Jessica, et al. 2012. "'Why won't You Be My Facebook Friend?': Strategies for Managing Context Collapse in the Workplace." Pp. 555–57 in *Proceedings of the 2012 iConference*, edited by Jens-Erik Mai. Toronto: ACM.

Vitak, Jessica, et al. 2015. "Balancing Audience and Privacy Tensions on Social Network Sites: Strategies of Highly Engaged Users." *International Journal of Communication* 9:1485–504.

Walther, Joseph. 1996. "Computer-mediated Communication: Impersonal, Interpersonal, and Hyperpersonal Interaction." *Communication Research* 23(1):3–43.

Walther, Joseph. 2011. "Theories of Computer-mediated Communication and Interpersonal Relations." Pp. 443–79 in *The SAGE Handbook of Interpersonal Communication*, edited by Mark L. Knapp and John A. Daly. 4th ed. Thousand Oaks, CA: SAGE.

Walther, Joseph, Jeffrey Anderson, and David Park. 1994. "Interpersonal Effects in Computer-mediated Interaction: A Meta-analysis of Social and Antisocial Communication." *Communication Research* 21(4):460–87.

Walther, Joseph, et al. 2009. "Self-generated versus Other-generated Statements and Impressions in Computer-mediated Communication: A Test of Warranting Theory Using Facebook." *Communication Research* 36(2):229–53.

Zhao, Shanyang. 2003. "Toward a Taxonomy of Copresence." *Presence: Teleoperators and Virtual Environments* 12(5):445–55.

Zhao, Shanyang. 2005. "The Digital Self: Through the Looking Glass of Telecopresent Others." *Symbolic Interaction* 28(3):387–405.

Zhao, Shanyang, and David Elesh. 2008. "Copresence as 'Being With.'" *Information, Communication & Society* 11(4):565–83.

Zhao, Shanyang, Sherri Grasmuck, and Jason Martin. 2008. "Identity Construction on Facebook: Digital Empowerment in Anchored Relationships." *Computers in Human Behavior* 24(5):1816–36.

CHAPTER 18

SYMBOLIC INTERACTIONISM AND RELIGION

ANDREA SALVINI AND IRENE PSAROUDAKIS

A Brief Overview of the Relevance of Religion in the Social Sciences

RELIGION has its particular relevance within the social sciences. This topic was undoubtedly central in classical sociology at the turn of the nineteenth and twentieth centuries and maintained its importance until the last decades of the previous century, when scientific interest in religious phenomena was restricted within specific disciplinary boundaries such as the sociology and psychology of religion. To some extent, the disciplinary confinement of religious studies appears to have coincided with the reduction of religions' role in Western societies; in recent decades, however, there has been a renewed interest in new forms of spirituality, which have attracted the attention of many scholars. Symbolic interactionism has devoted limited attention to these issues, with rare exceptions. This circumstance appears unintelligible if we consider that much of the conceptual assets expressed by symbolic interactionism can play an essential role in the empirical and theoretical understanding of religious phenomena. This chapter aims to discuss how symbolic interactionism can take the opportunity to draw on its conceptual corpus to shed light on the new forms of religiosity expressed in contemporary social processes.

Religion has been a central theme in sociology. Although classical authors have approached the subject in different ways, they pointed out a clear link between religious phenomena and societies' development, not only in Western contexts, as Max Weber's studies have highlighted.

Positivist sociology considered religion as a critical dimension in its framework, to strongly affirm the superiority of the new scientific spirit over the old forms of knowledge influenced by metaphysics and religious beliefs, but simultaneously recognizing religion as a powerful vehicle for socialization and social integration—a dimension that will never abandon the attention of scholars even in the following decades. Durkheim, in his careful exploration of the elementary forms of religious life (1915), observes that even within the decisive rationalizing factors of the modern world, societies cannot renounce the sacred. Indeed, the religious element—even in its various forms, even secular—is incorporated into society itself. In a completely different epistemological and conceptual framework, Weber considers religion as an influential factor in the ordering of the world and as a response to the timeless social and relational problems posed by *theodicy*—that is, the search for individual and collective answers to suffering and human fortune. The conflict between reason and religion marks both the development of social structures in modernity and the scientific theorization on that development.

The dialogue between reason and religion, or society and religion, continues in the following decades involving well-known (Parsons) and less well-known authors (Troeltsh, Sombart). However, the structure of the reflection remains substantially unchanged: religion, and religions, play an essential role as factors of social integration, regulation of individual and collective behavior, response to the great questions of meaning, nurturing hope, promoting cohesion, and possibly obfuscating consciences and bits of intelligence (Marx). The destiny of religion is closely connected with the destiny of societies of which religions are powerful levers of development and order; at the same time, God—whatever the name is assigned to deity—is brought back to the dimensions that pertain to divine entities, that is, the theological and metaphysical spheres. During their consolidation, sociology and other social sciences gradually replaced theological explanations and specialized in correspondence with the increasing degrees of complexity that characterize modern and contemporary life. Consequently, the speculation on the role of religion in social development is gathered in a specific disciplinary field—that of the sociology of religion, which is populated with theories, methods, and schools of thought increasingly refined and diversified. The wide-ranging reflections on religion's contribution as a factor of structuring and changing social, cultural, and economic systems that were typical of classical authors are gradually being abandoned. Research experiences are increasing, aiming to penetrate the empirical manifestations of religious phenomena, in terms of both the changes affecting religious institutions and how references to religious beliefs influence individuals' and groups' conduct. It is also worth noting how the sociology of religion—and, more generally, the attention of the social sciences to religious phenomena—has been relegated to a niche position in the division of scientific work, as if the fate of that disciplinary segment followed the very fates of the loss of the centrality of religion in social life. The current picture, however, exhibits a considerable variety of theoretical references that guide scholars in their experiences of empirical investigation, which revolve around some central concepts. We will remember, for their particular relevance, those of secularization and post-secularization, privatization and deprivatization, civil religion and embodiment—but the list could continue. The current—and transitory—outcome of these elaborations can be summarized in the preliminary consideration that the religious legitimation of the world has lost its plausibility and that religion seems to assume an increasingly individualized nature. God changes the form of his presence in the world, becomes a "property" of individuals, who, in the continuous search for the ultimate meaning of their existence, multiply their explorations in new fields, not subject to the influence of the organized orthodoxy of revealed religions. Religion becomes religiosity, that is, secular tension toward answering individual questions, subjected to a sort of "do-it-yourself." These answers are not embedded in institutionalized belief systems preserved by the churches, but in continuous processes of negotiation and experimentation that also involve the corporeal and emotional dimension and the possibility of self-reflecting the coherence of such experiences with one's own needs and identity. This picture was described as "religions" without churches (Lemert 2015), which manifest themselves in many ways and across many spheres of daily life (in sports, music, spiritual movements), generating new symbols and new meanings. These meanings are transformed according to individuals' needs during the never-ending process of building their own social identities and negotiated in belonging to more or less formalized groups (such as denominations in the United States or spiritual movements in Europe). It is precisely on this level that scholars inspired by symbolic interactionism make their most significant contribution.

They have preferred to capture the relationship of individuals with the sacred within the broader dynamics of constructing and negotiating the meanings they are engaged to in daily life. Consequently, rather than dedicating a formal, specific corpus of concepts to religion, symbolic interactionists have preferred to read religiosity as a significant dimension of the strategies through which human beings interact and generate meanings and organize, regulate, and transform their daily existence. Institutionalized religions and systems of regulation based on faith become symbolic universes to which individuals may refer in order to find confirmations or operate distancing within their own experience of meaning-making. Therefore, the interest in religions no longer concerns the role they play in terms of social integration (or conflict) in vast societies only, but also the way religion is a reference system for individual and collective conduct, negotiated in the light of the life contingencies of social actors.

The one described is a brief reconstruction that does not account for the wealth of contributions that have been made in the field of the sociology of religion, but it can help to highlight that the main interpretative pictures through which religious phenomena are read use concepts that belong to or derive from the interactionist tradition. This derivation, however, is rarely made explicit by scholars. Consequently, even in the sociology of religion, symbolic interactionism does not present itself as an autonomous and coherent perspective of reference for empirical investigations, although many draw on its conceptual heritage.

Symbolic Interactionism and Religious Phenomena

The study of religion was prominent in the works of classical European sociologists and in the American pragmatist tradition, from which symbolic interactionism flourished. Both William James and John Dewey have devoted special attention to religion—dedicating volumes of intense depth of thought, which, in the light of today's sensibilities, exhibit an extraordinary capacity for the anticipation of issues and analytical perspectives. William James does not consider religion as beliefs crystallized in revealed faiths, nor as religious institutions, but as a set of guiding principles whose role is to guide individuals in the practical choices of everyday life (2002). Therefore, religion becomes "religious experience" that includes all dimensions of the human being, particularly those that involve the emotional and spiritual level—which he calls "ecstatic"—that, at the end, are lived in an essentially individual experiential dimension. According to James, religious experience is lived by individuals in solitude, as they enter a relationship with any "divine" entity; this allows the reconstruction of a horizon of meaning useful to orient their choices and give sense to their destiny. John Dewey (2013) emphasizes the practical dimension of religion, which, because of its close connection with individual existence becomes *religiosity*, sensitivity to the spiritual dimension in the existential sphere.

Moreover, this spiritual dimension constitutes a frame of meaning that opens up to a sort of universal humanism—an element that evokes reasons that can be found in Comte's religion of great humanity, albeit in a different epistemological framework. The reflection on religion and religiosity will find moments of further development in the pragmatist tradition (also in the European one, as well documented by Romania 2018). The approach introduced by James and Dewey—centered on the existential experience of individuals in their relationship with the sacred—certainly offers interesting stimuli to penetrate the contemporary dynamics of "privatization" of religion or "post-secularization." However, what seems relevant is that this approach has strongly influenced the way symbolic interactionism has dealt with the topic we are discussing in this chapter.

In the 1960s, Luckmann (1967) already emphasized how religion, seen as the result of individualization's historical and social processes, should be analyzed in the individual dimension, as a social actor's perspective on daily existence, or instead as his/her perception about the world. According to Luckmann, individuals' worldview can be considered a form of religion. In other words, religion represents (is) the personal and subjective experience of humanity as a universe (a framework) full of meaning. Religion as a worldview transcends the individual level in terms of meaning; because of this, within the broader concept of religiosity, it is possible to include various forms of implicit or explicit sacralization, which do not always refer to the "divine" element or the "deity."

In the interactionist tradition, therefore, studies that refer to religious phenomena introduce and combine the interest in religious conduct within the more consolidated conceptual frameworks of the perspective, such as those that refer to identity, the construction of meanings, the dynamics of presentation and transformation of the self, and the forms of belonging as an expression of joint action, more or less organized.

Precisely for this reason, it is difficult to find in the texts that have constituted over time the essential references for the development of perspective, a systematic and coherent treatment dedicated explicitly to religion. Religious phenomena are considered as expressions of broader processes concerning mainly identity construction.

In other words, there are, in the interactionist tradition, many essays and studies dealing with issues related to religion and religiosity, but there is no systematic reconstruction of the contribution offered by perspective to this theme as a specific topic. This circumstance has led some observers to state that the interest of symbolic interactionism toward religion has been relatively scarce, discontinued, or fragmented (Nuti 2012). It should perhaps be said that the interest in religious phenomena has been developed through a significant investment in empirical research situated in terms of space-time coordinates, often aimed at advancing arguments for the development of conceptual areas more connoted in terms of interactionist frameworks. The next paragraph offers a significant glimpse of the wealth of this production. However, it should be noted that today there is a lack of systematic effort in the study of religious phenomena that enhances that wealth and draws useful indications for the further development of the interactionist perspective.

A brief survey of the handbooks that were recently published and aim to present the essential characteristics of symbolic interactionism offers significant insights to support our previous statements. In the most extensive and monumental text available today, edited by Reynolds and Herman-Kinney (2003), a chapter is dedicated to religious institutions, within a part related to "Institutions" by A. Shupe (2003). The chapter offers a useful reflection, which seems to be circumscribed precisely because of its location— on the relationship between faith and religious organization. Through the analysis of phenomena concerning the dynamics of religious belonging and leadership (and its legitimacy) within religious institutions, the author underlines how the interactionist perspective can provide useful conceptual frameworks that integrate mainstream interpretative proposals (especially those offered by social exchange theory) to understand the motivational processes that govern the choices of belonging by believers. In the part of the handbook dedicated to "substantive areas," the research interests of interactionist scholars have been addressed and divided into many analytical areas (such as "sport and leisure," "race and ethnic relations," "occupations and professions," and many others of extreme interest); this part does not include any specific reference to the dynamics of religiosity.

Even in the excellent and recent manuals *The Social Self* (Charmaz, Harris, and Irvine 2019) and *Sociologies of Interaction* (Dennis, Philburn, and Smith 2013), there are no specific chapters or paragraphs dedicated explicitly to the interactionist contribution to the dynamics of religiosity, as is also the case for the valid but less recent texts *Interactionism* (Atkinson and Housley 2003) and *Symbolic Interactionism: An Introduction, An Interpretation, An Integration* (Charon 2007); the more broad topic of spirituality—a trait that appears relevant and controversial in identity construction processes in contemporary societies—is also absent in the volumes just mentioned. "Religion," "religiosity," and "spirituality" are also absent in the index of the recent *The Routledge International Handbook of Interactionism* (vom Lehn, Ruiz-Junco, and Gibson 2021).

On the contrary, in the well-known and widespread book *Symbols, Selves and Social Reality* (Sandstrom, Martin, and Fine 2006), the authors refer to religiosity in different parts of the text, especially regarding the formation of social movements of a religious nature, through the analysis of the processes of belonging and recruitment.

The authors cite two studies that analyzed the recruitment processes in two religious organizations, by John Lofland on the Unification Church of Sun Myung Moon (Lofland 1966) and by David Snow and Cynthia Phillips on the Buddhist movement (Snow and Phillips 1980). The analysis of these studies shows how membership of these religious movements derives from different backgrounds and dynamics. In the first case, affiliation is the concluding step of the new members' search for a context that provides spiritually oriented solutions to the problems experienced in their daily lives. In contrast, in the second case, membership is the ending of an articulated process based on the construction of emotionally intense and engaging links by "veterans" to new members. Both studies offer interpretative proposals that are relevant from the methodological and theoretical points of view about the processes of approaching and belonging to religious movements and churches. As shown, however, the interest in these religious dimensions is combined with the more general interest in the study of social movements from an interactionist point of view.

The circumstance that religious phenomena are approached in combination with other aspects more typically consolidated in the interactionist tradition also appears clearly in the text *The Production of Reality: Essays and Readings on Social Interaction* (O'Brien 2006), where the topic of individual religiosity is addressed through reference to an essay by Jodi O'Brien, centered on the construction processes of queer Christian identities. The author points out that one of the most accredited theories regarding the attitude of individuals toward religion is the one that highlights the "shopping mentality" (Roof 1999) so that they would search, in the market of congregations, for those who can meet their personal needs more adequately. On the contrary, in the case of individuals with queer Christian identities, they are motivated by the desire for forms of re-integration within the Christian tradition—and only at this point do they seek a congregation to welcome them (Roof 1999:462). The author's interest in the dynamics of individual religiosity is part of a broader interest in identity construction processes, especially in the contradictions and conflicts that characterize those processes.

Finally, in the text *Negotiating Identity*—which is not a handbook, but an excellent interactionist essay on the topic of identity—Susie Scott dedicates an interesting part to those religious and spiritual communities that constitute one of the forms in which the so-called reinventive institutions (R.I.) express themselves (Scott 2015). Differently from total institutions (T.I.), the R.I.s are material, discursive or symbolic structures in which voluntary members actively seek to cultivate a new social identity, role or status. This is interpreted positively as a process of reinvention, self-improvement or transformation (Scott 2011:3).

The author argues that in this type of community, the object of worship is not the sacredness of a transcendental god but self-identity of the members, "as idealized potential." The self's sacralization is analyzed through reference to different contemporary spiritual communities and constitutes a phenomenon that contributes to redefining the conceptual categories with which religious dynamics have been interpreted in recent decades. Even in this case, however, the interest in such religious phenomena is part of a theoretical effort oriented to redefine—in an interactionist perspective—the complexity of the ways and forms of identity-building processes in our contemporary times.

This exploration of handbooks on symbolic interactionism is not meant to be exhaustive or complete; however, this examination confirms the argument that interactionist reflection has developed a consistent interest in religious phenomena, but in combination with, and support of, broader interests that concern themes considered more central to the interactionist framework. In the following paragraphs, we will try to systematize in a more clear and coherent way the relationship between religiosity and the conceptual framework of symbolic interactionism.

Symbolic Interactionists' Contributions to the Study of Religion and Religiosity

In terms of a general theory, religiosity has been investigated by the sociological discipline several times: it has been studied as a process of socialization, communication, regulation, rules and norms, social change, welfare and civic activities, and more. Within this conceptual framework, social constructionism may offer multiple reasons for reflection and in-depth analysis, as notably demonstrated in contemporary research about religious groups and individual members, new religious movements, or how religion has been developed and experienced in particular settings (Beckford 2015). Symbolic interactionism (S.I.) has never officially dealt with the phenomenon of religion as a theoretical stream. However, in the sociology of religion during the last twenty years, there was no lack of contributions directly inspired by the interactionist perspective or that used its main elements.

Redefining the concepts of religiosity (and spirituality) from a sociological point of view, and therefore discussing what kind of role religion plays in social and individual life, Borowik (2011) identifies three directions with which it is possible to understand and identify religious change: focusing the point of view (a) of individuals, (b) of social systems, and (c) of religion itself. In our discussion, these levels of interpretation are strictly connected and combined with the interactionist approach.

Symbolic interactionism and the sociology of religion share many concepts: identity, role, stigma, symbols, performance, and rituals, which are just a few of them. Moreover, the sociological conceptualization of religion and interactionist arguments—sometimes in addition to general social psychological perspectives (religion as a social actor)— show several links, mainly based on these elements. As suggested by Prus (2008), S.I. has the merit of developing "trans-contextual" concepts—ideas that allow for comparing underlying social processes within different situations. As a consequence, even if they are not directly conceptualized, religion, spirituality, and religiosity can be considered as "Open Sociological Questions" to which S.I. makes a contribution applying a micro-meso analysis approach, and it takes new contemporary challenges related to various areas of culture, and integrating the broader sociological discipline (Fine and Tavory 2019).

As follows, we examine some research experiences referred to as the typical "products" of symbolic interactionism, which have made the best use of methodological potential deriving from the application of qualitative methods in religious fields. In such studies, scholars use a wide range of qualitative methods. Interactionist concepts become tools for deepening the analyzed topics, developing them theoretically and empirically, and operating a linkage between self and society within religious and non-religion contexts because of their social construction. The identity question appears to be dominant as the common thread of most papers. Other levels of meaning are differently connected to the enucleated concepts.

Religiosity and the Self

Firstly, we include the concepts of religion and religiosity into a broader theory of the self, as a structural variant of symbolic interactionism (Stryker 1980). As Wimberley (1989), we can refer to a unidimensional and multidimensional process related to the individual religiosity framework about the identity questions. The unidimensional character is about "religious salience," or the importance religion has to someone and his/her different identities: for example, the position an individual has in a religious group, or in a situation of private ritualism in which personal devotional behavior does not match the expectations of others. Referring to Stark and Glock's (1965, 1968) "five dimensions of religious commitment" (orthodoxy of beliefs, ritual involvement, devotionalism, experience, and perception of divine and religious knowledge) and their operational definitions, the literature also describes the experiencing of "religious performance," a multidimensional phenomenon based on the positive adherence to norms and precepts: their internalization, fundamental in defining the self. It is about the cultural framework and the social structure of reference, and therefore to rules and related sanctions, whose impact influences role performance. By this, religiosity is an attribute of self and role identity, which are constructed in social interactions and must be conceived as a set of properties of a religious role identity. Religious salience and religious performance are strictly connected because (a) the degree of norm adherence depends on religious salience; (b) religious salience is influenced by the way religion and its beliefs are perceived as central to self, as essential elements in defining identity (there is a sort of religious consciousness establishing one's self-concept); (c) the result is a logical connection between salience and the dimensions of religiosity influencing individual's behaviors in ritualism, frequency, intensity, and devotion, and therefore the tricks social actors use to maintain faithful adherence to religion precepts (i.e., sacrifice, privation). Religious salience is not a dimension of religiosity, but the essence of this linkage—what relates them as different characteristics of religious beliefs and their importance.

Religiosity and Identity

If these arguments have been reconceptualized in terms of identity theory, they can be connected to interactionist typical ideas. How symbolic interactionism posed these questions provides a more than appropriate key for a more general understanding of religiosity. Role-taking dynamics respond to labeling processes since they conceptualize role expectations (Mead 1934), assumed as "moral" norms. Following Mead and his triadic definition of self, self is the outcome of various identities an individual has, including the religious one: it depends on the degree with which this partial identity is overwhelming the other possible identities composing the self. Religious identity is played as a role performance, experienced according to religious rules and behaviors, as expected by members of a religious group. Moreover, a similar dynamic of role relationship occurs between an individual and the deity (Wimberley 1989). The greater the relevance of religious identity, the greater the willingness to adhere to religious norms and to role requirements (expectations). According to Stryker (1980), a salience hierarchy acts in different situations, creating a sort of "structural overlap" of multiple identities, which sometimes conflict with one another. Thus, religious salience and performance can be analyzed by investigating the degree of centrality religion has in religious identity construction and norm adherence (religious role identity).

Religiosity—and therefore, how role identity is expressed through a role performance—is also explained in analyzing an ethical behavior, acted in organizational business structures and much more. For Weaver and Agle (2002), expectations about religious role, internalized as a religious identity, can influence behavior in relation to the degree of salience of religious identity, and religious motivational orientation (including belonging to a religious institution or particular religious categories). We know that empirical research in the psychology and sociology of religion affirms that religiosity does not automatically lead to ethical behavior, whether religiosity is defined according to the principles of a specific belief or in general. However, as noticed, interactionist theory helps to explain the development of religious identity concerning community/groups expectations (in terms of belief and knowledge, emotional statements, affect, ritual, devotion, and experience): they are expressed in the form of social roles, highlighting how the definition of the situation (and therefore the social setting) influence the salience of religious identity. This is useful in understanding how daily behavior conforms to religious self, and how individual reactions can be crucial in altering, disconfirming, or confirming established or planned religious behaviors, contributing or not to recognizing a "moral" attitude. This kind of consideration requires a more in-depth analysis, as different religious systems (and ethics) pose different kinds of role expectations and norms adherence.

The importance of social construction in religious dynamics is underlined by the impact they have on collective processes (e.g., memory) and on how some religions are intended as moral authorities because they create a moral framework through the use of narrative and rhetoric, the use of space, and the allocation of resources (van den Scott 2016).

In the same conceptual framework, the literature suggests analyzing how non-religious people give meaning to religious assumptions and norms to understand their experiences and identities. The authors discuss how non-religious people make sense of religion in their construction of non-religious selves, in sight of two elements: (1) in quantitative terms, their growing number (even organized as social movements), and their ever-greater capacity to mobilize collective actions also supported by new technologies; (2) in qualitative terms, the processes of marginalization and stigmatization they suffer, especially in the contemporary American society, which force them to perform particular practices of self in the backstage (Goffman 1959) through an "oppositional identity work." Morality and the moral career of individuals are intended as Goffman (1963), in the sense of socially constructed descriptions of human activity. The matter regarding which strategies of self are played by actors to define their "moral" identities, and others' too, as good or precious members of a collective situation (Sumerau 2012b) should be questioned.

The standpoint of Sumerau and Cragun (2016), consolidated by many contributions in the sociology of religion, is that non-religious people gain from "cultural instruments" of religion cultures (Swidler 1986) to establish plausible collective and individual identities. They act through social processes of moralization and demoralization of religion: emphasizing the positive aspects of religion, which facilitates the establishment of valuable selves, or vice versa underlining its negative aspects, to demonstrate how the absence of religion is essential in self-construction. By demoralizing religion, and by extension moralizing non-religion, atheists act positively in identity construction and normalize their selves. They mobilize perceptions of religious practices, sharing religious assumptions about the non-religious experiences with religious people; specifically, they consider their religious experiences in socialization as a background to draw from, to signify non-religion in its values and characters, and to build a "moral" practice (and therefore an identity) appearing alternative to religious self. In the end, non-religion is framed (Goffman 1974) as a moral identity. Authors demonstrate how these dynamics come from perceiving religion in its normative attributes (as obligatory and conformist, prejudicial, and stereotyping toward non-religious people). As a reason for marginalization, it encourages the labeling of "different people" rather than pursuing moral requirements. Furthermore, social interactions in religious contexts activated motivational processes, prompting atheists to seek meaning to their existence from other sources.

Religiosity and the Self-Other Dualism

Therefore, the dimension of other is relevant not only because of religious identity and religious role identity construction but also in adherence to norms (to a morality) defining in-group and out-group dynamics. While self is connected to the individual and the social, the degree to which identity is anchored in either "self" or "others" may vary. A balance should be negotiated, especially in collective processes of dependence and influence. Deepening the reflection on identity construction leads to interesting developments about the conception of the self as proposed by some particular religions. Immergut and Kaufman (2014) discuss the interactionist "dualism" self-other, which involves some implicit difficulties in managing self: it is "threatened" (influenced, oriented) by others, and it experiences a condition of constant anxiety (Cooley 1902; Mead 1934; Goffman 1959; Gekas 1982; Gergen 2009; Psaroudakis 2016). Keeping the concept of self as valid and relevant, despite the postmodern condition (Gubrium and Holstein 2000), and considering the self-object as an ongoing, reflexive process (Callero 2003), the authors explain how Buddhist philosophy, through its conceptions of "non-self" and interdependence (respectively, *anatta* and *prattyasamutp¯ada*), proposes an alternative interpretation of social interaction. Self is merely a label, occurring in constantly changing psycho-physical elements: everything changes and passes away—interactions too—so it is impossible to stabilize what has a variable nature. Self is a meaning, created and sustained in a symbolic demarcation by an interdependent "state of flowing" we are in. In sociology, this construct becomes real, and scholars naturalize the self-other dualism, essentializing the threatened self. On the contrary, Buddhism deconstructs this dualism as a misperception, a result of human imagination. Since stigma is a self-other duality premise, we assume this perspective is relevant because it offers symbolic interactionists a different (religious) lens used for the understanding the micro-interactional processes in which marginalized individuals are engaged.

Religiosity and Stigma

Stigma (Goffman 1963) is a frequent concept in studies of religion. Identities are strongly labeled at both a social and individual level. This happens in interactions between religious and non-religious people and particular categories of individuals and collective dynamics. For instance, Casey (2017) examines the intersection of religious out-group (non-Muslims, or dominant society) and in-group (other Muslims) religious stigma in the lives of Muslim Americans (O'Brien 2017), which experience the stigmatization process steps described by Link and Phelan (2001). A low degree of religiosity in Muslim Americans who have adopted Western cultural values (in role performance, role identity, and self-presentation) is considered a loss in status among other Muslims.

Moreover, in a study on disaffiliation narratives in religious groups (mostly new religious movements), Coates (2013) assumes the meaning that symbolic interactionism gives to notions of "self" and "others," finding people's motivations of disaffiliation among the gap between expectations of conformity and sense of autonomy, or between group ideals and the reality of group life. Many scholars consider disaffiliation as an extended and gradual process personally negotiated by single members through particular strategies of the self; in cases of doubts and dissonances that have become unsolvable, religious groups provide their members with appropriate scripts facilitating doubts resolution and acceptance. This is a "private" process, but sometimes collective factors step in, empirically realizing the interactionist conceptualization of personal uniqueness, as well as of a sense of belonging and social connectedness (Mead 1934; Holstein and Gubrium 2000). Belonging to a religious group is due to finding a stable "other" (a social self, built-in interaction), contributing to the construction of a more robust perception of one's own identity. Another reason for membership is the desire to emotionally relate to others to create a protected self, motivated by the disconfirmation of the previous identity and the willingness to change it according to group expectations. Social selves, or protected selves, often solve doubts or dissonances. Exit strategies from a religious group occur when there is the possibility to negotiate and reconstruct an alternative identity, finding an identity solution to religious identity preeminence as compared to other identities. Consistent with the symbolic interactionist perspective about the role of discursive resources in identity construction, other non-group identity resources became available and useful in interpreting an individual's experiences as "primary others" influencing the sense of self (Holstein and Gubrium 2000; Gubrium and Holstein 2001). However, religious disaffiliation can also occur in a crisis or trouble—a dissonance in identity, sometimes representing a potential "loss" of self. It happens when an inner request for a self-change becomes unsustainable compared to the desire for authenticity and to be perceived as autonomous and independent individuals. We refer here to the reconstruction of previous identity, and reconnection to the so-called true self (Hochschild 1983).

The criterion of authenticity, conceptualized by scholars either as feeling true to a perceived internal self, or in distinction among true-false selves (Psaroudakis 2016), differs based on various interpretations given by communities, times, and interactions. According to Fuist and McDowell's (2019) essay dedicated to identity in Christian counterculture, the authenticity framework is defined by five dimensions related to sincerity, integrity, the social setting we live in, consumption, and lived experience. This concept is situational and negotiated by individuals or groups: it depends on others' recognition (it means to be respected and defined as authentic persons), but its significance emerges from its social construction, even in the religious context. For these authors, the sense of authenticity—and therefore the "idea" about a religious person—regard about the way diverse groups construct their understanding of society, drawing on both religion and politics, ultimately shaping their joint action (Blumer 1969).

In-group and out-group dynamics are about norms and behaviors and connected to role performativity: how social actors perform their beliefs on everyday life stages (Goffman 1959), the performative nature of prayer utterances in social interactions, or the use of prayer expressions in conversations in private and public life. The act of praying can provide motivations for social action, while prayer expressions provide individuals with tools to act in different ways, aligning their behaviors to cultural norms, values, and expectations in given situations (Stokes and Hewitt 1976). Religious talk in everyday life helps individuals face social interactions or interactions with imaginary audiences, even in non-religious settings. Using qualitative media-analysis methods

(Altheide 1996), and foreseeing further developments in conversation analysis and ethnomethodology, Sharp (2013) follows the current trend in the sociology of religion in studying religion out of the standard borders of religious institutions: his research suggests that insights from philosophy of language are useful theoretical tools for understanding religious discourse in social interactions.

The Social Construction of Religiosity

Even though a lot of interactionist research is dedicated to religious selves, the way spirituality and divinity are socially constructed is explored very little. Some studies focus on what a deity should be or use religious expressions and performances to justify certain social phenomena. Sometimes natural experiences are "relocated" in conversational strategies, in a framework with a supernatural meaning (Wooffitt 1992) or different settings. We can find examples of narrative resources in constructing spiritual identities (a fusion between "I" and "me") in particular non-religious contexts, such as in artistic performances (Barton and Hardesty 2010).

Performativity is also related to rituals of belief, understood as status passages (Glaser and Strauss 1968, 1971; McCallion 2007; Burton 2020), providing for a series of temporal properties as activity (Mead 1932). About the initiation process, McCallion and Maines (2002) studied the duration of rites of Christian initiation of adults, which "turn" non-Catholic adults into Catholic, and the role of coordinators who function as spiritual gatekeepers. They are rituals working through periods and steps, allowing the initiates to discern their calling to faith, and involving the community. As for Glaser and Strauss, these processes require duration because they are not events, and individuals involved in status passages attend to time as a social object. However, the duration can be experienced as a problem because of tension between a prescriptive and sacred temporal order (to establish covenantal relations and the full absorption into the Catholic spiritual community) and secular, temporal orders.

Symbolic interactionism is therefore useful in investigating religious work and the social construction of religiosity, to understand both individuals experiencing religion and the role of divinity and belief interpretation (meaning) in influencing daily practices. Combining the sociology of religion studies with the interactionist perspective allows us to decline the concept of symbol in a specific way. The process of deity construction is a symbolization made through an individual and collective "deity work": social actors give meaning to deities and spirituality as well as to themselves, to others, or to social phenomena related to deities, in a joint action that aims at creating supernatural phenomena relevant to their social lives. Sumerau, Nowakowski, and Cragun (2016) conceive symbolization as a sort of identity work, as well as a dynamic of coding, since individuals are engaged in strategies (a) whereby they signify the existence of deities and themselves, as acts of their affirmation as religious selves (in body, emotions, and ideology), and (b) whereby they may establish the existence of deities in social interaction. People define specific forms of self and others through dramaturgical work and signify deity by symbolic material mobilization. Three steps are needed to maintain the collective belief in the existence of shared meanings: (1) defining (deities are perceived as elements of social life, having recognizable qualities), (2) coding (there are rules, norms, or codes individuals use to show their real existence: e.g., prayer as a form of coding, stories as a demonstration of deity's effect upon natural life), and (3) affirming (people show deity reality using expressions, language, ceremonies, and giving and receiving support).

As Blumer affirmed (1969), people construct and signify their existence and characteristics in everyday life; according to symbolic interactionist premises, individuals define particular objects as spiritual and legitimize an intersubjective reality (Berger and Luckmann 1966) by using subjective and normative strategies through a symbolization process. Ghidina (2018) studied how crop circles of grain gained spiritual significance for believers in forms of New Age spirituality. Also Waskul and Eaton (2018), analyzed the supernatural's role in identity construction and the consequent commercialization of the supernatural, based on the standpoint that religion is an institutionalized "cultural authority" validating and legitimizing religious phenomena.

Summary and Perspectives

This chapter focused on how the application of some typical symbolic interactionist concepts may contribute to the sociology of religion, developing and combining the theoretical and methodological potential of both perspectives. Although the emphasis of symbolic interactionism's contribution is firmly placed on identity, this concept is linked to other questions, such as role taking, others' expectations, recognition (also in terms of stigma), performance, processes of symbolization, and attribution of meaning. Further developments in methodology can be multiple, as shown by the cited literature. We hope for an even more generous application of qualitative methods. In investigating religiosity, research often refers to the methodological tradition of grounded theory (Charmaz 2006), which seems to be an adequate solution. Grounded-theory data analysis does not limit religion by describing religious phenomena at a superficial level, but rather makes it possible to take the perspective of research co-participants, investigating the meanings that social actors attribute to experiences and their sense of everyday life. Through fieldwork, life histories, social narratives, guided conversations, and in-depth semi-structured interviews, grounded theory goes "beyond data" by seizing details and undertones, and develops medium and wide-ranging theories (Glaser and Strauss 1967; Corbin and Strauss 1993; Charmaz 2006). The same approach has to be pursued in ethnographic investigations, and in qualitative media analysis, to collect the meaning construction processes and identity performances (Altheide 1996; Healey 2010).

In this direction, we underline the possibility of in-depth studies about specific themes, including the increasing development of new religious movements and incorporating spiritual philosophies into sociological theories about self, identity, and more. Sharing sensitizing concepts with S.I. can be useful in studying and comparing religious experiences and religiosity within some specific groups (niches or minorities), such as in LGBT communities (Sumerau 2012a, 2012b; Sumearu et al. 2016), in individuals having no religious background, or in particular social settings such as total institutions. We cite the study of Hicks (2008) on the role played by prison chaplains in identity process management, concerning both their "corrective" occupational dimension and religious precepts. In addition to its implications for identity research, religion may be relevant in understanding the dynamics of non-religious people and the role religion (or non-religion) plays in contemporary societies. The most recent studies about cremation (understood as a personal identity choice, also in contrast with the salience of religious self) can be an example (Salvini 2015; Salvini and Biancheri 2020). In the end, we have to recognize the geographical polarization of these kinds of studies: they mainly focus on analyzing Western, American societies, whereas it would be interesting to deepen their application into other cultural and social contexts.

REFERENCES

Altheide, David L. 1996. *Qualitative Media Analysis.* Thousand Oaks, CA: SAGE.
Atkinson, Paul, and William Housley. 2003. *Interactionism.* London: SAGE.
Barton, Bernadette, and Constance L. Hardesty. 2010. "Spirituality and Stripping: Exotic Dancers Narrate the Body Ekstasis." *Symbolic Interaction* 33(2):280–96.
Beckford, James A. 2015. "The Sociology of Religion. A Modest Social Constructionist View." *Nanzan Institute for Religion & Culture Bulletin* 39:9–25.
Berger, Peter L., and Thomas Luckmann. 1966. *The Social Construction of Reality.* New York: Doubleday and Co.
Blumer, Herbert. 1969. *Symbolic Interactionism: Perspective and Method.* Englewood Cliffs, NJ: Prentice Hall.
Borowik, Irena. 2011. "The Changing Meanings of Religion: Sociological Theories of Religion in the Perspective of the Last 100 Years." *International Review of Sociology* 21(1):175–89.
Burton, M. Diane. 2020. "Status Passages." In *The Blackwell Encyclopedia of Sociology,* edited by G. Ritzer. https://doi.org/10.1002/9781405165518.wbeoss258.pub2.
Callero, Peter L. 2003. "The Sociology of the Self." *Annual Review of Sociology* 29:115–33.
Casey, Patrick Michael. 2017. "Stigmatized Identities: Too Muslim to Be American, Too American to Be Muslim." *Symbolic Interaction* 41(1):100–19.
Charmaz, Kathy. 2006. *Constructing Grounded Theory: A Practical Guide Through Qualitative Research.* London: SAGE.
Charmaz, Kathy, Scott Harris, and Leslie Irvine. 2019. *The Social Self and Everyday Life. Understanding the World Through Symbolic Interactionism.* Oxford: Wiley Blackwell.
Charon, Joel M. 2007. *Symbolic Interactionism: An Introduction, An Interpretation, An Integration.* 9th ed. Upper Saddle River: Pearson Prentice Hall.
Coates, Dominiek D. 2013. "Disaffiliation from a New Religious Movement: The Importance of Self and Others in Exit." *Symbolic Interaction* 36(3):314–34.
Cooley, Charles Horton. 1902. *Human Nature and the Social Order.* New York: Scribners.
Corbin, Juliet, and Anselm Strauss. 1993. *Methods of Qualitative Research.* Thousand Oaks, CA: SAGE.

Dewey, John. 2013. *A Common Faith*. New Haven, CT: Yale University Press. (Original work published: 1934).

Dennis, Alex, Rob Philburn, and Greg Smith. 2013. *Sociologies of Interaction*. Cambridge: Polity.

Durkheim, Emile. 1915. *The Elementary Forms of Religious Life*. London: Allen & Unwin.

Fine, Gary Alan, and Iddo Tavory. 2019. "Interactionism in the Twenty-First Century: A Letter on Being-in-a-Meaningful-World." *Symbolic Interaction* 42(3):457–67.

Fuist, Todd Nicholas, and Amy D. McDowell. 2019. " 'Jesus Would Turn the Tables Over': Five Dimensions of Authenticity Applied to Countercultural Christianity." *Symbolic Interaction* 42(3):374–94.

Gekas, Viktor. 1982. "The Self-Concept." *Annual Review of Sociology* 8:1–33.

Gergen, Kenneth J. 2009. *Relational Being: Beyond Self and Community*. New York: Oxford University Press.

Ghidina, Marcia J. 2018. "Finding God in Grain: Crop Circles, Rationality, and the Construction of Spiritual Experience." *Symbolic Interaction* 42(2):278–300.

Glaser, Barney, and Anselm Strauss. 1967. *The Discovery of Grounded Theory: Strategies for Qualitative Research*. Mill Valley, CA: Sociology Press.

Glaser, Barney, and Anselm Strauss. 1968. *Time for Dying*. Chicago: Aldine.

Glaser, Barney, and Anselm Strauss. 1971. *Status Passage*. Chicago: Aldine-Atherton.

Goffman, Erving. 1959. *Presentation of Self in Every-day Life*. Garden City, NY: Doubleday Anchor.

Goffman, Erving. 1963. *Stigma: Notes on the Management of Spoiled Identity*. New York: Simon & Schuster.

Goffman, Erving. 1974. *Frame Analysis: An Essay on the Organization of Experience*. Cambridge: Harvard University Press.

Gubrium, Jaber F., and James A. Holstein. 2000. "The Self in a World of Going Concerns." *Symbolic Interaction* 23(2):95–115.

Gubrium, Jaber F., and James A. Holstein James, eds. 2001. "Introduction: Trying Times, Troubled Selves." Pp. 1–20 in *Institutional Selves: Troubled Identities in a Postmodern World*. New York: Oxford University Press.

Healey, Kevin. 2010. "The Pastor in the Basement: Discourses of Authenticity in the Networked Public Sphere." *Symbolic Interaction* 33(4):526–51.

Hicks, Allison M. 2008. "Role Fusion: The Occupational Socialization of Prison Chaplain." *Symbolic Interaction* 31(4):400–21.

Hochschild, Arlie Russell. 1983. *The Managed Heart: Commercialization of Human Feelings*. Berkeley: University of California Press.

Holstein, James A., and Jaber F. Gubrium. 2000. *The Self We Live by. Narrative Identity in a Postmodern World*. New York: Oxford University Press.

James, William. 2002. *The Varieties of Religious Experience*. London: Routledge. (Original work published: 1902).

Immergut, Matthew, and Peter Kaufman. 2014. "A Sociology of No-Self: Applying Buddhist Social Theory to Symbolic Interaction." *Symbolic Interaction* 37(2):264–82.

Lemert, Charles C., 2015. "Defining Non-Church Religion." *Review of Religious Research* 16(3):186–97.

Link, Bruce G., and Jo C. Phelan Jo. 2001. "Conceptualizing Stigma." *Annual Review of Sociology* 27:363–85.

Lofland, John. 1966. *Doomsday Cult*. Englewood Cliffs: Prentice Hall.

Luckmann, Thomas. 1967. *Invisible Religion: The Problem of Religion in Modern Society*. New York: Macmillan.

McCallion, Micheal J. 2007. "Status Passages." In *The Blackwell Encyclopedia of Sociology*, edited by G. Ritzer. https://doi.org/10.1002/9781405165518.wbeoss258.

McCallion, Michael J., and David R. Maines. 2002. "Spiritual Gatekeepers: Time and the Rite of Christian Initiation of Adults." *Symbolic Interaction* 25(3):289–302.

Mead, George Herbert. 1932. *The Philosophy of the Present*. LaSalle, IL: Open Court.

Mead, George Herbert. 1934. *Mind, Self and Society from the Standpoint of a Social Behaviorist*. Chicago, IL: University of Chicago Press.

Nuti, Carolina. 2012. "Symbolic Interactionism and Religion." Pp. 93–102 in *The Present and Future of Symbolic Interactionism*, vol. 2, edited by A. Salvini, D. Altheide, and C. Nuti. Milan: FrancoAngeli.

O'Brien, Jodi. 2006. "Wrestling the Angel of Contradiction: Queer Christian Identities." Pp. 450–64 in *The Production of Reality. Essays and Readings on Symbolic Interaction*, edited by Jodi O'Brien, 4th ed. Thousand Oaks, CA: Pine Forge Press.

O'Brien, John. 2017. *Keeping It Halal: The Every-day Lives of Muslim American Teenage Boys*. Princeton, NJ: Princeton University Press.

Prus, Robert. 2008. "Authenticity, Activity, and Conceptuality: Generating a Pluralist, Humanist, and Enduring Social Science." *Studies in Symbolic Interaction* 32:19–36.

Psaroudakis, Irene. 2016. "La costruzione dell'identità nella società contemporanea." Pp. 79–101 in *Interazioni Inclusive, Maggioli Editore*, edited by Andrea Salvini. Santarcangelo di Romagna: Maggioli Editore.

Reynolds, Larry T., and Nancy J. Herman-Kinney, eds. 2003. *Handbook of Symbolic Interactionism*. Walnut Creek: Altamira Press.

Roof, Wade Clark. 1999. *Spiritual Marketplace: Baby Boomers and the Remaking of American Religion*. Princeton: Rutgers University Press.

Romania, Vincenzo. 2018. "Pragmatism, Religion and Ethics: A Review Essay." *Sociologica* 12(3): 93–109.

Salvini, Andrea, and Rita Biancheri, eds. 2020. *Donne e Cremazione*. Pisa: Pisa University Press.

Salvini, Andrea, ed. 2015. *La cremazione a Pisa. Le ragioni di una scelta*. Pisa: Pisa University Press.

Sandstrom, Kent L., Daniel D. Martin, and Gary A. Fine. 2006. *Symbols, Selves and Social Reality*. 2nd ed. Los Angeles: Roxbury Publishing Company.

Scott, Susie. 2015. *Negotiating Identity. Symbolic Interactionist Approaches to Social Identity*. Cambridge: Polity.

Scott, Susie. 2011. *Total Institutions and Reinvented Identities*. Basingstoke: Palgrave.

Sharp, Shane. 2013. "How to Do Things with Prayer Utterances." *Symbolic Interaction* 36(2):159–76.

Shupe, Anson. 2003. "The Religious Institution." Pp. 625–35 in *Handbook of Symbolic Interactionism*, edited by Larry T. Reynolds and Nancy J. Herman-Kinney. Walnut Creek: Altamira Press.

Snow, David, and Cynthia Phillips. 1980. "The Lofland-Stark Conversion Model: A Critical Reassessment." *Social Problems* 47(4):430–47.

Stark, Rodney, and Charles Y. Glock. 1965. *Religion and Society in Tension*. Chicago: Rand McNally.

Stark, Rodney, and Charles Y. Glock. 1968. *American Piety*. Berkeley: University of California Press.

Stokes, Randall, and John P. Hewitt. 1976. "Aligning Actions." *American Sociological Review* 41(5):838–49.

Stryker, Sheldon. 1980. *Symbolic Interactionism. A Social Structural Version*. Menlo Park, CA: Benjamin/Cummings.

Sumerau, J. Edward, and Ryan T. Cragun. 2016. "'I Think Some People Need Religion': The Social Construction of Nonreligious Moral Identities." *Sociology of Religion: A Quarterly Review* 77(4):386–407.

Sumerau, J. Edward. 2012a. "'That's What a Man Is Supposed to Do': Compensatory Manhood Acts in an LGBT Christian Church." *Gender & Society* 26(3):461–87.

Sumerau, J. Edward. 2012b. "Mobilizing Race, Class, and Gender Discourses in a Metropolitan Community Church." *Race, Gender, and Class* 19(3–4):93–112.

Sumerau, J. Edward, Ryan T. Cragun, and Lain A. B. Mathers. 2016. "Contemporary Religion and the Cisgendering of Reality." *Social Currents* 3(3):293–311.

Sumerau, J. Edward, Alexandra C. H. Nowakowski, and Ryan T. Cragun. 2016. "An Interactionist Approach to the Social Construction of Deities." *Symbolic Interaction* 39(4):577–94.

Swidler, Ann. 1986. "Culture in Action: Symbols and Strategies." *American Sociological Review* 51:273–86.

van den Scott, Lisa-Jo K. 2016. "Collective Memory and Social Restructuring in the Case of Traditional Inuit Shamanism." *Symbolic Interaction* 40(1):83–100.

vom Lehn, Dirk, Natalia Ruiz-Junco, and Will Gibson, eds. 2021. *The Routledge International Handbook of Interactionism*. New York: Routledge.

Waskul, Dennis, and Marc Eaton. 2018. *The Supernatural in Society, Culture, and History*. Philadelphia: Temple University Press.

Weaver, Gary R., and Braley R. Agle. 2002. "Religiosity and Ethical Behavior in Organizations: A Symbolic Interactionist Perspective." *The Academy of Management Review* 27(1):77–97.

Wimberley, Dale W. 1989. "Religion and Role-Identity: A Structural Symbolic Interactionist Conceptualization of Religiosity." *The Sociological Quarterly* 30(1):125–42.

Wooffitt, Robin. 1992. *Telling Tales of the Unexpected: The Organization of Factual Discourse*. New York: Rowman & Littlefield.

PART III

POWER AND INEQUALITIES

CHAPTER 19

MARKEDNESS AND UNMARKEDNESS IN IDENTITIES AND SOCIAL INTERACTION

WAYNE H. BREKHUS

SYMBOLIC interactionism (SI) is often criticized for its lack of attention to structural social problems, power, and inequalities. As an important corrective to the structural-functionalist theories of its time, early SI emphasized the ways that meaning is constructed in everyday interactions. SI was a radical alternative to functionalist theorizing, but even this radical alternative had its own conservative blind spots. Like other longstanding theoretical traditions in sociology, SI developed in a context where sociologists gave greater epistemological weight to the ideas of scholars who represented unmarked, privileged social standpoints (e.g., white, Anglo-European/colonizer, male), rather than to those of scholars who represented marked positions of marginality (W. E. B. Du Bois, for example). Similar in this regard to structural-functionalism, SI too privileged the unmarked epistemological standpoints of Anglo-European/colonizer, white men, and as a result undertheorized the types of intersectional identities and interactional inequalities that theorists from marked social standpoints have prioritized as more central epistemological concerns. By privileging the epistemological concerns arising from unmarked social standpoints, SI has limited the full potential of its radical promise. Today we can realize the full promise of SI theorizing by expanding our canonical influences and our orienting concerns to analyze the interplay between unmarked social power and privilege and culturally marked aspects of identity and interaction.

Despite its historical blind spots, SI is uniquely situated to address intersectional identities and inequalities, particularly if we move beyond narrow allegiance to Mead and Blumer to expand the canon and the scope of symbolic interactionism. While still drawing upon the importance of Mead's and Blumer's insights on the self, and on the interactional production of meaning, we can also become more intentional about emphasizing the role of power and inequalities in shaping intersectional selves and in jointly reproducing social reality. An expansive vision of symbolic interactionism recognizes the central role of power and inequalities in shaping social identities and social interaction (DeGloma, Brekhus, and Force, this volume). Today researchers who are aligned with symbolic interactionist approaches are heavily invested in studying inequalities, especially structural and interactional inequalities associated with race, gender, sexuality, and class. Such researchers have become particularly interested in the role of structural and linguistic power, especially insofar as such forces influence social identities and shape perception and performance in everyday interactions.

In this chapter, I show how cultural markedness and unmarkedness shape perception, performance, and identity, and I address the implications for symbolic interactionist theory and research. In doing so, I highlight the sensitizing concepts of the marked and the unmarked, argue for a diverse and intersectional SI theoretical canon that can further orient us to the importance of connecting identity and interaction to power asymmetries in intersectional marked and unmarked relationships, and demonstrate the analytic importance of markedness and unmarkedness for sharpening our critical focus.

MARKED AND UNMARKED: SENSITIZING CONCEPTS FOR A SYMBOLIC INTERACTIONISM FOCUSED ON POWER AND COMPLEX INEQUALITIES

Eviatar Zerubavel (this volume) reminds us that one of Blumer's important contributions was to introduce the idea of *sensitizing concepts*. Sensitizing concepts, Zerubavel argues, are the "metaphorical 'lenses' through which researchers access the empirical world," and it is our attentional socialization to specific concepts that allows us to see things that come into focus that we would otherwise miss. The concepts of the marked and the unmarked are two important sensitizing concepts that inform a power-focused symbolic interactionism. Increasingly sociologists of identity have become interested in the ways that marked positions of stigma and disadvantage shape identity within contexts of unmarked structural privilege and advantage. More recently still, sociologists of identity have become interested in how privilege itself shapes identity as well as how the intersection of privilege and disadvantage influences identity. Recognizing the semiotic asymmetry between marked and unmarked attributes, identities, and phenomena is critical to understanding inequalities in identity and interaction.

The marked/unmarked contrast was originally introduced in linguistics to note how one variant is actively accented with a mark and treated as specialized or unique, while the other variant is passively defined as standard or generic by its absence of a mark (see Jakobson 1972; Trubetzkoy and Jakobson 1975; Waugh 1982). Linda Waugh (1982) developed a broader semiotic framework extending this same logic to social contrasts across different semiotic pairs such as homosexuality/heterosexuality, Black/white, and woman/man. These concepts have since become sensitizing concepts in sociology, particularly with respect to the sociology of identity (see Brekhus 1996, 2020; Zerubavel 2018).

Social marking delineates a semiotic distinction between parts of a contrast that are actively accentuated as *socially specialized* and those that are taken-for-granted as *socially generic* (Brekhus 1996:500, 2020:25). Along a broad range of contrasts some elements are marked while others are unmarked. For example, gay is marked, heterosexual or "straight" is unmarked; Black is marked, white is unmarked; immigrant is marked, native is unmarked; blind is marked, sighted is unmarked; transgender is marked, cisgender is unmarked; felon is marked, non-felon is unmarked; children or "minors" are marked as are elderly people or "senior citizens," but thirty-seven-year-old adults are neither marked as "majors" relative to minors or "junior citizens" relative to the elderly. In these contrasts, the marked elements are given far greater *semiotic weight* (Mullaney 1999; Zerubavel 2018:12) than the unmarked. This imbalance of semiotic weight is sometimes even codified as when hypodescent rules of racial ancestry make explicit that one's Black or indigenous heritage weighs more than one's white ancestry in determining one's racial classification. The "one-drop rule" (see Davis 1991), for example, goes so far as to codify that a "single drop" of Black ancestry weighs more than an "entire ocean" of white ancestry. The extreme imbalance in semiotic weight between the marked and the unmarked in hypodescent rules is a codified example of the unevenness in the markedness relationship that is often present, but only rarely spelled out so directly.

Because the marked carries greater semiotic weight, it disproportionately attracts social attention. People are far more likely to notice someone is a wheelchair user than a pedestrian or to be socially attentive to how a transgender person became transgender than to how a cisgender person became cisgender. The specification of marked categories as socially distinct also contributes to the mistaken perception that marked categories are more internally consistent and homogenous than unmarked ones. It is easier for people to conceptualize Latino culture, Southern culture, gay culture, and deaf culture as coherent cultural entities than to imagine, for instance, Anglo, Northern, heterosexual, or hearing culture as well-formed consistent entities.

Although the marked attracts disproportionate social attention and focus, "the most powerful element of the contrast is not the item that is accentuated with a marked social value but rather the item whose social value is implicitly constructed as normative, 'normal,' and positive through its absence of a mark" (Brekhus 2023:34, see also Brekhus 1996:502). The item which goes unremarked, unaccented, largely unnoticed, and taken for granted, becomes the cognitive default (Zerubavel 2018:14), and this naturalizes it as the unquestioned center of social reality. Marking some foods as "ethnic" draws our attention to Mexican, Chinese, Afghan, Ethiopian, and Thai foods as specialized cuisines while also doing the work of naturalizing the equally ethnic foods that remain ethnically unmarked and therefore tacitly defined as non-ethnic "general" cuisine. The social power of unmarked defaults is especially significant in how we generalize from social categories. When generalizing from representatives of marked categories we often make particularistic, category-specific generalizations, whereas when generalizing from representatives of unmarked categories we often make general, universal generalizations (Brekhus 1998:40). Take, for example, how empirical studies of tribes like the Yanomami, the Sambia, or the Nuer are considered the realm of tribe-specific anthropology, while empirical studies of Westerners (who are not marked as a specific cultural tribe) are considered the realm of generic human psychology. Anthropologist Joe Henrich and his colleagues (Henrich, Heine, and Norenzayan, 2010) note that "Behavioral scientists routinely publish broad claims about human psychology and behavior in the world's top journals based on samples drawn entirely from Western, Educated, Industrialized, Rich, and Democratic (WEIRD) societies. Researchers—often implicitly—assume that either there is little variation across human populations or that these 'standard subjects' are as representative of the species as any other population." They go on to demonstrate in a series of studies that Westerners are among the least representative "tribes" within the human species and that as such they are no more generically human, or less anthropologically unique, than other human populations.

Understanding the powerful semiotic relationship between marked and unmarked identities and attributes can be a focal point that allows SI scholars to develop a critical intersectional symbolic interactionism that examines how people negotiate structures of oppression and balance dimensions of social privilege and disadvantage. A sensitivity to the ways that we are multiply marked and unmarked along various axes can enrich our understanding of the various ways social agents navigate identity. Later in this chapter I will highlight scholars who are advancing a critical intersectional SI that analyzes the complex interplay of marked and unmarked attributes in identity presentation and social interaction, but first it is worth examining how an understanding of markedness and unmarkedness requires us to reconsider the canon of SI theorists who guide the orienting assumptions of SI scholars.

Challenging Unmarked Power and Epistemic Exclusion: The Shifting SI Canon

By exercising social power through unmarked defaults, we significantly shape social reality. The problem of generalizing from marked categories to group-specific assumptions, and from unmarked categories to general universal assumptions is not just a problem in everyday reality, but also a problem in the sociological production of knowledge. Julian Go (2020) argues that racialized exclusions pervade the development of sociological thought in terms of both what counts as important general theoretical knowledge and whose observations contribute to that knowledge. Because sociology emerged in the context of US imperialism, the exclusionary logics of empire created an epistemic structure wherein thinking in terms of binary oppositions between universalism and particularism and between objectivity and provincialism was built into the epistemology of the discipline (Go 2020:83). Seamster and Ray (2018:324) similarly assert that "ethnography began as a colonial project" whereby anthropologists employed binaries of "savagery" and "civilization" to help manage socially marked populations. Within this epistemic structure, universalism and objectivity were racialized as tied to the socially unmarked experiential standpoints of white Anglo-Europeans (Go 2020). Early twentieth-century sociologists, in effect, deployed the imperial binary to jettison non-whites from the status of general knowledge producers (Go 2020:85). This historical legacy continues to shape the epistemic contours of sociology today. A variant of the "savagery" and "civilization" binary, for example, can still be found in urban ethnographies of African-American and Latino/a populations where such communities are studied as "socially specialized" "deviant" populations set apart from the "civilized" world of unmarked "normality" (Seamster and Ray 2018:324) and where researchers erect "epistemological ghettos" around these spatial communities by developing group-specific theories about the specialized "deviant" populations or "tribes" that they study (Brekhus 1998:38–43).

We must ask ourselves if the racialized production of some populations (unmarked white Anglo-European colonizers) as the "objective producers" of knowledge and other populations as the studied "subjects" of anthropological and group-specific ethnographic findings in the early 20th century has affected the orienting questions built into the theoretical canon of symbolic interactionist research. Following from Go's (2020:84) observation that early sociology staked its claim to science based on the faulty colonial logic that white Anglo-Europeans were the only rational, impartial producers of knowledge, and that non-white analysts were inherently particularistic and subjectively shaped by their specialized social standpoint, it is worth noting how these logics may have narrowed our canon to exclude orienting perspectives useful to interactionist theorizing. Scholars have elsewhere discussed how the exclusion of Du Bois (see Morris 2015) and a range of women founders (see Lengermann and Niebrugge-Brantley 1998) from the mainstream sociological theory canon have created epistemological blind spots in our orienting theoretical frameworks. We should consider how the early twentieth-century marginalization of non-white and women theorists may have contributed to canonical foundations about the self, identity, and interaction that do not fully account for processes of oppression, power, and intersectionality and that may have ignored cultural paradigms that were simply rendered invisible.

Contemporary symbolic interactionism is shaped by the late twentieth-century reflexive turn in qualitative research spurred by feminist, queer, and racial and ethnic standpoint theorists. With a strong interest in the lived experiences of people from marked social categories, standpoint theorists emphasize the importance of race, class, gender, and sexuality to one's identity and one's negotiation of self in relation to others. Taking the experiences of people from marked social statuses as important to theorizing about interaction and the self provides an important corrective to symbolic interactionist perspectives that assume a generic social actor. Sheldon Stryker (2008:18) asserts that "Mead's concept of 'generalized other' erases distinctions among social structures within societies, despite variations consequential for social interaction." What is needed, then, to build upon Mead's insights about the self, is to bring an emphasis on these social structures (and the consequent variations in social standpoint arising from them) more centrally into the core of symbolic interactionism. A more nuanced and multidimensional symbolic interactionism that centers the dynamics of power, inequality, and intersectionality offers significant promise for the future study of interactional processes. We need to rethink and broaden the SI canon to address the realities of twenty-first-century social problems and the critical perspectives of today's more diverse and critically oriented symbolic interactionist scholars. The power-oriented concerns of many of today's interactionist researchers require a more inclusive canon that broadens the analytic scope of symbolic interactionism.

Many of the concerns of today's scholars parallel the concerns of earlier scholars from socially marked identity standpoints who were once marginalized as group-specific sociologists outside of the "general" canon, precisely because they focused on issues of race and gender that were perceived at the time as particularistic rather than general issues. The marginalization of non-white theorists has potentially established a canon of sociological theorists whose social standpoints are somewhat limited by their particularistic experiences as members of multiply privileged social identity groups. Mead, for example, saw society as relatively undifferentiated, and the self as largely singular, undivided, and coherent (Stryker 2008:18) in part, because his standpoint at the top of many hierarchies of invisible social privilege made the idea of a coherent general self, not troubled with competing statuses of marginality, appear unproblematic. Insomuch as SI scholars think as originalists who must maintain the tradition of accepting Mead and Blumer as the two overarching foundational theorists of the paradigm, we risk reproducing epistemic structures of the early twentieth century as our own contemporary structures. The canonization of founders can be related to enduring analytic features in their theories that stand the test of time, but it is also tied to geopolitical, cultural, and organizational dimensions that shape whose ideas get highlighted and whose get ignored or suppressed.

Go (2020:93) argues that "canonization is . . . the universalization of the provincial" and that it is usually the provincial standpoint of the unmarked that we universalize, citing for example how Max Weber's canonical theory about the force of ideas in social action arose out of "the parochial concerns of a handful of men in Germany in the early twentieth century" and that Parson's "grand theory" was parochial as he "thought in terms of the category 'social action' (and relatedly 'social order') rather than, say, capitalism, racialized violence, or the processual unfolding of gendered structures." Sociology's epistemic structures also provincialize the universal when developing "epistemological ghettos" (Brekhus 1998) around the lived experiences of people with marked identities. Ethnographers studying marked communities often make group-specific generalizations about their seemingly "socially specialized" subjects when the lived experiences of people in marked social categories reveal broad generic processes just as well as the lives of people in unmarked social categories. The biography-related concerns of African American theorists such as Du Bois present us with general theoretical canonical value to understand broad social processes including identity construction, performing for different social audiences, power relations, resistance, and the production of social inequalities, just as the biography-related concerns of Weber, Parsons, Simmel, Cooley, and Mead reveal general processes.

As the features of racism, sexism, classism, and colonialism structure social worlds, sociologists concerned with these issues and their interactional consequences are increasingly drawing inspiration from additional SI founders. This does not require an abandonment of Mead and Blumer, but it does require a broadening of the canon to incorporate a more analytically diverse range of foundational concerns. To this end, sociologists with interactionist theoretical concerns are beginning to draw from a broader range of foundational thinkers. Mary Jo Deegan (2016) challenges the epistemic exclusion of Jane Addams from conventional accounts of the development of the symbolic interactionist perspective. Tim Hallett and Greg Jeffers (2008) similarly argue for the contemporary relevance of Annie Marion MacLean, who conducted ethnographies that gave voice to her informants and explored the micro dynamics of status and gender at a time when ethnography was mostly colonial and ethnocentric. The tracing of SI's development to Mead, Dewey, Blumer and the men of the Chicago School in many accounts of the perspective's founding, dismisses as non-theoretical the normative social change oriented perspectives of Addams, MacLean, and other women of the Chicago School from the founding corpus of SI theorizing. Similar to the marginalization of Du Bois in his historical time, Addams's work was regarded as less theoretical because it focused on "particularistic" issues and lacked the appearance of a neutral, objective, distant social standpoint—the kind of standpoint that was upheld as more theoretical because it came from seemingly dispassionate theorists hailing from multiply unmarked identity perspectives.

The rigid divide between "objective" "dispassionate sociological theory" and a "subjective" normative commitment to studying social inequality with an eye toward social change, privileged unmarked social standpoints as appearing more scientific and more universal. Increasingly, however, "dispassionate distance" is itself recognized as a normative commitment, although one that is often unmarked and hidden. Today's SI theorists often blend analytic interest in the dynamics of interaction with a commitment to reveal social hierarchies and to potentially challenge and disrupt those hierarchies in order to reduce social inequalities. The orienting concerns of Addams, MacLean, and other women of the Chicago School to empirically document socially produced human pain with an eye toward reforming inequitable social arrangements (Lengermann and Niebrugge 1998:244–52) are consistent with the contemporary concerns of interactionist sociologists focused on intersectionality and structures of inequality.

Categorization and generalization are central to meaning-making and boundary maintenance processes (Timmermans and Tavory 2020) and thus how people navigate those categories is critical to understanding social interaction. Critical standpoint theorists analyze the consequences of living through categorical discrimination with a particular emphasis on how people in marginalized and structurally oppressed categories offer distinctive vantage points from which to observe the structuring of society (e.g. Crenshaw 1991; Collins 2019). Symbolic interactionism, with its focus on lived experience in interactional contexts, is analytically situated to illuminate the consequences of categorical discrimination and to address power and inequalities as central features of social life if it embraces the concerns of critical theorists as general theoretical concerns. To do so, it is important to recognize that Du Bois's observations about Black identity and the Black social self in the early twentieth century are general theoretical observations about identity management and the social self that should be as much a part of the foundational core of interactionist theorizing as Mead's ideas about the social self. The white founders of SI and other theoretical perspectives largely ignored race as a central issue (Zuckerman 2004; Morris 2015) because it was segregated from their daily vision and thus segregated from their epistemological vision. Du Bois recognized the central role of race in social life because it was a palpable feature in his everyday interactions. Today, especially given many of the visible social problems of our time, even white scholars understand that race is an issue of general, not particularistic, sociological interest.

José Itzigsohn and Karida Brown (2015) argue that Du Bois's linking of the macro structure of the racialized world with self-formation provides important understandings of the self that are missing from the self-formation theories of Mead, Cooley, and James. They point out that while Mead, Cooley, and James considered the negative effects of lack of recognition, they paid little attention to the many Black people who lived with this daily reality. It was an aside or endnote in their work. Du Bois, on the other hand, took on the color line and the sense of twoness created in the double consciousness of Black people, who intersubjectively constructed a Black world behind the veil while dealing with the dehumanizing lack of recognition from the white world, as an important part of understanding self-formation in everyday social interactions structured by racial inequalities (Itzigsohn and Brown 2015). Because of his own social standpoint within a racist society, Du Bois's theory of the self is more analytically intersectional and conscious of the role of racialization in self-formation. He recognizes the analytic benefits of marginality that a marked social identity provides, and the analytic blinders of unmarked privilege, when he observes, "Had it not been for the race problem early thrust upon me and enveloping me, I should have probably been an unquestioning worshiper at the shrine of the social order and economic development into which I was born. But just that part of the order which seemed to most of my fellows nearest perfection, seemed to me most inequitable and wrong" (Du Bois 1940/1984:27).

The observations Du Bois developed from the orienting concerns of his own positionality are just as important to general theorizing as the orienting concerns that Mead and Cooley derived from their more unmarked standpoints. Itzigsohn and Brown (2015) state "Du Bois is thought to be a scholar of race, and he is indeed that. But his work goes beyond treating race as a discrete concept and instead situates the process of *racializing* and *racialization* (i.e., the process of intersubjectively constructing racial categories and meanings that structure the experiences of groups and individuals) at the core of the formation and the organization of the modern world." These observations while important to the study of race are also general theoretical observations about social life. And Du Bois's (1897) analysis of the twoness of Black Americans having to balance two competing identities: their "Blackness," marginalized to less than a full citizen, and their "Americanness," emphasizes the general complex dynamics of the interplay of marked and unmarked identities that are critical to many forms of identity navigation.

What does an expanded SI canon that recognizes Du Bois's contributions to our orienting concerns offer us? We can start to see some of the benefits to understanding the complexity of social interaction around central issues of racialization in some exemplary SI theories today. Margaret Hagerman (this volume) extends the symbolic interactionism of Du Bois by examining the processes of racializing and racialization in white families. Emphasizing the ways that interactional constructions of racialized meanings are produced at the micro level in a dialectical relationship with "powerful meso and macro-level historical and institutional structures of oppression that perpetuate racial hierarchies and inequalities," Hagerman centers power and racialization in a critical symbolic interactionist perspective that builds upon Du Bois's orienting general conceptual sociological concerns. In order to show how racist categorizations are socio-semiotically produced and challenged in everyday racist social interactions, Timmermans and Tavory (2020) draw upon Du Bois's (1935/1962) understanding of whiteness as a form of capital that shields its unmarked power in the organization of social institutions. Starting with these works which begin to point the direction to a critically intersectional, power-focused symbolic interactionism, and relating them to other works that interrogate the intersections of unmarked privilege and marked difference, I outline the benefits of a broadened symbolic interactionist framework.

A CRITICAL INTERSECTIONAL SYMBOLIC INTERACTIONISM: THE POWER OF THE UNMARKED

Hagerman (2018, this volume) connects the study of unmarked white racial practices directly to symbolic interactionism through her critical research on white racial socialization. Challenging the perception that white families are not "racial" (see Burton et al. 2010) and that therefore racial socialization only happens in non-white families, Hagerman explores the subtle everyday interactional socialization of white kids into living and reproducing (as well as sometimes challenging) unmarked white privilege through a range of racialized choices such as where to live, what activities to participate in, and where to send their children to school. These choices to organize family routines in racially segregated ways are heavily racialized yet because they are choices made by white parents without explicitly acknowledging race, they have often been understood as "generic" and unraced rather than racialized practices.

Hagerman demonstrates that many white parents express "colorblind" racial discourse, but that white children learn about race primarily through their interactions. White children learn for example who lives in what neighborhoods by looking out the car window, as well as learning what racial identities are marked and unmarked by what neighborhoods their parents avoid and what neighborhoods they frequent. Young people "make sense of race through patterns they notice in their social environment" through their encounters and interactions with family and peers (Hagerman, this volume; see also Hagerman 2018; Van Ausdale and Feagin 2001). Further contributing to the invisibility of white racialized decisions, white parents often mark even mentioning the "specialized" topic of race as itself an act of racism (Hagerman 2018).

Employing a semiotic approach to trace the dynamic processes of specification and generalization in racist encounters, Timmermans and Tavory (2020) provide a complex, sophisticated approach to understanding the interactional navigations of intersecting marked and unmarked categorizations in racist encounters. Using racist encounters as a site for the construction and performance of racialized and racist understandings, they analyze the markedness dynamics of *upshifting* (generalizing or abstracting broader conclusions from a specific example) and *downshifting* (personalizing or singularizing events). One key dynamic they witness is that the person initiating a racist encounter upshifts to define the target of their racism as a marked social type representing stereotypical behaviors and features. In response, the targeted victim attempts to redefine their individual humanity by downshifting to recast the situation, asserting their identity as an individual rather than as a marked social type. But to present themselves as an individual they often must not only downshift, but typify "themselves as members of a different, *unmarked* category" (Timmermans and Tavory 2020:305). Thus, for example, they may define themselves as a "working person," a "citizen," a "family man," a "regular person," or similar types of categories to make a strategic "semiotic move toward humanization and unmarked categorization" (Timmermans and Tavory 2020:305).

As we see here, members of marked social categories can situationally deploy unmarked attributes to wield the semiotic power of the unmarked in attempts to override their marked attributes. In recognizing unmarkedness and markedness as creative strategic semiotic resources tied to larger structures of discourse, power, and oppression, a critical intersectional symbolic interactionism offers a complex understanding of power that has much to contribute to intersectionality theories.

One of the major developments in twenty-first-century sociology is the rise of intersectionality theory first introduced as a metaphor by Kimberlé Crenshaw (1991) in legal studies and championed and developed into a sociological paradigm by Patricia Hill Collins (1990/2000, 2019) and others. Intersectionality theory with its roots in Black feminism has organized its theoretical project around studying members of multiply marginalized categories (e.g., Black women) in order to recover silenced voices (Nash 2008:10). Intersectional theory as a paradigm focusing on systems of oppression along intersecting axes of race, gender, sexuality, and class, and the ways that multiply marginalized individuals negotiate these systems, has contributed much to our understanding of social power and identity. At the same time, the analytic power of intersectionality can be sharpened further by giving greater epistemological weight to the ways in which people manage their unmarked categories of privilege as well as their multiply marginalized categories (Nash 2008; Brekhus 2020:104–6, 2023:41–42). While intersectionality theory has generally been resistant to studying the privileged and the non-multiply marginalized (Nash 2008:10), the analytic advantages of ethnographically studying unmarked privilege as well as marked marginality allow us to see how systems of oppression and categorization are reproduced in interactional and discursive practice.

A complex intersectional SI lens recognizes that intersectionality involves not only managing multiply marginalized standpoints *but negotiating the interplay of the marked and the unmarked*. Examining how people with a marked attribute on one axis and an unmarked attribute on another axis downshift to deploy their unmarkedness can reveal the semiotic structuring of oppressive systems.

Ruth Frankenberg (1993) introduced unmarked "whiteness" as an unexamined but important aspect of white women's identities arguing that their often unacknowledged racial identity shapes white women's lives just as much as their marked gender identity. White women often expressed whiteness as a hollow, flavorless, empty, and formless identity rather than a set of racialized cultural practices that usually go unnamed and unmarked (Frankenberg 1993). Like Hagerman's white families, they engaged in a play of humility to downplay the power of whiteness. Unlike the ostentatious displays of white nationalists who wield white supremacy as a visible weapon, Frankenberg's humble white women describe themselves as bland and devoid of culture, symbolically conceding the terrain of "culture" to members of marked racial groups. Similarly, Brekhus (2003:75–77) found that white, middle-class, suburban gay men humbly described themselves as boring, ordinary, uninteresting, average Joe, and regular guy and foregrounded "generic" identities like neighbor and good person.

Whiteness, middle-classness, and suburbanness are often deployed as privileging discursive and interactional resources even when they are not explicitly named. Angela Stroud's (2015) ethnographic analysis of "good guys with guns" uses an intersectional critical race perspective to demonstrate the power of multiply unmarked identities in navigating a moral identity. White, middle-class gun owners defined themselves as moral citizens and "good guys with guns." There is no direct racial or class statement in the label "good guys with guns" but this identity was connected to a claim that they are civically engaged men who will render aid to anyone in need but that such need only applies to "good parts of town"; in "bad parts of town" one's guard should always be up because anyone seeking assistance is likely setting them up to be a victim (Stroud 2015:109–10). Through the seemingly unraced, unclassed position of a "good guy" these men articulate a potentially lethal moral order where rendering life-saving aid and rendering life-ending violence are opposite sides of the same moral coin depending on whether one has similarly semiotically unmarked statuses or a weightier "dangerous" marked status.

In another important study, Braden Leap's (2017) intersectional analysis of the survival narratives of rural, white, heterosexual men who traveled to the city similarly demonstrates how men with intersecting unmarked identities (white, heterosexual, male) constructed moral identities for themselves using their unmarked statuses. These men never explicitly mentioned whiteness in their narratives, but they constructed their moral identities as "good guys" who were savvy and able to navigate the city and its array of "dangerous urban figures" who they coded as deviant, exotic, and morally suspect. Their survival tales revealed a raced, classed, gendered, regioned, and sexualized intersectionality and "an intersectional ideal of what it meant to be a good rural man" even while never saying that the ideal rural man was white, working- to middle-class, and heterosexual (Leap 2017:18).

The study of the interactional production of whiteness as a powerful unmarked identity is among the most developed areas of research into the power of the unmarked, but there are other avenues of studying unmarked power dynamics as well. In a study that particularly emphasizes the importance of understanding the relationship between unmarked social structures of privilege and everyday interaction, for example, C. J. Pascoe (2007) ethnographically analyzes the interactional reproduction of heteronormative privilege in a United States high school, demonstrating that the primary "informal sexuality curriculum" produced in school assemblies, routine interactions, classroom pedagogy, school decorations, and major events like prom is compulsory heterosexuality. Unmarked heterosexuality is reproduced as normative, compulsory, and expected at almost every interactional level within the high school that Pascoe studied and presumably in many US high schools. Similarly J. E. Sumerau (Sumerau, Cragun, and Mathers 2016; Sumerau and Holway 2022) and Lain A. B. Mathers (2017) are developing a symbolic interactionist sociology of "cissexism" and the "cisgendering of reality," demonstrating, for example, how interactional practices are structured in ways that define transgender people as "interactional problems" or "deviations" to be managed as "exceptions" rather than as ordinary social actors themselves integral to the fabric of social reality. An important feature of interactionist studies that examine the production and reproduction of unmarked power is that they tie micro face to face interactions with more enduring meso- and macro-level social structures that shape and constrain creative human agency. While actors do have agency within social structures, attending to the ways that interaction and socialization are shaped by the often hidden and taken-for-granted social structures brings power and a critical edge more centrally into the symbolic interactionist tradition.

In an especially nuanced analysis of "doing" multidimensional social identities, Julie Bettie (2014) brings a critical intersectional analysis to the performance of raced, classed, and gendered subcultural identities. She argues that race/ethnicity and class "are too often presented as 'categorical' variables, essentially *there* rather than *created*" and that greater attention should be paid to the ways that they are performed and constructed through gender and subculture (Bettie 2014:35). Taking up this challenge, Bettie examines the embodied performance of raced class identities through the formation of cliques with differing subcultural styles. The informal peer hierarchy in high schools is centered around cliques that organize in terms of taste styles; these performances of subcultural style are fundamentally balancing acts of expressing marked difference and striving for social inclusion. One unique aspect of Bettie's approach is to bring class in as a performative identity of social structure through subcultural style. Performances of "rockers" or "preps" or "*las chicas*" ("the girls") or cholas ("hard cores") are expressed as subcultural identities but are also unstated performances of social class (Bettie 2014), just as performances of "good guys" or "regulars guys" or "neighbors" are often unstated performances of race. An intersectional lens focused on the ways people balance their marked and unmarked attributes allows symbolic interactionism to examine the ways power structures shape performance and the ways that performance shapes power.

CONCLUSION

Symbolic interactionism has long been an important perspective for understanding how meaning is creatively constructed and negotiated in everyday life. Blumer's interest in how people construct meanings in interaction, and Mead's interest in how the self is socially formed, are among the central orienting concerns for SI research and remain useful. They are, however, only one particularized part of a potentially broader SI canon. Many themes raised by Du Bois, including double consciousness, conflicted selves, and racialization and the construction of racial meanings in daily interaction, are also issues of central general theoretical concern today. I have argued in this chapter that SI is well positioned to address social inequalities and the kinds of concerns with power, social structure, marginality, and privilege that have become central to the discipline.

Formed as an alternative to structural-functionalism, SI has significantly shaped the discipline of sociology and given it a more critical edge. But SI as a perspective was itself also shaped by the particular historical and political circumstances of its formation and the epistemological structures of the time in which it emerged. While developing a critical lens to better address human agency and meaning-making at the micro-level, it at the same time continued to reproduce the unmarked privileging of white, Anglo-European/colonizer, male social standpoints. Along with this, the analytic concerns of SI were less focused on dimensions of structural inequality than they could have been had they more directly considered and advanced the orienting concerns of scholars like Du Bois whose theoretical observations and orienting concerns about inequality were marginalized at the time. We can improve SI approaches, as some recent scholars are doing, by analyzing the central role of unmarked normative power and the performative dimensions of markedness and unmarkedness in social interaction. In this chapter, I have highlighted markedness and unmarkedness as orienting concepts to access dimensions of categorization and social power. Employing these concepts contributes to a critical intersectional symbolic interactionism rooted in understanding complex inequalities. Symbolic interactionism, focused on how people interactionally navigate interlocking structures of oppression and privilege through their marked and unmarked statuses and identity performances, offers an important analytic lens for interpreting and understanding social inequalities and social problems.

REFERENCES

Bettie, Julie. 2014. *Women without Class: Girls, Race, and Identity*. Oakland: University of California Press.

Brekhus, Wayne H. 1996. "Social Marking and the Mental Coloring of Identity: Sexual Identity Construction and Maintenance in the United States." *Sociological Forum* 11(3):497–522.

Brekhus, Wayne H. 1998. "A Sociology of the Unmarked: Redirecting Our Focus." *Sociological Theory* 16(1):34–51.

Brekhus, Wayne H. 2003. *Peacocks, Chameleons, Centaurs: Gay Suburbia and the Grammar of Social Identity*. Chicago: University of Chicago Press.

Brekhus, Wayne H. 2020. *The Sociology of Identity: Authenticity, Multidimensionality, and Mobility*. Cambridge, UK; Medford, MA: Polity Press.

Brekhus, Wayne H. 2023. "Marked and Unmarked: A Semiotic Distinction for Concept-Driven Sociology." Pp. 31–51 in *Interpretive Sociology and the Semiotic Imagination*, edited by A. Cossu and J. Fontdevila. Bristol, UK: Bristol University Press.

Burton, Linda M., Eduardo Bonilla-Silva, Victor Ray, Rose Buckelew, and Elizabeth Hordge Freeman. 2010. "Critical Race Theories, Colorism, and the Decade's Research on Families of Color." *Journal of Marriage and Family* 72(3):440–59.

Collins, Patricia Hill. 1990/2000. *Black Feminist Thought: Knowledge, Consciousness, and the Politics of Empowerment*. New York: Routledge.

Collins, Patricia Hill. 2019. *Intersectionality as Critical Social Theory*. Durham, NC: Duke University Press.

Crenshaw, Kimberlé. 1991. "Mapping the Margins: Intersectionality, Identity Politics, and Violence against Women of Color." *Stanford Law Review* 43(6):1241–99.

Davis, F. James. 1991. *Who is Black?: One Nation's Definition*. University Park: Pennslyania State University Press.

Deegan, Mary Jo. 2016. "Jane Addams, The Chicago Schools of Sociology and the Emergence of Symbolic Interaction, 1889–1935." Pp. 57–76 in *The Astructural Bias Charge: Myth or Reality (Studies in Symbolic Interaction, Vol. 46)*, edited by G. Musolf. Bingley, UK: Emerald Publishing.

Du Bois, W. E. B. 1897. The Conservation of Races. The American Negro Academy of Occasional Papers, No 2. Washington DC: Published by the Academy.

Du Bois, W. E. B. 1935/1962. *Black Reconstruction in America: 1860–1880*. New York: Russell and Russell.

Du Bois, W. E. B. 1940/1984. *Dusk of Dawn: An Essay toward an Autobiography of a Race Concept*. New Brunswick: Transaction Books.

Frankenberg, Ruth. 1993. *White Women, Race Matters: The Social Construction of Whiteness*. Minneapolis: University of Minnesota Press.

Go, Julian. 2020. "Race, Empire, and Epistemic Exclusion: Or the Structures of Sociological Thought." *Sociological Theory* 38(2):79–100.

Hagerman, Margaret A. 2018. *White Kids: Growing Up with Privilege in a Racially Divided America*. New York: New York University Press.

Hallett, Tim, and Greg Jeffers. 2008. "A Long-Neglected Mother of Contemporary Ethnography: Annie Marion MacLean and the Memory of a Method." *Journal of Contemporary Ethnography* 37(1):3–37.

Henrich, Joseph, Steven J. Heine, and Ara Norenzayen. 2010. "The Weirdest People in the World?" *Behavioral and Brain Sciences* 33(2–3):61–83.

Itzigsohn, José, and Karida Brown. 2015. "Sociology and the Theory of Double Consciousness: W. E. B. Du Bois's Phenomenology of Racialized Subjectivity." *Du Bois Review: Social Science Research on Race* 12(2):231–48.

Jakobson, Roman. 1972. "Verbal Communication." *Scientific American* 227:72–80.

Leap, Braden. 2017. "Survival Narratives: Constructing an Intersectional Masculinity through Stories of the Rural/Urban Divide." *Journal or Rural Studies* 55:12–21.

Lengermann, Patricia M., and Jill Niebrugge-Brantley, eds. 1998. *The Women Founders: Sociology and Social Theory, 1830-1930: A Text/Reader*. Boston, MA: McGraw Hill.

Mathers, Lain A.B. 2017. "Bathrooms, Boundaries, and Emotional Burdens: Cisgendering Interactions Through the Interpretation of Transgender Experience." *Symbolic Interaction* 40(3):295–316.

Morris, Aldon D. 2015. *The Scholar Denied: W. E. B. Du Bois and the Birth of Modern Sociology*. Oakland: University of California Press.

Mullaney, Jamie L. 1999. "Making It 'Count': Mental Weighing and Identity Attribution." *Symbolic Interaction* 22(3):269–83.

Nash, Jennifer C. 2008. "Re-Thinking Intersectionality." *Feminist Review* 89(1):1–15.

Pascoe, C. J. 2007. *Dude, You're a Fag: Masculinity and Sexuality in High School*. Berkeley: University of California Press.

Seamster, Louise, and Victor Ray. 2018. "Against Teleology in the Study of Race: Toward the Abolition of the Progress Paradigm." *Sociological Theory* 36(4):315–42.

Stroud, Angela. 2015. *Good Guys with Guns: The Appeal and Consequences of Concealed Carry*. Chapel Hill: University of North Carolina Press.

Stryker, Sheldon. 2008. "From Mead to a Structural Symbolic Interactionism and Beyond." *Annual Review of Sociology* 34(1):15–31.

Sumerau, J. E., Ryan T. Cragun, and Lain A. B. Mathers. 2016. "Contemporary Religion and the Cisgendering of Reality." *Social Currents* 3(3):293–311.

Sumerau, J. E., and Giuseppina Valle Holway. 2022. "Transgender Possibilities and the Cisgendering of Family among Cisgender Women." *Symbolic Interaction* 45(2):167–88.

Timmermans, Stefan, and Iddo Tavory. 2020. "Racist Encounters: A Pragmatist Semiotic Analysis of Interaction." *Sociological Theory* 38(4):295–317.

Trubetzkoy, Nikolaj, and Roman Jakobson. 1975. *N. S. Trubetzkoy's Letters and Notes*. The Hague; Paris: Mouton.

Van Ausdale, Debra, and Joe Feagin. 2001. *The First R; How Children Learn Race and Racism*. Lanham, MD: Rowman and Littlefield.

Waugh, Linda R. 1982. "Marked and Unmarked: A Choice between Unequals in Semiotic Structure." *Semiotica* 38(3–4):299–318.

Zerubavel, Eviatar. 2018. *Taken for Granted: The Remarkable Power of the Unremarkable*. Princeton, NJ: Princeton University Press.

Zuckerman, Phil. 2004. *The Social Theory of W. E. B. Du Bois*. Thousand Oaks, CA: Pine Forge Press.

CHAPTER 20

THE APPEARANCE OF NOTHINGNESS
Concealed Strategic Actions

CARMELO LOMBARDO AND LORENZO SABETTA

INTRODUCTION: DO YOU BELIEVE IN NATURAL APPEARANCES?

Two Types of Social Nothingness

The enterprise of seeing sociologically the realm of everyday interactions and events, too trivial for striking either academic or layperson attention, owes much to the work of Erving Goffman and Harold Garfinkel, whose contribution in legitimizing this previously suspicious kind of study has been immense.[1] This does not imply, of course, that their perspectives can be conflated or lumped together. It may be surprising, even for informed readers, to find out that Garfinkel, back in the 1950s, did not publish his first theoretical manuscript *because of* Goffman's enthusiastic encouragements to do so, deciding to bring it out only in 2006 at Anne W. Rawls' insistence. Oddly (and simply) enough, to Garfinkel, Goffman's endorsement was a motive *not* to publish (Rawls 2006:3–4). This counterintuitive, reversed appraisal of Goffman's advice is a captivating issue, but it will remain untouched here.[2] We will rather present only one facet of the complex relationship between their approaches they disagreed on (and, indeed, only as a starting point for a different analysis). Goffman and Garfinkel were both obsessed with the various ways in which people are plunged into the taken-for-granted attitude toward daily practices (see Travers 1994; Misztal 2015:49–59). They also concurred on the inconspicuous, mostly nameless, and almost invisible character of the multitude of mundane actions that compose the background of social reality.[3] That is, they more or less agreed that a normal situation "constitutes but a mere non-event" (Zerubavel 2015:7) for those who are within it. In this respect, Ten Have (1990:29) talked about "the invisibility of common sense": a things-as-usual situation is not recognized as an episode in itself, and this uneventfulness is constitutive of habitual behavior (see Goffman 1971:239; Garfinkel 1974:16; Garfinkel and Livingston 2003:25). From "nothing special is happening" to "nothing is happening at all" is but a short step, since the characteristics of what is normal are those of what is invisible (Brighenti 2007:326). Still, what Goffman and Garfinkel assumed to be lying before and behind these daily nothing-is-up situations differs in a profound way. Rawls provides some valuable interpretive assistance:

> For Goffman the world of action was essentially messy and lacking order. It was the actor's job to create the appearance of order—a thin veneer of consensus. For Garfinkel, by contrast, the world of embodied practice—created and lived in by groups of actors (. . .) – was ordered in and through their efforts and had coherence and meaning only in and through (. . .) recognizable orders of practice. This could not be a fictional, or messy, order; and the consensus, or "trust" underlying it needed to be real and substantial, not thin or only apparent.
>
> (Rawls 2006:4)

Amazed by everyday life's patterned coherence, Garfinkel only trusted accounts uncompromisingly faithful to the witnessable details of practical activities; "it is the actual, routine communicative efforts of actors that Garfinkel seeks to theorize—'things done, said, heard, felt'" (Baehr 2019:89). Though equally amazed by the same phenomenon,[4] Goffman often looked at it obliquely, in attempting to fathom how the innocent façade of social situations can conceal a different underlying reality. In this regard, Goffman's definition of man as "*homo fabricator*" (Burns 1992:260) is radically alien to Garfinkel, who dubbed this vaguely Machiavellian stance as "Goffman's 'naughty' view" (1967:174), deeming it too concerned with the hypothetical presence of some dissembling calculations. This distrustful attitude could lead to probing inquiries and inquisitor questions, both misguided for Garfinkel: "in the empirical applications of Goffman's notions one is continually tempted to press the informant with exasperation, 'Oh come on now, you must know better than that. Why don't you confess?'" (Garfinkel 1967:174). Although actually filled with a stunning variety of ethnomethods and micro dynamics, Garfinkel's routine activities are surrounded by an aura of authentic social nothingness. To account for how they unfold or why they are attuned to each other, there is no need to dig into a deeper psychological level: there are no hidden intentions to disclose or conspiracies to uncover. The sense of nothingness that normalcy may engender represents, indeed, a reassuring collective achievement. Far from being Sartrean, this means "nothing to worry about" and refers to the smoothness of intersubjectivity. Perceiving a situation as normal (i.e., not like a we-have-a-situation situation) fosters trusting intentions toward others (Misztal 2001:314), enabling people to mind their business. For the same reason, however, this perception is susceptible to contrivance and lends itself to being made up, instrumentally used to misrepresent situations under a cloak of inadvertent ordinariness. After all, "the appearance of normality counts for more than its actual occurrence" (Misztal 2015:50)—here comes Goffman's demon: "the most innocent-looking situation may be for this very reason the best one for [wrongdoers, or anyone else for that matter] to create" (Goffman 1971:280). Natural appearances, when nothing is out of ordinary, could portend something ominous.

A distinction may be drawn, in this view, in the endless landscape of "the social life of nothing" (Scott 2019), akin to the acts of omission/acts of commission difference (Scott and Stephens 2018). In the final line of his poem *The Snow Man* (1921), Wallace Stevens cryptically distinguished between the "nothing that is not there and the nothing that is," somehow postulating the existence of two different kinds of "nothingness" (meaning "nothing unusual is happening": see Emerson 1970). One could say that "the nothing that is there" is the Garfinkelian one, which indicates actual uneventful absence. This type of, so to speak, veracious nothing does not enshroud anything deliberately intentional behind itself—it is not a veil to be pierced. The "nothing that is not there" is presupposing a typical Goffmanesque scenario. Nothingness, here, may well be just a surface layer or a fictional guise, the effect of a maneuver conceived to affect other people's behavior and making them act on the basis of this projected (non)meaning. Neither staged nor schemed, Garfinkel's everyday life routines are what they seem. Uninteresting from the viewpoint of their own practitioners (Garfinkel 1967:7), these actions and situations are disregarded and can feel like nothing, but a kind of nothing *with nothing behind it*, with no recondite motive to unmask. An explanation of these non-situations in terms of intentional agents would be meaningless, since no hidden puppeteer is pulling the strings behind the scenes. Rather differently, Goffman's approach is more cautious in drawing "the line between ordinary activity and fabrications" (Goffman 1986:118). The "overdetermination of normalcy" (Goffman 1971:256) leaves open the possibility of interpreting those same empty moments as deliberately built for strategic purposes. Nothingness, in such cases, is just a perception, an appearance that someone set up (if so, intentions matter).

This second type of social nothingness, which is only exterior and in fact deliberately arranged, is the topic of this chapter.[5] Following Goffman's analysis of normal appearances, our purpose is to illustrate how the "appearance of nothingness" can be conceived as a symbolic social object, intentionally displayed for inducing other actors to feel that nothing is happening. We begin by introducing the concept of concealed strategic actions, actions that first disguise the very existence of a strategic action whatsoever, giving to their audience the impression that nothing is going on. Some Goffmanian concepts (secret exhibition, given/given off information, and of course normal appearances) are used and connected among each other; the notion of pseudo-unintentional evidence is analyzed. Then, we hone in on Thaler's and Sunstein's nudge theory as a current and influential example of strategic concealed action. The hypothesis is that certain nudges (e.g., default options) are more effective insofar as they denote interventions that do not seem interventions; the same may apply to the program of libertarian paternalism, interpreted here as a version of paternalism that, staying in the background, is not experienced as such. We conclude our discussion by exploring, from an interactionist point of view, the relationship between strategic actions (concealed or not) and their reception by targeted audiences, trying to make an argument about the relevance of reactions both for social action theory and symbolic interactionism. Our feeling is that concealed strategic actions continue to hold promise (since Goffman, and even more so considering the recent body of interactionist literature—associated with the writings of Brekhus, Friedman, Scott, and Zerubavel—on nothingness, unmarked default, and cultural blind spots) for infusing SI with new verve and vitality, and possibly for reworking its precepts and confronting questions arising within other subfields (e.g., the sociology of culture and cognition).

Giving the Given Off, or: How to Influence Without Appearing To

Reading Goffman, one is constantly reminded of the many ways (lies, pranks, shenanigans, frauds, falsehoods, etc.) through which "the individual can be caused to be out of touch with what it is that is really going on" (Goffman 1986:111). To assume that people are as they appear, and things are as they claim to be, is to disregard the lurking presence of efforts to concoct activities so that others will be induced to have a false belief about them. These efforts seek to dupe others by manipulating their assumptions about actualities and appearances, usually through some moves that do not openly display themselves as such and hide the calculation that went into their construction (see Ytreberg 2010). Some advertisements do not look like advertisements (e.g., some radio programs, at least in Italy and in the United States, have the talk-show host read the ad in such an insouciant manner that it does not appear to be an ad, but just the host's next statement on the show), and recent policy regulations, not by chance, require social media influencers to disclose sponsored content (there is a growing literature on this issue: Evans et al. 2017; Shan, Chen, and Lin 2020). A scam, by definition, does not present itself as a swindle (on the contrary, it comes in the guise of con games). A number of technological systems dissimulate by design and are built to provide a false sense of outward neutrality that conceals secondary, unseen functions (see Monahan 2016). Even a noticeable act of mass persuasion like propaganda, under certain conditions, may not be seen for what it is. Felt by the audience as non-instrumental while altogether instrumentally oriented, Kate Smith managed to sell 39 million dollars of war bonds through the pretense of authenticity and friendship; Merton (1946) called this process "pseudo-gemeinschaft," the feigning of intimacy with others in order to bend them to one's own advantage (see Fleck 2021). Make-believe, pretense, and deceptive appearances are also central to art and works of fiction (Walton 1990). To achieve a reality effect, a text can draw attention away from itself as text, so as to generate a feeling of unmediated contact with the real (see Barthes 1975). It is said, in this regard, that *ars est celare artem*, art lies in concealing art.[6] This does not only imply that true art conceals the means by which it is achieved, meaning that is aesthetically better to keep the process of composition below the surface of artworks. The saying rather suggests a kind of oxymoron, something like artificial naturalness or calculated spontaneity, that is, a painstakingly arranged impression of nothing contrived. Engineering an appearance of nothingness amounts to projecting an elusive, self-eliding definition of the situation according to which there is no "situation" at all in the first place. The act of setting up such pseudo-normal, faux-unmarked situations might be defined as concealed strategic action (henceforth, CSA). Whereas lies and falsehoods hide the truth but do not necessarily hide themselves as statements or gestures (they might well have the appearance of something, just impostering and pretending to be different from what they really are: see Vogel, Moats, Woolgar, and Helgesson 2021), the crucial feature of CSAs is that they strategically conceal their own existence. These actions, dissembling their presence, manage to avoid presenting themselves upon the audience notice, and yet affect their behavior. CSAs are also different from the " 'situation as normal' interaction tactics" explored by Glaser and Strauss (1964:672), which consist of turning a blind eye to something unusual and act as if it had not happened. CSAs intentionally introduce a change but keep this intention from being detected. If they are successfully carried out, CSAs are experienced as non-actions (they are meant to be so), in the context of non-situations.[7] Although the idea of structuring situations without triggering deliberate modes of cognition is not new (see Harvey 2010:190–91) and Goffman has expatiated on analogous subjects (Goffman 1971:238–333), the kind of strategic actions executed without any sign that a plan to do so is involved is still undertheorized. Many questions (all quite relevant to symbolic interactionism) can be raised about CSAs: What is the mechanism by which they are performed? What is the point of performing such phantasmal actions? Are there any actual instances of CSAs with some practical importance? What, if any, is their sociological or theoretical relevance? By recourse to some of Goffman's concepts, we start from the first issue.

At the beginning of the essay "Expression Games: An Analysis of Doubts at Play," Goffman briefly examines an anecdotal story that epitomizes several of his abiding interests—expressions, social illusion, impression management, spies and espionage, the definition of the situation. Goffman borrows the story from Alexander M. Orlov, a colonel in the Soviet secret police and KGB defector, who illustrates a device employed by the People's Commissariat for Internal Affairs (*Narodnyy Komissariat Vnutrennikh Del*, NKVD). To confirm her fake persona, an agent who believes she will be investigated for identity check can leave behind herself a set of negligible traces associated with her undercover identity. The gimmick, a counter-uncovering technique named "secret exhibition" (SE), consists of a series of *seemingly banal* clues (for example, a couple of old postcards or railway tickets in her apartment) which have been, in fact, carefully scattered in advance, but in such a way as to pass off as undevised and ingenuous. SEs exploit the belief that trace-like, trivial hints are informative and insightful because they have been produced without any thinking and, therefore, should reveal something about their producers; "once an agent suspects that he will be inspected for minor cues of authentication, he can provide some that might not otherwise have been sought. He can fabricate just those little leavings of the self that shrewd observers might use as a check upon official but false presentations" (Goffman 1969:25–26). An SE, basically, is an exhibition that does not seem like an exhibition, a process that screens itself behind an ostensibly unmarked semblance, and SEs are an example of CSAs. These actions are manipulative, but even though manipulated persons do not usually realize the way in which they are being influenced, forms of overt manipulation exist (Barnhill 2014:58–59). CSAs, instead, are not only covert, but nonexistent from the perspective of their audience. They work on certain aspects (those that sustain the appearance of nothing) that no one would expect to be the target of any work (e.g., in Goffman's words, minor cues, little leavings of the self). CSAs are a bit more sophisticated than the typical backstage/frontstage relationship, in the classic sense of preparing the frontage while in the backstage. Here, *the backstage work aims at erasing the very idea that there is any stage (and anything staged) at all*. CSAs, in other words, conceal both the facts of the matter and the fact itself that something is concealed (see Goffman 1971:262). Attending to worthless trifles and negligible parts of the scene (who would bother to counterfeit them?), SEs fabricate the appearance that there is not anything special going on. Speaking of social appearances and "simulating artlessness," Barbara Carnevali observed that "the illusion is close to perfection insofar as it acts upon those details which the audience believes to be spontaneous" (2012:14). From this perspective, the appearance of nothingness achieved by SEs is an appearance of unintentionality. Rather than empty or void, "nothing" in this case means random and inadvertent, casual—nothing organized. Preparing what will seem unprepared, SEs make use of certain information that gives the impression of being accidentally exuded but is, in fact, intentionally communicated, like a trail of phony footprints. In this vein, Goffman distinguished (1959:2) between deliberately "given" and unwittingly "given off" information, reformulating elsewhere (1969:5–6) the same distinction and separating "expressed" (produced without anticipating their future information value) from "transmitted" (produced to affect other actors' beliefs) information.[8] SEs play on this double level of information and communicate purposefully what will appear inadvertently transpired, that is, giving the given off.

There is a fine line between calculated and not calculated information, and anything in the environment that by being noticed changes our minds about something that may have been displayed on purpose. Yesterday's unintentional evidence can become today's intentional evidence: "the movements, looks, and vocal sounds we make as an unintended by-product of speaking and listening never seem to remain innocent (…). We look simply to see, see others looking, see we are seen looking, and soon become knowing and skilled in regard to the evidential uses made of the appearance of looking" (Goffman 1981:2). Moreover, hypothetically foolproof cues are the most vulnerable precisely because of their trustworthy, innocent character. Their seeming bona fide nature makes them subject to misuse: "the most reliance-inspiring conduct on the subject's part is exactly the conduct that it would be most advantageous for him to fake if he wanted to hoodwink the observer" (Goffman 1969:62) and the "best evidence could also be the worst evidence" (Goffman 1971:327). Commenting on this, Philip Manning (2000) observed that Goffman was, at once, a theorist of deception and a theorist of trust. Such endeavors are two sides of the same interactional coin. Sincerity and mimicry—honesty and bad faith—share the same wardrobe: that of credibility. To manifest reliability, actors cannot but employ the same means that can also be used for betrayal: "however we convince others that we are as we appear to be, we use the same resources confidence tricksters use to deceive people" (Manning 2000:288). Since truth tellers and hoaxers are both characterized by the intention of appearing credible, this intention could not be considered discriminating. Indeed, the opposite is true. When perceived by the audience, the very desire to be convincing is potentially suspicious (more on this below), if only because deception always requires some degree of intentionality, while authenticity does not. Hence the stratagem of SEs, which not only transmit apparently unintentional information, but also give the impression that no information is given at all. SEs try to stay invisible in the sense of being "there without being an object" (Merleau-Ponty 1968:229), conserving the state of the environment's invisibility characteristic of normality while in fact molding it.

SEs are a purely Goffmanian example of CSAs. Byzantine and convoluted, CSAs seem a spy novel trope (SEs are similar to the purposeful leak of supposedly revealing information) unlikely to take place throughout the mundanity of daily life. In the next paragraph, we argue that exactly the unremarkable backstage of normal situations (i.e., situations *where "the action" usually isn't*, to paraphrase Goffman) is well suited for concealing actions strategically oriented. In so doing, we also maintain that an expanded symbolic interactionist framework is uniquely equipped to illuminate microeconomic concepts.

The Discreet Charm of Nudges: Does a Default Option Feel Like an Option?

Ever since it was proposed by Richard Thaler and Cass Sunstein a decade ago, nudge theory has been widely discussed, criticized, endorsed, and put into use. The idea has been undeniably successful. Thaler was awarded the Nobel Prize in Economic Science in 2017, and Sunstein was put in charge of the White House Office of Information and Regulatory Affairs during the Obama administration; the informal label "nudge unit" has become the shorthand for policy teams who apply behavioral insights to government policy. Boiled down to its nuts and bolts, the theory claims that nonintrusive inputs might work better than rigid commands when it comes to affecting and changing people's behavior. To nudge is, literally, to poke gently in the ribs, and one who nudges intends to mildly alert or warn another. Adverbs like "mildly" or "gently" are crucial since, to count as a nudge, the intervention must be easily avoidable and should not forbid any other option. By the same token, mandates and prohibitions are opposed to nudges (Thaler and Sunstein 2008:10), which are defined accordingly as any aspect of the choice architecture (i.e., any element of the environment that can encourage people to act in certain ways) that alters people's behavior without drastically modifying their incentives or enforcing any law. In sum, the aim is to influence actors to make decisions while leaving intact their freedom of choice, a political stance called "libertarian paternalism," a softer version of paternalism that does not undermine citizens' free will (Thaler and Sunstein 2008:4–6). Nudging, then, seems like pushing without pushing too much, steering but not coercing, guiding without determining—what is the point of these gracious limitations?

The reasons that make nudging intriguing for policymakers (realizing collective optimal outcomes is beneficial, gaining compliance without enforcement is cheap, and the freedom of disregarding nudges and acting otherwise is liberty-preserving) are the same reasons that make its functioning analytically puzzling. That mild, non-invasive, and effortlessly evitable interventions are more effective than injunctions is not a self-evident rationale. Yet, to break down nudge theory's logic is not immediate, since the set of policies that fall under the umbrella term of nudge is interminable and, for example, there is no clear-cut distinction between nudging and simply informing. Like Moliere's Monsieur Jourdain, who discovers that he has been speaking prose for his whole life, we might suddenly become aware of how pervasive nudging is in daily life. Calorie counters, tobacco packaging warning messages, acoustic fasten-seat-belt reminders, automatic enrollments, interface design of websites, voting ashtrays that invite users to cast their vote on a topic by disposing of their cigarette butt, geolocation services, text-message reminders, etched images of houseflies into urinals, and menu compositions, as well as many others—always framing situations so as to promote specific types of conduct. This stunning variety indicates that the mechanisms of nudges' success (or lack thereof) may be of different orders (Caraban et al. 2019; Engelen 2019), and the relationship of causality between each nudge and the output they brought about may not always be the same. For argument's sake, we focus only on the specific example of nudge theory represented by so-called default options (from now on, DO), the preset selection of a choice automatically followed unless explicitly modified, that is, the "option that will obtain if the chooser does nothing" (Thaler and Sunstein 2008:83). Considered as "unquestionably the most prominent of [nudge theory] significant successes" (Loewenstein and Chater 2017:27), DOs have been used in the form of automatic enrollment or generic settings, across many domains: insurance policies, retirement plans, organ donation, end-of-life care, environmental management, digital platforms, and so on (see Madrian and Shea 2001; Johnson and Goldstein 2003). What is peculiar to DOs is that they require no effort at all from the individual, who does not need to do anything in order to be defaulted. DOs establish the path of least resistance, and, because of inertia, chances are that they will stick in spite of people's preferences. This objection, conceded by Sunstein himself (2015), is one of the many that have been raised to the nudge theory, claiming that it considers individuals as cognitive misers and users of shortcuts (Bovens 2009; Goodwin 2012), impinges on their autonomy (Grüne-Yanoff 2012; White 2013), has mostly short-term effect and neglects the structural reasons behind social problems (John et al. 2011; Leggett 2014), and does not preserve freedom of choice (Wilkinson 2013). Most of the criticism concentrates on moral issues and political consequences of the nudge program that are not directly relevant here.[9] It seems significant, though, that nudging has often been considered linked to non-deliberative psychological faculties, phenomenologically opaque and linguistically tacit. This is not the case for autonomously chosen nudges (like GPS driving directions or alarm clocks), whose users are voluntarily nudging themselves, but with heteronomous nudges (such as shelf placement of products or autoplay features on streaming services) it is even unclear whether they are experienced by their audiences *as nudges at all*. DOs in particular, given their no-action-needed character, may well go completely unnoticed and still steer individuals without their awareness (hence something associable with quickly and automatically executable cultural schemas that can have effects outside individuals' control: see Boutyline and Soter 2021). Actually, thanks to their implicit and backdrop-like character, DOs can avoid reactance and work best when individuals do not realize they have been nudged, being more effective insofar as they represent *interventions that do not seem interventions*. If one does not know to be enrolled in a plan, it is complicated (though technically easy and costless) to opt out of it: "the less overt these modes of influencing are the less an individual is in a position of reversing the default option" (Rebonato 2014:369). This mechanism has been hypothesized (and praised: see Smith, Goldstein, and Johnson 2013) early on and empirically tested as well, but discordant results have been obtained (see Loewenstein et al. 2015; Bruns et al. 2018; Arad and Rubinstein 2018). Whether transparency makes nudging ineffective, or less effective, is still an open question, perhaps bound to remain so. It seems unreasonable to expect that an *experimentum crucis* could resolve the matter since there are many ways of flagging nudges, and soft disclosures (pointing only to the existence of a nudge) have different effects than full ones do (plainly explaining, maybe in cynical terms, the whole mechanism behind a nudge and its goal). Besides, DOs could work even when flagged because people might interpret them, again, not as an option but as a fait accompli, or like an indication of what most users want.[10] To figure that the option you choose simply by not choosing is only one of the alternatives, and actually a choice, remains tricky.

Aptly enough, Sunstein (2014:14) has defined choice architecture also as "the background against which choices are made." From a sociological perspective, backgroundness is an aspect of social reality characterized as generic and nondescript. Its cardinal feature is to not be expressly construed as such, being rather apprehended like an in-between realm outside the spotlight (see Zerubavel 2015). Sunstein himself argued that "even essential parts of the social background are so taken for granted that they are unnamed, unnoticed, and invisible" (2014:14). While his point is that nudges are everywhere and defaulting is inevitable (bottom line: let's nudge deliberately), the emphasis on choice architecture's inconspicuousness gives a whole new meaning to the core principle of nudge theory, according to which "small and apparently insignificant details can have major impacts on people's behavior" (Thaler and Sunstein 2008:3). DOs' apparent insignificance represents a gnoseological virtue, not a small-changes-big-impact causal puzzle; it explains why their gentle pressure is not felt like pressure and does not become a special object of attention. Perceptually marginal and relegated to the background of commonplaces scenes, DOs (like the banal cues of secret exhibitions) have a "non-thing-like quality" (Zerubavel

2015:12) that enables them to fly below the radar, affecting people's choices without arousing harsh feelings. Speaking of which, Thaler observed that "paternalism stirs strong emotions. Many people abhor it. They think that human beings should be able to go their own way, even if they end up in a ditch" (2014:3). Thus, following Rebonato (2014:392), a mischievous interpretation (a "naughty view," to borrow Garfinkel's quip on Goffman) of libertarian paternalism would say that people do not experience this version of paternalism as such, and this is its real strength. While previous forms of paternalism were easily recognizable *and therefore* prone to originate defiance, this dissembled version (a form of paternalism that stays in the background) is far less glaring and more round-about, in accordance with the general principle of the actions that conceal themselves—antagonistic reactions need a perceived action to be provoked.

INTENTIONS, REACTIONS, AND INTERACTIONS

Just one more remark on nudging. Elaborating on the reasons that make nudges less effective than policy makers anticipate, Sunstein cautioned: "people might show reactance to some nudges, rejecting an official effort to steer *because it is an official effort to steer*" (Sunstein 2017:21, italics added). To affect others' behavior or modify their beliefs can be hard precisely because of the very effort to do so; defiance, reactance, and the urge of behaving differently than what one has been told are well-known psychological phenomena (see Burgoon et al. 2002).[11] Muscularly pressured to embrace a certain attitude, an individual can act in the exact opposite direction: anti-alcohol warnings, anti-smoking campaigns, and violent videogames labels may induce oppositional behavior, arousing interest precisely in booze, cigarettes, and first-person shooters among the target audience (Ringold 2002; Grandpre et al. 2003; Bijvank et al. 2009). The forbidden-fruit mechanism is just one of the ways in which boomerang effects are caused by influence processes and sensed encroachments on individuals' freedom. Blatant or bold attempts to affect others' behavior may also instigate doubts and some all-too-human questions about influencers' perceived motives (What do you want from me? Why do you care? What's your angle?). By contrast, certain actions wind up being convincing only to the extent that they are *not* experienced as impatient to convince anyone. Making sense of euergetism (the ancient usage of high-status individuals distributing part of their wealth to the community, a practice embraced by Roman emperors among others), Paul Veyne argued that it was an effective propaganda tool only because it was not viewed as an effective propaganda tool. Roman plebeians felt that all the emperor wanted was to showcase his excellence and quasi-divine nature, not to buy people's loyalty—yet, this is what he eventually gained (Veyne 1976:679). Veyne also noted that a direct path to influence others may be counterproductive:

> Why do we believe in the existence of microbes or foreign cities we have never been to? Because we trust tribe elders, microbiologists, geographers, and travel agencies,

given that we do not see what interest they may have in cheating us. But if they seemed too eager or anxious to make us believe that, we would start to be suspicious. (1976:668–69).[12]

Taking his cue from Veyne, Elster (1981) conjectured that the production of some psychological and social effects is slowed down (and actually altogether halted) when individuals try to bring them about on purpose—nothing more unimpressive than heavy-handed efforts to impress others, nothing less worthy of reverence than one who demands venerability, and so on. Elster claimed that these states are by-products that can never be ingenerated by design. No matter how advantageous these by-products are, they remain essentially side effects, "willing what cannot be willed" (1981:436). For instance, from the fact that non-instrumental attitudes may be instrumentally beneficial does not follow that one can instrumentally fake non-instrumentality: this would alter the dynamic, fatally corrupting it. This argument is in keeping with Bourdieu's analyses on "objectives which could have been attained (. . .) only if they were not declared as objectives" (1988:151): for example, autodidacts and parvenus fail to achieve distinction because of the very anxiety to pull that off, "betraying their exclusion by their eagerness to prove their membership" (Bourdieu 1984:84). They try too hard, the antithesis of the nonchalance that would do it. That pursuing a specific goal may lead, precisely because of this, to its renunciation seems paradoxical, and, indeed, it has been called "the essential paradox of human action" (Merton 1936:903). However, there is nothing intrinsically self-defeating in agency. The truism is that social actions are not a solitaire and how they are interpreted in the cultural situation where they take place matters a great deal to their eventual outcome:

> with the complex interaction which constitutes society, action ramifies, its consequences are not restricted to the specific area in which they were initially intended to center, they occur in interrelated fields explicitly ignored at the time of action. Yet it is because these fields are in fact interrelated that the further consequences in adjacent areas tend to *react* upon the fundamental value-system.
>
> (Merton 1936:903, emphasis in original)

Oppositions, objections, counteracts, counterattacks, counterweights, and backlash (in a word, adverse reactions) are an integral part of actions' fate, especially when their recipients are not just distant counterparts or detached audiences, but the immediate target that is supposed to be affected (convinced, beguiled, etc.) and guided accordingly. If it is easy to poorly predict (not to say pilot) others' reactions in advance, it is also because the very scope of the initial, purposive, action might speak against itself—and, again, instrumental actions in particular, variously indisposing their receivers and breeding collisions of wills, have a tendency to be counterproductive. Since usually its addressees are not (or do not see themselves as) beneficiaries, instrumental behavior can create its own enemies among those people whose conduct is essential for a successful outcome. Even rational actions share this unfortunate inclination. When patently enacted, they can be judged as coldly calculating, aggressive, or annoyingly cunning and condescending: *paradoxically inconsiderate*, they can ignite negative responses from other actors that preclude the occurrence of what was intended, becoming "hyperrational" (Elster 2009). In this sense, it does not seem the intention behind an action (instrumental or not) to be self-destructive per se, but its recognition by the audience that could set off antagonistic reactions. CSAs, thus, cloak themselves with ordinariness and unintentionality to make this recognition unlikely to happen: since a reaction needs an action to occur, actions that are not viewed as such may benefit from the absence of responses, which is usually reserved to everyday activities (i.e., the ubiquitous and tacit green-lighting process through which others' activities are seen but unnoticed). To be clear, CSAs' aspiration of marshaling reactance-proof strategies may well be ephemeral, if not just a fantasy. Secrets demand a compartmentalized structure that is burdensome to keep going (see Gibson 2014; Costas and Grey 2016), and even the most extreme of totalitarian regimes cannot maintain total control over the backstage (Bail 2015:100). CSAs, then, can be conceived as a rather diachronic phenomenon, relatively obsolescent. Nudges are eventually identified as such, seemingly "inadvertent nothings" are later recognized as "purposeful some-things," and "once-secret techniques become familiar and thereby less effective" (Goffman 1969:27). However impermanent and dramaturgically difficult "acting natural" may be (Goffman 1971:268), on the edge of oxymoronic tasks (communicating without apparent communication, impinging upon others without seeming to), the tactic of relying on "unalarming and uninteresting" strategies (Goffman 1971:268) is technically possible. Moreover, environment-mediated CSAs (as in the case of SEs and DOs) could be easier to perform than vis-à-vis ones. On that note, future CSAs can be expected to take place especially in online contexts, considering that the work of bots, algorithms, and artificial intelligence greatly improves when not spotted or felt as such. Thus, the "kind of social negotiation" associated with "the interpretative dance of predator and prey, or, in a Goffmanian world, of con man and mark" could stop being "a protracted social interaction (Handler 2012:185), becoming something handled beforehand and then kept out of sight.

Any strategy or strategic behavior has the ambition of directing a course of actions in advance, or at least heavily influence it, but CSAs' effort to entirely "resolve" the interaction ahead of the interaction itself, by making it reactance-proof, seems peculiar. At a first glance, CSAs represent a (quite standard) interplay of the three Blumerian premises of symbolic interactionism (Blumer 2004). Rather than an inherent feature of social situations, the feeling that nothing is going on, caused by unremarkable or natural appearances, could be, in fact, a meaning intentionally attached to the situation by one of the parties involved in the interaction (second pillar), in order to get the other party to act toward this meaning (first pillar) in a way that is dynamic and could change at any time (third pillar). But to impede adverse reactions, whether this is possible or not, is to take the interactional out of actions, and reactance-proof actually means interaction-proof. As Tavory and Fine have recently underscored, the incumbency of disruptions upon social situations is not a sword of Damocles or an embarrassing aspect of spoiled experiences, but a key feature of genuine intersubjectivity. In this view, the smoothness of successful CSAs is the opposite of "the "roughness" of interaction" (Tavory and Fine 2020:382); that is the whole point of CSAs and also what makes them eerie. Reactions canonically rhyme with reactionary (see Hirschman 1991) or reactive (see Starobinski 2003; Brigenti 2019), but they also refer to a core property of human agency: the capacity to resist external influences and act otherwise.

Notes

1. Although this piece is equally co-written, Italian academic bureaucracy demands precise authorship specifications: to comply with that, we state that Carmelo Lombardo wrote the sections "Introduction. Do You Believe in Natural Appearances? Two Types of Social Nothingness" and "Intentions, Reactions, and Interactions," while Lorenzo Sabetta wrote the sections "Giving the Given Off, or: How to Influence Without Appearing to" and "The Discreet Charm of Nudges. Does a Default Option Feel Like an Option?" As for matters less pedantic, earlier versions of this essay were presented during two seminars at the Institute for Analytical Sociology (Linköping University, November 2019) and at the Bar Ilan Center for Cultural Sociology (Bar-Ilan University, January 2020): we are grateful to members of both audiences for helpful comments and questions. We are also very grateful to Christian Borch, Wayne Brekhus, Dmitri Shalin, and Hizky Shoham for their insightful feedback and first-rate opinions.
2. To cover all the similarities and dissimilarities between Garfinkel's and Goffman's perspectives would require a separate paper. Rawls's works, however, constitute an excellent guide for that purpose: see Rawls 1987, 1989, 1990; see also Heritage 2001 and Dennis 2011.
3. See Brekhus 1998 and 2000; Zerubavel 2015 and 2018; Scott 2018 and 2019; Lombardo and Sabetta forthcoming.
4. Goffman was even more amazed, on a meta-level, by the fact that the constant orderliness of everyday life was anything but amazing to social actors (see, for example, Goffman 1971:288).
5. Of course, our necessity of simplifying complexities and schematizing in a binary fashion should not open the door to facile conclusions. Indeed, the very notion that there is something definitive going on in a situation is open to question.
6. The phrase is medieval, but it is often erroneously attributed to Ovid. Actually, in his *Metamorphoses* there is a similar passage: Pygmalion carved a statue out of ivory that was so lifelike and vivid that he himself, the sculptor, comes to think of it as a real woman. Thus, "ars adeo latet arte sua," to such an extent artistry lies hidden by means of its own artistry (Jones 2007:223).
7. CSAs are latent for the audience, but, obviously, they are manifest for the leading agent(s) who orchestrated them. As Coleman (1990:27) and Giddens (1990:102–3) pointed out, things are not either manifest or latent for everyone, and it is always possible to specify for whom a certain function is intended and recognized and for whom the same function is unintended and unrecognized.
8. This dichotomy between intended and unintended information can be found also in Marc Bloch (1953:61, "voluntary witnesses" vs. "witnesses in spite of themselves"), Raymond W. Gibbs (1999:115, "authorized inference" vs. "unauthorized inference"), Diego Gambetta (2009:xv–xvi, "signals" vs. "signs"), and Carlo Ginzburg (2016, "deliberate evidence" vs. "unintentional evidence").

9. These concerns are nonetheless relevant in general, especially so for nudge theory's fathers. Arguing that nudging does not inevitably entail malevolent ethical implications has become a full-time job for Sunstein in particular (see, for example, Sunstein 2015a, 2015b, 2015c, 2016a, 2016b; Sunstein et al. 2019; see also Thaler 2018).

10. Examining the power of DOs and the types of heuristics involved, even Thaler and Sunstein observed that "these behavioral tendencies toward doing nothing will be reinforced if the default option comes with some implicit or explicit suggestion that it represents the normal or even the recommended course of action" (2008:83).

11. Though not eternal ones: some of the points we are making here could surely use some historicizing, including the "natural" resistance to being told what to do, which seems natural today but was not always the case (patronizing tones and assertive injunctions were commonly, and efficaciously, used in former times).

12. This passage is abridged in the English version of *Bread and Circuses*, which is some 250 pages shorter than the original one; we have translated this excerpt from the French edition.

REFERENCES

Arad, Ayala, and Ariel Rubinstein. 2018. "The People's Perspective on Libertarian-Paternalistic Policies." *Journal of Law and Economics* 61(2):311–33.

Baehr, Peter. 2019. *The Unmasking Style in Social Theory*. New York: Routledge.

Bail, Christopher A. 2015. "The Public Life of Secrets: Deception, Disclosure, and Discursive Framing in the Policy Process." *Sociological Theory* 33(2):97–124.

Barnhill, Anne. 2014. "What Is Manipulation?". Pp. 51–72 in *Manipulation: Theory and Practice*, edited by Christian Coons and Michael Weber. Oxford: Oxford University Press.

Barthes, Roland. 1975. *S/Z*. London: Jonathan Cape.

Bijvank, Marije N. et al. 2009. "Age and Violent-Content Labels Make Video Games Forbidden Fruits for Youth." *Pediatrics* 123(3):870–76.

Bloch, Marc. 1953. *The Historian's Craft*. New York: Random House.

Blumer, Herbert G. 2004. *George Herbert Mead and Human Conduct*. Walnut Creek, CA: AltaMira Press.

Bourdieu, Pierre. 1984. *Distinction: A Social Critique of the Judgement of Taste*. Cambridge, MA: Harvard University Press.

Bourdieu, Pierre. 1988. *Homo Academicus*. Stanford, CA: Stanford University Press.

Boutyline, Andrei, and Laura K. Soter. 2021. "Cultural Schemas: What They Are, How to Find Them, and What to Do Once You've Caught One." *American Sociological Review*, online first.

Bovens, Luc. 2009. "The Ethics of Nudge". Pp. 207–19 in *Preference Change: Approaches from Philosophy, Economics and Psychology*, edited by Till Grüne-Yanoff and Sven Ove Hansson. Berlin: Springer.

Brekhus, Wayne H. 1998. "A Sociology of the Unmarked: Redirecting our Focus." *Sociological Theory* 16(1):34–51.

Brekhus, Wayne H. 2000. "A Mundane Manifesto." *Journal of Mundane Behavior* 1(1):89–106.

Brighenti, Andrea. 2007. "Visibility: A Category for the Social Sciences." *Current Sociology* 55(3):323–42.

Brighenti, Andrea. 2019. "The Reactive. Social Experiences of Surface and Depth". Pp. 194–210 in *Imitation, Contagion, Suggestion. On Mimesis and Society*, edited by Christian Borch. New York: Routledge.

Bruns, Hendrik et al. 2018. "Can Nudges Be Transparent and Yet Effective?" *Journal of Economic Psychology* 65:41–59.

Burgoon, Michael et al. 2002. "Revisiting the Theory of Psychological Reactance". Pp. 213–32 in *The Persuasion Handbook: Developments in Theory and Practice*, edited by James P. Dillard and Michael Pfau. Thousand Oaks, CA: SAGE.

Burns, Tom. 1992. *Erving Goffman*. New York: Routledge.

Caraban, Ana et al. 2019. "23 Ways to Nudge: A Review of Technology-Mediated Nudging in Human-Computer Interaction." *Proceedings of the 2019 CHI Conference on Human Factors in Computing Systems* 503:1–15.

Carnevali, Barbara. 2012. *Le apparenze sociali: Una filosofia del prestigio*. Bologna: Il Mulino.

Coleman, James S. 1990. "Robert K. Merton as Teacher". Pp. 97–110 in *Robert Merton: Consensus and Controversy*, edited by Jon Clark, Celia Modgil, and Sohan Modgil. London-New York: Falmer Press.

Costas, Jana, and Christopher Grey. 2016. *Secrecy at Work: The Hidden Architecture of Organizational Life*. Stanford, CA: Stanford University Press.

Dennis, Alex. 2011. "Symbolic Interactionism and Ethnomethology." *Symbolic Interaction* 34(3):349–56.

Elster, Jon. 1981. "States that are essentially by-products." *Social Science Information* 20(3):431–73.

Elster, Jon. 2009. *Reason and Rationality*. Princeton: Princeton University Press.

Emerson, Joan P. 1970. "Nothing Unusual Is Happening." Pp. 208–22 in *Human Nature and Collective Behavior: Papers in Honor of Herbert Blumer*, edited by Tamotsu Shibutani. Englewood Cliffs, NJ: Prentice Hall.

Engelen, Bart. 2019. "Nudging and rationality: What is there to worry?" *Rationality and Society* 31(2):204–32.

Evans, Nathaniel J. et al. 2017. "Disclosing Instagram Influencer Advertising: The Effects of Disclosure Language on Advertising Recognition, Attitudes, and Behavioral Intent." *Journal of Interactive Advertising* 17(2):138–49.

Fleck, Christian. 2021. "A Mertonian Breviary for Cultural Sociologists." Forthcoming in *The Anthem Companion to Robert K. Merton*, edited by Charles Crothers and Lorenzo Sabetta. London: Anthem.

Gambetta, Diego. 2009. *Codes of the Underworld: How Criminals Communicate*. Princeton: Princeton University Press.

Garfinkel, Harold. 1967. *Studies in Ethnomethodology*. Englewood Cliffs, NJ: Prentice Hall.

Garfinkel, Harold. 1974. "The Origins of the Term 'Ethnomethodology." Pp. 15–18 in *Ethnomethodology: Selected Readings*, edited by Roy Turner. New York: Penguin.

Garfinkel, Harold, and Eric Livingston. 2003. "Phenomenal Field Properties of Order in Formatted Queues and Their Neglected Standing in the Current Situation of Inquiry." *Visual Studies* 18(1):21–28.

Gibbs, Raymond W. 1999. *Intentions in the Experience of Meaning*. Cambridge: Cambridge University Press.

Gibson, David R. 2014. "Enduring Illusions: The Social Organization of Secrecy and Deception." *Sociological Theory* 32(4):283–306.

Giddens, Anthony. 1990. "R. K. Merton on Structural Analysis." Pp. 97–110 in *Robert Merton: Consensus and Controversy*, edited by Jon Clark, Celia Modgil, and Sohan Modgil. London-New York: Falmer Press.

Ginzburg, Carlo. 2016. "Unintentional Revelations: Reading History against the Grain." *24th Annual Eugene Lunn Memorial Lecture*, University of California–Davis, April 18.

Glaser, Barney G., and Anselm L. Strauss. 1964. "Awareness Contexts and Social Interaction." *American Sociological Review* 29(5):669–79.

Goffman, Erving. 1959. *The Presentation of Self in Everyday Life*. Garden City, NY: Doubleday Anchor Books.

Goffman, Erving. 1969. *Strategic Interaction*. Philadelphia: University of Pennsylvania Press.

Goffman, Erving. 1971. *Relations in Public: Microstudies of the Public Order*. New York: Basic Books.

Goffman, Erving. 1981. *Forms of Talk*. Philadelphia: University of Pennsylvania Press.

Goffman, Erving. 1986. *Frame Analysis: An Essay on the Organization of Experience*. Boston: Northeastern University Press.

Goodwin, Tom. 2012. "Why We Should Reject 'Nudge.'" *Politics* 32(2):85–92.

Grandpre, Joseph et al. 2003. "Adolescent Reactance and Anti-Smoking Campaigns: A Theoretical Approach." *Health Communication* 15(3):349–66.

Grüne-Yanoff, Till. 2012. "Old Wine in New Casks: Libertarian Paternalism Still Violates Liberal Principles." *Social Choice and Welfare* 38(4):635–45.

Handler, Richard. 2012. "What's Up, Doctor Goffman? Tell Us Where the Action Is!" *Journal of the Royal Anthropological Institute* 18(1):179–90.

Harvey, Daina C. 2010. "The Space for Culture and Cognition." *Poetics* 38:184–203.

Heritage, John. 2001. "Goffman, Garfinkel and Conversation Analysis." Pp. 47–56 in *Discourse Theory and Practices: A Reader*, edited by Margaret Wetherell, Stephanie Taylor, and Simeon J. Yates. London: SAGE.

Hirschman, Albert O. 1991. *The Rhetoric of Reaction. Perversity, Futility, Jeopardy*. Cambridge, MA: Belknap Press of Harvard University Press.

John, Peter et al. 2011. *Nudge, Nudge, Think, Think: Experimenting with Ways to Change Civic Behaviour*. London: Bloomsbury.

Johnson, Eric J., and Daniel Goldstein. 2003. "Do Defaults Save Lives?" *Science* 302(5649):1338–39.

Jones, Peter. 2007. *Reading Ovid: Stories from the Metamorphoses*. Cambridge: Cambridge University Press.

Leggett, Will. 2014. "The Politics of Behaviour Change: Nudge, Neoliberalism and the State." *Policy & Politics* 42(1):3–19.

Loewenstein, George et al. 2015. "Warning: You Are About To Be Nudged." *Behavioral Science & Policy* 1(1):35–42.

Loewenstein, George, and Nick Chater. 2017. "Putting Nudges in Perspective." *Behavioural Public Policy* 1(1):26–53.

Lombardo, Carmelo, and Lorenzo Sabetta, eds. Forthcoming. *Against the Background of Social Reality: Defaults, Commonplaces, and the Sociology of the Unmarked*. New York: Routledge.

Madrian, Brigitte C., and Dennis F. Shea. 2001. "The Power of Suggestion: Inertia In 401(k) Participation and Savings Behavior." *Quarterly Journal of Economics* 116(4):1149–87.

Manning, Philip. 2000. "Credibility, Agency, and the Interaction Order." *Symbolic Interaction* 23(3):283–97.

Merleau-Ponty, Maurice. 1968. *The Visible and the Invisible*. Evanston, IL: Northwestern University Press.

Merton, Robert K. 1936. "The Unanticipated Consequences of Purposive Social Action." *American Sociological Review* 1(6):894–904.

Merton, Robert K. 1946. *Mass Persuasion. The Social Psychology of a War Bond Drive*. New York: Harper.

Misztal, Barbara A. 2001. "Normality and Trust in Goffman's Theory of Interaction Order." *Sociological Theory* 19(3):312–24.

Misztal, Barbara A. 2015. *Multiple Normalities: Making Sense of Ways of Living*. Basingstoke: Palgrave.

Monahan, Torin. 2016. "Built To Lie: Investigating Technologies of Deception, Surveillance, and Control." *The Information Society* 32(4):229–40.

Rawls, Anne W. 1987. "The Interaction Order Sui Generis: Goffman's Contribution to Social Theory." *Sociological Theory* 5(2):136–49.

Rawls, Anne W. 1989. "Language, Self, and Social Order: A Reformulation of Goffman and Sacks." *Human Studies* 12(1–2):147–72.

Rawls, Anne W. 1990. "Emergent Sociality: A Dialectic of Commitment and Order." *Symbolic Interaction* 13(1):63–82.

Rawls, Anne W. 2006. "Respecifying the Study of Social Order: Garfinkel's Transition from Theoretical Conceptualization to Practices in Details." Pp. 1–97 in *Seeing Sociologically: The Routine Grounds of Social Action*, by Harold Garfinkel. Boulder, CO: Paradigm.

Rebonato, Riccardo. 2014. "A Critical Assessment of Libertarian Paternalism." *Journal of Consumer Policy* 37(3):357–96.

Ringold, Debra J. 2002. "Boomerang Effects in Response to Public Health Interventions: Some Unintended Consequences in the Alcoholic Beverage Market." *Journal of Consumer Policy* 25(1):27–63.

Scott, Susie. 2018. "A Sociology of Nothing: Understanding the Unmarked." *Sociology* 52(1):3–19.

Scott, Susie. 2019. *The Social Life of Nothing. Silence, Invisibility and Emptiness in Tales of Lost Experience*. New York: Routledge.

Scott, Susie, and Neil Stephens. 2018. "Acts of Omission and Commission in the Embodied Learning of Diasporic Capoeira and Swimming." *Qualitative Research* 18(5):565–79.

Shan, Yan, Kuan-Ju Chen, and Jhih-Syuan Lin. 2020. "When Social Media Influencers Endorse Brands: The Effects of Self-influencer Congruence, Parasocial Identification, and Perceived Endorser Motive." *International Journal of Advertising* 39(5):590–610.

Smith, N. Craig, Daniel G. Goldstein, and Eric J. Johnson. 2013. "Choice Without Awareness: Ethical and Policy Implications of Defaults." *Journal of Public Policy & Marketing* 32(2):159–72.

Starobinski, Jean. 2003. *Action and Reaction: The Life and Adventures of a Couple*. New York: Zone Books.

Sunstein, Cass R. 2014. *Why Nudge? The Politics of Libertarian Paternalism*. New Haven: Yale University Press.

Sunstein, Cass R. 2015a. "The Ethics of Nudging." *Yale Journal of Regulation* 32:413–50.

Sunstein, Cass R. 2015b. *Choosing Not to Choose: Understanding the Value of Choice*. Oxford: Oxford University Press.

Sunstein, Cass R. 2015c. "Nudges, Agency, and Abstraction: A Reply to Critics." *Review of Philosophy and Psychology* 6(3):511–29.

Sunstein, Cass R. 2016a. *The Ethics of Influence: Government in the Age of Behavioral Science*. Cambridge: Cambridge University Press.

Sunstein, Cass R. 2016b. "Do People Like Nudges?" *Administrative Law Review* 68(2):177–232.

Sunstein, Cass R. 2017. "Nudges That Fail." *Behavioural Public Policy* 1(1):4–25.

Sunstein, Cass R., et al. 2019. "Trusting Nudges? Lessons from an International Survey." *Journal of European Public Policy* 26(10):1417–43.

Tavory, Iddo, and Gary A. Fine. 2020. "Disruption and the Theory of the Interaction Order." *Theory and Society* 49(3):365–85.

Ten Have, Paul. 1990. "Methodological Issues in Conversation Analysis." *Bulletin of Sociological Methodology/Bulletin de méthodologie sociologique* 27:23–51.

Thaler, Richard H. 2018. "Nudge, Not Sludge." *Science* 361(6401):431.

Thaler, Richard H., and Cass R. Sunstein. 2008. *Nudge: Improving Decisions About Health, Wealth, and Happiness.* New Haven, CT: Yale University Press.

Travers, Andrew. 1994. "Destigmatizing the Stigma of Self in Garfinkel's and Goffman's Accounts of Normal Appearances." *Philosophy of the Social Sciences* 24(1):5–40.

Veyne, Paul. 1976. *Le pain et le cirque. Sociologie historique d'un pluralisme politique.* Paris: Seuil.

Vogel, Else, David Moats, Steve Woolgar, and Claes-Fredrik Helgesson. 2021. "Thinking with Imposters: The Imposter as Analytic." Pp. 1–30 in *The Imposter as Social Theory: Thinking with Gatecrashers, Cheats and Charlatans,* edited by Steve Woolgar, Else Vogel, David Moats, and Claes-Fredrik Helgesson. Bristol, UK: Bristol University Press.

Walton, Kendall L. 1990. *Mimesis as Make-believe: On the Foundations of the Representational Arts.* Cambridge, MA: Harvard University Press.

White, Mark D. 2013. *The Manipulation of Choice: Ethics and Libertarian Paternalism.* New York: Palgrave MacMillan.

Wilkinson, T. Martin. 2013. "Nudging and Manipulation." *Political Studies* 61(2):341–55.

Ytreberg, Espen. 2010. "The Question of Calculation. Erving Goffman and the Pervasive Planning of Communication." Pp. 293–312 in *The Contemporary Goffman,* edited by Michael H. Jacobsen. New York: London.

Zerubavel, Eviatar. 2015. *Hidden in Plain Sight: The Social Structure of Irrelevance.* Oxford: Oxford University Press.

Zerubavel, Eviatar. 2018. *Taken for Granted: The Remarkable Power of the Unremarkable.* Princeton: Princeton University Press.

CHAPTER 21

POWER AND INTERACTION

MICHAEL L. SCHWALBE AND KELSEY MISCHKE

INTRODUCTION

George Herbert Mead and Herbert Blumer are not usually thought of as among sociology's preeminent theorists of power. Indeed, many sociologists might dismiss Mead, Blumer, and the symbolic interactionism they inspired as being of little use for understanding power in sociological terms; for that, they are more likely to turn to Karl Marx, Max Weber, or Robert Michels. Or they might grant that symbolic interactionism can give us insight into how power operates in face-to-face interaction but not on larger scales. We agree, of course, that symbolic interactionism can do the former, as we will show. But we disagree that its value is limited to the so-called micro level of analysis. By showing us how power operates in interaction, symbolic interactionism can illuminate the ontological roots of power as it operates on larger, structural scales.

The first sticking point in all sociological discussions of power is the matter of definition. Many review pieces begin by lamenting the lack of disciplinary consensus about precisely what power is (see, e.g., Margolis 1989; Rogers 1974; Roscigno 2011; Wrong 1968). Our tack here, rather than begin by sorting through a morass of competing definitions, is to use Mead to establish a generic view of power and to draw on Blumer for advice about how to see it empirically. We will then apply this perspective to analyzing the exercise of power in interaction. Finally, we will consider how a symbolic interactionist analysis of power in interaction can, with some conceptual additions, be used to understand what other sociologists might call the exercise of power on a structural level.

Though we begin with Mead and Blumer, locating our treatment of power firmly in symbolic interactionism, we construe the interactionist camp more broadly. Any compatible approach that gives us theoretical purchase on matters of meaning, symbol use, interpretation, and the interactional creation of social order is a potential resource. We thus draw on concepts from dramaturgy, ethnomethodology, the sociology of emotion, and social constructionism. This allows us to develop a fuller analytic account of power,

A Meadian Definition of Power

How, then, can Mead help us understand power? It would appear that Mead himself said little about power. The term does not appear in the index of *Mind, Self, and Society*, *The Philosophy of the Present*, or *The Philosophy of the Act*. Nor does it appear in the index of David Miller's (1980) *George Herbert Mead: Self, Language, and the World*. Yet it can be argued that Mead wrote about power in other terms. When Mead speaks of the capacity of organisms to adjust their environments to meet organismic needs (Mead 1934:96–100, 117–34), he is referring to power in the most elementary sense. In this view, the capacity to modify an environment—to make it more amenable to satisfying an organism's needs—is what we might otherwise call "power." This definition, consistent with Mead's monistic ontology, does not treat power as evident only in conscious human action; it is, rather, a feature of life itself.[1]

We are primarily concerned, however, with conscious human action, and so it is necessary to translate power, in the Meadian sense articulated above, into something we can see. For this purpose, we draw on Blumer. In his 1969 essay "The Methodological Position of Symbolic Interactionism," Blumer advises us to try to see the forms of action, or forms of doing, that correspond to the abstract concepts of which sociological theories are made (Blumer 1969:44–46; see also Blumer 1956). What this advice implies is that if we define power as a matter of human beings modifying their environments to satisfy their needs and desires, we need to take another step and ask what this looks like in action. We need to ask, How do people, individually and collectively, modify their environments to satisfy their needs and desires? Answering that question is how we make power visible.

The advantage of the Meadian definition is that it allows us to avoid getting bogged down, at the start, in trying to distinguish among power, authority, compulsion, coercion, influence, and related notions. Instead, we can see these as terms used to label variations of what is essentially the same thing: the exercise of capacities to modify the external world, or some part of it, so as to satisfy needs and desires. To use a physical analogy: explosions, fire, and rust appear to be distinct phenomena, and indeed they can have vastly different consequences; yet they are all instances of oxidation, occurring more or less rapidly. Likewise, we can look at the various ways people modify their environments and count them all as manifestations of power—or, more precisely, as instances of exercising a capacity that we call, for convenience, "power."

Another advantage of the Meadian definition is that it lets us put power exercised vis-à-vis the physical world, and power exercised vis-à-vis the social world, under the same conceptual roof. A person who picks and eats a ripe apple—thus modifying the environment—is exercising power in relation to the physical world. A person who starts a fruit company, hires workers to plant and tend trees and harvest a crop, and then corners the market on apples, is exercising power in the social world. Both cases involve modifying part of the world to satisfy needs and desires. In the first case, power is used to move a nonconscious physical object from tree to gullet; in the second case, power is used to move people. As sociologists, our interest is in the latter type of cases. The key question, then, is, How are people moved? Or, How is cooperation elicited? The answer will reveal how power works, in face-to-face interaction and on larger scales.

Readers familiar with prior symbolic interactionist writings on power may have noticed that we have so far only briefly alluded to the long-running critique of symbolic interactionism as paying insufficient attention to power. The critique dates from the 1970s, coming from both outside (Huber 1973; Kanter 1972; Lichtman 1970) and inside (Hall 1972; Meltzer, Petras, and Reynolds 1975) symbolic interactionism. In the decades since, many symbolic interactionists have accepted this criticism, in its milder form, usually as preface to their own writing about power (Athens 2015; Hall 1972, 1985; Luckenbill 1979; Musolf 1992; Prus 1999; Ruiz-Junco 2016). Although it is fair to say that symbolic interactionism does not have a strong tradition of studying power in the manner of political or economic sociologists (but see Blumer 1954), we reject the notion that symbolic interactionism is inherently unable to come to grips with power beyond the level of face-to-face-interaction. We concur with Dennis and Martin's (2005) argument that symbolic interactionists *have* examined power (e.g., Becker 1963:15–18; Denzin 1977; Farberman 1975), though not in ways recognized by sociologists who operate with a reified concept of social structure (see also Maines 2001). We also agree, however, with Ruiz-Junco's (2016) claim that symbolic interactionism is still in need of its own theory of power. We hope to oblige.

To summarize: our working definition of power, derived from Mead, is the *capacity* to modify an environment, including nonconscious physical objects and people, to satisfy needs and desires. To actually do the modifying is to *exercise* power. Though we have taken our cues from Mead and Blumer, this way of defining power is not peculiar to symbolic interactionism; most sociological definitions converge on the idea that power is the ability to bring about a desired state of affairs. So we are on the same page as most other sociologists who have examined power. We turn in a distinctly symbolic interactionist direction, however, in focusing on how the cooperation of others is elicited, given that this is essential to making things happen when dealing with self-conscious social beings. Humans can, of course, be treated as mere physical objects, but this is different from mobilizing them to act as minded creatures in the service of a goal.

The quality of mindedness is an important part of the picture (Mead 1934:303–19). Humans are not the only creatures with minds; but ours, arising out of a massively complex central nervous system, can perceive and respond to more than brute physical stimuli. We can also perceive and respond to signs, symbols, and configurations of symbols (such as this sentence). We can respond to images of the external world— past, present, and future—that we conjure in our minds. We can use these mental images of objects, including ourselves, to guide action and solve problems. We can also use language to call forth responses in ourselves and induce new thoughts and feelings. What this Meadian view of human minds implies for understanding power is that mobilizing people to make things happen in the social world requires the use of signs and symbols to create meanings, shape definitions and perceptions of reality, limit or extend imagination, and induce or quash emotions. A symbolic interactionist approach to power calls for trying to see how these things are done, face to face and at a distance, to elicit cooperation, mobilize others, coordinate action, and thereby modify the social world.

Resistance, Exploitation, and Consciousness

Before proceeding, we need to comment on how our conception of power bears on several issues that often arise in sociological discussions of power. One issue is whether we can speak of power in the absence of resistance. If there is no resistance to the will of a person or group, it has been argued, then there is no evidence of power (Buckley 1967; Dahl 1957; Gamson 1968; Weber 1910–14/1946; Wrong 1968). It is of course hard to see how power is *exercised* absent its exertion against a resistant environment. Yet we can still examine power as a latent capacity. We can ask, What gives a person or group this capacity? This question directs our attention to the material and symbolic resources available to and usable by a person or group seeking to modify the social environment. Occasions when such resources are deployed against resistance are opportunities for studying the *exercise* of power, but they are not our only opportunities for studying the *bases* of power (cf. Rogers 1974).

Capacity should also be understood as depending not simply on qualities "inside" a person or group. The capacity to modify an environment is a function of the relationship between capacities and the environment; capacities adequate to modify one environment might not be adequate to modify another. This, too, is a basic insight we take from Mead (1934:125–31). To understand power as a capacity, we must therefore consider the relationship between an organism—a person or group, in the present case—and its environment. Likewise, to see the exercise of power, we must consider what an organism can do in a particular environment. The same principle applies to individual or collective human actors: deploying capacities to modify the environment—that is, exercising power—depends on the efficacy of those capacities in relation to the obdurate features of an environment, be they physical or social.

A related issue is whether the exercise of power inherently involves exploitation. In our terms, this would refer to one person or group modifying the social environment to satisfy needs and desires at someone else's expense. If this is not the case—if all affected parties can be shown to benefit both subjectively and objectively—can we speak of power being exercised? The answer, in our view, is yes. Exercising the capacity to modify the social environment is distinct from the results of its exercise. These results might be beneficial to some and harmful to others, beneficial to all, or possibly harmful to all. Our view of power adds useful complexity by calling for distinct analytic attention to capacities, the use of these capacities, and the results that follow in any given case. In short, the existence of power does not depend on the quality of its effects.

A third issue is whether the exercise of power necessarily involves conscious awareness of the resources that are being deployed to modify the social environment. Here we would answer no. People can modify the behavior of others, even dominate others, without full awareness of precisely how they are doing it. For example, diffuse status characteristics (e.g., race, gender, age) might be part of what underlies one actor's ability to elicit the cooperation of others, yet the actor might be unaware that this is happening (Ridgeway 2011). On the other side of the equation, those whose behavior is being influenced can be unaware of precisely why they feel moved to cooperate or comply. To limit our attention to cases in which there is conscious awareness of power being exercised strategically would be to see only a thin slice of social life.

Finally, to return to our definition of power as the capacity to modify the social environment by eliciting the cooperation of others, we want to clarify that "cooperation," as we mean it, does not necessarily entail conscious agreement. It *might*, as in cases where resistance leads to negotiation and eventual agreement. Often enough, however, cooperation can occur as a matter of habit, without reflection on the whys and wherefores, or even the possibility of resistance. Cooperation can be elicited, as Mead might say, based on social conditioning; actors seeking to modify the social environment wield signs and symbols that evoke conditioned responses, which might never be questioned by those whose minds and behavior are affected. The exercise of power, in other words, is a social process that can operate beneath the conscious awareness of those who are caught up in it. Unpacking the process sociologically requires attention to more than what actors realize they are doing.

Exercising Power in Interaction

To what, then, does a symbolic interactionist perspective on the exercise of power in interaction direct our attention? To understand how power operates in interaction, what should we look for? Earlier we suggested that symbolic interactionism highlights the importance of symbol use, meanings, interpretation, negotiation, and emotion. And indeed it does, in general terms. To be more specific, however, we propose that it directs our attention to five forms of action: (1) crafting virtual selves; (2) using normative and procedural rules; (3) establishing frames and definitions of reality; (4) managing emotions; and (5) invoking extra-situational relationships or "nets of accountability." We will consider each of these in turn.

Crafting Virtual Selves

A virtual self is not a psychological entity; it is the self, or essential character, imputed to an actor by an audience, based on the audience's interpretation of the actor's expressive behavior. This is the dramaturgical conception of the self developed by Erving Goffman in *The Presentation of Self in Everyday Life* (Goffman 1959) and other works. According to Goffman, the virtual self is what matters in interaction because it is what an audience responds to. A virtual self of high social value elicits respect and deference, while a virtual self of low social value—a *stigmatized* virtual self—elicits disdain, revulsion, pity (Goffman 1967:47–95, 97–112). Actors who can craft virtual selves of high social value can move others; they can elicit not only ritual deference but possibly also compliance with requests and demands. Crafting a high-value virtual self is thus one way of exercising power in interaction.

The importance of signifying status in interaction is certainly not a matter recognized only by dramaturgists. Weber recognized the importance of prestige or social honor in moving others. Contemporary social psychologists, some identified with symbolic interactionism (Fine 1984; Hallet 2007), others with the expectation states tradition (Ridgeway 2011, 2019), have pointed to status as a crucial component of actors' ability to elicit the compliance of others. The underlying principle is that, presuming a shared cultural framework of social valuation, humans tend to defer to those whom they perceive as of higher social value or rank. Here we can say that the ability to muster and wield signs of rank—and thus to signify a self that will be seen as owed deference in a situation—is part of exercising power in interaction (see also Goffman 1951).

A related idea is that elites, those who can mobilize the necessary material and symbolic resources, can craft "powerful virtual selves," or what might better be called selves that are seen as capable of compelling compliance and as worthy of obedience (Hall 1972; Schwalbe et al. 2000). Strictly speaking, the virtual self being crafted—as an impression in the minds of an audience—is not itself powerful; it is, rather, an illusion that has the effect of inducing others to cooperate. *Belief* in the special virtue or competence of the person crafting a powerful virtual self is what motivates compliance or elicits cooperation. Instilling such a belief, through skilled manipulation of symbols and controlled expressive behavior, is another part of the process of exercising power in interaction.

As we noted earlier, wielding signs and symbols that induce cooperation can be a matter of habit. This is true in the case of crafting virtual selves. For example, a male body and light skin are signifiers that are not necessarily wielded consciously, yet in some contexts they will be taken as indicators of social value that shape the virtual self imputed to an individual and help to elicit cooperation. This is part of what confers "skin-color privilege." It is a phenomenon often denied by those who benefit from it, because it is not consciously sought (Johnson 2005).

Other signifiers of status—speech, adornment, gesture—can function similarly; they can form an ensemble of expressive behaviors, occurring as a matter of habit, that shape virtual selves and elicit the compliance of others (Schwalbe and Shay 2014). Power can thus be exercised in ways that escape the awareness of those exercising it and those being affected by it. When this occurs, what we are seeing is how inequalities that are part of society as a whole, so-called structural inequalities, invisibly underlie the exercise of power in face-to-face interaction. Although this idea is more often associated with Bourdieu's (1977) notion of habitus, it is easily assimilated to a symbolic interactionist analysis of power (Hallett 2007).

Using Normative and Procedural Rules

The concept of "rules," as used by dramaturgists and symbolic interactionists to explain patterned interaction, is often misunderstood. Some rules—about how interactional tasks can and should be done—may indeed be discursive; one can speak them aloud or write them down and put them in a handbook. This is the popular understanding of rules. For the most part, however, interactional rules exist as tacit knowledge, or as shared, nondiscursive understandings about how to do things together (procedural rules) and about how things should be done so as to display good character (normative rules). For example, normative rules tell us when apologies are necessary and why we should offer them; procedural rules tell us how to formulate proper apologies.

This view of rules treats them as symbolic resources that we use to get things done together in mutually sensible, reasonably efficient, and morally acceptable ways (cf. Giddens 1979, 1984). Without such rules, social interaction would be chaotic, unpatterned, and emotionally dangerous. As Goffman put it, these rules are like the "ground rules of a game, the provisions of a traffic code or the rules of syntax of a language" (1983:5). By drawing on them we make interaction orderly and meaningful, and we avoid excess risk to the feelings attached to the images of ourselves that we create in interaction.

Rules are linked to the exercise of power in that they can be used as resources to elicit the cooperation of others and, sometimes, coordinate the action of many others. To know procedural rules is to know how to do things together; it is to be able to say, in effect, "Here is how we can orchestrate ourselves to get done what will satisfy our individual and collective needs and desires." To be able to invoke practical rules that others will accept as suited to a situation is to be able to channel human energy toward desired ends. Such rules—when communicated, understood, and accepted—enable the playing of games. "Game" is also a metaphor here; in reality, the games of capitalism, politics, and criminal justice, ones that we play every day, can be matters of life and death.

Normative rules prescribe actions that accord with shared moral principles and values. These rules, too, can be used to elicit cooperation. To invoke them is to say, One should do X, not necessarily because X is efficient, but because it is the right thing to do, and doing X displays good character. Cooperation can be elicited by invoking a normative rule and noting, however subtly, the consequences of ignoring it: stigmatization, shame, and possibly ostracism as well (this is part of what gives force to nets of accountability, as discussed later). Given a general human desire to avoid such consequences, the ability to invoke normative rules can be an effective way to leverage compliance (Branaman 2003). Which is to say, an effective way to exercise power.

The self is again implicated here. Inasmuch as we act to protect the feelings attached to cherished images of ourselves—images created and affirmed in interaction—we are inclined to embrace the normative rules that enable us to display good character (Goffman 1967:5–45). Cooperation can thus be elicited by strategic use of normative rules. What is communicated in interaction is that if one wishes to be seen as a good person, if one wishes to have this self-image affirmed, and if one wishes to protect the feelings attached to this image, then it is necessary to comply with normative rules—to do as one has been taught and told to do. The reward for cooperation, to turn the equation around, is affirmation of good moral character, positive self-regard, and avoidance of emotional damage (Schwalbe and Shay 2014).

A final point is that procedural rules often have a normative valence, making them even more compelling. It is not, for example, that rules about queuing tell us only how best to line up for this or that purpose; these rules can also bear on character, in that failure to use them signifies a disregard for fair play. In many situations, a willingness to use mutually understood procedural rules signifies not only concern for efficiency but also respect for others. The ability to tap this shared understanding—to communicate that one must accept established ways of doing things together not just for the sake of efficiency but also to be a good person, respectful of others, and thus deserving of respect in return—can, and often is, used to elicit cooperation and compliance. It is another ability that underlies the exercise of power in interaction.

Establishing Frames and Definitions of Reality

Every occasion of face-to-face interaction, if it is to come off smoothly, requires an answer to the question, What is going on here? The answer tells us what kind of situation we are in and what kind of conduct is called for, presuming the situation is a familiar one. How this question is answered—how a situation is *framed* (Goffman 1974)—on any given occasion is related to the exercise of power. The ability to establish a frame that "sticks" is an ability that can be used to elicit cooperation and coordinate the action of others (cf. Molotch and Boden 1985).

People gather to play, fight, flirt, learn, celebrate, mourn, govern, work, and worship, among other things. How an occasion of interaction is framed means that different normative and procedural rules will be used to guide conduct. Getting others to accept one's preferred set of rules, a power tactic we discussed above, can depend on getting others to accept one's preferred frame (Goffman 1974:321–24). "We are here to *work*—to accomplish a task on which everyone's welfare depends," an actor might propose, thereby implying that cooperation is mandatory, lest everyone suffer, and that a boss is needed to efficiently direct the collective effort. The success of this strategy will depend, in turn, on shared understandings of what a "work" frame implies for joint action, and whether this frame prevails over others. Getting one's preferred frame accepted, as a way to elicit cooperation, is part of exercising power (Hall 1972).

Once a frame is established, we know what kind of situation we are in and, given our identity in the situation, what is expected of us. But how big is a situation? Many symbolic interactionists and social psychologists who study small-group dynamics might define "situation" as the setting in which co-presence occurs. For purposes of understanding how power is exercised in interaction, this is an overly narrow definition. We propose that "situation" is more usefully defined to include external conditions that affect actors' willingness to cooperate. Actors' understandings of these conditions are their operative definitions of reality, and these too can be manipulated as part of exercising power (Prus 1999:9–10, 152–54).

Most people are reluctant to take up arms against others and try to kill or maim them. This is, for politicians and militarists, a hard kind of cooperation to elicit (Grossman 2009). It becomes easier, however, if the right definition of reality can be established at a societal level. If masses of people can be led to believe that they are about to be attacked by potent, savage enemies, they might eagerly put on uniforms and march to war. There is, of course, nothing hypothetical about this example; such manipulation, typically undertaken by political and economic elites seeking to preserve their privileges at the expense of others, has been evident throughout history, up to the present day.

Our point, however, is not political but analytic: establishing the broader definitions of reality that actors bring with them to situations is part of exercising power in situations. Describing how this is done—using the apparatuses of the state, education, mass media, and so on—is beyond the scope of this chapter (but see Alexander [2017] for a compatible analysis). Yet it is crucial to acknowledge that it *is* done, and that these definitions of reality are resources that can be used to exercise power situationally (Becker 2003:661; Rogers 1977). Recruiting people for war is one example. Eliciting cooperation for any kind of mass undertaking similarly depends on the definitions of reality that are constructed to make cooperation with elite demands seem imperative (Welsh 1991; Young 1990).

To establish a frame is to establish a definition of situated reality—an answer to the *what-is-going-on-here?* question, which implies answers to the *which-rules-apply?* and *how-shall-we-behave?* questions. To establish societal definitions of reality is to shape actors' understandings of the background conditions—including threats and opportunities—that intelligent situated action must take into account. Framing, to put it another way, shapes understandings of situations; defining reality shapes understandings of the larger world. The ability to elicit cooperation depends on the construction and strategic use of both kinds of understandings. Humans live, as symbolic interactionism holds, in a symbolic world, and the ability to craft that world of symbols confers the ability to move minds and bodies.

Managing Emotion

At one time, it would have been fair to say that symbolic interactionism suffered from a pro-cognitive bias, stemming perhaps from Blumer's premise that human behavior is guided by meanings. In Blumer's treatment (1969:2–21), these meanings seem to be consciously recognized, handled, and altered. The thinking mind seems very much in charge. As the foregoing discussion suggests, this heavily cognitive view spills over into considerations of how power is exercised: symbols are wielded to craft virtual selves, rules are invoked to elicit cooperation, frames and definitions of reality are established. But what, then, of emotion?

Emotion, as the Latin root of the word reminds us, is about movement, suggesting that the ability to induce emotion has long been seen as crucial for moving people to cooperate. This idea is also deeply woven into the symbolic interactionist perspective (Hochschild 1979; Shott 1979). As we noted earlier, feelings attached to self-images can be exploited to elicit cooperation; positively enhancing such feelings, or threatening them with damage, can be strategies for compelling behavior. Indeed, feelings attached to any kind of object (abstract, material, social) can be used in a similar way to mobilize or demobilize people. The ability to wield symbols that can induce feelings of ecstasy, anger, fear, hope, pride, and shame might well be the crucial ability underlying the exercise of power in interaction (Kemper 2006; Wasielewski 1985).

Here again much of this process can occur beneath conscious awareness. As the social psychology of emotion has taught us, feelings can be induced by signs and symbols before those feelings are recognized, interpreted, and labeled (Thoits 1989). This may be part of how signs of status operate, inducing positive or negative feelings—"emotional energy," in Randall Collins's (2004) terms—that lead people to comply with the wishes of higher-status others. Even those wielding these signs and symbols need not be aware of how this occurs. Such emotional manipulation can, of course, be conscious and strategic, undertaken with intent to mobilize or paralyze others. In such cases, we might examine the resources used to induce emotion, the skill with which these resources are deployed, and the conditions that make such deployment effective.

Our earlier discussion of crafting powerful virtual selves can be extended to include the idea of crafting emotional fronts that induce cooperation. This might involve fronts—emotional displays—that evoke fear or awe. It might also involve seemingly *non*-emotional fronts that imply unshakeable rationality. For example, Fields, Copp, and Kleinman (2006) suggest that the learned ability to repress emotional display can be used to legitimate men's claims to be better suited to positions of leadership, presuming that the best leaders are those who can stay cool in a crisis. Others have made similar arguments, stressing that it is emotional *display* that is controlled to create an impression of hyper-rationality, and thereby mask a pursuit of domination that is fundamentally driven by emotion (Cohn 1987; Sattel 1976).

Managing emotion is closely related to the more cognitive activities of establishing frames and definitions of reality. It is hard, for example, to induce fear without establishing that there is, in fact, a threat that warrants fear. So, too, with anger: it must be established that there is a person, group, event, or condition that calls for this emotion. It would be correct to say that all emotions depend on accepting some construal of reality, and that managing perceptions of reality and managing emotions are two sides of the same process. The results of the process are not just that people are made to feel a particular way or experience a particular emotion but also that they are led to cooperate, whether this means acting or doing nothing.

Invoking Extra-situational Relationships

It is impossible to understand the exercise of power in a situation by looking at nothing but the situation. Ideas, cultural values, rules, and skills that originate outside a situation are brought to a situation where they are used to elicit the cooperation of others (Hall 1972, 1985, 1997). Power depends as much on these resources as on what we can see happening in face-to-face interaction. Here, then, we want to call attention to how actors invoke extra-situational relationships to compel cooperation and compliance. These relationships have been called "control chains" (Collins 1981:993) or, from a more explicitly symbolic interactionist perspective, "nets of accountability" (Schwalbe 2015, 2016, 2019).

A net of accountability is a set of relationships that constrains behavior by promising, and/or delivering, rewards for cooperation and punishments for non-cooperation. Actors whose communication and behavior constitute the "net" hold each other accountable for following normative and procedural rules. To fail to follow an agreed-upon rule is to risk being seen as incompetent, immoral, or possibly insane—and thus to potentially lose a relationship that provides valued resources. This is what it means to be "held accountable" in a consequential way (Garfinkel 1967; Heritage 1984; Hollander 2013). To fail to give an adequate account for violating an agreed-upon rule is to risk losing one's place in a system or organization that provides essential material and emotional rewards. It is to risk being ejected from the game.

Interaction in a classroom provides a familiar example. If a student refuses to do a required assignment, a teacher can hold the student accountable as a student, perhaps by saying, "As a student, you should be glad to do work that will add to your knowledge and skill." This rhetorical tack invokes ideas about what it means to be a good student. But the student might think otherwise ("Being a good student means not wasting time on stupid assignments"), and so a different tack is needed. The teacher might say, "Look, if you don't do the assignment, you'll fail the course and fail to graduate." This strategy invokes realities beyond the situation in an attempt to elicit cooperation within it.

In the example above, the teacher symbolically invokes a net of accountability: a set of rule-governed relationships among teachers, school staff, administrators, parents, employers, and perhaps others. Given how these relationships are known to operate, the student is being told of the damage that will ensue from non-cooperation. Promising such damage by plausibly invoking a net of accountability is a strategy for eliciting cooperation. A student who understands that the net can in fact be *activated* through the teacher's communication with others outside the classroom—to produce real consequences—is likely to comply with the teacher's wishes. Cooperation is thus not merely a result of the teacher's charisma or status. It results from a complex set of accountability relationships in which many people, near and far, are enmeshed (see also Dennis and Martin 2005:209).

The same principles of accountability underlie the exercise of power in other situations. Workers comply with the demands of bosses because of nets of accountability that include other employees of the company, police, lawmakers, creditors, spouses, and children. The rule-governed relationships among these actors ensure that the worker who does not cooperate, like the resistant student, will suffer negative consequences (e.g., loss of a home, loss of ability to support a family, loss of respect from friends). Again, the exercise of power in a situation of face-to-face interaction depends on realities—in this case, relationships that operate in predictable, consequential ways—that exist beyond the situation but that can be invoked to leverage compliance within the situation (Hall 1997; Hall and McGinty 2002).

The concept of nets of accountability illuminates the extra-situational realities that enable the situational exercise of power. Just as establishing a frame or definition of reality is done by building on shared cultural knowledge brought to a situation, invoking a net of accountability likewise depends on shared cultural knowledge of how these nets encompass a situation. Actors who can wield these nets—by invoking them symbolically and, when necessary, activating them—can elicit the cooperation of others who understand, or can be made to understand, how they are caught in the net. This conceptualization also suggests that nets can vary in strength. When accountability relationships among extra-situational actors are highly rule governed, when actors fear that unmet accountability demands can mean the loss of valued resources, and when it is easy to communicate across situations, the net is tight indeed.

Symbolic Interactionism's Contributions

The claim that symbolic interactionism is not useful for studying power was never true, even if, as noted earlier, some symbolic interactionists seemed to agree. This claim was based on the notion that studying power sociologically meant studying political and economic "structures" that somehow existed apart from situated joint action. But if we define power as the capacity to modify an environment to satisfy needs and desires, and if we grant that doing this requires eliciting the cooperation of others, then symbolic interactionism gives us strong analytic purchase on how power works. It points to specific forms of action through which cooperation is elicited and things are made to happen in the social world.

We would go further and say that symbolic interactionism is more than a "micro" perspective useful mainly for studying power in face-to-face interaction. As symbolic interactionists (Becker 1986; Dennis and Martin 2007; Maines 1977; Schwalbe 2016) and others (Collins 1981; Giddens 1984) have argued, what we typically think of as "social structures" consist of people doing things together in recurrent, orderly ways. This patterned joint action is maintained, day to day, by securing the cooperation of many social actors in many linked situations (cf. Blumer 1969:58–59). The routine cooperation that gives us a "structured" social world is secured through the forms of action we have discussed here: crafting virtual selves, using normative and procedural rules, establishing frames and definitions of reality, managing emotion, and invoking nets of accountability. The implication is that symbolic interactionism can well illuminate the interactional roots of the large-scale social arrangements we call, metaphorically, social structures.

The concept of nets of accountability is especially useful for seeing how power operates on larger scales. A corporate CEO, for example, elicits the cooperation not only of the relative few people with whom face-to-face interaction is possible, but of all those caught downstream in the organization's net of accountability—a net that can reach beyond the formal bounds of the corporation to include actors in other organizations and realms of life. In this way, the exercise of power is never just "micro" or merely situational; it always draws on a complex set of rule-governed extra-situational relationships, and it always involves communicatively linked situations. By calling our attention to this, symbolic interactionism helps us see how the foundations of power are broad and diffuse, and how its exercise is related to the concerns of organizational, economic, and political sociology.

A symbolic interactionist perspective also helps us see how power can be exercised without conscious awareness or intent. The person who occupies a high-status position, or who possesses bodily signifiers of high status, can often elicit deference without effort. Part of this may owe to conditioned emotional responses evoked by the signs and symbols wielded by a high-status actor. Part of it may owe to how a high-status actor's mere presence establishes an interactional frame or definition of reality (cf. Goffman 1959:3–4). Another part of it may owe to tacit understandings of the nets of accountability that can be activated by a high-status actor—or by any actor who occupies a key position in a network of rule-governed relationships. We need not, given this view of how power operates, debate whether power exists if an actor is unaware of exercising it. If an actor, consciously or unconsciously, as a matter of habit or strategy, can modify the social environment by eliciting the cooperation of others, power is operating. Our task, then, becomes an empirical one: examining the forms of action through which this occurs.

Another potential contribution of symbolic interactionism lies in unpacking what Lukes (2005) calls the "third face" of power. The first face of power is usually defined as coercion in cases of overt conflict; the second, more gentle face is defined as control exercised through agenda-setting. The third face is defined as securing consent by shaping consciousness—a strategy that aims to preclude the need for coercion and organizational wrangling. Lukes argues that this third face of power, though perhaps the most common, is hardest to see. Symbolic interactionism can help by illuminating the third-face forms of action we have discussed in this chapter (see also Hall 1985:341). We can thus see that the third face of power is more complex than has often been realized, yet it is not empirically inscrutable.

Finally, a symbolic interactionist take on power can help us see how it is nurtured, undermined, and resisted. If power is the capacity to modify the environment to satisfy needs and desires by eliciting the cooperation of others, then efforts at one time to diminish this capacity—by withholding resources or denying opportunities to develop skills—can undermine the power of an individual or group at a later time. Conversely, providing resources and nurturing skills at one time can enhance the power of an individual or group at a later time. This view reminds us that power and its exercise have historical dimensions. To understand power, we must examine how it is developed as a capacity and how the conditions that enable its exercise take shape over time.

A symbolic interactionist perspective also helps us see how power, no matter how durable it might seem, can be resisted. If power is a matter of eliciting the cooperation of others, it can be resisted by disrupting the processes through which cooperation is attained. The powerful virtual selves of elites can be strategically discredited; rules, frames, and definitions of reality can be challenged; dissident emotions can be cultivated; new extra-situational accountability relationships can be created. Ultimately, resisting power by disrupting cooperation is a matter of using symbols to remake perceptions of and feelings about socially constructed realities. Guns can be useful tools for eliciting cooperation, but guns still must be wielded by human hands. Power, the symbolic interactionist view leads us to understand, does not come from the tool but from what can be done to the mind of its user.

Conclusion

We began in an unusual place for theorists of power: with G. H. Mead and Herbert Blumer. Drawing on Mead, we defined power as the *capacity* of an organism—for our purposes, the capacity of a person or group—to modify its environment to satisfy needs and desires. This definition, we said, allows us to deal with power generically, avoiding dubious debates about whether it is distinct from authority, influence, compulsion, coercion, and so on. We argued that *exercising* power—modifying the social world to satisfy needs and desires—means eliciting the cooperation of others. We then applied Herbert Blumer's advice to try to understand "analytical elements" (i.e., abstract concepts) in terms of action or forms of doing. Taking this approach to our Meadian concept of power, we asked, What are the forms of action through which cooperation is elicited?

Our attempt to answer this question was situated, first, in a general symbolic interactionist perspective that sees signs, symbols, meanings, and interpretation as central to the patterned, minded behavior that constitutes human social life. We deliberately construed symbolic interactionism broadly (some might say too broadly) to include elements of dramaturgy, ethnomethodology, sociology of emotions, and social constructionism. This approach led us to identify five forms of action through which power is exercised by eliciting the cooperation of others: crafting powerful virtual selves, using normative and procedural rules, managing emotion, establishing frames and definitions of reality, and invoking extra-situational relationships or "nets of accountability."

What this approach gains us is not only theoretical clarity about the nature of power but also the possibility of a firmer grip on how it is exercised. Each of the forms of action through which cooperation is elicited is amenable to study. By looking at how these actions are undertaken—the resources and strategies used by whom, vis-à-vis whom, under what conditions—we can see power at work. In a sense, a symbolic interactionist perspective makes power mundane. It is not an occult force resistant to empirical exposure; it is a universal capacity, the exercise of which occurs, albeit with greater or lesser effect, as an ordinary part of everyday life.

Finally, we hold that even while symbolic interactionism demystifies power and makes visible its exercise in interaction, it also helps us see how power operates on larger scales. Every organization and institution—every government, every economy, every world system—is held together by the daily eliciting of cooperation; which is to say, by the exercise of power in concrete situations. This requires the continual crafting of virtual selves, the use of normative and procedural rules, the managing of emotions, the establishment of frames and definitions of reality, and the use of nets of accountability. By directing our analytic attention to these forms of action, a symbolic interactionist perspective on power shows us more than how cooperation is elicited situationally. It shows us how a highly unequal world, a world fraught with political, economic, and status inequalities, is made, reproduced, and changed.

NOTE

1. Mead's concept of mind as emergent from natural evolutionary processes and shaped by an organism's interaction with its environment parallels the philosophical anthropology articulated by Marx in *The Economic and Philosophic Manuscripts of 1844* (1844/1988). The key point of convergence lies in seeing human bodies and minds as products of continual efforts to transform nature in the interest of survival. To engage in this process is, for Marx and for Mead, to exercise power, though it is not only nature that can be transformed by minded behavior but also social relationships—the latter point being one Marx considered more fully in *The German Ideology* (1846/1998). This convergence suggests that even perspectives thought of as paradigmatically "macro" are premised on some understanding of power as an essential part of everyday human existence. It is this understanding, we contend, that can be enriched by Mead, and, moreover, in a way that is compatible with many macro perspectives. For further exploration of the relationship between Marx's and Mead's ideas, see Goff (1980) and Schwalbe (1986).

REFERENCES

Alexander, Jeffrey C. 2017. *The Drama of Social Life*. Malden, MA: Polity Press.
Athens, Lonnie. 2015. *Domination and Subjugation in Everyday Life*. New York: Routledge.
Becker, Howard S. 1963. *Outsiders*. New York: Free Press.
Becker, Howard S. 1986. *Doing Things Together*. Evanston, IL: Northwestern University Press.
Becker, Howard S. 2003. "The Politics of Presentation: Goffman and Total Institutions." *Symbolic Interaction* 26(4):659–69.

Blumer, Herbert. 1954. "Social Structure and Power Conflict." Pp. 232–39 in *Industrial Conflict*, edited by Arthur Kornhauser, Robert Dubin, and Arthur M. Ross. New York: McGraw Hill.

Blumer, Herbert. 1956. "Sociological Analysis and the 'Variable.'" *American Sociological Review* 21(6):68–690.

Blumer, Herbert. 1969. *Symbolic Interactionism: Perspective and Method*. Englewood Cliffs, NJ: Prentice Hall.

Bourdieu, Pierre. 1977. *Outline of a Theory of Practice*. Cambridge, UK: Cambridge University Press.

Branaman, Ann. 2003. "Interaction and Hierarchy in Everyday Life: Goffman and Beyond." Pp. 86–126 in *Goffman's Legacy*, edited by A. J. Treviño. Lanham, MD: Rowman & Littlefield.

Buckley, Walter. 1967. *Sociology and Modern Systems Theory*. Englewood Cliffs, NJ: Prentice Hall.

Cohn, Carol. 1987. "Sex and Death in the Rational World of Defense Intellectuals." *Signs: Journal of Women in Culture and Society* 12(4):687–718.

Collins, Randall. 1981. "On the Microfoundations of Macrosociology." *American Journal of Sociology* 86(5):984–1014.

Collins, Randall. 2004. *Interaction Ritual Chains*. Princeton, NJ: Princeton University Press.

Dahl, Robert. 1957. "The Concept of Power." *Behavioral Science* 2(3):201–15.

Dennis, Alex, and Peter J. Martin. 2005. "Symbolic Interactionism and the Concept of Power." *British Journal of Sociology* 56(2):191–213.

Dennis, Alex, and Peter J. Martin. 2007. "Symbolic Interactionism and the Concept of Social Structure." *Sociological Focus* 40(3):287–305.

Denzin, Norman. 1977. "Notes on the Criminogenic Hypothesis: A Case Study of the American Liquor Industry." *American Sociological Review* 42(6):905–20.

Farberman, Harvey. 1975. "A Criminogenic Market Structure: The Automobile Industry." *Sociological Quarterly* 16(4):438–57.

Fields, Jessica, Martha Copp, and Sherryl Kleinman. 2006. "Symbolic Interactionism, Inequality, and Emotions." Pp. 155–78 in *Handbook of the Sociology of Emotions*, edited by Jan E. Stets and Jonathan H. Turner. New York: Springer.

Fine, Gary Alan. 1984. "Negotiated Orders and Organizational Cultures." *Annual Review of Sociology* 10:239–62.

Gamson, William A. 1968. *Power and Discontent*. Homewood, IL: Dorsey Press.

Garfinkel, Harold. 1967. *Studies in Ethnomethodology*. Englewood Cliffs, NJ: Prentice Hall.

Giddens, Anthony. 1979. *Central Problems in Social Theory*. Berkeley, CA: University of California Press.

Giddens, Anthony. 1984. *The Constitution of Society*. Berkeley, CA: University of California Press.

Goff, Tom W. 1980. *Marx and Mead: Contributions to a Sociology of Knowledge*. London: Routledge.

Goffman, Erving. 1951. "Symbols of Class Status." *British Journal of Sociology* 2(4):294–304.

Goffman, Erving. 1959. *The Presentation of Self in Everyday Life*. Garden City, NY: Anchor.

Goffman, Erving. 1967. *Interaction Ritual*. New York: Pantheon.

Goffman, Erving. 1974. *Frame Analysis*. New York: Harper & Row.

Goffman, Erving. 1983. "The Interaction Order." *American Sociological Review* 48(1):1–17.

Grossman, Dave. 2009. *On Killing*. New York: Back Bay Books.

Hall, Peter M. 1972. "A Symbolic Interactionist Analysis of Politics." *Sociological Inquiry* 42(3–4):35–75.

Hall, Peter M. 1985. "Asymmetric Relationships and Processes of Power." *Studies in Symbolic Interaction*, Supplement 1:309–44.

Hall, Peter M. 1997. "Meta-Power, Social Organization, and the Shaping of Social Action." *Symbolic Interaction* 20(4):397–418.

Hall, Peter M., and Patrick J. W. McGinty. 2002. "Social Organization across Space and Time: The Policy Process, Mesodomain Analysis, and Breadth of Perspective." Pp. 303–22 in *Structure, Culture, and History: Recent Issues in Social Theory*, edited by Sing C. Chew and J. David Knottnerus. Latham, MD: Rowman and Littlefield.

Hallett, Tim. 2007. "Between Deference and Distinction: Interaction Ritual Through Symbolic Power in an Educational Institution." *Social Psychology Quarterly* 70(2):148–71.

Heritage, John. 1984. *Garfinkel and Ethnomethodology*. Cambridge, UK: Polity.

Hochschild, Arlie. 1979. "Emotion Work, Feeling Rules, and Social Structure." *American Journal of Sociology* 85:551–75.

Hollander, Jocelyn. 2013. "'I Demand More of People': Accountability, Interaction, and Gender Change." *Gender and Society* 27(1):5–29.

Huber, Joan. 1973. "Symbolic Interactionism as a Pragmatic Perspective: The Bias of Emergent Theory." *American Sociological Review* 38(2):274–84.

Johnson, Allan. 2005. *Privilege, Power, and Difference*. 2nd ed. New York: McGraw Hill.

Kanter, Rosabeth M. 1972. "Symbolic Interactionism and Politics in Systemic Perspective." *Sociological Inquiry* 42(3–4):77–92.

Kemper, Theodore D. 2006. "Power and Status and the Power-Status Theory of Emotions." Pp. 87–113 in *Handbook of the Sociology of Emotions*, edited by Jan E. Stets and Jonathan H. Turner. New York: Springer.

Lichtman, Richard T. 1970. "Symbolic Interactionism and Social Reality: Some Marxist Queries." *Berkeley Journal of Sociology* 15:75–94.

Luckenbill, David F. 1979. "Power: A Conceptual Framework." *Symbolic Interaction* 2(2):97–114.

Lukes, Steven. 2005. *Power: A Radical View*. 2nd ed. New York: Palgrave Macmillan.

Maines, David R. 1977. "Social Organization and Social Structure in Symbolic Interactionist Thought." *Annual Review of Sociology* 3:235–59.

Maines, David R. 2001. *The Faultline of Consciousness: A View of Interactionism in Sociology*. New York: Aldine.

Margolis, Diane R. 1989. "Considering Women's Experience: A Reformulation of Power Theory." *Theory and Society* 18(3):387–418.

Marx, Karl. 1844/1988. *The Economic and Philosophic Manuscripts of 1844*. Amherst, NY: Prometheus.

Marx, Karl. 1846/1998. *The German Ideology*. Amherst, NY: Prometheus.

Mead, George H. 1934. *Mind, Self, and Society from the Standpoint of a Social Behaviorist*. Edited by Charles W. Morris. Chicago: University of Chicago Press.

Meltzer, Bernard N., John W. Petras, and Larry T. Reynolds. 1975. *Symbolic Interactionism: Genesis, Varieties, and Criticism*. London: Routledge and Kegan Paul.

Miller, David L. 1980. *George Herbert Mead: Self, Language, and the World*. Chicago: University of Chicago Press.

Molotch, Harvey L., and Deirdre Boden. 1985. "Talking Social Structure: Discourse, Domination, and the Watergate Hearings." *American Sociological Review* 50(June):273–88.

Musolf, Gil Richard. 1992. "Structure, Institutions, Power, and Ideology: New Directions Within Symbolic Interactionism." *Sociological Quarterly* 33(2):171–89.

Prus, Robert. 1999. *Beyond the Power Mystique: Power as Intersubjective Accomplishment*. Albany, NY: State University of New York Press.

Ridgeway, Cecilia L. 2011. *Framed by Gender*. New York: Oxford University Press.

Ridgeway, Cecilia L. 2019. *Status: Why Is It Everywhere? Why Does It Matter?* New York: Russell Sage Foundation.

Rogers, Mary F. 1974. "Instrumental and Infra-Resources: The Bases of Power." *American Journal of Sociology* 79(6):1418–33.

Rogers, Mary F. 1977. "Goffman on Power." *American Sociologist* 12(April):88–95.

Roscigno, Vincent. 2011. "Power, Revisited." *Social Forces* 90(2):349–74.

Ruiz-Junco, Natalia. 2016. "The Persistence of the Power Deficit? Advancing Power Premises in Contemporary Interactionist Theory." *Studies in Symbolic Interaction* 46:145–65.

Sattel, Jack. 1976. "The Inexpressive Male: Tragedy or Sexual Politics?" *Social Problems* 23:469–77.

Schwalbe, Michael L. 1986. *The Psychosocial Consequences of Natural and Alienated Labor.* Albany, NY: SUNY Press.

Schwalbe, Michael L. 2015. *Rigging the Game: How Inequality Is Reproduced in Everyday Life.* 2nd ed. New York: Oxford University Press.

Schwalbe, Michael L. 2016. "Overcoming Aprocessual Bias in the Study of Inequality: Parsing the Capitalist Interaction Order." *Studies in Symbolic Interaction* 46:95–122.

Schwalbe, Michael L. 2019. "Upscaling Goffman: Four Principles of Neostructural Interactionism." Pp. 30–44 in *Critical and Cultural Interactionism*, edited by Michael Hviid Jacobsen. New York: Routledge.

Schwalbe, Michael L., Sandra Godwin, Daphne Holden, Douglas Schrock, Shealy Thompson, and Michelle Wolkomir. 2000. "Generic Processes in the Reproduction of Inequality." *Social Forces* 79(2):419–52.

Schwalbe, Michael L., and Heather Shay. 2014. "Dramaturgy and Dominance." Pp. 155–80 in *Handbook of the Social Psychology of Inequality*, edited by Jane D. McLeod, Edward J. Lawler, and Michael L. Schwalbe. New York: Springer.

Shott, Susan. 1979. "Emotion and Social Life: A Symbolic Interactionist Analysis." *American Journal of Sociology* 84(6):1317–34.

Thoits, Peggy A. 1989. "The Sociology of Emotions." *Annual Review of Sociology* 15:317–42.

Wasielewski, Patricia. 1985. "The Emotional Basis of Charisma." *Symbolic Interaction* 8(2):207–22.

Weber, Max. 1910–14/1946. *From Max Weber: Essays in Sociology.* Edited by Hans H. Gerth and C. Wright Mills. New York: Oxford University Press.

Welsh, John F. 1991. "Dramaturgy and Political Mystification: Political Life in the United States." Pp. 399–410 in *Life as Theater*, 2nd ed., edited by Dennis Brissett and Charles Edgley. New York: Aldine.

Wrong, Dennis H. 1968. "Some Problems in Defining Social Power." *American Journal of Sociology* 73(6):673–81.

Young, T. R. 1990. *The Drama of Social Life.* New Brunswick, NJ: Transaction.

CHAPTER 22

RACIAL SOCIALIZATION AND RACISM

MARGARET A. HAGERMAN

"Race is not something we are born with (in that it is not a genetic or biological fact) but something that is mapped onto us from the first moments of life (with the listing of race on the birth certificate). Racial identities do not automatically follow from these early external racial assignments. They take shape over time, through multiple interactions with those who are the same and those who are different. We learn ways to categorize ourselves and others... [and] what it means to belong to one race rather than another. Race then is not a real or innate characteristic of bodies but a set of signifiers projected onto these bodies—signifiers we must learn about and negotiate in order to successfully move through the social world."

(Lewis 2003:6)

INTRODUCTION

Theorizing about race and racism requires negotiating between the micro-level, interpretive, and interactional meaning-making processes involved in the social construction of race and the powerful meso- and macro-level historical and institutional structures of oppression that perpetuate racial hierarchies and inequality. Despite debates about how to best theorize race,[1] theoretical "work is best when we focus both on the construction of race and the rootedness of racism" within institutions (Golash-Boza 2013:998). Even when theories about race differ in key ways, race theorists generally seek to account for the dialectical relationship between micro- and macro-level processes as well as how these different levels mutually reinforce each other (Holt 1995).

When researching and writing about racial socialization and racism from a micro-level perspective, it is important to not lose sight of the mutually sustaining relationship between the shared meaning-making processes that unfold in everyday life and the big, broad structures that shape and reinforce those meanings. This is particularly true when thinking about theories of how the newest members of a society, through an interpretive process, come to understand the concept of race. Understanding how children learn about race requires taking into account how this learning process is shaped by both micro-level meaning-making and macro-level structures. And this is a key theoretical principle of symbolic interactionism.

Although many scholars of race and racism do not strongly identify as "interactionists," much of the theoretical work on how people interpret racial meanings and produce racial ideological perspectives is clearly inspired by interactionist principles. In this sense, scholarship on racial socialization and racism should be recognized as contributing to the field of symbolic interactionism. Similarly, scholars who do directly develop general interactionist theories of identity, micro-interaction, socialization, and so forth ought to be aware of this body of scholarship on racial socialization and racism, which can inform symbolic interactionism more generally.

In the following pages, I will explore how race as a concept develops for young people through processes of social interaction within particular contexts—or a learning process commonly referred to as "racial socialization." Overall, this chapter hopes to offer an interpretive, micro-level, sociological framework for thinking about racial socialization that is grounded in historical and structural understandings of race as a social project. And in addition, this chapter illustrates key connections between the traditional field of symbolic interactionism and the study of racial socialization and racism.

RACE AS A SOCIAL CONSTRUCTION

In the early twentieth century, W. E. B. Du Bois used empirical findings about black life in the United States to challenge sociologists' stereotypical and racist theorizing of the day, which often identified racial differences as being connected to biology (Du Bois 1995; Du Bois 2014). Although his contributions as a black scholar have not always been taken seriously by the discipline (Morris 2017), the work of Du Bois was crucial in moving toward an understanding of race as a social construct rather than an inherent biological trait, which was a dominant way of thinking about race during the nineteenth century. Although some would argue that a biological and essentialist view of race persists to this day (Roberts 2011), most sociologists agree that race is a socially constructed phenomenon.

As the philosopher Charles Mills (2010) describes, "the reality of race is basically a reality that is socially created—it not an intrinsic reality of the nature of the human race." Race is "a way of 'making people up'" (Omi and Winant 2015:105) and "signifies and symbolizes sociopolitical conflicts and interests in reference to different types of human bodies" (Winant 2000:172). Racial categories shift over time as demonstrated by frequent changes to the U.S. Census (Cornell and Hartmann 2006), inconsistent Supreme

Court case decisions about who counts as white over time (Haney López 1996), and research on comparative racialization, which explores how meanings attached to race vary tremendously across place.

In their development of racial formation theory, Omi and Winant (2015) introduced and advanced the concept of "racialization," or the "extension of racial meaning to a previously racially unclassified relationship, social practice, or group" (p. 13). Racialization occurs at the individual level of human bodies but also at the level of institutional practices. They argue that these "racial projects" represent ongoing contestation, and they describe "how race [is] part of the state and also how large-scale meaning becomes part of our common sense—what race means, what categories mean, who belongs to which—and lead to ongoing interpretation of our experience in racial terms" (Lewis, Hagerman, and Forman 2019:32).

Although these ideas about race are socially constructed, they are real in their consequences, as the famous Thomas theorem states (Thomas and Thomas 1928:571–72). "Race is strategic; race does ideological and political work" and is not simply an illusion (Omi and Winant 2015:111). As such, a large and important body of scholarship documents the existence and impact of racism in contemporary society along with the production and reproduction of, as well as resistance to, this ideological and political work.[2]

LEARNING RACE AND RACISM: AN INTERACTIONAL AND INTERPRETIVE PROCESS

Given that race is a social construction with real consequences, how then do people come to understand the meanings attached to the categories we know as "races"? How do people learn to categorize themselves? How do people learn what it means to belong to a particular racial group? How do people learn racial hierarchies? And how do people learn their own position within these hierarchies? Principles of symbolic interaction are helpful in answering these questions.

Herbert Blumer, the scholar who coined the term "symbolic interaction" in 1937, offers a general theory on these fundamental questions about how people make meaning. He argues that "human society consists of people engaging in action . . . culture as a conception, whether defined as custom, tradition, norm, value, rules or such like, is clearly derived from what people do. Similarly, social structure in any of its aspects . . . refers to relationships derived from how people act toward each other" (Blumer 1969:6–7). As humans interact with each other, they develop and reproduce meanings about various aspects of their social world, such as meanings attached to social categories and positions within social hierarchies. This meaning-making process is central to the symbolic interactionist approach to sociology and vital to understanding not only how race is socially constructed but also how the very concept of race is learned.

Blumer also wrote explicitly about race (1958). He argued that racial prejudice, for example, is not simply about an individual's feelings toward another person at the psychological level (a common assumption); instead, individual-level expressions of prejudice are linked to a collective and relational meaning-making process in which one feels that their social group's position is being challenged. This argument is laid out in Blumer's (1958) famous essay, "Race Prejudice as a Sense of Group Position." As Bobo (1999) writes in his elaboration of Blumer's work,

The social phenomenon of racial prejudice is not just a story of bad ideas and a biased reading of relevant social information; it is not just a story of noxious socialization and reverence for the symbols of the tribe; it is also, and perhaps principally, *a story of self as positioned in a racialized and stratified social world.* (p. 468, emphasis added)

Here, Bobo clearly draws attention to the key point that racial actors are individuals situated within hierarchies of power and are part of collective groups. They develop their ideas about themselves and others from a collective position within a broader social context and through social interactions with others.

In thinking more about the connection between micro-, symbolic interactionist, meaning-making processes, on the one hand, and the larger, macro-level racial structure of a society, on the other hand, Feagin (2006) argues that racism is systemic and a "material, social, and ideological reality that is well-embedded in major US institutions" (2). Specifically, he states that racism is "foundational to and deeply ingrained in US history and is operational throughout society levels—group relations, institutions, organizations, power structures" (Feagin and Elias 2013:936). Leading race scholar Eduardo Bonilla-Silva (1997) also answers this question in his call for a structural interpretation of racism. As he writes, in a racialized social system, "differential economic, political, social, and even psychological rewards [are distributed] to groups along racial lines; lines that are socially constructed." Once this has happened, or once a society has "become racialized . . . a set of social relations and practices based on racial distinctions develops at all society levels" (p. 474). He argues that "on the basis of this structure, there develops a racial ideology (what analysts have coded as racism). This ideology . . . becomes the organizational map that guides actions of racial actors in society. It becomes as real as the racial relations it organizes." Although he applies this theory to any racialized society,

Bonilla-Silva argues that we need to focus on the collective nature of racial consciousness and understanding. In laying out the racial ideology paradigm, Bonilla-Silva demonstrates how ideas about race are deeply tied to the organization of social relations and are not the free-floating creations of individuals. (Lewis, Hagerman, and Forman 2019:37).

Learning racial ideologies involves interpreting and internalizing the norms of a society and the symbolic meanings that help us make sense of the world around us. Although this process occurs throughout the life course, many studies on this topic focus specifically on children and youth as racial ideologies, and meaning-making processes are learned at the earliest periods of development in an individual's life course.

As a result of this emphasis on childhood, most research on the topic of how people learn race as a concept focuses on two institutions in which most children are deeply embedded: families and schools. These are both areas of enormous scholarship, and this essay cannot do justice to the entire vast range of important work that exists. As such, I will seek to pull out key examples of research about racial socialization and racial learning that engage directly with symbolic interactionist approaches.

RACIAL SOCIALIZATION PROCESSES
IN FAMILIES

Drawing on the framework of symbolic interactionism, "racial socialization" refers to race-based communications that occur within families. This process is understood to be interactional: "children's racial knowledge and attitudes are formed and reformed through ordinary social interaction and conversations with their parents" (Hughes and Chen 1999:470). This area of research is large and interdisciplinary and includes sociological approaches, although much of this work is situated within disciplines of child development and family studies. Much of the research on this topic explores differences in how parents approach these communications about race with their children as well as the outcomes across a range of measures related to positive racial identity development (Hughes and Chen 1999), increased self-esteem (Phinney and Chavira 1995), improved educational outcomes (Bowman and Howard 1985), and increases in overall wellbeing (Hughes and Johnson 2001).

It is essential to point out that this body of scholarship emerged from questions posed specifically by black social scientists about how parents raising black children in a racist society like that of the United States prepare their children for potential and likely experiences of discrimination or even racial violence (Bowman and Howard 1985; Peters 1985). As such, a number of studies have examined how parents raising black children engage in explicit and implicit forms of racial socialization (Brega and Coleman 1999; Constantine and Blackmon 2002; Dow 2019; Thomas and Blackmon 2015; Threlfall 2016; Whitaker and Snell 2016; Winkler 2008, 2012). For excellent reviews of the research in this area, see Hughes et al. (2006).

Studies of racial socialization have broadened in scope over the last few decades, and scholars have documented how racial socialization operates among a range of families of color including Latino families (Douglass and Umaña-Taylor 2015; Hughes 2003; Quintana and Vera 1999; Rivas-Drake 2010), Asian American families (Chao 1994; Gartner, Kiang, and Supple 2014; Juang, Yoo, and Atkin 2017), multiracial families (Chancler, Webb, and Miller 2017; Orbe 1999; Rockquemore and Laszloffy 2005; Rollins and Hunter 2013), and to a limited extent American Indian families (Cheshire 2001; Yasui et al. 2015). Overall, studies of racial socialization in families of color document the messages conveyed to children as well as the mechanisms parents draw upon to convey these ideas. While some of these mechanisms may appear to be subtle, overall, the literature shows that many parents raising children of color are consciously, explicitly, and deliberately working to teach their kids how to navigate the existing racial landscape. Specifically, families teach their children lessons about race with the goal of helping them develop strategies for countering racism and building resilience while providing tools of empowerment (Brega and Coleman 1999; Knight et al. 1993; Phinney and Chavira 1995). Critical research on racial socialization processes in white families is very limited in large part due to the long-standing assumption that white families do not "have" race" (Burton et al. 2010). In recent years, this has become a growing area of scholarship.

Racial socialization research overwhelmingly considers how parents report participating in sending their kids messages about race with less attention paid to how children interpret or make meanings of these messages. Often, approaches to childhood socialization in general suggest that this is something that happens *to* young people—that young people are uncritical, empty vessels that adults fill with their own knowledge. This passive view of socialization is "associated with the theoretical tradition of structural functionalism [and] emphasizes the conformity and adaptation of individuals to the formal and informal norms of the specific groups and society to which individuals belong" (Settersten, Jr. 2002:13). As the famous gender scholar Barrie Thorne writes in her call for child-centered research methods, "children don't necessarily see themselves as 'being socialized'" (Thorne 1993:13). This structural functionalist approach is thus quite deterministic and does not leave room for children's agency or own interpretive work. As such, it is critiqued for an overemphasis on outcomes of socialization and a lack of attention to how children are active participants in their own social learning processes (Corsaro 2011:11). Furthermore, psychologists Diane Hughes and Deborah Johnson point out that this deterministic model does not account for the transactional nature of socialization between parent and child—for instance, when a child introduces a new topic to the family or influences how a parent thinks about something rather than the other way around (Hughes and Johnson 2001). Given these concerns, William Corsaro, a sociologist renowned for his contributions to the New Sociology of Childhood, states,

> Socialization is not only a matter of adaptation and internalization but also a process of appropriation, reinvention, and reproduction. Central to this view of socialization is the appreciation of importance of collective, communal activity—how children negotiate, share, and create culture with adults and each other.
>
> (Corsaro 2011:11)

An alternative view of socialization, then, is "associated with the theoretical tradition of symbolic interaction and its offshoots [and] instead emphasizes how aspects of individual development, such as self-concept, attitudes, and dispositions are created and re-created through interaction in social settings" (Settersten 2002:14). This view of how the newest members of society develop their understandings of the social world has become more dominant in recent years and has specifically been elaborated upon by sociologists. Perhaps the most famous is Corsaro's (2011) theory of "interpretive repro-duction." Focusing on the symbols of language and the everyday cultural routines of kids, this approach to understanding socialization acknowledges "how children nego-tiate, share, and create culture with adults and each other" (Corsaro 2011:20). As young people develop their own understandings of the world through social action with other people, "children come to collectively produce their own peer worlds and cultures" through a dialectical process of both reproduction and reinvention (Corsaro 2011:27). Examples of interpretive reproduction can be seen through how young children play imaginative games or how children refashion dominant ideologies (Hagerman 2016). Gender scholars have explored how kids participate in their own gender socialization on playgrounds (Thorne 1993), and political sociologists have used this socialization model to understand with more accuracy and nuance how kids develop political viewpoints, demonstrating, for instance, that kids do not simply parrot those of their parents, an often taken-for-granted assumption (McDevitt and Chaffee 2002).

Scholars who specifically address racial socialization have applied this approach in their recent research. Erin Winkler (2012) takes the position that children are active participants in what she calls "comprehensive racial learning." As she writes,

> Children develop their ideas about race in the context of systems, structures, institutions, government, and culture, all of which are racialized within the US con-text. Not only their parents, but schools, media, religious institutions, neighbors, po-lice, peers, place, and a whole host of other forces enter into the process.
>
> (Omi and Winant 1994; Van Ausdale and Feagin 2001) (1)

Winkler (2012) documents empirically through a study with African American children and their parents how kids are "active, critical participants in making sense of ideas about race" (1). In her research, Winkler explores how kids conceive of race based on meanings of place specifically—how growing up in Detroit sends messages about race to children. Furthermore, she observes how children notice race and develop understandings about racial difference after leaving Detroit to visit a different place, the children picking up on cues from the social environment or differences in patterns around them as they travel.

Hagerman (2018) builds on the work of Winkler and explores how white chil-dren growing up in communities of race and class privilege develop understandings about race, racism, inequality, and privilege through their social interactions and interpretations of the social context in which they are embedded. She argues that children develop their ideas about the world from within a particular "racial context of childhood" that is shaped by not only what parents say to their kids about race (as well documented by scholars like Underhill 2017 and Vittrup 2018) but also the choices parents make about where to live, where to send their kids to school, what media to consume, and so on. Young people make sense of race through patterns they notice in their social environment, which is especially important in families that claim to be "colorblind" and in which parents rarely speak openly with children about race. Kids growing up in these white families are still learning about race implicitly, however, regardless of the explicit racial discourse surrounding them. For instance, children look out the window in the car and notice who lives in different parts of the community and what those people look like. Subsequently, kids map racialized ideas about class, safety, homelessness, and whether a part of town is "good" or "bad" on to their observations of patterns and develop common-sense, taken-for-granted ideas about why these patterns exist. Often, interactions with parents, siblings, and peers reinforce and shape these notions. A symbolic interactionist approach to understanding racial socialization explains why and how this process works. Both Winkler and Hagerman demonstrate how through interacting with place, parents, peers, and more, kids interpretively reproduce the social world around them and develop ideas through their interpretations of messages and cues in their social environment.

Though not the central focus of this chapter, it is important to note briefly that a qualitative methodological approach is required for this kind of research; quantitative methods do not allow the researchers to understand the "complexities and nuances" of participants' experiences and do not allow for an inductive approach in which the researcher comes to understand the views of the participant. This is important for understanding the experiences and viewpoints of marginalized groups as told by them (Collins 2008) and for accessing the actual ideas of white respondents who engage in survey non-response practices and other avoidance tactics when it comes to answering survey questions about race (Alexander 2017). As Emerson (2001) writes, qualitative methods, and particularly participant observation and interviewing,

> d[o] not seek to represent social "things in themselves" . . . but things as they are grasped and shaped through the meaning-conferring response of members. Ethnographic descriptions of the social world . . . identify and convey the meanings that actions and events have for actors in that world. (30)

Certainly, these qualitative, ethnographic approaches are ideal for researching racial socialization and racial learning processes. And these approaches are informed directly by and dependent upon principles of symbolic interactionism.

Schools as Sites for Racial Learning

Although parents play a primary role in shaping (but not determining) the social ideas about race that children produce, reproduce, and sometimes rework, so too do schools play a major role in young people's racial learning. One of the most compelling accounts of how schools are race-making institutions and play a powerful role in the process of racial formation is put forth in the work of Amanda Lewis. Based on ethnographic research in three elementary schools, Lewis (2003) argues that race and racial inequality are reproduced in day-to-day life in schools. "Schools are arguably one of the central institutions involved in the drawing and redrawing of racial lines . . . schools are settings where people acquire some version 'of the rules of racial classification' and of their own racial identity" (Omi and Winant 1994:60). Lewis describes how schools in both direct and indirect ways teach young people racial lessons and how schools "fram[e] ideas about race . . . and serve as a sorting mechanism" (p. 7). Based on research with fourth graders, Lewis (2010) also examines how young people produce racial discourse in the context of school.

In other research, Lewis and her colleague John Diamond provide a powerful ethnographic look at how one high school community reproduces race and racism by examining how "*structural inequalities, institutional practices*, and *racial ideologies* mutually reinforce each other" and collectively serve to perpetuate racial inequality within the school (Lewis and Diamond 2015:8). This work connects directly to existing research on racialized tracking in schools—how messages about worth, intelligence, ability, and so on are communicated to children through how schools are organized along racial lines (Oakes 2005; Tyson 2011). When white kids are disproportionately represented in honors classes, for instance, they learn something not only about themselves as being "smarter" than other kids but they also make associations between who is smart "like them" and who is not. Indeed, research shows that the very designations of kids into gifted and talented programs hinges upon racialized (and racist) understandings of children and their abilities (Carman 2011; Roda 2015).

These studies only scratch the surface of an important body of school-based research that demonstrates how schools participate in shaping young people's ideas about race and racialized outcomes through processes like tracking, school discipline, and racialized/racist understandings of kids (see, for instance, Bettie 2002; Carter 2005; Gilliam and Shahar 2006; Kozol 2012; Ladson-Billings and Tate 2006; Lee and Zhou 2015; Lewis and Manno 2011; Meiners 2007; Morris 2005; Noguera 2003; Oeur 2018; Posey-Maddox 2014; Skiba et al. 2011). However, even this brief discussion speaks directly to how meaning-making processes connected to race extend beyond family-based contexts and include other institutions, especially schools. Furthermore, this work within families and schools provides a clear example of how to bridge the micro-level of interpretation to the meso-level of institutions and to the macro-level of power structures as discussed at the outset of this chapter.

THE RACIAL IDEAS OF CHILDREN

In addition to studying how the process of racial learning works, social scientists have also long been interested in the content of children's racial ideas and how these ideas develop across different ages in childhood. Again, this area of inquiry is informed by principles of symbolic interactionism. These researchers are interested broadly in how children as human actors utilize these ideas in ways that affirm and/or challenge the prevailing racial order in everyday life.

Research shows that kids begin to make meaning about race during the early childhood years. In the early 1940s, black psychologists Mamie and Kenneth Clark conducted a series of studies with young black children and dolls in order to understand empirically how racism impacts kids' sense of self and others (Clark and Clark 1939). This research served to bolster arguments against school segregation as part of the 1954 *Brown v. Board of Education* the United States Supreme Court case. More recently, child-development researchers and others have conducted a wide range of studies that explore young children's racial understandings. This research shows that kids as young as three months old can categorize people by race (Kelly et al. 2005). By three years of age, children can express explicit forms of racial bias (Aboud 2008). Van Ausdale and Feagin (2001), two sociologists conducting research in the context of a child-care facility, find that children between the ages of three and six speak directly about race and understand racial hierarchy and that these kids' ideas are connected to the messages adults at the center present to them, including "correctives" provided to children who deviate from social norms. Research also demonstrates that by age five, black and brown kids are conscious of existing racist stereotypes about their groups and are negatively impacted by these racist ideas (Hirschfeld 2008). By age eight, white kids learn that it is socially unacceptable to express explicit forms of racial bias—and instead exhibit an increase in implicit forms of prejudice (Raabe and Beelmann 2011). These are only some examples of the important research in this area. (For an excellent review of research on children's ideas in early childhood, see Quintana 1998.)

In middle childhood, children begin to think in more ideological terms (Meece and Daniels 2007) and tend to exhibit more prejudice toward members of groups with less power (Raabe and Beelmann 2011). As kids have more interactions outside of their family and spend more time at school, with their peers (Adler and Adler 1998) during extracurricular activities (Andrews et al. 1997), or at summer camp (Moore 2002), they continue to produce ideas about race as they interpret the social environment around them. Research shows that as children get older, they "pick up on the ways in which whiteness is normalized and privileged in the U.S. society" (Winkler 2012:10–11). For example, for one group of white children interviewed and observed over time, their ideological positions on race become more cemented as they moved from middle childhood to adolescence (Hagerman 2019), and their ideas did not change much as they got older. Similarly, Mueller (2017), Byrd (2017), and Warikoo and de Novais (2015) find that it is often difficult for young adults to shift their ideological views on race developed in the pre-college years of their lives.

Conclusion

Overall, this chapter outlined some of the key issues related to the topic of racial socialization. How people develop "common-sense" understandings of race at the everyday level is crucial for understanding the reproduction of, or for challenging, the prevailing racial order. And this chapter has highlighted how principles of symbolic interactionist principles inform the study of racial socialization. As Lewis, Hagerman, and Forman (2019) write,

> The stories we tell (or feel comfortable listening to) about race are about how we understand, explain, justify and contest racial hierarchies and therefore, what kind of solutions we propose to pressing social challenges. In a context like the United States, founded on principle [*sic*] of equality, ways of making *sense* of entrenched racial hierarchies have always been key to those who wish either to challenge or sustain current arrangements. (p. 30)

Studying micro-level interactions and racial meaning-making processes of children is therefore crucial to understanding how racial injustice is experienced, how it persists, and how it might be challenged. In order to do this work, scholars must draw upon the central principles provided by the field of symbolic interactionism. And in turn, research on racial socialization and racism has the potential to inform the field of symbolic interactionism in general.

NOTES

1. See *Ethnic and Racial Studies* 36(6) for a debate about how to best theorize racism, including most centrally a debate about Omi and Winant's theory of racial formation (Omi and Winant 2013, 2015) and Feagin's theory of systematic racism (Feagin 2013; Feagin and Elias 2013), as well a call for intersectional approaches (Wingfield 2013).
2. This is a wide field of study with far too many citations to adequately reference in this short chapter. It may be useful to know, however, that studies of race and racism are conducted across a range of fields to address an equally wide range of topics such as education, the criminal justice system, sports, the economy, the child welfare system, healthcare, access to food, and more. Such research is conducted at micro-, meso-, and macro-levels.

REFERENCES

Aboud, F. 2008. "A Social-Cognitive Developmental Theory of Prejudice." Pp. 55–71 in *Handbook of Race, Racism, and the Developing Child*, edited by S. M. Quintana and C. McKown. Hoboken, NJ: John Wiley & Sons.

Adler, Peter and Patricia Adler. 1998. *Peer Power: Preadolescent Culture and Identity*. English Language edition. New Brunswick, NJ Rutgers University Press.

Alexander, Elizabeth C. 2017. "Don't Know or Won't Say? Exploring How Colorblind Norms Shape Item Nonresponse in Social Surveys." *Sociology of Race and Ethnicity* 4(3):400–16.

Andrews, David L., Robert Pitter, Detley Zwick, and Darren Ambrose. 1997. "Soccer's Racial Frontier: Sport and the Suburbanization of Contemporary America." Pp. 261–81 in *Entering the Field: New Perspectives on World Football*, edited by G. Armstrong and R. Giulianotti. Oxford: Berg.

Bettie, Julie. 2002. "Exceptions to the Rule: Upwardly Mobile White and Mexican American High School Girls." *Gender & Society* 16(3):403–22.

Blumer, Herbert. 1937. "Social Psychology." Pp. 144–97 in *Man and Society: A Substantive Introduction to the Social Science*, edited by Emerson Peter Schmidt. New York: Prentice Hall, Inc. https://brocku.ca/MeadProject/Blumer/Blumer_1937.html.

Blumer, Herbert. 1958. "Race Prejudice as a Sense of Group Position." *Pacific Sociological Review* 1(1):3–7.

Blumer, Herbert. 1969. *Symbolic Interactionism: Perspective and Method*. Berkeley: University of California Press.

Bobo, Lawrence D. 1999. "Prejudice as Group Position: Microfoundations of a Sociological Approach to Racism and Race Relations." *Journal of Social Issues* 55(3):445–72.

Bonilla-Silva, Eduardo. 1997. "Rethinking Racism: Toward a Structural Interpretation." *American Sociological Review* 62(3):465–80.

Bowman, Phillip J., and Cleopatra Howard. 1985. "Race-Related Socialization, Motivation, and Academic Achievement: A Study of Black Youths in Three-Generation Families." *Journal of the American Academy of Child Psychiatry* 24(2):134–41.

Brega, Angela G., and Lerita M. Coleman. 1999. "Effects of Religiosity and Racial Socialization on Subjective Stigmatization in African-American Adolescents." *Journal of Adolescence* 22(2):223–42.

Burton, Linda M., Eduardo Bonilla-Silva, Victor Ray, Rose Buckelew, and Elizabeth Hordge Freeman. 2010. "Critical Race Theories, Colorism, and the Decade's Research on Families of Color." *Journal of Marriage and Family* 72(3):440–59.

Byrd, W. Carson. 2017. *Poison in the Ivy: Race Relations and the Reproduction of Inequality on Elite College Campuses*. New Brunswick, NJ: Rutgers University Press.

Carman, Carol A. 2011. "Stereotypes of Giftedness in Current and Future Educators." *Journal for the Education of the Gifted* 34(5):790–812.

Carter, Prudence L. 2005. *Keepin' It Real: School Success Beyond Black and White*. Oxford: Oxford University Press.

Chancler, Lover L. M., Farrell J. Webb, and Chiquita Miller. 2017. "Role of the Black Grandmother in the Racial Socialization of Their Biracial Grandchildren." *Marriage & Family Review* 53(5):444–64.

Chao, Ruth K. 1994. "Beyond Parental Control and Authoritarian Parenting Style: Understanding Chinese Parenting through the Cultural Notion of Training." *Child Development* 65(4):1111–19.

Cheshire, Tamara. 2001. "Cultural Transmission in Urban American Indian Families." *American Behavioral Scientist* 44:1528–35.

Clark, Kenneth B. and Mamie K. Clark. 1939. "Segregation as a Factor in the Racial Identification of Negro Pre-School Children." *The Journal of Experimental Education* 8(2):161–63.

Collins, Patricia Hill. 2008. *Black Feminist Thought: Knowledge, Consciousness, and the Politics of Empowerment*. New York: Routledge.

Constantine, Madonna G. and Sha'Kemas M. Blackmon. 2002. "Black Adolescents' Racial Socialization Experiences Their Relations to Home, School, and Peer Self-Esteem." *Journal of Black Studies* 32(3):322–35.

Cornell, Stephen E., and Douglas Hartmann. 2006. *Ethnicity and Race: Making Identities in a Changing World*. 2nd edition. Thousand Oaks, CA: Pine Forge Press.

Corsaro, William. 2011. *The Sociology of Childhood*. 3rd ed. Los Angeles: Pine Forge Press.

Douglass, Sara, and Adriana J. Umaña-Taylor. 2015. "Development of Ethnic–Racial Identity among Latino Adolescents and the Role of Family." *Journal of Applied Developmental Psychology* 41:90–98.

Dow, Dawn Marie. 2019. *Mothering While Black*. Berkeley: University of California Press.

Du Bois, W. E. B. 2014. *The Philadelphia Negro (The Oxford W. E. B. Du Bois)*. Oxford: Oxford University Press.

Du Bois, W. E. B. 1995. *W. E. B. DuBois on Sociology and the Black Community*. Edited by D. S. Green and E. D. Driver. Chicago: University of Chicago Press.

Emerson, Robert M. 2001. *Contemporary Field Research: Perspectives and Formulations*. 2nd ed. Prospect Heights, IL: Waveland Press Inc.

Feagin, Joe. 2013. *Systemic Racism: A Theory of Oppression*. New York: Routledge.

Feagin, Joe, and Sean Elias. 2013. "Rethinking Racial Formation Theory: A Systemic Racism Critique." *Ethnic and Racial Studies* 36(6):931–60.

Feagin, Joe R. 2006. *Systemic Racism: A Theory of Oppression*. New York: Routledge.

Gartner, Meaghan, Lisa Kiang, and Andrew Supple. 2014. "Prospective Links between Ethnic Socialization, Ethnic and American Identity, and Well-Being among Asian-American Adolescents." *Journal of Youth and Adolescence* 43(10):1715–27.

Gilliam, Walter S., and Golan Shahar. 2006. "Preschool and Child Care Expulsion and Suspension: Rates and Predictors in One State." *Infants & Young Children* 19(3):228.

Golash-Boza, Tanya. 2013. "Does Racial Formation Theory Lack the Conceptual Tools to Understand Racism?" *Ethnic and Racial Studies* 36(6):994–99.

Hagerman, Margaret A. 2018. *White Kids: Growing Up with Privilege in a Racially Divided America*. New York: New York University Press.

Hagerman, Margaret A. 2019. "Racial Ideology and White Youth: From Middle Childhood to Adolescence:" *Sociology of Race and Ethnicity*. doi: 10.1177/2332649219853309.

Hagerman, Margaret Ann. 2016. "Reproducing and Reworking Colorblind Racial Ideology Acknowledging Children's Agency in the White Habitus." *Sociology of Race and Ethnicity* 2(1): 58–71.

Haney López, Ian. 1996. *White by Law: The Legal Construction of Race*. New York: New York University Press.

Hirschfeld, Lawrence A. 2008. "Children's Developing Conceptions of Race." Pp. 37–54 in *Handbook of Race, Racism, and the Developing Child*, edited by S. M. Quintana and C. McKown. Hoboken, NJ: John Wiley & Sons.

Holt, Thomas C. 1995. "Marking: Race, Race-Making, and the Writing of History." *The American Historical Review* 100(1):1–20.

Hughes, Diane. 2003. "Correlates of African American and Latino Parents' Messages to Children about Ethnicity and Race: A Comparative Study of Racial Socialization." *American Journal of Community Psychology* 31(1–2):15–33.

Hughes, Diane, James Rodriguez, Emilie P. Smith, Deborah J. Johnson, Howard C. Stevenson, and Paul Spicer. 2006. "Parents' Ethnic-Racial Socialization Practices: A Review of Research and Directions for Future Study." *Developmental Psychology* 42(5):747–70.

Hughes, Diane, and Lisa Chen. 1999. "The Nature of Parents' Race Related Communications to Children: A Developmental Perspective." Pp. 467–90 in *Child Psychology: A Handbook of Contemporary Issues*, edited by L. Balter and C. S. Tamis-LeMonda. Philadelphia: Taylor and Frances Group.

Hughes, Diane, and Deborah Johnson. 2001. "Correlates in Children's Experiences of Parents' Racial Socialization Behaviors." *Journal of Marriage and Family* 63(4):981–95.

Juang, Linda P., Hyung Chol Yoo, and Annabelle Atkin. 2017. "A Critical Race Perspective on an Empirical Review of Asian American Parental Racial-Ethnic Socialization." Pp. 11–35 in *Asian American Parenting*. Champaign, IL: Springer.

Kelly, D., P. Quinn, A. Slater, K. Lee, A. Gibson, M. Smith, L. Ge, and O. Pascalis. 2005. "Three-Month-Olds, but Not Newborns, Refer Own-Race Faces." *Developmental Science* 8:31–36.

Knight, George P., Martha E. Bernal, Camille A. Garza, Marya K. Cota, and Katheryn A. Ocampo. 1993. "Family Socialization and the Ethnic Identity of Mexican-American Children." *Journal of Cross-Cultural Psychology* 24(1):99–114.

Kozol, Jonathan. 2012. *Savage Inequalities: Children in America's Schools*. Reprint ed. New York: Broadway Books.

Ladson-Billings, Gloria, and William F. Tate. 2006. *Education Research in the Public Interest: Social Justice, Action, and Policy*. New York: Teachers College Press.

Lee, Jennifer, and Min Zhou. 2015. *The Asian American Achievement Paradox*. Russell Sage Foundation.

Lewis, Amanda E. 2003. *Race in the Schoolyard: Negotiating the Color Line in Classrooms and Communities*. New Brunswick, NJ: Rutgers University Press.

Lewis, Amanda E., and John B. Diamond. 2015. *Despite the Best Intentions: How Racial Inequality Thrives in Good Schools*. New York: Oxford University Press.

Lewis, Amanda E., Margaret A. Hagerman, and Tyrone A. Forman. 2019. "The Sociology of Race & Racism: Key Concepts, Contributions and Debates." *Equity & Excellence in Education* 52(1):29–46.

Lewis, Amanda E. and Michelle J. Manno. 2011. "The Best Education for Some: Race and Schooling in the United States Today." Pp. 93–109 in *State of White Supremacy: Racism, Governance, and the United States*, edited by M.-K. Jung, J. C. Vargas, and E. Bonilla-Silva. Stanford, CA: Stanford University Press.

Lewis, R. L'Heureux. 2010. "Speaking the Unspeakable: Youth Discourses on Racial Importance in School." Pp. 401–21 in *Children and Youth Speak for Themselves*. Vol. 13, *Sociological Studies of Children and Youth*, edited by H. Beth Johnson. Bingley, U.K: Emerald Group Publishing Limited.

McDevitt, Michael, and Steven Chaffee. 2002. "From Top-Down to Trickle-Up Influence Revisiting Assumptions about the Family in Political Socialization." *Political Communication* 19(3):281–301.

Meece, Judith, and Denise H. Daniels. 2007. *Child and Adolescent Development for Educators*. 3rd ed. New York: McGraw Hill.

Meiners, Erica R. 2007. *Right to Be Hostile: Schools, Prisons, and the Making of Public Enemies*. New York: Routledge.

Mills, Charles. 2010. "The Racist Roots of Liberalism." Presented at the University of King's College lecture series "Conceptions of Race in Philosophy, Literature and Art," Halifax.

Moore, Valerie Ann. 2002. "The Collaborative Emergence of Race in Children's Play: A Case Study of Two Summer Camps." *Social Problems* 49(1):58–78.

Morris, Aldon. 2017. *The Scholar Denied: W. E. B. Du Bois and the Birth of Modern Sociology*. 1st ed. Oakland: University of California Press.

Morris, Edward W. 2005. " 'Tuck in That Shirt!' Race, Class, Gender, and Discipline in an Urban School." *Sociological Perspectives* 48(1):25–48.

Mueller, Jennifer C. 2017. "Producing Colorblindness: Everyday Mechanisms of White Ignorance." *Social Problems* 64:219–38.

Noguera, Pedro A. 2003. *City Schools and the American Dream: Reclaiming the Promise of Public Education*. New York: Teachers College Press.

Oakes, Jeannie. 2005. *Keeping Track: How Schools Structure Inequality*, 2nd rev. ed. New Haven, CT: Yale University Press.

Oeur, Freeden Blume. 2018. *Black Boys Apart: Racial Uplift and Respectability in All-Male Public Schools*. Minneapolis: University of Minnesota Press.

Omi, Michael, and Howard Winant. 1994. *Racial Formation in the United States: From the 1960s to the 1990s*. 2nd ed. New York: Routledge.

Omi, Michael, and Howard Winant. 2013. "Resistance Is Futile?: A Response to Feagin and Elias." *Ethnic and Racial Studies* 36(6):961–73.

Omi, Michael, and Howard Winant. 2015. *Racial Formation in the United States*, 3rd ed. New York: Routledge.

Orbe, M. P. 1999. "Communicating About 'Race' in Interracial Families." Pp. 167–80 in *Communication, Race, and Family: Exploring Communication in Black, White, and Biracial Families*, edited by T. J. Socha and R. C. Diggs. Mahwah, NJ: Routledge.

Peters, Marie F. 1985. "Racial Socialization of Young Black Children." Pp. 159–73 in *Black Children: Social, Educational, and Parental Environments*, edited by H. P. McAdoo and J. L. McAdoo. Newbury Park, CA: SAGE.

Phinney, Jean S., and Victor Chavira. 1995. "Parental Ethnic Socialization and Adolescent Coping With Problems Related to Ethnicity." *Journal of Research on Adolescence* 5(1):31–53.

Posey-Maddox, Linn. 2014. *When Middle-Class Parents Choose Urban Schools: Class, Race, and the Challenge of Equity in Public Education*. Chicago: University of Chicago Press.

Quintana, Stephen M. 1998. "Children's Developmental Understanding of Ethnicity and Race." *Applied and Preventive Psychology* 7(1):27–45.

Quintana, Stephen M., and Elizabeth M. Vera. 1999. "Mexican American Children's Ethnic Identity, Understanding of Ethnic Prejudice, and Parental Ethnic Socialization." *Hispanic Journal of Behavioral Sciences* 21(4):387–404.

Raabe, T., and A. Beelmann. 2011. "Development of Ethnic, Racial, and National Prejudice in Childhood and Adolescence: A Multinational Meta-Analysis of Age Differences." *Child Development* 82(6):1715–37.

Rivas-Drake, Deborah. 2010. "Ethnic-Racial Socialization and Adjustment Among Latino College Students: The Mediating Roles of Ethnic Centrality, Public Regard, and Perceived Barriers to Opportunity." *Journal of Youth and Adolescence* 40(5):606–19.

Roberts, Dorothy. 2011. *Fatal Invention: How Science, Politics, and Big Business Re-Create Race in the Twenty-First Century*. New York: The New Press.

Rockquemore, Kerry, Ann and Tracey A. Laszloffy. 2005. *Raising Biracial Children*. Lanham, MD: AltaMira Press.

Roda, Allison. 2015. *Inequality in Gifted and Talented Programs: Parental Choices about Status, School Opportunity, and Second-Generation Segregation*. New York: Springer.

Rollins, Alethea, and Andrea G. Hunter. 2013. "Racial Socialization of Biracial Youth: Maternal Messages and Approaches to Address Discrimination." *Family Relations* 62(1):140–53.

Settersten, Richard A. Jr. 2002. "Socialization and the Life Course: New Frontiers in Theory and Research." *Advances in Life Course Research* 7:13–40.

Skiba, Russell J., Robert H. Horner, Choong-Geun Chung, M. Karega Rausch, Seth L. May, and Tary Tobin. 2011. "Race Is Not Neutral: A National Investigation of African American and Latino Disproportionality in School Discipline." *School Psychology Review* 40(1):85–107.

Thomas, Anita Jones, and Sha'Kema M. Blackmon. 2015. "The Influence of the Trayvon Martin Shooting on Racial Socialization Practices of African American Parents." *Journal of Black Psychology* 41(1):75–89.

Thomas, William I., and Dorothy S. Thomas. 1928. *The Child in America: Behavior Problems and Programs*. New York: Knopf.

Thorne, Barrie. 1993. *Gender Play: Girls and Boys in School*. New Brunswick, NJ: Rutgers University Press.

Threlfall, Jennifer Mary. 2016. "Parenting in the Shadow of Ferguson: Racial Socialization Practices in Context." *Youth and Society*. 50(2): 255–73.

Tyson, Karolyn, ed. 2011. *Integration Interrupted: Tracking, Black Students, and Acting White after Brown*. 1st ed. New York: Oxford University Press.

Underhill, Megan. 2017. "Parenting during Ferguson: Making Sense of White Parents' Silence. " *Ethnic and Racial Studies* 41(11):1934–1951.

Van Ausdale, Debra, and Joe R. Feagin. 2001. *The First R: How Children Learn Race and Racism*. Lanham, MD: Rowman & Littlefield Publishers.

Vittrup, Brigitte. 2018. "Color Blind or Color Conscious? White American Mothers' Approaches to Racial Socialization." *Journal of Family Issues* 39(3):668–92.

Warikoo, Natasha K., and Janine de Novais. 2015. "Colour-Blindness and Diversity: Race Frames and Their Consequences for White Undergraduates at Elite US Universities." *Ethnic and Racial Studies* 38(6):860–76.

Whitaker, Tracy R., and Cudore L. Snell. 2016. "Parenting While Powerless: Consequences of 'the Talk.'" *Journal of Human Behavior in the Social Environment* 26(3–4):303–9.

Winant, Howard. 2000. "Race and Race Theory." *American Review of Sociology* 26:169–85.

Wingfield, Adia Harvey. 2013. "Comment on Feagin and Elias." *Ethnic and Racial Studies* 36(6):989–93.

Winkler, Erin N. 2008. "'It's Like Arming Them': African American Mothers' Views on Racial Socialization." Pp. 211–41 in *The Changing Landscape of Work and Family in the American Middle Class: Reports from the Field*, edited by E. Rudd and L. Descartes. Lanham: Lexington Books.

Winkler, Erin N. 2012. *Learning Race, Learning Place: Shaping Racial Identities and Ideas in African American Childhoods*. New Brunswick, NJ: Rutgers University Press.

Yasui, Miwa, Thomas J. Dishion, Elizabeth Stormshak, and Alison Ball. 2015. "Socialization of Culture and Coping with Discrimination Among American Indian Families: Examining Cultural Correlates of Youth Outcomes." *Journal of the Society for Social Work and Research* 6(3):317–41.

CHAPTER 23

GENDER AND EMBODIMENT AS NEGOTIATED RELATIONS

S. L. CRAWLEY AND ASHLEY GREEN

RECENTLY, the *New York Times* published an article on "How Queer Women Powered the Suffrage Movement" (Salam 2020). Attempting to redress the erasure from history of participation by women with same-sex intimate relationships, the article offers a laudable effort to write an inclusive history of suffrage. The problem is "queer women" most certainly did not participate in the suffrage movement. The term *queer women* is a late twentieth-century invention. While women with same-sex intimate partnerships of the early twentieth century ought to be documented, they would not have called themselves queer—an epithet of an earlier era, which queer theorists and activists have tried to reclaim nearly a hundred years later. This anachronism points to a common tendency to assume the fixity of sexual and gender identities across time. Indeed, it points to the very need to trace the malleability of sexual and gender identity lexicons, demonstrating how gender and embodiment are negotiated, relational, localized, and constantly in flux. This chapter begins by tracing the twenty-first-century gender-identity revolution and its historical underpinnings to waves of intellectual movements, illustrating the interpretive character of identity work. We then trace the development of gender theory including some of the theoretical skirmishes among gender scholars that are also common throughout sociology and across disciplines. We conclude by briefly suggesting potential future directions.

IDENTITY PROLIFERATION, NEGOTIATION, AND RESISTANCE

In the everyday world, gender is often referenced as an identity—a personal characteristic. Yet for interpretive[1] scholars, it is identity *work*—the practice of announcing "I am non-binary" or being held accountable to "you are a woman"—which constitutes gendered embodiments. Gender then is constituted by pervasive and thoroughgoing situational organizing practices of meaning-making in our worlds that are always relational and emergent among people in institutional contexts at historical moments, and not a feature of individuals. Identities do not denote types of people but, rather, comprise organizing practices constantly produced between and among us—which can be normalizing or resistant. Every day interactively, people make meaning of the bodies and embodiments we encounter. Of course, gendered embodiment is also always intersectional, transnational, racializing, and class based, and it comprises complex connections between bodies, language, and practices under governmental and medical surveillance. Gender, sexuality, and bodies reference different yet connected concepts in complex, historically specific, and localized ways. The recent proliferation of identity terms demonstrates how gender is constantly in flux, processual, and subject to resistance, though deeply connected to local stocks of knowledge and intertwined with academic lexicons. Here, we ask: what can the changing lexicon of non-heteronormative identities tell us about identity work?

A basic premise of queer theory is that identities emerge in history relative to the discursive and material context of moments (Crawley and Broad 2008; D'Emilio 1993; Foucault 1978). Terms emerge as self-reference, epithets, and/or markers of collective identity. Figure 23.1 (below) shows a Timeline of the (US) "Queer" Lexicon, which—though not exhaustive—demonstrates the propinquity between modernist science and mundane identities. "Thought bubbles" place academic ideas chronologically in relation to (US) identities taken up in everyday usage over about 150 years. The timeline demonstrates the inextricable links between genders, sexualities, and bodies (wherein the terms above the timeline are related to gender, the terms below it are related to sexuality or bodies, and the italicized terms emerge from racial minority communities). This timeline shows waves, recessions, and sometimes recursions of identities in moments.

In the late 1860s, newly minted modernist scientists "discovered" *hermaphrodites* (a term now recognized as an epithet, referred to by the 1990s as *intersex*)—people whose bodies do not fit the binary medical classification system of female and male (Dreger 1998). About the same time, the *homosexual* was "invented" followed by the classification of the *heterosexual* in early 1890s (Foucault 1978). Female *sexual inverts* were recognized about the same era but not referred to as *lesbian* until about the 1920s, roughly in coincidence with Freud's "discovery" that women have sexual desire (Faderman 1991). In the 1930s and 1940s, as the early homophile movement began advocating that homosexuals were good people deserving of civil rights, *gay*—meaning all things pleasurable—became associated with male communities who practiced drag, camp, and "impersonation," but who were not referred to as *gay men*—until after WWII (Chauncey 1994). *Butch* and *femme* were self-references as well as erotic identities and community-organizing devices, among primarily white lesbians about the same era (Kennedy and Davis 1993). Masculine African American women often used *stud* and *bulldagger*—an epithet turned self-reference—rather than *butch*. In the 1950s, doctors began using medical science to manipulate bodies and subsequently defined the term *transsexual*—an

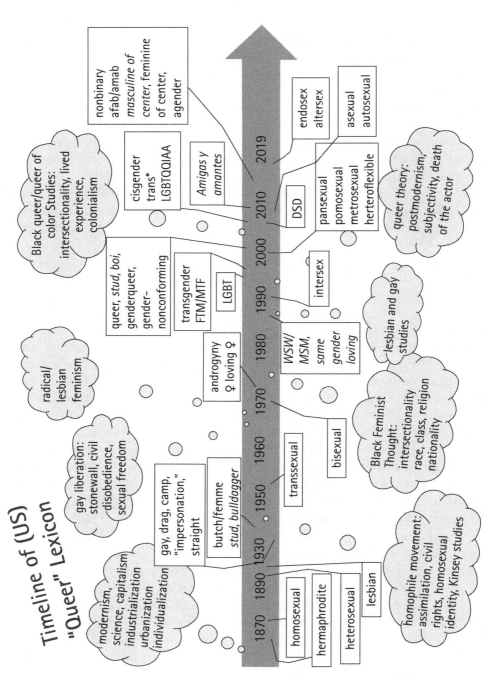

FIGURE 23.1. Timeline of (US) "Queer" Lexicon

early medicalizing term that recognized disjunctures between essentialized notions of bodies and self-definition (Stryker 2008). As it becomes clear that gender and sexual identities emerge and change in historical context, subsequent monikers illuminate how academic lexicons also pave the way for new identity categories and identity work.

Both feminisms and self-styled gay and lesbian studies developed through the 1970s and 1980s. Radical or lesbian feminisms generated women-centered, politicized identities such as *women-loving women* and *androgyny*—political strategies to fight patriarchy, even against gay men (Faderman 1991). Women's and men's communities were often separate, until the AIDS epidemic coalesced women and men to fight for their lives—resulting in references to *gay and lesbian* communities, which by the mid-1990s had morphed into *LGBT* (adding *bisexual* and *transgender*). *Transgender* (as opposed to *transgendered*) indicates that gender identity is a pervasive and thoroughgoing identity, not an adjectival modifier or a variable characteristic. *MTF* or *FTM* recognized that the gender experiences of trans people are different based on sex assigned at birth.

Meanwhile, though Black feminist thought (Hill Collins 1990; hooks 1989; Lorde 1984) was catching on in the academy even among many white academics, African American communities wishing to distance themselves from racism within white LGBT communities instead used terms such as *WSW* and *MSM* (women-seeking-women and men-seeking-men) and *same gender loving*—terms used to avoid totalizing identities and rather focused on desire and sexual practices. Especially during the early part of the AIDS epidemic, clinical care workers often focused on those terms to entice the widest audience possible to see themselves potentially at risk and get testing and treatment. Today some men reject the MSM subjectivity because it seems to come from healthcare workers more so than community members (Liu 2020).

Around the early 1990s, as a critique of Western binary thinking and normalizing regimes of power, queer theory encouraged the proliferation of identities as well as the refusal to claim identity. Counterintuitively, *queer* became an anti-identity along with *genderqueer* and *gender nonconforming*. Terms for sexuality like *pomosexual* (postmodern, unclassifiable sexuality) and *pansexual* (which points to sexual freedom) rejected focus on a desired body/object. Intersex activism began in earnest about that time, recognizing that embodiment exists in nuances far beyond the binary medical classificatory scheme of female versus male, later morphing into terms such as *DSD* (differences of sex development), which purposefully desexualizes the body generated to quell fears of parents of intersex children (Davis 2015).

Subsequent to queer theory's wide reception in academia, by the late 2000s identity terms included not only *queer* and *transgender* but *trans** (the asterisk referencing online search nomenclature), *cisgender* (people whose gender matches their expectations assigned at birth [Schilt and Westbrook 2009]), and *asexual* and *autosexual* (those not in search of a partner; taking pleasure in one's own body), and the community acronym grew to *LGBTQQIAA+* (lesbian, gay, bisexual, transgender, queer, questioning, intersex, asexual, allies, and more). Building on Black feminist thought, critiques of the whiteness of queer scholarship such as Black queer studies (Cohen 1997; Johnson and Henderson 2005) and queer of color studies (Ferguson 2004; Muñoz 1999) as well as work focused on transnational migration and coloniality pointed out the insularity of US scholarship (Patil 2018) by introducing terms like *amigas y amantes* ("sexually nonconforming Latinas" [Acosta 2013]) among many other important works. As of the mid 2010s, even more common terms include *non-binary* (which rejects "the binary" as one who is neither man nor woman but may be masculine or feminine appearing), *AFAB/AMAB* (assigned female or male at birth), *masculine-* or *feminine-of-center,* and *agender* (no gender identity, rather than one at odds with gender assigned at birth), which seem to point directly to gender theory. While some terms common from the mid-1990s like *MTF* (male to female) and *FTM* (female to male) seem to have retracted from common usage, new terms like *cisgender* and *endosex* (not intersex) arise to mark the previously unmarked category (Brekhus in this volume), and other terms reference the production of identities within virtual realities like *altersex* (imaginative, fictional, and fantastical body types that are not physically possible). And, of course, after the mid-2000s and beyond, one should never assume a pronoun, as public discourse and etiquette now regularly draws on frames of gender neutrality and gender inclusivity (Saguy and Williams 2019).

Though *straight* emerged in the early 1940s, the unmarked identities of *heterosexual* woman and man are not included on this timeline, in part because the lexicon of the neutral category has not changed considerably. What is understood to comprise normative femininity and masculinity, however, has changed dramatically over 150 years, becoming somewhat more egalitarian, flexible, and fluid, as exemplified by the newer terms *metrosexual* (urban straight men who dress fashionably) and *heteroflexible* (largely but not entirely straight-identified). It is telling that the heteronormative lexicon remains unchanged while the normative expectations of the unmarked category change demonstrably.

This timeline demonstrates *gender identity as negotiated relations* specific to historical moments and specific communities. Ultimately about negotiating a livable life in a culture of normativity and surveillance, identity work can engage accommodation to normativity or political resistance (Cook 2006). We return to this point shortly, but first outline a very brief history of gender theory in sociology.

The Origins of Gender Sociology, or Why "Socialization" and "Gender Roles" Don't Work

Rooted in structural functionalism, early theories of gender focused on "socialization," which was purported to result in two distinct "gender roles" (Parsons 1943), claiming that agents of socialization such as families, peers, schools, and the media teach children from an early age what is expected of them based on their sex assigned at birth—women as gentle, quiet, caregivers; men as strong, leaders and breadwinners of the family—and no recognition of variability. Under the socialization model, roles are purportedly necessary in order to keep the family unit in a state of equilibrium (Jackson and Scott 2002), are characterized by assumed "innate processes" that are overly deterministic (Stanley and Wise 1983:277), and presume consensus by individuals to the roles and between women and men (Stacey and Thorne 1985). None of this can explain varied gendered expectations by culture and across time, widely varying individual practice, or even social change within the United States. Further, the socialization model continues to put the focus on gender acquisition as individual development rather than recognizing the social ordering and production of gender (Connell 1987, 1995; Thorne 1993). More determinist of a binary notion of (heteronormative) gender than explanatory of extant variability (and entirely silent on sexuality), there was little "social" about the androcentric sociological gender theory of the early twentieth century. Challenging these functionalist perspectives, early feminist sociologists argued that gender is much more pervasive throughout social experience—not simply consensus-based gender roles. Following the critical turn, feminist scholars challenged early androcentric sociology, seeking to theorize ways in which gender is ordered by power dynamics, interactionally, institutionally, and structurally (Mann 2012).

Opening a now vast literature about women and work, Komarovsky (1946) identified inconsistencies in women's "sex roles" between that of the homemaker and the "career girl." Bernard (1972, 1976) examined the restructuring of sex roles, challenging the assumption that roles could be preassigned at birth, and recognized that marriage for men was more beneficial than marriage for women. Smith (1974, 1987) critiqued mainstream sociological theorizing as implicitly gendered because, as a conceptual practice, it is abstracted from material, situated practices in everyday life, especially the feeding, cleaning, and healthcare of bodies, which is typically prescribed as women's work. Smith (1990:18–19) explains:

> It has been a condition of a man's being able to enter and become absorbed in the conceptual mode, and to forget the dependence of his being in that mode upon his bodily existence, that he does not have to focus . . . upon his bodily existence. . . . At almost every point women mediate for men . . . the relationship between the conceptual mode of action . . . and the actual material conditions upon which it depends.

Some of the most productive early critiques of androcentric and individualist gender theory came in terms of unsettling beliefs in the supposed naturalness of bodies and practices by microsociologists. Not so much interested in gender as in writing a unique theory of self, Goffman (1979) articulated the performance of gender—a social arrangement that was not of individual choice or volition but of ritualized "impression management" (Brickell 2006; Treviño 2003:10–11). Gender was simply one empirical example shoring up Goffman's thesis of how the "interaction order" is established through cooperative performances. Using his dramaturgical metaphor (Goffman 1959), gender was unhinged from expectations of innate expression or personal choice and taken up as constitutive of the interaction order.

Similarly, Garfinkel's (1967) ethnomethodology contributes to gender theorizing via his archetypal case of Agnes: a young male-bodied person who lived successfully as a woman (e.g., West and Zimmerman 1987; Stokoe 2006; O'Brien 2016). Garfinkel's goal was not to study bodies or gender but rather *to create a new sociology*—one that focuses on how people as active and pragmatic agents use common-sense reasoning to make sense of their worlds. Hence, his interest in Agnes was not whether she "really" was or was not a woman, but the illustrative case of social order superseding what had been seen as putatively biological: that is, how it was possible for anyone *to accomplish* woman or man. Assuming no inherent truth, Garfinkel's focus on Agnes allowed him to "understand how membership in a sex category is sustained across a variety of practical circumstances and contingencies, at the same time preserving the sense that such membership is a natural, normal moral fact of life" (Zimmerman 1992:195). Ethnomethodology offered just the theory needed for gender scholars to overturn essentialist logics of the innateness of gender. Rather than servants to a functionally necessary survival system, people produce gender relationally and in situated social contexts (O'Brien 2016). Though neither theorized with feminist intentions, Goffman's and Garfinkel's new schools of thought— both based in everyday life—offered much for feminist scholars seeking to articulate a critique of gender, and nascent feminist gender theory began to proliferate.

GENDER AS INTERACTIONAL ACCOMPLISHMENT

Following Garfinkel, Kessler and McKenna (1978) explicitly utilized ethnomethodology to show how people make gender attributions every time they meet someone new—assuming that the person is either a man or a woman based on perceived characteristics, such as manner of dress, length of hair, and body size and shape. Pushing beyond Garfinkel and turning the "science" of gender on its head, Kessler and McKenna (1978:163) posit that "our seeing of two genders leads to the 'discovery' of biological, psychological, and social differences."

Subsequently engaging a combination of Goffman's and Garfinkel's insights, West and Zimmerman (1987:137) explicate a comprehensive theory of "doing gender" as pervasive, everyday accomplishment in which gender as a practice is "unavoidable" because it is not just individual but *relational*. Gender is not *what one is* but *what one does* in coordination with others. Gender is a relational engagement wherein each of us produces gender displays or performances—that is, "doing gender"—of which *others* take account and hold us accountable—hence, it is interactional—between us, among us. Because the physiology of our actual bodies typically cannot be known in everyday interaction unless stated outright (or unless people are unclothed such as during sex or a medical examination), others tend to base gender attribution not on actual physiology but rather based on assumed "sex category"—a binary assumption of maleness or femaleness. Once sex category is assigned (regardless of its alignment with bodily features), individuals are then *held accountable by others* for engaging in appropriate displays of gender and giving accounts of gender appropriateness (Hollander 2013). "The man 'does' masculinity by, for example, taking the woman's arm to guide her across a street, and she 'does' being feminine by consenting to be guided and not initiating such behavior with a man" (West and Zimmerman 1987:135). Additionally, West and Zimmerman claim that, by doing gender, men and women are in fact reinforcing that idea that sex-based differences are natural. West and Zimmerman never specifically take opinion on the "realness" of so-called biological sex, except to note that male and female are merely medical classifications. Individuals can offer conformist gender displays or they can resist, however, they will be assessed in every instance. Now-classic ethnographies demonstrate *gender as an accomplishment* in a wide variety of situated practices, especially schooling (Cahill 1986; Thorne 1993).

Judith Butler and Queer Theory

Gaining notoriety at nearly the same time as ethnomethodological gender theories, queer theory turned toward an even more radical, poststructuralist approach to the influence of language and discourse, calling into question categories like "woman" altogether (Butler 1990). Whereas early feminist theorists championed the importance of women's standpoint, Butler argued that it was the (compulsory) discursive practice of reiteratively citing gendered categories that produced their existence. Queer theory is situated in a poststructuralist project that seeks to deconstruct regulatory discourses, in which power is situated, especially with regard to sexuality (Foucault 1975).[2] Borrowing from speech-act theory, Butler (1990, 1993) defined gender performativity as more than merely performing what one understands to be traits attributed to "man" or "woman." Rather, it is the continual repetition of such acts and the citing of such acts as "naturally" binary that produce the perception that gender feels innate, thus reinforcing the discourse. Outlining gender as "a kind of imitation for which there is no original" (Butler 1991:20–21), Butler points out that there is no authentic, bodily origin of gender: only reiterations of discursive practices. The "limits [of gendered possibilities] are always set within the terms of a hegemonic cultural discourse predicated on binary structures" (Butler 1990:13)—hence, it is gender *performativity* that creates the belief in the thing we call sex difference. Butler's work has received wide appeal among feminists outside sociology and some appeal within sociology. Still some sociological critics argued that Butler's largely literary focus falls short of understanding how gender is actively produced *as practice in interaction* especially as relational, joint action, rather than individual, discursive acts (Burkitt 1998; Jackson and Scott 2000).

GENDER AS INSTITUTION OR SOCIAL STRUCTURE

The linguistic and performative focus of both queer and ethnomethodological work caused more traditional sociologists to balk, suggesting that such work is limited to a micro-level analysis. In particular, some theorists argue that, by analyzing gender as a social institution, sociologists can better understand the pervasiveness of gender as a structural system of oppression. Lorber (1994:1) argues that gender is "an institution that establishes patterns of expectations for individuals, orders the social processes of everyday life, is built into the major social organizations of society . . . and is also an entity in and of itself." Though not disagreeing with interactionist theorists, Lorber (1994:10) argues that "real change would mean a conscious reordering of the organizing principles of social life . . . [and that] change is unlikely to be deep-seated unless the pervasiveness of the social institution of gender and its social construction are made explicit." Similarly, Risman (2004:433) refers to gender as social structure, stating that it "has consequences on three dimensions: (1) At the individual level, for the development of gendered selves; (2) during interaction as men and women face different cultural expectations even when they fill the identical structural positions; and (3) in institutional domains where explicit regulations regarding resource distribution and material goods are gender specific." Thus, Risman (2004) argues that it is not enough to merely look at gender as an interactional achievement, sociologists of gender must also attend to the ways in which gender exists as part of a larger social structure rooted in power dynamics. Flipping the causal direction, Ridgeway and Smith-Lovin (1999) claim that gender as a social institution has created an unequal relationship between men and women, which always permeates gendered interactions as a result. Ridgeway and Correll (2004) argue that, like all social institutions, gender is internalized and thus reconstituted through interaction, which is what allows it to persist across time.

Though an institutional focus is warranted, many criticisms of the ethnomethodological focus of West and Zimmerman's definitional article are wrongheaded, seemingly based on various misreadings of the theoretical underpinnings of ethnomethodology.[3] Some readings of ethnomethodology falsely dichotomize it as merely a micro theory. However, ethnomethodology was always focused on the connections between interaction and broader social order, in particular presuming that face-to-face interactions are always already of the institutional order (Fairchild 2004; Hollander 2013; West and Zimmerman 2009). Similarly, a series of criticisms focusing on "undoing gender" (Deutsch 2007; Risman 2009) wrongly critiqued ethnomethodology for focusing only on gender conformity, suggesting that it left no room for understanding social change or resistance. These critiques tend to fall into a language that assumes a liberal, rational, individuated actor making willful choices. Ethnomethodology does not assume a rational actor, but rather a different vision of the social actor—*a practical actor*—one who uses available mundane, common-sense truth narratives but puts them together in artful ways: *in practice, in interaction, relationally.*

More productive approaches might be termed synthesis approaches in which gender is envisioned as *process and practice*, which connects interaction to institutional settings. Martin (2004) argues that a mutually constitutive understanding of institutions and interactions should be included in the criteria for establishing "gender as social institution," positing that it is imperative to deconstruct the false binary created between micro and macro theories in order to understand how gendered expectations are embedded in institutionalized systems of power. For Martin, social institutions are organized by rules

GENDER AND EMBODIMENT AS NEGOTIATED RELATIONS   411

and norms, ordered by power relations, and internalized and embodied by members of social groups, hence persist across time yet also constantly changing. Similarly, Connell (1995:71) articulates "gender as a structure of social practice" in which, imbedded in historical process, "Gender is social practice that constantly refers to bodies and what bodies do, it is not social practice reduced to the body." In this rendering, gender importantly is understood as an order of relations, not individualized acts.[4] Because gender as practice remains a salient direction for gender theory, we turn to some of the specificities of practices of femininities and masculinities before we return to future directions for gender theory.

HEGEMONIC MASCULINITY AND EMPHASIZED FEMININITY AS RELATIONAL PRACTICE

What specifically does it mean to "do" masculinity or femininity? In what ways can masculinity and femininity reinforce or subvert gendered expectations? Much current scholarship builds on Raewyn Connell's (1987) concepts of *hegemonic masculinity* and *emphasized femininity* as relational practice. Centering the critique around the Gramscian concept of hegemony, hegemonic masculinity is a practice of masculinity as the accepted form of patriarchal dominance to which both women and men acquiesce. In any setting, the specific practice of masculinity is simply the commonly assumed (hence, hegemonic) form for that setting. Connell (1987:183) asserts, "there is an ordering of versions of femininity and masculinity at the level of the whole society . . . [and] their interrelation is centered on a single structural fact, the global dominance of men over women," thus recognizing both the dominance of masculinity as well as its necessary *relation* to practices of femininity as a world order. Connell (1987:183) argues that subordinate masculinities are constructed in relation to hegemonic masculinity—some that are compliant and others that are subordinated or marginalized—while no form of femininity can be hegemonic because femininities are either "defined around compliance with this subordination [to men]" or defined by "strategies of resistance or forms of noncompliance."

Hegemonic and Subordinate Masculinities

Specifically, masculinity as practice encourages boys and men to constantly and consciously measure their physical embodiment against each other, especially through the requisite teaching of sports (Connell 1983:19, 27, emphasis added):

> To be an adult male is distinctly *to occupy space*, to have a physical presence in the world. Walking down the street, I square my shoulders and covertly *measure myself* against other men . . . what it means to be masculine is, quite literally, *to embody force, to embody competence*.

Further, *masculinity as homophobia* is the practice and surveillance of a specific masculine ideal by men for men (Kimmel 1994), not homophobia in the traditional sense of fear or hatred of homosexuals, but men's fear that other men will emasculate them. Importantly, masculinity is not only in hegemonic form but rather multiple experiences of masculinity produced as a result of struggles in relations to the hegemonic standard—"white, middle-class, early middle aged, heterosexual men with a recent record in sports" (Kimmel 1994:125), as well as attempts to resist normative gendered expectations. Some forms of masculinity may be complicit in maintaining the dominance of the gender system without replicating hegemonic masculinity. For example, Crawley (1998, 2011; Crawley, Foley, and Shehan 2008) coins the term *vicarious masculinity* to describe non-athletic men's propensity to align themselves with elite male athletes' bodies to suggest some connection, not of actual physical ability but simply by virtue of maleness. Importantly, the relational character of the concept of hegemony suggests that there is no fixed substance of hegemonic masculinity; it is simply the agreed-upon standard of dominance within a particular cultural space (Messerschmidt 2019)—which ensures the flexibility of practices as well as their nimbleness to retain dominance. For example, Ward (2015) points out that many common practices among men who identify as heterosexual involve touching other men's genitals, all the while vehemently declaring they are "not gay."

Yet there is room for resistance. Connell (1992:748) argues that homosexual masculinity resists normative expectations of hegemonic masculinity. Gay men's masculinity is a form of resistance—"in these men's lives a condition of freedom" (Connell 1992:748)—that subverts normative, hegemonic expectations of masculinity. However, this subversion of hegemonic masculinity has its limitations. Connell (1992) also notes that gay men still upheld gendered expectations by doing traditional masculinity in other ways, particularly by engaging in monogamous relationships, and by being dismissive or hostile toward feminists. Drawing on the Bhabhian notion of "hybridity," Demetriou (2001:348) offers up the concept of "hybrid masculinities," which are a "constant appropriation of diverse elements from various masculinities that makes the hegemonic bloc capable of reconfiguring itself and adapting to the specificities of new historical conjunctures." An example of one such hybrid masculinity is suggested by Bridges (2014:79) in his study of straight men who "appear to blur the boundaries between gay and straight through assimilating a variety of gay aesthetics," though he cautions against seeing this as "an indication of declining levels of gender and sexual inequality." Additionally, scholars such as Halberstam (1998:9) have theorized female masculinity as having the potential to "challenge hegemonic models of gender conformity," as has Crawley (2002) and Crawley and Willman (2018).

Whereas homosexual masculinity may be posited as subverting hegemonic masculinity, homophobia impacts in the "appropriate" doing of masculinity. In her study of high school boys, Pascoe (2007:13) found that "masculinity is an identity that respondents think of as related to the male body but as not necessarily specific to the male body." In other words, respondents believe masculinity can only be achieved in relation to "male-ness," but not all people who are perceived as male-bodied can achieve masculinity. More specifically, those who are not able to achieve this goal of masculinity are faced with "the threatening specter of the fag" (Pascoe 2007:81). While this devalued understanding of masculinity is often feminized, it is not always related to sexual identity. According to Pascoe (2007:58), "while it was not necessarily acceptable to be gay, at least a man who was gay could do other things that would render him acceptably masculine. A fag, by the very definition of the word, could not be masculine."

An important advantage in theorizing gender as practice(s) is the potential for engaging intersectionality to focus on the specificity of practices across genders as they intersect with race, class, sexuality, religious background, nation/location, age, ability, and so forth. Building on the work of Connell (1992) and Bridges (2014), scholars have analyzed Black masculinity (Dow 2016), emotions and masculinity in migrant men from Guatemala in the United States (Montes 2013), understandings of Western masculinity outside of Western contexts (Liu 2019), and the relationship between women and the construction of masculinity in Mexico (Gutmann 1997), just to name a few. Collectively, these scholars challenge the notion of a static masculinity, demonstrating instead that understandings of masculinities are constantly changing and being renegotiated in relation to a hegemonic ideal as well as femininities and many other forms of masculinities.

Femininities

Quite the opposite of bodily empowerment, the embodiment of *emphasized femininity* is *inhibited intentionality* (Young 1980)—the tendency of girls to concentrate motion in one body part, rather than fully extending the entire body. Young (1980:153) posits, "The girl learns actively to hamper her movements. She is told that she must be careful not to get hurt, not to get dirty, not to tear her clothes." Whereas masculinity is the competitive control and acquisition of space, femininity is intended to be passive compliance in favor of becoming an object to be viewed, not an active agent. Femininity, then, is not hegemonic but rather an emphasized display of beauty that serves as an ideal relation to hegemonic masculinity. Similarly, it is not requisite practice for all women but rather establishes a normative, hierarchal relation with those who do not achieve it.

A number of scholars have theorized power relations that exist within and between differing experiences of femininity. Schippers (2007:94) theorizes what they term *hegemonic femininity* that "consists of the characteristics defined as womanly that establish and legitimate a hierarchical and complementary relationship to hegemonic masculinity and that, by doing so, guarantee the dominant position of men and the subordination of women." Schippers (2007) offers up three pariah femininities: the Lesbian, the Bitch, and the Slut. Pariah femininities are "simultaneously stigmatized and feminized" (and notably all sexualized) and are regarded as "contaminating to the relationship between masculinity and femininity" (Schippers 2007:95–96); "When a woman is authoritative, she is not masculine; she is a bitch—both feminine and undesirable" (2007:95). Pariah femininities are neither feminine nor masculine, because when a woman takes on traits that are associated with masculinity, they are no longer desirable. However, Schippers's "pariah femininities" are limited to white, Western understandings of femininity.

Pyke and Johnson (2003:50–51) posit that there is a hegemonic femininity among other femininities that is racialized as white. The Korean-American and Vietnamese-American women they interviewed "treat gender as a racialized feature of bodies" and resist the racialized stereotypes of Asian women by conforming to the hegemonic standard (Pyke and Johnson 2003:50). Hamilton et al. (2019) attempt a pivot away from Connell's notion of gender order by arguing that Connell's work cannot accommodate intersectional relations. Instead, they posit theories of white femininities as domination among women and some men based on Hill Collins's notion of the matrix of domination. Messerschmidt (2020) responds by arguing that Hamilton and colleagues (among others) critique Connell's work improperly based on a misreading that Connell's work was always only about gender as a single axis form of oppression, citing many ways in which Connell's work has been read and used as relations among women and men in variously intersectional contexts. Similarly, both Bettie (2003) and Trautner (2005) explicate unequal relations of class among women's embodiments of femininities. Offering a transnational, intersectional lens, Lara (2005:12) argues that "*la bruja*" has been constructed by colonizers as evil, in which " '*la bruja*' [is] a female practitioner of spiritual, sexual, and healing knowledge" that "symbolizes power outside of patriarchy's control that potentially challenges a sexist status quo." This construction of femininity resists colonial constructions of *la bruja* in a way that embraces positive representations of femininity. Other scholars have focused on racialized femininity in the context of embodiments of nationalism (Balogun 2012), as well as commodification of femininity and Brazilian "body culture" by Brazilian women entrepreneurs (Malheiros and Padilla 2014).

Furthermore, scholars have theorized resistance and embodied femininity in relation to non-heterosexual identities. According to Eves (2004:481), "the status of butch/femme as the most recognizable lesbian archetype is important in establishing lesbian visibility and space." But when embodied by bi or queer women who are not in relationships with women, femininity can lead to invisibility of their queer identity. In her study on cisgender women who are in relationships with trans men, Pfeffer (2014:31) demonstrates that "many cis women participants described being (mis) recognized as heterosexual as not only personally invalidating but as alienating from queer communities of social support and belonging." Daly, King, and Yeadon-Lee (2018) found that some bisexual women are "style chameleons" who often switch between what participants referred to as "lesbian" style and femininity, depending on the setting or who they are dating at the time. To a lesser extent, the concept of "femme-ness" has been theorized as a conscious embodiment of femininity by those who do not seek to fit the hetero/cis-normative ideal (Hoskin 2017; Nestle 1992). According to Hoskin (2017:100), "femme is the abnormal occupation of feminine normality, meaning femininity embodied by those to whom recognition as feminine is culturally denied or who do not comply with norms of 'proper womanhood.'" Specifically, Hoskin (2017:99) is referring to "sassy queer men; unapologetically sexual straight women; trans women; crip bodied femmes who refuse to be desexualized or degendered; and femmes of colour who refuse to approximate white beauty norms," as well as the cisgender lesbian women who have historically identified as femme (Nestle 1992).

ARE WE STILL DOING GENDER?: THE EMERGENCE OF TRANS, NON-BINARY, AND GENDERQUEER RESISTANCE

Our timeline above illustrates that, subsequent to the introduction of queer theory, scholars and activists alike returned to Garfinkel's original move by critiquing normative embodiment by viewing it through the lens of those understood as non-normative. Gender theory turned to intersex, trans, and queer embodiments to discuss and disrupt presumed connections between bodies and notions of essentialism. Kessler (1998) and Fausto-Sterling (1993, 2000, 2005) turned the lens on how scientists and medical doctors produce normative, binary notions about bodies and biologies that then constitute medical "truths." Kessler studied not intersex people, but rather the ways doctors and medical texts construct "natural" bodies as binary femaleness and maleness, thus erasing the fairly common natural birth of people who are not easily medically classifiable as female or male. Preves (2003) and Davis (2015) interviewed intersex people about their lived experiences of being medicalized by doctors, often in compliance with parents. A biologist who foregrounds the body as a system rather than a collection of separable parts, Fausto-Sterling (1993, 2000, 2005) offered an entire body of work that challenged such notions as two definitive sexes, the existence of a natural body unmarked by social experience, hormones as sex-specific and relegated to "sex organs," and the belief in bodily difference as uncommon. All this work had great impact on how people envision and practice gender in recent decades.

In the late 1990s and early 2000s, the term *genderqueer* began to grow in popularity as a way to describe gendered experiences that did not fall within the man/woman (masculine/feminine) binary. The earliest use of the term in academic literature was the anthology *GenderQueer: Voices from Beyond the Sexual Binary*, edited by Joan Nestle, Clare Howell, and Riki Wilchins (2002). In the decade and a half since, a number of studies have been published on people who articulate genderqueer identities or nonbinary identity, among other identities such as agender, bigender, and genderfluid, to name a few (Barbee and Schrock 2019; shuster 2019; zamantakis 2019). For example, Darwin (2017) writes about the potential of online spaces, such as a genderqueer specific subreddit (a popular social-media site), which can serve as a backstage for non-binary-identified individuals to try out strategies for doing non-binary gender and foster collective identity. However, Darwin (2017:330) also notes that non-binary individuals "are held accountable to binary misconceptions of transgender during their interactions with others and even within their own internal dialogues." Similarly, Saguy and Williams (2019) offer analyses of institutional attempts to assert gender neutrality in news media and in the law (Saguy, Williams, and Rees 2020). Recently, Hord (2020:1) argues that pairing "non-binary lesbian" as non-specific gender identity with specified sexual identity, rather than shoring up essentialist notions of bodies, has the potential to unhinge identity projects more broadly from "sanctioned identities built on exclusions."

Following the pervasiveness of West and Zimmerman's (1987) classic article, several theorists offered up the case of transgender people as exemplars of the potential to expand beyond binary gender (R. Connell 2009; C. Connell 2010; Nordmarken 2019; Schilt and Connell 2007; Pfeffer 2017; Vidal-Ortiz 2002). The recent theoretical turn that has placed an increased emphasis on transgender individuals' experiences of gender has occurred in juxtaposition to previous theories of transsexuals[5] as deviant (Schilt and Lagos 2017). The "gender difference paradigm" that gained prominence in the 1990s "challenged the framing of transgender as a deviant gender identity . . . and called for empirical documentation of the ways in which . . . cisgender people are constituted in the cultural practices of everyday life" (Schilt and Lagos 2017:430). Westbrook and Schilt (2014) demonstrate how violence enacted on trans people at the point of bodily exposure, often during sex, demonstrates the implicit heteronormativity within practices of doing gender, as West and Zimmerman outlined. C. Connell (2010) and Schilt (2006), separately and together (2007), note the ways in which trans people unsettle normative gender practices in work settings. Vidal-Ortiz (2009) offers the figure of the trans woman of color to critique the assumed whiteness of normative gender theory.

Trans theorists have offered a critique of queer theorists' failure to account for the lived experiences of transgender individuals (Namaste 1996; Rubin 1999), arguing that sociologists must "learn to theorize a desire for realness or authenticity rather than critique it" (Rubin 1999:190). Many theorists heeded a call for more empirical documentation of the range of gender identities and practices that could challenge, shift, or reproduce normative constructions of gender in order to make space for transgender experiences beyond those that purport an essentialized or medicalized narrative (Mason-Schrock 1996; Namaste 1996; Rubin 1999). For example, Schilt and Westbrook (2009:451) analyze how transgender individuals disrupt gendered expectations within interactional contexts, finding that "both cisgender men and women treat transmen as socially male in nonsexualized public interactions," however, during sexualized interactions, "cisgender women regulate transmen's sexualized behaviors through talk and gossip, whereas cisgender men police transwomen through aggressive verbal harassment [and/or violence]" (Schilt and Westbrook 2009:459). Additionally, Snorton (2017:8) theorizes experiences rooted in "twinned" histories of anti-Blackness and anti-transness. Other avenues of research within transgender scholarship focus on inclusion of transgender individuals in "queer spaces" (Stone 2013), the affirmation of transgender youth's identities by parents (Rahilly 2015; Meadow 2018), and the construction of families between transgender men and cisgender women (Pfeffer 2017). While some may argue that narratives of trans identities resist binary, essentialist constructions of gender, this scholarship also highlights the ways in which transgender individuals are still held accountable to binary gender expectations rooted in biological understandings of sex assigned at birth. Pfeffer (2017) notes the difficulty of definitions of sexuality and sexual orientation among trans men and their partners when one's body is transitioning.

Though frequently regarded as resisting traditional gendered expectations, there are others who suggest that transgender men and women who identify within the binary of male and female are actually reinforcing gendered expectations. This is, in part, a result of essentializing language often used in describing trans experience. Narratives of identity often reflect traditional "coming out" formula stories, which tell the narrative of "discovering a truth" (Plummer 1995:83). The "discovery narrative" is often present in transgender life stories (Johnson 2016). Indeed, Mason-Schrock's (1996:179) earlier study on transsexuals' personal narratives found that the construction of the "true self" was most often achieved through learning to tell "childhood stories" of "actual or fantasized cross-dressing experiences," "getting caught cross-dressing," and "participation in sports." At first glance, the use of discovery narratives appears to be operating as a regulatory regime that reinforces an understanding of gender identity as something that is natural or inherent, however it must also be noted that the process of medicalizing trans bodies requires providing a recognizable account of trans-ness in order to gain access to services. Johnson (2016) refers to this coerciveness to conform to medicalized models as transnormativity. Differentiating between trans folks who conform to one gender as opposed to those who wish to remain non-binary, Garrison (2018) analyzes the ways in which non-binary individuals make use of discovery narratives in an attempt to be recognized as "trans enough." According to Garrison (2018:615) "in order to claim public identities as trans, non-binary respondents are often motivated to present accounts that closely reflect prevailing understandings of trans experience (e.g., the 'born in the wrong body' narrative), even when these accounts fail to capture the nuance of their experiences." Yet, paradoxically "those who claim identities aligned with the existing [binary] system have the freedom to present more complicated, boundary-challenging accounts of their experience, although they may claim less personal investment in doing so" (2018:633).

WE ARE ALL TRANS(ITIONING): THE PERVASIVE AND NEGOTIATED EMBODIMENT OF GENDER

Taking gendered embodiment seriously across the breadth of this literature demonstrates that all gender is meaning-making practice that becomes identity-forming (Connell 2012; Crawley, Foley, and Shehan 2008; Crawley and Willman 2018; Meadow 2018). We all are subject to accounts, accountabilities, and performativities every day—every moment—throughout our lives. In short, we negotiate meanings in and as relations with each other. Gender is a constant and emergent production enveloping all of social life. When theorists and actors in everyday life focus only on transgender or non-binary cases, we leave the unmarked category—heteronormative gender—unquestioned. If trans is transitioning, in motion, engaging negotiation, then we must recognize that everyone engages gender practices—sometimes confirming and sometimes resisting heteronormative discourses. Heteronormative, cisgender people engage daily practices of bodily shaping (working out, nutrition practices, and cosmetic work including breast augmentation, labioplasty, penile implants, anti-aging creams, taking pharmaceuticals for erectile disfunction, or hormone replacement) to maintain performances of binary gendered embodiment—that is, to keep looking masculine or feminine. This is especially true as people age. Rather than relaxing comfortably into bodily change, the typical response to aging is to work ever harder to maintain the youthful appearances that define normative, binary gender. This is no less active and no less emergent than what is referred to as gender transition among people who identify as transgender—and it is no less lifelong. We are all imminently transitioning. Indeed, shoring up our focus on gender as relational, Meadow's (2018) recent study of trans children and their parents posits that gender is now more salient in everyday interaction, as parents often actively work to advocate for their gender-variant children and work in concert to resist gender conformity with them.

In sum, we suggest that theorists and activists *re-focus on identities as negotiated social relations.* In particular, framing our work more transparently from interpretive epistemologies, we might call into question whether social theory has made too much of a so-called micro and macro divide, whether we must only envision willful individuated actors or the so-called death of the subject, and how a social scientific focus on counting or measuring types of people obscures relations. A renewed focus on relations among gender practices enables us to see analytical connections of gender and embodiment across time and space from particular embodiments to transnational dynamics as well as engaging intersectional analysis more consistently, strengthening rather than dividing our academic movements. Methodologies that focus on relations such as Smith's (2005) institutional ethnography could offer productive directions for analysis.

Given what we have summarized, there are some engaging areas where the field may be going. One compelling direction is the radical potential offered up by "femme" embodiment as resistance, particularly given that femininity has historically been devalued, not only in heteronormative spaces, but also in LGBTQ + spaces. New theorizations of femininity as resistance tend to be inclusive of trans and non-binary femininities and intersectional, as embodiments of femininity are always racialized and classed, and intersect with sexuality, age, and ability. Another interesting direction considers how "doing" gender happens in virtual environments. Future avenues of research should explore the ways in which online spaces can be used as sites of identity negotiation and resistance, or possibly serve to further regulate gendered practices. An additional challenge remains in seeing connections between local, interactional practices and transnational contexts. Patil's (2018) call to understand *webbed connectivities* and the way the heterosexual matrix is connected across gender, race, class, sexuality, and nation over time is an expansive model that begins this task.

As our timeline demonstrates, identities do not denote types of people but, rather, comprise relational organizing practices of meaning-making in specific historical moments constantly produced between and among us—which can be normalizing or resistant. Recognizing gender as relational and constantly in production for everyone, whether trans-identified, non-binary, or cisgendered, illustrates the value of interpretive theories in understanding intersectional gender and embodiment as negotiated relations.

ACKNOWLEDGMENTS

Earlier versions of this chapter were presented at the American Sociological Association 2019 meetings in New York and the Sociologists for Women in Society 2020 Winter Meeting in San Diego, CA.

Notes

1. We use the term *interpretive social theory* to invoke an epistemological alignment of several schools of thought (constructionism, ethnomethodology, symbolic interactionism, phenomenology, among others), rather than symbolic interactionism specifically, in part because both Goffman and Garfinkel defined their work as different from Herbert Blumer, who coined *symbolic interactionism*.
2. For a summary of queer theory as it intersects sociology, see Crawley and Broad 2008.
3. While we suggest both misreadings and a general under-utilization of ethnomethodology in sociology more generally, an exhaustive critique of this issue in the history of the discipline is beyond the scope of this article. Crawley is pursuing a more in-depth critique in a forthcoming article.
4. Both Martin's (2004) and Connell's focus on *practice* as within institutions has strong affinities with ethnomethodological ideas, but neither has a specific discussion of ethnomethodology. Both rely epistemologically on critical realism rather than interpretivism. In a forthcoming work, Crawley discusses how interpretivist epistemological bases might advance this work.
5. This term has fallen out of use in both academic and activist circles, as it was previously used to indicate individuals who had undergone some form of medical transition, an experience that not all transgender individuals want or have access to.

References

Acosta, Katie L. 2013. *Amigas Y Amantes: Sexually Nonconforming Latinas Negotiate Family*. New Brunswick, NJ: Rutgers University Press.

Balogun, Oluwakemi. 2012. "Idealized Femininity and Embodied Nationalism in Nigerian Beauty Pageants." *Gender & Society* 26(3):357–81.

Barbee, Harry, and Douglas Schrock. 2019. "Un/gendering Social Selves: How Nonbinary People Navigate and Experience a Binarily Gendered World." *Sociological Forum* 34(1):572–93.

Bernard, Jessie. 1972. *The Future of Marriage*. New York: Bantam Books.

Bernard, Jessie. 1976. "Change and Stability in Sex-Role Norms and Behavior." *Journal of Social Issues* 32(3):207–23.

Bettie, Julie. 2003. *Women Without Class: Girls, Race, and Identity*. Berkeley: University of California Press.

Brickell, Chris. 2006. "The Sociological Construction of Gender and Sexuality." *The Sociological Review* 54(1): 87–113.

Bridges, Tristan. 2014. "A Very 'Gay' Straight?: Hybrid Masculinities, Sexual Aesthetics, and the Changing Relationship between Masculinity and Homophobia." *Gender & Society* 28(1):58–82.

Burkitt, Ian. 1998. "Sexuality and Gender Identity: From a Discursive to a Relational Analysis." *The Sociological Review* 46(3):483–504.

Butler, Judith. 1990. *Gender Trouble*. New York: Routledge.

Butler, Judith. 1991. "Imitation and Gender Insubordination." Pp. 13–31 in *Inside/Out: Lesbian Theories, Gay Theories*, edited by D. Fuss. New York: Routledge.

Butler, Judith. 1993. *Bodies That Matter: On the Discursive Limits of Sex*. New York: Routledge.

Cahill, Spencer E. 1986. "Language Practices and Self-Definition: The Case of Gender Identity Acquisition." *Sociological Quarterly* 27(3):295–311.

Chauncey, George. 1994. *Gay New York*. NY: BasicBooks.

Cohen, Cathy. 1997. "Punks, Bulldaggers, and Welfare Queens: The Radical Potential of QueerPolitics?" *GLQ* 3(4):437–65.

Connell, Catherine. 2010. "Doing, Undoing, or Redoing Gender? Learning from the Workplace Experiences of Transpeople." *Gender & Society* 24(1):31–55.

Connell, Raewyn. 1983. *Which Way Is Up? Essays on Sex, Class and Culture*. Sydney, Australia: George Allen and Unwin.

Connell, Raewyn. 1987. *Gender and Power: Society, the Person and Sexual Politics*. Stanford, CA: Stanford University Press.

Connell, Raewyn. 1992. "A Very Straight Gay: Masculinity, Homosexual Experience, and the Dynamics of Gender." *American Sociological Review* 57(6):735–51.

Connell, Raewyn. 1995. *Masculinities*. Berkeley: University of California Press.

Connell, Raewyn. 2009. "Accountable Conduct: 'Doing Gender' in Transsexual and Political Retrospect." *Gender & Society* 23(1):104–11.

Connell, Raewyn. 2012. "Transsexual Women and Feminist Thought: Toward New Understanding and New Politics." *Signs* 37(4):857–81.

Cook, K. J. 2006. "Doing Difference and Accountability in Restorative Justice Conferences." *Theoretical Criminology* 10(1):107–24.

Crawley, S. L. 1998. "Gender, Class and the Construction of Masculinity in Professional Sailing: A Case Study of the America3 Women's Team." *International Review for the Sociology of Sport* 33(1):33–42.

Crawley, S. L. 2002. "'They *Still* Don't Understand Why I Hate Wearing Dresses': An Autoethnographic Rant on Dresses, Boats and Butchness." *Cultural Studies↔↔Critical Methodologies* 2(1):69–92.

Crawley, S. L. 2011. "Visible Bodies, Vicarious Masculinity, and 'The Gender Revolution': Comment on Paula England." *Gender & Society* 25(1):108–12.

Crawley, S. L., and K. L. Broad. 2008. "The Construction of Sex and Sexualities." Pp. 545–66 in *The Handbook of Constructionist Research*, edited by J. Holstein and J. Gubrium. New York: Guilford Press.

Crawley, S. L., Lara J. Foley, and Constance L. Shehan. 2008. *Gendering Bodies*. Lanham, MD: Rowman & Littlefield Publishers, Inc.

Crawley, S. L., and Rebecca K. Willman. 2018. "Heteronormativity Made Me Lesbian: Femme, Butch and the Production of Sexual Embodiment Projects." *Sexualities* 21(1–2):156–73.

Daly, Sarah, Nigel King, and Tracey Yeadon-Lee. 2018. "'Femme It Up or Dress It Down': Appearance and Bisexual Women in Monogamous Relationships." *Journal of Bisexuality* 18(3):257–77.

Darwin, Helana. 2017. "Doing Gender Beyond the Binary: A Virtual Ethnography." *Symbolic Interaction* 40(3):317–34.

Davis, Georgiann. 2015. *Contesting Intersex: The Dubious Diagnosis*. New York: NYU Press.

D'Emilio, John. 1993. "Capitalism and Gay Identity." Pp. 467–76 in *The Lesbian and Gay Studies Reader*, edited by H. Abelove, M. A. Barale, and D. M. Halperin. New York: Routledge.

Demetriou, Demetrakis. 2001. "Connell's Concept of Hegemonic Masculinity: A Critique." *Theory and Society* 30(3):337–61.

Deutsch, Francine M. 2007. "Undoing Gender." *Gender & Society* 21(1):106–27.

Dow, Dawn Marie. 2016. "The Deadly Challenges of Raising African American Boys." *Gender & Society* 30(2):161–88.

Dreger, Alice Domurat. 1998. *Hermaphrodites and the Medical Invention of Sex*. Cambridge, MA: Harvard University Press.

Eves, Alison. 2004. "Queer Theory, Butch/Femme Identities and Lesbian Space." *Sexualities* 7(4):480–96.

Faderman, Lillian. 1991. *Odd Girls and Twilight Lovers*. New York: Penguin.

Fairchild, Emily. 2004. "Examining Wedding Rituals through a Multidimensional Gender Lens: The Analytic Importance of Attending to (In)consistency." *Journal of Contemporary Ethnography* 43(3):361–89.

Fausto-Sterling, A. 1993. "The Five Sexes: Why Male and Female Are Not Enough." *The Sciences* 33(2):20–25.

Fausto-Sterling, A. 2000. *Sexing the Body: Gender Politics and the Construction of Sexuality*. New York: Basic Books.

Fausto-Sterling, A. 2005. "The Bare Bones of Sex: Part 1 – Sex and Gender." *Signs* 30(2):1491–527.

Ferguson, Roderick. 2004. *Aberrations in Black: Toward a Queer of Color Critique*. Minneapolis: University of Minnesota Press.

Foucault, Michel. 1975/1995. *Discipline and Punish: The Birth of the Prison*. New York: Vintage Books.

Foucault, Michel. 1978. *The History of Sexuality*, vol. 1: *An Introduction*. New York: Pantheon Books.

Garfinkel, Harold. 1967. *Studies in Ethnomethodology*. Englewood Cliffs, NJ: Prentice Hall.

Garrison, Spencer. 2018. "On the Limits of Trans Enough: Authenticating Trans Identity Narratives." *Gender & Society* 32(5):613–37.

Goffman, Erving. 1959. *The Presentation of Self in Everyday Life*. New York: Double Day, Anchor.

Goffman, Erving. 1979. *Gender Advertisements*. New York: Harper & Row.

Gutmann, Matthew. 1997. "The Ethnographic (G)ambit: Women and the Negotiation of Masculinity in Mexico City." *American Ethnologist* 24(4):833–55.

Halberstam, Jack. 1998. *Female Masculinity*. Durham, NC: Duke University Press.

Hamilton, Laura T., Elizabeth A. Armstrong, J. Lotus Seeley, and Elizabeth M. Armstrong. 2019. "Hegemonic Femininities and Intersectional Domination." *Sociological Theory* 37(4):315–41.

Hill Collins, Patricia. 1990. *Black Feminist Thought*. New York: Routledge.

Hollander, Jocelyn A. 2013. "'I Demand More of People': Accountability, Interaction, and Gender Change." *Gender & Society* 27(1):5–29.

Hooks, bell. 1989. *Talking Back: Thinking Feminist, Thinking Black*. Boston, MA: South End.

Hord, Levi C. R. 2020. "Specificity Without Identity: Articulating Post-Gender Sexuality through the 'Non-binary Lesbian.'" *Sexualities* (early online release).

Hoskin, Rhea Ashley. 2017. "Femme Theory: Refocusing the Intersectional Lens." *Atlantis* 38(1):95–109.

Jackson, Stevi, and Sue Scott. 2000. "Putting the Body's Feet on the Ground: Towards a Sociological Reconceptualization of Gendered Embodiment." Pp. 9–24 in *Constructing Gendered Bodies*, edited by K. Beckett-Milburn and Linda McKie. New York: Palgrave.

Jackson, Stevi, and Sue Scott. 2002. "Introduction." Pp. 1–26 in *Gender: A Sociology Reader*, edited by S. Jackson and S. Scott. London: Routledge.

Johnson, Austin H. 2016. "Transnormativity: A New Concept and Its Validation Through Documentary Film About Transgender Men." *Sociological Inquiry* 86(4):465–91.

Johnson, E. Patrick, and Mae Henderson. 2005. *Black Queer Studies: A Critical Anthology*. Durham, NC: Duke University Press.

Kennedy, Elizabeth Lapovsky, and Madeline D. Davis. 1993. *Boots of Leather, Slippers of Gold: The History of a Lesbian Community*. New York: Routledge.

Kessler, Suzanne J. 1998. *Lessons from the Intersexed*. New Brunswick, NJ: Rutgers University Press.

Kessler, Suzanne J., and Wendy McKenna. 1978. *Gender: An Ethnomethodological Approach*. New York: Wiley.

Kimmel, Michael. 1994. "Masculinity as Homophobia: Fear, Shame, and Silence in the Construction of Gender Identity." Pp. 119–41 in *Theorizing Masculinities*, edited by H. Brod and M. Kaufman. Newbury Park, CA: SAGE.

Komarovsky, Mirra. 1946. "Cultural Contradictions and Sex Roles." *American Journal of Sociology* 52(3):184–89.

Lara, Irene. 2005. "Bruja Positionalities: Toward a Chicana/Latina Spiritual Activism." *Chicana/Latina Studies* 4(2):10–45.

Liu, Chuncheng. 2020. "'Red is not the only color of the rainbow': The Making and Resistance of the 'MSM' Subject among Gay Men in China." *Social Science & Medicine* 252:112947.

Liu, Monica. 2019. "Devoted, Caring, and Home loving: A Chinese Portrayal of Western Masculinity in Transnational Cyberspace Romance." *Men and Masculinities* 22(2):317–37.

Lorber, Judith. 1994. *Paradoxes of Gender*. New Haven, CT: Yale University Press.

Lorde, Audre. 1984. *Sister Outsider: Essays and Speeches*. Trumansburg, NY: Crossing.

Malheiros, Jorge, and Beatriz Padilla. 2014. "Can Stigma Become a Resource? The Mobilisation of Aesthetic-Corporal Capital by Female Immigrant Entrepreneurs from Brazil." *Identities: Global Studies in Culture and Power* 22(6):687–705.

Mann, Susan Archer. 2012. *Doing Feminist Theory: From Modernity to Postmodernism*. New York: Oxford University Press.

Martin, Patricia. 2004. "Gender as Social Institution." *Social Forces* 82(4):1249–73.

Mason-Schrock, Douglas. 1996. "Transsexuals' Narrative Construction of the 'True Self.'" *Social Psychology Quarterly* 59(3):176–92.

Meadow, Tey. 2018. *Trans Kids: Being Gendered in the Twenty-First Century*. Berkeley, CA: University of California Press.

Messerschmidt, James W. 2019. "The Salience of 'Hegemonic Masculinity.'" *Men and Masculinities* 22(1):85–91.

Messerschmidt, James W. 2020 "And Now, the Rest of the Story . . .: A Critical Reflection on Paechter (2018) and Hamilton et al. (2019)." *Women's Studies International Forum* 82:1–10.

Montes, Veronica. 2013. "The Role of Emotions in the Construction of Masculinity: Guatemalan Migrant Men, Transnational Migration, and Family Relations." *Gender & Society* 27(4):469–90.

Muñoz, Jose Esteban. 1999. *Disidentifications: Queers of Color and the Performance of Politics*. Minneapolis: University of Minnesota Press.

Namaste, Ki. 1996. "'Tragic Misreadings': Queer Theory's Erasure of Transgender Subjectivity." Pp. 183–203 in *Queer Studies: A Lesbian, Gay, Bisexual, and Transgender Anthology*, edited by G. Beemyn and M. Eliason. New York: NYU Press.

Nestle, Joan. 1992. *The Persistent Desire: A Femme-Butch Reader*. New York: Alyson Books.

Nestle, Joan, Clare Howell, and Riki Wilchins. 2002. *GenderQueer: Voices from Beyond the Sexual Binary*. Los Angeles: Alyson Books.

Nordmarken, Sonny. 2019. "Queering Gendering: Trans Epistemologies and the Disruption and Production of Gender Accomplishment Practices." *Feminist Studies* 45(1):36–66.

O'Brien, Jodi. 2016. "Seeing Agnes: Notes on a Transgender Biocultural Ethnomethodology." *Symbolic Interaction* 39(2):306–29.

Parsons, Talcott. 1943/1954. "The Kinship System of the Contemporary United States." Pp. 177–96 in *Essays in Sociological Theory*. New York: Free Press.

Pascoe, C. J. 2007. *Dude, You're a Fag: Masculinity and Sexuality in High School*. Berkeley: University of California Press.

Patil, Vrushali. 2018. "The Heterosexual Matrix as Imperial Effect." *Sociological Theory* 36(1):1–26.

Pfeffer, Carla. 2014. "'I Don't Like Passing as a Straight Woman': Queer Negotiations of Identity and Social Group Membership." *American Journal of Sociology* 120(1):1–44.

Pfeffer, Carla. 2017. *Queering Families: The Postmodern Partnerships of Cisgender Women and Transgender Men*. New York: Oxford University Press.

Plummer, Ken. 1995. *Telling Sexual Stories: Power, Change, and Social Worlds*. New York: Routledge.

Preves, Sharon K. 2003. *Intersex and identity: The contested self*. New Brunswick, NJ: Rutgers University Press.

Pyke, Karen, and Denise Johnson. 2003. "Asian American Women and Racialized Femininities: 'Doing' Gender across Cultural Worlds." *Gender & Society* 17(1):33–53.

Rahilly, Elizabeth. 2015. "The Gender Binary Meets the Gender-Variant Child: Parents' Negotiations with Childhood Gender Variance." *Gender & Society* 29:338–61.

Ridgeway, Cecilia, and Lynn Smith-Lovin. 1999. "The Gender System and Interaction." *Annual Review of Sociology* 25:191–216.

Ridgeway, Cecilia, and Shelley Correll. 2004. "Unpacking the Gender System: A Theoretical Perspective on Gender Beliefs and Social Relations." *Gender & Society* 18(4):510–31.

Risman, Barbara. 2004. "Gender as a Social Structure: Theory Wrestling with Activism." *Gender & Society* 18(4):429–50.

Risman, Barbara. 2009. "From Doing to Undoing: Gender as We Know It." *Gender & Society* 23(1):81–84.

Rubin, Henry. 1999. "Trans Studies: Between a Metaphysics of Presence and Absence." Pp. 173–92 in *Reclaiming Genders: Transsexual Grammars at the Fin de Si`ecle*, edited by K. More and S. Whittle. New York: Cassell.

Saguy, Abigail C., and Juliet A. Williams. 2019. "Reimagining Gender: Gender Neutrality in the News." *Signs* 44(2):465–89.

Saguy, Abigail C., Juliet A. Williams, and Mallory Rees. 2020. "Reassessing Gender Neutrality." *Law & Society Review* 54(1):7–32.

Salam, Maya. 2020. "How Queer Women Powered the Suffrage Movement." *The New York Times* (August 14). https://www.nytimes.com/2020/08/14/us/queer-lesbian-women-suffrage.html?smid=em-share.

Schilt, Kristen. 2006. *Just One of the Guys?: Transgender Men and the Persistence of Gender Inequality*. Chicago: University of Chicago Press.

Schilt, Kristen, and Catherine Connell. 2007. "Do Workplace Gender Transitions Make Gender Trouble?" *Gender, Work and Organization* 14(6):596–618.

Schilt, Kristen, and Danya Lagos. 2017. "The Development of Transgender Studies in Sociology." *Annual Review of Sociology* 43:425–43.

Schilt, Kristen, and Laurel Westbrook. 2009. "Doing Gender, Doing Heteronormativity: 'Gender Normals,' Transgender People, and the Social Maintenance of Heterosexuality." *Gender & Society* 23(4):440–64.

Schippers, Mimi. 2007. "Recovering the Feminine Other: Masculinity, Femininity, and Gender Hegemony." *Theory and Society* 36(1):85–102.

shuster, stef. 2019. "Generational Gaps or Othering the Other? Tension between Binary and Non-Binary Trans People." Pp. 309–22 in *Expanding the Rainbow: Exploring the Relationships of Bi, Pan, Queer, Ace, Intersex, Trans, Poly, and Kink People*, edited by B. Simula, A. Miller, and J. E. Sumerau. Boston: Brill/Sense.

Smith, Dorothy E. 1974. "Theorizing as Ideology." Pp. 41–44 in *Ethnomethodology*, edited by R. Turner. Middlesex, England: Penguin Books.

Smith, Dorothy E. 1987. *The Everyday World as Problematic*. Boston: Northeastern University Press.

Smith, Dorothy E. 1990. *The Conceptual Practices of Power*. Boston: Northeastern University Press.

Smith, Dorothy E. 2005. *Institutional Ethnography: A Sociology for People.* Lanham, MD: AltaMira Press.

Snorton, C. Riley. 2017. *Black on Both Sides: A Racial History of Trans Identity.* Minneapolis: University of Minnesota Press.

Stacey, Judith, and Barrie Thorne. 1985. "The Missing Feminist Revolution in Sociology." *Social Problems* 32(4):301–16.

Stanley, Liz, and Sue Wise. 1983/2002. "What's Wrong with Socialization?" Pp. 273–79 in *Gender: A Sociology Reader,* edited by S. Jackson and S. Scott. London: Routledge.

Stokoe, E. 2006. "On Ethnomethodology, Feminism, and the Analysis of Categorical Reference to Gender in Talk-In-Interaction." *The Sociological Review* 54 (3):468–94.

Stone, Amy. 2013. "Flexible Queers, Serious Bodies: Transgender Inclusion in Queer Spaces." *Journal of Homosexuality* 60(12):1647–65.

Stryker, Susan. 2008. *Transgender History.* Berkeley, CA: Seal Press.

Thorne, Barrie. 1993. *Gender Play: Girls and Boys in School.* New Brunswick, NJ: Rutgers University Press.

Trautner, Mary Nell. 2005. "Doing Gender, Doing Class: The Performance of Sexuality in Exotic Dance Clubs." *Gender & Society* 19(6):771–88.

Treviño, A. Javier. 2003. "Introduction: Erving Goffman and the Interaction Order." Pp. 1–49 in *Goffman's Legacy,* edited by A. Javier Treviño. Lanham, MA: Rowman and Littlefield.

Vidal-Ortiz, Salvadore. 2002. "Queering Sexuality and Doing Gender: Transgender Men's Identification with Gender and Sexuality." Pp. 181–233 in *Gendered Sexualities,* edited by P. Gagné and R. Tewksbury. New York: Elsevier Press.

Vidal-Ortiz, Salvadore. 2009. "The Figure of the Trans-Woman of Color through the Lens of 'Doing Gender.' " *Gender & Society* 23(1):99–103.

Ward, Jane. 2015. *Not Gay: Sex between Straight White Men.* New York: NYU Press.

West, Candace, and Don H. Zimmerman. 1987. "Doing Gender." *Gender & Society* 1(2):125–51.

West, Candace, and Don H. Zimmerman. 2009. "Accounting for Doing Gender." *Gender & Society.* 23(1):112–22.

Westbrook, Laurel, and Kristen Schilt. 2014. "Doing Gender, Determining Gender: Transgender People, Gender Panics, and the Maintenance of the Sex/Gender/Sexuality System." *Gender & Society* 28(1):32–57.

Young, Iris. 1980. "Throwing like a Girl: A Phenomenology of Feminine Body Comportment Motility and Spatiality." *Human Studies* 3(2):137–56.

zamantakis, alithia. 2019. " 'I Try Not to Push It Too Far': Trans/Nonbinary Individuals Negotiating Race and Gender in Intimate Relationships." Pp. 293–307 in *Expanding the Rainbow: Exploring the Relationships of Bi, Pan, Queer, Ace, Intersex, Trans, Poly, and Kink People,* edited by B. Simula, A. Miller, and J. E. Sumerau. Boston: Brill/Sense.

Zimmerman, Don. 1992. "They Were All Doing Gender, but They Weren't All Passing: Comment on Rogers." *Gender & Society* 6(2):192–98.

CHAPTER 24

SEX AND SEXUALITY

CIRUS RINALDI

INTRODUCTION

MOST of our sexual activity originates in the body, to the extent that as beings, we are and we have in common a body, much like we respond to external inputs through our organs of perception. However, it would not be possible to comprehend fully the range of biological and physiological reactions, nor their effects, unless we were able to employ a series of meanings used to describe those particular situations that are usually referred to as sexual situations (Weinberg 2015:xiii). Sociological essentialist and positivist approaches to sexuality justify the status quo and consider it as provided with a reality *sui generis* (Plummer 2007:16); accordingly, this "reality" is defined as a series of characteristic features that are deemed natural and that would reproduce themselves mechanically through social structures and hierarchies involving the body itself, such as ability, ethnicity, race, class, and age, as well as people's own sense of themselves as sexual beings (Plante 2006:95). These approaches fail to problematize the interactions of the biological, psychological, and physiological level and the social, cultural, and contextual dimensions in which they are embedded. The implicit risk is that we are led to consider sexuality as a direct and mechanical product of "nature," whose representations are able to transcend time, society, and history (Rubin 1984:275). In turn, sociological analysis grounded in essentialism risks invoking "nature" or defining a particular conduct as "natural," thereby positing a particular social and cultural object as essentially "true." It follows that sex/sexuality is conceived of as a universal, abstract category that can be applied to any social context across time and space (Padgug 1992:54). Whereas "essentialist" or "naturalist" perspectives view sex/sexuality as something "given," as a set of immutable, "natural," fixed characteristics (Weeks 1985), symbolic interaction(ism) engages with the idea that human sexuality is fundamentally unstable and variable. By definition, "sex" is the effect of society and of culture, one of many variables that are the effect of different arrangements and structures (like, for instance, gender, age, class, ethnicity, ability)—it is one element interconnected with many other factors defining society. Interactionist analysis allows us to grasp the full range of human sexualities as the result of the production, organization, negotiation, and transformation processes that occur in the social realm (Plummer 2002:1). This chapter aims to outline the ways in which symbolic interactionism shifts the focus of inquiry into sex from *being sexual* toward *becoming sexual*, which takes into account how sexualities are *done*, rather than tracing their origins in an immutable (conception of) nature. Symbolic interactionism is mostly concerned with analyzing language and its capacity to typify, to classify, and to share experiences and events. It pays particular attention to the social reality of social-sexual worlds, conceived as the result of social interaction and negotiation, as well as of the *production of meanings* (DeLamater and Hyde 1998).

Symbolic Interactionism and Sexuality: A Short Outline

The predicament of symbolic interactionism is that, beginning with the process of social learning through which we employ and negotiate a "repertoire" of meanings that subjects can perform, we develop a specific language, a series of names, and meanings defined as "sexual" that we employ to talk about and label a particular set of sensations, situations, subjects, and traits (Gecas and Libby 1976). Symbolic interactionism developed within the work of the pragmatists at the Chicago School in the 1920s. The idea of *process* and of the possibility of multiple forms that a single process can take is central to symbolic interactionism. It follows that, as a theory, symbolic interactionism is concerned with the interactions, forms of adjustment, and the mutual influences between social actors and *environment(s)*, where both human and social life are seen as *emerging processes* (Mead 1934/1962). Key thinkers of this tradition, including George H. Mead and Robert E. Park, never dealt specifically with issues of sexuality; others, like William I. Thomas, produced works that touched on this subject tangentially, drawing from secondary sources mostly borrowed from anthropology that presented rather stereotyped notions of gender differences (Thomas 1907). It is only in recent times that the role of the Chicago School has been reassessed, shedding light on its contribution to urban studies more generally, and specifically to understanding the city as "sexual laboratory" (Heap 2003:459), as well as to the study of sexual subcultures (Mumford 1997; Rubin 2002; Heap 2009). In addition to unpublished research and reports,[1] in their canonical texts the Chicago School group has tended to focus more or less explicitly on sexual themes, though they did so within a moralist and pathologizing framework that ultimately failed to broaden the scope of a theory of sexualities in a meaningful way. Having said this, the group never really treated the subject of sex without bespeaking their prudish discomfort, arguably springing from their position inside the academy, and from the predominant views on sexuality within the studies of the time, which focused exclusively on exploring (and condemning) social deviance.

The work of Florian Znaniecki is a case in point. In a paper he presented at the first International Congress for Sexual Research (Berlin, October 10–16, 1926), he argued that "a sexual act is a social act when it bears upon a human being as its object and tends to provoke a conscious reaction of this being" (Znaniecki 1927:222), hence taking into account a series of strictly regulated activities. Conversely, and in the midst of the then emerging taxonomic approach to human sexuality, mainly through the influential work of Alfred C. Kinsey, some key figures of the pragmatist and social interactionist schools elaborated more nuanced understanding of the subject. E. W. Burgess, for instance, argued that human sexuality, unlike that of animals (which remained the product of instincts), was the result of attitudes and values emerging from particular groups and social environments. He went on to claim that it was therefore impossible to speak of sexual behavior; rather, sexuality was a matter of "conduct," namely, of "behavior as prescribed or evaluated by the group. It is not simply external observable behavior, but behavior which expresses a norm or evaluation" (Burgess 1949:229). Herbert Blumer was the leading theorist in this approach to human sexuality. His famous study, *Movies and Conduct*, met the censure of the authorities. This work had been developed as part of the Payne Fund Studies, a series of researches published between 1933 and 1935 devoted to the theme of "motion pictures and youth"; the author never published his "Private Monograph on Movies and Sex" (see Jowett, Jarvie, and Fuller 1996) and just dealt with the topic in a review of *Sexual Behavior in the Human Male* of Alfred C. Kinsey and colleagues (Kinsey, Pomeroy, and Martin 1948), which first appeared in a nonspecialist journal (Blumer 1948), and in which he criticized the authors' exclusive focus on quantitative data, since they were interested in the mere distribution of sexual outlets and the biological occurrences of orgasm. By doing so, Blumer believed that these authors were failing to consider that orgasm should be placed within a "framework of social definition and social practice" in order to grasp its social nature, while also allowing to recognize its different meanings according to a specific situation. It was not until the quantitative interactionist school of Iowa's Manford H. Kuhn published his theories on quantitative social interactionism that a symbolic interaction view of sexuality emerged, however incomplete. For Kuhn, sexual actions, not unlike any other type of actions, are more carefully understood as social objects that determine the range of responses by social actors. Actors apply a predefined vocabulary of meanings based on the particular group to which they belong, as well as on the language and sexual motives borrowed from their own social roles. This also explains why meanings cannot be fully comprehended through the mere application of physiological factors to account for sexuality (Kuhn 1954:123). John H. Gagnon and William Simon's work is one of the most comprehensive studies of sexuality in the postwar period. At the end of 1950, the two met at the University of Chicago, which was a leading institution in the fields of symbolic action and interactionist theories. They met again toward the mid-1960s at Alfred C. Kinsey's Institute for Sex Research, where they elaborated their "theory" of sexual scripts by building upon dominant interactionist approaches, as shown in their volume *Sexual Conduct: The Social Sources of Human Sexuality*. The "theory" of sexual scripts represented a further improvement of American pragmatism, bringing together a number of approaches, among them George Herbert Mead's theory of social roles, the influence of literary critic Kenneth Burke's dramatism (Burke 1945, 1965), and Wright Mills' theory of motives (Mills 1940), as well as key interactionist concepts, primarily the idea of "career" first introduced by Everett Hughes (Hughes 1971) and reworked later on by Howard Becker (Becker and Strauss 1956; Becker 1966) and Erving Goffman (Goffman 1961). Gagnon and Simon's work led to a major change in sociological inquiry, through shifting the analytical framework of research on human sexuality away from biological, psychological, and medical approaches. Specifically, the two authors replaced the idea(s) of impulses and physiological activities that were typical of a bio-medical approach with that of *symbolic actions*. In other words, sexuality was no longer seen as an "independent variable" but rather as a "dependent" one, influenced by social categories such as age, gender, class, ethnicity, and sexual orientation. For Gagnon and Simon, there are three distinct types of sexual scripts: first, *cultural scripts*, which refer to orientations, maps of instructions, and repertoires of meanings available in social life guiding individuals toward a suitable choice of specific roles to perform within a given relationship; second, *interpersonal scripts*, which refer to the ways in which individuals apply a certain cultural scenario based on a specific cultural of interactional context or situation, and finally, the so-called *intrapsychic scripts*, which conjure the desiring dimensions of subjects' intimate lives (Simon and Gagnon 1986). Sexual conduct therefore results from the combination of the three kinds of scripts. However, for the most part, a certain relationship can be considered satisfactory only to the extent that it employs specific cultural codes as defined by cultural scripts. Although it is possible to proceed with an analytical definition of sexual scripts, each script is interrelated with the others. The theory of sexual scripts thus allows exploring subjects' own organization and building of individual sexual meanings and behaviors. Rather than merely responding to physiological and sexual sensations, subjects are motivated by their own symbolic system, which plays a fundamental role in the social organization of their sexual experience. The theory of sexual scripts has been subject to criticism on several grounds. Some have argued against its lack of consideration for more structural issues (Green 2008a, 2008b); others have claimed that it does not adequately consider, for instance, the difficulties in predicting intrapsychic scripts due to the changing nature of people's desires (Green 2014:52); still others have added that this indeterminacy also extends to the possibility that unexpected sexual meanings may occur (Walby 2012:2, 28–31). Despite this criticisms, sexual scripts nonetheless have offered a deeper understanding of the fact that there are more reasons to be sexual than ways of being sexual (Simon and Gagnon 1986). Furthermore, the theory of sexual script has made it possible to move beyond what can be viewed as more simplistic aspects typical of a Freudian approach to sexuality that either naturalizes the sexual or sees it as the founding aspect of social behavior, while failing to consider that "social roles are not vehicles for the expression of sexual impulse but that sexuality becomes a vehicle for expressing the needs of social roles" (Gagnon and Simon 1973/2005:33). Following from what has been discussed so far, the theory of sexual scripting shares a series of common traits with symbolic interactionism, including the following: (a) sexual meanings originate in our social interactions and that we learn about them and how to use them through others, not through our individual experiences; (b) sexual meanings are neither static, nor are they assigned to things, people, and objects once and for all, but rather, they change much like our perceptions of them; (c) the attribution of sexual meanings is not an automatic action, but rather, it is always the result of a self-reflexive and interpretative process, which also involves creativity; (d) we are always positioned within interactions soliciting our search for the "correct sexual meaning" of events, which is also the most appropriate in terms of context; (e) individuals become fully human through interacting with others, and furthermore, becoming sexual is part of the development of the social self, of communicative processes, and of the forms of social organization; (f) all kinds of behavior, including sexual conduct, is the result of instincts, urges, and objects that we find in our environment, as well as of the definitions we use to describe them; (g) we refer to a set of rules and ways of feeling, which not only allow us to frame our actions as members of a particular group within the context of the available cultural models, but also provide us with a repertoire of feelings that may be seen as desirable in a particular context; and (h) it follows that our shaping of sexual behaviors is not based exclusively on physiological and biological impulses, but rather emerges from the different contexts in which we are involved, as well as from the very processes of building, negotiating, and establishing the meaning of a certain situation with others. A number of both classic and more recent theoretical perspectives (Plummer 1982; Longmore 1998) and anthologies (Steele 2004; Weinberg and Newmahr 2015) have assessed the influence of symbolic interactionism within a constructionist framework. As demonstrated by these works, symbolic interactionism remains one of the most compelling analytical perspectives for the study of human sexualities, even in the context of its interrelations with other approaches. The next sections in this chapter will discuss the key aspects of becoming sexual from an interactionist perspective. More specifically, the analysis will focus on the role of language and of naming in *saying oneself sexually*, the processes of socialization and learning, and the status passages involved in *constructing the sexual self* and *doing sexual things together* in the shaping of sexual performances.

TALKING SEX(UALLY): THE PRODUCTION OF SEXUAL MEANINGS AND NAMING DESIRES

Sexuality is built upon meanings that are not necessarily sexual, much in the same way as the language we use to produce and to communicate sexual meanings is not based solely on sexuality itself. Whenever people use words in their daily interactions, they are not just shaping their own sexual identity, but rather, and as a matter of fact, they are doing many more things (Cameron and Kulick 2006:xi–xii). When we *say* something sexual, we are saying many things at once: something that has the power to do (or not to do) something else ("You can't be back home so late at night. You're a girl!"), a form of mastery ("You like this, don't you? Shut up and get it"), a form of intimacy ("Doing this with you feels so different. . . I've never felt like this before"), something about race ("Those migrant bitches like it that way; they never say no/refuse"), something about social status and class ("Do you really fancy her? Can't you see she's just a wench, she's not for you!"), and so on. Social actors use language to make sense of what they do, what they expect to be doing, and what they should do as they are presented with something they view as sexual. If we did not refer to language, to systems of meanings, and to symbolic and culture mediation, *there could be no sex/sexuality as we know it*: if we conceived sexuality as mere natural and organic product, we would end up having a series of "uncoordinated erections and lubrifications, of sexuality without rule or fantasy, of fumbling inabilities to interpret acts, orgasms, objects or people as sexual" (Plummer 1984:38). Our ability to interpret, which allows us to produce meaning, is not ensuing from the fact that we have sexual organs and a sexual apparatus: the materiality of instincts, urges, and physiological reactions—and here, one can think of ejaculating or having an erection—are telling us very little (if anything at all) about socio-sexual meanings, other than that we share some kind of biological "baggage." What is referred to as nature fails to predict our own uses of this baggage (and there are many), in both social and symbolic terms. It follows that any attempt to think of sexuality as a set of predefined elements including where we have sex, when, with whom or what, and how is doomed from the start. All these aspects are the product of society, culture, and the symbolic; they require establishing relationships within the context of dynamics that involve power, status, toles, meanings, rules, and representations alongside specific sexual configurations (Berger and Luckmann 1966:100). As a consequence, we find ourselves providing meanings and "names" to instincts, urges, and sensations so that *all* things, including sexuality, may function properly. Although they are regularly appearing as "crude" characteristics, as objective and universal facts, their meaning changes based on the social group to which they refer, the social context, and the different historical moments when they occur (Brekhus 2015). If we succeed in interpreting an "urge" (for example, an erection) and in giving it the necessary meanings in order to be able to "feel something" or "to do something" (having an orgasm), then this is only because, in the meantime, we have learned to assign certain names and to respond to specific urges; we also learn a series of techniques and modalities with regard to what we should feel and how we should experience pleasure, thus matching our "desires" and "fantasy." Yet, this is also the case because we learn how to self-stimulate adequately, to identify the attending effects, and to feel satisfied about a specific outcome and for a particular reason (often, these exceed the sexual). In other words, we learn to give a name to what happens to us, to others, and to us when we are with others.

The very moment we use a sexual definition or label, we are also adding on qualities and expectations to the thing or person we are referring to, somehow drawing the boundaries (Strauss 1959:19), organizing our sensorial experiences based on categories available from cultural models that are currently in use in our social world and in the groups to whom we belong. When a person or a thing is referred to as "masculine" or "feminine," for instance, something from the surrounding reality is at stake: we would not expect to call "masculine" a male subject who wears a miniskirt or some makeup.

Along the same lines, a high-pitched tone of voice is read a sign of a lessened masculinity, or at least as gender ambiguousness; or else, a male subject acting arrogantly may be read as someone who "knows his own way," whereas a woman subject with the same characteristic is likely to be read as a "no-good." It is necessary to be able to understand the range of definitions and names people use to refer to objects, acts, individuals, and relationships available in their contexts in order to grasp sexual conducts. Furthermore, these definitions are highly dependent on context, while also bringing forth specific social and sexual worlds. Consequently, a particular sexual name is used or someone or something is defined as "sexual" based on the uses and semiotic repertoires available in a specific social and sexual world; this also changes according to the definition we employ when referring to a particular situation, itself a rather ambiguous process. The ensuing repertoires of meanings inform the names we give to people/things, the reasons we use a particular name to refer to something or someone, the subjects and actions we identify, and the times we decide to call them by sexual names. So, for instance, a man from Nicaragua is called a "macho" or "man-man" (*hombre-hombre*) if he is the penetrative sexual partner with either women or men; by contrast, a man who performs as the receptive partner is called "chochòn," which is not always used to denigrate him. This allows drawing the confines of sexual categories and practices that do not align themselves with our (Western) *situated* conceptualization of homosexuality (Lancaster 1992). Sexual meanings orient people's actions in the sphere of social life. When they act, people draw from the repertoires that are constituted by these meanings, also through adapting them dynamically or creatively. By doing so, people become legitimate, competent sexual actors. These meanings collect stories and semiotic systems through which we all receive information about the requirements and practices needed to perform our own roles (what Gagnon has termed the sexual "who, what, where, and why"; see Gagnon 1977). We learn our *lines* and to *improvise* certain actions according to what is required by a given situation as well as to our resources. Suffice it to think that defining the meaning of "having sex" is highly problematic, and it varies according to the meanings provided within the different groups. For example, if we stress the role of penetrative sex (penis-vagina) by viewing it as the quintessential sexual practice, as well as the most rewarding one—namely, as "real sex" or "normal sex"—then, we may end up considering any other sexual practice as not strictly, or not fully, sexual (e.g., fellatio or anal intercourse; Sanders and Reinisch 1999). Alternatively, these other practices may be defined "immoral" or "dirty sex." By the same token, to associate a woman's loss of her virginity with her first penetrative sexual act is to deny those women who do not want to experiment with it the status of "former virgins" (Carpenter 2001:136; Medley-Rath 2007).

SEXUAL LABELING AND DESIRE

Not only are these practices of naming and labeling used to navigate the world of social relationships, but they are also used to "let it all work out properly," that is, as a way for subjects to ensure that (their own and the others') expectations are met. When we manage our bodily sensations and physiological urges, we are also, at the same time, performing individual and collective actions like giving names, labels, and meanings to ourselves and to others. In other words, we are creating sensorial and corporeal codes that allow us not only to assign meanings to our actions, desires, and sensations, but also to interpret other people's perceptive behavior (Schwalbe and Mason-Schrock 1996:115; Snow and Anderson 1987). When we bring in our senses to the so-called social-sexual interactions (touch, sight, hearing, smell, and taste) we are enacting a series of practices and reflexive processes, rather than just responding to external inputs or urges. In this case, we are making these inputs, urges, and desires *meaningful*, which would otherwise remain vague and ambiguous, just like we are *signifying* our "shared common socio-physiological natural capacities" (Mead 1962:139n, cit. in Dingwall, Nerlich, and Hillyard 2015:75). We could paraphrase Becker and say that *our sensorial and physical experiences of sexual inputs emerge from our conceptualization of sexuality and its uses, within the development of our experiences of what is socially defined as sexual* (Becker 1966:42). There are no universal inputs and urges that produce general, universal, homogenous responses, because we all depend on the dynamic, complex interrelations of culture, interaction, and subjectivity. This is not to deny the materiality of our perceptive organs, but rather to argue that sexual arousal originates within cultural and symbolic contexts, and that through interpreting meanings we enrich our physiology. In other words, we experience sexual arousal only as the product of a mediation involving social structures, cultures, interactions, and social contexts. Our sexual conducts are shaped and organized according to culturally mediated inner experiences (Lindesmith, Strauss, and Denzin 1975): individuals must become aware of what is happening to them—that is to say, they must learn to develop a vocabulary in order to name their (and other people's) sensations and actions, as well as to provide answers if required. Our physiological reactions constitute the raw material subject to processes of interpretation involving the shared common experiences of a particular group; as such, they *can be perceived* only according to certain modalities, and they "function" *only when* endowed with symbolic meanings. We are not reacting suddenly to a given input; rather, we are providing meanings to what is happening *inside* (as well as *outside*) ourselves, whereby we translate these sensations into names, labels, and linguistic categories. Nothing can be seen as inherently or ontologically sexual that belongs to social and human life (Parker 2010:58). This also applies to solitary sex and related masturbatory fantasies, in that they both originate in erotic imaginary, language, names, and labels that are internalized, together with social influences and previous experiences, as well as future projects. All these aspects perform a regulatory function on social behavior and, by extension, sexual behavior. Subjects are always in the position to be able to somehow control their own internal symbolic processes; this means that, to varying degrees, their sexual responses and reactions can always be accelerated, slowed down, or inhibited completely (Lindesmith, Strauss, and Denzin 1975:506). In one way or another, even when we think we are surrendering to desire in its most solitary and intimate form, we are transforming our culture into the internal language of symbolic mediation, which is also to say that we are creating, more or less deliberately, an (absent) audience for our own activity (Goffman 1959:170–75). We are dealing with cultural repertoires that are acted upon in two different ways: on the one hand, we learn and internalize them as part of the values, norms, and sexual codes available within a particular historical context; on the other, we mobilize our internal resources to influence and be influenced by them. At times, these internal resources can be experienced as and manipulated into professional imaginaries, as in the case of pornography. From this point of view, the projection of sexual fantasies is based on enacting (verbal or visual) scripts that produce collective or individual scenes (fantasy), for instance, by drawing from hegemonic imaginaries where the codes of masculinity are represented by specific forms of heterosexuality (which entail, among others, the sexual availability of women, whereby they are expected to synchronize with and to respond promptly to males' sexual demands). It is not by chance, then, that the few sociological inquiries into sexual fantasies have shown their different production between males and females, beginning with the language and narrative strategies that are being used. And so, if a higher degree of *sensual imagination* is detected in women, full of emotional details and romantic elements, *sexual imagination* is a characteristic feature of men, who tend to define themselves as active, aggressive sexual actors, as the instigators of sexual activity through making explicit reference to specific sexual practices (Kimmel and Plante 2004). The analysis carried out so far is evidence of the fact that fantasies and intra-psychic processes are firmly embedded in personal contexts and cultural scenarios that are symbolically mediated by actors (in this case, by referring to gendered structures). These fantasies and processes are responsible for the differential sexual standard: whereas boys are educated to become proactive subjects when searching for or experiencing their own sexuality, girls are subject to more severe forms of control, which leads them to internalize a passive or receptive role—a process that first takes place in childhood and increases with menstruation. The meanings attached to gender roles and their social construction contribute, though always in nondeterministic terms, to the defining construction of sexual fantasies and desires, and to the kinds of feeling rules that must be displayed by competent gendered subjects. This also extends to the compromises within what is defined as *identity (hetero)sexual work* whereby, for instance, a couple may develop strategies to indicate the partner's sexual availability and to prevent women from displaying their desire(s) openly (Duncombe and Marsden 1996:227, cit. in Kimmel and Plante 2004:63). Cultural scenarios allow for varying degrees of specialization of males' fantasies with regard to gender(ed) roles, in that heterosexual males usually learn to give sexual meanings to women's bodies and physical attributes ("I like butts," "I am crazy about breasts"), but we do not hear very often the same or similar comments made by women *in public* ("I like a particular kind of penis").

THE DEFINITION OF THE SEXUAL SITUATION AND THE SEXUAL DEFINITION OF THE SITUATION

Is the patient standing naked in front of their gynecologist doing anything sexual? If a guy has an erection as he climbs a tree, are we led to assume that he is doing something sexual? Is a naked couple sunbathing on the beach doing something sexual? And what about a clerk working for a mortuary, reassembling, washing, and undressing a corpse? Is he, too doing something sexual? For the most part, the answers to the above questions varies according to our *definition of the situation* that we are observing, the names we give to what is being described, the type of expert figures labeling the behaviors and traits indicated, and the moral judgement that we hold with regard to the above; they also vary according to our social status, the time when we make this assessment, and who we make it with, as well as to our religion, ethnicity, and so on. Our actions must be in accordance with those of others for any kind of social action to be possible; this requires a *shared common definition of the situation*. Contrasting interpretations may occur, for instance, in the adult world. A case in point is adults' tendency to view children's manipulation of their genitals as something "sexual," even though boys and girls alike do not give the same (sexual) meaning to what they are doing (Gagnon and Simon 1973/2005:10, 30; Plummer 1975:31–32). We would not be dealing with anything sexual at all in the absence of the elements required *to give us* a "sexual" name, *to give others* a "sexual" name, *to define the situation* in a particular way, to give a specific *name* to the sexual actors involved and their aims, *to sketch* a particular behavior, and *to anticipate* its effects as well as the effects of the others' *expectations*. For the most part, our social experiences are "translated" in sexual terms—they are "sexualized." Furthermore, it could also be the case that a wide range of sexual conducts may not have an exclusively "sexual" origin, or they may be justified by referring to a number of reasons to support the idea that sexuality is highly influenced by culture (Meston and Buss 2007).

Some people have sex in return for money; others see sexuality as a boost to their self-esteem and a means to reproduce a successful form of masculinity; still others view masturbation as a way to relieve stress. There are also males who have sex with other males to create and to reinforce a gender(ed) bond. In the past, there were forms of sex work and group sex verging on the sacred. Some people may have sex in order to establish a relationship with others; some others may do it in order to prove that they have finally succeeded in changing their status ("Now that I am 18, I finally made it!"); still others instead are having group sex to be allowed to enter a confraternity. Some people may use violence to conquer and to subordinate others (as in the case of ethnic rape in times of war). The proposed shift toward the definition of the situation allows us to understand that the actions we perform are not abstract or *decontextualized*, but rather they inform our conducts in general, and our sexual conducts in particular, which are always *situated*. Furthermore, attempts at defining a situation require the ability to grasp or to predict the actions performed by others, as well as the ability to see ourselves in terms of a particular image emerging within a particular context. Here suffice it to think of the kind of definition at stake in those situations when we are asked to show those body parts usually hidden from the other's gaze like, for instance, during a meeting with a urologist or gynecologist whose gender may differ from the one we identify with. In this case, the definition of a situation should take into account the existence of *nonsexual motives*, that is, it needs to be "de-sexualized". Furthermore, all the roles involved in the situation (doctor, staff, patient) must act in concert to maintain this specific definition in order to minimize if not neutralize altogether the potential risks of eroticization of subjects' conducts, as well as to draw the boundaries between those who *show* "the body" and those who *observe* or examine it (Henslin and Biggs 1978). Given that we are dealing with a context where nudity is involved (Douglas 1977; Weinberg 1965, 1966, 1967), they also need to avoid using forms of *civil inattention* or, more precisely, *studied inattention* (Goffman 1963; Douglas 1977:108; "I am sharing the same nudist space and as she is talking to me I try to look right into her eyes; I am pretending this man standing naked in front of me and who's making me blush and who may turn me on *is not actually standing in front of me*, I am faking it while strolling on the beach, I look disinterested and even quite bored"). This brings us to focus on the situated dimension of sexuality and its components, which do not coalesce to produce a static, fixed dimension. In other words, if our capacities include *being sexualized*, they also extend to creating the conditions according to which a certain context may be *desexualized*. As a result, sexuality emerges as a dependent variable that we can adjust and adapt to specific situations, which are going to be with us across our lifetime as *sexual becomings*.

Constructing the Sexual Self

Our socialization takes place within cultural contexts that over time have provided a "vocabulary of sexual motives" we are all asked to learn more or less directly and implicitly, yet which we can also reject. This vocabulary is not necessarily associated with a specific sexual activity, but it has socialized us into a series of analogies, associations, and meanings. This process happened way earlier than our first contact with sexuality. Here suffice it to think, for instance, of informal expressions and slang we have heard or may hear at school, in the street, or those writings on the wall whose meaning exceeds their application to a specific sexualized situation (even though they anticipate the majority of dominant social values).

A female adolescent who is thought to be sexually emancipated, with a particular appearance, or her dress code may be addressed as "whore." A shy, effeminate, male classmate or who does not play soccer may be called "queer." Also, expressions like "suca" ("suck my cock"), which are very common in Mediterranean Europe, or "ti ho fottuto"

("I fucked you," used to imply a person's shrewdness and ability to cheat others) may be used as a joke within a group of males. This set of examples refers to forms of *decontextualized meanings* and their indirect application; however, they produce effects on a subject's sexual image of themselves and others, or even addressed deliberately to others. These expressions do not immediately call into question a sexual practice, but they function informally as practices of sexual socialization where sexuality is a tool to *say* and to *mean* something that is not strictly sexual (much in the same way as gender roles, subordination, differential power relationships, etc.).

In contrast to functionalist theories (Parsons and Bales 1955/1974) that look at socialization as the mechanical reproduction of a given social system, symbolic interactionism rejects the idea that sexual socialization may be grounded upon *predictable* and *automatic* phases, but rather, it frames it within the context of a dynamic, multidimensional, and above all mutual process. Any social-sexual interaction is such that subjects learn and are provided instructions: the people involved learn how to adapt as required to the different situations, as well as to coordinate their actions with (those of) the others with regard to their objectives, hence shaping new scenarios. In any society at any given time, *people become sexual just like they become anything else*: beginning with their human interactions within their social environment, context, and group they learn and collect meanings, much in the same way as they do skills and values with regard to sexuality (Gagnon 1977:2). There is early evidence that constructing a sexual self is an open process in their interrelatedness with gender belongings, defined as the labels attached as part of a process of sociocultural attribution of roles. Gender belongings are first filtered through the expectations of meaningful ones, such as parents, who provide instructions on what is required to be appropriate females or males across the key stages of child development. It follows that, instead of looking at the early stages of individual life as phases in the emergence of a "natural" sexuality, they should be dealt with as the timeframe within which most of the preparatory work aimed at sexuality is being carried out (Gagnon and Simon 1973/2005:22). Here we are dealing with the very phases when parents reproduce their normative expectations about gender roles—with regard to children's appearance, bodies, and conducts—while also projecting onto them sexual meanings from the adult world, thus causing children's feelings of embarrassment, anxiety, pride, anger, or unease. These processes represent the means through which the sexual norms people internalize and the feeling rules and emotion they formulate are prefiguring informal social processes that will control the people's future sexual development (Hochschild 1979). They also entail verbal and nonverbal sanctioning of girls' and boys' explorations of their own bodies, such as the following: "You shouldn't do this!," "Stop touching," "You'll get dirty!," or "Stop touching down there!" These reproaches contribute to children's development of a *vocabulary of motives* (Mills 1940/1971), including both *emotional* and *sexual motives*, providing them with answers, justifications, and excuses that are instrumental to the adults' sexual scripts, without constituting a particular sexual script they can apply to a given context (Gagnon and Simon 1973/2005: 26). At this stage, children still receive rather scant, "nontargeted" information from their interactions with parents. Girls and boys codify this information, which will be used in their different learning contexts, *even those that are not strictly sexual*, given that the information is not expressed *through explicit sexual terms*, but in more general ones involving the moral sphere ("dirty," "good," "naughty"). As a consequence, it is possible to think of gender and sexual socialization within the context of a wider sexual-emotional socialization process, involving the following: (a) receiving and providing emotional responses according to our own relationships with meaningful ones; (b) receiving instructions as to *what we should feel* about something we do, or feel, and so on; (c) learning the emotional reactions we should expect from others following a certain gesture or action; (d) beginning to look at our actions based on our own and other people's feelings; (e) learning what we should feel at a given time or due to a specific action, as well as how to express this (Hochschild 1979); and (f) developing romantic norms and emotional roles with regard to the love stories as they should be (Simon, Eder, and Evans 1992; this relates to intragender groups in general, specifically to women's groups). Drawing from Spencer Cahill's notion of "emotional capital" (Cahill 1999), there seems to be a particular *sexual-emotional capital* we accumulate over the period from childhood to adulthood, which refers to a set of resources that we learn to gather (as we do) and to apply to the emotional and sexual requests we received during the course of life. In the next phases, in particular pre-adolescence and adolescence, this kind of information, and the attendant values, moral codes, sexual cultures, and emotions, are provided by groups of peers and other socialization agencies. Peer cultures are usually divided along gender lines, allowing their members to develop a moral code through which to produce specific images of the (sexual) self and gender(ed) performances. The development of a masculine moral code inside male peer groups strengthens homosocial bonds between members through the idealization of toughness, emotional self-control, competition, and the celebration of masculine aggressiveness (Fine 1987). Through committing themselves to speak about sexuality for reasons that are not purely sexual, young males subscribe to dominant values and self-validate their masculine status, also involving the management of other people's ideas about them (Goffman 1959).

Generally, the construction of male homosocial bonds is produced through using the language of violence, emotional control, and other violent conducts further improved by the acquisition of misogynistic and homophobic attitudes, the celebration of masculine power, and the public display of a hegemonic (heterosexual) masculinity. Most of the reference points for the construction of hegemonic sexual roles originate from the performance of male sexual identarian codes, which need to distance themselves from the opposing poles (as in the case of homosexuals, "inadequate" males, and females). This constitutes the definition of performance strategies for amplifying masculinity. More specifically, and as compared to their female peers, boys are less inclined to limit their freedom and sexual explorations, whereas the former learn at a very young age that being able to manage feelings of shame and guilt is what is at stake in their "proper" management of sexuality (Gagnon and Simon 1973/2005:31). The process of social-sexual learning for girls involves their adoption of a reactive sexual role and their learning how to display reluctance and privacy, while preventing them from receiving specifically sexual instructions beyond a punitive, sanctioning framework. The types of informal control of female sexualities are best exemplified by different types of derogatory expressions usually referred to as "slut talk" or "slut shaming"; these include modes of address, such as "bitch" and other forms of definition whose moral contours contribute to the shaping of their sexual behavior and gendered presentations along the lines of class, racial, and ethnic belongings (Armstrong et al. 2014; Sweeney 2014). The same line of thought may be applied to the use of other derogatory terms, such as "queer" and "fag." Just like the above, in this case the performance of masculinity is played out alongside the threat of using *fag talk* in order to ensure that boys conform to hegemonic masculine codes. *Calling someone a whore* has got nothing to do with actual sexual conduct in the same way as *calling someone a queer* or *fag* is used neither to define their sexual identity, nor to observe specific sexual practices that may actually be carried out. Both instances represent the use of discursive mechanisms aimed at discipling oneself and others (Pascoe 2007:54).

Sexual Choreographies and Performances

The aspects discussed in the previous sections stimulate a reflection on how, in the first instance, our *being sexual* varies according to the rituals and performances in which we are involved as part of our daily lives. Such is the case any time we perform a role to communicate our identity to one or more audiences from communicative, expressive, aesthetic, and verbal points of view. From a symbolic interactionist approach, our being sexual is more likely something we do, a *doing (oneself) sexual(ly)*. It follows that, like other spheres of social life, sexuality is based on a *performative imperative*, whereby *we must necessarily appear to (female or male) others* (Edgley 2015:56), or at least a competent and plausible sexual(ized) social actor. The moment we take *center stage* from the *backstage* and stand in front of an audience lends itself to an understanding of the ways that social actors "dress up for" a particular role or, conversely, "take off" their clothes (Goffman 1959); the same is true for the reverse movement from one's presence onstage to their retreat backstage. Any kind of social-sexual interaction must be somehow staged and "tuned" in order to reach a balance of actions and therefore to get at a common shared definition. Having sex means *doing some things with others*; what is more, we succeed in understanding certain techniques and in performing certain acts only by rehearsing them in conversation with ourselves as much as in interactions with others. We are still doing something with others when we have a sexual fantasy, due to the particular culture we have internalized. These elements can be seen at work rather easily in BDSM scenes: their dramaturgies provide an understanding of sexuality and eroticism as something that can be *performed*. Similarly, it is possible to use the ensuing representations and organizations to get at the more "natural," immediate, and pristine parts of our self, while also questioning the belief that eroticism is one of the most "authentic" spheres of our daily lives (Newmahr 2013:261).

These are the reasons why our sexual identities change according to our ways to confront the different contexts in which we happen to be situated. They can refer either to strategies to valorize certain resources in specific situations, or else, to find one's own way in time and space, while managing accurately the so-called *auxiliary characteristics and marks* (Brekhus 2015:117), or conversely, finding a hierarchical organization to discern *which specific resources* are more *salient* for our self (Stryker 1980). If our tendency is to view a certain identity as more salient, then it is likely to be the driving our interpretation of a given situation, so that we are able to interact with others and/or to coordinate one another's actions. Our interpretation of some of our sexual characteristics allows us to provide to our different selves a degree of identity salience, and consequently to organize the different features of identity, relationships, lifestyles, values, and social networks in which we are likely to be involved. In Brekhus's ethnography of gay men, for instance, different values and varying degrees of relevance are placed upon one's homosexual self. As shown by his gay male interviewees, there are numerous and diverse ways to express a (homo)sexual identity; furthermore, subjects (both homosexual and non-homosexual) create a number of identitarian strategies, caught in the midst of individual choices and structural constraints (Brekhus 2003, 2012). This explains why, within an interactionist framework, changes in life occupy such a crucial role in the sequence of scenes leading to the achievement of a particular status or identity (Strauss 1959). There is no space for an etiology of sexual conducts; instead, symbolic interactionism stresses the acquisition of meaning for sexualities as they are subjectively organized and transformed into (a series of) active roles, that is, in social criteria for the attribution of a certain status (Glaser and Strauss 1971). For this reason, our sexual identities can be explained within the context of an ongoing series of changes in status, where subjects are undergoing biographical (identity) transformations that produce reconfigurations of the self. They also produce new forms of socialization involving the subject's newly discovered conceptualization of the self and the forms of recognition from others. It could be that one is becoming gay; another is becoming an ex-virgin; still another is experimenting with new forms of sexuality at an old age; it could be that a sex worker is leaving their activity—in all these cases, as well as in many others, we are about to perform a different role and to refuse the previous one(s). This requires our involvement in forms of role exiting (Ebaugh 1988) that will lead us to define new perceptions of our sexual self, to manage our impressions ensuing from a different status, and to learn how to introduce our new roles. One of the most productive concepts in the field of sociological studies of sexualities is the notion of career, hinting at a model of investigation into processes constituted by phases that are not necessarily chronologically arranged, and which take into account both the subjective dimension and the role of structural constraints (Becker 1966; Goffman 1961). It follows that every form of sexual socialization or entrance into social-sexual worlds, or sexual subcultures, can be seen through the lens of sexual careers (see, among others, the renowned study of identity works and homosexuality in Plummer 1975). As part of their careers, subjects undergo cognitive changes; they learn how to speak of themselves in new ways, and to retell the story of their life using a new vocabulary (in a kind of sexual retrospective interpretation); but they also learn to redefine themselves, and as in the case of transsexualism, to prepare, shape, and redefine their own bodies—a proper example of reflexive transembodiment (Schrock and Boyd 2005). Similarly, those subjects involved in certain sexual subcultures, especially stigmatized subcultures, find themselves involved in identity works (Schwalbe and Mason-Schrock:141–42) that are required to manage their own visibility and to avoid control. However, these works can also be useful for new negotiations of sexual meanings and the constructions of additional ones, through a process of resignification involving the practices, meanings, and codes of the broader subculture to which they belong in unforeseen ways. Let us illustrate this by making some examples: *queer* groups provide an alternative articulation of derogatory terms like "queer" by turning their meaning upside-down (Rinaldi 2016); normative homosexual males, such as *clones*, re-articulate the canons of a hyper-virile normative masculinity to take their distance from age-old stereotypes targeting effeminate gay men (Rinaldi 2015); more organized groups, such as swingers, reverse some of the (normative) meanings such as, among others, sexual monogamy and privacy (even though they continue to draw from conventional society, for instance, when men control their women partner's sexual activity or force them to realize their own erotic or pornographic fantasies; see Welzer-Lang 2005:92). Other examples include the following: in barebacking (anal sex performed without a condom), subjects who willingly exchange HIV-infected bodily fluids are defining new forms of social organization and unforeseen "acquired" kinship structures for which the fluid-virus exchange is combined with the myth of the "patient zero" (Dean 2009, 2012); southern Italian sex workers who define themselves heterosexual and look for homosexual clients are involved in a *performative production* of sexual activity requiring that they exhibit "authentic" sexual signs (e.g., erection or orgasm), which are realized through a series of learning strategies (first, learning to find pleasure and to discern its positive effects; Rinaldi 2020). In this case, belonging to a deviant subculture allows subjects to construct situated meanings and interactional rules, to develop situational competences, and to perform newly emerged *identitarian configurations* through which they can remain "males" and therefore avoid a possible contamination from their cultural enemy ("the queer [man]"; Seidman 2005).

Sex Is Never "Just Sex": Conclusion

Normative and positivistic perspectives that have dealt with sexuality have often employed a simplistic and homogeneous notion of the issues. They have produced *exoticized* and *deviantized* sexual subjects belonging to a distinct category, and they have reinforced an idea of (sexual) normality that has seldom been interrogated and that ultimately remains "unmarked" (Zerubavel 2018). An interactionist approach allows understanding that we learn how to *become sexual* and to use sexual meanings just like we learn any other kind of meaning (Rinaldi 2016). After all, we should pay attention to the terms under which people are offering, requesting, having, or otherwise employing sex as people who are developing a joint action (Blumer 1969). Following Blumer, this could be defined as a *joint sexual action*: even when we believe that we are comfortably placed in a hermit's cell, the mind is always a place of hospitality and intercourse (Cooley 1992: 97)—we are always making *sexual things* together with others.

Therefore symbolic interactionists look at all forms of sexualities as "unnatural" (Gagnon and Simon 2019), since just like any other human behavior they do not include a set of predetermined, fixed forms and contents; as any other human behavior, sexuality is a complex condition originating from the purely human capacity/ability to think, to act, and to remember, as well as from people's needs to live with other human beings.

NOTE

1. These are mostly PhD and MA theses, ethnographic notes, or even just life stories, which are collected and then transcribed. The vast majority is held at the Regenstein Library, University of Chicago, and at the Ernest W. Burgess Fund, Special Collections Research Center of the University. See Heap 2003:458n5 and Heap 2009.

REFERENCES

Armstrong, Elizabeth A., Laura T. Hamilton, Elizabeth M. Armstrong, and J. Lotus Seeley. 2014. "'Good Girls': Gender, Social Class and Slut Discourse on Campus." *Social Psychology Quarterly* 77(2):100–22.

Becker, Howard S., and Anselm L. Strauss. 1956. "Careers, Personality and Adult Socialization" *American Journal of Sociology* 62:253–63.

Becker, Howard S. 1966. *Outsiders: Studies in the Sociology of Deviance*. New York: The Free Press.

Berger, Peter L., and Thomas Luckmann. 1966. *The Social Construction of Reality*. New York: Anchor Books.

Blumer Herbert. 1948. "A Sociologist looks at the 'Kinsey Report': Sexual Behavior in the Human Male by Alfred C. Kinsey, Wardell B. Pomeroy, Clyde E. Martin." *Ecology* 29(4):522–24.

Blumer, Herbert. 1969. *Symbolic Interactionism: Perspective and Method*. Englewood Cliffs: Prentice Hall.

Brekhus, Wayne H. 2003. *Peacocks, Chameleons, Centaurs: Gay Suburbia and the Grammar of Social Identity*. Chicago: University of Chicago Press.

Brekhus, Wayne H. 2012. "Gay pendolari, gay integranti: Strategie Identitarie dei gay di periferia bell'Era Post-Closet." Pp. 187–214 in *Alterazioni: introduzione alle sociologie delle omosessualità*, edited by Cirus Rinaldi. Milan: Mimesis

Brekhus, Wayne H. 2015. *Culture and Cognition*. Malden, MA: Polity.

Burgess, Ernest W. 1949. "The Sociological Theory of Psychosexual Behaviour." Pp. 227–43 in *Psychosexual Developments in Health and Disease*, edited by Paul Hoch and Joseph Zubin. New York: Grunn and Stratton.

Burke, Kenneth. 1945. *A Grammar of Motives*. New York: Prentice Hall.

Burke, Kenneth. 1965. *Permanence and Change: An Anatomy of Purpose*. Indianapolis: Bobbs-Merrill.

Cahill, Spencer E. 1999. "Emotional Capital and Professional Socialization: The Case of Mortuary Science Students (and Me)." *Social Psychology Quarterly* 62:101–16.

Cameron, Deborah, and Don Kulick. 2006. "General Introduction." Pp. xi–xii in *The Language and Sexuality Reader*, edited by Deborah Cameron and Don Kulick. New York: Routledge.

Carpenter, Laura M. 2001. "The Ambiguity of 'Having Sex': The Subjective Experience of Virginity Loss in the United States." *Journal of Sex Research* 38(2):127–39.

Cooley, Charles H. 1992. *Human Nature and Social Order*. New Brunswick: Transaction Publisher.

Dean, Tim. 2009. *Unlimited Intimacy. Reflections on the Subculture of Barebacking*. Chicago: University of Chicago Press.

Dean, Tim. 2012. "La cultura della 'fecondazione'. Barebacking, bugchasing, giftgiving." Pp. 273–92 in *Alterazioni. Introduzione alle sociologie dell'omosessualità*, edited by Cirus Rinaldi. Milano-Udine: Mimesis.

DeLamater, John D., and Janet S. Hyde. 1998. "Essentialism vs. Social Constructionism in the Study of Human Sexuality." *Journal of Sex Research* 35(1):10–18.

Dingwall, Robert, Brigitte Nerlich, and Samantha Hillyard. 2015. "Determinismo Biologico e Interazionismo Simbolico: correnti eraditarie e percorsi culturali." Pp. 55–82 in *L'interazionismo simbolico: caratteristiche e prospettive*, edited by Raffaele Rauty. Calimera: Kurumuny.

Douglas, Jack D. 1977. *The Nude Beach*. Beverly Hill: SAGE.

Duncombe, Jean, and Dennis Marsden. 1996. "Whose Orgasm Is This Anyway? 'Sex Work' in Long-Term Heterosexual Couple Relationship." Pp. 220–58 in *Sexual Cultures: Communities, Values and Intimacy*, edited by Jeffrey Weeks and Janet Holland. New York: Macmillan.

Ebaugh, Helen R. 1988. *Becoming an Ex: The Process of Role Exit*. Chicago: University of Chicago Press.

Edgley, Charles. 2015. "Sex as Theatre: Action, Character and the Erotic." Pp. 55–72 in *Selves, Symbols and Sexualities: An Interactionist Anthology*, edited by Thomas S. Weinberg and Staci Newmahr. Thousand Oaks: SAGE.

Fine, Gary A. 1987. *With the Boys: Little League Baseball and Preadolescent Culture*. Chicago: University of Chicago Press.

Gagnon, John H., and William Simon. 1973/2005. *Sexual Conduct: The Social Sources of Human Sexuality*. Chicago: Aldine Publishing Company.

Gagnon, John H., and William Simon. 2019. *Outsiders Sessuali. Le Forme Collettive della Devianza Sessuale*, edited by S. Grassi and C. Rinaldi. Aprilia: Novalogos.

Gagnon, John H. 1977. *Human Sexualities*. New York: Scott, Foresman and Co.

Gecas, Viktor, and Roger Libby. 1976. "Sexual Behavior as Symbolic Interaction." *The Journal of Sex Research* 12(1):33–49.

Glaser, Barney G., and Anselm L. Strauss. 1971. *Status Passage*. London: Aldine Transaction.

Goffman, Erving. 1959. *The Presentation of Self in Everyday Life*. Garden City, NY: Doubleday.

Goffman, Erving. 1961. *Asylums*. New York: Anchor Books.

Goffman, Erving. 1963. *Behavior in Public Places: Notes on the Social Organization of Gatherings*. New York: The Free Press.

Green, Adam I. 2008a. "The Social Organization of Desire: The Sexual Fields Approach." *Sociological Theory* 26(1):25–50.

Green, Adam I. 2008b. "Erotic Habitus: Toward a Sociology of Desire." *Theory and Society* 37(6):595–626.

Green, Adam I. 2014. "The Sexual Fields Framework." Pp. 25–66 in *Sexual Fields: Toward a Sociology of Collective Sexual Life*, edited by Adam I. Green. Chicago: University of Chicago Press.

Heap, Chad. 2003. "The City as a Sexual Laboratory: The Queer Heritage of the Chicago School." *Qualitative Sociology* 26(4):457–87.

Heap, Chad. 2009. *Slumming. Sexual and Racial Encounters in American Nightlife, 1885–1940*. Chicago: University of Chicago Press.

Henslin, James M., and Mae A. Biggs. 1978. "Dramaturgical Desexualization; The Sociology of Vaginal Examination." Pp. 141–70 in *The Sociology of Sex: An Introductory Reader*, edited by James M. Henslin and Edward Sagarin. New York: Schocken Books.

Hochschild, Arlie R. 1979. "Emotion Work, Feeling Rules and Social Structure." *American Journal of Sociology* 85(3):551–75.

Hughes, Everett C. 1971. *The Sociological Eye: Selected Essays*. New Brunswick, NJ: Transaction.

Jowett, Garth S., Ian C. Jarvie, and Karhryn H. Fuller. 1996. *Children and the Movies: Media influence and the Payne Fund Controversies*. New York: Cambridge University Press.

Kimmel, Michael S., and Rebecca F. Plante. 2004. "Introduction." Pp. xi–xvi in *Sexualities: Identities, Behaviors and Society*, edited by Michael S. Kimmel and Rebecca F. Plante. New York: Oxford University Press.

Kinsey, Alfred C., Wardell B. Pomeroy, and Clyde E. Martin. 1948. *Sexual Behavior in the Human Male*. Philadelphia: W.B. Sanders Co.

Kuhn, Manford. 1954. "Kinsey's View on Human Behaviour." *Social Problems* 1(4): 119–25.

Lancaster, Roger N. 1992. *Life Is Hard: Machismo, Danger and the Intimacy of Power in Nicaragua*. Berkeley: University of California Press.

Lindesmith, Alfred R., Anselm L. Strauss, and Norman K. Denzin. 1975. *Social Psychology*. Hinsdale: The Dryden Press.

Longmore, Monica A. 1998. "Symbolic Interactionism and the Study of Sexuality." *The Journal of Sex Research* 35(1):44–57.

Mead, George H. 1934/1962. *Mind, Self, and Society*, edited by Charles W. Morris. Chicago: University of Chicago Press.

Medley-Rath, Stephanie R. 2007. "Am I Still a Virgin?: What Counts as Sex in Twenty Years of Seventeen." *Sexuality and Culture* 11:24–38.

Meston, Cindy M., and David M. Buss. 2007. "Why Humans Have Sex?" *Archives of Sexual Behavior* 36:477–507.

Mills, Charles W. 1940/1971. "Situated Actions and Vocabularies of Motive." *American Sociological Review* 5(6):904–13. doi: 10.2307/2084524

Mumford, Kevin. 1997. *Interzones: Black/White Sex Districts in Chicago and New York in the Early Twentieth Century*. New York: Columbia University Press.

Newmahr, Staci. 2013. "Sadomasochistic Selves: Dramaturgical Dimensions of SM Play." Pp. 261–75 in *The Drama of Social Life: A Dramaturgical Handbook*, edited by Charles Edgley. Farnham: Ashgate.

Padgug, Robert A. 1992. "Sexual Matters: On Conceptualizing Sexuality in History." Pp. 43–67 in *Forms of Desire: Sexual Orientation and Social Constructionist Controversy*, edited by Edward Stein. New York: Routledge.

Parker, Richard. 2010. "Reinventing Sexual Scripts: Sexuality and Social Change in the Twenty-First Century." *Sexuality Research and Social Policy* 7:58–66.

Parsons, Talcott, and Robert F. Bales. 1955/1974. *Family, Socialization an Interaction Process.* Glencoe: The Free Press.

Pascoe, Cheri J. 2007. *Dude. You're a Fag: Masculinity and Sexuality in High School.* Berkley: University of California Press.

Plante, Rebecca F. 2006. *Sexualities in Context: A Social Perspective.* Boulder, CO: Westview.

Plummer, Ken. 1975. *Sexual Stigma. An Interactionist Account.* London/New York: Routledge/ Paul Kegan.

Plummer, Ken. 1982. "Symbolic Interactionism and Sexual Conduct: An Emergent Perspective." Pp. 223–41 in *Human Sexual Relations: Toward a Redefinition of Sexual Politics,* edited by Michael Brake. New York: Pantheon Books.

Plummer, Ken. 1984. "The Social Uses of Sexuality: Symbolic Interaction, Power and Rape." Pp. 37–55 in *Perspectives on Rape and Sexual Assault,* edited by June Hopkins. London: Harper and Row.

Plummer, Ken. 2002. "General Introduction, Sexualities: Critical Concepts." Pp. 1–24 in *Sociology,* vol. 1: *Making a Sociology of Sexualities,* edited by Ken Plummer. New York: Routledge.

Plummer, Ken. 2007. "Queer, Bodies, and Postmodern Sexualities: A Note on Revisiting the 'Sexual' in Symbolic Interactionism." Pp. 16–30 in *Sexual Self,* edited by Michela Kimmel. Nashville, TN: Vanderbilt University Press.

Rinaldi, Cirus. 2015. "'Rimani maschio finché non ne arriva uno più maschio e più attivo di te.' La costruzione delle maschilià omosessuali tra normalizzazione, complicità e consumo." *Ragion Pratica* 2:443–62.

Rinaldi, Cirus. 2016. *Sesso, Sè, e Società. Per una Sociologia delle Sessualità.* Milan: Mondadori.

Rinaldi, Cirus. 2020. *Uomini che si Fanno Pagare. Genere, Identità e Sessualità nel Sex Work Maschile tra Devianza e Nuove Forme di Normalizzazione.* Rome: DeriveApprodi.

Rubin, Gayle S. 1984. "Thinking Sex: Notes for a Radical Theory of the Politics of Sexuality." Pp. 267–319 in *Pleasure and Danger: Exploring Female Sexuality,* edited by Carole S. Vance. Boston: Routledge and Kegan Paul.

Rubin, Gayle S. 2002. "Studying Sexual Subcultures: Excavating the Ethnography of Gay Communities in Urban North America." Pp. 17–68 in *Out in Theory: The Emergence of Lesbian and Gay Anthropology,* edited by Ellen Lewin and William Leap. Urbana: University of Illinois Press.

Sanders, Stephanie A., and June M. Reinisch. 1999. "Would You Say You 'Had Sex' If . . . ?" *Journal of American Medical Association* 281(3):275–77.

Schrock, Doug P., and Emily M. Boyd. 2005. "Reflexive Transembodiment." Pp. 51–66 in *Body/Embodiment: Symbolic Interactionism and the Sociology of the Body,* edited by Dennis Waskul and Philip Vannini. Aldershot: Ashgate.

Schwalbe, Michael L., and Douglas Mason-Schrock. 1996. "Identity Work as Group Process." *Advances in Group Processes* 13:113–47.

Seidman, Steven. 2005. "From Polluted Homosexual to the Normal Gay: Changing Patterns of Sexual Regulation in America." Pp. 39–61 in *Thinking Straight: The Power, the Promise and the Paradox of Heterosexuality,* edited by Chrys Ingraham. New York: Routledge.

Simon, Robin W., Donna Eder, and Cathy Evans. 1992. "The Development of Feeling Norms Underlying Romantic Love among Adolescent Females." *Social Psychology Quarterly* 55(1):29–46.

Simon, William, and John H. Gagnon. 1986. "Sexual Scripts: Permanence and Change." *Archives of Sexual Behavior* 15:97–120.

Snow, David A., and Leon Anderson. 1987. "Identity Work among the Homeless: The Verbal Construction and Avowal of Personal Identities." *American Journal of Sociology* 92:1336–71.

Steele Tracey L., ed. 2004. *Sex, Self, and Society: The Social Context of Sexuality*. Belmont, CA: Thomson Wadsworth.

Strauss, Anselm L. 1959. *Mirrors and Masks: The Search for Identity*. Glancoe: Free Press.

Stryker, Sheldon. 1980. *Symbolic Interactionism: A Social Structural Version*. Reading: Cummings.

Sweeney, Brian N. 2014. "Masculine Status, Sexual Performance and the Sexual Stigmatization of Women." *Symbolic Interaction* 37(3):369–90.

Thomas, William I. 1907. *Sex and Society: Studies in the Social Psychology of Sex*. Chicago: University of Chicago Press.

Walby, Kevin. 2012. *Touching Encounters: Sex, Work and Male-for-Male Internet Escorting*. Chicago: University of Chicago Press.

Weeks, Jeffrey. 1985. *Sexuality and Its Discontents*. London: Routledge.

Weinberg, Martin S. 1965. "Sexual Modesty, Social Meanings and the Nudist Camp." *Social Problems* 12(3):311–18.

Weinberg, Martin S. 1966. "Becoming a Nudist." *Psychiatry* 29(1):15–24.

Weinberg, Martin S. 1967. "The Nudist Camp: Way of Life and Social Structure." *Human Organization* 26(3):91–99.

Weinberg, Thomas S., and Staci Newmahr. 2015. *Selves, Symbols and Sexualities*. Thousand Oaks: SAGE.

Weinberg, Thomas S. 2015. "Introduction." P. xiii. in *Selves, Symbols and Sexualities*, edited by Thomas S. Weinberg and Staci Newmahr. Thousand Oaks: SAGE.

Welzer-Lang, Daniel. 2005. *La planéte échangiste. Les sexualités collectives en France*. Paris: Payot.

Zerubavel, Eviatar. 2018. *Taken for Granted: The Remarkable Power of the Unremarkable*. Princeton: Princeton University Press.

Znaniecki, Florian. 1927. "The Sexual Relation as a Social Relation and Some of Its Changes." Pp. 222–30 in *Verhandlungen des I Internationalen Kongresses für Sexualforschung, Berlin, vom 10 bis 16 Oktober 1926*, edited by Max Marcuse. Berlin: A. Marcus & W. Weber.

CHAPTER 25

....

DEVIANT SELVES, TRANSGRESSIVE ACTS, AND MORAL NARRATIVES

The Symbolic-Interactionist Field of Transgression, Crime, and Justice

....

THADDEUS MÜLLER

INTRODUCTION: THE SOCIAL CONSTRUCTION OF MORAL MEANINGS

....

THE symbolic-interactionist field of transgression, crime, and justice focuses on the dynamic interactional meaning-making process that shapes the moral narratives of a range of actors such as perpetrators, police, and judges. Moral narratives include different meaning-making processes such as labeling, stigmatization, criminalization, normalization, and neutralization. These processes are about (1) degrading, dominating, controlling, and excluding, and (2) their narrative counterparts, which focus on resisting the othering claims of moral narratives and constructing alternative narratives.

In this chapter, I will discuss a wide range of studies within the symbolic-interactionist field of transgression, crime, and justice that deepen our understanding of the social construction of moral meanings and focus on the interrelation among deviant selves, transgressive acts, and moral narratives. This field is vast and complex. It covers a century of studies starting with the Chicago School ethnographies after the First World War. I will focus here on two fundamental contributions of symbolic interaction to this field: the labeling perspective, and more specifically the social construction of moral narratives, and the ethnographic approach to studying the social constructions of moral meanings during everyday interactions in the field of transgression, crime, and justice.[1]

This field changed fundamentally in the 1960s because of the publication of deviance studies embracing the labeling perspective. These studies were essentially shaped by symbolic interactionism and centered on the following questions: who defines what kind of behavior as criminal, how does this process take place, and how does this shape the definitions of self and subsequently the career of deviants and criminals?[2]

An equally significant contribution of symbolic interactionism has been its ethnographic focus on studying the perspectives of rule breakers and developing an understanding of how this shapes and is shaped by their everyday social life. This approach stems from ethnographic studies of the Chicago School in 1918–38. The notion of studying "the natural social world of every-day experience," as Blumer described it (1954:7), has been the guideline for the best ethnographic studies in the field of transgression, crime, and justice.

This chapter consists of two parts. In the first part, I will focus on deviance studies, starting with Becker's contribution and the subsequent developments within this perspective in 1960–80. In the second part, I will pay attention to symbolic-interactionist studies in the field of transgression, crime, and justice since the so-called death of deviance studies (1980–2020). Here I will discuss several subfields that use different interrelated conceptual frames, such as stigma, moral panic, and social problems, and I will focus on two subthemes: (1) violence, the perspective of the "badass," and (2) the criminal-justice system as a labeling machine.

In the conclusion, I will highlight the methodological and theoretical strength of the symbolic-interactionist angle studying the field of transgression, crime, and justice and how this can be used to further develop our understanding of this field.

Deviance Studies (1960–80)

Outsider: Studies in the Sociology of Deviance by Howard Becker (1963) was groundbreaking within sociology and criminology, because it emphasized a new perspective on crime and justice. Becker proposed to look at the social significance of labeling.

> *social groups create deviance by making rules whose infraction creates deviance*, and by applying those rules to particular people and labelling them as outsiders. (...) The deviant is one to whom that label has been successfully applied; deviant behaviour is behaviour that people so label. (Becker 1963:9)

Becker showed the consequences of being labeled: when the label of a criminal becomes his or her master status, it will dominate the way people perceive and characterize him or her. The exclusion from respectable society will trigger a deviant career, which confirms the image people have of a person. In sum, societal reaction, and especially the formal institutional reactions of the criminal-justice system, particularly its othering moral narratives, are crucial in understanding the experienced moral degradation and the development of a deviant career of becoming an outsider.

Becker's *Outsiders* is also groundbreaking because he suggested paying attention to those whose work it is to label certain behavior as deviant: moral entrepreneurs. Becker focused on one example of the work of moral entrepreneurs: the natural history of *The Marihuana Tax Act*. Becker explained how in the 1930s the *Bureau of Narcotics* influenced the media by feeding them atrocity stories concerning "reefer madness": sane young people who are intoxicated by cannabis go on a killing spree. These publications were instrumental in convincing Congress to criminalize the use of cannabis.

Becker did also focus on how outsiders create a counternarrative in relation to their societal position. He described the cultural process of becoming deviant as acquiring and developing a set of moral meanings by looking at the process of becoming a marihuana user. He puts this in the social and cultural context of a specific group: the dance musician. He describes different elements that constitute this social world and its moral counternarratives, such as how musicians label themselves ("special," "gifted," and "free"), and how they perceive and label the middle-class people they play for, "squares," whom they see as their moral opposites. Becker's work shows that *accounts*, such as excuses and justifications (Scott and Lyman 1968, 1970) and *techniques of neutralization* (Sykes and Matza 1957) play a crucial role in the social construction of counternarratives that outsiders use to resist and neutralize labeling.

Becker is the first one to point out that *Outsiders* is shaped by the Chicago School tradition. He refers to (1) scholars who emphasized the importance of societal reaction, such as Tannenbaum, Lemert, Kitsuse, and Goffman, and (2) scholars who produced ethnographic studies of the social worlds of outsiders, such as immigrants, deviant subcultures, and criminal groups and their moral narratives (for a more detailed account of the social production of *Outsiders*, see Müller 2014).

Tannenbaum (1938) used the concept "dramatization of evil" to describe what he called the "process of tagging." He stated that this process is crucial in the transformation of a delinquent child into a criminal: a gradual process in which a person becomes characterized as an evil immoral person: "the person becomes the thing he is described as being" (Tannenbaum 1938:20). Lemert's *Social Pathology* (1951) is the first study that systematically focuses on deviance and highlights the importance of societal reaction. "The deviant person is one whose role, status, function, and self-definition are importantly shaped by how much deviation he engages in, by the degree of its social visibility, by the particular exposure he has to the societal reaction, and by the nature and strength of the societal reaction" (Lemert 1951:23).

Later Lemert also developed the important distinction between primary and secondary deviation, which emphasized the crucial importance of labeling. He stated that when there is no formal reaction to the criminal-justice system, the discussed public labeling process will not take place, and one can speak of primary deviation. In case of a formal reaction, we can speak of secondary deviation: the development of a deviant career as a result of labeling shaped by the criminal-justice system and subsequently by wider society (Lemert 1951:76). The transition from primary to secondary deviance is further shaped by social-economic differences: persons belonging to the middle and upper classes have more resources to (1) control the social visibility of their transgression and hide their rule-breaking, and (2) when caught they have more resources to limit societal reaction and prevent prosecution and punishment (e.g., Chambliss 1973; Müller 2016; Piliavin and Briar 1964).

Kitsuse (1961) and Goffman (1959) each published significant articles on the processes by which persons come to be defined as deviants. Both authors shaped the symbolic-interactionist field of deviance with later publications: *Asylums* (Goffman 1961), *Stigma* (Goffman 1963b), and *Constructing Social Problems* (Spector and Kitsuse 1977), which I will discuss later in this chapter.

As mentioned before, the work of Becker and other deviance scholars is to be traced back to the work of Chicago sociologists who published many outstanding urban ethnographies on marginal or deviant groups, such as *The Hobo: The Sociology of The Homeless Man* (Anderson 1923), *The Gang: A Study of 1,313 Gangs in Chicago* (Thrasher 1926), and *The Jack-Roller: A Delinquent Boy's Own Story* (Shaw 1930). For the Chicago sociologists, it was crucial to see how the people they studied gave moral meanings to their social worlds because that shaped their behavior. This stance is known as the Thomas theorem: "if a person perceives a situation as real, it is real in its consequences" (Thomas and Thomas 1928). This became one of the core principles for the labeling theory: the criminal label defines how we see and interact with an offender. The other core principle that relates to the self-perception of the perpetrator is Cooley's *Looking Glass Self*: our expectations and interpretation of the way people see and judge us, shapes the way we see ourselves and defines our moral worth (Cooley 1902).

An excellent example of the early labeling perspective is the study of Piliavin and Briar (1964) on policing and how it creates social injustice. The authors show that officers use different elements in the juveniles' self-presentation to evaluate their moral character. This depends on whether they belong to marginalized and stigmatized groups— "Negroes, youths with well-oiled hair, black jackets, and soiled denims or jeans" (Piliavin and Briar 1964:210)—and whether they are cooperative and respectful during the interrogation. The authors explain that because African American juveniles have structural negative discriminative experiences with the police, they react in a hostile and noncooperative way during the questioning. They conclude: "He is a delinquent because someone in authority has defined him as one, often on the basis of the public face he has presented to officials rather than of the kind of offence he has committed" (Piliavin and Briar 1964:214). This publication shows that while middle-class youth tend to get away with an informal caution, marginal youth tend to end up in court, receiving a sentence and a criminal record that will shape their life (see also Chambliss 1973; Emmerson 1969).

In the same year that *Outsiders* was published, two other classic studies were published that shaped the symbolic-interactionist field of transgression, crime, and justice: *Stigma* (Goffman 1963b) and *Symbolic Crusade* (Gusfield 1963).

Stigma is a form of moral degradation and reduces a person "in our minds from a whole and usual person to a tainted, discounted one" (p. 3). Goffman's focus is on a wide range of activities and categories that are stigmatized, which he relates to physical deformities, moral transgression, and marginalized groups because of race, ethnicity, and/or religion. Goffman is not overly interested in the social construction of moral narratives around stigma or in counternarratives of those who are stigmatized. His focus is on social order and how different actors, stigmatized and non-stigmatized, participate in managing stigma in social encounters and thus try to maintain social order. A classic example of the early application of stigma is *Sexual Stigma* by Ken Plummer (1975) in which he presents an interactionist account of the stigma of being gay.

Gusfield's work is a prime example of the constructionist approach, studying the activities of moral entrepreneurs in how they create criminalizing moral narratives. Where Goffman ignored this and Becker hinted at this process, Gusfield made it the centerpiece of his work. In *Symbolic Crusade: Status Politics and the American Temperance Movement*, Gusfield (1963) develops a "dramatistic theory" in which he focuses on status and symbolic issues in politics. He focuses specifically on the intersection of immigration and the social construction of law, relating the temperance movement to the effort to maintain cultural and political dominance in reaction to the mass immigration that took place in the United States during the second half of the nineteenth century. He argues that the temperance movement defined the presence of the new immigrants as a threat to American society and sought to preserve the cultural dominance of Protestant rural communities.

Jack Douglas played an important role in the further development of deviance studies with his focus on power, conflict, and the brute being, a concept derived from Merleau-Ponty. It emphasizes the significance of strong "brute" emotions, such as pleasure, lust, disgust, and shame, in how individuals and groups construct moral meanings in their daily existence. Douglas also stressed that researchers should use their brute emotions to understand their field, a revolutionary concept that was first discussed and developed by Johnson in his classic *Doing Field Research* (1975).

With his first monograph *The Social Meanings of Suicide* (1967), Douglas rejects Durkheim because his analysis is not supported by how individuals in everyday life construct moral meanings. Douglas discovers that integration plays a crucial role in the processes of defining the meaning of death in official records. Those who are well integrated have family and or friends who put an effort into defining the cause of death as anything but suicide, because of overwhelming "brute" feelings of shame and pain related to this social act. Douglas shows in this work the complexity of meaning-making in relation to such morally charged acts as suicide. He states that the only way to understand this "is by studying the specific meanings of real-world phenomena of this socially-defined type as the individuals involved construct them . . ." (1967:253). In the beginning of the seventies, Douglas advances the field of transgression by integrating power, inequalities, and oppression in his work on deviance and the social construction of moral meanings (1971). Another crucial contribution is what Douglas called the "multi-perspectival picture of society" (1976:55). While most ethnographic studies focus on one community or group, Douglas stated that in order to understand the plural and conflicted character of society, one has to research how different parties construct their moral narratives in the public arena of conflict and politics.

All these innovative themes, such as the brute being, a focus on conflict, and the multiperspective approach, were combined in the highly original and pioneering *The Nude Beach* (Douglas, Rasmussen, and Flanagan 1977). It describes a range of conflicting perspectives on nudity, such as those of the regular casual nude beachers, the gay scene, the swinging scene, the police, and the property owners who are against the nude beach. There are two dominant perspectives on the nude beach: (1) the nude beachers' view that it was a natural and pleasant place where sex played a secondary role and (2) their opponents' view that the beach was in fact a public carnal orgy. His conclusion is that both parties are constructing a set of meanings—shaped by their interests and brute feelings such as shame, disgust, lust, and pleasure—neither of which is in line with the observations of the nude beach. For example, Douglas and his co-researchers provide many descriptions of "brute" sexual behavior that might discredit the nude beach. They confirm that sex acts do take place on the beach, but at the same state that there is "always some degree of concealment, so they are not simply "open to plain view" . . . (1977:106; for a more detailed discussion of Douglas's work on crime and justice, see Müller 2019c).

Two other symbolic-interactionist-inspired perspectives that changed the field of transgression, crime, and justice pay attention to (1) moral panics and (2) social problems. Both tend to pay attention to those who have narrative power, such as moral entrepreneurs and claims makers, to construct moral narratives. Inspired by the interactionist approach in American deviance studies, Cohen further developed this field in *Moral Panics and Folk Devils: The Creation of the Mods and the Rockers* (1972) by describing how media creates moral narratives resulting in mass stigmatization. A moral panic is a distorted representation of social reality, created by moral entrepreneurs, consisting of journalists, citizens, politicians, and experts. They define the behavior of a certain category of citizens, *folk devils*, as a threat to society. This process of "symbolization" also consists of a prediction that if nothing is done there will be grave consequences. Cohen associates the construction of *moral panics* and *folk devils* with swift societal changes. He relates it to a structural social transformation from a postwar society with an emphasis on discipline and collectivism to one in which consumerism and individualism are highlighted.

Inspired by scholars such as Gusfield, Becker, and Blumer Spector and Kitsuse (1977) develop a coherent approach to the natural history of the meaning-making process of social problems. Their innovative contribution to the field of transgression, crime, and justice in *Constructing Social Problems* is the introduction of a method and theory that focuses on the narrative construction of social problems and not on social conditions as the explaining factor. Their radical innovation is to research systematically "the activities of individuals or groups making assertions of grievances and claims with respect to some putative conditions" (Spector and Kitsuse 1977:75). In their classic publication, they introduce new terminologies such as claims making and claims makers, with which they focus on a wide range of examples of normalization, stigmatization, and criminalization.

Deviance studies were criticized because, according to a range of scholars, it was too descriptive, did not pay attention to the role of power, and did not explain crime[3] (e.g.,

Gouldner 1968; Liazos 1972; Taylor, Walton, and Young 1973; Gove 1975).[4] When one pays close attention to deviance studies, it becomes clear that power and social tension play a significant role. For instance, Becker stated: "Differences in the ability to make rules and apply them to other people are essentially power differentials (either legal or extra-legal)" (1963:18.) In a later version of *Outsiders*, Becker states that his intention was never to "propose solutions to the etiological questions" (1972:179). He reaffirmed that labeling "cannot possibly be conceived as the sole explanation of what alleged deviants actually do" (1973:179).

The heydays of symbolic interactionism in the 1960s and 1970s within sociology and criminology produced a respectable range of well-received books in a relatively short period (which sadly I cannot discuss here), such as *Wayward Puritans* (Erikson 1966), *Hustlers, Beats and Others*[5] (Polsky 1967), *Becoming Deviant* (Matza 1969), *Deviance: The Interactionist Perspective* (Rubington and Weinberg 1968), and *Deviance and Identity* (Lofland 1969). Some have stated that since the late 1970s deviance studies lost their significance or even proclaimed its death, but something else has happened: the thriving of the symbolic-interactionist field of transgression, crime, and justice (Best 2004; Sumner 1994; Dellwing, Kotarba, and Pino 2014)

THE THRIVING OF THE SYMBOLIC-INTERACTIONIST FIELD OF CRIME AND JUSTICE (1980–2020)

Studies in the field of transgression, crime, and justice inspired by symbolic interactionism developed since the late seventies in roughly two directions: (1) studies that focus on the work of moral entrepreneurs and its outcome: stigmatizing and criminalizing moral narratives and (2) ethnographic studies on subcultures, interactions, and situations. The thriving of symbolic interactionism has resulted in a wide range of significant studies that because of the scope and angle of this chapter I cannot discuss here such as *Hookers, Rounders, and Desk Clerks: The Social Organization of The Hotel Community* (Prus and Irini 1980), *Deviance and Medicalization: From Badness to Sickness* (Conrad and Schneider 1980), *The Culture of Public Problems: Drinking-Driving and the Symbolic Order* (Gusfield 1981), *Abortion and the Politics of Motherhood* (Luker 1984), *The Alcoholic Self* (Denzin 1987), *Down on Their Luck: A Study of Homeless Street People* (Snow and Anderson 1993), *Passing By: Gender and Public Harassment.* (Gardner 1995), *Sidewalk* (Duneier 1999), *Courting Disaster: Intimate Stalking, Culture and Criminal Justice* (Dunn 2002), *Accounts of Innocence: Sexual Abuse, Trauma and Self* (Davis 2005), and *On The Run* (Goffman 2015).

In this second part, I will touch upon this thriving field and discuss five interconnected subfields: stigma, moral panic, social problems, existential sociology, and cultural criminology. I will also focus on two themes: (1) violence as labeling: the perspective of the "badass," and (2) the criminal-justice system as a labeling machine: multiple perspectives.

The stigma concept has become one of the most influential symbolic-interactionist concepts in the field of transgression, crime, and justice. In several ways the process of stigmatization and labeling are similar, and in many publications they are used to describe and analyze similar processes. For instance, Schur combines labeling and stigma in *The Politics of Deviance* (1980) in which he focuses on the role of power shaping what he calls *stigma contests* in relation to for example abortion, gay liberation, and rape. Stigma is applied to a wide range of groups, such as LGBTQ+, sex workers, and former prisoners. More recently there is a focus on the agency of stigmatized person and their ability to resist stigma. Discussing this in more detail is impossible considering the scope of this chapter. For a more detailed discussion of recent developments in relation to stigma, I would like to refer to an issue of *Symbolic Interaction* (Müller 2020) and *Stigma Revisited* (Hannem and Bruckert 2012).

The concept of moral panic has been become, just like stigma, a common concept in criminology and sociology (Altheide 2009). It has been used to analyze how the media constructs public fears concerning topics such as drugs, immigration, and child abuse. This approach has been further developed by Goode and Ben-Yehuda (1994), who focus on the following characteristics: heightened public concern, hostility toward marginalized groups, consensus among those who have narrative power, disproportionality or exaggeration, and volatility or temporality. These are quite similar to Cohen's original definitions, though Goode and Ben-Yehuda put more emphasis on a measurable objective indication of exaggeration, where Cohen focuses more on neglect or denial of more fundamental social-justice issues (see also Cohen 2001). Scholars who use the moral-panic concept tend to focus on the perspective and activities of moral entrepreneurs with narrative power, though some do pay attention to how folk devils resist hegemonic stigmatizing and criminalizing narratives (Ferrell 1993; McRobbie and Thornton 1995; Müller 2019a; De Young 2004; Lumsden 2009; Griffiths 2010).

The social-problem perspective focuses on the claims-making process and has resulted in many significant publications (see Best 2013; Loseke 2011; Holstein and Miller 2003). I will discuss here two classic examples in more detail. Joel Best (1987) describes in *Rhetoric in Claims-Making: Constructing the Missing Children Problem*, the characteristics of moral narratives, and their recurring elements (see also Johnson 1989 and Best 1990). For example, they contain broad including definitions, to increase the public attention to a problem: in the case of missing children, it includes runaways, child-snatching by noncustodial parents, and abduction by strangers. The narrative also tends to refer to a growing number to emphasize the grave and pressing nature of the problem; at some moment claims makers stated that 50,000 children were abducted by strangers. These numbers were contested by the *Denver Post*, whose journalists discovered that this took place between 100 and 200 times per year.

Donileen Loseke (1987) compares the official moral narrative of wife abuse with the narratives of women who are living in a shelter (see also Loseke 1992). In the official moral narrative, there is a "correct" description of the actors (the man as abuser and the woman as the pure victim) and the act (repetitive, intended, extreme physical violence that produces psychological injuries). According to these narratives, women first have to internalize the label of abused wife, before they are able to empower themselves. But not all women agree, as Loseke observed in what see called "reality-definition contests." For instance, women resist the label of abused wife because they see it as discrediting. Recent studies tend to focus on a multi-perspective approach to social problems emphasizing the presence of competing for moral narratives (e.g., Best and Harris 2013).

Scholars inspired by existential sociology (Douglas and Johnson 1977) focus on (1) "brute" emotional existential aspects of transgression, crime, and justice, and (2) the social construction of moral narratives and how this creates injustice. Examples are studies on drug dealing (Adler 1985), self-harm (Adler and Adler 2011), *Bureaucratic Propaganda* (Altheide and Johnson 1980), wife abuse (Ferraro and Johnson 1983), *Death Penalty Myths* (Gerber and Johnson 2007), justice (Altheide 1992; Johnson 1995), and crime, fear, and media (Altheide 2002, 2006). Here I will focus on three examples.

Wheeling and Dealing

Adler (1985) is a classic ethnographic study on upper-level drug traffickers in southern California. In order to explain their commitment to this dangerous transgressive career, Adler specifically focuses on their brute being. The smugglers choose a highly hedonistic lifestyle, thus revolting against rationalized and conventional society. They are motivated by hedonistic materialism and living the fast Dionysian life. Only by paying attention to their emotional drive can their on-the-edge behavior be understood.

Johnson explains in his hallmark publication on justice (1995) that symbolic-interactionist studies show that justice is not a rational abstract construct removed from everyday existential life. In contrast, justice is enacted in daily existence. It is fundamentally emotional, related to judgments of fairness and equality. Justice is guided and shaped by strong emotions such as envy, vengeance, compassion, and kindness. Justice is gendered, dynamic, and related to the ways we interact with others: "justice is in the doing" (1995:202). Social actions are shaped by how we use language to construct moral narratives about crime and justice. These narratives have ramifications for how we see ourselves, how we define our communities, who belongs to them, and who is excluded. In sum, justice is not an abstract, rational, and distant virtue or principle: "It is a common property of our everyday lives" (1995:203).

In *Terrorism and the Politics of Fear*, Altheide (2017) describes how fear is used in moral narratives favoring American politics such as the occupation of Iraq and expanding forms of surveillance. After 9/11 the American media constructed a narrative that highlighted the moral and social superiority of the United States, which was crucial in creating support for the attack on Iraq. In this hegemonic fear narrative, there is a clear division between us versus them, the evil barbaric Muslim other who is threatening democracy and freedom. Altheide points out that this discourse is shaped by the ecology of communication, which refers to the structure, organization, and accessibility of information technology. For instance, during the Iraq war, the American government scrutinized the information the media gained to prevent images that might disrupt the support at home, as happened during the Vietnam War. Only a handful of journalists were willing to bypass this and create a critical stance toward the policy of the Bush Administration.

Altheide also shows that a specific group of conservative moral entrepreneurs belonging to the thinktank Project for the New American Century (PNAC) constructed the hegemonic moral narrative that made the Iraq War possible:

> The dominant frameworks that guided the messages originated with a very conservative think tank, the PNAC. The PNAC shaped fundamental foreign policy changes that led up to the invasion of Iraq. This was accomplished when several of its members joined the Bush administration as cabinet members or close advisors. This conservative think tank also contributed heavily to the propaganda campaign to justify the war, as well as working with major news media to redirect dissent within War Programming.
>
> (Altheide and Grimes 2005:623)

The work of Becker, Cohen, Katz, and other symbolic-interactionist scholars forms an inspiration for authors who identify with cultural criminology and pay attention to the social construction of meaning in relation to transgression and crime. Cultural criminology focuses on three intertwined fields of interest that are closely linked to symbolic interactionism: (1) subcultures resisting marginalization and stigmatization, (2) the representation of crime in (social) media and how it shapes everyday life, and (3) the situational foreground in which transgression takes place (see, for a more detailed discussion of cultural criminology and symbolic interaction, Müller 2019b).

Ferrell is one of the grounding scholars with his ethnographic studies on marginalized and criminalized groups (1993, 2006, 2018). In *Crimes of Style* he describes the culture of writing graffiti and the excitement of its transgression. Ferrell refers in this work to labeling and moral panic in relation to the criminalization of graffiti by the city of Denver. This is constructed by the local political and business elites who have a direct interest (political and moral gain) and an indirect one (real estate value). The anti-graffiti campaign represents graffiti writers as folk devils who need to be controlled and reformed. Still, Ferrell highlights that the writers were able to resist the campaign by creating a counternarrative that attracted new writers and using the media attention to attract commissioners (local business) for their graffiti pieces.

Within cultural criminology, the concept of transgression replaces deviance, because it is not in line with diversity in late modernity and tends to disregard agency, the pleasure of transgression, and its cultural and social empowerment. In sum, transgression focuses on symbolic meanings—similar to deviance studies—and celebrates its excitement and transcendent quality, resisting the bureaucratic and disciplining forces of neoliberal society (Ferrell et al. 2015; Young 2007).

Staci Newmahr's *Playing on the Edge: Sadomasochism, Risk, and Intimacy* (2011) is one the best examples of an ethnographic study on transgression. Newmahr gives an insider account of the symbolic meaning of pain in the SM community she was a member of.

Most of the participants see themselves as outsiders who feel deeply connected to their SM community. Newmahr gives rich descriptions of participants enacting master/slave narratives while balancing pain, pleasure, degradation, and domination. She shows that this subculture is based on trust and thus creates intimacy between the SM partners, resulting in the emotional gratifying "brute" satisfaction of transcendence.

Within and beyond these five perspectives, there are many significant themes studied with a symbolic-interactionist frame, such as drug use, media, and crime and white-collar crime. I will restrict myself here to discussing two themes: violence and the criminal-justice system.

Violence as Labeling: The Perspective of the "Badass"

Since the 1980s several groundbreaking symbolic-interactionist studies on violence have been published, which I will discuss here in brief (Anderson 1990; Athens 1992; Collins 2008; and Katz 1988). Though these publications refer to different forms of violence, here I will focus on one element they all share: the perspective of the "badass."

Lonnie Athens's violentization theory focuses on three elements: violent dominant encounters, violent socialization, and violent communities (2017). Here I will describe his work on the becoming of dangerous violent men. Athens discovered that their biographical narratives center around the moral meaning of domination and degradation. They have developed a strong emotional sensitivity toward signs of (dis)respect. Violence is used to restore a threatened sense of self, for instance when they experience that their reputation is in danger. With violence they label themselves as strong and respectful and others as weak and worthless.

These men grew up in abusive households, in which they were structurally degraded and labeled as socially and morally insignificant through physical, verbal, and emotional abuse. They learned that when faced with shame and humiliation, the right way to restore one's self-image is the use of violence. In their childhood, they started dominating and degrading others by using violence, through which they redefined themselves as strong and domineering and which gave them satisfaction, pleasure, and pride. At the same time, they gain a reputation in their community for being a "badass," for their ability to hurt and subjugate others. Because of this reputation, they feel pushed and even entitled to use violence when they sense that others do not respect them. They also become experts in using violence, which gives them an immediate advantage over others who are not used to violence. Violence has become a form of self-labeling, a goal in itself, and is inherently related to a positive experience of power and dominance, degrading others, and inflating self-esteem.

Jack Katz's *Seduction of Crime* (1988) is about the morally sensual attraction of crimes, such as cold-blooded "senseless" murders and stickups. Katz states that it is crucial to pay attention to the "seductive qualities of crimes: those aspects in the foreground of criminality that make its various forms sensible, even sensually compelling, ways of being" (Katz 1988:3). Katz focuses in his book on the foreground: a path of action, a line of interpretation, and an emotional process. Katz shows that violent acts are ways of overcoming degrading situations. The violent perpetrators Katz discusses are driven by "brute" moral emotions such as "humiliation, righteousness, arrogance, ridicule, cynicism, defilement, and vengeance" (Katz 1988:9). Comparable to Athens's work is the existential emphasis on the brute being of perpetrators: the emotional satisfaction and fulfillment they gain by dominating and degrading others and how this is crucial for a positive labeling of themselves as being morally right in their plight of gaining respect and creating a reputation of a "badass."

Randal Collins's approach focuses on the emotional development during violent situations for which he compares a wide range of cases such as police violence, domestic violence, military violence, riots, gang violence, stick-ups, and robberies (2008). Observing videos and photographs and including ethnographic data, he states that the dominant emotion during violent encounters is not anger, but confrontational tension/fear (ct/f), which makes violence difficult to pursue. There are five pathways that circumvent ct/f, of which choosing a weak victim is common in street crime, which I will discuss here. Choosing a weaker victim or a person in a situationally weaker position creates a situation of "emotional dominance" in which ct/f becomes better to manage. In these situations violent perpetrators gain "emotional energy," which makes them feel good and entails feelings of pride, pleasure, empowerment, satisfaction, and accomplishment. Especially in situations where there is an audience, reputation is at stake, and one is forced to act as a "badass." For those who use violence regularly, dominating others generates an emotional high. The habitual violent perpetrator becomes "an addict of situational dominance, a prisoner of his own interactional skills" (Collins 2008:186).

Elijah Anderson has published several classic ethnographies on inner-city communities and crime in which respect, dominance, and degradation play a crucial role (1978, 1990, 1999). Here I will focus on his most famous study *Code of The Street: Decency, Violence, and The Moral Life of The Inner City* (1999). It describes how minute details of interactions in the street can lead to violent confrontations. Inspired by Goffman, Anderson describes a reverse of Goffman's representation of public life that is shaped by civil inattention (Goffman 1963a): any sign of subordination can be exploited on the street. One has to present oneself as strong and as a person who can stand up for him/herself. Any transgression of the code of the street can be read as a sign of disrespect. This can be the tone of one's voice, the phrasing of a question, and the way one looks at the other. If one does not respond with force, one can be seen as weak and as prey for a robbery or a beating. Retaliation can restore one's status position as a "badass," but can also lead to deadly violence. The code of the street is a form of street justice where the police are absent. Anderson shows that a minority is actively involved in this kind of justice, but everybody, including the majority of the families that detest street culture, needs to act on the code of the street in order to be able to navigate safely the public space of their neighborhoods.

Many publications have been inspired by these four outstanding classic studies. I will discuss here three examples in short. Robert Garot formulates gang identity as a creative and sensual performance (2007) enacted during an interaction ritual called "Being hit up." This is the intimidating approach of an African American man between fifteen and twenty-five who is suspected to be a member of a rival gang. This interaction starts with the objectifying question: "where you from." Garot shows that this interaction ritual can be used as a resource to show one's resilience, create action, and construct one's identity as a badass.

Stretesky and Pogrebin (2007) focus on the relationship between gun violence and gangs. The authors show that gun violence adds to the reputation of gang members, with which they demonstrate their definition of masculinity. Gun violence, as in shooting and killing rival gang members, is for them the appropriate reaction in a situation of identity denial that results in the degrading experience of disrespect. The authors conclude that guns are crucial in self-labeling and thus are strategies to protect one's social and physical self in the ghetto.

Jacobs (2013) describes in his article on carjacking how carjackers use emotions to define the situation in such a way to gain full compliance from their victims. Enacting the code of the street, they scan the public for those who might challenge them and those who might be easy to subjugate. They will act haphazardly when they see someone as weak and therefore as easy prey. Coercion is minimal in these situations, as the victim tends to cooperate fully. In other situations, especially when their victims embrace street culture, they have to expressively present the consequences of threat in order to gain compliance. The interactional approach of the foreground of crime shows in a detailed way how the experience of fear and coercion are constructed by the self-presentation of the carjackers.

The Criminal-Justice System as a Labeling Machine: Multiple Perspectives

Since 1980 many studies inspired by symbolic interaction have focused on the criminal-justice system as a labeling machine as well as on those who resist and fight labeling. This system consists of a diverse range of institutions and actors such as the police, judges, and parole officers who enact degrading and othering moral narratives while presenting themselves as legitimate and credible (e.g., Burns and Peyrot 2008; Comfort 2003; Conti 2009; David et al. 2018; Dunn 2010; Flower 2018; Frohmann 1991; Gatthings and Parrotta 2013; Greer 2002; Harris 2008; Hunt and Manning 1991; Kenney and Clairmont 2009; Marx 1988; Manning 1988; Manning and Van Maanen 1978; Traverse 2007, 2012; Van Maanen 1984). Here I will discuss three studies that cover policing, court, and prison that also include divergent perspectives on resistance and justice.

Schneider shows in his groundbreaking *Policing and Social Media: Social Control in an Era of New Media* (2016) that the changing logic of social media has a huge impact on the police and the way they construct moral narratives. In the past they could rely on controlling the narrative by informing the media with firsthand observations and comments by experienced police officers. This has changed by the presence of a new landscape of digital recording, which creates online imagery of policing. Schneider shows that the shared and uploaded images counter their desired narrative and discredit their societal position. One of the cases discussed in Schneider's book is the shooting of Sammy Yatim in Toronto in the summer of 2013. He was killed in an empty tram, holding a knife, by a police officer who fired nine bullets. Schneider examines the online communication process as it unfolds and describes when and how meanings are produced and negotiated in relation to the death of Sammy Yatim.

A recording by a bystander was put on YouTube within minutes after the incident. The police lost control over the narrative, and the video became the frame of reference used in the public debate, which centered around the theme of "armed victim." The digital sense-making process that took place in the YouTube comments constructed mixed meanings of different elements of the shooting such as knife (itty bitty/sword), police force (justified/excessive), and moral character (thug/teenager). Posts of the Facebook page "Sammy's Fight Back for Justice" organized by friends and family presented him in a positive moral narrative as a reliable, hard-working student who would never harm anybody. Mainstream media used this page to construct his moral character while using a picture that portrayed him as the boy next door. Yatim was subsequently portrayed in a positive light and that "he was most undeserving of his fate." Schneider shows that the police were mere bystanders in this online collective meaning-making process. In 2015 the Toronto police tried to regain control over police narratives by starting to wear body cameras showing the perspective of police officers. Still they have to continue to deal with competing narratives on crime and justice. The police officer who shot Sammy was arrested, convicted, and sent to prison.

The court is in itself the primal institution of labeling, in which verdicts are shaped by moral narratives on transgressive acts and moral selves. As a result of this, court cases are performances of moral contests in which participants try to present themselves as credible actors enacting moral narratives favoring themselves and discrediting the adversary party. Controlling one's feelings and avoiding the presentation of negative emotions are essential here. Konradi examines this process of emotion management in *"I Don't Have to Be Afraid of You": Rape Survivors' Emotion Management in Court* (1999). She focuses on what rape survivors do with and about their emotions and shows that this is a crucial aspect of their experience in court (see also Konradi 2007). In this excellent publication, Konradi shows how the interactional meaning-making process is shaped by brute feelings such as fear, anger, shame, and frustration. These are mainly related to "recalling the rape experience, encountering the defendant, and having the defense attorney make interaction difficult" (Konradi 1999:51). The accounts of the interviewed women show that court is a site for empowerment and resistance, but also a place where they feel at a loss and humiliated—especially when the defense attorney attacks their testimony, provokes negative emotions, and tries to "expose them in wrong face to the jury" (Konradi 1999:47), which goes against the women's claims of being a victim, of their moral worth. Konradi shows that the women are not passive victims of their own feelings and that they have strategies, such as deflecting, suppressing, and cultivating emotions to protect their threatened self and present themselves as reliable and credible in court. By paying close attention to the voices of the interviewed women, Konradi was able to demonstrate that they have agency in their fight for justice navigating situations of moral contest and emotional upheaval.

Imprisonment is the ultimate consequence of being labeled a criminal in court. In her study on female prisoners, Jill A. McCorkel (1998) uses Goffman's concept of total institution to describe their experience of a rehab program. The moral narrative of the program is that the addicted women have made bad moral choices, have an immoral character, and need to leave their addicted self behind. The program is characterized by strict surveillance, control, and publicly degrading rituals. In contrast to Goffman's total institution, free space is not admitted by staff. McCorkel's superb publication shows that even in this *totalitarian* institution, women are able to construct a critical space, which they call "going to the crackhouse." This is a social space (not a specific physical one), in which they are able to complain about the program and in which they can manifest who they really are in their eyes. Another form of resistance is public transgression: breaking the rules and facing the negative consequences:

> I did this because there's only so far you can degrade a person before she either breaks or rebels. Right now, I'm rebelling for myself. I did this, and now she and I both know that they haven't got me. There's still a part of me that wants to fight in here.
> (McCorkel 1998:245)

McCorkel concludes that the assiduous surveillance of the prison rehab program is countered by the social construction of a critical space in which the women are able to share moral narratives in which they redefine themselves as respectable individuals and claim a positive definition of pre-institutional self (see also McCorkel 2013).

CONCLUSION: WHOSE SIDE ARE WE ON?

In this chapter I have described studies that focus on the interrelation among deviant selves, transgressive acts, and moral narratives. These narratives shape definitions of self and subsequently behavior in relation to transgression, crime, and justice. This chapter shows that these narratives are dynamic; they transform over time and are interpreted depending on the developing situation. Moral entrepreneurs with "narrative power" (Plummer 2020), shaped by access to and the control of financial, cultural, social, and political resources, play a crucial role in this meaning-making process. But this does not mean that others take these narratives for granted and embrace them as the truth. Many studies I have touched upon here show that marginalized groups do have agency in entering "critical space," resisting moral narratives, and creating counternarratives.

The studies I have discussed here demonstrate how morality and self, as in degradation, boosting self-esteem, and "brute" transcendence of the normative gaze, shape the social field of transgression, crime, and justice. This can be related to the code the street, but also to strategies of rape survivors in court cases, the resistance of female prisoners, and the on-the-edge experiences during graffiti writing and SM. Studies discussed here show that transgressive and criminal acts play a fundamental role in moral narratives embraced to uphold an aspired self. This can be seen in a wide range of criminal acts, such as white-collar crime, terrorism, and domestic violence, but also in the activities of moral entrepreneurs, such as rule makers and rule enforcers. Moral meanings concerning crime and transgression shape social scripts that sustain the aspired moral self of a person, as someone who is respected and who is recognized for what he or she does as valuable. But in the field of transgression, crime, and justice, these scripts are contested, and as a result moral selves are being threatened, which requires a form of moral repair for which one can use different verbal and nonverbal strategies, such as accounts, neutralization strategies, transgression, and violence.

Studies inspired by symbolic interaction have been able to describe and analyze these conflicting meaning-making processes, such as stigmatization, criminalization, and normalization. These studies have focused on (1) narratives of moral entrepreneurs who criminalize or normalize certain forms of behavior, and how this relates to their social-economic position, interests, and definitions of self. Studies inspired by symbolic interaction have also paid attention to (2) the (counter)narratives of those who face the consequences of narratives of criminalization and stigmatization, their interests, and how this shapes their self-perceptions, social worlds, and their reaction toward dominant moral narratives.

This chapter shows that, as Johnson explained, justice is not an abstract concept related to court and formal legal procedures. Justice is a daily activity, guided by moral narratives and strong emotions. If our moral selves are threatened, we feel hurt, anxious, and enraged and try to defend ourselves, resisting moral degradation. At the same time, justice is also about protecting the moral selves of marginalized others, how we engage with them, and how we treat their selves as sacred by showing deference and demeanor (Goffman 1967:91).

Symbolic-interactionist researchers contribute to these narratives and are part of these narratives. This triggers the question posed by Becker over fifty years ago: *Whose Side Are We On?* (Becker 1967). If we cannot be bothered by this question, we sustain the status quo, in which exclusion, marginalization, stigmatization, and social injustice are a common experience for many. A critical and mildly skeptical approach embraces a more active public position in which we as researchers submerge in social life, critically, with rigor, passion, and an eye for (social) justice. Symbolic interactionists have developed an arsenal of concepts and methods to do this work, gaining thick descriptions of social life and a deep understanding of how persons give meaning to it. We are able to describe and analyze moral narratives, with concepts such as moral entrepreneurs, claims making, folk devils, and horror stories. We are able to analyze the dynamics of meaning-making processes in relation to societal themes that evolve around justice and crime, such as the criminalization of drugs, the death penalty, and the Iraq War. Symbolic interactionism is able to debunk the moral narratives of the established as supporting their own interest and as ways of controlling, stigmatizing, and excluding marginalized groups.

462   THADDEUS MÜLLER

This chapter shows that because of its theoretical and methodological tools, symbolic-interactionist studies are well equipped to listen to and represent voices of marginalized groups in depth and show their humanity and agency in how they fight for justice.

NOTES

1. Symbolic interactionists have made important contributions to studying victims/survivors (see Ferraro and Johnson 1983; Holstein and Miller 1990; Dunn 2010), but sadly, I cannot discuss this within the scope of this chapter.
2. Here I am using transgression and deviance for acts of moral transgression (breaking a social norm), in general without victims, such as drug use and sexually deviant behavior, and criminal I use for breaking criminal law, in general with victims (see Adler and Adler 1994:7–9). The difference between transgression and deviance is discussed later in this chapter.
3. A later critique was that the labeling perspective did not pay attention to the labeling of women and their role as perpetrators or victims (Schur 1984).
4. For a detailed reaction to this critique, see Plummer (1979) and Rock (1979).
5. Becker initiated this book and supervised its completion (Polsky 1967:xii).

REFERENCES

Adler, Patricia A. 1985. *Wheeling and Dealing: An Ethnography of an Upper-Level Drug Dealing and Smuggling Community*. New York: Columbia University Press.
Adler, Patricia A., and Peter Adler. 1994. *Constructions of Deviance: Social Power, Context, and Interaction*. Belmont, CA: Wadsworth Publishing Company.
Adler, Patricia A., and Peter Adler. 2011. *The Tender Cut: Inside the Hidden World of Self-injury*. NYU Press, 2011.
Altheide, David L., and John M. Johnson. 1980. *Bureaucratic Propaganda*. Boston: Allyn & Bacon.
Altheide, David L. 1992. "Gonzo justice." *Symbolic Interaction* 15(1):69–86.
Altheide, David L. 2002. *Creating Fear: News and the Construction of Crisis*. Hawthorne, NY: Aldine de Gruyter.
Altheide, David L. 2017. *Terrorism and the Politics of Fear*. New York: Rowman & Littlefield.
Altheide, David L. 2006. *Terrorism and the Politics of Fear*. Alta Mira Press.
Altheide, David L. 2009. "Moral panic: From Sociological Concept to Public Discourse." *Crime, Media, Culture* 5(1):79–99.
Altheide, David L., and Jennifer N. Grimes. 2005. "War Programming: The Propaganda Project and the Iraq War." *The Sociological Quarterly* 46(4):617–43.
Anderson, Elijah. 1978. *A Place on the Corner*. Chicago: University of Chicago Press.
Anderson, Elijah. 1990. *Streetwise: Race, Class, and Change in an Urban Community*. Chicago: University of Chicago Press.
Anderson, Elijah. 1999. *Code of the Street: Decency, Violence, and the Moral Life of the Inner City*. New York: W. W. Norton & Company.
Anderson, Niels 1923. *The Hobo: The Sociology of the Homeless Man*. Chicago: University of Chicago Press.

Athens, Lonnie H. 1992. *The Creation of Dangerous Violent Criminals*. Urbana: University of Illinois Press.

Athens, Lonnie H. 2017. "Applying Violentization: From Theory to Praxis." *Victims & Offenders* 12(4):497–522.

Becker, Howard S. 1963. *Outsiders: Studies in the Sociology of Deviance*. New York: The Free Press.

Becker, Howard S. 1967. "Whose Side Are We On?" *Social Problems* 14(3):239–47.

Best, Joel. 1987. "Rhetoric in Claims-Making: Constructing the Missing Children Problem." *Social Problems* 34(2):101–21.

Best, Joel. 1990. *Threatened Children: Rhetoric and Concern About Child-Victims*. Chicago: University of Chicago Press.

Best, Joel. 2004. "Deviance May Be Alive, But Is It Intellectually Lively? A Reaction to Goode." *Deviant Behavior* 25(5):483–92.

Best, Joel. 2013. *Social Problems*. New York: W. W. Norton & Company.

Best, Joel, and Scott R. Harris, eds. 2013. *Making Sense of Social Problems: New Images, New Issues*. Boulder/London: Lynne Rienner Publishers.

Blumer, Herbert. 1954. "What Is Wrong with Social Theory?." *American Sociological Review* 19(1):3–10.

Burns, Stacy Lee, and Mark Peyrot. 2008. "Reclaiming Discretion: Judicial Sanctioning Strategy in Court-Supervised Drug Treatment." *Journal of Contemporary Ethnography* 37(6):720–44.

Chambliss, William J. 1973. "The Saints and the Roughnecks." *Society* 11(1):24–31.

Cohen, Stanley. 1972. *Folk Devils and Moral Panics: The Creation of the Mods and Rockers*. Oxford: Martin Robertson.

Cohen, Stanley. 2001. *States of Denial States of Denial: Knowing about Atrocities and Suffering*. Cambridge: Polity Press.

Collins, Randall. 2008. *Violence: A Micro-sociological Theory*. Princeton, NJ: Princeton University Press.

Comfort, Megan L. 2003. "In The Tube at San Quentin: The 'Secondary Prisonization' of Women Visiting Inmates." *Journal of Contemporary Ethnography* 32(1):77–107.

Conrad, Peter, and Joseph Schneider. 1980. *Deviance and Medicalization: From Badness to Sickness*. St Louis, MO: Mosby.

Conti, Norman. 2009. "A Visigoth System: Shame, Honor, and Police Socialization." *Journal of Contemporary Ethnography* 38(3):409–32.

Cooley, Charles H. 1902. *Human Nature and Social Order*. New York: Charles Scribner's Sons.

David, Gary C., Anne Warfield Rawls, and James Trainum. 2018. "Playing the Interrogation Game: Rapport, Coercion, and Confessions in Police Interrogations." *Symbolic Interaction* 41(1):3–24.

Davis, Joseph E. 2005. *Accounts of Innocence: Sexual Abuse, Trauma and Self*. Chicago: University of Chicago Press.

Dellwing, Michael, Joe Kotarba, and Nathan Pino. 2014. *The Death and Resurrection of Deviance: Current Ideas and Research*. London: Palgrave and Macmillan.

Denzin, Norman. 1987. *The Alcoholic Self*. Newbury Park, CA: SAGE.

De Young, Mary. 2004. *The Day Care Ritual Abuse Moral Panic*. London: McFarland.

Douglas, J. D. 1967. *The Social Meanings of Suicide*. Princeton, NJ: Princeton University Press.

Douglas, J. D. 1971. *American Social Order: Social Rules in a Pluralistic Society*. New York: Free Press.

Douglas, J. D. 1976. *Investigative Social Research*. Beverly Hills, CA: SAGE.

Douglas, J. D., and J. M. Johnson, eds. 1977. *Existential Sociology*. Cambridge: Cambridge University Press.

Douglas, J. D., P. K. Rasmussen, and C. A. Flanagan. 1977. *The Nude Beach*. Beverly Hills, CA: SAGE.

Duneier, Mitchell. 1999. *Sidewalk*. New York: Macmillan.

Dunn, Jennifer L. 2002. *Courting Disaster: Intimate Stalking, Culture and Criminal Justice*. New York, NY: Aldine de Gruyter.

Dunn, Jennifer L. 2010. *Judging Victims: Why We Stigmatize Survivors, and How They Reclaim Respect*. Boulder, CO: Lynne Rienner Publishers.

Emerson, Robert M. 1969. *Judging Delinquents: Context and Process in Juvenile Court*. Chicago: Aldine.

Erikson, Kai. 1966. *Wayward Puritans*: A Study in the Sociology of Deviance. New York: John Wiley & Sons.

Ferraro, Kathleen J., and John M. Johnson. 1983. "How Women Experience Battering: The Process of Victimization." *Social Problems* 30(3):325–39.

Ferrell, Jeff. 1993. *Crimes of Style: Urban Graffiti and the Politics of Criminality*. New York: Garland.

Ferrell, Jeff. 2006. *Empire of Scrounge: Inside the Urban Underground of Dumpster Diving, Trash Picking, and Street Scavenging*. New York: NYU Press.

Ferrell, Jeff. 2018. *Drift: Illicit Mobility and Uncertain Knowledge*. Berkeley: University of California Press.

Ferrell, Jeff, Keith Hayward, and Jock Young. 2015. *Cultural Criminology: An Invitation*. Los Angeles: SAGE.

Flower, Lisa. 2018. "Doing Loyalty: Defense Lawyers' Subtle Dramas in the Courtroom." *Journal of Contemporary Ethnography* 47(2):226–54.

Frohmann, Lisa. 1991. "Discrediting Victims' Allegations of Sexual Assault: Prosecutorial Accounts of Case Rejections." *Social Problems* 38(2):213–26.

Gardner, Carol Brooks.1995. *Passing by: Gender and Public Harassment*. Berkeley: University of California Press.

Gathings, M. J., and Kylie Parrotta. 2013. "The Use of Gendered Narratives in the Courtroom: Constructing an Identity Worthy of Leniency." *Journal of Contemporary Ethnography* 42(6):668–89.

Gerber, Rudolph Joseph, and John M. Johnson. 2007. *The Top Ten Death Penalty Myths: The Politics of Crime Control*. Westport, CT: Greenwood Publishing Group.

Goffman, Erving. 1959. "The Moral Career of the Mental Patient." *Psychiatry* 22(2):123–42.

Goffman, Erving. 1961. *Asylums: Essays on the Social Situation of Mental Patients and Other Inmates*. New York: Doubleday Anchor.

Goffman, Erving 1963a. *Behavior in Public Places: Notes on The Social Organization of Gatherings*. New York: The Free Press.

Goffman, Erving. 1963b. *Stigma: Notes on the Management of Spoiled Identity*. Englewood Cliffs, NJ: Prentice Hall.

Goffman, Erving. 1967. *Interaction Ritual: Essays on Face-to-face Interaction* Chicago: Aldine.

Goffman, Alice. 2015. *On The Run: Fugitive Life in an American City*. Chicago: Chicago University Press.

Goode, Erich, and Nachmann Ben-Yehuda. 1994. *Moral Panics: The Social Construction of Deviance*. Oxford: Blackwell.

Gouldner, Alvin W. 1968. "The Sociologist as Partisan: Sociology and the Welfare Atate." *The American Sociologist* 3:103–16.

Gove, Walter R. 1975. *The Labelling of Deviance: Evaluating a Perspective*. London: John Wiley & Sons.

Griffiths, Richard. 2010. "The Gothic Folk Devils Strike Back! Theorizing Folk Devil Reaction in the Post-Columbine Era." *Journal of youth studies* 13(3):403–22.

Greer, Kimberly. 2002. "Walking an Emotional Tightrope: Managing Emotions in a Women's Prison." *Symbolic Interaction* 25(1):117–39.

Gusfield, Joseph R. 1963. *Symbolic Crusade: Status Politics and the American Temperance Movement*. Urbana: University of Illinois Press.

Gusfield, Joseph.1981. *The Culture of Public Problems: Drinking-Driving and the Symbolic Order*. Chicago: University of Chicago Press.

Hannem, Stacey, and Chris Bruckert. 2012. *Stigma revisited: Implications of the Mark*. Ottawa: University of Ottawa Press.

Harris, Alexes. 2008. "The Social Construction of 'Sophisticated' Adolescents: How Judges Integrate Juvenile and Criminal Justice Decision-Making Models." *Journal of Contemporary Ethnography* 37(4):469–506.

Holstein, James A., and Gale Miller, eds. 2003. *Challenges and Choices: Constructionist Perspectives on Social Problems*. Hawthorne, NY: Aldine de Gruyter.

Holstein, James A., and Gale Miller. 1990. "Rethinking Victimization: An Interactional Approach to Victimology." *Symbolic Interaction* 13(1):103–22.

Hunt, Jennifer, and Peter K. Manning. 1991."The Social Context of Police Lying." *Symbolic Interaction* 14(1):51–70.

Jacobs, Bruce. 2013. "The Manipulation of Fear in Carjacking." *Journal of Contemporary Ethnography* 42(5):523–44.

Johnson, John M. 1975. *Doing Fieldwork*. New York: The Free Press.

Johnson, John M. 1995 "In Dispraise of Justice." *Symbolic Interaction* 18(2):191–205.

Johnson, John M. 1989. "Horror Stories and the Construction of Child Abuse," Pp. 5–19 in *From Images of Issues: Typifying Contemporary Social Problems*, edited by Joel Best. Hawthorne, NY: Aldine de Gruyter.

Katz, Jack. 1988. *Seductions of Crime: Moral and Sensual Attractions in Doing Evil*. New York: Basic Books.

Kenney, J. Scott, and Don Clairmont. 2009. "Using the Victim Role as Both Sword and Shield: The Interactional Dynamics of Restorative Justice Sessions." *Journal of Contemporary Ethnography* 38(3):279–307.

Konradi, Amanda. 1999. "'I Don't Have to Be Afraid of You': Rape Survivors' Emotion Management in Court." *Symbolic Interaction* 22(1):45–77.

Konradi, Amanda. 2007. *Taking the Stand: Rape Survivors and the Prosecution of Rapists*. Westport, CT: Greenwood Publishing Group.

Kitsuse, John I. 1961 "Societal Reaction to Deviant Behavior: Problems of Theory and Method." *Social Problems.* 9:247–56.

Lemert, Edwin M. 1951. *Social Pathology; A Systematic Approach to the Theory of Sociopathic Behavior*. New York: McGraw Hill.

Liazos, Alexander. 1972 "The Poverty of the Sociology of Deviance: Nuts, Sluts, and Preverts." *Social Problems* 20(1):103–20.

Lofland, John. 1969. *Deviance and Identity*. Englewood Cliffs: Prentice Hall Inc.

Loseke, Donileen R. 1987. "Lived Realities and the Construction of Social Problems: The Case of Wife Abuse." *Symbolic Interaction* 10(2):229–43.

Loseke, Donileen R. 1992. *Battered Woman and Shelters: The Social Construction of Wife Abuse*. New York: SUNY Press.

Loseke, Donileen R. 2011. *Thinking About Social Problems: An Introduction to Constructionist Perspectives*. New York: Transaction Publishers.

Luker, Kristen. 1984. *Abortion and the Politics of Motherhood*. Berkeley: University of California Press.

Lumsden, Karen. 2009. "'Do We Look Like Boy Racers?' The Role of the Folk Devil in Contemporary Moral Panics." *Sociological Research Online* 14(1):1–12.

Manning, Peter K. 1988. *Symbolic Communication: Signifying Calls and the Police Response*. Cambridge, MA: MIT Press.

Manning, Peter K., and John Van Maanen. 1978. *Policing: A View From the Street*. Santa Monica, CA: Goodyear Publishing Company.

Marx, Gary T. 1988 *Undercover: Police Surveillance in America*. Berkeley: University of California Press.

Matza, David. 1969. *Becoming Deviant*. Englewood Cliffs, NJ: Prentice Hall Inc.

McCorkel, Jill A. 1998. "Going to the Crackhouse: Critical Space as a Form of Resistance in Total Institutions and Everyday Life." *Symbolic interaction* 21(3):227–52.

McCorkel, Jill A. 2013. *Breaking Women: Gender, Race, and the New Politics of Imprisonment*. New York: NYU Press.

McRobbie, Angela, and Sarah L. Thornton. 1995. "Rethinking 'Moral Panic' for Multi-mediated Social Worlds." *British Journal of Sociology* 46(4):559–74.

Müller, Thaddeus. 2014. "Chicago, Jazz and Marijuana: Howard Becker on Outsiders." *Symbolic Interaction* 37(4):576–94.

Müller, Thaddeus. 2016. "We Do Not Hang Around: It Is Forbidden." *Erasmus Law Review* 9(1):30–38.

Müller, Thaddeus. 2019a. "Cannabis, Moral Entrepreneurship, and Stigma: Conflicting Narratives on the 26 May 2016 Toronto Police Raid on Cannabis Shop." *Qualitative Sociology Review* 15(2):148–71.

Müller, Thaddeus. 2019b. "Cultural Criminology and Its Incitement for Symbolic Interactionism: Transgression, Marginalisation, Resistance and Media in the Wider Context of Power and Culture in Late Modernity." Pp. 210–27 in *Critical and Cultural Interactionism: Insights from Sociology and Criminology*, edited by Michael Hviid Jacobsen. London: Routledge.

Müller, Thaddeus. 2019c. "Jack Douglas and the Reinvention of Society and Sociology: Creative Deviance, the Construction of Meaning and Social Order." Pp. 191–211 *Forgotten Founders and Other Neglected Social Theorists*, edited by C. T. Conner, N. M. Baxter, and D. R. Dickens. London: Rowman & Littlefield.

Müller, Thaddeus. 2020. "Stigma, the Moral Career of a Concept: Some Notes on Emotions, Agency, Teflon Stigma, and Marginalizing Stigma." *Symbolic Interaction* 43(1):3–20.

Newmahr, Staci. 2011. *Playing on the Edge: Sadomasochism, Risk, and Intimacy*. Bloomington: Indiana University Press.

Piliavin, Irving, and Scott Briar. 1964. "Police Encounters with Juveniles." *American Journal of Sociology* 70(2):206–14.

Plummer, Ken. 1975. *Sexual Stigma: An Interactionist Account*. London: Routledge and Kegan.

Plummer, Ken. 1979. "Misunderstanding Labelling Perspectives." Pp. 85–121 in *Deviant Interpretations* edited by David Downes and Paul Rock. Oxford: Martin Robertson.

Plummer, Ken. 2020. "'Whose Side Are We On?' Revisited: Narrative Power, Narrative Inequality, and a Politics of Narrative Humanity." *Symbolic Interaction* 43(1):46–71.

Polsky, Ned. 1967. *Hustlers, Beats, and Others*. Chicago: Aldine Publishing Comp.

Prus, Robert C., and Styllianoss Irini. 1980 *Hookers, Rounders, and Desk Clerks: The Social Organization of the Hotel Community*. Toronto: Gage Publishing Ltd.

Rock, Paul. 1979 "The Sociology of Crime, Symbolic Interactionism and Some Problematic Qualities of Radical Criminology." Pp. 52–84 in *Deviant Interpretations* edited by David Downes and Paul Rock. Oxford: Martin Robertson.

Scott, Marvin B., and Stanford M. Lyman. 1968. "Accounts." *American Sociological Review* 33:46–62.

Scott, Marvin B., and Stanford M. Lyman. 1970. "Accounts, Deviance and Social Order." Pp. 89–119 in *Deviance and Respectability. The Social Construction of Moral Meanings*, edited by Jack Douglas. New York: Basic Books.

Schur, Edwin M. 1980. *The Politics of Deviance: Stigma Contests and the Uses of Power*. Englewood Cliffs, NY: Prentice Hall.

Schur, Edwin M. 1984. *Labeling Women Deviant: Gender, Stigma, and Social Control*. New York: Random House.

Schneider, Christopher J. 2016. *Policing and Social Media: Social Control in an Era of New Media*. Lanham: Lexington Books.

Shaw, Clifford R. 1930. *The Jack-Roller: A Delinquent Boy's Own Story*. Chicago: University of Chicago Press.

Snow, David A., and Leon Anderson. 1993. *Down on Their Luck: A Study of Homeless Street People*. Berkeley: University of California Press.

Rubington, Earl, and Martin S. Weinberg. 1968 *Deviance: The Interactionist Perspective*. New York: The Macmillan Company.

Spector, Malcolm and John I. Kitsuse 1977. *Constructing Social Problems*. San Francisco: Cumming Pub Co.

Stretesky, Paul B., and Mark R. Pogrebin. 2007. "Gang-Related Gun Violence: Socialization, Identity, and Self." *Journal of Contemporary Ethnography* 36(1):85–114.

Sumner, Colin. 1994. *The Sociology of Deviance: An Obituary*. Buckingham: Open University Press.

Sykes, Gresham M., and David Matza. 1957. "Techniques of Neutralization: A Theory of Delinquency." *American Sociological Review* 22(6):664–70.

Tannenbaum, Frank. 1938. *Crime and Community*. New York: Ginn.

Taylor, Ian, Paul Walton, and Jock Young. 1973. *The New Criminology: for a Social Theory of Deviance*. London: Routledge and Kegan Paul.

Thomas, William Isaac, and Dorothy Swaine Thomas. 1928. *The Child in America: Behavior Problems and Programs*. New York: Knopf.

Thrasher, Frank M. 1926. *The Gang: A Study of 1,313 Gangs in Chicago*. Chicago: University of Chicago Press.

Travers, Max H. 2007. "Sentencing in the Children's Court: An Ethnographic Perspective." *Youth Justice* 7(1):21–35.

Travers, Max H. 2012. *The Sentencing of Children: Professional Work and Perspectives*. Washington, DC: New Academia Publishing.

Van Maanen, John. 1984. "Making Rank: Becoming an American Police Sergeant." *Urban Life* 13(2):155–76.

Young, Jock. 2007. *The Vertigo of Late Modernity*. Los Angeles: SAGE.

CHAPTER 26

MEDICINE, HEALTH, AND ILLNESS

GIUSEPPINA CERSOSIMO

PREMISE. SYMBOLS AND THE INTERPRETATION OF MEDICAL KNOWLEDGE

HAVING worked for twenty years as a faculty of medicine and surgery, I have come to appreciate that applying an interactionist method to research, diagnosis, and therapy needs to become as much a part of curricula as medical statistics. Unlike the current sporadic manner in which interactionist insights are integrated, it is important that symbolic interactionists make their contribution within teams working in different medical divisions and health systems; only then will we see the improvement of diagnosis, treatment, and therapy in healthcare systems. My interest in using interactionist insights to improve healthcare systems is what drives me to write this chapter. In the chapter, I focus on how symbolic interactionism with its sensitizing concepts, grounded theory, and a holistic approach centered on everyday life interactions has contributed to the study of healthcare and I take a forward focus, emphasizing the growing potential for symbolic interactionism to address new frameworks of doctor and patient interactions and new technologies that shape the contemporary medical landscape.

The approach described in this chapter is to be found in a form of sociological analysis called symbolic interaction, which was very influential in the United States from the 1940s to the 1970s. This was especially true among sociologists interested in the micro worlds of social life. Among many of the detailed aspects of social life that these writers explored was the experience of illness. What the interactionists put into play was a consideration of the impact of how people thought of symptoms, managed them, and related to others despite and because of the definition given to them. What this sociological perspective has shown is that the effects of symptoms have gone far beyond biochemical changes in the body to affect almost all aspects of daily life. One of the most intriguing observations, which became clear once a number of diseases were examined in this way, was the fact that from a social point of view different diseases had remarkably similar social and psychological sequelae, despite the symptoms, the etiology and the prognosis being quite different, such as cancer, rheumatoid arthritis, hepatitis, diabetes, and epilepsy. Illness has a profound impact on oneself—on a person's sense of who and what they are—in ways that are strikingly similar regardless of the disease and the illness situation definition.

Interaction among individuals is based on symbols. Individuals act in connection with the meaning they attribute to objects (Blumer 1969:10–11). This meaning is not innate, but, instead, it is engendered by individuals' experience and interpretations (Blumer 1969:2).

Symbolic interactionism sets a theoretical basis to help us better understand how groups and individuals can influence the results of treatments through their symbolic interactions. Despite the growing interest in alternatives to face-to-face clinical encounters, contact between patients and health professionals remains, for many individuals, a privileged and essential part of self-identity. In contrast to a paternalistic model of medical care, in which the power of decision making will be entirely delegated by the doctor, this highlights the fact that every individual has his or her own personal orientations and prerogatives, and therefore changes the predominant view of sick people as passive or unarmed in the face of disease. Within the tradition of interactionism, two versions (Goffman's and Strauss's) differed in their perspective of the patient. Strauss focuses on the patient as an active subject, while Goffman seems to be more interested in the patient as a victim of social evaluation and stigmatization. In both versions we can note that the role of the doctor is built alongside that of the patient in an interactive construction made up of meanings and interpretations. The study of interaction in healthcare is based on a deep analysis of verbal and nonverbal conversations since most healthcare professionals and patients exchange information, and they talk to each other on the basis of their social worlds and the symbolic systems through which they interpret their lives. However, it is necessary to highlight that to some extent the order in healthcare interaction is unique, less flexible, and more assertive than in daily life (Charmaz and Belgrave 2013). In other words, in doctor-patient interaction "asymmetry is interactively achieved" (Maynard 1991:449), so interaction is the very means by which participants enact patterns of authority, distinctions of class, discursive formation, and other institutional features that form their social surroundings (Maynard 1991). Cersosimo (2017) noted that during the interaction, the different social actors have interactive manners, and different ways of interpretation, derived from their symbolic universes. Cersosimo also found that when observing situations, doctors, interns, students, and patients behaved differently on the basis of age, gender, and experience. Older doctors tended to act in a more paternalistic way, and patients had a more reverential attitude towards them. This was not the case for interns, who tended to prefer pro-active patients and for students who tended to discuss appropriate sharing and division of work and responsibility among colleagues and patients. The meaning of "taking care," with reference to the context in which doctors are educated or are studying, has different nuances because it can correspond to applied methods and means for treating the disease or to promote health with new forms of relationships. Older doctors tend to consider treatment as a synonym for therapy, whereas younger doctors tend to include the concepts of prevention, literacy, and information sharing. Healthcare, therefore, means taking care of people in a holistic manner (Cersosimo 2017).

We can try to explain this through three propositions: symbol, interaction, and interpretation. A "symbol" can be, for instance, a brochure with the illustration of an education plan for a new lifestyle, or the presence of a more or less invasive technology with which the diagnosis is performed. When diagnosing a disease, doctors emerge as leaders by using the symbols embedded in health policies and public health systems. As a consequence, patients tend to define their doctor as the person able to diagnose their disease, prescribe their therapy, perform their surgery, explain their medication, or indicate how to follow a particular regime. In other words, patients legitimize the power attributed to doctors through symbols—from drugs to new technology, and through invasive and less invasive practices. This highlights our social inheritance, that of treating doctors as superior beings rather than ordinary people. After meeting with a doctor, the trend is to pathologize the patient who receives the diagnosis or for the patient to self-pathologize, fascinated by medicalization. The superior role our society assigns to doctors is strengthened and upheld by the uniform ("the scrubs") as well as by the presence of medical and technical, laparoscopic, and ecographic devices that set the stage where the interaction occurs. The meaning of the term "doctor" is deeply embedded in our mind through symbols. This is also referenced in our understanding of their omnipresence, from birth to death, it is common sense that... *we come into the world and we die in our doctors' hands.*

The study of symbols helps us interpret and explain how we view the doctor's role and how doctors take leading roles. In the case of patients following new medical prescriptions, adopting new dietary lifestyles, or being instructed on how to care for themselves after hospitalization (tertiary prevention), success can be achieved through an interactive relationship where symbols are useful to help define healthcare roles and their functions.

Studies of this type are not lacking in the literature; think for example of the study of sexual habits and behaviors linked to HIV and AIDS among African American women. Symbolic interactionism has been used as a theoretical perspective and method to examine the social experiences and behaviors of African American women and to guide and structure understanding of the processes used by African American women in behaviors, and social and intimate interactions to avoid infecting one's partners (Hunter and Tilley 2015).

THE DEVELOPMENT AND PERSPECTIVE OF SYMBOLIC INTERACTIONISM AND STUDIES ON HEALTHCARE

Interactionist studies of health, mental health, illness, and chronic disease have been applied to work and further research in healthcare. In fact, the introduction of symbolic interactionism transformed research methodology in the field of healthcare. Symbolic interactionism has made three great contributions. The first is its orientation toward dynamic sensitizing concepts (Blumer 1969) that direct research and focus the researcher on particular analytic questions rather than simply providing empirical answers. The second is the prioritization of qualitative methods and an appreciation for the logic of grounded theory. The third is interactionism's holistic approach to interfacing with the everyday life of patients.

Over the years, several researchers have developed the interactionist approach within their studies on health and disease.

First Line of Studies: Disease as Social Construction

Lemert (1951) and Goffman (1961) were the first interactionists who defined an approach to mental illness as more centered upon social processes as compared to psychiatric theories. By this token, the issues related to the course of disease become mobility and *status* problems, while diagnosis and treatment become, at the sociological level, the entry into and exit from the *status* of mentally ill patient. Moreover, the issues related to conditions and circumstances under which psychiatric internment starts and ends take on the meaning of "career contingencies" (here Goffman supports Lemert's argument that social circumstances, external to the patient, can be decisive for admission to the hospital). This perspective highlights a situation of mortification and the initiation into a new moral career of the ill subjects that causes a "reduction of the self" within the barriers erected by the institution between the inpatient and the outer world. On the other hand, even the modes in which they are received and the rules of behavior, because of their impact upon the subject, are significant factors of loss of or threat upon the individual's identity. It is a violation of the lived experience (of the individual) that is "enacted" as soon as he or she enters the places of admission by means of the aseptic and bureaucratic recording of news about his or her private world. Such a violation of the individual private space, then heightened by processes of bodily degradation and humiliation, takes place continuously through the contamination among subjects coming into physical contact unintentionally, since the organization of time and space imposed by the doctor and by the chief medical officer obliges them to comply with the demands of the organizational structure.

Second Line of Studies: Patient's Negotiation of His/Her Status

We can begin by recalling studies by Glaser and Strauss (1965, 1968), (Strauss et al. 1975) on death and dying and chronic disease. The most relevant interactionist approach to disease, present in Anselm Strauss's studies, was his recognition of the patient as one capable of negotiating their own social status, and participating in and arriving at a medical diagnosis. This line of research has been taken up in the investigations of Stewart and Sullivan (1982), relating to the participation of patients in the formulation of their diagnosis with Multiple Sclerosis. In this interactionist model, the patient is consistently active in the process of interpretation with regard to the concept of pathology. This process was summarized in the formulation given by Charmaz, who assigns the chronically ill person the role of innovator, an active creator of new ways of living with the illness, by renewing his or her personal identity (Charmaz 1987).

Third Line of Studies: Healthcare Professions

Another line of relevant studies has been put forth in relation to the socialization of healthcare professions (Hughes 1961), in particular the reorganization of work and care times; or as in the approach of Goffman (1963) and Freidson (1965), who introduced the notions of stigma and disability, a stable awareness of the presence of deviance in modern society. Erving Goffman's observation study of patients in a mental hospital revealed that an individual's behavior in a mental hospital is a response to his/her definition of the context (rules, regulations, expectations) of the hospital. Symbolic interactionists believe that health and illness cannot be viewed as separate from the social context in which we live. Medical knowledge is also socially constructed, and so it is not objective, and it is fallible. Instead Freidson ascribed the responsibility of the social construction of such social realities as health and disease to the category of physicians who, once they become professionals, wield their power to consider and treat disease as a deviation from the norm. In other words, the practice of medicine entails the social risk that a deviancy, originally ascribed to the biological order only, is "dragged" toward a dimension whose cultural traits are perceived as a distancing from social norms. The "social construction" of the disease is shaped precisely by the re-organization and restructuring of specific relations between the subjects and the medical profession in its various forms. Freidson (1970) argued that the doctor tends to perceive the patient and their needs through the categories of the doctor's specialized knowledge, linked to his or her professional autonomy. On the contrary, the patient tends to perceive his or her disease considering their daily life needs and in accordance with their social world. In Freidson's model there is no a priori consensus between the doctor and the patient and the latter is not passive, because the patient-doctor interaction embraces a plurality of configurations. Of course the active-passive configuration is more likely to prevail when the patient's social status is low and if their disease is stigmatized as is the case for alcoholism or mental disorders.

Fourth Line of Studies: Trajectories and Autobiographies

Subsequently Robert Dingwall in 1976 and Michael Bury, a few years later (1982), developed a specific strand of studies and research with the approach of symbolic interactionism applied to the themes of health and disease. Their work, inspired by the interactionist school, was influenced by the "objective" on the part of the British sociologists to distance themselves and to be independent somehow from American interactionism. These British interactionists saw a distinction between trajectory and biography, viewing trajectories consequences in terms of direct, singular, and subjective experiences of the sick person, and the biographical aspects as those that can be experienced by the spouse and other family members. When the disease is out of control due to an acute phase or crisis, a tendency emerges to consider not so much its trajectory, but more the biographical concerns and their social impact (Bury 1982; Dingwall 1976). Bury (1982) showed chronic disease as a destructuring of the biography of a chronically ill subject. Such a distinction has never been taken into consideration by Corbin and Strauss: "Our interviews suggest that even under the most routine conditions of illness and everyday life, but even more so during critical periods of the illness, there is a tug-of-war between the requisites of trajectory management and those of everyday life and biography" (Corbin and Strauss 1988:233).

> Here we find conceptions of the self and of time; people's lives are seen through the prism of disease. In this sense chronic and terminal disease compound the problems of adult reality and accelerate the ageing process. Both problems come into stark relief. Bury (1982) viewed chronic illness as a destructuring of the biography, unlike Corbin and Strauss (1988), who saw disease as a moment in which all the threads of the patient's biography become interwoven because caregiving activities at home mark their own and their family's life by increasing collaboration between the spouses (pp. 234–36). Their care work extends to the hospital too, where families are expected to monitor therapies and complete the nurse's task.
> (Strauss et al. 1982)

Many studies followed these various groundbreaking contributions throughout the 1980s and beyond. In one of the first, Jaber Gubrium (1980) studied elderly patients in a nursing home environment. Using interactionism as a method, he highlighted "strategic interaction" among clinical staff and patients as the process of planned actions favorable to both professionals and patients leading to a higher degree of collaboration and inclusion. Later, Corbin and Strauss (1988) considered illness as a time to renew the crucial phases of the patient's biography, and the care work at home was seen as significant in the lives of patients as well as the family by way of increasing the collaboration between participants (Corbin and Strauss 1988:234–36) in a new and symbolic universe.

Fifth Line of Studies: Interpretations of Suffering

Taking another interactionist approach to the study of disease, some researchers began to look at the interpretation of suffering as a means of understanding various forms of social isolation, thus giving a voice to those who generally remain unheard: patients, family members, caregivers, and care assistants. Strauss's first contributions sought to end this silence (1965). Charmaz (1995) followed in this path with a qualitative and ethnographic work on chronic disease that also contributed to a nascent sociology on the body and suffering (Charmaz 1995; Olesen 1994). Charmaz was particularly interested in the repercussions of chronic diseases on the identity of those affected, as well as on the impact of physical pain, psychological distress, and the deleterious effects of medical procedures, which cause the chronically ill to suffer as they experience their illnesses. However, a narrow medicalized view of suffering, solely defined as physical discomfort, ignores or minimizes the broader significance of the suffering experienced by debilitated and chronically ill patients. I contend that the nature of that suffering is the *loss of self* felt by so many individuals with a chronic illness (Charmaz 1983:168).

Sixth Line of Studies: Improving in Different Levels of Practices for Healthcare

In another study carried out on the subject of emergency care, Wayne Mellinger (1994) pointed to doctor-nurse communication as a key to patients' survival in the emergency room. Communication is characterized as the process by which doctors and nurses give and receive information, as well as their ability to collaborate and decide what action to take. This process is a type of interactive negotiation as the meaning of the situation (and, especially, the patient's condition) is defined before the action takes place (Mellinger 1994).The emerging model sets a *turn-by-turn* interaction, and the creation of meaning results from progressive negotiations amongst healthcare professionals. In this sense, Mellinger's analysis (1994) echoes Blumer's assumptions on meaning and interaction. However, Mellinger went beyond simply assuming the specific role of interpretation, meant to simplify what in practice is a complex dynamic process of creation and action in meaning, and follows Anselm Strauss's idea of negotiated order (1978, 1993). The interaction among individuals gives meaning according to specific situations and shapes participants' mental processes (Blumer 1969) in a continuous process of cognitive evolution that facilitates communication.

Carol Heimer and Lisa Staffen (1998) also argued, in their study on neonatal intensive care, that clinical professionals induced parents' willingness and capacity to optimize their children's health. Lutfey found that "patient adherence and provider roles [...] evolve in tandem" (2005:444), as clinicians not only selectively provide patients and caregivers with the opportunities and tools to be more involved in medical care, but also shape the circumstances under which such involvement could take place more or less successfully. Therefore, the interactionist framework allowed the researchers to see that providers not only induce certain kinds of patient behavior, but also contribute to the development of behavioral skills—appropriate to new lifestyles—when a disease is diagnosed and then treated. Some years later, Joseph Kotarba (2014) elaborated interactionism's overall holistic approach to interfacing with everyday life in the evaluation of an NIH-funded, translational medical research program. The qualitative component of this research has provided interactionist-inspired insights into translational research, such as examining cultural change in medical research in terms of changes in the form and content of formal and informal discourse among scientists delineating the impact of significant symbols. Symbolic interaction provides three great resources to do this. The first symbolic interactionism, as shown from Kotarba's work, has its orientation toward dynamic sensitizing concepts that direct research and ask questions instead of supplying a priori and often impractical answers. The second is its orientation to qualitative methods, and appreciation for the logic of grounded theory. The third is interactionism's overall holistic approach to interfacing with the everyday life world.

Some years later, another study used the holistic interactionist model to analyze a new relationship between doctors and patients, evaluating that over the last years communication between physicians and patients has become more and more complex. The patient-doctor relationship has been transformed into a network of relations in which every contact is characterized by deep and continuous social and technological changes. This study showed a new way of communicating between doctors and patients, which restructured and redefined old and new issues on health and disease and a new form of interaction (Cersosimo 2017). Pennanen and Mikkola (2018) observed and described empowerment as emerging through the social interactions that take place in hospital administrative group meetings, based on observation and analysis of seven administrative group meetings in a Finnish hospital. Pennanen and Mikkola showed that responsibility is constructed by creating co-responsibility among participants, taking individual responsibility, and defining non-responsibility. Action, role, and task responsibilities emerged from the interactions of these group meetings. To support employees' involvement in the process of defining responsibilities, Pennanen and Mikkola found that healthcare professionals must be provided with sufficient resources to deal with their associated responsibilities so that they can manage those different dimensions. These insights can be used to further improve administrative groups in healthcare settings.

All of these observations have deepened our ability to consider how the axioms of symbolic interactionism can provide both theoretical insight and empirical focus to better understand administrative decision making, the behavior of doctors and nurses, relationships within healthcare organizations, patients' experiences, feedback, and disease management strategies, thereby pushing healthcare theory towards a perspective focused on knowledge and interaction among all who are involved in the healthcare universe.

Today's New Framework for the Interaction between Doctors and Patients

Today, we must rethink the previous theories we used to explain the complex relationships between physicians, health systems, health professionals, and patients. Medicine, while significantly determining its own course, is greatly influenced by the customs, values, economic considerations and politics within the social transformations of which it is a part. The boundary between the field of medicine and society itself has been redefined, taking on complex characteristics such as the power of advertising and the media, cultural preferences and shared desires, and the change of a symbolic universe enriched by innovations.

The use of social media allows Internet users' active contribution to online contents, thereby increasing the production and sharing of information among patients through forums, communities, blogs and websites (Boyd 2011; Lupton 2013; Koteyk et al. 2015). Many Internet-based applications "allow the creation and exchange of User Generated Content" (Kaplan and Haenlein 2010:61).

In health organization, communication follows several patterns given the heterogeneity and constantly changing backgrounds as well as changing means of communication.

In a contemporary world where information abounds, the relationship between patient and doctor is different. The "modern" patient is an informed "consumer" who can sit on symmetric communication with the doctor as a result of now-open access to information previously restricted to doctors. The idealized encounter is a cooperative interaction that brings patient and doctor together in a kind of handshake agreement about what ails the former and what the latter can do in response. Nevertheless, it is not always so simple, particularly as the encounter between patient and doctor is about far more, and points out more than a simple classification of disease; is most important not to draw attention away from the care of the person who is ill and of her/his social world.

An ever-more-informed patient revises his or her symbolic and value system, hence they are not willing to accept the doctor-patient relationship in which the former prescribes and the latter complies totally with prescriptions. However, the symbolic interactions in the doctor's rooms are strongly framed by what it means both to be a patient and a doctor. An example of this can be a diagnosis that may go counter to the patient experience as is the contemporary diagnosis of obesity. Many patients and advocacy groups refute that obesity is a disease and maintain that the medicalization of obesity is evidence of size discrimination rather than of biophysical dysfunction (Gard and Wright 2005, Campos et al. 2006). Both individual and collective action in the case of disputed diagnoses has resulted in reconsideration in some cases, and removal, in others, of the disease label. The fat acceptance movement has both advocated for and succeeded to a certain extent in the demedicalization of some aspects of obesity biology. Patients' direct participation in healthcare decisions has become a symbol to perplex, or at least a question. At such an advanced and favorable point for health services, it feels natural to give this touch of quality, but it is worth debating if patient participation in the decisions and choices related to their care directly and substantially benefits the process, or if it is better avoided. Healthcare has not been in *good health* for some time.

Interpreting the Contemporary Medical Scene: Technologies, Media, and Groups

The medical scene has been transformed by new actors with a specific and preponderant goal—mass communication—changing the relationship that also changed its meaning and interpretation. In fact, the excess of information, and the accessibility of information, is not always positive. It can stimulate individuals to play a more active role in decisions about their own health, but it can also become a source of confusion and disorientation. Mass media often provide contradictory or partial information. Media accounts are not always supported by scientific evidence, and this creates a certain level of anxiety and often false hopes and expectations among patients. Moreover, the declaration of the "right to health" has changed the relationship between health professionals and patients. The citizen, informed and protected in their rights, becomes a profane expert. He or she is no longer in care or custody, but rather claims an equal role. These examples are contrasted by doctors who view traditional helping as relationship renewal—transformed and sometimes devalued. In this way, the informed patient becomes a challenge. When patients wield their knowledge, appointments take longer, and the patient becomes (or is experienced as) nagging and overbearing. Patients may believe they know everything while understanding only parts of the available information (often with journalistic or virtual origins). The effect may be a crisis in the experience of traditional relational expectations, and the professionalism of the doctor.

In the communication of health issues, a participatory technology, the World Wide Web is clearly an unprecedented opportunity, and a form of interactive progress that can allow healthcare information to become accessible for people all over the world. This means rethinking the ultimate goals of medicine, social and individual values, and institutional dynamics. This goes hand in hand with the need to re-read issues related to the relationship and communication between doctor and patient, as well as between doctors and other health professionals (Tellis and Tellis 1984; Larson 1999). However, reproposing new models and reinterpreting the myriad of relationships within the healthcare environment and between various subjects requires a confrontation with problems that are not easy to solve.

Therefore the relationship between those who provide assistance and those who receive it changes completely. Health professionals are given the right to recognize—based on their expert knowledge—that a certain condition or disease can determine, initiate, or sanction an unhealthy person to the official, social role of the patient. The patient appeals to the professional to be listened to and understood, expecting that professional to empathize, to assume—even if for only a moment—his or her role, in order to obtain the complete meaning in the communication exchange. The relationship thus becomes one of negotiation, an exchange between two subcultures, a process that selects the symptoms, their perception and interpretation, and the way of proceeding throughout the therapeutic relationship in relation to the overall system of care. The reality is that communication between healthcare professionals and patients has become highly complex, within a relational network characterized in all its components by growing contingencies and changes. As people's needs change, their definition of health and disease also changes. The patient, in a contradictory way, increases his or her expectations toward the doctor and other healthcare provider. At the same time, the patient loses trust in them because of his or her self-obtained information and self-medication practice. The professional medical models change, as well as their action and control constraints. The whole structure of the socio-health system changes as well, while the relationship between patients and practitioners becomes more impersonal, hasty, superficial, almost extraneous. The technologies and procedures that mediate those relationships also change; doctors and health professionals increasingly use technical instruments and equipment such as optical fibers, electronic circuits, silicon chips, robotics, and nanotechnology, which further distance them from their clients.

New Forms of Interaction and the Role of E-Health

The birth and affirmation of e-health and other similar tools has changed the internal interactions of health institutions, helping to determine and renew contexts, processes and relationships on the basis of new information on health issues and care.

E-health technologies are aimed at both patients and healthcare professionals. This is a relationship without precedent for the various sites and e-networks that offer health information and claims.

The virtual presence of health organizations has profoundly influenced the ways in which people understand the themes of health and disease and engage in the healthcare system. Patients are invited to use information and services interactively, orienting themselves in research on diagnoses and treatments, information about prescriptions, notices from health professionals and patients with similar pathologies, the offering and receiving of social support, and the ability to keep family and friends informed about their condition. This online communication network increasingly affects the healthcare world as patients are provided with information about their health through online medical journals, quite different from traditional reading materials.

In the field of information specialists, it becomes a question of developing an integrated system through which a patient's profile can interact with the individual's educational orientation in relation to well-being. The network can also allow for contact between professionals, enabling the exchange of information and the organization of groups of patients—especially useful in the treatment of chronic pathologies—to change behaviors by removing subjects from the terrible individualization of a particular uncommon disease. This results in the breakdown of the centralization of information and creates a new care process and work group based on the collaboration of professionals rather than on the re-proposal of traditional hierarchies.

The experience of chronic disease has also taken on a public, interactive dimension that highlights the relationship between individuals and virtual communication. Now we can grasp the communicative processes evoked in blogs, social media, online networks, and other forms of communication. The sick are able to produce online illness blogs as a way to share their own illness narratives and connect with others going through similar processes. In a reversal of roles, disease has lost its character as a private experience, becoming an increasingly public experience to be described and written about, and to be reproduced in images which are always traceable and can be referenced. Blogs have been used extensively to self-document the intimate and often intensive experiences of living with serious illness, charting treatment often over many years, connecting with others, and drawing attention and concern along the way. The value of blogs help the patients in the role-taking, form of identity and affect management, network-enabling in generating online spaces for shared experience and support, and it is helpful to reinterpretation of new life conditions (see Wilson et al. 2015; Ross et al. 2018; Levonian et al. 2021).

An indication of this change is represented by the emergence of disease subcultures and social movements related to pathologies, which are becoming a driving force behind the self-empowerment of various cultures in the field of chronic diseases and beyond. The experience of chronic disease has also taken on an interactive public dimension. It was shared earlier only with family and friends but now includes the people met virtually in a public realm. This can be understood today through the communication processes evoked on blogs, online, and by way of the myriad forms of communication we experience from institutional to social. Diagnosis is focused on how the Internet community seems to build new identities for chronically ill patients who perform a supporting function, and are perceived in terms of an alternative medical culture, giving importance to the subjective experiences of the sick protagonist (Jutel 2009). In this new context, the social construction of ways of living with chronic disease takes place in a way that explores new identities, values, behaviors, feelings, and emotions. It is an experience of a new self, one that recognizes its body as sick, but also expresses a new and substantially different idea about being chronically ill—*being successfully ill*, having an active and meaningful life, despite the disease and its constraints.

This transformation has had implications on relationships within the healthcare system. We can observe on one side patients' excessive initiatives in terms of medication, self-surveillance, and self-management, and on the other side specific features satisfying doctor-patient interactions, such as (Cersosimo 2019):

- Knowledge of medical issues and terms linked to the understanding of scientific knowledge and health culture (meaning, doctors are less likely to be interrupted when visiting with patients)
- The skills to communicate health-related information to providers in a medically intelligible and efficient manner (this implies efficiency)
- Knowledge of what information is relevant to healthcare personnel
- An enterprising disposition and a proactive stance towards health, both of which presuppose a sense of mastery and self-efficacy
- The ability to take an instrumental attitude toward one's own body
- An orientation toward the future and its control through calculation and action

- A sensitivity to interpersonal dynamics and the ability to adapt one's own style of interaction

On the other hand, it is about health literacy, as defined by Marcia Ratzan and Scott Parker "the degree to which individuals have the capacity to obtain, process, and understand basic health information and services needed to make appropriate health decisions" (Ratzan and Parker 2000:vi). Ten years later, health literacy has been defined ". . .health literacy includes a variety of skills— reading and writing certainly, but also a facility with numbers and calculations (numeracy) and the ability to understand spoken health information and to describe one's health needs. In addition, health literacy is dynamic and essentially resides at the intersection of patient abilities and the demands of the particular situation" (Weser, Rudd, and DeJong 2010:590). As such, health literacy is crucial in interactions in order to ensure the correct functioning of the healthcare environment. Indeed, when health literacy is insufficient, it can contribute to social disparities in care quality as well as to wasteful inappropriate health services. Other features that impact on interaction with health professionals include self-efficacy, mastery, control, and self-esteem (e.g., Bandura 1997, 2004), all referring to a "core belief that one has the power to produce desired changes by one's actions" (Bandura 2004:144). Health literacy and selectivity add another element to the discussion since they indicate the ways, be they direct or indirect/symbolic or functional, in which these resources contribute to the rationalization of health systems with a series of interaction and actions, a greater sharing of information, and answers to doubts and questions that could improve communication, treatment compliance, and care. In this case, interaction and symbols act like knowledge capital (Bourdieu 1977), to which a distinction and positive approval is given, and re-compensated as such. This double nature of interaction, both functional and symbolic, offers a conceptual processing of existing notions on health literacy. In other terms, interaction in healthcare is based on a deep analysis of verbal and symbolic conversations since most health operators and patients exchange information and talk to each other starting from their social worlds and symbolic systems through which they interpret their lives.

Interactionist Methods in the Holistic Perspective

Interactionist methods have always maintained an intimate stance toward the everyday-life world, and its concerns, theories, languages, and narratives. Symbolic interactionism has always shown analytical and policy concern for what are commonly referred to as social problems. Symbolic interactionism's development of labeling theory and its close sibling, social constructivism, has led interactionists to heed Howard Becker's observation that "Invariably, we all label ourselves and others to signal different aspects of our identities. . . Labels that have been allocated to us either during childhood or later on in life are generally internalised thus imposing boundaries and defining us into categories" (Becker 1973:2). Finally, symbolic interactionism's holistic orientation both culminates in and is illustrated by, a respect for, if not always strict adherence to, grounded theory (Charmaz 2006).

In research, narrative interaction helps to develop a patient-centered agenda and generate new hypotheses (Greenhalgh and Hurwitz 1999). Therefore, communication within the healthcare organization cannot have a single paradigm. This is not only because the news and the recipients are different, but also because they affect multiple aspects such as the characteristics of those who must disclose, and the influences on the sources from which the information originates. Interactionist methods in holistic perspective of care and role theory as one field of study fills the gap of previous qualitative studies, which focused on a given role rather than on the different actors, roles and situations in the healthcare system. Symbolic interactionism offers a way to end the perceived incongruity between qualitative and quantitative methodologies by offering a theoretical perspective that can embrace both approaches. For researchers who use multiple method designs, symbolic interactionism provides a theoretical perspective for conceptually clear and soundly implemented research about human health behavior. The use of symbolic interactionism as a theoretical perspective for multiple method designs in healthcare research offers the hope of a richer, fuller understanding of doctors and of the individuals who are the recipients of healthcare.

Therefore symbolic interactionism can make use in medical and biomedical research of its different modes to observe and explain health and disease, treatment, and inequalities in healthcare systems.

Symbolic interactionism emphasizes the creation of meanings in life and human actions, underlining the pluralistic nature of society, the cultural and social relativism of ethical and social norms and rules, and the vision of the self as socially structured. This approach deals above all with the social interaction that takes place in people's daily lives. Symbolic interactionism has, over time, influenced the medical sciences and research methodology. It refers to questions about the knowledge of realities that subject experience, as well as to its definition as a method or criterion for the analysis of the meaning of existence that leads to action.

A related point is the lasting, capable, and attentive presence, in the fieldwork, of ways that elements of symbolic interactionism are involved in grounded theory, ethnomethodology, conversational analysis, and discourse analysis in the research of Everett Hughes, Barney Glaser and Anselm Strauss, Harold Garfinkel, and Aaron Cicourel. Thus, when working within this framework, a researcher not only must understand the definition of achievable objectives, the choice of methods, and the attention to the dynamics of research, but also evaluate, from beginning to end, all phases of the research process.

The value of research and its relationship with interactionism will likely be exalted by future researchers, as has repeatedly happened depending on whether the methods adopted are capable "to be faithful to the complexity of everyday life" (Atkinson 2015:38), and of the global context, seizing its existential and problematic dimensions. This tends to further validate the theoretical and practical premises indicated, effectively transferring them to the choices made within research, assigning renewed legitimacy to those methods, and reiterating the positive theoretical substance of the theoretical orientation considered. The application of symbolic interactionism to research in healthcare systems functions in ways substantially connected to the questions and the issues of the researcher, leading to the adequate although the also problematic formulation of answers, perhaps beyond the horizons of advanced questions in the initial phase of only evidence-based medicine.

Social sciences within the field of medical research are systematically confronted with the genealogy of cultural ideas around three key issues: experience, social inequalities, and social action. In other words, the social sciences are tasked with giving voice to unheard questions about public health.

A possible model for addressing unheard questions should include analyzing the actions, reactions, communication, and consequential effects of the "back stage." Theoretically, on "the back stage," the dynamics of unchecked roles and "role-taking" in healthcare systems create a hyperactive circle—a barrier—around the patient, who ultimately ends up spending more time alone than is realized by the actors in the home. The evolution of healthcare systems can be energized and taken to the next stage by including the study of role dynamics and symbolic interaction among the patient, the family, clinical personnel, managers, and hospital administrators in order to better serve the patients and their families. The application of the roles and symbolic interactionism frameworks can start moving healthcare system research from reporting statistics and costs to gaining theoretical understanding and theory development. The roles framework provides a methodology to discern the different actors and the multiple roles they play; symbolic interactionism provides a methodology that connects meaning, interaction, and interpretation to the roles and actions individuals take while fulfilling the obligations of the temporal roles they occupy. The methodological and theoretical fusion applied in this study highlight the impact each individual (family, staff, clinical, and management) has on the experience of the patient, family, and healthcare-system personnel.

Symbolic interactionism's approach involves the use of methods that appear most suitable for the type of research being conducted, granting the researcher the freedom to simultaneously use any methodological tool for research. Consider, for example, the following research question: After a bariatric surgery, how does the patient's quality of life change, and how does the demand for visits by the health system decrease? The answer may result from face-to-face interviews, individual interviews, a focus-group discussion, and/or the suggestions of those involved in the clinical trials (Santonicola et al. 2021).

The approaches just outlined are guidelines for the application of symbolic interactionism to medical/clinical research and do not pose questions with obvious answers but rather explore broad research areas. This method is oriented toward the formulation of clear, focused, concise, complex, and arguable research questions around which one can center a hypothesis.

Another guideline for this type of research is the establishment of a working group for the simplification and standardization of terminology to improve data collection in the field, the management of logistics, coordination, and decision making. Examples of questions connected to the application of SI research in a clinical setting may be, What research question can be asked? What methods and research design can be applied? Who are the key research team members? What do we want to know, and what previous knowledge do we have? Choosing research methods and cultural practices, a researcher must decide what actions to take and which research methods to employ: Should they be qualitative? How should we blend methodologies, and which programs of sensitization to the community must we employ to be aware of and be responsive to certain ideas, events, situations, or experiences?

Medical understanding is not a neutral and objective construction of reality, but rather an interpretation of definitions that shape reality, as critical as the experience that made the subject sick. This does not mean that we abandon the biomedical model, but rather that we integrate it with a narrative approach. The narrative approach can allow us to recognize the importance of sensitizing concepts. Think, for example, of how Kathy Charmaz defines identifying moments as "telling moments filled with new self-images . . . telling because they spark sudden realizations [and] reveal hidden images of self" (Charmaz 1991:207) and on how this sensitizing concept adopted from her work on chronic illness, can illuminate our understanding of disease narratives.

RELEVANCE OF NEGOTIATED INTERPRETATIONS. AN EXAMPLE: THE INTENSIVE CARE UNIT

Today the relationships and interactions between doctors, health professionals, patients, and family members are mainly based on negotiation. Negotiation is a process by which two or more parties dispute a scarce resource and seek an agreement. Negotiation therefore is not about the exclusion of this priority or that recommendation, but rather a synthesis of intentions and precedence. Any successful negotiation between social actors cannot ignore communications made by way of knowledge, cultural understanding, social and/or political mediation, differentiation of roles and status, or of a shared linguistic and symbolic universe.

Interaction in healthcare is based on a deep analysis of symbolic conversations. This is because most healthcare professionals and patients exchange information and speak to each other from the standpoint of the social worlds and symbolic systems through which they interpret their lives. These analyses are connected to the general structure of the actors' activities and to the different sequence of clinical contexts in which they occur, in relation to specific interactions and strategies (Cersosimo 2019:311–12).

Therefore, the logic of negotiation has its own roots into symbolic interactionism and role theory (Blumer 1969). Meaning is derived from social interactions and it is the result of an interpretative process which pushes the individual toward an inner conversation: during this communication he or she "selects, checks, suspends, regroups, and transforms meaning in the light of the situation in which he is placed and the direction of his action" (Blumer 1969:5). This kind of interpretation is not the result of predefined meanings, but rather derives from a creative process in which the meaning is often revised.

Keeping in mind these premises of symbolic interactionism (Blumer 1969), diseases can therefore be treated from a new—interactionist—perspective, one in which daily life is populated by individuals interacting through relationships in which doctors' implicit roles emerge and influence patients daily lives as well as their healthcare system management.

In other words, negotiation is the opposite of a pure self-interest doctrine: it is a way to ensure that healthcare facilities are malleable, flexible spaces through which the results of symbolic interaction can be shared between patients, doctors, and healthcare professionals.

Organizations are not seen as formations structured by univocal, standardized rules since reflection and dialogue, individuals and collectives, are necessary to modify, maintain, and reproduce them. Their very existence depends on their continuous reconstruction through action, interpretation, and meaning. Their objectives and strategies can be discussed, and the agreements reached can take various forms, including the intentional or tolerated coexistence of many disparate objectives. From time to time the same social actors attribute the purpose and possible success of the exchange process to situations deriving from the experience of everyday life. In evaluating the interaction of patients in a coma or intensive care unit, we are interested not only in social rules and other structural conditions, but also in the tendencies of interaction that separate from our regulated forms and open new modes of interaction and new interpretation.

It is helpful in this context to think specifically in terms of the experience of Intensive Care and Emergency Care departments. Healthcare workers in these positions are perhaps more emblematic than others. They are at the center of social and cultural changes that medical practices are more generally experiencing today. In Intensive Care units, the pace of instrumental innovations has been remarkable. At the same time, we have witnessed a constant and progressive increase in specialist, technical, and sectoral knowledge, becoming increasingly capable of intervening effectively in extreme conditions. The Intensive Care physician is often in a paradoxical position, being the administrator of an imposing and increasingly effective scientific and technological apparatus of which he or she controls only a specific sector. A doctor who performs this role is increasingly required to meet the growing expectations related to their ability to prolong life, and to respond to requests for the permission to die—to be released from suffering. This position requires negotiations of the most intimate dimensions with respect to the patient and their family. The medical and nursing staff within these units are increasingly aware that successful communication depends on their ability to communicate and negotiate their role between their own team and the patient's family.

In Intensive Care and Resuscitation Units, the double meaning of communication is not always clear. There are discrete communications that must be undertaken relating to the services provided (internal health communication), as well as those regarding the information shared about clinical decisions related to specific patients, and communication concerning lifestyles, future prospects, safety, and so on that are provided to guarantee the future health of patients (external health communication). These are distinct communication processes with profound implications. The negotiation process is not, as it may seem, a collateral issue with the preeminent objective being the protection of health through therapeutic, concrete, and operational interventions, but rather a successful negotiation implies a productive dialogue.

A dialogue takes place when meaningful interaction is fostered, that is if the transmission and receiving of information and the receiving of that information takes place in a comprehensible and acceptable way by the patient and family. In a case when a patient is not conscious, direct communication is not possible, so healthcare workers must effectively communicate with the family. A further complication to this process is how the various roles of staff members within the Intensive Care unit cooperate or negotiate with each other. The process of verbal and non-verbal communication often involves not a single doctor and patient, but an entire team and family members that are distributed over several shifts. It has been observed that there are profound differences between the information that doctors and nurses are authorized to share and what they feel they are able to communicate (Krimshtein et al. 2011).

In preparing to communicate with families in this situation, it may be useful to be aware of the most frequent and important questions they may have. Certainly their view of the patient and the disease is quite different from that of the doctor (Peigne et al. 2011). Relatives are the ones charged with the demanding and painful task of caring for and making decisions on behalf of a seriously ill patient, a task that becomes more complex if they are unable to express their preferences regarding treatment. In addition to the information that the doctor must provide on the patient's condition and prognosis, information on their choices regarding those treatments are vitally important. This approach requires an ability to negotiate and share roles as well as medical information with the family, and this requires that all team members have good communication skills so they can assist families in understanding and interpretating the consequences and benefits of each choice while attempting to interpret the patient's will.

Role-taking helps us to decipher these roles while individuals perform their actions. Symbols, meanings, interactions, and interpretations can clarify some health topics since language (defined as "by naming something, we classify our knowledge"), Strauss (1959) can be considered as an equal representation of our thoughts, values, and norms. Interactionism shows how a series of words that could mislead patients (unconscious, functional disease, pharmacological coma) can be reformulated through symbols to give a piece of information or instill empathy and self-determination when choosing the best way of life to protect one's health.

Healthcare can be intelligible and interesting for patients and patients' families, if they can see how to reduce costs and supplements, and transform themselves into an active part of the process meant to appropriately manage their health. Thus, a symbolic interaction could have a different meaning once a patient or their family members interpret the interaction and apply it to their own reference framework.

Interaction and symbols offer a consistent framework to help us understand the impact of important changes such as the complex dynamics of medical interaction, and the relink between healthcare and broader social relationships. They allow us to make the most of the resources provided in medical encounters, those being flexible and variable behaviors and features that benefit patients as well as the healthcare system.

Final Remarks

A symbolic interactionist framework reveals that behavior is connected to the ways a person defines other individuals who are significant for them, the physical settings that they are in, and all of the elements that in a particular situation they consider relevant. Examining health treatments through the lens of symbolic interactionism allows for a deeper analysis of the strategic interactions among various stakeholders. Symbolic interactionism can help us so that service quality is higher, unnecessary hospitalizations are limited, and requests are better distributed across local health services. The application of symbolic interactionism as a research methodology in health-system administrations can trigger deep conversations and change, related to the optimization of appropriate medical care, while reducing disparities within the healthcare system.

Acknowledgment

I thank Rosalba Perrotta and Wayne Brekhus for valuable comments, but responsibility for the arguments made in the chapter remains, however, with the author alone.

References

Atkinson, Paul. 2015. *For Ethnography*. London: SAGE.
Bandura, Albert 1997. *Self-Efficacy: The Exercise of Control*. W.H. Freeman: New York.
Bandura, Albert. 2004. "Health Promotion by Social Cognitive Means." *Health Education and Behavior* 31:143–64.
Becker, Howard S. 1973. "Outsiders: Studies in the Sociology of Deviance." New York: Free Press.
Blumer, Herbert. 1969. *Symbolic Interactionism: Perspective and Method*. Englewood Cliffs, NJ: Prentice Hall Inc.
Bourdieu, Pierre. 1977. *Outline of a Theory of Practice*, Cambridge, Cambridge University Press.
Boyd, Danah M. 2011. "Social Network Sites as Networked Publics: Affordances, Dynamics, and Implications." Pp. 39–58 in *Networked Self: Identity, Community, and Culture on Social Network Sites*, edited by Z. Papacharissi. New York: Routledge.
Bury, Michael. 1982. "Chronic Illness as Biographical Disruption." *Sociology of Health and Illness*, 4:137–69.

Campos, Paul, Abigail Saguy, Paul Ernsberger, Eric Oliver, and Glenn Gaesser. 2006. "The Epidemiology of Overweight and Obesity: Public Health Crisis or Moral Panic?" *International Journal of Epidemiology* 35(1):55–60. https://doi.org/10.1093/ije/dyi254

Cersosimo, Giuseppina. 2017. "Improving Health Communication through Renewed and Enlarged Social and Technological Interactions." *Sociologia e Ricerca Sociale* 114:117–37. http://dx.doi.org/10.3280/SR2017-114006

Cersosimo, Giuseppina. 2019. "Interaction and Symbolism in Health Care Systems." *Italian Sociological Review* 9(2):305–59.

Charmaz, Kathy. 1983. "Loss of Self: A Fundamental Form of Suffering in the Chronically Ill." *Sociology of Health and Illness* 5(2):168–95.

Charmaz, Kathy. 1987. "Struggling for a Self: Identity Levels of the Chronically Ill." Pp. 283–321 in *Research in the Sociology of Health Care. A Research Annual. The Experience and Management of Chronic Illness*, edited by J. A. Roth and P. Conrad. Greenwich–London, JAI Press.

Charmaz, Kathy. 1991. *Good Days, Bad Days: The Self in Chronic Illness and Time*. New Brunswick, NJ: Rutgers University Press.

Charmaz, Kathy. 1995. "The Body, Identity and Self." *Sociological Quarterly* 36:657–80.

Charmaz, Kathy. 2006. *Constructing Grounded Theory: A Practical Guide Through Qualitative Analysis*. London: SAGE.

Charmaz, Kathy, and Linda. L. Belgrave. 2013. "Modern Symbolic Interaction Theory and Health." Pp. 11–39 in *Medical Sociology on the Move*, edited by W. Cockerham. Dordrecht: Springer.

Corbin, Juliet, M., and Anselm Strauss. 1988. *Unending Work and Care: Managing Chronic Illness at Home*. San Francisco: Jossey-Bass Publishers.

Dingwall, Robert. 1976. *Aspects of Illness*. London: Martin Robertson.

Freidson, Eliot. 1965. "Disability and Social Deviance." Pp. 71–99 in *Sociology and Rehabilitation*, edited by M. Sussman. American Sociological Association, Washington, DC.

Friedson, Eliot. 1970. *Profession of Medicine*. New York: Harper and Row.

Gard, Michael, and Jan Wright. 2005. *The Obesity Epidemic. Science, Morality and Ideology*. London: Routledge.

Glaser, Barney. G., and Anselm, L. Strauss. 1965. *Awareness of Dying*. Chicago: Aldine.

Glaser Barney, G., and Anselm, L. Strauss. 1968. *Time for Dying*. Chicago: Aldine.

Goffman, Erving. 1961. *Asylums: Essays on the Social Situation of Mental Patients and Other Inmates*. Doubleday Broadway Publishing Group, Random House, Inc.

Goffman, Erving. 1963. *Stigma: Notes on the Management of Spoiled Identity*. Englewood Cliffs, NJ: Prentice Hall.

Greenhalgh, Trisha, Brian Hurwitz. 1999. "Narrative Based Medicine: Why Study Narrative." *British Medical Journal* 318(7175): 48–50. doi.org/10.1136/bmj.318.7175.48

Gubrium, Jaber F. 1980. "Patient Exclusion in Geriatric Staffings." *The Sociological Quarterly* 21(3):335–47.

Heimer, Carol, A., and Lisa, R. Staffen 1998. *For the Sake of the Children: The Social Organization of Responsibility in the Hospital and the Home*. Chicago: University of Chicago Press.

Hughes, Everett. C. 1961. "Education for a Profession." *The Library Quarterly: Information, Community, Policy* 31(4):336–43.

Hunter, Teresa S., and Donna S. Tilley. 2015. "A Grounded Theory Study of the Process Used to Negotiate Condom Use Among African-American Women: Review of the Literature." *Journal of Cultural Diversity* 22(1/ Spring):23–29. PMID: 26288909.

Jutel, Annemarie. 2009. "Sociology of Diagnosis: A Preliminary Review." *Sociology of Health and Illness* 31(2):278–99.

Kaplan, Andrea M., and Michale Haenlein. 2010. "Users of the World, Unite! The Challenges and Opportunities of Social Media." *Business Horizons* 53(1):59–68.

Kotarba, Joseph. 2014. "Symbolic Interaction and Applied Social Research. A Focus on Translational Science Research." *Symbolic Interaction* 37(3):412–25. doi/10.1002/symb.111

Koteyko, Nelya, Daniel Hunt, and Barrie Gunter. 2015. "Expectations in the Field of the Internet and Health: An Analysis of Claims about Social Networking Sites in Clinical Literature." *Sociology of Health & Illness* 37(3):468–84. doi/10.1111/1467-9566.12203

Krimshtein, Nina S., et al. 2011. "Training Nurses for Interdisciplinary Communication with Families in the Intensive Care Unit: An Intervention." *Journal of Palliative Medicine* 14(12):1325–32.

Larson, Elaine. 1999. "The Impact of Physician-Nurse Interaction on Patient Care." *Holistic Nursing Practice.* 13 (2/January):38–46. doi: 10.1097/00004650-199901000-00007

Lemert, Edwin. 1951. *Social Pathology: A Systematic Approach to the Theory of Sociopathic Behavior.* New York: McGraw Hill.

Levonian, Zachary, et al. 2021. "Patterns of Patient and Caregiver Mutual Support Connections in an Online Health Community." *Proceedings of the ACM on Human-Computer Interaction* 4(CSCW3):1–46.

Lupton, Deborah. 2013. "Quantifying the Body: Monitoring and Measuring Health in the age of mHealth Technologies." *Critical Public Health* 23(4):393–403.

Lutfey, Karen. 2005. "On Practices of 'Good Doctoring': Reconsidering the Relationship between Provider Roles and Patient Adherence." *Sociology of Health and Illness* 27:421–47.

Maynard, Douglas W. 1991. "Interaction and Asymmetry in Clinical Discourse." *American Journal of Sociology* 97:448–495.

Mellinger, Wayne M. 1994. "Negotiated Orders: The Negotiation of Directives in Paramedic-Nurse Interaction." *Symbolic Interaction* 17(2):165–85.

Olesen, Virginia. 1994. "Problematic Bodies: Past, Present and Future." *Symbolic Interaction* 7:231–37.

Peigne, Vincent, et al. 2011. "Important Questions Asked by Family Members of Intensive Care Unit Patients." *Critical Care Medicine* 39(6):1365–71.

Pennanen, Evelina, and Leena Mikkola. 2018. "Constructing Responsibility in Social Interaction: An Analysis of Responsibility Talk in Hospital Administrative Groups." *Qualitative Research in Medicine & Healthcare* 2(3):154–64.

Ratzan, Scott C., and Ruth M. Parker. 2000. "Introduction." Pp. v–vi, in *National Library of Medicine Current Bibliographies in Medicine: Health Literacy*, edited by C. R.Selden and M. Zorn. National Institutes of Health, U. S. Department of Health and Human Services.

Ross, Emily, Tineke Broer, Anne Kerr, and S. Cunningham-Burley. 2018. "Identity, Community and Care in Online Accounts of Hereditary Colorectal Cancer Syndrome." *New Genetics and Society* 37(2):117–36.

Santonicola, Antonella, Giuseppina Cersosimo, Luigi Angrisani, Mario Gagliardi, Luca Ferraro, Paola Iovino. 2021. "Nonadherence to Micronutrient Supplementation After Bariatric Surgery: Results from an Italian Internet-Based Survey." *Journal of the American College of Nutrition* 30(March):1–9. https://doi.org/10.1080/07315724.2020.1830003

Stewart, David C., and Thomas J. Sullivan. 1982. "Illness Behavior and the Sick Role in Chronic Disease: The Case of Multiple Sclerosis." *Social Science and Medicine* 16:1397–1404.

Strauss, Anselm. 1959. *Mirrors and Masks: The Search for Identity.* New York: Aldine de Gruyter.

Strauss, Anselm, et al. 1975. *Chronic Illness and the Quality of Life*. Saint Louis: Mosby.

Strauss, Anselm 1978. *Negotiations: Varieties, Contexts, Processes, and Social*. San Francisco: Jossey-Bass.

Strauss, Anselm, et al. 1982. "The Work of Hospitalised Patients." *Social Science and Medicine* 16: 977–86.

Strauss, Anselm. 1993. *Continual Permutations of Action*. New York: Aldine de Gruyter.

Tellis-Nayak, Michael, and Vivian Tellis-Nayak. 1984. "Games that Professionals Play: The Social Psychology of Physician-Nurse Interaction." *Social Science and Medicine* 18:1063–69. 10.1016/0277-9536(84)90166-7

Weser, Susan, K., Riman E. Rudd, and William DeJong. 2010. "Quantifying Word Use to Study Health Literacy in Doctor-Patient Communication." *Journal Health Communication* 15(6):590–602.

Wilson, Eelena, Amanda Kenny, Virginia Dickson-Swift. 2015. "Using Blogs as a Qualitative Health Research Tool." *International Journal of Qualitative Methods* 14(5):1–12.

PART IV

ENVIRONMENT, DISASTERS, AND RISK

CHAPTER 27

INTERACTIONIST TOOLS FOR ASSESSING COMMUNITY RESILIENCE

BRADEN LEAP

INTRODUCTION

SOCIO-ECOLOGICAL resilience theory has increasingly been utilized by scholars, development officials, and policy makers to assess whether and how communities can be sustained in response to disruptions related to a range of socio-ecological processes such as floods, epidemics, climate change, and economic downturns (Walker and Cooper 2011; Brown 2014; Cretney 2014). Academics have argued that social theories should be utilized to better assess the social dynamics of resilience (Berkes and Ross 2013; Fabinyi et al. 2014; Leap 2018). Nevertheless, and paralleling the neglect of micro-sociological perspectives within environmental sociology (Brewster and Bell 2009; Brewster and Puddephatt 2017), resilience scholars have eschewed explicit engagements with symbolic interaction even as there have been calls to utilize interpretivist theoretical traditions (e.g., Tidball 2014; Hobman and Walker 2015; Stojanovic et al. 2016; Muhar et al. 2017).

I contend that classic and contemporary research by symbolic interactionists, and those in closely related theoretical traditions, can provide an effective toolkit for enriching assessments of how resilience unfolds in practice. This is especially important if we hope to develop and implement policies and programs that have a greater potential for enhancing communities' abilities to effectively respond to socio-ecological disruptions (Stojanovic et al. 2016). After introducing resilience theory, I address how interactionist work on institutions as well as interactions between humans and nonhumans—what I refer to as (non)human interactions—can enrich considerations of resilience. Paralleling others who advocate employing multiple theoretical traditions to better assess the intricate complexities of resilience (e.g., Stone-Jovicich et al. 2018), instead of arguing that symbolic interaction should supplant other approaches to studying resilience, I emphasize that symbolic interactionism can complement and extend existing research on resilience.

SOCIO-ECOLOGICAL RESILIENCE THEORY

Borrowing from new ecology's focus on the emergent relations between organisms that create positive feedback loops and nonlinear changes within ecosystems (Holling 1973), socio-ecological resilience focuses on whether communities can be sustained through novel rearrangements of the (non)human things and beings that comprise them (Gunderson 2000). Resilience scholars and practitioners do not focus on whether a community can return to an ideal equilibrium in response to an acute event such as a disaster or chronic changes such as shifting climatic conditions. Instead, they consider whether the socio-ecological interconnections comprising a community can be reorganized in emergent manners so that it is sustained (Adger 2000; Folke 2006; Berkes and Ross 2013; Herman 2016).

Scholars across the social sciences generally agree on the following three points concerning the social dynamics of resilience.

1) The interconnected tensions between agency and social structures are centrally important to reorganizing and sustaining communities (Berkes et al. 2003b; Davidson 2010, 2013; Westley et al. 2013; Cretney 2014; Stone-Jovicich 2015; Clarke and Mayer 2017; Leap 2018; Leap and Thompson 2018). Resilience emerges—or fails to emerge—from individuals and groups creatively navigating and reworking social structures such as institutions and social norms.

2) Linkages among (non)human things, beings, and institutions across scales of space and time impact whether and how communities are reorganized and sustained (Adger 2000; Peterson 2000; Berkes et al. 2003a; Chaffin and Gunderson 2016). Resilience is informed by (non)human interactions that take place across multiple geographic scales and whose consequences, which reverberate into the future, are informed by (non)human interactions that have taken place previously in both immediate and distant spaces and times.

3) Socio-ecological heterogeneities and inequalities inform—and are informed by— resilience (Cote and Nightingale 2012; Turner 2013; Fabinyi et al. 2014; Olsson et al. 2014; Biermann et al. 2015; Ingalls and Stedman 2016; Leap 2018). (Non) humans have divergent degrees of power and capacities to inform resilience, and individuals and groups are differentially advantaged by rearrangements of their socio-ecological communities.

Case studies concerning a wide array of topics such as agriculture (Cafer 2018; Carr 2019), aquaculture (Hoque et al. 2017), food systems (Lever et al. 2019), oil spills (May

2018), collective identities (Leap and Thompson 2018; Thompson 2019), urban planning (Meerow and Newell 2019), and shifting animal migration patterns (Leap 2019) illustrate that whether communities are sustained in response to shifting socio-ecological conditions is contingent on how unequal relations among (non)humans are creatively rearranged across scales of both space and time. A social theory must be able to account for these interrelated dynamics if it is suitable for studying resilience.

Political ecology (Peterson 2000; Turner 2013; Fabinyi et al. 2014; Ingalls and Stedman 2016; Hoque et al. 2017), actor-network theory (Zimmerer 2011; Dwiaratama and Rosin 2014; Stone-Jovicich 2015), and feminist theory (Leap 2018) have been utilized to explore the social dynamics of socio-ecological resilience, but symbolic interaction has not received explicit engagement from resilience scholars. This is unfortunate because the theoretical tradition can enrich our understanding of how resilience is achieved in practice, which is particularly significant if we hope to develop and implement policies and programs that have a greater probability of enhancing sustainability (Stojanovic et al. 2016). The following sections detail how symbolic interaction can effectively address, and in some cases extend, our understandings of how communities are—or are not—reorganized in response to socio-ecological disruptions.

Emergent, Creative Interactions Among (Non)Humans

Creative interactions among (non)humans are centrally important to resilience because the ability to respond to socio-ecological disruptions is generally dependent on rearranging communities in innovative manners (Berkes et al. 2003b; Davidson 2010, 2013; Leap 2018). For a social theory to be suitable for resilience scholars, it must be able to consider (non)human interactions *and* how creativity informs these interactions. Symbolic interaction not only is capable of accounting for (non)humans' innovative actions and interactions, but also provides an exceptionally strong toolkit for considering the intricacies of these interactions.

Although Mead has been critiqued for reductive portrayals of nonhumans (Irvine 2004, 2017; Jerolmack 2009), scholars generally conclude that symbolic interactionism can be utilized to effectively study (non)human interactions (Sanders 2003; Irvine 2004, 2017; Capek 2006; Smith and Bugni 2006; Weigert 2008; Jerolmack 2013; Leap 2015; Brewster and Puddephat 2016). Research by interactionists concerning how people relate to landscapes is illustrative and especially notable because the ability to reorganize relationships with landscapes is centrally important to whether and how communities are sustained as shifting socio-ecological conditions render previous ways of interacting with particular socio-ecologies untenable (Adger et al. 2011; Eaton et al. 2019; Leap 2019; Masterson et al. 2019). Following the core interactionist insight that how we organize our relationships with other beings and things is contingent on our continued interactions with them (Mead 1934; Blumer 1969), symbolic interactionists hold that how people relate to landscapes is not a static condition determined by either the physical qualities of places or our ways of interpreting them. Paralleling the broader literature on place (Freudenburg et al. 1995; Gieryn 2000; Stedman 2003; Tsing 2005; Masterson et al. 2019), symbolic interactionists emphasize that how people understand and use landscapes is dependent on ongoing (non)human interactions (Greider and Garkovich 1994) that are informed by the meanings and materialities of the beings and things interacting (Weigert 2008; Leap 2015). Consequently, different individuals and groups can have radically different perceptions of the same place and how people ought to relate to it (Fine 1997; McLachlan 2009; Shtob 2019), and ways of relating to a place can be reorganized in response to shifting socio-ecological conditions (Leap 2015, 2019).

Symbolic interactionists also contend that creativity is centrally important to (non) human interactions. According to interactionists, we are constantly reconstructing our selves, communities, and societies through ongoing interactions. Attention to innovation is built into the very core of the theoretical tradition. Stryker (2008:17) explains:

> Society is continuously created and recreated as humans inevitably meet new challenges. Thus, change is a constant in the social process, as is emergence: the occurrence of new, unpredictable experience that necessitates creative adaptation. Stated differently, novel solutions to problems emerge as persons adapt existing meanings and behaviors to deal with unforeseen contingencies in the social process.

In fact, and as I will address in greater detail later in this chapter, there has been considerable debate as to whether interactionism might grant *too much* weight to the significance of creativity (Maines 1977; Wood and Wardell 1983; Musolf 1992).

Symbolic interactionism and related traditions have more to offer resilience scholars than just an ability to account for innovative (non)human interactions. Interactionist theories provide a particularly strong set of tools for deepening our understanding of these interactions—effectively differentiating interactionism from other theoretical traditions, such as actor-network theory, that have been championed by resilience scholars that also consider (non)human interactions (Zimmerer 2011; Dwiaratama and Rosin 2014; Stone-Jovicich 2015). Research on temporality, impression management, and conversations is illustrative.

Temporality: Fusing the Past and Future in the Present

Interactionists have repeatedly explored the significance of temporality since the very beginning of the theoretical tradition. Mead (1934) drew particular attention to the significance of anticipation. He argued that everything from interacting to organizing complex societies was contingent on humans' abilities to anticipate how other (non)humans will react to potential futures. Playing baseball effectively, for example, is contingent on individuals' abilities to anticipate how others playing the various positions will react to particular scenarios that could arise during gameplay (Mead 1934). Extending the significance of anticipating how a range of others occupying interrelated roles will react, Mead (1934:155) explains:

> The complex co-operative processes and activities and institutional functionings of organized human society are also possible only in so far as every individual involved in them or belonging to that society can take the general attitudes of all other such individuals with reference to these processes and activities and institutional functionings, and to the organized social whole of experiential relations and interactions thereby constituted—and can direct his own behavior accordingly.

The ability to reproduce communities and societies is contingent on having communities of individuals who can anticipate how others are likely to interact in the future.

But what informs anticipations of futures? In short, individuals anticipate futures by actively interpreting their pasts and present. The past, present, and future are constantly fused as individuals interpret their pasts to anticipate their futures as they interact in the present (Mead 1932; Maines et al. 1983; Katovich and Couch 1992). But reducing temporality to individuals interpreting and anticipating is somewhat misleading because how the past, present, and future are fused is social. Maines et al. (1983:168) stress:

> It is critically important to recognize that pasts and futures in Mead's formulation are public in nature. The imagined future of an act is public rather than locked in individual consciousness; likewise, the reconstructed past is public rather than existing solely and forever in individual memory. Futures arise out of attempts to create forms which can serve as goals for common action in the present.

The convergence of the past, present, and future, and the consequences therein, is contingent on countless individuals and groups acting upon multiple anticipations of the future that are generated through ongoing interactions embedded in institutions and communities structured by power and inequalities. Research concerning perceptions of and responses to risks, or negative outcomes that could happen in the future, is illustrative.

From Beck's (1992, 2009) conceptualization of risk society to survey research on perceptions of a range of socio-ecological risks such as pollution and climate change (Klineberg et al. 1998; McCright and Dunlap 2011), scholars have repeatedly shown the significant social determinants and ramifications of risk perceptions. Beyond perceptions, case studies of occupations such as wildland firefighting (Desmond 2007) and community responses to pollution (Hochschild 2016), tsunamis (Shtob 2019), nuclear development (Ashwood 2018), and climate change (Leap 2019) illustrate that responses to risks are informed by individuals actively reinterpreting their pasts within particular institutional and community settings that shape perceptions of the past and responses to futures containing a multitude of risks. Severe weather forecasts distributed by the national weather service, for example, emerge from teams of meteorologists working together to predict the future while juggling institutional goals and authority structures, individual and collective memories, and computer-generated weather models (Fine 2007).

Scholars have repeatedly shown that how "futures are remembered" (Shtob 2019) can both enable and undermine resilience (McIntosh et al. 2000; Davidson 2010; Wilson 2013; Messer et al. 2015). Individual and collective rememberings can provide avenues for coping with the emotional shocks of socio-ecological disruptions (Bennett 2009; Sherman 2009), support economies through nostalgic tourist industries (Beel et al. 2017), and help mobilize collective challenges to socio-ecological exploitation (Banerjee and Steinberg 2015). The literature is also replete with examples of state and corporate institutions promoting rememberings that inhibit preparedness for (Colten and Sumpter 2009) and collective responses to socio-ecological disasters (Scott 2010). Auyero and Swistun (2009), for example, show that state-corporate actors subdued collective efforts to challenge pollution in an Argentine shantytown by purposefully cultivating uncertainty about both the past and future.

By considering how the past, present, and future are fused in practice, symbolic interactionists provide resilience scholars with a conceptualization of (non)human interactions that is attuned to the significance of temporality. Beyond an active understanding of temporality that recognizes how individuals and groups creatively fuse the past, present, and future, interactionists also recognize that temporality is "public" (Maines et al. 1983). How the past, present, and future are entangled, and the consequences therein, are informed by individuals' and groups' abilities to leverage disproportionate degrees of authority and previously legitimated interpretations of the past and future as they navigate convoluted mixes of institutions, collective memories, and obligations that come with belonging to communities (Fine 2007; Shtob 2019; Leap 2019).

Impression Management

Goffman (1959) famously illustrated that impression management is centrally important to how individuals interact as they go about their lives. We are constantly presenting particular versions of ourselves to others in an attempt to manage the impressions they have of us. Impression management is centrally important to how individuals organize their (non)human relationships (Griskevicius et al. 2010; Brick et al. 2017; Swim et al. 2019). Participating in energy conservation, recycling, meat eating, dog poop disposal, and invasive species control are all impacted by individuals' efforts to cultivate favorable impressions for others in their communities (Brough et al. 2016; Hargreaves 2016; Gross and Horta 2017; Machum 2017; Niemiec et al. 2018).

Impression management can both facilitate and undercut individual and collective efforts to respond to shifting socio-ecological conditions. Individual, household, and collective responses to socio-ecological crises are impacted by individuals managing their gender presentations for others in their households and communities, for example

(Heather et al. 2005; Sherman 2009; Alston and Whittenbury 2012; Larkins 2018; Leap 2018, 2019). Research has also repeatedly shown that efforts to resist polluting industries are undermined when actively resisting such industries contradicts locally accepted ways of interacting with people and landscapes (Shriver et al. 2000; Bell and York 2010; Scott 2010; Messer et al. 2015; Filteau 2016; Lewin 2017). Even when individuals feel compelled to actively resist the industrialized destruction of their communities, the social pressures to do otherwise, which are regularly cultivated by polluting industries themselves, can dissuade individuals from even speaking out against industrial exploitation (Bell 2016; Adams et al. 2019; Lewin 2019).

In short, resilience is enabled whenever adaptations permit individuals to present favorable versions of themselves to others. However, resilience can be undercut when responding to socio-ecological crises in manners that would sustain communities puts individuals' reputations at risk. Although exploring dramaturgical concepts such as actors, audience, back stage, front stage, scripts, stigma, roles, role strain, and role distance in greater detail is beyond the scope of this chapter (see Goffman 1959, 1961b, 1963, 1977), it seems clear that all have potential for greater use by resilience scholars. By employing such concepts, behaviors like participating in a social movement to purposefully reorganize a community are framed as interactive processes informed by impression management as opposed to purely individual choices and behaviors.

The Complexities and Significance of Conversations

Symbolic interactionists generally hold that verbal communication is centrally important to how we go about our lives and organize our communities (e.g., Mead 1934). Conversation analysts, while distinct from symbolic interactionists, provide a detailed approach to interpersonal talk. In contrast to an understanding of conversations as being free-wheeling discussions in which individuals say whatever comes to mind whenever they want, conversation analysts illustrate that conversations tend to be structured (Sacks et al. 1974; Schegloff 1992; Holstein and Gubrium 2000). Individuals generally take turns while talking with each other. When in a group conversation, individuals also tend to address what the most immediately preceding speaker said as opposed to saying something completely random or addressing something that was said before the immediately preceding speaker. These structures of talk are important to group decision-making processes because they impact the decisions that emerge from group discussions. Gibson (2011:406) explains:

> The perception of a correct answer, of a way forward, is an interactional outcome, something achieved through conversation and subject to its rules and vicissitudes rather than merely discovered by means of it.

The choice to quarantine Cuba during the Cuban Missile Crisis, for example, was informed by the conversational norms mediating discussions during meetings between

Kennedy and his advisors (Gibson 2011). Talk does not simply provide a means for arriving at a course of action. The structures of talk mediate, or transform, decisions generated through talk.

Scholars have increasingly emphasized that the complexities of conversations impact individual and community responses to socio-ecological disruptions (e.g., Leap 2019). Analyzing the lack of collective, political action in response climate change in a Norwegian community, Norgaard (2011) found that conversational norms dissuaded residents from even discussing the potentially disastrous dimensions of climate change. Examining anti-fracking activists in Southern Illinois, Buday (2017) illustrates how activists' commitment to an informal decision-making process enabled particular individuals to dominate group meetings and the decisions that emerged from them. Environmental sociologists have also increasingly illustrated how face-to-face conversations can be integrally important to mobilizing collective responses to socio-ecological challenges facing communities. These interactions can help build solidarity among individuals (Bell 2016), promote awareness of problems (Auyero et al. 2017), and help generate solutions that employ the partial, situated knowledges of various individuals and constituencies in a community (Ashwood et al. 2014).

Further exploring how conversations inform responses to socio-ecological disruptions could prove especially useful for resilience scholars. By drawing on foundational research by conversation analysts and other contemporary works incorporating attention to the significance of talk, resilience scholars could better consider how communities generate and implement strategies for addressing socio-ecological challenges. Scholars, policy makers, and development practitioners could also promote spaces and/or events amenable to conversations capable of generating solutions to challenges (see Ashwood et al. 2014).

ORGANIZATIONS AND INSTITUTIONS: SIMULTANEOUSLY CONSIDERING AGENCY, STRUCTURE, AND POWER

Interactionists' work on temporality, impression management, and conversations allude to their awareness that interactions are shaped by social structures patterning behaviors. Nevertheless, because interactionists approach reality as something that is constantly renegotiated through ongoing (non)human interactions, the theoretical tradition has been critiqued for presenting an overly fluid version of social life that is devoid of attention to the social structures in which these interactions are embedded. Some dispute whether this was ever a valid critique of the theoretical tradition (Maines 1977, 1988), but, after decades of refinement in response to this critique, it is clear that symbolic interaction is capable of considering social structures, power, and inequalities (Musolf

1992; McGinty 2014). Interactionists' work on organizations and institutions is illustrative and especially noteworthy because organizations and institutions are centrally important to efforts to reorganize and sustain communities when they are disrupted by shifting socio-ecological conditions.

Echoing research that illustrates how responses to shifting socio-ecological conditions are influenced by both informal and formal organizations and institutions (Acheson 1988; Dietz et al. 2003; Bryan 2004; Burley et al. 2007), scholars have repeatedly shown that organizations and institutions impact resilience (Foxon et al. 2009; Cosens et al. 2014; Chaffin and Gunderson 2016). There is general agreement that organizations spanning spatial scales can promote resilience by maintaining flexibility at all organizational levels, devolving sufficient control to more localized levels of the organization, building trust between individuals within and outside the organization, and providing technical and material resources to communities (Tompkins and Adger 2004; Young and Lipton 2006; Tompkins et al. 2008; Amundsen et al. 2010; Dumaru 2010; Becken et al. 2013; Thorn et al. 2015; Leap 2019). Organizations are less likely to enhance resilience if their informal and official arrangements inhibit flexible responses to shifting socio-ecological conditions and if they do not incorporate local networks and knowledges into policy formulation and implementation processes (Smithers and Smit 1997; Tompkins and Adger 2004; Thomas and Twyman 2005; Sobel and Leeson 2006; Colten et al. 2012; McNeeley 2012). Such insights are crucially important, but resilience scholarship would benefit from analyses that better consider the mundane intra/inter-organizational processes impacting resilience (Dovers and Hezri 2010; Leap 2019). Research on co-management conservation strategies, which seek to administer resources through partnerships between conservation organizations and stakeholders impacted by the management of such resources, exemplifies these broader trends in the literature on resilience.

Co-management does not necessarily produce beneficial or sustainable socio-ecological outcomes (Coggins 1999). However, co-management strategies are more likely to promote resilience when there are social ties and feelings of solidarity among officials and stakeholders (Pretty 2003; Sandström and Rova 2010; Leap and Thompson 2018); conservation organizations distribute material and technical resources to diverse stakeholders (Adger et al. 2006); heterogeneous, situated knowledges are incorporated into policy development and implementation processes (Andrews et al. 2018); and sufficient decision-making power is devolved to those working and living at the community level. In such arrangements, those with in-depth, place-specific socio-ecological knowledges can more effectively leverage heterogeneous resources to flexibly respond to emerging socio-ecological challenges (Carlsson and Berkes 2005; Armitage et al. 2009). In spite of a tremendous amount of research on co-management, the dynamic, on-the-ground *processes* of attempting to co-manage resources are relatively understudied. Paralleling research on resilience more generally, greater attention needs to be granted to how co-management emerges—or fails to emerge—through the shifting, power-laden interactions of heterogeneous (non)humans that comprise communities and conservation organizations (Carlsson and Berkes 2005; Hoffman 2009; Fischer et al. 2014; Leap 2019).

Interactionists have repeatedly studied organizations and institutions (e.g., Goffman 1961a; Becker et al. 1968; Hall 1972; Strauss 1982; Fine 1984, 2007), and while there are some dissimilarities (McGinty 2014), they tend to share a core set of assumptions that would enable resilience scholars to better consider how intra/inter-organizational processes impact resilience. Like other areas of social life, interactionists conceptualize organizations and institutions as entities that are constantly being reworked through ongoing (non)human interactions. Interactionists emphasize that individuals are constantly interpreting, bending, breaking, and rewriting the norms and rules guiding organizational processes. The inhabited institutions approach, for example, focuses direct attention on the people working in organizations and how they constantly transform organizational outputs (Hallett and Ventresca 2006; Hallett 2010; Hallett and Meanwell 2016). Instead of being robotic conduits for implementing mandates that delineate exactly how to respond to every possible situation, individuals with different, and at times conflicting, objectives creatively interpret procedures while carrying out their work. In contrast to the emotionless, impersonal officials working in Weber's (1946) ideal type bureaucracy, individuals in organizations are also recognized as what they really are—emotional beings navigating interpersonal relationships complicated by histories that often include convoluted mixtures of trust, obligation, ambition, hope, fear, uncertainty, and dominance (Leap 2019).

Although interactionists acknowledge the significance of individuals creatively navigating institutions, interactionists also stress that ongoing interactions within organizations are shaped by both informal and formal rules, authority structures, and organizational cultures. Hall's conceptualization of "meta-power" is notable. According to Hall (1997, 2003), meta-power refers to interactions that impact subsequent interactions in distant spaces and times. He further explains:

> Meta-power refers to the *shaping* of social relationships, social structures, and *situations* by altering the matrix of possibilities and orientations within which social action occurs (i.e., to remove certain actions from actors' repertoires and to create or facilitate others). Meta-power refers to altering the type of game actors play; it refers to changing the distribution of resources or the conditions governing interaction.
>
> (Hall 1997:405, emphasis in original)

Meta-power is not enacted in symmetrical manners within organizations, nor is it a resource that is used in a uniform fashion independent of the situation of its enactment. The ability to impact subsequent interactions across distant spaces and times is asymmetrical and contingent on the creativity of those interacting as well as a litany of situational factors such as individuals' locations within organizational hierarchies, formalized operating procedures, and the interpersonal histories of those interacting (Hall 1997, 2003). Meta-power, in other words, is emergent and contingent on individuals' and groups' abilities to creatively leverage and/or subvert existing formal and informal organizational arrangements and resources.

Interactionist approaches to organizations and institutions could be especially useful for resilience scholars. Beyond considering the significance of linkages across scales of both space and time, interactionist approaches to organizations and institutions account for the dynamic, emergent tensions among agency, structure, and power. This is particularly significant because sustaining communities in response to socio-ecological disruptions is contingent on how differentially empowered individuals and groups creatively leverage, modify, and subvert both informal and formal social structures as they adapt (Davidson 2010; Leap 2018). By simultaneously acknowledging the significance of those who inhabit institutions and the organizational arrangements of those institutions, interactionist approaches would enable resilience scholars to better open the black boxes of organizations and institutions.

Conclusion

Scholars have increasingly emphasized that social theory should be utilized to better explore the social dynamics of socio-ecological resilience. Political ecology, actor-network theory, and feminist theory have received increasing attention, but resilience scholars have not explicitly engaged symbolic interaction. This is an oversight. Like other theoretical traditions, symbolic interaction can effectively address tensions between agency and structure; linkages across scales of space and time; and inequalities among (non) humans.

Symbolic interaction can do more than just align itself with previous theoretical considerations of resilience. By focusing on the significance of everyday, mundane (non)human interactions that are embedded within organizations and institutions, interactionist theory can enrich our considerations of the dynamic processes that determine whether communities are sustained in response to socio-ecological processes such as floods, hurricanes, epidemics, and climate change. The black boxes of organizations and institutions can be opened, the transformative consequences of conversations can be explored, and activities such as recycling are reframed as interactive processes linked to impression management and anticipated futures. In short, interactionist theory holds tremendous promise for greater use by resilience scholars because it presents a set of concepts and tools that could strengthen our understandings of the dynamic processes that enable and undermine responses to shifting socio-ecological conditions.

References

Acheson, James M. 1988. *The Lobster Gangs of Maine.* Hanover: University Press of New England.

Adams, Alison E., Thomas E. Shriver, Laura A. Bray, and Chris M. Messer. 2019. "Petrochemical Pollution and the Suppression of Environmental Protest." *Sociological Inquiry.* doi: 10.1111/soin.12321

Adger, W. Neil. 2000. "Social and Ecological Resilience: Are They Related?" *Progress in Human Geography* 24(3):347–64.

Adger, W. Neil., Jon Barnett, F.S. Chapin III, and Heidi Ellemor. 2011. "This Must Be the Place: Underrepresentation of Identity and Meaning in Climate Change Decision-Making." *Global Environmental Politics* 11(2):1–24.

Adger, W. Neil, Katrina Brown, and Emma L. Tompkins. 2006. "The Political Economy of Cross-Scale Networks in Resource Co-Management." *Ecology and Society* 10(2):9.

Alston, Margaret and Kerri Whittenbury. 2012. "Does Climate Crisis in Australia's Food Bowl Create a Basis for Change in Agricultural Gender Relations?" *Agriculture and Human Values* 30(1):115–28.

Amundsen, Helene, Frode Berglund, and Hege Westskog. 2010. "Overcoming Barriers to Climate Change Adaptation—a Question of Multilevel Governance?" *Environment and Planning C* 28:276–89.

Andrews, Evan J., Maureen G. Reed, Timothy D. Jardine, and Toddi A. Steelman. 2018. "Damming Knowledge Flows: POWER as a Constraint on Knowledge Pluralism in River Flow Decision-making in the Saskatchewan River Delta." *Society and Natural Resources* 31(8):892–907.

Armitage, Derek R., Ryan Plummer, Fikret Berkes, Robert I. Arthur, Anthony T. Charles, Lain J. Davidson-Hunt, Alan P. Diduck, Nancy C. Doubleday, Derek S. Johnson, Melissa Marschke, Patrick McConney, Evelyn W. Pinkerton, and Eva K. Wollenberg. 2009. "Adaptive Co-management for Social-Ecological Complexity." *Frontiers in Ecology and the Environment* 7(9):95–102.

Ashwood, Loka. 2018. *For-Profit Democracy*. New Haven, CT: Yale University Press.

Ashwood, Loka, Noelle Harden, and Michael M. Bell. 2014. "Linked and Situated: Grounded Knowledge." *Rural Sociology* 79(4):427–52. doi: 10.1111/ruso.12042

Auyero, Javier and Debora Swistun. 2009. *Flammable*. New York: Oxford University Press.

Auyero, Javier, Maricarmen Hernandez, and Mary Ellen Stitt. 2017. "Grassroots Activism in the Belly of the Beast: A Relational Account of the Campaign Against Urban Fracking in Texas." *Social Problems*. doi: 10.1093/socpro/spx035.

Banerjee, Damayanti, and Sheila L. Steinberg. 2015. "Exploring Spatial and Cultural Discourses in Environmental Justice Movements: A Study of Two Communities." *Journal of Rural Studies* 39:41–50.

Beck, Ulrich. 1992. *Risk Society*. Translated by Mark Ritter. Thousand Oaks, CA: SAGE.

Beck, Ulrich. 2009. *World at Risk*. Translated by Ciaran Cronin. Malden, MA: Polity.

Becken, Susanne, Ana Kumari Lama, and Stephen Espiner. 2013. "The Cultural Context of Climate Change Impacts: Perceptions among Community Members in the Anapurna Conservation Area, Nepal." *Environmental Development* 8:22–37.

Becker, Howard S., Blanche Geer, David Riesman, and Robert Weiss. 1968. *Institutions and the Person*. Chicago: Aldine de Gruyter.

Beel, David E., Claire D. Wallace, Gemma Webster, Hai Nguyen, Elizabeth Tait, Marsaili Maclead, and Chris Mellish. 2017. "Cultural Resilience: The Production of Rural Community Heritage, Digital Archives, and the Role of Volunteers." *Journal of Rural Studies* 54:459–68.

Bell, Shannon Elizabeth. 2016. *Fighting King Coal*. Cambridge, MA: MIT Press.

Bell, Shannon Elizabeth and Richard York. 2010. "Community Economic Identity: The Coal Industry and Ideology Construction in West Virginia." *Rural Sociology* 75(1):111–43.

Bennett, Katy. 2009. "Telling Tales: Nostalgia, Collective Identity and an Ex-Mining Village." Pp. 187–205 in *Emotion, Place, and Culture*, edited by Mick Smith, Joyce Davidson, Laura Cameron, and Liz Bondi. Burlington, VT: Ashgate.

Berkes, Fikret and Helen Ross. 2013. "Community Resilience: Toward an Integrated Approach." *Society and Natural Resources* 26:5–20.

Berkes, Fikret, Johan Colding, and Carl Folke. 2003a. *Navigating Social-Ecological Systems.* New York: Cambridge University Press.

Berkes, Fikret, Johan Colding, and Carl Folke. 2003b. "Synthesis: Building Resilience and Adaptive Capacity in Socio-ecological Systems." Pp. 352–87 in *Navigating Social-ecological Systems*, edited by Fikret Berkes, Johan Colding, and Carl Folke. New York: Cambridge University Press.

Biermann, Maureen, Kevin Hillmer-Pegram, Corrine Noel Knapp, and Richard E. Hum. 2015. "Approaching a Critical Turn? A Content Analysis of the Politics of Resilience in Key Bodies of Resilience Literature." *Resilience* 4(2):59–78.

Blumer, Herbert. 1969. *Symbolic Interactionism.* Berkeley: University of California Press.

Brewster, Bradley H., and Antony J. Puddephatt. 2016. "George Herbert Mead as a Socio-Environmental Thinker." Pp. 144–164 in *The Timeliness of George Herbert Mead*, edited by Hans Joas and Daniel R. Huebner. Chicago: University of Chicago Press.

Brewster, Bradley H. and Antony J. Puddephatt. 2017. "Introduction: awakening micro-theoretical perspectives in environmental sociology." Pp. 1–16 in *Microsociological Perspectives for Environmental Sociology*, edited by Bradley H. Brewster and Antony J. Puddephatt. New York: Routledge.

Brewster, Bradley H. and Michael Mayerfeld Bell. 2009. "The Environmental Goffman: Toward an Environmental Sociology of Everyday Life." *Society and Natural Resources* 23(1):45–57.

Brick, Cameron, David K. Sherman, and Heejung S. Kim. 2017. "'Green To Be Seen' and 'Brown To Keep Down': Visibility Moderates the Effect of Identity on Pro-environmental Behavior." *Journal of Environmental Psychology* 51:226–38.

Brough, Aaron R., James E. B. Wilkie, Jingjing Ma, Mathew S. Isaac, and David Gal. 2016. "Is Eco-Friendly Unmanly? The Green-Feminine Stereotype and Its Effects on Sustainable Consumption." *Journal of Consumer Research* 43(3):567–82.

Brown, Katrina. 2014. "Global Environmental Change I: A Social Turn for Resilience?" *Progress in Human Geography* 38(1):107–17.

Bryan, Todd A. 2004. "Tragedy Averted: The Promise of Collaboration." *Society and Natural Resources* 17:881–96.

Buday, Amanda. 2017. "The Home Rule Advantage: Motives and Outcomes of Local Anti-fracking Mobilization." *Social Currents* 4:575–93.

Burley, David, Pam Jenkins, Shirley Laska, and Traber Davis. 2007. "Place Attachment and Environmental Change in Coastal Louisiana." *Organization and Environment* 20(3):347–66.

Cafer, Anne M. 2018. "Khat: Adaptive Community Resilience Strategy or Short-Sighted Money Maker?" *Rural Sociology* 83(4):772–98.

Capek, Stella M. 2006. "Surface Tension: Boundary Negotiations around Self, Society, and Nature." *Symbolic Interaction* 29(2):157–81.

Carlsson, Lars and Fikret Berkes. 2005. "Co-management: Concepts and Methodological Implications." *Journal of Environmental Management* 75:65–76.

Carr, Edward R. 2019. "Properties and Projects: Reconciling Resilience and Transformation for Adaptation and Development." *World Development* 122:70–84.

Chaffin, Brian C., and Lance H. Gunderson. 2016. "Emergence, Institutionalization and Renewal: Rhythms of Adaptive Governance in Complex Socio-ecological Systems." *Journal of Environmental Management* 165:81–87.

Clarke Hannah E., and Brian Mayer. 2017. "Community Recovery Following the Deepwater Horizon Oil Spill: Toward a Theory of Cultural Resilience." *Society and Natural Resources* 30(2):129–44.

Coggins, George C. 1999. "Regulating Federal Natural Resources: A Summary Case against Devolved Collaboration." *Ecology Law Quarterly* 25(4): 602–610.

Colten, Craig E., and Amy R. Sumpter. 2009. "Social memory and resilience in New Orleans." *Natural Hazards* 48: 355–364.

Colten, Craig E., Jenny Hay, and Alexandra Giancarlo. 2012. "Community Resilience and Oil Spills in Coastal Louisiana." *Ecology and Society* 17(3):5. doi: 10.5751/ES-05047-170305.

Cosens, Barbara, Lance Gunderson, and Brian Chaffin. 2014. "The Adaptive Water Governance Project: Assessing Law, Resilience and Governance in Regional Socio-ecological Water Systems Facing a Changing Climate." *Idaho Law Review* 51(1):1–28.

Cote, Muriel, and Andrea J. Nightingale. 2012. "Resilience Thinking Meets Social Theory: Situating Social Change in Socio-ecological Systems (SES) Research." *Progress in Human Geography* 36(4):475–89.

Cretney, Raven. 2014. "Resilience for Whom? Emerging Critical Geographies of Socio-ecological Resilience." *Geography Compass* 8(9):627–40.

Davidson, Debra J. 2010. "The Applicability of the Concept of Resilience to Social Systems: Some Sources of Optimism and Nagging Doubts." *Society and Natural Resources* 23:1135–49.

Davidson, Debra J. 2013. "We Still Have a Long Way to Go, and a Short Time to Get There: A Response to Fikret Berkes and Helen Ross." *Society and Natural Resources* 26:21–24.

Desmond, Matthew. 2007. *On the Fireline*. Chicago: University of Chicago Press.

Dietz, Thomas, Elinor Ostrom, and Paul C. Stern. 2003. "The Struggle to Govern the Commons." *Science* 302:1907–12.

Dovers, Stephen R., and Adnan A. Hezri. 2010. "Institutions and Policy Processes: The Means to the Ends of Adaptation." *WIREs Climate Change* 1:212–31.

Dumaru, Patrina. 2010. "Community-Based Adaptation: Enhancing Community Adaptive Capacity in Druadrua Island, Fiji." *WIREs Climate Change* 1:751–63.

Dwiaratama, Angga, and Christopher Rosin. 2014. "Exploring Agency beyond Humans: The Compatibility of Actor-Network Theory (ANT) and Resilience Thinking." *Ecology and Society* 19(3):28.

Eaton, Weston M., Morey Burnham, Katrina Running, C. Clare Hinrichs, and Theresa Selfa. 2019. "Symbolic Meanings, Landowner Support, and Dedicated Bioenergy Crops in the Rural Northeastern United States." *Energy Research and Social Science* 52:247–57.

Fabinyi, Michael, Louisa Evans, and Simon J. Foale. 2014. "Social-ecological Systems, Social Diversity, and Power: Insights from Anthropology and Political Ecology." *Ecology and Society* 19 (4):28. doi:10.5751/ES-07029-190428.

Filteau, Matthew R. 2016. "'If You Talk Badly About Drilling, You're a Pariah': Challenging a Capitalist Patriarchy in Pennsylvania's Marcellus Shale Region." *Rural Sociology* 81(4):519–44.

Fine, Gary Alan. 1984. "Negotiated Orders and Organizational Cultures." *Annual Review of Sociology* 10:239–62.

Fine, Gary Alan. 1997. "Naturework and the Taming of the Wild: The Problem of 'Overpick' in the Culture of Mushroomers." *Social Problems* 44(1):68–88.

Fine, Gary Alan. 2007. *Authors of the Storm*. Chicago: University of Chicago Press.

Fischer, Anke, Dereje Tadesse Wakjira, Yitbarek Tibebe Weldesemaet, and Zelealem Tefera Ashenafi. 2014. "On the Interplay of Actors in the Co-Management of Natural Resources—A Dynamic Perspective." *World Development* 64:158–68.

Folke, Carl. 2006. "Resilience: The Emergence of a Perspective for Social-ecological Systems Analyses." *Global Environmental Change* 16:253–67.

Foxon, Timothy J., Mark S. Reed, and Lindsay C. Stringer. 2009. "Governing Long-Term Social-Ecological Change: What Can the Adaptive Management and Transition Management Approaches Learn from Each Other?" *Environmental Policy and Governance* 19:3–20.

Freudenburg, William R., Scott Frickel, and Robert Gramling. 1995. "Beyond the Nature/Society Divide: Learning to Think About a Mountain." *Sociological Forum* 10(3):361–92.

Gibson, David R. 2011. "Avoiding Catastrophe: The Interactional Production of Possibility during the Cuban Missile Crisis." *American Journal of Sociology* 117(2):361–419.

Gieryn, Thomas F. 2000. "A Space for Place in Sociology." *Annual Review of Sociology* 26:463–96.

Goffman, Erving. 1959. *The Presentation of Self in Everyday Life*. New York: Anchor Books.

Goffman, Erving. 1961a. *Asylums*. New York: Anchor Books.

Goffman, Erving 1961b. *Encounters*. Indianapolis: Bobbs-Merrill.

Goffman, Erving 1963. *Stigma*. Englewood Cliffs: Prentice Hall.

Goffman, Erving 1977. "The Arrangement Between the Sexes." *Theory and Society* 4:301–31.

Greider, Thomas and Lorraine Garkovich. 1994. "Landscapes: The Social Construction of Nature and the Environment." *Rural Sociology* 59(1):1–24.

Griskevicius, Vladas, Jashua M. Tybur, and Bram Van den Bergh. 2010. "Going Green To Be Seen: Status, Reputation, and Conspicuous Conservation." *Journal of Personality and Social Psychology* 98(3):393–404.

Gross, Mathias, and Ana Horta. 2017. "Dog Shit Happens: Human-Canine Interactions and the Immediacy of Excremental Presence." Pp. 143–60 in *Microsociological Perspectives for Environmental Sociology*, edited by Bradley H. Brewster and Antony J. Puddephatt. New York: Routledge.

Gunderson, Lance H. 2000. "Ecological Resilience—In Theory and Application." *Annual Review of Ecology and Systematics* 31:425–39.

Hall, Peter M. 1972. "A Symbolic Interactionist Analysis of Politics." *Sociological Inquiry* 42(3-4):35–75.

Hall, Peter M. 1997. "Meta-Power, Social Organization, and the Shaping of Social Action." *Symbolic Interaction* 20(4):397–418.

Hall, Peter M. 2003. "Interactionism, Social Organization, and Social Processes: Looking Back and Moving Ahead." *Symbolic Interaction* 26:33–55.

Hallett, Tim. 2010. "The Myth Incarnate: Recoupling Processes, Turmoil, and Inhabited Institutions in an Urban Elementary School." *American Sociological Review* 75(1):52–74.

Hallett, Tim, and Emily Meanwell. 2016. "Accountability as an Inhabited Institution: Contested Meanings and the Symbolic Politics of Reform." *Symbolic Interaction* 39(3):374–96.

Hallett, Tim, and Marc J. Ventresca. 2006. "Inhabited Institutions: Social Interactions and Organizational Forms in Gouldner's *Patterns of Industrial Bureaucracy*." *Theory and Society* 35:213–36.

Hargreaves, Tom. 2016. "Interacting for the Environment: Engaging Goffman in Pro-Environmental Action." *Society and Natural Resources* 29(1):53–67.

Heather, Barbara, Lynn Skillen, Jennifer Young, and Theresa Vladicka. 2005. "Women's Gendered Identities and the Restructuring of Rural Alberta." *Sociologia Ruralis* 45(1–2):86–97.

Herman, Agatha. 2016. "'More-than-Human' Resilience(s)? Enhancing Community in Finnish Forest Farms." *Geoforum* 69:34–43.

Hobman, Elizabeth V., and Iain Walker. 2015. "Stasis and Change: Social Psychological Insights into Social-ecological Resilience." *Ecology and Society* 20(1):39.

Hochschild, Arlie Russell. 2016. *Strangers in Their Own Land*. New York: New Press.

Hoffman, David M. 2009. "Institutional Legitimacy and Co-management of a Marine Protected Area: Implementation Lessons from the Case of Xcalak Reefs National Park, Mexico." *Human Organization* 68(1):39–54.

Holling, C. S. 1973. "Resilience and Stability of Ecological Systems." *Annual Review of Ecology and Systematics* 4:1–23.

Holstein, James A., and Jaber F. Gubrium. 2000. *The Self We Live By*. New York: Oxford University Press.

Hoque, Sonia F., Claire H. Quinn, and Susannah M. Sallu. 2017. "Resilience, Political Ecology, and Well-Being: An Interdisciplinary Approach to Understanding Social-ecological Chance in Coastal Bangladesh." *Ecology and Society* 22(2):45. doi: 10.575/ES-09422-220245

Ingalls, Micah L., and Richard C. Stedman. 2016. "The Power Problematic: Exploring the Uncertain Terrains of Political Ecology and the Resilience Framework." *Ecology and Society* 21(1):6. doi:10.5751/ES-08124-210106.

Irvine, Leslie. 2004. *If You Tame Me*. Philadelphia: Temple University Press.

Irvine, Leslie. 2017. "Wild Selves: A Symbolic Interactionist Perspective on Species, Minds, and Nature." Pp. 128–42 in *Microsociological Perspectives for Environmental Sociology*, edited by Bradley H. Brewster and Antony J. Puddephatt. New York: Routledge.

Jerolmack, Colin. 2009. "Humans, Animals, and Play: Theorizing Interaction When Intersubjectivity is Problematic." *Sociological Theory* 27(4):371–89.

Jerolmack, Colin. 2013. *The Global Pigeon*. Chicago: University of Chicago Press.

Katovich, Michael A., and Carl J. Couch. 1992. "The Nature of Social Pasts and Their Use as Foundations for Situated Action." *Symbolic Interaction* 15(1):25–47.

Klineberg, Stephen L., Matthew McKeever, and Bert Rothenback. 1998. "Demographic Predictors of Environmental Concern: It Does Make a Difference How It's Measured." *Social Science Quarterly* 79(4):734–53.

Larkins, Michelle L. 2018. "Complicating Communities: An Intersectional Approach to Women's Environmental Justice Narratives in the Rocky Mountain West." *Environmental Sociology* 4(1):67–78.

Leap, Braden. 2015. "Redefining the Refuge: Symbolic Interactionism and the Emergent Meanings of Environmentally Variable Spaces." *Symbolic Interaction* 38(4):521–38.

Leap, Braden. 2018. "Not a Zero-Sum Game: Inequalities and Resilience in Sumner, Missouri, the Gooseless Goose Capital of the World." *Gender, Place and Culture*. 25(2):288–308.

Leap, Braden T. 2019. *Gone Goose*. Philadelphia: Temple University Press.

Leap, Braden, and Diego Thompson. 2018. "Social Solidarity, Collective Identity, Resilient Communities: Two Case Studies from the Rural U.S. and Uruguay." *Social Sciences* 7:250. doi: 10.3390/socsci7120250.

Lever, John, Roberta Sonnino, Fiona Cheetham. 2019. "Reconfiguring Local Food Governance in an Age of Austerity: Towards a Place-Based Approach?" *Journal of Rural Studies* 69:97–105.

Lewin, Philip G. 2017. "'Coal is Not Just a Job, It's a Way of Life': The Cultural Politics of Coal Production in Central Appalachia." *Social Problems*. doi: 10.1093/socpro/spx030

Lewin, Philip. 2019. "'I Just Keep My Mouth Shut': The Demobilization of Environmental Protest in Central Appalachia." *Social Currents*. doi: 10.1177/2329496519852947

Machum, Susan. 2017. "Sorting the Trash: Competing Constructions and Instructions for Handling Household Waste." Pp. 161–77 in *Microsociological Perspectives for Environmental Sociology*, edited by Bradley H. Brewster and Antony J. Puddephatt. New York: Routledge.

Maines, David R. 1977. "Social Organization and Social Structure in Symbolic Interactionist Thought." *Annual Review of Sociology* 3:235–59.

Maines, David R. 1988. "Myth, Text, and Interactionist Complicity in the Neglect of Blumer's Macrosociology." *Symbolic Interaction* 11:43–57.

Maines, David R., Noreen M. Sugrue, and Michael A. Katovich. 1983. "The Sociological Import of G.H. Mead's Theory of the Past." *American Sociological Review* 48(2):161–73.

Masterson, Vanessa A., Johan P. Enqvist, Richard C. Stedman, and Maria Tengo. 2019. "Sense of Place in Social-ecological Systems: From Theory to Empirics." *Sustainability Science* 14(3):555–64.

May, Candace K. 2018. "Governing Resilience through Power: Explaining Community Adaptations to Extreme Events in Coastal Louisiana." *Rural Sociology*. doi: 10.1111/ruso.12252

McCright, Aaron M., and Riley E. Dunlap. 2011. "Cool Dudes: The Denial of Climate Change among Conservative White Males in the United States." *Global Environmental Change* 21:1163–72.

McGinty, Patrick J. W. 2014. "Divided and Drifting: Interactionism and the Neglect of Social Organizational Analyses in Organization Studies." *Symbolic Interaction* 37(2):155–86.

McIntosh, Roderick J., Joseph A. Tainter, and Susan Keech McIntosh. 2000. "Climate, History, and Human Action." Pp. 1–44 in *The Way the Wind Blows: Climate, History, and Human Action*, edited by Roderick J. McIntosh, Joseph A. Tainter, and Susan Keech McIntosh. New York: Columbia University Press.

McLachlan, Carly. 2009. " 'You Don't Do a Chemistry Experiment in Your Best China': Symbolic Interpretations of Place and Technology in a Wave Energy Case." *Energy Policy* 37:5342–50.

McNeeley, Shannon M. 2012. "Examining Barriers and Opportunities for Sustainable Adaptation to Climate Change in Interior Alaska." *Climatic Change* 111:835–57.

Mead, George H. 1932. *The Philosophy of the Present*. LaSalle: Open Court.

Mead, George H. 1934. *Mind, Self, and Society*. Edited by Charles W. Morris. Chicago: University of Chicago Press.

Meerow, Sara, and Joshua P. Newell. 2019. "Urban Resilience for Whom, What, When, Where, and Why?" *Urban Geography* 40(3):309–29.

Messer, Chris M., Thomas E. Shriver, and Alison E. Adams. 2015. "Collective Identity and Memory: A Comparative Analysis of Community Response to Environmental Hazards." *Rural Sociology* 80(3):314–39.

Muhar, Andreas, Christopher M. Raymond, Riyan J. G. van den Born, Nicole Bauer, Kerstin Bock, Michael Braito, Arjen Buijs, Courtney Flint, Wouter T. de Groot, Christopher D. Ives, Tamara Mitrofanenko, Tobias Plieninger, Catherine Tucker, and Carena J. van Riper. 2017. "A Model Integrating Social-Cultural Concepts of Nature into Frameworks of Interaction between Social and Natural Systems." *Journal of Environmental Planning and Management*. doi: 10.1080/09640568.2017.1327424

Musolf, Gil Richard. 1992. "Structure, Institutions, Power, and Ideology: New Directions within Symbolic Interactionism." *The Sociological Quarterly* 33(2):171–89.

Niemiec, R. M., N. M. Ardoin, F. K. Brewer, S. Kung, and K. Lopez. 2018. "Increased Neighbor Interaction and Fear of Social Sanctions: Associates with Resident Action to Control the Invasive Little Fire Ant." *Society and Natural Resources* 31(10):1149–168.

Norgaard, Kari Marie. 2011. *Living in Denial*. Cambridge, MA: MIT Press.

Olsson, Per, Victor Galaz, and Wiebren J. Boonstra. 2014. "Sustainability Transformations: A Resilience Perspective." *Ecology and Society* 19(4):1. doi:10.5751/ES-06799-190401

Peterson, Garry. 2000. "Political Ecology and Ecological Resilience: An Integration of Human and Ecological Dynamics." *Ecological Economics* 35:323–36.

Pretty, Jules. 2003. "Social Capital and the Collective Management of Resources." *Science* 302:1912–14.

Sacks, Harvey, Emanuel A. Schegloff, and Gail Jefferson. 1974. "A Simplest Systematics for the Organization of Turn-Taking for Conversation." *Language* 50(4):696–735.

Sanders, Clinton R. 2003. "Actions Speak Louder than Words: Close Relationships between Humans and Nonhuman Animals." *Symbolic Interaction* 26(3):405–26.

Sandström, Annica, and Carl Rova. 2010. "Adaptive Co-management Networks: A Comparative Analysis of Two Fishery Conservation Areas in Sweden." *Ecology and Society* 15(3):14.

Schegloff, Emanual A. 1992. "Repair after Next Turn: The Last Structurally Provided Defense of Intersubjectivity in Conversation." *American Journal of Sociology* 97(5):1295–1345.

Scott, Rebecca. 2010. *Removing Mountains*. Minneapolis: University of Minnesota Press.

Sherman, Jennifer. 2009. *Those Who Work, Those Who Don't*. Minneapolis: University of Minnesota Press.

Shriver, Thomas E., Sherry Cable, Lachelle Norris, and Donald W. Hastings. 2000. "The Role of Collective Identity in Inhibiting Mobilization: Solidarity and Suppression in Oak Ridge." *Sociological Spectrum* 20:21–64.

Shtob, Daniel A. 2019. "Remembering the Future: Natural Disaster, Place, and Symbolic Survival." *Rural Sociology* 84(1):123–47.

Smith, Ronald W., and Valerie Bugni. 2006. "Symbolic Interaction Theory and Architecture." *Symbolic Interaction* 29(2):123–55.

Smithers, John, and Barry Smit. 1997. "Human Adaptation to Climate Variability and Change." *Global Environmental Change* 7(2):129–46.

Sobel, Russell S., and Peter L. Leeson. 2006. "Government's Response to Hurricane Katrina: A Public Choice Analysis." *Public Choice* 127:55–73.

Stedman, Richard C. 2003. "Is It Really Just a Social Construction?: The Contributions of the Physical Environment to Sense of Place." *Society and Natural Resources* 16:671–85.

Stojanovic, Tim, Hilda M. McNae, Paul Tett, Tavis W. Potts, J Reis, Hance D. Smith, and Iain Dillingham. 2016. "The 'Social' Aspect of Social-ecological Systems: A Critique of Analytical Frameworks and Findings from a Multisite Study of Coastal Sustainability." *Ecology and Society* 21(3):15. doi: 10.5751/ES-08633–210315.

Stone-Jovicich, Samantha. 2015. "Probing the Interfaces between the Social Sciences and Social-ecological Resilience: Insights from Integrative and Hybrid Perspectives in the Social Sciences." *Ecology and Society* 20(2):25.

Stone-Jovicich, Samantha, Bruce E. Goldstein, Katrina Brown, Ryan Plummer, and Per Olsson. 2018. "Expanding the Contribution of the Social Sciences to Social-ecological Resilience Research." *Ecology and Society* 23(1):21.

Strauss, Anselm. 1982. "Interorganizational Negotiation." *Urban Life* 11:350–67.

Stryker, Sheldon. 2008. "From Mead to a Structural Symbolic Interactionism and Beyond." *Annual Review of Sociology* 34:15–31.

Swim, Janet K., Ashley J. Gillis, and Kaitlynn J. Hamaty. 2019. "Gender Bending and Gender Conformity: The Social Consequences of Engaging in Feminine and Masculine Pro-Environmental Behaviors." *Sex Roles*. doi: 10.1007/s1119

Thomas, David S. G., and Chasca Twyman. 2005. "Equity and Justice in Climate Change Adaptation amongst Natural-Resource-Dependent Societies." *Global Environmental Change* 15:115–24.

Thompson, Diego. 2019. "Community Identity, Governance, and Resilience under Agri-environmental Shifts in Two Communities of Southwestern Uruguay." *Community Development*. doi: 10.1080/15575330.2019.1659383

Thorn, Jessica, Thomas F. Thornton, and Ariella Helfgott. 2015. "Autonomous Adaptation to Global Environmental Change in Peri-urban Settlements: Evidence of a Growing Culture of Innovation and Revitalization in Mathare Valley Slums, Nairobi." *Global Environmental Change* 31:121–31.

Tidball, Keith G. 2014. "Seeing the Forest for the Trees: Hybridity and Social-ecological Symbols, Rituals and Resilience in Postdisaster Contexts." *Ecology and Society* 19(4):25.

Tompkins, Emma L., and W. Neil Adger. 2004. "Does Adaptive Management of National Resources Enhance Resilience to Climate Change?" *Ecology and Society* 9(2):10.

Tompkins, Emma L., Roger Few, and Katrina Brown. 2008. "Scenario-Based Stakeholder Engagement: Incorporating Stakeholders Preferences into Coastal Planning for Climate Change." *Journal of Environmental Management* 88:1580–92.

Tsing, Anna Lowenhaupt. 2005. *Friction*. Princeton: Princeton University Press.

Turner, Matthew D. 2013. "Political Ecology I: An Alliance with Resilience?" *Progress in Human Geography* 38:1–8.

Walker, Jeremy, and Melinda Cooper. 2011. "Genealogies of Resilience: From Systems Ecology to the Political Economy of Crisis Adaptation." *Security and Dialogue* 42(2):143–60.

Weber, Max. 1946. "Bureaucracy." Pp. 196–244 in *From Max Weber: Essays in Sociology*, translated and edited by H. H. Gerth and C. Wright Mills. New York: Oxford University Press.

Weigert, Andrew W. 2008. "Pragmatic Thinking about Self, Society, and Natural Environment: Mead, Carson, and Beyond." *Symbolic Interaction* 31(3):235–58.

Westley, Frances R., Ola Tjornbo, Lisen Schultz, Per Olsson, Carl Folke, Beatrice Crona, and Örjan Bodin. 2013. "A Theory of Transformative Agency in Linked Social-ecological Systems." Ecology and Society 18(3):27. doi:10.5751/ES-05072–180327

Wilson, Geoff A. 2013. "Community Resilience, Social Memory and the Post-2010 Christchurch (New Zealand) earthquakes." *Area* 45(2):207–15.

Wood, Michael, and Mark L. Wardell. 1983. "G. H. Mead's Social Behaviorism vs. The Astructural Bias of Symbolic Interactionism." *Symbolic Interaction* 6(1):85–96.

Young, Kenneth R., and Jennifer K. Lipton. 2006. "Adaptive Governance and Climate Change in the Tropical Highlands of Western South America." *Climatic Change* 78:63–102.

Zimmerer, Karl S. 2011. "The Landscape Technology of Spate Irrigation amid Development Changes: Assembling the Links to Resources, Livelihoods, and Agrobiodiversity-food in the Bolivian Andes." *Global Environmental Change* 21(3):917–34.

CHAPTER 28

ECO-UNCERTAINTY AS A FRAME AND WAY OF LIFE

DAINA CHEYENNE HARVEY

FRAMING THE ENVIRONMENT

WHILE many concepts within symbolic interaction have enjoyed widespread use outside of the paradigm, framing has held particular sway among both interactionists and non-interactionists. Framing has been at the heart of many hallmark studies within symbolic interaction and social movement studies (Benford and Snow 2000; Goffman 1974). Framing has been especially useful for understanding claims about the environment and disputes over which theoretical lens is best for understanding environmental issues. For example, those who imply a *treadmill of production* frame tend to stress the negative impact of economic growth, while those who employ an *ecological modernization* frame stress the environmental potential of economic development. Frame analysis can also help us grasp different ways of articulating the root causes of environmental problems. For instance, those who employ a *population and scarcity* frame will interpret environmental problems to stem from the presence of too many people in the world, while those who employ a *critical anti-capitalist frame* will usually emphasize the unequal distribution of otherwise abundant resources. We even see framing disputes play out in popular media where there are contestations over whether climate change is anthropogenic or natural, or heated debates pitting environmental sustainability against jobs and economies (Barbosa 2009; Foster, Clark, and York 2010). Different sides to every debate tend to frame the same issue differently, leading to different interpretations of reality and, by implication, different courses of action.

Frames seeks to both articulate and define reality and cultural meanings (Snow et al. 1986). They also seek to provide logical solutions to issues (Benford and Snow 2000). And while much work has been done to illuminate framing disputes (like those mentioned above), despite Snow's (2003) positioning of frames as potentially uncertain, the idea of framing disputes or multiple frames causing uncertainty has been underexplored. In a rare exception, Daub's (2010) work on the Communication, Energy, and the Paperworkers Union of Canada shows how framing both involves a borrowing from master frames and is a negotiation. They explain how the "self-negotiation" of frames depends on individual views and perceptions and results in an interpretative process where frames can be combined and transformed (see also Benford and Snow 2000). Here frames are manipulated so that they fit with what would be competing cognitive schema. As Daub (2010:136) notes, this self-negotiation of frames, which involves a good amount of cognitive dissonance, is probably common as regards environmental issues (i.e., white people seeing racism as an environmental issue; Lewis Jr. et al. 2021) or the collective-action problem that exists in asking countries with very small carbon footprints (> 1 percent) to do their part in the allocation of global funds for climate mitigation (Brechin 2016).

Likewise, the effects of framing on understanding are often taken for granted. In their work on risk communication, Pilnick and Zayts (2014) show how uncertainty can hinder interactions, but can also be used as a cognitive tool to mitigate diagnoses in doctor-patient interactions. Here uncertainty works as a strategy for interaction on the part of both doctors who do not want to convey bad news, and also patients so they do not have to deal with bad news. Likewise, Auyero and Swistun (2009a) show how confusion and uncertainty can limit social movements. In their study of Flammable, a shantytown in Argentina besieged by chemical refineries, residents exhibit "toxic uncertainty" (p. 91) due to both the deliberate practices of Shell and other corporate actors, and the cognitive strategies of the residents themselves. Residents use their healthy bodies to condemn the sick and blame them for poor parenting practices and poverty in daily interactions. Likewise, Shell interacts with the community by sponsoring local sports teams and providing some jobs, thus purchasing silence, but more importantly by creating uncertainty.

In this chapter, I build on this work to show how dominant actors use frames to mitigate their responsibility for environmental inequality and to confuse the dominated, as well as also how the dominated reproduce uncertainty to mitigate their involvement in social movements. In the process, I show how a symbolic interactionist perspective can be used to illuminate framing work and frame disputes, which are rooted in social interaction, and show how such disputes create uncertainty in general, and eco-uncertainty in particular. To contextualize my case study of the post-Katrina Lower Ninth Ward in New Orleans, Louisiana, I first review the related literature on environmental inequality.

ENVIRONMENTAL INEQUALITY IS RACIAL INEQUALITY

Most issues of environmental justice have historically involved race or the racialization (Omi and Winant 1986) of environmental ills, like garbage (Pellow 2002), pollution (Sze 2007), or chemicals (Voyles 2015). Thus, environmental inequality is, quite directly, an extension of racism. For example, corporations or governments deliberately target certain racialized communities for locally unwanted land uses (LULUs), resulting in the unequal distribution of toxins and hazardous wastes (Bryant 1995) along the intersecting lines of race and class. In *Dumping in Dixie*, Bullard (1990) provides one of the first studies to look at environmental racism in a systematic way. What began as an analysis of landfill sites in Houston, Texas, in the case of *Bean v. Southwestern Waste Management Corp.*, eventually resulted in documenting widespread patterns of environmental racism in the South (e.g., Bullard and Wright 1986, 2012). In Houston, for example, Bullard found that all of the dumps and the majority of landfills and incinerators were in black-majority neighborhoods, whereas the black population of Houston composed only 25 percent of the total population. Many other studies have produced similar findings, namely that race is the most significant predictor of the location of waste facilities (e.g., Mohai and Bryant 1992; Morello-Frosch and Lopez 2006; Roberts and Toffolon-Weiss 2001).

Environmental justice struggles often take place in "fenceline communities"—those communities that border hazardous sites or are built on toxic landfills or dumps—which have become, or are on their way to becoming, environmental sacrifice zones. These zones are often the legacy of weapons productions or mining, or due to the presence of heavy industries (oil/gas). Historically, the United States recognized these sites if they were contaminated with radioactive pollutants, but recently there has been a push to extend the definition to include all areas that are sites of, or adjacent to, heavily polluted areas. The idea behind sacrifice zones is that the health of a community (and that of its individual members) is being sacrificed for extensive chemical production or extreme extractions (as has become known in communities impacted by hydraulic fracturing, or "fracking"). Steve Lerner (2010) documents many of these sites in *Sacrifice Zones: The Front Lines of Toxic Chemical Exposure in the United States*. As Taylor (2014) and others (Pellow 2002; Sze 2007) have shown, minority communities are often rooted in sacrifice zones.

While the "race versus class" debate over environmental inequalities continues within environmental sociology (Mascarenhas 2009), other literature on risk (Tierney 2014) and climate justice (Harlan et al. 2015), for instance, has found that race is still the primary determinant of environmental inequality. More clear, however, are the effects of race on recovery from environmental inequality. Here the literature is demonstrative. Non-whites have more difficulty escaping and recovering from disasters and other environmental peril (Fothergill et al. 1999; Barrios 2017). Indeed, as the work on Katrina discussed below suggests, race has been the key variable for understanding what it means to live with constant environmental issues (Johnson 2011; Loyd 2007; Marable 2006; Sanyika 2009).

The Ecological Precariat and Ecological Suffering

Living in sacrifice zones creates environmental suffering (Auyero and Swistun 2009a). As Auyero and Swistun note, "the simple fact [is] that the poor do not breathe the same air, drink the same water, or play on the same soil as the nonpoor do" (2009a:18). Furthermore, this inequality produces "toxic wor(l)ds" in that one's entire existence occurs amid toxicity and that toxicity structures understandings and meaning-making with regard to the world itself. The hallmark of this suffering, they argue, is doubt, confusion, and uncertainty.

Elsewhere I have used Auyero and Swistun's work on environmental suffering and toxic wor(l)ds to show how a community's entire ecology can result in suffering (Harvey 2016). The people who are forced to endure this suffering I call the ecological precariat (Harvey 2016). While others have noted how environmental traumas can produce "communities of sufferers" (Fritz 1961/1996:29; Erikson 1976), the suffering in most cases is often temporarily bracketed. That is, the suffering occurs during the disaster and for some time after the disaster. The precariat live with suffering. They never know when the next disaster will hit; they are not fully aware of the environmental peril they live with or what it is doing to their bodies or those of their family. Suffering becomes one's habitus. The environment itself is precarious.

Interactions are important for constructions of the ecological precariat. As Auyero and Swistun explain, residents engage in a "discursive repertoire" with others whereby meaning-making activities occur (2009a:81). This repertoire can be understood as a discursive performance that results from "specific situations, relational settings, and available cultural representations" (Auyero and Swistun 2009a:159). Here, as symbolic interactionists have shown us, culture is used to form detailed scripts or ways of being that we use to interact as members of certain communities (DeGloma 2009; Grazian 2007; Harvey 2015, 2017a). These discourses and vocabularies not only signal to others our membership in the community, but also provide a framework of socialization to outsiders who wish to join or simply communicate with the community (DeGloma 2009).

HURRICANE KATRINA AND NATUREWORK

The aftermath of Hurricane Katrina revealed that environmental inequalities impacted who died, who suffered, and who was able to rebuild. In general, the social and economic history of a community affects its resiliency (Fothergill and Peek 2004). In New Orleans, the built environment radiated out from the French Quarter to the battures—low-level areas that had been swamps. This meant that the wealthier and whiter areas were elevated above sea level, while black neighborhoods and those with low socioeconomic standing were placed much farther below sea level. Likewise, neighborhoods like the Lower Ninth Ward, which pre-Katrina was 98 percent black, had been made more vulnerable by the construction of various canals and poorly made levees, which ultimately increased the amount of flood water in the neighborhood (Freudenburg et al. 2009). This meant that water stayed in those neighborhoods longer and caused more damage (Finch, Emrich, and Cutter 2010).

Environmental inequality also affected the social process and dynamics of returning home. Because of the amount of environmental destruction and the toxic pollution of the Lower Ninth Ward, residents were not allowed to return for almost a year. One hundred percent of the houses in the Lower Ninth Ward were declared uninhabitable. During Katrina there were reports of 575 oil spills, resulting in 8 million gallons of oil that seeped into the soil. Citywide there was enough debris to cover a thousand football fields six stories high (Godsil, Huang, and Solomon 2009). In the long-term aftermath, the Army Corps of Engineers revealed a plan to store much of this toxic debris from Katrina and industrial pollution in the Lower Ninth Ward (Harvey 2017b).

Previous research has examined how different communities understand these risks and hazards (i.e., environmental pollution and climate change), and how these hazards may impact their communities (Kroll-Smith, Couch, and Marshall 1997; Jones and Rainey 2006; Paolisso et al. 2012). While much of the literature on environmental risk stresses uncertainty (i.e., Clarke 2006; Tierney 2014), the *lived experience* of uncertainty remains underexplored within both environmental studies and symbolic interactionism (for exceptions see Auyero and Swistun 2009a, b; Button 2010; Norgaard 2011). Indeed, as Čapek writes, the environment has traditionally had a limited role in symbolic interaction, and yet it is actively interpreted in ways that are both contested and problematic (2006; Weigert 2008). Most environmental interactionist work posits knowing actors (Weigert 1997; Statham 1995; Zabestoski 2003), and therefore does not leave room for uncertainty. Within environmental sociology, Norgaard's (2011) work on climate denial in Norway and Auyero and Swistun's (2009a, b) work on environmental suffering in Argentina both show how uncertainty is used to mitigate the possibility of social action or reduce cognitive dissonance in places marked by environmental inequality.

Čapek's (2006:158) concept of "surface tension" as "the fluid, negotiated, and often contradictory quality of narratives about nature and self" is useful for thinking about uncertainty in the environment within the symbolic interactionist tradition. For Čapek surface tensions develop through meaning-making between nature and the self as the boundaries and borders of the two change. Here interactions are thrown together in ways that contradict previous interactions or imagined interactions (2006:165). In her work, the way we related to nature or the environment or environmental actors (i.e., egrets) can change over time, and this change can produce tension. While she does not use work in cognitive sociology, she writes that these tensions can exist within the same eco-self (for example, think vegetarians who still eat fish or climate scientists who regularly eat meat). Her surface tension is less about uncertainty (though that it is there) and more about the process of becoming—of forming an eco-self—but she does note that the eco-self is capable of dissonance.

This dissonance is of course more common than we imagine if we think of our conceptualization of nature as a version of Mead's (1934) generalized other (Čapek 2006; Weigert 1997). As Weigert (1997) explains, the conceptualization of the other involves the generation of a generalized environmental other (GEO). The generalized other forms through interactions with others in our immediate communities. Here Zerubavel's (1997) use of "thought community" is helpful (Fleck 1979). Zerubavel notes that we rarely think about the social world in a universal way or, much as we imagine, as solitary individuals. Rather our thoughts are intersubjective. Our thoughts are formed by our memberships in various groups and communities and our interactions with social actors in those groups and communities. Thought communities foment and solidify both intentions and meanings within interactions. Thus, the way that we think about the environment is formed by our associations and interactions with other groups we belong to—and one might add aspirational groups that we imagine ourselves interacting with or belonging to. Such community affiliations give rise to a shared and abstracted notion of the environment that functions as a collective moral voice or actor shaping our conception of self in relation to the world.

The relationship between symbolic interaction and the communities that influence us can be seen in Fine's seminal work on mushroom culture (1997, 1999). Here Fine details how we use cultural templates to define our relationship(s) to the environment (see also Tsing 2015). These templates, which can be in competition with one another, come from the various subcultures of which we are participants. Fine calls this "naturework." Naturework involves the process by which we translate environmental objects/subjects/actions into meaningful symbols—where nature becomes culture (1997:69).

Symbolic interaction is thus a vital lens for analyzing and understanding how we interact with or make sense of the environment. The basic tenants of symbolic interaction and concepts like GEOs and naturework reveal why/how *ecological dissonance* or *eco-uncertainty* would be common. Symbols can of course be interpreted in contrasting ways by different groups, or they can take on different meanings over time (especially in the context of settled vs. unsettled periods; Swidler 1986). Likewise, groups can use these symbols in opposing ways (keeping with the geographical context, oil as income vs. oil as a threat).

DUSTING THE LOWER NINTH WARD

For many, Hurricane Katrina and the federal levee failures were an exceptional disaster because of the number of people affected, the death and destruction the storm caused, and for the unique insights into social aspects of life that are usually obscured.[1] As a result, Katrina has been framed by academics as a breakdown in civil society (Dynes and Rodriguez 2007), as a militarized event (Tierney and Bevc 2006), as a racialized event (Dyson, 2006; Marable, 2006; Johnson 2011), as a toxic event (Godsil, Huang, and Solomon 2009), as urban spectacle (Gotham 2007), and as disaster capitalism (Klein 2007; Gunewardena and Schuller 2008; Adams et al. 2009). These divergent, and sometimes contrasting, frames reflect contested meanings and understandings of Hurricane Katrina. These frames, however, have continued to structure understandings of the environment in the long-term aftermath of Katrina. In particular, for the focus of this chapter, these frames clouded understandings of an environmental disaster five years after Katrina in the Lower Ninth Ward.

Around 2:00 a.m. on September 6, 2010, the Chalmette Refinery,[2] located in the parish adjacent to the Lower Ninth Ward, suffered a power outage and as a result released chemicals into the air.[3] The refinery initially framed the "accident" as part of normal operations.[4] Residents of Cancer Alley know that the refineries burn off gases and chemicals escape from the plumes in order to release pressure during the refinery process. The refinery was using that knowledge to mitigate claims regarding the severity of the accident. The refinery initially maintained that the accident resulted in an "undetermined amount" of chemicals released. They also maintained that the powdery substance that was part of the release was not hazardous[5] and said that residents could safely wash it from cars, buildings, and other surfaces;[6] "there was no emergency condition related to this release and the resulting community exposures would not be expected to have acute or chronic health impacts."[7] According to those officials, Chalmette Refining employees handled the catalyst dust without the use of protective equipment. Residents of the Lower Ninth Ward were told that in any event, the neighborhood had not been affected as the substances did not travel beyond the perimeter of the facility.

A few days later the refinery released a communication that stated that the toxins released included one ton of catalyst and 2,000 pounds of sulfur dioxide.[8] This was supported by the Louisiana Department of Environmental Equality, which has long suffered industry capture, meaning that it is run by former executives of the various refinery companies, which reported releases of: "SO_2, H_2S, NO_x, and MSDS solids—spent cracking catalyst [as a result of] power loss to multiple units throughout refinery which resulted in temporary pressure imbalance in the FCC regenerator, which allowed a loss of catalyst . . . [9]"—but went on to frame the event as a nuisance.[10] While local officials played off the seriousness of the event the next day, stating it looked like "confectioner's sugar,"[11] by Friday they advised that children, the elderly, and those with compromised immune systems not to come into contact with the powdery substance. They also for the first time included the Lower Ninth Ward in the affected area and warned residents not to touch the hazardous chemicals.

Toward the end of the week, as news of the accident spread throughout the community, residents were informed through the media that the refinery had dramatically increased their original estimates of released chemical to 19 tons of catalyst and 105,869 pounds of sulfur dioxide.[12]. Residents were, however, informed that the refinery was once again saying that the Lower Ninth was not affected. As the threat of a class-action lawsuit surfaced, residents were informed that the chemicals released posed no threat and the refinery walked back claims regarding children, the elderly, and the immune-compromised.[13]

The refinery, supported by the LDEQ, framed the event as a routine release, a minor incident, a chemical accident, and subsequently again as a routine release, all within a single week. Environmental organizations such Bridge the Gulf, familiar with this cycle, framed the event as business as usual:

> But parish officials downplayed the effects of catalyst despite recommendations of the Material Safety Data Sheet and failed to alert residents of the other chemicals involved in the accident even though they had that information on hand.[14]

ECO-UNCERTAINTY AS A FRAME AND WAY OF LIFE 519

This framing of the issue by the community project Bridge the Gulf is common among environmental organizations within Cancer Alley that depict refineries and their political allies consistently using contradictory messaging and denials of injury despite knowing better.

Fieldnote September 8, 2010

> A city official in an unmarked car stopped by Deborah's house to ask if any of us had heard about the accident in Chalmette. We replied we had. He went on to explain that it was not really a big deal and that since we worked outside we would not be affected since any chemicals would have dispersed rapidly in the air. We nodded and at lunch told PJ and few others who still had eye and throat irritations that the DEQ said they were faking.

The exchange[15] with the official was by that time contradictory to the new information released by the refinery. This is a tactic created by the oil and gas industry in Cancer Alley; it produces eco-uncertainty.

Additionally, environmental organizations framed the accident in ways that echoed the long-term aftermath of Katrina, where residents needed to consult with experts. The Sierra Club, which had an official in the Lower Ninth Ward, invited a lawyer to the next meeting of the Holy Cross Neighborhood Association. Flyers were placed around the community, and conversations regarding the lawsuit could be heard at the gas station and the sole food truck/restaurant in the community. Attendance at the monthly meeting went from a few dozen to close to a hundred residents. Several residents noted that this was similar to meetings during Katrina and the BP oil disaster. Here a symbolic interactionist perspective focused on local interaction is quite useful; it shows how local communicative dynamics contrast the official authority of "experts" and other powerful actors with the voices of everyday residents, which generates anger, skepticism, and even dismissiveness among locals, allowing uncertainty and confusion to take place (Harvey 2016). A symbolic interactionist perspective thus allows the researcher to see the day-to-day unfolding of an environmental disaster though local frames that have been used to continuously frame both disasters and everyday accidents; it also sheds light on local manifestations of complex discursive acts of power and harm. Without an interactionist-informed ethnographic approach, it would be nearly impossible to glean any insight evident in these fieldnotes.

For example, Paul, who was a regular fixture at the neighborhood meeting, focused on the back-and-forth messaging from the refinery.

> We don't count, what you mean we don't count? How can they tell us that? You gonna let white folks make claims, but then just dismiss us out [of] hand? We don't count. You know how long that Parish been telling us that.

In order to make sense of the events that night, Paul focused on "counting." Residents of the neighborhood were already upset that Chalmette Parish had been able to attract development after Katrina, but the Lower Ninth Ward had not. When the Lower Ninth Ward had put in a bid for a Wal-Mart, they were told the population was too low. When they inquired if they could combine their population with Chalmette's population as residents from Chalmette would likely use the Wal-Mart, the city said no. Chalmette, however, was allowed to "count" the Lower Ninth Ward's population in their own bid. Likewise, residents felt as if the Lower Ninth Ward had been the archetype neighborhood for the destruction and suffering wrought by Katrina, but had been left out of rebuilding. Residents would often ask rhetorical questions when city officials visited the neighborhood, such as, where is the money we raised—we don't count? Residents were also quick to point out that because the neighborhood had not been economically redeveloped since Katrina, they were not eligible for money they assumed was pouring into neighboring areas from the British Petroleum/Deepwater Horizon oil disaster.[16]

The "counting" also had an ontological connotation as in "not mattering." This has a racial aspect to it as well, as Gladys notes below:

> This ain't the first time, won't be the last. This is what they do to us, because they can. Ain't no one going to say it, but it's because we're Black. If this was Uptown or the Garden District they ain't saying that, they [white neighborhoods] wouldn't have it.

Chalmette was formed by white flight from the Lower Ninth Ward when the city forced an elementary school in the Lower Ninth to integrate. There was a long-standing understanding that it was a white place. In the immediate aftermath, Chalmette passed a law that no one could rent to or sell to anyone not living in Chalmette pre-Katrina. While the town argued that the law prevented flipping houses or large-scale real estate development, the law was a dog whistle calling to mind land deeds and racial covenants of the twentieth century.

The framing of the dusting as "not counting," combined with the racial connotation, made sense to residents who felt that they had been abandoned in other disasters. It highlighted the continuous environmental peril that residents dealt with on a daily basis. The literal "not counting" of people served as both a meaning-making tool for residents and framed for sympathetic outsiders why residents had been abandoned both during Katrina and in the long-term aftermath.[17]

Underscoring the constant environmental issues residents dealt with, many residents seemed underwhelmed by the dusting. One resident, whom I followed out of the meeting regarding the class-action lawsuit, noted that she may or may not join the suit. She mentioned that she had not received anything for her "Katrina Cough," so she assumed she would not receive anything for the dusting.

> I don't know what made me sick. I had the "Katrina Cough" for years. Some people say this place was polluted before then, though. Then they telling us that we sick from the chemicals plant. I got symptoms, but my children don't. And they be outside more. It don't make no sense. They need to get straight before they come to us. It's every day, though; every day like this baby; it don't stop.

Bettie dismissed the class-action lawsuit, as many did, as something that was part of their ongoing suffering. Likewise, Lee, whom I spoke to on a daily basis, when I asked the next day where he had been (i.e., why he had not attended the meeting), commented, "that was Tuesday, Wednesday was just as bad." Lee further explained that the lawsuit would not go anywhere.

> Man, that's a waste of time. What they [the lawyers] gonna get? Half of nothing. It'll go on for years and years and then they will come to us and say take this settlement, like it's nothing, it'll be nothing. Or, or they just tell us that there is nothing they can do because we were all sick before that. You know. How do you know you were sick from the dusting and not from breathing the chemicals they release the day before. Maybe this just aggravated what happened to you in Katrina or . . . you know how they do it. They smart. You live here for forty, fifty years, you don't know what made you sick.

As someone who had suffered internal and external issues—from swimming in and consequently swallowing toxic water when the breach in the walls of the Industrial Canal flooded the Lower Ninth Ward during Katrina, Lee had met with many lawyers and been told because of the contamination and pollution of the Lower Ninth Ward, it would be difficult to clearly illustrate the cause of his environmental suffering.

Residents' myriad interactions with media, officials, environmental organizations and other nonprofits, and eventually lawyers resulted in residents like Lee and Bettie taking on an understanding of events but also framing their situation for others through a master-frame of *eco-uncertainty*. Eco-uncertainty is the not knowing of one's ecological future. It entails existential anxiety about one's personal and social future due to uncertainty about one's ecological situation. Residents of the Lower Ninth Ward, for example, do not know if their community will be safe or what their ecological future might hold for them. Most are certain that because of climate change they will experience more severe environmental crises, but many do not know when a crisis might occur or even the specific nature of that crisis (Harvey 2016). Because they are below sea level, they worry that the community may not be sustainable. Some residents have made preparations by raising their homes. Because they live in Cancer Alley, they worry that their environment may be making them sick. Others, however, are unsure whether their homes were rebuilt with toxic drywall or if the mold remediation was done properly. Most, however, live with the uncertainty of what would happen to them and their community if another Katrina occurred. Furthermore, they realize that they cannot trust or count on the government to protect them or alleviate their suffering from future environmental crises.

Eco-uncertainty should be seen as a soft tactics used to create dominance over a subjugated population (Auyero 2010; Auyero and Swistun 2007, 2009b). Uncertainty bounds and limits actions to rectify environmental risks and future catastrophes. As Auyero and Swistun (2007) demonstrate in their study of environmental suffering, doubt, confusion, and mistakes, are created by agents of power (petro-chemical companies or government agencies) to effectively limit possible recourses to remedy their toxic environment. In their work this translates into an "endless waiting time," "a temporal domination," where residents wait for the government or oil companies to move them or pay for their medical care (Auyero and Swistun 2007, 2009a, 2009b; Harvey 2015). In the Lower Ninth Ward, eco-uncertainty also creates prolonged periods of waiting, but it also misdirects responses and mitigates social movements from occurring (Harvey 2016, 2017b). Here residents like Lee and Bettie adopt the same frame that industry uses to mitigate economic and moral culpability, to mitigate their personal involvement in social action.

Most importantly for this chapter, eco-uncertainty becomes a way of knowing and a way of explaining life to others. It is the basis for both action and inaction. It is formed and buttressed through interactions with residents and with other social actors. It is a form of both knowing and not-knowing. It becomes a master frame for interpreting not only environmental ills but also social life itself. Without a symbolic interactionist– informed framework, eco-uncertainty would go unnoticed or seem unimportant.

Eco-uncertainty exists because, as Čapek (2006) explains, our eco-self is a process that can be inherently contradictory as boundaries change between nature and self. Likewise, as Zerubavel (1997) notes, the groups and communities we belong to shift over time and at times overlap or are in contradiction with one another. In a place like the Lower Ninth Ward, with a changing environment (one that might be relatively more safe at certain times than others) that shifts in the way residents think about the environment due to interactions with community groups or environmental groups, eco-uncertainty seems not only plausible, but most likely the dominant frame that people use to make sense of their environment.

Conclusion

While past work on environmental racism and environmental justice highlights the negative externalities that poorer communities of color (Bullard and Wright 2012; Pellow 2002; Roberts and Toffolon-Weiss 2001; Sze 2007), and disproportionately, women (Fothergill 2004; Lerner 2010) often face on a day-by-day basis, or in the aftermath of disaster, missing from these frameworks is the physical and mental toll of uncertainty (for a rare exception see Auyero and Swistun 2007, 2009a, 2009b). Not knowing when something will go wrong or whether the state will offer relief or "make it right" can be as harmful as the actual environmental peril. This uncertainty is at the heart of what Erikson (1994), and others (Picou, Marshall, and Gill 2004; Miller 2006) have noted transforms a community into a "corrosive community" in the aftermath of a disaster.

Communities that have access to resources to demand environmental protection or ensure their resiliency in the aftermath of environmental peril have security in the knowledge that they are, for the most part, protected from uncertainty. This knowledge is a form of environmental privilege—a privilege that has historically belonged to white, middle- to upper-class communities. As Roberts and Toffolon-Weiss (2001) note, the most vulnerable have also been the most cautious in participating in the environmental justice movement—particularly in Louisiana. Their uncertainty in what is going on in their neighborhood is also in part determined by the uncertainty regarding who they can trust. The failure of the government to remunerate those who were most affected from Katrina and the ongoing environmental suffering has exacerbated the uncertainty of residents of the Lower Ninth Ward. People living with eco-uncertainty lack the ontological security that environmental privilege affords the middle class and wealthy. With eco-uncertainty, as residents in the Lower Ninth Ward remind us, you never know what might happen. And yet, as seen through a symbolic interactionist–informed ethnography, while de-mobilizing, it can also be used to interpret events and explain suffering.

Acknowledgments

The author thanks the Rutgers University Initiative on Climate and Society, The Horowitz Foundation for Social Policy and The Natural Hazards Center at the University of Colorado at Boulder, and the Public Entity Risk Institute with support from the National Science Foundation and Swiss Re for funding portions of this research. Thomas DeGloma and Janet Lorenzen offered valuable comments on an earlier draft of the chapter.

Notes

1. Elsewhere I have written about the dusting as a secondary violence (Harvey 2017b).
2. The Chalmette Refinery was owned by ExxonMobil in 2010.
3. The Chalmette refinery is a well-known polluter. From 2005 to 2009, it released 6 million pounds of airborne pollutants and 12 million gallons of pollutants into local waters.
4. Refineries regularly burn off chemicals through a process known as flaring—whereby materials not captured or recycled are burned in a flare out of smokestacks. And thus is normal. It is also normal in the sense that the Chalmette Refinery is part of an area that environmental activists call "Cancer Alley." There are over 150 petrochemical plants along a stretch of land from New Orleans to Baton Rouge. These plants are responsible for 129 million pounds of toxic releases each year (Louisiana Department of Environmental Quality 2000). This area has the highest incidence of cancer in the country. As such, the releases, accidental or intentional, have become "normalized."
5. https://thelensnola.org/2011/02/24/refinery-hf-alternative/
6. https://bridgethegulfproject.org/blog/2010/beyond-bp-chalmette-refinery%E2%80%99s-labor-day-accident-and-cover
7. http://www.louisianarefineryaccidentdatabase.org/refineryyear.php?refinery=BB005&year=2010
8. https://neworleanscitybusiness.com/blog/2010/10/08/leak-persists-at-chalmette-refinery-where-worker-died/
9. http://www.louisianarefineryaccidentdatabase.org/refineryyearcitcomp.php?refinery=BB005&year=2010
10. https://www.nola.com/news/article_ae9e1739-2f77-5b58-8560-f878cb919432.html

11. https://idisaster.wordpress.com/tag/exxonmobil/
12. https://thelensnola.org/wp-content/uploads/2011/02/report.pdf
13. http://www.labucketbrigade.org/blog/exxonmobils-chalmette-refining-dumps-1-ton-catalyst-community-another-accident-beleaguered-oil
14. https://bridgethegulfproject.org/blog/2010/beyond-bp-chalmette-refinery%E2%80%99s-labor-day-accident-and-cover
15. I spent fourteen months from 2010 to 2011 doing ethnographic field work, interviews, and participant observation in the Lower Ninth Ward. This involved working with a consortium of nonprofits, community and neighborhood groups, local government, and academics.
16. BP disaster claims were overwhelmingly made by small business owners who had to demonstrate economic losses caused by BP. Residents thus felt that they had not been counted twice—once for economic development and then for economic losses that would have resulted if that development had occurred.
17. Social abandonment was a common frame that residents used to convey the state of the neighborhood to newly arrived volunteers (Harvey 2016).

REFERENCES

Adams, Vincanne, Taslim Van Hattum, and Diana English. 2009. "Chronic Disaster Syndrome: Displacement, Disaster Capitalism, and the Eviction of the Poor from New Orleans." *American Ethnologist* 36:615–36.

Auyero, Javier, and Débora Swistun. 2009a. *Flammable: Environmental Suffering in an Argentine Shantytown*. New York: Oxford University Press.

Auyero, Javier, and Débora Swistun. 2009b. "Tiresias in Flammable Shantytown: Toward a Tempography of Domination." *Sociological Forum* 24(1):1–21.

Auyero, Javier, and Débora Swistun. 2007. "Confused Because Exposed: Towards an Ethnography of Suffering *Ethnography* 8(2):123–44.

Auyero, Javier. 2010. "Patients of the State. An Ethnographic Account of Poor People's Waiting." *Latin American Research Review* 46(1):5–29.

Barbosa, Luiz C. 2009. "Change by Necessity: Ecological Limits to Capitalism, Climate Change, and Obstacles to Transition to an Environmentally Sustainable Economy." Presented at the 59th Annual Meeting of The Society for the Study of Social Problems, August 7–9, 2009, in San Francisco, CA.

Barrios, Roberto E. 2017. *Governing Affect: Neoliberalism and Disaster Reconstruction*. Lincoln: University of Nebraska Press.

Benford, Robert D., and David A. Snow. 2000. "Framing Processes and Social Movements: An Overview and Assessment." *Annual Review of Sociology* 26:611–39.

Brechin, Steven R. 2016. "Climate Change Mitigation and the Collective Action Problem: Exploring Country Differences in Greenhouse Gas Contributions." *Sociological Forum* 31(S1):846–61.

Bryant, Bunyan. 1995. "Pollution Prevention and Participatory Research as a Methodology for Environmental Justice." *Virginia Environmental Law Journal* 14(4):589–613.

Bullard, Robert D. 1990. *Dumping in Dixie: Race, Class, And Environmental Quality*. New York: Routledge.

Bullard, Robert D., and Beverly Hendrix Wright. 1986. "The Politics of Pollution: Implications for the Black Community." *Phylon* 47(1):71–78.

Bullard, Robert, and Beverly Wright. 2012. *The Wrong Complexion for Protection: How the Government Responds to Disaster Endangers African American Communities*. New York: New York University Press.

Button, Gregory. 2010. *Disaster Culture: Knowledge and Uncertainty in the Wake of Human and Environmental Catastrophe*. Walnut Creek: Left Coast Press.

Čapek, Stella. 2006. "Surface Tension: Boundary Negotiations Around Self, Society, and Nature in a Community Debate Over Wildlife." *Symbolic Interaction* 29(2):157–81.

Clarke, Lee. 2006. *Worst Cases: Terror and Catastrophe in the Popular Imagination*. Chicago: University of Chicago Press.

Daub, Shannon J. 2010. "Negotiating Sustainability: Climate Change Framing in the Communications, Energy and Paperworkers Union." *Symbolic Interaction* 33(1):115–40.

DeGloma, Thomas. 2009. "Expanding Trauma Through Space and Time: Mapping the Rhetorical Strategies of Trauma Carrier Groups." *Social Psychology Quarterly* 72(2):105–22.

Dynes, Russel R., and Havidán Rodríguez. 2007. "Finding and Framing Katrina: The Social Construction of Disaster." Pp. 25–36 *The Sociology of Katrina: Perspectives on a Modern Catastrophe*, edited by David Brunsma, David Overfelt, and J. Steven Picou. Lanham: Rowman & Littlefield.

Dyson, Michael Eric. 2006. *Come Hell or High Water: Hurricane Katrina and the Color of Disaster*. New York: Basic Civitas Books.

Erikson, Kai. 1976. *Everything in Its Path: Destruction of Community in the Buffalo Creek Flood*. New York: Simon & Schuster.

Erikson, Kai. 1994. *A New Species of Trouble: The Human Experience of Modern Disasters*. New York: Norton.

Fine, Gary Alan. 1997. "Naturework and the Taming of the Wild: The Problem of 'Overpick' in the Culture of Mushroomers." *Social Problems* 44(1):68–88.

Fine, Gary Alan. 1999. *Moral Tales: The Culture of Mushrooming*. Cambridge, MA: Harvard University Press.

Fleck, Ludwik. 1979. *Genesis and Development of a Scientific Fact*. Chicago: University of Chicago Press.

Fothergill Alice, Enrique G. M. Maestas, and JoAnne DeRouen Darlington. 1999. "Race, Ethnicity and Disasters in the United States: A Review of the Literature." *Disasters* 23(2):156–73.

Fothergill Alice, and Lori A. Peek. 2004. "Poverty and Disasters in the United States: A Review of Recent Sociological Findings." *Natural Hazards* 32:89–110.

Fothergill, Alice. 2004. *Heads above Water: Gender, Class, and Family in the Grand Forks Flood*. New York: SUNY Press.

Freudenburg, William, Robert Gramling, Shirley Laska, and Kai Erikson. 2009. "Disproportionality and Disaster: Hurricane Katrina and the Mississippi River-Gulf Outlet." *Social Science Quarterly* 90(3):497–515.

Fritz, Charles. 1961/1996. *Disasters and Mental Health: Therapeutic Principles Drawn From Disaster Studies*. Historical and Comparative Disaster Series No. 10. Newark: University of Delaware Research Center.

Finch, Christina, Christopher Emrich, and Susan Cutter. 2010. "Disaster Disparities and Differential Recovery New Orleans." *Population and Environment* 31:179–202.

Foster, John Bellamy, Brett Clark, and Richard York. 2010. *The Ecological Rift: Capitalism's War on the Earth*. New York: Monthly Review Press.

Grazian, David. 2007. "The Girl Hunt: Urban Nightlife and the Performance of Masculinity as Collective Activity." *Symbolic Interaction* 30(2):221–43.

Godsil, Rachel, Albert Huang, and Gina Solomon. 2009. "Contaminants in the Air and Soil in New Orleans After the Flood." Pp. 115–38 in *Race, Place, and Environmental Justice After Hurricane Katrina*, edited by Robert Bullard and Beverly Wright. Boulder, CO: Westview Press.

Goffman, Erving. 1974. *Frame Analysis: An Essay on the Organization of Experience*. Cambridge: Harvard University Press.

Gotham, Kevin F. 2007. "Critical Theory and Katrina: Disaster, Spectacle, and Immanent Critique." *City* 11:81–99.

Gunewardena, Nandini, and Mark Schuller. 2008. *Capitalizing on Catastrophe: Neoliberal Strategies in Disaster Reconstruction*. Lanham: Alta Mira Press.

Harlan, Sharon L, David N. Pellow, and J. Timmons Roberts. 2015. "Climate Justice and Inequality." Pp. 127–63 in *Climate Change and Society: Sociological Perspectives*, edited by R. Dunlap and R. Brulle. New York: Oxford University Press.

Harvey, Daina Cheyenne. 2017a. " 'Gimme a Pigfoot and a Bottle of Beer': Performance of Food in the Aftermath of Hurricane Katrina." *Symbolic Interaction* 40(4):498–522.

Harvey, Daina Cheyenne. 2017b. "Secondary Violences as Social Policy in the Aftermath of a Disaster: A Corollary to Naomi Klein's Disaster Capitalism." *Humanity and Society* 41(3):333–54.

Harvey, Daina Cheyenne. 2016. "The Discourse of the Ecological Precariat: Making Sense of Social Disruption in the Lower Ninth Ward in the Long-term Aftermath of Hurricane Katrina." *Sociological Forum* 31(S1):862–84.

Harvey, Daina Cheyenne. 2015. "Waiting in The Lower Ninth Ward in New Orleans: A Case Study on the Tempography of Urban Marginalization." *Symbolic Interaction* 38(4):539–56.

Johnson, Cedric. 2011. *The Neoliberal Deluge: Hurricane Katrina, Late Capitalism, and the Remaking of New Orleans*. Minneapolis: University of Minnesota Press.

Jones, Robert Emmet, and Shirley A. Rainey. 2006. "Examining Linkages Between Race, Environmental Concern, Health, and Justice in a Highly Polluted Community of Color." *Journal of Black Studies* 36(4):473–96.

Klein, Naomi. 2007. *The Shock Doctrine: The Rise of Disaster Capitalism*. New York: Picador.

Kroll-Smith, Steve, Stephen R. Couch, and Brent K. Marshall. 1997. "Sociology, Extreme Environments and Social Change." *Current Sociology* 45(3):1–18.

Lerner, Steven. 2010. *Sacrifice Zones: The Front Lines of Toxic Chemical Exposure in the United States*. Cambridge: MIT Press.

Lewis Jr., Neil A., Dorainne J. Green, Ajua Duker, and Ivuoma N. Onyeador. 2021. "Not Seeing Eye to Eye: Challenges to Building Ethnically and Economically Diverse Environmental Coalitions." *Currents Opinions in Behavioral Sciences* 42:60–64.

Louisiana Department of Environmental Quality. 2000. *Toxic Releases Inventory 1998*, 10th edn. Baton Rouge: LDEQ.

Loyd, Jenna. 2007. "Katrina: A Racist Disaster." *Capitalism Nature Socialism* 18:122–29.

Marable, Manning. 2006. "Katrina's Unnatural Disaster: A Tragedy of Black Suffering and White Denial." *Souls: A Critical Journal of Black Politics, Culture, and Society* 8:1–8.

Mascarenhas, Michael. 2009. "Environmental Inequality and Environmental Justice." Pp. 127–41 in *Twenty Lessons in Environmental Sociology*, edited by K. Gould and T. Lewis. New York: Oxford University Press.

Mead, George H. 1934. *Mind, Self, and Society*. Chicago: University of Chicago Press.

Miller, DeMond Shondell. 2006. "Visualizing the Corrosive Community." *Space and Culture* 9(1):71–73.

Mohai, Paul, and Bunyan Bryant 1992. "Race, Poverty and the Distribution of Environmental Hazards: Reviewing the Evidence." *Race, Poverty, and the Environment* 2(3/4):3, 24–27.

Morello-Frosch, Rachel, and Russ Lopez. 2006. "The Riskscape and the Color Line: Examining the Role of Segregation in Environmental Health Disparities." *Environmental Research* 102(2):181–96.

Norgaard, Kari Marie. 2011. *Living in Denial: Climate Change, Emotions and Everyday Life*. Cambridge: MIT Press.

Omi, Michael, and Howard Winant. 1986. *Racial Formation in the United States*. New York: Routledge.

Paolisso, Michael, Ellen Douglas, Ashley Enrici, Paul Kirshen, Chris Watson, and Matthias Ruth. 2012. "Climate Change, Justice, and Adaptation among African American Communities in the Cheaspeake Bay Region." *Weather, Climate, and Society* 4(1):34–47.

Pellow, David N. 2002. Garbage Wars: The Struggle for Environmental Justice in Chicago. Cambridge: MIT Press.

Picou, Steven, Brent K. Marshall, and Duane A. Gill. 2004. "Disaster, Litigation, and he Corrosive Community." *Social Forces* 82(4):1493–1522.

Pilnick, Alison, and Olga Zayts. 2014. "'It's Just a Likelihood': Uncertainty as Topic and Resource in Conveying 'Positive' Results in an Antenatal Screening Clinic." *Symbolic Interaction* 37(2):187–208.

Roberts, J. Timmons, and Melissa Toffolon-Weiss. 2001. *Chronicles From the Environmental Justice Frontline*. New York: Cambridge University Press.

Sanyika, Mtangulizi. 2009. "Katrina and the Condition of Black New Orleans: The Struggle for Justice, Equity, and Democracy." Pp. 87–111 in *Race, Place, and Environmental Justice after Hurricane Katrina*, edited by R. Bullard and B. Wright. Boulder, CO: Westview Press.

Snow, David A., E. Burke Rochford, Steven K. Worden, and Robert D. Benford. 1986. "Frame Alignment Processes, Micromobilization, and Movement Participation." *American Sociological Review* 51(4):464–81.

Snow, David A. 2003. "Social Movements." Pp. 811–33 in *Handbook of Symbolic Interactionism*, edited by L. T. Reynolds and N. J. Herman-Kinney. Walnut Creek: AltaMira.

Statham, Anne. 1995. "Environmental Identity: Symbols in Cultural Change." Pp. 207–40 in *Studies in Symbolic Interaction*, vol. 17, edited by N. K. Denzin. New York, NY: JAI.

Swidler, Ann. 1986. "Culture in Action: Symbols and Strategies." *American Sociological Review* 51(2):273–86.

Sze, Julie 2007. *Noxious New York: The Racial Politics of Urban Health and Environmental Justice*. Cambridge: MIT Press.

Taylor, Dorceta. 2014. *Toxic Communities: Environmental Racism, Industrial Pollution, and Residential Mobility*. New York: New York University Press.

Tierney, Kathleen. 2014. *The Social Roots of Risk: Producing Disasters, Promoting Resilience*. Stanford: Stanford University Press.

Tierney, Kathleen, and Christine A. Bevc, 2006. "Disasters as War: Militarism and the Social Construction of Disaster in New Orleans." Pp. 37–54 in *The Sociology of Katrina: Perspectives on a Modern Catastrophe*, edited by David Brunsma, David Overfelt, and J. Steven Picou. Lanham: Rowman & Littlefield.

Tsing, Anna L. 2015. *The Mushroom at the End of the World: On the Possibility of Life in Capitalist Ruins*. New Jersey: Princeton University Press.

Voyles, Traci Brynne. 2015. *Wastelanding: Legacies of Uranium Mining in Navajo Country*. Minneapolis: University of Minnesota Press.

Weigert, Andrew J. 1997. *Self, Interaction, and Natural Environment*. Albany: State University of New York.

Weigert, Andrew J. 2008. "Pragmatic Thinking about Self, Society, and Natural Environment: Mead, Carson, and Beyond." *Symbolic Interaction* 31(3):235–58.

Zavestoski, Stephen. 2003. "Constructing and Maintaining Ecological Identities: The Strategies of Deep Ecologists." Pp. 297–315 in *Identity and the Natural Environment*, edited by S. Clayton and S. Opotow. Cambridge, MA: MIT.

Zerubavel, Eviatar. 1997. *Social Mindscapes: An Invitation to Cognitive Sociology*. Cambridge: Harvard University Press.

CHAPTER 29

....

DISASTERS

....

MARGARETHE KUSENBACH AND GABRIELA B. CHRISTMANN

INTRODUCTION

....

IN everyday language, "disaster" does not refer to minor or individual problems but to critical events that severely disturb "normal" social life and may even threaten a community's very existence. A more complex characterization can be found in social science discourse. Here, according to Tierney (2019:4), disasters are generally understood as

> the juxtaposition of physical forces—geological, atmospheric, technological, and other forces—and vulnerable human communities. The severity of a disaster is measured not by the magnitude of the physical forces involved, but rather by the magnitude of its societal impacts.

In both these understandings, disasters have been disrupting communities since the dawn of human social organization, and human concern with their causes, dynamics, and impacts dates back just as far.

Meanwhile, the birth of disaster research as an academic subject can be located in the early days of the Cold War in the United States, meaning the late 1940s (Tierney 2019:15). Today, over seven decades later, disaster research is firmly institutionalized at many leading universities and anchored by numerous research centers all over the world—for instance, the *Natural Hazards Center* at the University of Colorado Boulder, USA; the *Centre of Natural Hazards and Disaster Science* at Uppsala University, Sweden; and the *Asian Disaster Reduction Center* in Kobe, Japan, to name just a few. Today, there are numerous organizations—for example, the Research Committee "Sociology of Disasters" (RC39) of the *International Sociological Association* and many scholarly journals (such as *Disasters, Natural Hazards, Natural Hazards Review*, the *International Journal of Mass Emergencies and Disasters*, or the *International Journal of Disaster Risk Reduction*) that promote and circulate disaster research. Undoubtedly, since its inception, disaster research has matured into the interdisciplinary field of "disaster studies."

In 1963, less than twenty years after the birth of disaster research, the very first institution devoted to this area—the *Disaster Research Center* (DRC), originally at Ohio State University but currently housed at the University of Delaware—was cofounded by three sociology professors. It may not be common knowledge that one of the DRC's founders, Enrico (Henry) Quarantelli (1924–2017), while a graduate student at the University of Chicago, was significantly influenced by Herbert Blumer. In her seminal new book, Kathleen Tierney (2019:17–25) argues that in its early years, through this particular as well as some other connections, disaster research was significantly inspired *methodologically* by the Chicago School and the paradigm of symbolic interactionism (SI), as personified by Herbert Blumer and others. Quarantelli and his colleagues at the DRC believed in the value of direct field observations, and in the collection of qualitative, open-ended data in close interaction with affected populations (Quarantelli and Perry 2005). Indicating another influence of the Chicago School, these early disaster scholars were also interested in unexpected collective processes, such as social solidarity and supports that arise during disasters, particularly in urban contexts.

Given these early connections, it may be puzzling to today's observers that SI has not played (and still does not play) a larger role in the *theoretical* foundation of disaster studies, even though the use of qualitative methods still continues today, side by side with quantitative inquiry. Instead, in its early stages, disaster research was strongly shaped by structural functionalism and systems theory (Tierney 2019:18), while over the past two decades, conflict theory and political-economy frameworks have come to dominate the field. Beyond the commonplace catchphrase that disasters are somehow "socially constructed" rather than natural events, which may suggest a strong influence of social-constructionist thinking, many key ideas and insights rooted in the paradigm of SI—such as those pertaining to meaning, interaction, performance, identity, narrative, discourse, and culture—are still notably *absent* from the vast majority of today's disaster research. We believe this is unfortunate and warrants remedial efforts.

Before proceeding with our description of the existing interfaces between SI and disaster research, we would like to make two brief comments. First, disaster research has always been an *applied* field of study, meaning that it is outcome oriented. The definitive goal of disaster research is to help protect people from adverse impacts and, ultimately, save lives in the real world. This orientation makes disaster research a much more pragmatic and policy-oriented discipline than sociology. Thus, SI, like any other theoretical paradigm, is only relevant in disaster studies to the extent that it can contribute to practical knowledge and real-world applications, if not solutions, that address pressing social problems. It is not, nor should it be, the goal of disaster research to promote conceptual thinking and abstract modeling solely for theoretical purposes. However, this does not mean that disaster research, as a social science, can exist or reach its goals without paying careful attention to epistemology and theory (Tierney 2007).

The second point relates to labels and contexts. We take "symbolic interactionism" (SI) to be the North American name for a widely used twentieth-century social-science paradigm that is frequently called something else in other disciplines and in other parts of the world. While not completely interchangeable, SI overlaps with what European sociologists call the "sociology of knowledge" or, more broadly, "interpretive social theory," "social hermeneutics," or "social phenomenology," and what social scientists in other disciplines and countries might refer to as "social constructionism" or "social constructivism." Likewise, in the United States, one may hear terms such as "Chicago School," "ethnography," or "interpretivism" used interchangeably with SI. Other common names for this school of thought may simply be "qualitative sociology" or "qualitative inquiry." The study of disasters, as an interdisciplinary, global, and applied field, is rife with conceptual untidiness regarding the proper use of these labels, and we therefore do not limit our discussion to those publications which are referencing the SI paradigm correctly and explicitly.

Rather, our aim here is to discuss studies that are influenced by some of the above-mentioned *key ideas* circulating within the larger cloud of symbolic-interactionist theory or social constructionism more broadly. The main goals of this chapter are to document the insights that SI-inspired thinking and research have, thus far, brought to disaster studies, as well as to suggest how the SI paradigm might further inform and move forward disaster research in the future.

Symbolic Interactionist Influences in Disaster Studies

In this main section, we discuss a variety of constructionist and interactionist contributions to disaster studies, both theoretical and empirical, based on a (necessarily limited) selection of readings from the larger literature that we consider particularly relevant and inspiring. After a general look at sociological theory in disaster studies, we discuss the advantages of conceptualizing disasters from a social-constructionist standpoint in public and political discourse. In the next subsection, we continue our review by turning to constructionist and interactionist thinking (or lack thereof) with regard to disaster perception at the micro level. Next, we consider the importance of culture when studying disasters, a stronghold of interpretive social research. We conclude our review by assessing constructionist framings of vulnerability and resilience, two key concepts in the field of disaster studies. Overall, we strive to show that the symbolic-interactionist or interpretive perspective—exemplified through ideas such as the social construction of reality; the structures of the life world; the primacy of knowledge, meaning, and interpretation; the importance of human agency; a social self that is generated through interaction and socialization; and the immense impacts of narratives, discourse, culture, and history—can help disaster scholars answer important research questions and solve problems in the real world.

Sociological Theory in Disaster Studies

For its first several decades, disaster research was an activity for academic specialists operating out of the limelight and away from grand theoretical debates. However, to the limited degree that disaster research was (and still is) theoretical, it drew, by and large, on sociological paradigms (Tierney 2019:65). As mentioned above, in the early days, disaster research was most strongly influenced theoretically by structural functionalism and systems theory, the dominating frameworks at the time (Tierney 2019:18). As a field nearly exclusively populated by white men, practitioners (over)emphasized social consensus and collaboration in the aftermath of disasters, rather than examining the emergence of conflicts and the persistence of social inequalities—which, today, are considered the root causes of disaster vulnerability in the first place. Perhaps as a consequence of these early orientations, mainstream, traditional notions of realism and scientific knowledge continued to guide disaster research for a long time, until at least the 1980s.

Beginning in the 1990s, disaster researchers—later than scholars in most other social science fields—began to question previous certainties. The terrorism crisis of 9/11 in 2001, the Indian Ocean Tsunami in 2004, the triple Tohoku-Fukushima disaster in 2011, and most certainly Hurricane Katrina in 2005 functioned as watershed events that brought intense public scrutiny and academic attention to disaster research (Picou and Marshall 2007). Along with the demographic profile of disaster scholars, theories and research questions in the field have diversified over the past two or three decades. Today, the social-structural inequalities of race, ethnicity, class, and gender—as well as, increasingly, age, health/disability, and sexuality—that underlie disasters have come to occupy center stage in the discipline (see, e.g., Enarson and Morrow 1998; Fothergill 2004; Fothergill and Peek 2004; Hartman and Squires 2006; Tierney 2005).

Correspondingly, conflict-theory and political-economy frameworks have become the dominating paradigms in the field. In today's sociology of disasters, most researchers craft their agendas, in line with the most influential discourses in the field, to address concerns over "vulnerability" and "resilience"—a concept pair rooted in social inequalities, disparate distributions of resources, as well as dynamics of power and exclusion. In Tierney's words (Tierney 2019:66), what unites these efforts and approaches is their analytic devotion to the *social production* of disasters, to "how social structure and social processes operate to create the conditions that make geological, meteorological, and other physical events disastrous."

These recent theoretical shifts in disaster research have not fully embraced symbolic interactionism as another well-established sociological approach. But how could this be true, if virtually all social science researchers in this field believe disasters to be "socially constructed" and "social constructionism" (a paradigm largely identical with

SI) is considered to be one of the major theoretical approaches in disaster research (Tierney 2019)? We believe that this view is not entirely correct. In our view, many disaster scholars have embraced social constructionism only superficially and have not completely understood or integrated the many insights that interpretive sociology in general, and symbolic interactionism in particular, can offer. Despite its recent growth, disaster studies is still a comparatively small area of inquiry, especially in sociology. Within this field, an even smaller number of scholars, perhaps as few as two or three dozen, have fully incorporated symbolic-interactionist thinking and ideas.

Before we proceed, a clarification is in order. We do not argue in this essay that the different paradigms guiding the study of disasters (Tierney 2019) are in competition with one another or that any single approach can, or should, be used at the total expense of any other. To the contrary, we believe that a holistic understanding of disasters requires the combination of various theories, methods, and frameworks that balance the strengths and weaknesses of one another. In this vein, we argue that, in the future, disaster scholars will benefit from paying more attention to the social dynamics surrounding meaning, agency, identity, interaction, culture, and many other ideas developed and applied in existing symbolic-interactionist and constructionist scholarship. In our view, without a more in-depth accounting of these issues, we cannot effectively implement the many excellent mitigation, protection, and adaptation strategies that our colleagues in the natural sciences are already offering. Moreover, we believe there is a large capacity for critical, emancipatory reflection and action within symbolic-interactionist or social-constructionist frameworks that is too often overlooked by today's dominant theoretical approaches (see, e.g., Denzin 2016).

Disasters as Social Constructions

Today, a common statement in disaster studies, and the title of a well-known book (Hartman and Squires 2006), is that "there is no such thing as a natural disaster." Note that this deviates from how disasters are understood in the everyday world, where they are frequently viewed as acts of God, or acts of nature, meaning events that humans cannot control or fully understand, nor carry any responsibility for. Behind the academic statement stands the idea that a natural (or technological) event only becomes a disaster when it profoundly implicates human actions and impacts human communities. In this view, all disasters must be social phenomena because human vulnerability and suffering are what makes them disasters in the first place.

As Tierney (2019:66 ff.) insightfully argues, the social nature of disasters applies to processes both of "production" and "construction." Disaster research conducted within the frameworks of conflict theory and political economy is primarily concerned with how human vulnerability, as the root cause of disasters, is socially *produced* through power dynamics and social structural inequalities. Where people live, which homes they occupy, and what resources they can access in daily life, as well as crisis situations, are profoundly unequal and expressive of power differences—insights that disaster researchers share with colleagues who study environmental justice (Bullard 2000; Taylor 2014) as well as many other issues.

However, saying that disasters are "socially constructed" aims at something different. As Tierney states (2019:66), a deeper understanding of disasters as socially constructed entails a focus on "how ideas and assumptions about hazards and disasters—and our own understandings—are shaped by narratives, discourses, institutional practices, and other factors." Borrowing from the vocabulary of symbolic interactionism, we might add that some of the "other factors" mentioned by Tierney include interactions, identities, and cultures, and that the "ideas," "assumptions," and "understandings" in Tierney's quoted comment may also be described as social meanings or forms of knowledge.

In the social-constructionist framework, if members of a society share the opinion that certain phenomena are serious assaults on society and therefore deserve to be labeled disasters, catastrophes, or calamities—regardless of measurable impacts—they *become* disasters in their consequences. Conversely, if members of a society do not develop this interpretation of an adverse event, it is not treated as disaster and, in many ways, *is* not a disaster, even if factual evidence to the contrary exists. This collective, interpretational work through which social actors define and, consequently, construct what counts as real was first described by Peter Berger and Thomas Luckmann (1966) in their well-known book *The Social Construction of Reality*, which offers a general sociological theory of knowledge. Although the authors did not elaborate specifically on the social construction of disasters, they laid the groundwork for such an understanding, even if it took a while for this key idea to take root in disaster studies. And, as is common for other areas of research that have undergone a more or less pronounced "constructionist" turn, Berger and Luckmann's views were often incorporated only partially and sometimes were even outright misunderstood (Pfadenhauer and Knoblauch 2019).

An early example of a constructionist understanding of disasters can be found in Spector and Kitsuse's (1977) seminal book on social problems, in which the authors discussed the dual interpretation of floods as natural events, on the one hand, and as caused by human action, on the other, while offering a powerful illustration of the social-constructionist framework's potential when examining disasters. Likewise, in the 1990s, environmental sociologist Hannigan (1995) argued that environmental problems, including disasters, must be considered as both a *material reality* and a *social reality*. For members of a society, disasters only exist on the basis of socially constructed, shared structures of knowledge that allow them to interpret a material reality within the context of their shared social reality. This is particularly true for how members of a society view the factors that contribute to the emergence of environmental problems and disasters, how they assess the societal impacts of disastrous events, and—not least— how they develop and implement measures to prevent, minimize, and overcome a devastating catastrophe (e.g. Leap 2019). Hannigan emphasized that it is typically in public discourse, particularly in media accounts, where societal knowledge about environment and disasters is produced. Public and media discourse strongly influence collective perceptions of, and responses to, adverse events.

Publicly labeling one, but not the other, adverse event as a disaster is extremely consequential in symbolic and materials respects. Moreover, it is a highly political act. For instance, in the United States, the president must issue a disaster declaration that will then trigger governmental rescue efforts and financial supports. This declaration will convince many experts, the media, and citizens that a disaster has indeed occurred. In today's highly divisive political climate, partisan beliefs and interests shape public perceptions of disasters at the most elemental level, strongly influencing disaster-recovery efforts or policies that may save lives or put lives in peril (Cooper and Block 2007).

To give one example of an important case study that is well known outside of disaster studies, Klinenberg (2002) shockingly revealed that a 1995 heat wave killed hundreds of people in Chicago, yet was never officially recognized, nor responded to, as a disaster. Arguably, this neglect was due to the demographic profile of the majority of victims (non-white, poor, elderly) as well as the absence of (newsworthy) material destruction and/or economic losses that are typical of extreme heat. At a more general level, Cerulo (2006) examines the strong preference in American society for "positive asymmetry," a pervasive bias toward envisioning only the best possible outcomes and the most positive events in all areas of social life, including the institutions of science and politics, which gets in the way of envisioning and perceiving negative and catastrophic incidents.

A brief look at today's news media reveals that even when disasters are scientifically evident and recognized by parts of the public, a politically motivated framing of an event as nonexistent or as "natural," rather than human-induced, can stand in the way of all manners of response, recovery, preparedness, and mitigation. It is difficult to underestimate the significance of the act of publicly constructing (or labeling, or framing) an event as a disaster, as countless constructionist studies in the areas of social problems and social movements have shown (Benford and Snow 2000). Without a constructionist perspective and the analytic tools it provides (such as frames, narratives, discourse, and many others), disaster scholars would be unable to comprehend the practical politics of disasters and assess their material impacts on communities. However, going beyond a framing of disasters as socially constructed in the public sphere, the symbolic-interactionist framework offers insights into many other topics of concern. In the next section, we delve more deeply into what could be described as the social construction of disasters at the micro level, where it is typically discussed as a matter of "perception"—a term that glosses over the active meaning-making and interpretational work that is part and parcel of perceiving anything.

Disaster Perception: Meaning Making, Agency, and Identity

For obvious reasons, in the applied field of disaster studies, human perception of disasters is an important topic of study. Nonetheless, despite immense efforts, current scholarly knowledge on disaster perception and, in extension, disaster-related decision making (for instance, whether to evacuate or not), is inadequate. Scholars have discovered a startling gap: the "considerable divergence" (Peacock et al. 2005:131; also see Garvin 2001; Margolis 1996; and Siegrist and Cvetkovich 2000) between expert or "objective" assessments of disasters as measurable, and to some extent predictable, events, on the one hand, and non-expert or "subjective" understandings of disasters, on the other. In disaster studies, there is a pressing need to account for "paradoxic" human factors in disasters (Wachinger et al. 2013), which follow a very different logic than non-human factors and evidently are difficult to calculate. After all, people make decisions and act based on what they *believe* is going on, rather than what *is* going on from a scientific or expert point of view. This is not a huge revelation to symbolic-interactionist scholars, and here is where they have an opportunity to make significant contributions.

Interpretive scholars know that ordinary people perceive the reality of risks and hazards within a different province of reality, the "everyday-life world," which is dominated by practical issues and concerns that typically lie outside the realm of expert knowledge (Schütz and Luckmann 1973; also see Garvin 2001). Viewed from this perspective, experts overlook what is "relevant" (to recall a concept used by Alfred Schütz) to ordinary people and what ultimately motivates their actions. A review of the literature on disaster perception and related actions reveals that the exact impact of social-structural variables, such as class, gender, age, and race/ethnicity, is inconclusive. By themselves or even in combination, these factors cannot explain why or how people know something or decide what to do. This may suggest the significance of other social dynamics.

In an overview article on risk perception, Wachinger and colleagues (Wachinger et al. 2013:1049) state that:

> [p]erceptions may differ depending on the type of risk, the risk contexts, the personality of the individual, and the social context. Various factors such as knowledge, experience, values, attitudes, and emotions influence the thinking and judgment of individuals about the seriousness and acceptability of risk.

Viewed from a symbolic-interactionist point of view, it makes perfect sense that "personal experience" and "trust or distrust in authorities" have emerged as the two most important factors in predicting personal interpretations of disasters (Wachinger et al. 2013) rather than one's age, income, racial, or gender category—even though these and other structural factors most certainly play a significant role in shaping personal experiences and trust in institutions. Symbolic interactionism could further explain that the general meanings and interpretations that determine hazard and risk perception are embedded in larger culture and transmitted to individuals through socialization and interaction. However, these processes vary considerably from one person to the other due to context and situational circumstances, even if they have some characteristics in common.

This insight could lead experts to believe that when people have experienced a disaster, they will be more likely to prepare, for instance, by stockpiling supplies or planning for evacuation. However, this is not always the case, indicating that the factors leading to disaster preparedness are even more complicated in real life. In some cases, previous disaster experience will increase someone's willingness to plan ahead, while in other cases, disaster experience evidently decreases concern and preparation. Wachinger and her colleagues (2013) aptly call this disconnect the "risk perception paradox," implying the existence of many intervening variables and complex social processes that play a role in this puzzle of human perception and decision making.

Overall, "the relationships between perception and behavioral response relative to preparedness is still unclear and controversial" (Wachinger et al. 2013:1063). And even though evacuation, as one important behavioral response, has been studied extensively (see Dash and Gladwin 2007, for an overview), past research has predominantly focused on testing the effects of social-structural variables rather than developing a larger conceptual framework to disentangle the interplay of human interpretation, decision making, and action in relation to disasters. Consequently, "for as much research as has been conducted on the issue of evacuation, our understanding of evacuation is extremely limited" (Dash and Gladwin 2007:72). In short, research on the important topics of disaster perception and decision making at the micro level is still grappling with finding the right questions to ask, and quite far from finding satisfying answers. Disaster researchers have yet to develop a detailed theoretical framework to these problems, beyond a hunch that "experience" and "trust in authorities" play some sort of role (Wachinger et al. 2013). To move forward, it will be essential to better understand what perception actually means regarding hazard risk, personal vulnerability, and resilience, and how it is linked to action. This can be accomplished by applying a symbolic-interactionist framework.

For example, Kusenbach's (2017) article focuses on exactly how personal experience, identities, and cultural beliefs, as well as practical constraints, shape perceptions of hazard risk and personal vulnerability, along with decision making (evacuation), among mobile home residents in Florida, a group that is already considered highly vulnerable overall from a structural point of view. She found that most participants do not believe that they are particularly vulnerable to disaster, after having made some preparations and while comparing themselves with others in their personal networks. Some appear to think that evacuation amounts to running away, a cowardly act that is incompatible with their strong sense of personal agency and resilience. Overall, people's sense of vulnerability and related actions were deeply embedded in their personal and collective identities, as well as being influenced by (seemingly unrelated) practical concerns (also see Kusenbach and Christmann 2013).

Compared with perceptions of personal vulnerability and resilience, we know a bit more about the ways in which hazard risk is perceived, or not perceived, at various levels of society, including in everyday life. Rayner (2012) explains that acknowledging the existence of a problem can be avoided through various strategies, such as denial, dismissal, diversion, and displacement. For instance, in their analysis of a slow-onset chemical disaster in Buenos Aires, Auyero and Swistun (2009) aptly refer to the local's various strategies of denial and misperception as a "labor of confusion." Norgaard's (2011) careful study of how Norwegians perceive climate change is an excellent example of denial. Norgaard found that even though people personally experienced and observed signs of climate change, they could not admit to themselves the full extent of what was going on, because it was too painful emotionally, and ultimately not reconcilable with the fact that Norway's economic prosperity and national identity is rooted in the exploitation of fossil fuels (which contributes to climate change). Her work shows that, also at the personal level, obvious truths can be ignored, denied, or buried when they are uncomfortable, similar to what we can readily observe in public and political discourse.

In sum, while it would be incorrect to say that considerations of meaning making, human agency, and identity have been completely absent from disaster research in the past, these ideas are currently not well developed, and much more research and theorizing building on SI and social-constructionist theory remains to be done in the future in order to address current gaps. Next, we turn to how a social-constructionist understanding of "culture," a term that is often contrasted with "social structure," has been incorporated in disaster studies.

The Role of Culture

Tierney (2019:40–41) argues that, in disaster research, attention to culture is paid mainly due to the efforts of anthropologists. There is no doubt that the works of many outstanding disaster anthropologists have been influential in this very regard (see Hoffman and Oliver-Smith 2002 and Barrios 2017 for overviews). Anthropological research on disasters, especially in non-Western societies, is indeed an essential part of the field, not least due to the much higher levels of mortality and destruction attributed to disasters in these regions. Regardless of location, anthropologists' deep familiarity with their field settings and their focus on indigenous knowledge, symbols, meanings, and cultural practices make valuable contributions to our global understanding of disasters (for recent examples, see Browne 2015; Button 2016; and Marino 2015). In the early 1980s, it fell to anthropologists Mary Douglas and Aaron Widavsky (1983) to emphasize that differences in patterns of risk perception between societies were rooted in their specific cultures. Their approach—referred to as the "cultural theory of risk"—argues that it is the cultural way of life in a specific society that determines what is considered to be endangered and thus worthy of protection, and that these views are deeply embedded in social institutions.

While anthropologists typically receive the most recognition for using in-depth ethnographic methods in their research on disasters, qualitative scholars in other disciplines, including sociology, are also emphasizing cultural contexts and processes in research on disasters. These include a (small) number of disasters scholars who incorporate symbolic interactionist and constructionist theories in their work (on SI contributions to cultural sociology, see Denzin 2016). Let us take a brief look at some prominent examples.

Erikson (1976) offered an early and well-known sociological treatment of cultural contexts in disaster recovery. His research on the aftermath of a devastating flood in the Appalachian Mountains (United States) focuses on the "collective trauma" among the survivors of the disaster. It is grounded in a thorough cultural history of the region. The idea of "cultural trauma," developed by Alexander and colleagues (Alexander 2004), offers another culturally and historically sensitive concept that can explain collective identity formation in the aftermath of devastating events more broadly.

A somewhat newer and powerful example of a cultural disaster analysis in sociology is Vaughan's (1996) brilliant book on the explosion of space shuttle Challenger right after its launch in 1986 (see also Vaughan 2004). Via a thorough historic ethnography, Vaughan shows that the Challenger explosion was not a technological accident at all but rather a logical, and perhaps inevitable, consequence of the prevailing institutional culture at NASA at the time. The organization was characterized by the "normalization of deviance," a "culture of production" (rather than precaution), and "structural secrecy" that influenced decision making in ways that severely compromised safety and eventually led to the fateful launch. Even though Vaughan's findings were discussed at the highest level of government and officials attempted to make changes at NASA, the very same cultural conditions culminated in the explosion of a second space shuttle, Columbia, in 2003 upon its return to Earth. Lastly, while not framed as a disaster study, Hochschild's (2018) most recent book carefully unravels the cultural narrative or "deep story" that has guided politically conservative Louisiana residents to shrug off the severe environmental degradation and its disastrous impacts on their communities while prioritizing economic well-being and fatalistic world views.

A different, contemporary cultural approach to disasters can be found in Heimann's (2019) examination of climate-change perceptions across several European countries in which culture is theorized as a "relational space." Heimann (2019) argues that different cultural value systems, beliefs, and identities can explain the varying perceptions of problems and potential solutions, as well as disparate preferences for mitigation and adaptation strategies. Heimann's perspective is partially rooted in communicative constructivism (Knoblauch 2019), a new branch of social-constructionist theory increasingly influential in Europe, in which particular emphasis is paid to mediatization and institutionalization in communication. Due to lack of space, we cannot comment more extensively on interactionist and constructionist contributions in the area of culture, however, some authors and studies (i.e., Norgaard 2011; Cerulo 2006) mentioned elsewhere in our review are also pertinent in this regard. Overall, it can be noted that research on culture and how it permeates social-life at the macro and micro levels, as well as their interfaces, is one of the frontiers in disaster studies where symbolic-interactionist scholarship can make immense contributions in the future, building on groundwork laid by well-known and novice scholars alike. Next, in the last subsection, we turn to symbolic-interactionist insights regarding two core concepts within disaster studies: vulnerability and resilience.

Vulnerability and Resilience in Symbolic Interactionist View

Since the 2000s, the concepts of vulnerability and resilience have evolved as the key concerns of social science disaster research (see Adger 2006; Pelling 2003; Medd and Marvin 2005; Coaffee et al. 2008; Christmann and Ibert 2012; Christmann and Kusenbach 2017). A thorough analysis of conceptual approaches to vulnerability and resilience reveals that, over time, these concepts, although originating in the natural sciences, have become firmly rooted in social science-based thinking about disasters. This is particularly obvious when scholars speak of "social" vulnerability and resilience. The concept of social vulnerability (see Prowse 2003; Blaikie et al. 2004; Kusenbach et al. 2010) takes into consideration the fact that the distribution of risk in a society is a reflection of social inequalities, for instance, in terms of class, age, gender, race/ethnicity, migration, disability, and sexuality. Morrow (2008:4) explains that "simply stated, social vulnerability occurs when unequal exposure to risk is coupled with unequal access to resources." The corresponding concept of social resilience (see, e.g., Adger 2000; Keck and Sakdapolrak 2013) is also, essentially, defined around the capabilities of individuals and groups to cope with different types of dangerous events.

Although the prevailing conceptual approaches to vulnerability and resilience are rooted in the social sciences and center on analyses of social inequalities, most of them are, to some degree, "essentialist" in nature insofar as they state that some people simply "are" vulnerable based on measurable indicators and assume strong relationships between factual variables. In contrast, when following a constructionist logic, vulnerability cannot simply mean the physical exposure of a structurally disadvantaged social group to certain hazards. Rather, it must account for people's personal interpretive "perceptions" of risk and exposure to a hazard, and their own relative location, as well as examine the impacts of situational and larger cultural contexts.

To our knowledge, Christmann and Ibert (2012) are the only scholars, thus far, to suggest concepts of vulnerability and resilience that address this missing perspective by incorporating social-constructionist ideas, paired with insights from actor-network theory. Their work is grounded in Berger and Luckmann's (1966) already mentioned premise according to which people and entire societies construct their own realities by attributing meaning to objects. Latour's (2005) actor-network theory expands this approach by stating that not only the (symbolic) interactions between various social actors are crucial in the process of socially constructing vulnerability and resilience but also those exchanges happening between actors and *objects* located in an actor network. According to actor-network theory, it is the existence of objects that ultimately enables humans to act, and, consequently, "objects too have agency" (Latour 2005:63).

Taking these perspectives into account, Christmann and Ibert (2012:267) define *vulnerability* as the result of a process of social construction in the course of which members of a society judge potential threats and negotiate them via discourse. In the course of this process, they often select one aspect (for instance, an object, a place, a symbol, or a social group) that is considered particularly valuable and worthy of protection, which is made the focus of consideration. Social actors then estimate the connections between this valued aspect and other components in the network that exert potentially negative impacts, which constructs vulnerability. Relatedly, *resilience* is understood as a social construction emphasizing proactive or reactive actions to protect the valued aspect within the network. From the point of view of actors, resilience constructions aim at changing the interconnections of all components in ways that will reduce the vulnerability of the centrally valued aspect, in order to preserve its functions and maintain its integrity. Regardless of these details, our larger point is that current understandings of vulnerability and resilience lack essential social aspects due to their failure to incorporate a constructionist emphasis on perceptions and interactions within systems, and due to a lack of attention to objects and their affordances. An example might be helpful.

Christmann and coauthors (2019) offer an empirical application of these ideas in their comparative study of Lübeck and Rostock, two neighboring cities on Germany's Baltic Sea coast. It was found that even though both cities share very similar physical, material, and demographic characteristics, their collective views of climate change differed dramatically, based on distinct cultural, historical, and social patterns. Perceptions of risk varied in the two cities based on what locals considered to be the valued but endangered object (i.e., the historic city core in one case, the sea itself in the other) and the source of its endangerment (i.e., the stormy sea in one case, the changing climate in the other). Perceptions of vulnerability and resilience also differed drastically, based on the city's distinct identities, which were grounded in their particular cultural, political, and economic history and development. In short, applying social-constructionist and actor-network theoretical ideas produced a deep understanding of the very different views and actions of these neighboring cities for which no other explanation could be found.

Similarly, there is evidence in other studies that different groups threatened by the same natural hazard often interpret their vulnerability in quite different ways (cf. Bulkeley 2013; Gotham and Greenberg 2014). Discourse-analysis studies in particular have pointed out that the way in which the vulnerabilities of climate change are perceived depends on the respective social and cultural systems within which this threat is negotiated (Boykoff 2008; Cannon and Müller-Mahn 2010), thereby emphasizing micro-macro links. However, researchers in this area (e.g., Carvalho and Burgess 2005; Trumbo 1996) typically do not draw theoretical conclusions from their findings and do not use a social-constructionist framing of vulnerability and resilience.

In sum, we see, again, that while many disaster studies result in findings that strongly support social-constructionist and symbolic-interactionist ideas, explicit theoretical framings and definitions of concepts in these traditions are much rarer to come by. Lastly, our—necessarily incomplete—review of symbolic-interactionist thinking and influences in contemporary disaster research concludes with a brief view toward the future.

FUTURE DIRECTIONS

Building on the work discussed in this essay and similar efforts, we are hopeful that the influence of symbolic-interactionist thinking in disaster scholarship will grow in the decades to come. As a conclusion, we briefly discuss four future directions for disasters studies and touch on the continued contributions SI research and theorizing may be able to make.

First, we see a clear trend toward merging the two fields of disaster studies and environmental studies, and we expect this combined field to grow into one of the largest and most active subfields of sociology in the future. In the age of anthropomorphic climate change, there is strong evidence that extreme meteorological events (i.e., storms, heat waves, wildfires, droughts, floods), geological events (i.e., earthquakes, volcanic eruptions), and biological events (i.e., epidemics) are becoming more frequent, more severe, and less predictable overall (Tierney 2019:223ff.). The global COVID-19 pandemic is a terrifying case in point. Combined with explosive population growth and the rapid rise in human settlement in coastal and otherwise vulnerable locations, disaster-induced losses are expected to rise sharply. The unfolding climate crisis is now viewed as part of a much broader environmental crisis nearing existential proportions.

As the links among climate change, environmental impacts, and disasters are becoming increasingly undeniable (one might think that they already are), disaster studies will become more influenced by theories, methods, and topics currently dominant in environmental studies. Here, we can observe a growing popularity of theories that break apart the long-standing dualism of culture and nature, of human subjects and non-human objects. Environmental scholars are increasingly developing "systemic," "relational," and "hybrid" theoretical approaches to society and environment. For instance, in recent years, actor-network theory and, in particular, the work of Bruno Latour have provided convincing and important theoretical impulses in this subfield (see Brewer et al. 2013). Symbolic interactionist-inspired theorizing and research about perception, interaction, and agency, especially when expanded to include nonhuman beings and objects (e.g., Cerulo 2009; Irvine 2008, 2009; Jerolmack 2013), can deliver considerable direction and momentum in this regard.

Second, we anticipate that disaster scholars will increasingly turn their attention to newly evolving forms of human interaction, sociality, and identity in relation to the meteoric rise of digital technologies and social media. If anything, we can be certain that new technologies, new media, and new forms of knowledge and social relationships will continue to rapidly transform all provinces of the social world in the future. On the one hand, virtual reality and social media may strengthen collaborative resilience building (Goldstein 2012) through broadening and speeding up channels of information and communication that can aid during disaster preparedness, impact, and recovery. On the other hand, it can be observed that entirely new technological disasters emerge due to the digitization of systems and institutions, and our increasing reliance on technology (see Boin and McConnell 2007 on critical infrastructure failures; Mitchell and Townsend 2005 on cyber-criminality). In particular, the combination of extreme natural events and "cyber disasters" may generate domino effects that can exacerbate the size, length, and impact of calamities. While the complex interactions between social action and digital technologies in the context of disasters have been recognized, they have not yet been fully understood. Further theoretical conceptualization and empirical research are urgently needed, and here is where symbolic-interactionist studies of digital interaction and cyberspace discourse and culture can offer important insights. As many chapters in this volume show, SI has been at the forefront of examining new forms of social interaction and developing new conceptual tools to grasp emerging social problems and issues.

Third, and closely related to the first two trends, there is a general awareness of the increasing global interdependence of people, places, and systems in disaster studies that is occasionally described as a "global turn." We are beginning to understand that, in addition to global ecological impacts, many disasters (such as COVID-19) have social, political, and economic repercussions that reach far beyond national and regional borders. In many respects, we have already developed a rich scholarly understanding of the human determinants of disasters, and we know quite well which technological solutions exist or must be developed. However, despite ongoing efforts, we are severely lacking an understanding of how to translate scientific and technical knowledge into relevant policy and political action. In order to address disasters on a global scale, researchers must develop much better models of disaster perception and decision making in governance and politics, as well as in everyday life. We cannot save lives and strengthen resilience until we find effective ways of using and applying scientific knowledge in the real world.

Based on the populist wave that has gripped many countries, it is becoming increasingly obvious that *new* political coalitions and policy solutions, external to national governments, must be found to reduce suffering and vulnerability on a global level. Effective disaster management and prevention call for a high degree of coordinated action both locally and across national borders. However, it is still largely unclear which social movements and what kind of new governance models have been, or will be, successful in making societies more resilient against disasters. People who lack essential means of survival in daily life will not devote time and resources to preparing for disasters (Tierney 2019:228), and thus we must address structural inequalities while also attending to the dynamics of knowledge, interaction, and identity in moving toward the goal of building resilience. Symbolic-interactionist approaches can help disaster scholars develop theoretical frameworks that link material with ideational factors, connect experiential life worlds with social structures, and spur change and transformation at local, regional, and global levels.

Lastly, globalization and global effects of climate change have strongly increased our need to better account for cultural frameworks and cultural differences in all areas of disaster research. As already mentioned, different societies as well as social groups within them are likely to develop contrasting, even conflicting, vulnerability and resilience perceptions with regard to disasters, and these various perceptions cannot be pushed aside or integrated without considerable debate. Thus far, as mentioned above, these differences have been explained via approaches such as "culture theory" (Douglas and Wildavsky 1983). What is still missing, however, is empirical research on the questions of exactly how culture affects perceptions of disasters (i.e., risk, vulnerability, and resilience), how societies ascribe meaning to natural (and technological) phenomena within the context of their specific history and environment, and how they sometimes manage to modulate or ignore dangers and risks forecasted by experts (e.g., Hochschild 2018; Leap 2019). Above all, it is crucial to understand how mechanisms of denial can be weakened, how cultural distortions can be ironed out, and how cultural resources can be used to overcome selective awareness and positive asymmetry (Cerulo 2006). In disaster research, working with cultural frameworks will also require a much higher degree of critical reflexivity regarding one's *own* cultural knowledge, norms, and biases (Marino 2015).

Perhaps it is here where research on emotions and identities, a contemporary stronghold of symbolic-interactionist research and thinking, can be called upon to forge connections between the micro worlds of experience and the macro contexts of culture, media, and politics (e.g., Barrios 2017). It is here where social constructionists, symbolic interactionists, narrative scholars, discourse analysts, and a multitude of their colleagues operating within the interpretive paradigm can offer up existing frameworks, and develop new understandings, that will further deepen our understanding of the social construction of disasters and assist disaster scholars in their ultimate quest to prevent suffering and save lives.

References

Alexander, Jeffrey C. 2004. "Toward a Theory of Cultural Trauma." Pp. 1–29 in *Cultural Trauma and Collective Identity*, edited by Jeffrey C. Alexander, Ron Eyerman, Bernard Giesen, Neil J. Smelser, and Piotr Sztompka. Berkeley: University of California Press.

Auyero, Javier, and Debora A. Swistun. 2009. *Flammable: Environmental Suffering in an Argentine Shantytown*. Oxford: Oxford University Press.

Adger, Neil W. 2000. "Social and Ecological Resilience: Are They Related?" *Progress in Human Geography* 24(3):347–64.

Adger, Neil W. 2006. "Vulnerability." *Global Environmental Change* 16:268–81.

Barrios, Robert E. 2017. *Governing Affect: Neoliberalism and Disaster Reconstruction*. Lincoln: University of Nebraska Press.

Benford, Robert D., and David A. Snow. 2000. "Framing Processes and Social Movements: An Overview and Assessment." *Annual Review of Sociology* 26:611–39.

Berger, Peter L., and Thomas Luckmann. 1966. *The Social Construction of Reality*. Garden City, NY: Doubleday.

Blaikie, Piers, Terry Cannon, Ian Davis, and Ben Wisner. 2004. *At Risk: Natural Hazards, People's Vulnerability and Disasters*. New York: Routledge.

Boin, Arjen, and Allan McConnell. 2007. "Preparing for Critical Infrastructure Breakdowns: The Limits of Crisis Management and the Need for Resilience." *Journal of Contingencies and Crisis Management* 15(1):50–59.

Boykoff, Maxwell T. 2008. "The Cultural Politics of Climate Change Discourse in UK Tabloids." *Political Geography* 27(5):549–69.

Brewer, Graham, Aiobheann McVeigh, and Jason von Meding. 2013. "An Evaluation of the Usefulness of Actor Network Theory in Understanding the Complexities of Vulnerability and Resilience in Post-Disaster Reconstruction." *International Journal of Architectural Research* 7(3):80–92.

Browne, Katherine E. 2015. *Standing in the Need: Culture, Comfort, and Coming Home after Katrina*. Austin: University of Texas Press.

Bulkeley, Harriet. 2013. *Cities and Climate Change*. London: Routledge.

Bullard, Robert. 2000. *Dumping in Dixie: Race, Class, And Environmental Quality. Third Edition*. London: Routledge.

Button, Gregory. 2016. *Disaster Culture: Knowledge and Uncertainty in the Wake of Human and Environmental Catastrophe*. London: Routledge.

Cannon, Terry, and Detlef Müller-Mahn. 2010. "Vulnerability, Resilience and Development Discourses in the Context of Climate Change." *Natural Hazards* 55(3):621–35.

Carvalho, Anabela, and Jacquelin Burgess. 2005. "Cultural Circuits of Climate Change in U.K. Broadsheet Newspapers, 1985–2003." *Risk Analysis* 25(6):1457–69.

Christmann, Gabriela B., and Oliver Ibert. 2012. "Vulnerability and Resilience in a Socio-Spatial Perspective: A Social-Scientific Approach." *Raumforschung und Raumordnung* 70(4):259–72.

Christmann, Gabriela B., Heiderose Kilper, and Oliver Ibert. 2019. "Resilient Cities: Theoretical Conceptulisations and Observations about the Discourse in the Social and Planning Sciences." Pp. 121–48 in *Resilience in Social, Cultural and Political Spheres*, edited by Benjamin Rampp, Martin Endreß, and Marie Naumann. Wiesbaden: Springer VS.

Christmann, Gabriela, and Margarethe Kusenbach. 2017. "Introduction to the Special Issue: Disaster Vulnerability and Resilience Building at the Social Margins." Special Issue, *International Journal of Mass Emergencies and Disasters* 35(2):1–6.

Cerulo, Karen A. 2006. *Never Saw It Coming: Cultural Challenges to Envisioning the Worst*. Chicago: University of Chicago Press.

Cerulo, Karen A. 2009. "Nonhumans in Social Interaction." *Annual Review of Sociology* 35:531–52.

Coaffee, J., D. M. Wood, and P. Rogers. 2008. *The Everyday Resilience of the City. How Cities Respond to Terrorism and Disaster*. London: Palgrave Macmillan.

Cooper, Christopher, and Robert Block. 2007. *Disaster: Hurricane Katrina and the Failure of Homeland Security*. New York: Macmillan.

Dash, Nicole, and Hugh Gladwin. 2007. "Evacuation Decision Making and Behavioral Responses: Individual and Household." *Natural Hazards Review* 8(3):69–77.

Denzin, Norman K. 2016. "Symbolic Interactionism's Contribution to the Study of Culture." Pp. 105–15 in *The SAGE Handbook of Cultural Sociology*, edited by David Inglis and Anna-Mari Almila. London: SAGE.

Douglas, Mary, and Aaron Wildavsky. 1983. *Risk and Culture: An Essay on the Selection of Technological and Environmental Dangers*. Berkeley: University of California Press.

Enarson, Elaine, and Betty H. Morrow. 1998. *The Gendered Terrain of Disaster: Through Women's Eyes*. Westport, CT: Greenwood.

Erikson, Kai. 1976. *Everything in Its Path: Destruction of Community in the Buffalo Creek Flood.* New York: Simon and Schuster.

Fothergill, Alice. 2004. *Heads Above Water: Gender, Class and Family in the Grand Forks Flood.* New York: State University of New York Press.

Fothergill, Alice, and Lori A. Peek. 2004. "Poverty and Disasters in the United States: A Review of Recent Sociological Findings." *Natural Hazards* 32(1):89–110.

Garvin, Teresa. 2001. "Analytical Paradigms: The Epistemological Distances between Scientists, Policy Makers, and the Public." *Risk Analysis* 21(3):443–55.

Goldstein, Bruce Evan, ed. 2012. *Collaborative Resilience. Moving Through Crisis to Opportunity.* Cambridge, MA: MIT Press.

Gotham, Kevin Fox, and Miriam Greenberg. 2014. *Crisis Cities: Disaster and Redevelopment in New York and New Orleans.* Oxford: Oxford University Press.

Hartman, Chester, and Gregory D. Squires. 2006. *There Is No Such Thing as a Natural Disaster: Race, Class, and Hurricane Katrina.* New York: Routledge.

Hannigan, John A. 1995. *Environmental Sociology: A Social Constructionist Perspective.* New York: Routledge.

Heimann, Thorsten. 2019. *Culture, Space and Climate Change: Vulnerability and Resilience in European Coastal Areas.* New York: Routledge.

Hochschild, Arlie Russell. 2018. *Strangers in Their Own Land: Anger and Mourning on the American Right.* New York: The New Press.

Hoffman, Susanna M., and Anthony Oliver-Smith, eds. 2002. *Catastrophe and Culture: The Anthropology of Disasters.* Santa Fe, NM: School of American Research Press.

Irvine, Leslie. 2008. *If You Tame Me: Understanding our Connection with Animals.* Temple University Press.

Irvine, Leslie. 2009. *Filling the Ark: Animal Welfare in Disasters.* Philadelphia, PA: Temple University Press.

Jerolmack, Colin. 2013. *The Global Pigeon.* Chicago: University of Chicago Press.

Keck, Marcus, and Patrick Sakdapolrak. 2013. "What Is Social Resilience? Lessons Learned and Ways Forward." *Erdkunde* 67(1):5–19.

Klinenberg, Eric. 2002. *Heat Wave: A Social Autopsy of Disaster in Chicago.* Chicago: University of Chicago Press.

Knoblauch, Hubert. 2019. *The Communicative Construction of Reality.* New York: Routledge.

Kusenbach, Margarethe. 2017. "'It's Not Where I'd be Running Like an Idiot for a Small One': Hurricane Perceptions and Evacuation Decision Making Among Florida Mobile Home Residents." *International Journal of Mass Emergencies and Disasters* 25(2):91–120.

Kusenbach, Margarethe, Jason L. Simms, and Graham A. Tobin. 2010. "Disaster Vulnerability and Evacuation Readiness: Coastal Mobile Home Residents in Florida." *Natural Hazards* 52(1):79–95.

Kusenbach, Margarethe, and Gabriela B. Christmann. 2013. "Understanding Hurricane Vulnerability: Lessons from Mobile Home Communities." Pp. 61–84 in *Disaster Resiliency: Interdisciplinary Perspectives*, edited by Naim Kapucu, Christopher Hawkins, and Fernando Rivera. New York: Routledge.

Latour, Bruno. 2005. *Reassembling the Social: An Introduction into Actor-Network Theory.* Oxford: Oxford University Press.

Leap, Braden T. 2019. *Gone Goose: The Remaking of an American Town in the Age of Climate Change.* Philadelphia, PA: Temple University Press.

Margolis, Howard. 1996. *Dealing with Risk.* Chicago: University of Chicago Press.

Marino, Elizabeth. 2015. *Fierce Climate, Sacred Ground: An Ethnography of Climate Change in Shishmaref, Alaska*. Fairbanks: University of Alaska Press.

Medd, Will, and Simon Marvin. 2005. "From the Politics of Urgency to the Governance of Preparedness: A Research Agenda on Urban Vulnerability." *Journal of Contingencies and Crisis Management* 13(2):44–49.

Mitchell, William J., and Anthony M. Townsend. 2005. "Cyborg Agonistes: Disaster and Reconstruction in the Digital Electronic Era." Pp. 313–34 in *The Resilient City. How Modern Cities Recover from Disaster*, edited by Lawrence J. Vale and Thomas J. Campanella. Oxford: Oxford University Press.

Morrow, Betty H. 2008. *Community Resilience. A Social Justice Perspective*. CARRI Research Report 4. Miami: Florida International University.

Norgaard, Kari M. 2011. *Living in Denial: Climate Change, Emotions, and Everyday Life*. Cambridge, MA: MIT Press.

Picou, Steven, and Brent K. Marshall. 2007. "Introduction: Katrina as a Paradigm Shift: Reflections on Disaster Research in the Twenty-First Century." Pp. 1–20 in *The Sociology of Katrina*, edited by D. L. Brunsma, D. Overfelt and J. S. Picou. London: Rowman and Littlefield.

Peacock, Walter Gillis, Samuel David Brody, and Wes Highfield. 2005. "Hurricane Risk Perceptions Among Florida's Single Family Homeowners." *Landscape and Urban Planning* 73(2–3):120–35.

Pelling, Mark. 2003. *The Vulnerability of Cities: Social Resilience and Natural Disaster*. London: Earthscan.

Pfadenhauer, Michaela, and Hubert Knoblauch, eds. 2019. *Social Constructivism as Paradigm? The Legacy of the Social Construction of Reality*. New York: Routledge.

Prowse, Martin. 2003. *Towards a Clearer Understanding of "Vulnerability" in Relation to Chronic Poverty*. Manchester, UK: Palgrave Macmillan.

Quarantelli, E. L., and R. W. Perry. 2005. "A Social Science Research Agenda for the Disasters of the Twenty-first Century: Theoretical, Methodological and Empirical Issues and their Professional Implementation." Pp. 325–96 in *What Is a Disaster? New Answers to Old Questions*, edited by R. W. Perry and E. L. Quarantelli. Philadelphia, PA: Xlibris.

Rayner, Steve. 2012. "Uncomfortable Knowledge: The Social Construction of Ignorance in Science and Environmental Policy Discourses." *Economy and Society* 41(1):107–25.

Schütz, Alfred, and Thomas Luckmann. 1973. *The Structures of the Life-World*, vol. 1. Chicago: Northwestern University Press.

Siegrist, Michael, and George Cvetkovich. 2000. "Perception of Hazards: The Role of Social Trust and Knowledge." *Risk Analysis* 20(5):713–20.

Spector, Malcolm, and John I. Kitsuse. 1977. *Constructing Social Problems*. London: Routledge.

Taylor, Dorceta. 2014. *Toxic Communities: Environmental Racism, Industrial Pollution, and Residential Mobility*. New York: NYU Press.

Tierney, Kathleen J. 2019. *Disasters: A Sociological Approach*. Medford, MA: Polity Press.

Tierney, Kathleen J. 2007. "From the Margins to the Mainstream? Disaster Research at the Crossroads." *Annual Review of Sociology* 33:503–25.

Tierney Kathleen J. 2005. "Social Inequality, Hazards, and Disasters." Pp. 109–28 in *On Risk and Disaster: Lessons from Hurricane Katrina*, edited by Ronald J. Daniels, Donald F. Kettl, and Howard Kunreuther. Philadelphia: University of Pennsylvania Press.

Trumbo, Craig. 1996. "Constructing Climate Change: Claims and Frames in US News Coverage of an Environmental Issue." *Public Understanding of Science* 5(1): 269–83.

Vaughan, Diane. 2004. "Theorizing Disaster: Analogy, Historical Ethnography, and the Challenger Accident." *Ethnography* 5(3):315–47.

Vaughan, Diane. 1996. *The Challenger Launch Decision: Risky Technology, Culture, and Deviance at NASA*. Chicago: University of Chicago Press.

Wachinger, Gisela, Ortwin Renn, Chloe Begg, and Christian Kuhlicke. 2013. "The Risk Perception Paradox: Implications for Governance and Communication of Natural Hazards." *Risk Analysis* 33(6):1049–65.

INDEX

For the benefit of digital users, indexed terms that span two pages (e.g., 52–53) may, on occasion, appear on only one of those pages.

Figures are indicated by *f* following the page number

A

abductive analysis, 10, 20n2
Aboujaoude, Elias, 94
actors. *See* social actors
Addams, Jane, 32, 42, 341
Adler, Patricia, 201, 454
Adler, Peter, 201
Aetius, 43
affective heritage embracement, 268
African Americans
  Chicago School dissertations
    on, 32–33
  double consciousness of, 342
  feminism and, 344, 405
  hip hop and, 199–200, 213
  HIV/AIDS among, 470
  labeling theory and, 449
  racial socialization among, 390, 392
  social self and identity of, 342, 343
  urban ethnographies of, 339
agency
  capacity for resistance and, 362
  constraints on, 129, 231, 346
  in cultural production, 230
  disaster perception and, 537, 538
  in doctrine of emergence, 197
  ephemerality in erosion of, 88
  human nature and, 93, 94
  in performance of self, 149
  power of, 231
  pragmatism and, 5, 9–10
  sensory incongruity as challenge to, 89
  in social constructionism, 165
  in socialization, 391

  in socio-ecological resilience, 494
  of technology users, 297
  transformation of intentions and, 128
Agle, Braley R., 322
Ahmed, Sarah, 229
AIDS/HIV, 168, 170, 405, 440, 470
Alexander, Jeffrey C., 8, 148, 197–198, 228, 229, 539
Altheide, David, 66, 261, 454–455
American pragmatism, 221, 223, 316–317, 427–428
American Sociological Association (ASA), 5, 9, 32–33
Ammerman, Nancy, 203
analytic bracketing, 168–169
Anderson, Elijah: Code of The Street: Decency, Violence, and The Moral Life of The Inner City, 457
Anderson, Ronald E., 95
Andrews, Molly, 186
animalistic infra-humanization, 93, 94
Antipater, 43
apparatgeist, 288
Arab Spring, 284
Aristotle, 43
artificial intelligence, 97, 98, 361
ASA (American Sociological Association), 5, 9, 32–33
Athens, Lonnie, 456
Atkinson, Paul, 188
attentional sensitization, 71, 72
attentional socialization, 76–77, 336
Atzmon, Thaddeus, 269
Aubert, Nicole, 83

audiences
  in dramaturgical perspective, 146–149,
    151–158
  emotional response of, 34
  invisible, 307–308, 310
  mass media and, 275, 278, 287
  music and, 259, 260, 264, 265
  new media and, 276, 287
  in online interactions, 30, 302, 305–311
  storytelling and, 177
Augé, Marc, 243–244
authenticity
  consumption and, 268
  of digital information, 91
  of emotions, 232, 233
  music and, 268
  occupations and, 200
  of online interactions, 304–306, 309, 311
  of performances, 147, 148, 151, 177
  religion and, 325
  subcultures and, 214, 216
autoethnography, 62, 180–181
Auyero, Javier, 498, 513–516, 521–522, 537
Averill, James, 226

B

"badasses," 456–458
Bakker, Arnold B., 86
balanced self, 263
Baldwin, James Mark, 28
Bamberg, Michael, 186
Banbury, Jonafa, 269
Barthes, Roland, 198, 210
Baudrillard, Jean: *The Consumer Society*, 243
Baumgartner, Thomas, 134
Baym, Nancy K., 82, 86, 300, 307
Bean v. Southwestern Waste Management
    Corp. (1979), 514
Beauvoir, Simone de, 34
Becker, Howard, 119n1
  Art Worlds, 133
  "Becoming a Marihuana User," 109
  career concept and, 428
  on conventions in the arts, 266
  Hughes as influence on, 32
  on inertia and conventions, 113
  institutional analyses of, 133

on labels, 480
on language across contexts, 39
*Outsider: Studies in the Sociology of
  Deviance*, 167, 447–448, 452
on patterned cooperation, 267
on representations of society, 117
on sexuality, 432
situation concept of, 227
on subcultures, 208–209, 259–260
on theoretical perspective selection, 44
Benjamin, Walter, 245
Bennett, Andy, 264–265
Ben-Yehuda, Nachmann, 453
Berger, Peter L.
  on paramount reality, 147
  on quantitative measurement, 114
  The Social Construction of Reality, 7, 74, 162,
    164–167, 225, 534
  on synthesis between Mead and Schutz, 35
Bernard, Jessie, 407
Best, Joel, 163, 167–169, 453
Bettie, Julie, 346–347, 414
bias. *See* discrimination and bias
Birmingham School (Centre for Contemporary
    Cultural Studies), 207–213, 217
bisexuals. *See* LGBTQ+ community
Black communities. *See* African Americans
Black feminism, 344, 405
Blalock, Hubert M.: *Social Statistics*, 116
blogs, 277, 283, 287, 302, 308, 476, 478–479
Blumer, Herbert
  on consumption, 247
  on empirical world, 60
  on ethnography, 447
  *Industrialization as an Agent of Social
    Change*, 135
  legacy of, 29–30
  macrostructural concerns of, 127, 137
  on meaning and meaning-making, 14, 376,
    388
  "The Methodological Position of Symbolic
    Interactionism," 70, 369
  Movies and Conduct, 427
  on power, 368, 369, 381
  premises of SI, 2, 4, 19, 64, 109, 125, 137, 361
  "Race Prejudice as a Sense of Group
    Position," 389

on research methodology, 49–52
on sensitizing concepts, 11, 16, 71, 258, 336
on sexuality, 427
SI as term coined by, 2, 4, 27–28, 388
situation concept of, 227
on social interactions, 199
on social organization, 124, 129
on social psychology, 28–30
Symbolic Interactionism: Perspective and Method, 27–28, 50, 125, 166
Bobo, Lawrence D., 389
Bonilla-Silva, Eduardo, 389
Bonner, T. N., 36
Borer, Michael Ian, 8, 17, 195
Borowik, Irena, 320
bots, 96–97, 361
Bottompley, Anne, 253
Botts, Tina Fernandes, 171
Bourdieu, Pierre
  on attaining objectives, 360
  Distinction, 230
  empirical research and, 64
  on habitus, 230n4 373
  hegemony and, 33
  subcultures and, 214
boyd, danah, 306, 307, 309–310
Boynton, G. R., 287
BP oil disaster (2010), 519, 521, 524n16
Brekhus, Wayne H., 1, 12, 13, 18–19, 335, 345, 439
Briar, Scott, 449
bricolage, defined, 27
Bridges, Tristan, 412, 413
British Sociological Association, 5
Brown, A. R. Radcliffe, 35
Brown, Karida, 342–343
Brown v. Board of Education (1954), 395
Buckley, Walter F., 134
Buday, Amanda, 500
Buddhism, 319, 324
Bullard, Robert: *Dumping in Dixie*, 514
Burgess, Ernest W., 2, 3, 30–31, 38, 124, 427
Burke, Kenneth, 151, 428
Burns, Tom R., 134, 151
Burr, Aaron, 40
Bury, Michael, 472–473
Butler, Judith, 13, 149, 409
Byrd, W. Carson, 395

C

Cahill, Spencer, 437
Callahan, Yesha, 171
Campbell, Scott W., 282
Campo, Enrico, 8, 17, 241
"Cancer Alley" (Louisiana), 518–521, 523n4
Čapek, Stella, 516, 522
capitalism. *See also* consumption
  Birmingham School on, 209
  Chicago School on, 41–42
  cultural forms of, 243
  environmental issues and, 512
  in hypermodern society, 83
  neoliberal, 251
Carnevali, Barbara, 355
Carr, Lowell J.: "Situational Sociology," 227
Carr, Nicholas, 89
Casey, Patrick Michael, 324
Caws, Peter, 112
celebrity sightings, 202
cell phones. *See* smartphones
Centre for Contemporary Cultural Studies (Birmingham School), 207–213, 217
Cersosimo, Giuseppina, 12, 19–20, 468, 469
Certeau, Michel de, 230
Cerulo, Karen A., 535
Challenger explosion (1986), 539
Chang, Johannes, 135
Charmaz, Kathy, 60, 472, 474, 483
Chattopadhyay, Sumana, 282
Chicago
  Great Fire in (1871), 31
  heat wave in (1995), 535
  Hull House in, 32
  music scene in, 259
  on sexuality, 426
  as urban laboratory, 3
Chicago School
  on capitalism, 41–42
  commitment to scholarship, 32
  disaster research and, 530
  dissertations on Black groups and institutions, 32–33
  divisiveness within, 30
  ethnographies and, 57, 134, 208, 447–449
  French advocates of, 33
  in history of SI, 1, 2, 4

552 INDEX

Chicago School (*cont.*)
  innate human nature rejected by, 29
  narrative studies and, 17, 177
  pragmatism and, 1, 9, 177, 426
  on sexuality, 426
  social ecology and, 3, 12, 31
  on social organization, 126
  on subcultures, 3, 7, 207–209, 211, 213, 217
  urban ethnography and, 3
  women and, 32, 341
children. *See also* socialization
  digital technologies and, 96
  domain of social influence for, 285
  racial ideas of, 394–395
  resilience and, 391
  role-taking by, 165
  transgender, 416, 418
  victimization of, 163, 167, 453
choice architecture, 356–358
Christianity, 269, 319, 325, 326
Christie, Bruce, 298
Christmann, Gabriela B., 20, 529, 540–541
Chrysippus, 43
Cicero, 43
Clair, Jeffrey, 269
Clark, Kenneth and Mamie, 395
Clarke, Adele, 60, 128, 227
class
  environmental issues and, 514–515
  femininity and, 414
  inequality and, 135
  performances of, 347
  shopping malls and, 245
  standpoint theories and, 339–340
  subcultural identity and, 213, 346
class struggle, 207, 210, 213
Cleanthes, 43
Clements, Frederic: *Plant Succession*, 31
climate change, 170, 497, 512, 521, 538–543
Coates, Dominiek D., 324
cognition
  analytical focus on, 119
  deliberate modes of, 354
  emotions and, 226
  impersonal aspect of, 76
  postmodernism and, 34
  software mindset and, 90–91

  Stoic views of, 43
cognitive dissonance, 513, 516
cognitive sociology, 11, 77, 104, 204n1 516
Cohen, Albert, 3
Cohen, Stanley: *Moral Panics and Folk Devils: The Creation of the Mods and the Rockers*, 451
Coleman, James S., 362n7
collective identity
  gender and, 403, 415
  new-media promotion of, 284
  performance of, 8, 148, 154
  of SI community, 4
collective trauma, 539
Collins, Patricia Hill, 14, 344, 414
Collins, Randall, 148, 377, 457
Comaneci, Catalina, 278
communication. *See also* language; mass media; new media; semiotics
  by drug users, 260, 261
  ecology of, 133
  by e-mail, 86, 88, 89, 93, 299, 300
  in grounded theory research, 61
  in healthcare, 474–483
  ICTs, 18, 296–301, 303
  institutionalization of, 539
  of meaning, 225
  normative structures of, 3
  out of character, 157–158
  power relations and, 63
  quantitative measurement and, 105, 110, 111
  reflexive self and, 2
  in scientific communities, 105, 117–119
  by texting, 86, 90, 93, 276, 282, 288
  VoIP services and, 281–282
communities
  building, 147, 283
  collective identity of, 4
  fenceline, 514
  group styles developed by, 8
  marginalized, 176
  meso-level, 12
  music and, 264–266
  portable, 267–268
  thought, 76, 106, 516–517
computer-mediated interactions. *See* online interactions

Comte, Auguste, 317
concealed strategic actions (CSAs), 19, 352–356, 361–362, 362n7
concept-driven research, 70–78
  attentional socialization in, 76–77
  cognitive skills used in, 78
  data-driven research vs., 70–71
  prepared mind in, 73–76
  sensitizing concepts in, 16, 71–72, 74–76
  thematic focus in, 72–73, 77
  theory-driven research vs., 70–71
conceptual ordering, 55–56
conflict theory, 530, 532, 533
connectivity syndrome, 86
Connell, C., 416
Connell, Raewyn, 411–414, 419n4
Conrad, Peter, 157
consciousness
  digital technologies and, 84
  double, 14, 342, 347
  Durkheim on society as, 7
  emotional manipulation and, 377
  false, 122, 210
  identity as element of, 165
  power and, 372, 380
  racial, 389
  self-consciousness, 9, 223, 224, 231
  in social psychology, 28, 224
  social-relational character of, 9
constructionism. *See* social constructionism
consumption, 241–253. *See also* shopping and shopping malls
  authenticity and, 268
  culture of, 241–244, 248
  hyperconsumption, 83
  identity and, 17, 209, 242
  meaning of, 243, 247, 251, 253
  as object of investigation, 241–244
  postmodern, 242
  as recreational activity, 246, 249
  seduced vs. sovereign consumers, 245
  semiotics and, 243
  SI perspectives on, 246–253
  spaces of, 8, 17, 242–248, 251–252
  subcultural patterns of, 214
conversation analysis, 36, 39, 176–179, 182–183, 326, 499–500

Cooley, Charles Horton
  Human Nature and the Social Order, 123
  on looking glass self, 41, 149, 449
  role in invention of SI, 28, 29, 124
  self as conceptualized by, 2
  Social Organization, 123
  Social Process, 123
  sympathy as described by, 29, 41
cooperation
  elicitation of, 12, 370–382
  patterned, 267, 379
  in performances, 146, 147, 151, 157
  quantitative measurement and, 113, 114, 117
  rewards for, 375, 378
  sympathy and, 29, 32
Copes, Heith, 216
Copp, Martha, 377
Corbin, Juliet, 55–56, 60, 473
Correll, Shelley, 410
Corsaro, William, 391–392
Côté, Jean-François, 134
Couch, Carl: Constructing Civilizations, 135
Cournut, Jean, 83
Covaleski, Mark A., 135
COVID-19 pandemic, 139–140n3, 282, 542
Cragun, Ryan T., 323, 326
Crass (band): "Punk is Dead," 217
Crawford, Margaret: "The World in a Shopping Mall," 244–245
Crawley, S. L., 13–14, 19, 402, 412, 419nn3–4
Crenshaw, Kimberlé, 344
Cressey, Donald, 3
Cressey, Paul, 208
crime and criminal justice system, 185, 446–462. *See also* deviance
critical theory
  encoding/decoding model and, 210
  feminism and, 5
  identity and, 6
  Marxism and, 12
  postmodernism and, 12, 34
Crossley, Nick, 134
CS. *See* cultural sociology
CSAs. *See* concealed strategic actions
Cuban Missile Crisis (1962), 499–500
cues-filtered-out model, 299
cultivation analysis, 279

554   INDEX

cultural capital, 106, 214, 231
Cultural Indicators Project, 279
cultural knowledge, 211, 379, 544
cultural norms, 17, 199, 214, 277, 281, 325
cultural sociology (CS), 5, 7–8, 196–204, 221–
    222, 228, 538
culture, 195–204. *See also* race and ethnicity;
    subcultures
  analytic value of, 195
  autonomy of, 197, 198
  codes and context of, 196–200
  of consumption, 241–244, 248
  definitions of, 196
  disassociation of social organization from,
    139n1
  disasters and, 538–539
  emotions and, 221–229, 232–234
  in everyday life, 201–203, 221
  generalized other and, 7, 8, 199
  idioculture, 8, 18, 258, 264, 266, 281
  meaning-making and, 198–200, 203–204
  organizational, 128, 133, 136, 502
  power in relation to, 213
  pragmatism and, 7, 8, 10, 21n3 148
  production of, 196–197, 213, 230, 392
  representations of, 228, 515
  scripts related to, 148–149, 428, 515
  as semiotic process, 228
  sexuality and, 434
  social constructionism and, 7, 8, 164–165,
    225
  social life in relation to, 197
  social psychology and, 7
  subjectivity and, 229–234
  transmission of, 276–277
Currie, Scott, 260
cyberactivism, 283–284
cyber self, 286, 305

D

Daft, Richard, 298
Daly, Sarah, 414
Damasio, Antonio, 88–89
Darwin, Charles, 29, 31, 32, 42
Darwin, Helana, 415
Dator, James A., 82, 97
Daub, Shannon J., 513

Davis, Fred, 261
Davis, Georgiann, 415
Davis, Jenny, 305, 308
Dawson, Lorne, 249
Deegan, Mary Jo, 341
deep fakes, 91
Deepwater Horizon oil disaster. *See* BP oil
    disaster
default options (DOs), 19, 357–359, 363n10
definition of the situation
  in dramaturgical perspective, 150–151, 154,
    158
  nothingness and, 354
  sexual, 434–435
  social constructionism and, 165
DeGloma, Thomas, 1
dehumanization, 92–95, 342
Demetriou, Demetrakis, 412
Dennis, Alex, 134, 370
DeNora, Tia, 263
Denzin, Norman, 33–35, 129, 136, 180, 181, 225
depression, 181
de-realization, 81, 85–92, 97–99, 98f
Derks, Daantje, 86
Descartes, René, 108
deviance
  criminalization of, 448
  gender identity and, 416
  literature review, 447–452
  in performances, 153
  primary vs. secondary, 448–449
  in reactivist perspective, 167
  sexuality and, 426, 440
  subcultures and, 208–209, 262, 440
Dewey, John
  on habit, 10, 21n3
  pragmatism and, 223, 270
  on religion, 317
  role in invention of SI, 28, 124
dialogues, as representations of society,
    117–118
Diamond, John, 394
digital self, 285, 302–303
digital technologies, 81–99. *See also* internet;
    online interactions; social media
  analytic power of, 91
  cyber-ostracism and, 87

dependence on, 84, 91, 92
de-realization and, 81, 85–92, 97–99, 98f
disasters involving, 542–543
ephemerality and, 87–88, 98
hypermodernism and, 16, 82–84, 89, 95
infra-humanization and, 81, 92–99, 98f
nonhuman agents and, 81, 96–97
personalization of, 91–92, 96
sensory incongruity and, 89–90
smartphones, 83–84, 86, 281–284, 286
software mindset and, 90–91
spatial detachment and, 88–89
subcultures and, 215–216
surveillance capabilities, 95–96, 98
temporal disorganization and, 85–87
VoIP services, 281–282
DiMaggio, Paul, 197, 204n1
Dingwall, Robert, 15, 27, 472–473
Diogenes, 43
Dirsmith, Mark, 134, 135
Disaster Research Center (DRC), 530
disasters, 529–544. See also specific disasters
Chicago School on, 530
culture and, 538–539
cyber, 543
ecological, 498
environmental, 282, 517–521
future research directions, 542–544
perceptions of, 534–538, 540–541
recovery from, 494, 514
resilience and, 532, 537, 540–544
SI perspectives on, 531–541
social construction of, 532–535
sociology of, 20, 529, 532–533
suffering following, 515
vulnerability to, 532, 533, 537, 540–544
discrimination and bias. See also racism
acritical, 125, 136
astructural, 125, 132, 136, 137
authorial, 212
categorical, 342
homophobia, 412, 437
imperial, 13
macro-deterministic, 2
microsociological, 127
positive asymmetry, 535, 544
pro-cognitive, 376

structural, 211
weight-based, 107, 476
disease. *See also* healthcare; medicine; *specific diseases*
autoethnography and, 180–181
interactive dimension of, 478–479
quantitative thresholds for, 112
sense of self affected by, 469, 474
as social construction, 19, 471, 472
suffering caused by, 473–474
trajectory management, 473
diversity. *See* culture; race and ethnicity
division of labor, 31, 40, 42, 129, 246
Dolezal, Rachel, 170
Domonoske, Camilia, 90
DOs (default options), 19, 357–359, 363n10
Douglas, Jack
The Nude Beach, 451
The Social Meanings of Suicide, 35
Understanding Everyday Life, 35
Douglas, Mary, 538
downshifting, 344, 345
dramatic realization, 153, 158
dramatism, 151, 227, 428, 450
dramaturgical perspective, 146–158. *See also* performances
apology ritual in, 148, 155, 156
audiences in, 146–149, 151–158
cooling out process in, 157
definition of the situation in, 150–151, 154, 158
dramaturgical circumspection, 153, 158
dramaturgical discipline, 148, 153, 158
dramaturgical loyalty, 154, 158
frontstage and backstage in, 152, 156, 355
hidden performances in, 156–158
impression management in, 146, 152–154, 156, 158
individual performances in, 151–154
interaction orders in, 146, 150, 151, 155, 157, 407
self-presentation in, 152–154, 157
social actors in, 3, 146–158
social transformations and, 64
stigmatization in, 156–157
teamwork in, 154–158
theatre in, 146–148, 152, 156, 158

DRC (Disaster Research Center), 530
drug use, 260–261, 456. *See also* marijuana
Du Bois, W. E. B., 6, 14, 18, 339, 341–343, 347, 387
Durkheim, Emile
    on impersonal aspect of cognition, 76
    Parsons influenced by, 2
    on religion, 148, 315
    The Rules of Sociological Method, 70
    on society as conscience and consciousness, 7
    statistics as used by, 111, 115
    Suicide, 111
Duverger, Maurice, 116

E

Eagleton, Terry, 196
Eaton, Marc, 327
Ebert, John David, 83–84
ecology
    of communication, 133
    language of, 31
    political, 495, 503
    social, 3, 12, 30–33
    urban, 207–209
economic inequality, 135
economy. *See also* capitalism
    environmental issues and, 512
    globalization of, 83
    gross domestic product and, 112–113
    market structures, 135–136, 139
    recessions in, 112, 283, 403
    service economy, 200
    sharing economy, 283
eco-self, 516, 522
eco-uncertainty, 20, 517, 519, 521–523
Edmonds, Beverly C., 136
educational socialization, 133, 393–394, 406
e-heath, 478–479
Eliasoph, Nina, 8, 199
Ellis, Carolyn, 62
    Final Negotiations: A Story of Love, Loss, and Chronic Illness, 180
Elster, Jon, 360
e-mail, 86, 88, 89, 93, 299, 300
Emerson, Robert M., 393
Emirbayer, Mustafa, 9–10

emotional capital, 437
emotions, 221–234
    authenticity of, 232, 233
    in autoethnography, 62
    brute, 450, 451, 454, 457–458
    culture and, 221–229, 232–234
    digital transmission of, 85
    elicitation of, 371, 377
    in everyday life, 222, 226, 229–231
    language and, 225–226
    management of, 376–377, 381, 382
    meaning of, 222, 229, 232
    postmodernism and, 34
    sexuality and, 436–437
    social constructionism and, 17, 225–228, 232
    sociology of, 11, 17, 229, 381
    subjectivity and, 230, 231, 234
    toxic online content and, 94
emphasized femininity, 411, 413
empirical research, 49–56, 63–66, 253, 304, 318, 322, 543–544
employment. *See* labor; occupations
encoding/decoding model, 210
environmental issues, 512–523
    climate change, 170, 497, 512, 521, 538–543
    disasters, 282, 498, 517–521
    eco-uncertainty and, 20, 517, 519, 521–523
    fracking, 500, 514
    framing of, 512–513
    inequality, 513–516
    naturework and, 517
    sustainability, 64, 283, 512
environmental justice, 513–514, 522, 523, 534
environmental privilege, 522–523
environmental racism, 513–514, 522
environmental sociology, 493, 514, 516
environmental suffering, 20, 514–516, 521–523
ephemerality, 87–88, 98
Erikson, Kai, 522, 539
essentialism, 53, 165, 387, 408, 415–416, 425, 540
Estes, Carroll L., 136
ethnicity. *See* race and ethnicity
ethnography
    autoethnography, 62, 180–181
    challenges of, 58–59
    Chicago School and, 57, 134, 208, 447–449
    comparative studies, 200

consumer spaces and, 248, 251
data collection and analysis in, 58
disaster research and, 538–539
epistemological ghettos in, 13, 339, 340
fieldwork in, 57, 114, 184, 327
on gender as accomplishment, 409
interpretive studies, 5
interviews in, 58
marked identities and, 13, 339–341
narrative, 62–63, 176, 178, 180–181, 184–185
net-ethnography, 66
organizational, 267
participant observation in, 57, 58, 259, 393
peopled approach to, 12, 198
pragmatism and, 10, 20n2
racial socialization and, 393–394
reflexive standpoint, 13
Simmelian methods of, 11
subcultures and, 208, 211–212, 217
urban, 3, 339, 449
ethnomethodology
on conversational exchanges, 155
gender and, 407–408, 410
language in, 36, 39
philosophical traditions of, 35–36
subcultures and, 214
under-utilization of, 419n3
euergetism, 359
Eves, Alison, 414
existential self, 262–263
existential urgency, 200
exploitation
consumption and, 246
in political situations, 209
power and, 371
secret exhibitions and, 354
in technocratic society, 95
extra-situational relationships, 378–381

F

Facebook
authenticity of profiles, 304
cross-cultural user studies, 282
as news source, 90–91
policing incidents on, 459
PTSD of moderators on, 94
self-presentation on, 303, 309

facework, 93, 153, 155, 157
families. *See also* children
gender socialization in, 406
inequality within, 135
mesodomain analysis of, 133
racial socialization in, 343–344, 390–393
Farberman, Harvey, 129, 136, 225
Faris, Ellsworth, 29, 124
Fausto-Sterling, A., 415
Feagin, Joe, 389, 395, 396n1
feelings. *See* emotions
female masculinity, 412
femininity, 406, 409, 411, 413–414, 418
feminism
Black, 344, 405
critical theory and, 5
encoding/decoding model and, 210
gender theory and, 407–409
intersectionality and, 13, 14
lesbian, 405
radical, 405
shopping malls and, 248–249
socio-ecological resilience and, 495, 503
structural functionalism challenged by, 5
Fenstermaker, Sarah, 13
Ferrara, Emilio, 96
Ferrell, Jeff: *Crimes of Style*, 455
Ferris, Kerry, 202
Fields, Jessica, 377
fieldwork, 55, 57, 61, 114, 184, 327, 481
Fine, Gary Alan
on analytical view of SI, 65
on blending of SI with other perspectives, 1
on future of SI, 129, 137, 139n2
Hughes as influence on, 32
on idioculture, 8, 266, 281
on intersubjectivity, 361
on local contexts, 199
on mesoanalyses, 133
on naturework, 517
on peopled ethnographic studies, 12, 198
on subcultures, 211
First Amendment, 253n1
Fleck, Ludwik, 74, 76
foggy mirror concept, 305
folk devils, 451, 453
Fontana, Andrea, 201

forbidden-fruit mechanism, 359
Force, William Ryan, 1, 8–9, 17, 207, 268
Forman, Tyrone A., 396
Foucault, Michel, 63, 64
Four Wishes, 29
fracking, 500, 514
Francis, Ara A., 8, 16, 162
Frank, Arthur: The Wounded Storyteller: Body, Illness, and Ethics, 181
Frankenberg, Ruth, 345
Frankfurt School, 197
Franks, David, 89–90, 222, 225
Frazier, E. Franklin, 32–33
Freidson, Eliot, 32, 472
Freud, Sigmund, 403
Friedman, Asia, 163, 164
Frye, Northrop, 11
Fuist, Todd Nicholas, 325
Fujimura, Joan, 170
Fuller, Celene, 16, 81
functionalism. *See* structural functionalism

G

Gagnon, John H.: Sexual Conduct: The Social Sources of Human Sexuality, 427–428
gangs, 457–458
Gardner, Robert Owen, 267
Garfinkel, Harold
    on background expectancies, 185
    on gender, 13, 407–408, 415
    intellectual influences on, 36
    on meaning as indexical, 211
    on nothingness, 19, 350–352
    on rule interpretation, 35
    Studies in Ethnomethodology, 74
Garot, Robert, 457–458
Garrison, Spencer, 417
Gauchet, Marcel, 88
gays. *See* LGBTQ+ community
GDP (gross domestic product), 112–113
Geertz, Clifford, 203–204, 221, 226
Geertz, Hildred, 225–226
gender, 402–418. *See also* LGBTQ+ community; men; transgender persons; women
    division of labor by, 246
    embodiments of, 19, 403, 415, 417–418

emotional displays and, 377
future research directions, 418
identity based on, 345, 402–403, 405–406, 415–417
inequality and, 412
as institution or social structure, 409–411
as interactional accomplishment, 408–409
language of, 403–406, 404*f*
meaning-making and, 403, 417
music and, 269
norms related to, 251
performances of, 8, 13, 149, 407, 409, 437
politics of, 170
practices of, 411–416
sexuality and, 433, 435–438
social construction of, 13, 171
socialization and, 392, 406–407
standpoint theories and, 339–340
subcultural identity and, 213, 346
theories of, 13, 406–409, 411, 415, 416
gender difference paradigm, 416
gender neutrality, 406, 415
genderqueer identity, 415
gender roles, 5, 43, 406–408, 433, 436
gender theory, 406–409, 411, 415, 416
generalized other
    culture and, 7, 8, 199
    defined, 7, 41
    environmental, 516
    mass media as, 280
    in music, 262
    in role-taking, 279
    shared meaning and, 7
    standpoint theories and, 340
generic social processes, 11, 128, 135, 136, 138
Gerbner, George, 279
gestures
    digital technologies and, 85, 89, 98
    in performances, 147, 149, 157, 158
    as signifiers of status, 373
    in social constructionism, 163, 226
    in social psychology, 224
Ghidina, Marcia J., 327
Gibson, David R., 499
Gibson, William, 260, 266
Giddens, Anthony, 5, 64, 362n7
Gilbertson, Scott, 92

Gill, Elizabeth, 129
Gitelman, Lisa, 111
Glaser, Barney, 20n2 60, 62, 151, 326, 354, 471
globalization
    disaster research and, 543–544
    economic, 83
    of media, 278, 288
    postmodernism and, 265
    of shopping malls, 251–252
    of SI perspective, 50
global warming. *See* climate change
Glock, Charles Y., 321
Go, Julian, 13, 338–340
Goffman, Erving. *See also* dramaturgical
    perspective
    *Asylums: Essays on the Social Situation of
        Mental Patients and Other Inmates*, 178,
        449
    career concept and, 428
    on communication, 86, 299
    on deviance, 449
    "Expression Games: An Analysis of Doubts
        at Play," 354
    "Felicity's Condition," 35
    Forms of Talk, 179
    Frame Analysis, 179
    on gender construction, 13
    Hughes's relationship with, 34
    on impression management, 153, 498
    on information control, 95
    institutional analyses of, 133
    on interactional hooks, 203
    on interaction orders, 150, 200, 213, 407
    narrative studies and, 177–179
    on nothingness, 19, 350–353
    on orderliness of everyday life, 362n4
    on patients and disease, 469, 471, 472
    on patterns of social difference, 13
    on performances, 3, 8, 152, 302, 407
    The Presentation of Self in Everyday Life, 177,
        373
    on rules, 374
    on secret exhibitions, 354–356
    situation concept of, 227
    on social interactions, 297, 301
    on social organization, 129
    on social relations, 247

*Stigma: Notes on the Management of Spoiled
    Identity*, 178, 449
    on stigmatization, 156–157, 178, 449–450
    on subcultures, 208, 211
    Warner as mentor to, 34–35
Goode, Erich, 453
Google, 90, 92, 95
Gordon, Steven L., 226
Goss, Jon, 245
Gottschalk, Simon, 16, 66, 81, 261, 267, 286
GPS technology, 89, 92, 358
Gramsci, Antonio, 209, 210
Great Recession (2007–2009), 283
Green, Ashley, 13–14, 19, 402
Greenblatt, Stephen, 231
Greenfield, Adam, 92
gross domestic product (GDP), 112–113
Grotius, Hugo, 42
grounded theory research
    analytic basis of, 20n2
    concept-driven research vs., 73
    data collection and analysis in, 55, 60, 61
    description of, 59–60
    fieldwork in, 61, 327
    formulations of, 41, 60, 62
    interviews in, 61
    pragmatism and, 10
    sensitizing concepts in, 60
    steps in, 60–62
group identity, 154, 181–182, 186, 268
Gubrium, Jaber F., 16–17, 168, 175, 182, 184, 187,
    270, 473
Guenther, Antony, 117
Gurwitsch, Aron, 36
Gusfield, Joseph R.: Symbolic Crusade: Status
    Politics and the American Temperance
    Movement, 450

H

Habermas, Jürgen, 5, 34, 64
habitus, 230n4 373, 515
Hacking, Ian, 112
Haedicke, Michael, 136
Haenfler, Ross, 212
Hagerman, Margaret A., 12, 14, 19, 343–344,
    386, 392–393, 396
Halberstam, Jack, 412

INDEX

Hall, Jeffrey, 301
Hall, Peter M., 126–131, 134, 136, 139n1 502
Hall, Stuart, 209–211, 215
Hallett, Tim, 133, 341
Hamilton, Alexander, 40
Hamilton, Laura, 414
Hannigan, John A., 534
Harland, Richard, 225
Harris, Scott, 135
Harvey, Daina Cheyenne, 12, 20, 512
Haslam, Nick, 93, 94
Hassan, Robert, 84
Hayek, Friedrich, 36, 40
healthcare, 468–486. *See also* disease;
    medicine
  awareness contexts in, 151
  communication in, 474–483
  e-heath, 478–479
  holistic approach to, 470, 474–475,
      480–483
  implications of SI for, 19–20
  intensive care units, 484–485
  negotiated interpretations in, 483–486
  patient autobiographies in, 473
  patient-doctor interactions in, 469–470,
      475–483
  patient's negotiation of status in,
      471–472
  practice improvements, 474–475
  professional socialization in, 472
  quantitative thresholds in, 112
  SI perspectives on, 470–475
  technologies in, 476–479
health literacy, 480
Hebdige, Dick, 210, 213, 215
hegemony
  Bourdieu on, 33
  femininity and, 413–414
  gender and, 409
  Gramsci on, 209, 210
  masculinity and, 214, 411–413, 433, 437
  moral narratives and, 454
  subcultures and, 212–214
Heimann, Thorsten, 539
Heimer, Carol, 474
Henrich, Joe, 338
Herman-Kinney, Nancy J., 318

hermeneutics, 198, 531
Hertzler, Joyce O., 28
Hess, David, 170
Hicks, Allison M., 328
hierarchies
  challenges to, 341
  as constraint on agency, 129
  of identities, 322
  peer, 346–347
  of power, 389
  racial, 343, 386, 395–396
  sexuality and, 425
  social constructionism on, 172
  subcultures and, 214
Highmore, Ben, 230
HIV/AIDS, 168, 170, 405, 440, 470
Ho, X. X. S., 269
Hochschild, Arlie R., 153, 226, 539
Hodgson, John, 148
Hogan, Bernie, 309
Hoggart, Richard, 209
Holmes, Christopher, 170
Holmes, Oliver Wendell, 223
Holstein, James, 168, 182, 187, 270
Holyfield, Lori, 268
homelessness, 182, 393
homophobia, 412, 437
homosexuality. *See* LGBTQ+ community
hooks, bell, 14
Hord, Levi C. R., 415
Horowitz, Ruth, 134, 135
Hoskin, Rhea Ashley, 414
Hughes, Diane, 391
Hughes, Everett
  career concept and, 428
  Chicago School and, 2, 30, 208
  Goffman's relationship with, 34
  institutional analyses of, 133
  role in invention of SI, 30
  on sociology of occupations, 31–32, 42
  structural interactionism of, 30
Hull House (Chicago), 32
Hume, David, 37, 40, 41, 118
Hurricane Katrina (2005), 515–523, 532
Hutcheson, Frances, 40
hydraulic fracturing (fracking), 500, 514
hypermodernism, 16, 82–84, 89, 95

I

Ibarra, Peter, 167, 169
Ibert, Oliver, 540–541
ICTs (information and communication technologies), 18, 296–301, 303
idealization, 153, 158, 303–306, 311, 437
identity. *See also* self
  Black, 342, 343
  collective (*see* collective identity)
  construction of, 8, 17–18, 165, 231, 246–251
  consumption and, 17, 209, 242
  critical theory and, 6
  deviant, 208
  disaster perception and, 537–538
  gender, 345, 402–403, 405–406, 415–417
  group, 154, 181–182, 186, 268
  marked (*see* marked identities)
  mass-media influences on, 280
  meaning-making and, 13–14
  moral, 323, 345–346
  music and, 17–18, 262–265, 269
  myth of, 249
  narrative, 11, 189
  new-media influences on, 285–286
  in non-places, 244
  performances of, 8, 13, 146–149, 154, 347, 348
  personal, 8, 11, 249, 270, 328, 472
  racial/ethnic, 170–171, 268, 344–345, 386, 390, 394
  religion and, 322–325
  sexual, 402, 405, 413–415, 429, 438–439
  social (*see* social identity)
  sociology of, 2, 337
  subcultural, 213, 346–347
  transgender, 170–171, 416–417
  transsexual, 182–183
  unmarked (*see* unmarked identities)
identity work
  gender and, 402–403, 405, 406
  narrative studies and, 183
  oppositional, 323
  sexuality and, 433, 440
  social performance and, 146
  symbolization as, 326
idioculture, 8, 18, 258, 264, 266, 281
illness. *See* disease
Immergut, Matthew, 324

impression management
  in dramaturgical perspective, 146, 152–154, 156, 158
  gender performance and, 407
  in online interactions, 304–306, 311
  in politics, 136, 154
  resilience and, 498–499, 503
  sexuality and, 439
improvisation, 148, 151, 199–200, 260, 266–267
Indian Ocean Tsunami (2004), 532
inequality
  disaster vulnerability and, 532, 533, 540
  double consciousness and, 14
  dynamics of, 6, 135, 340
  economic, 135
  eco-uncertainty and, 20
  environmental, 513–516
  in families, 135
  gender, 412
  interactional, 335, 336
  legitimization of, 149
  negotiated orders and, 135
  in new-media access, 283
  of power, 247
  racial, 134, 342–343, 386, 393–394, 513–514
  sexual, 412
  shopping and, 250
  social organization of, 130
  standpoint theories and, 12–13
  structural, 12, 134, 347, 373, 394, 532–533, 543
inertia, 113, 116–117, 357
influenza pandemic (1918), 36
information and communication technologies (ICTs), 18, 296–301, 303
infra-humanization, 81, 92–99, 98*f*
interaction orders, 13, 150–151, 155, 157, 200, 213, 407
interactions. *See* online interactions; social interactions
International Sociological Association, 5
internet. *See also* online interactions; social media
  access to, 85
  harassment on, 94
  music and, 260–261, 264, 267
  subcultures and, 215–216, 260–261
  third revolution, 91
  VoIP services and, 281–282

562   INDEX

interpersonal relationships, 2, 298, 502
interpersonal scripts, 428
interpretive reproduction theory, 392
interpretive social theory, 419n1. *See also*
    symbolic interactionism
intersectionality
    feminism and, 13, 14
    marked/unmarked identities and, 338,
        343–348
    SI and, 338, 343–348
intersubjectivity
    in concept-driven research, 76
    digital technologies and, 90, 92, 98
    disruptions upon social situations and, 361
    nothingness and, 351
    online disclosures and, 307
    of personal experiences, 17
    of quantitative measurement, 16, 104, 106,
        110, 113–119
    reality and, 98, 327
interviews, 54–56, 58, 61, 248, 327, 393
intrapsychic scripts, 428
Irwin, John, 211, 264
Islam and Muslims, 324
Itzigsohn, José, 342–343

J
Jackson, Kenneth, 244
Jacobs, Bruce, 458
Jago, Barbara J., 181
James, William
    on music-at-once, 262
    pragmatism and, 223
    on religion, 317
    role in invention of SI, 28, 124
    self as conceptualized by, 2
    on social relations, 247
Jauréguiberry, Francis, 86
Jaworski, G. D., 34
Jeffers, Greg, 341
Jefferson, Tony, 209
Jenner, Caitlyn, 170
Jerolmack, Colin, 202
Jews and Judaism, 203
Joas, Hans, 64
jobs. *See* labor; occupations
Johnson, Boris, 170

Johnson, Deborah, 391
Johnson, Denise, 414, 417
Joinson, Adam, 309

K
Kant, Immanuel, 7, 37–39
Karp, David, 269
    *Speaking of Sadness: Depression,
        Disconnection, and the Meanings of
        Illness*, 181
Kato, Yuki, 251
Katrina (hurricane 2005), 515–523, 532
Katz, Elihu, 277
Katz, Jack: *Seduction of Crime*, 456–457
Kaufman, Peter, 324
Kelvin, Lord (William Thomson), 118
Kempner, Joanna, 170
Kessler, Dave, 234
Kessler, Suzanne J., 408, 415
Kim, Pyungho, 284
King, Nigel, 414
Kinsey, Alfred, 112, 427
Kitsuse, John I., 449, 534
Kleinman, Sherryl, 211, 377
Klinenberg, Eric, 535
knowledge
    access to, 63
    as capital, 480
    cultural, 211, 379, 544
    empirical, 42
    generation of, 13, 61, 63, 338–339
    institutional, 185
    Kant on types of, 37
    logical structures of, 38
    marijuana-related, 109
    medical, 468–470, 472, 479
    racial, 390
    of reality, 37, 50–51, 56, 62, 64
    ritualized displays of, 214
    scientific, 170, 479, 532, 543
    self-knowledge, 231, 305
    shared, 12, 105, 113–114, 211, 374, 379, 534
    in social constructionism, 162–164, 167, 169,
        225
    sociology of, 223
    statistical, 117
    Stoic views of, 43

Komarovsky, Mirra, 407
Konradi, Amanda: "I Don't Have to Be Afraid of You": Rape Survivors' Emotion Management in Court, 459–460
Kotarba, Joseph A., 9, 17–18, 258, 261, 262, 268, 271, 474–475
Kroeber, Alfred, 31
Kuhn, Manford H., 427
Kula, Witold, 106
Kusenbach, Margarethe, 20, 529, 537

L

labeling theory, 260, 446–449, 452–460, 462n3 480
labor. *See also* occupations
    division of, 31, 40, 42, 129, 246
    feminized forms of, 216
    nets of accountability in, 378–379
    power structure and, 134
Langer, Suzanne K., 221
language. *See also* communication; conversation analysis
    of analysis, 12
    for categorization, 108
    causal, 40
    of ecology, 31
    emotions and, 225–226
    in ethnomethodology, 36, 39
    of gender, 403–406, 404f
    inter-group, 105
    of LGBTQ+ community, 403–406, 404f, 431
    oppositional, 214
    perception shaped by, 222
    philosophy of, 326
    power of, 336
    of quantification, 118
    reflective intelligence and, 224
    of role-taking, 165
    of sexuality, 403–406, 404f, 429–433
    shared meaning and, 163, 278
    of social constructionism, 170–171, 232
    as socially shared system, 38
    of sociology, 63, 113, 137
    of violence, 437
Lanier, Jaron, 97
Lara, Irene, 414

Latinos/Latinas
    communication preferences, 282
    music scenes and, 265, 266
    racial socialization among, 390
    urban ethnographies of, 339
Latour, Bruno, 170, 540, 542
Leap, Braden, 20, 346, 493
Leblanc, Lauraine, 212
Lee, Jooyoung, 199–200
Lefebvre, Henri, 230
Lemert, Edwin, 471
    Social Pathology, 448
Lengel, Robert, 298
Lepenies, Philipp, 112–113
Lerner, Steve: *Sacrifice Zones: The Front Lines of Toxic Chemical Exposure in the United States*, 514
lesbians. *See* LGBTQ+ community
Lever, Janet: *Soccer Madness*, 233
Lévi-Strauss, Claude, 27, 198
Lewis, Amanda, 393–394, 396
Leyens, Jacques-Philippe, 93
LGBTQ+ community. *See also* transgender persons
    coming-out narratives, 186
    feminism and, 405
    language of, 403–406, 404f, 431
    masculinity and femininity in, 412, 414
    racism within, 405
    religion and, 319, 328
    sexual identity expression in, 439
    stigmatization of, 453
    subcultures and, 213–214
    in suffrage movement, 402
Li, Qian, 9, 18, 296
libertarian paternalism, 352, 357, 359
Lichterman, Paul, 8, 199
Liebow, Elliot: *Tell Them Who I Am*, 182
life course model, 269–270, 389
life stories, 56, 177, 417
Link, Bruce G., 324
Lipsius, Justus, 42
literature, representation of society through, 117–118
Litt, Eden, 308
Liu, Sida, 32
Lofland, John, 319

564   INDEX

Lombardo, Carmelo, 19, 350
Longstaff, Howard P., 28
looking glass self, 41, 149, 297, 449
Lorber, Judith, 410
Loseke, Donileen, 186, 227, 453–454
Loughnan, Steve, 93
Luckenbill, David, 134
Luckmann, Thomas
  on paramount reality, 147
  on religion, 317
  The Social Construction of Reality, 7, 74, 162,
    164–167, 225, 534
  on synthesis between Mead and Schutz, 35
Lukes, Steven, 380
Lutfey, Karen, 474
Lyman, Stanford M., 154
Lynch, Michael Patrick, 95

M

Maclean, Annie Marion, 32, 341
macro phenomena, 125–139
  culture, 139n1
  inequality, 134–135
  market structures, 135–136, 139
  micro-macro divide, 122, 126, 127, 129, 138,
    139
  negotiated orders and, 127
  power structures, 134
  SI's capacity for analysis of, 125, 128, 131, 132,
    137, 139n3
  social change, 135, 139
  social networks, 133–134
  social organization, 132–133
  social policy, 136
Madison, James, 40
Mahmoud, Alessandro, 268
Maines, David R., 124, 126–127, 131, 137, 196,
    200, 326, 497
Malinowski, Bronislaw, 35
malls. *See* shopping and shopping malls
Manning, Philip, 355–356
Marder, Ben, 309
marginal self, 263–264
marijuana, 109–110, 209, 260, 448
marked identities, 335–348
  epistemological concerns and, 335, 338–342
  ethnography and, 13, 339–341

intersectionality and, 338, 343–348
  sensitizing concepts and, 336–338
  socialization and, 343–344
  standpoint theories and, 339–340
marriage, 135, 407
Martin, Patricia, 410–411, 419n4
Martin, Peter, 134, 370
Marvasti, Amir B., 16–17, 175
Marwick, Alice, 306, 309–310
Marx, Karl and Marxism
  challenges to, 33
  on class struggle, 207, 210, 213
  critical theory and, 12
  on false consciousness, 210
  neo-Marxism, 197, 209
  on power, 368
  psychoanalytic, 210
  semiotic, 211
  on subcultures, 207, 209–211, 213
masculinity. *See also* men
  displays of, 408–409
  female, 412
  of gang members, 458
  hegemonic, 214, 411–413, 433, 437
  as homophobia, 412
  homosexual, 412
  hybrid, 412
  normative, 406
  sexuality and, 433, 434, 437, 438
  subcultural practice and, 213–214, 216
  subordinate, 411
  vicarious, 412
Mason-Schrock, Douglas, 182–183, 417
mass media
  agenda-setting role of, 287
  cultural scripts and, 148–149
  defined, 275
  feedback channels, 287
  gatekeeping role of, 286
  as generalized other, 280
  healthcare and, 477
  interpretation of messages from, 277–278
  new-media influences on, 286–288
  power of, 210
  self and identity influenced by, 280
  SI perspectives on, 276–280, 288–289
  in social reality construction, 278–280

sociocultural influences on, 277–278
subcultures and, 215–216
uses of, 277
Mathers, Lain A. B., 346
Mayer-Schönberger, Viktor, 95
Mayhew, Henry: *Life and Labour of the London Poor*, 182
McCallion, Michael J., 326
McCarthy, E. Doyle, 17, 221, 225
McCorkel, Jill A., 460
McDowell, Amy D., 325
McGinty, Patrick J. W., 12, 16, 122, 136, 267
McKenna, Wendy, 408
Mead, George Herbert
  on anticipation, 496–497
  on consciousness, 9
  on cooperation, 372
  on emergence of meaning, 197
  on experience of time, 9
  on generalized other, 7, 41, 279, 340, 516
  German influences on, 36, 38
  on "I" and "me," 10, 149, 262
  on language of role-taking, 165
  legacy of, 29, 35, 223
  Mind, Self, and Society, 369
  The Philosophy of the Act, 369
  The Philosophy of the Present, 369
  on power, 368–371, 381, 382n1
  on reflexive self, 2, 3, 149, 188, 262
  role in invention of SI, 28, 29, 124
  situation concept of, 227
  on social organization, 123–124
  social psychology of, 4, 29–30, 166, 223–225
  on social relations, 247
  on social roles, 428
Meadow, Tey, 418
meaning. *See also* meaning-making; shared meaning
  analysis of, 58, 61
  co-construction of, 2
  of consumption, 243, 247, 251, 253
  emergence of, 197
  of emotions, 222, 229, 232
  in healthcare, 474
  as indexical, 211
  life course model of, 269–270, 389
  looking glass self and, 41

of marijuana use, 260
mediators of, 202
of music, 261–263
performance of, 4
polysemousness, 210
postmodern sources of, 263
quantitative measurement and, 12, 105, 108–113
racial, 213, 343, 347, 386–389, 394–396
religion and, 315–317, 327
as sensitizing concept, 196
settings in shaping of, 3
sexuality and, 425–432, 436, 440–441
social construction of, 167, 225
of social objects, 224
structural hermeneutics, 198
meaning-making
  categorization and generalization in, 341–342
  culture and, 198–200, 203–204
  disaster perception and, 538
  by ecological precariat, 515
  gender and, 403, 417
  identity and, 13–14
  moral narratives and, 446
  power relations and, 14
  quantitative measurement and, 12, 105
  race and, 386–389, 394–396
  in research process, 10, 16, 53–55
  as sensitizing concept, 196
  social interactions and, 4, 18–19, 109, 276, 296
  subcultures and, 17, 207, 211
  surface tensions and, 516
measurement. *See* quantitative measurement
mechanistic infra-humanization, 93–94, 96
media, 275–289. *See also* mass media; new media
Media Evolution Theory, 280–281
medicine. *See also* disease; healthcare
  knowledge of, 468–470, 472, 479
  paternalistic model of, 469
  sex and gender in, 403, 405, 415, 417
Mellinger, Wayne, 474
Meltzer, Bernard N., 29
men. *See also* gender; masculinity
  as "badasses," 456–458
  gender roles for, 406–407
  marriage for, 135, 407

Menchik, Daniel, 308
Merton, Robert, 74, 208, 353
mesodomain analysis, 127–128, 133, 138, 139n3
mesostructures, 126–127, 129, 196, 200
Messerschmidt, James W., 414
meta-power, 128, 134, 139, 502
Michels, Robert, 368
micro phenomena, 122, 125–127, 129, 136–139
Mikkola, Pennanen, 475
Milkie, Melissa A., 280
Mill, John Stuart, 41
Miller, Daniel: Shopping, Place, Identity, 250
Miller, David: George Herbert Mead: Self,
     Language, and the World, 369
Mills, C. Wright, 5, 178–179, 224, 428
Mills, Charles, 387
Mische, Ann, 9–10
Mischke, Kelsey, 12, 19, 368
Mises, Ludwig von, 36
Monachesi, Elio D., 28
Montesquieu
     Persian Letters, 118
     The Spirit of the Laws, 118
moral career, 157, 178, 323, 471
moral entrepreneurs, 168, 448, 450–453, 455,
     460–461
moral identity, 323, 345–346
moral narratives, 446, 448, 450–455, 458–461
moral order, 7, 183, 202, 209, 345
moral panics, 451, 453
moral self, 459, 461
moral transgression, 450, 462n2
Morrione, Thomas J., 127
Morris, Maeghan: "Things to Do with
     Shopping Centres," 248–249
Morrow, Betty H., 540
Mueller, Jennifer C., 395
Müller, Thaddeus, 12, 19, 263, 446
Murthy, Dhiraj, 310
music, 258–271. See also specific genres
     authenticity and, 268
     communities and, 264–266
     drug use and, 260–261
     gender and, 269
     heavy metal music, 213, 216, 261
     hip hop, 199–200, 213, 216, 269
     identity and, 17–18, 262–265, 269

idioculture and, 266
improvisation in, 199–200, 260, 266–267
internet and, 260–261, 264, 267
jazz music, 209, 259–260, 266
life-as-music approach, 270
life course model of, 269–270
meaning of, 261–263
punk music, 210, 212–213, 216–217, 261, 268
religion and, 269
rock music, 261, 263, 265
role in social life, 18, 258, 271
self and, 262–264, 270
sense of place and, 265, 267
sensitizing concepts and, 259, 270
social interactions and, 266–267
social organization and, 267–268
social scenes and, 264–265
subcultures and, 259–262
Muslims and Islam, 324
mystification, 156, 158
myths, 29, 127, 147–148, 175, 210, 249, 440

N

narrative identity, 11, 189
narrative studies, 175–189. See also stories and
     storytelling
     cautions regarding, 188–189
     conversational, 176, 177, 179, 182–185
     development of, 17, 176–179
     environment and, 62, 184–187
     ethnographic, 62–63, 176, 178, 180–181,
          184–185
     forms and aims of, 175–176
     of group identity, 181–182
     of power and practice, 186–187
     of self-construction, 179–186
     strategic, 176–179, 183, 186
Nash, Jeffrey and Dina, 269
Nass, Gilbert, 117
naturework, 517
negotiated orders
     in healthcare, 474
     inequality and, 135
     macro phenomena and, 127
     mesostructures and, 200
     social organization and, 124, 126–127, 129, 133
     social scene performance and, 151

net-ethnography, 66
networks. *See* social networks
neutralization, 448, 461
Newmahr, Staci: Playing on the Edge: Sadomasochism, Risk, and Intimacy, 455–456
new media. *See also* digital technologies
   agenda-setting role of, 287
   defined, 275–276
   feedback channels, 288
   interpretation of, 281–283
   mass media influenced by, 286–288
   research methodology and, 65, 66
   self and identity influenced by, 285–286
   SI perspectives on, 280–286, 288–289
   social change and, 283–284
   sociocultural influences on, 281–283
   uses of, 281–283
New Orleans
   Chalmette Refinery, 518–521, 523nn2–4
   Hurricane Katrina (2005), 515–523, 532
Nightingale, Florence, 27, 30
9/11 terrorist attacks (2001), 532
non-binary identity, 403, 406, 415, 417
Norgaard, Kari M., 500, 516, 537–538
norms. *See also* social norms
   acquisition through socialization, 7
   in consumer spaces, 245, 247, 248
   conversational, 499–500
   cultural, 17, 199, 214, 277, 281, 325
   gender-based, 251
   interaction orders and, 150
   for new-media interactions, 284
   religious, 320–323, 325
   sexual, 427, 433, 436
   speech-related, 199
   subcultural, 214, 216
   transgression of, 253
nothingness, 350–362
   CSAs and, 19, 352–356, 361–362, 362n7
   default options and, 19, 357–359, 363n10
   engineered appearances of, 353–356
   nudge theory and, 352, 356–361
   secret exhibitions and, 354–356, 358
   types of, 350–352
Novais, Janine de, 395

Nowakowski, Alexandra C. H., 326
nudge theory, 352, 356–361, 363n9

O

obesity, 107, 112, 476
O'Brien, Jodi, 319
occupations. *See also* labor
   prop objects and, 152
   sacralization of, 203
   service-related, 200, 259
   sociology of, 31–32, 42
Ocejo, Richard, 200
Olesen, Virginia, 27, 30, 35
Omi, Michael, 388, 396n1
Omtzigt, Pieter, 96
online interactions, 296–311
   audiences in, 30, 302, 305–311
   authenticity of, 304–306, 309, 311
   blurring of private and public spaces in, 309–310
   context collapse and, 308–310
   disadvantages of, 93–95
   future research directions, 311
   gleaning information through, 299–300
   idealization and, 303–306, 311
   impression management in, 304–306, 311
   meaning-making through, 296
   media and cue richness for, 298–299
   performances in, 302–303
   presence of others in, 297–302, 310
   self-disclosure in, 303, 304, 306, 309
   self-presentation in, 302–306, 309, 311
   semiotic tactics for use in, 299
   technical affordances and, 298, 301–302, 307, 309–310
Orcutt, James D., 95
organizational culture, 128, 133, 136, 502
organizational ethnography, 267
Orlov, Alexander M., 354
Ovid: *Metamorphoses*, 362n6

P

pandemics
   COVID-19, 139–140n3, 282, 542
   influenza (1918), 36
pariah femininities, 413
Pariser, Eli, 91–92

568 INDEX

Park, Namkee, 281–282
Park, Robert E.
Chicago School and, 2, 3, 31, 208
German influences on, 36–38
role in invention of SI, 28, 30, 124
on sexuality, 426
structural interactionism of, 30
Parker, Scott, 480
Parsons, Talcott, 2, 35, 340
participant observation, 57, 58, 259, 393
Pascoe, C. J., 346, 412–413
Pasteur, Louis, 74
paternalism, 352, 357, 359, 469
Patil, Vrushali, 418
Pawluch, Dorothy, 167–168
Peirce, Charles Sanders, 2, 10, 21n3 223
perceptions
Aristotle on, 43
of beauty, 270
of climate change, 539
of disasters, 534–538, 540–541
of gender, 409
in improvisation, 266
Kant on, 37–39
language in shaping of, 222
of marked/unmarked identities, 337
of nothingness, 351, 352
of place, 496
of poverty, 108
of presence of others, 297–298, 301–302, 310
of reality, 92, 278, 280, 371, 377
of religion, 323
of risk, 163, 497, 536–538, 540–541
self-perception, 35, 449, 461
of sex differences, 163–164
of shopping, 249
social nature of, 163–164
performances. *See also* dramaturgical
perspective; social actors
accounts of, 154
authenticity of, 147, 148, 151, 177
of class, 347
cynical, 148, 153, 155
defined, 147, 152
disclaimers regarding, 153–154
of gender, 8, 13, 149, 407, 409, 437
gestures in, 147, 149, 157, 158

hidden, 156–158
of identity, 8, 13, 146–149, 154, 347, 348
improvisation in, 148, 151
individual, 151–154
of meaning, 4
misrepresentation in, 156
in online interactions, 302–303
of race, 8, 347
religious, 321, 322
remedial interchanges in, 155–156
response cries in, 157
role distance in, 156, 158
of self, 3, 8, 16, 149
of sexuality, 8, 19, 437, 438
in shopping malls, 252
sincere, 148, 153, 155
slips out of character, 148, 157–158
social, 13, 16, 146, 148–149, 226
of social scenes, 146, 150–151
supportive interchanges in, 155
tact in, 146, 148, 155, 158
teamwork in, 154–158
tie signs in, 154–155
Perinbanayagam, R. S.: "Definition of the
Situation," 227
personal identity, 8, 11, 249, 270, 328, 472
personalization, 62, 91–92, 96, 298
Peterson, Pete, 264–265
Peterson, Richard, 197
Pfeffer, Carla, 414, 416
Phelan, Jo C., 324
Phillips, Cynthia, 319
Piaget, Jean, 87
pigeon flyers, 202–203
Piliavin, Irving, 449
Pilnick, Alison, 513
Piven, Frances Fox, 208
place
in interaction orders, 157
non-places, 243–244
perceptions of, 496
racial socialization and, 392–393
sense of, 18, 249, 250, 265, 267
Plummer, Ken
Narrative Power, 186–187
on narrative studies of self-construction,
185–186

Sexual Stigma, 450
on stories, 175, 182, 187, 188
poetry as representation of society, 117, 118
Pogrebin, Mark R., 458
Polanyi, M., 33
policing, 449, 457–459
politics
    of ambiguity, 77
    disasters and, 535, 543
    discourse of, 198
    ecology and, 495, 503
    of gender, 170
    impression management in, 136, 154
    post-truth, 170
    power structure in, 134
    of race, 170
    of SI tradition, 32
    of social constructionism, 169–172
    socialization and, 392
    subcultures and, 212
    temporal disorganization in, 85
    violence and, 213
positivism, 2, 5, 71, 314, 425, 440
postmodernism
    consumption and, 242
    critical theory and, 12, 34
    globalization and, 265
    in qualitative research, 10, 62–63
    self and, 285–286, 305
    social constructionism and, 34
    sources of meaning in, 263
    subjectivity and, 242
    theoretical expansion, 33–34
poststructuralism, 149, 227, 409
poverty, 31, 73, 107–108, 513
power, 368–382
    of agency, 231
    analytic, 91, 345
    as collective transaction, 134
    communication and, 63
    consciousness and, 372, 380
    culture in relation to, 213
    of default options, 363n10
    defined, 369–372, 379, 381
    disaster vulnerability and, 532, 533
    double consciousness of self and, 14
    dynamics of, 6, 15, 65, 340, 532

environmental suffering and, 521
exercise of, 369–382
exploitation and, 371
faces of, 380
of globalized media, 278, 288
hierarchies of, 389
inequality of, 247
of language, 336
latent, 209, 371
of mass media, 210
mesodomain analysis of, 127, 128
meta-power, 128, 134, 139, 502
of myths, 210
narrative studies of, 186–187
ontological roots of, 19, 368
in political processes, 134
of racial socialization, 19
resistance and, 371, 372, 381
of semiotics, 344
social, 12, 209, 335, 338, 345, 347
standpoint theories and, 12–13
subcultures and, 207
totalitarian, 83
unmarked identities and, 338–340, 343, 345, 346
pragmatism
    agency and, 5, 9–10
    American, 221, 223, 316–317, 427–428
    Chicago School and, 1, 9, 177, 426
    culture and, 7, 8, 10, 21n3 148
    in disaster research, 530
    ethnography and, 10, 20n2
    in mainstream sociology, 4–6
    religion and, 316–317
    renewed engagement with, 9–11
    sexuality and, 427–428
    social, 1, 17, 221, 223–224
    subjectivity and, 223, 224
prejudice. *See* discrimination and bias
Presser, Lois: "Violent Offenders, Moral Selves: Constructing Identities and Accounts in the Research Interview," 183–185
Preves, Sharon K., 415
Project Blowed (hip hop collective), 199–200
Project for the New American Century (PNAC), 455
Propp, Vladimir, 11

570 INDEX

Proust, Marcel, 72
Prus, Robert, 11, 43, 134, 249, 320
Psaroudakis, Irene, 18, 314
pseudo-gemeinschaft, defined, 353
psychology. *See also* social psychology
  cultural influences on, 222
  marked/unmarked identities in, 338
  of religion, 314, 322
  social constructionist movement in, 225
  temporal disorganization and, 85
  theoretical disputes with sociology, 29
Pufendorf, Samuel von, 42
Purcell, Kristen, 107
Pyke, Karen, 414

Q

qualitative research. *See also* ethnography;
    grounded theory research
  bottom-up approach to, 4
  data collection in, 55
  in disaster studies, 530
  interviews, 54–56, 58, 61, 248, 393
  legitimization of, 56, 64
  in mainstream sociology, 5
  meaning-making and, 16
  narrative studies, 17
  postmodernism in, 10, 62–63
  pragmatism and, 10
  prevalence of use in SI, 52
quantitative measurement, 104–119
  collective nature of, 106, 109–113
  communication through, 105, 110, 111
  conventions of, 106, 113, 114, 117
  inertia and, 113, 116–117, 357
  intersubjectivity of, 16, 104, 106, 110, 113–119
  meaning and, 12, 105, 108–113
  operationalization and, 50, 51
  representations of society and, 117–118
  rigid-mindedness of, 108
  single-mindedness of, 104, 107
  social life and, 109, 119
  as socio-cognitive process, 105–108
  splitting by measuring process, 104, 107
  statistical treatment of variables in, 53
quantitative research. *See also* quantitative
    measurement
  data collection in, 55

in disaster studies, 530
in mainstream sociology, 5, 105
positivist approaches to, 2
prevalence of use in SI, 52
rites of researchers in, 115
Quarantelli, Enrico (Henry), 530
Quarry, Neville, 249
queer theory, 403, 405, 409, 415, 416. *See also*
    LGBTQ+ community

R

race and ethnicity, 386–396. See also racism;
    specific racial and ethnic groups
  children's ideas of, 394–395
  femininity and, 414
  hierarchies and, 343, 386, 395–396
  identity based on, 170–171, 268, 344–345,
    386, 390, 394
  inequality and, 134, 342–343, 386, 393–394,
    513–514
  macro-level structures of, 14
  marked/unmarked identities and, 337, 343
  meaning and, 213, 343, 347, 386–389,
    394–396
  performances of, 8, 347
  politics of, 170
  racial formation theory, 388, 396n1
  skin-color privilege and, 373
  social construction of, 14, 171, 172, 386–389
  socialization and, 14, 19, 343–344, 390–396
  standpoint theories and, 339–340
  subcultural identity and, 213, 346
  transracialism, 170–172
  urban ecology on, 208
racism
  environmental, 513–514, 522
  institutional, 386, 389, 394
  justifications for, 171
  in LGBTQ+ community, 405
  meaning-making and, 389
  sense of self affected by, 395
  in social interactions, 343, 344
  strategies for countering, 391
Ramirez, Michael, 264
rape, 434, 459–460
Rapinoe, Megan (Maggie), 233–234
Ratzan, Marcia, 480

Rawls, Ann, 178–179, 350, 351, 362n2
Ray, Victor, 339
Rayner, Steve, 537
reality. *See also* social reality
  disasters and, 534
  empirical, 56, 60, 62, 123
  frames and definitions of, 375–377, 380–382, 512
  intersubjective, 98, 327
  knowledge of, 37, 50–51, 56, 62, 64
  multiform, 104, 107
  objective reflections of, 53, 55
  perceptions of, 92, 278, 280, 371, 377
  performance of, 147–149, 151
  postmodernism and, 34
  sexuality and, 425
  social constructionism and, 162–170, 225
  subcultures and, 209, 214
Rebonato, Riccardo, 359
recessions, 112, 283, 403
Redfield, Robert, 28, 31
Reed, Lou, 263
reflexive self, 2, 3, 11, 149, 188, 262
Reid, Thomas, 40
religion and spirituality, 314–328. *See also* *specific religions*
  dualism of self-other and, 323–324
  in everyday life, 203
  fundamentalism and, 83
  future research directions, 327–328
  identity and, 322–325
  literature review, 318–319
  meaning and, 315–317, 327
  music and, 269
  negative behavior held in check by, 94
  pragmatism and, 316–317
  privatization of, 317
  psychology of, 314, 322
  self and, 319–325
  social constructionism and, 320, 326–327
  sociology of, 314–316, 320, 322, 326, 327
  stigmatization and, 323–326
  taxonomies of, 38
  worship as collective practice, 148
research methodology, 49–66. *See also* qualitative research; quantitative research
  Blumerian orientation, 49–52

concept-driven, 16, 70–78
data collection and analysis, 55–56
empirical, 49–56, 63–66, 253, 304, 318, 322, 543–544
meaning-making and, 10, 16, 53–55
mixed methods, 56, 66
objectives of research and, 53–54
position of researcher and, 54–55
post-Blumerian, 56–63
surveys, 50–51, 77, 393, 497
theoretical propositions and, 56
theory-driven vs. data-driven, 70–71
resilience, 493–503
  children and, 391
  conversation analysis and, 499–500
  creative interactions and, 495–500
  disasters and, 532, 537, 540–544
  environmental inequalities and, 515
  environmental privilege and, 522
  impression management and, 498–499, 503
  institutional and organizational impacts on, 500–503
  interaction rituals and, 458
  socio-ecological theory of, 493–495
  temporality and, 496–498, 500
resistance
  default options and, 357
  of empirical world, 51
  to external influences, 362
  femininity as, 418
  homosexual masculinity as, 412
  to innovations, 116
  music as form of, 263
  political, 406
  power and, 371, 372, 381
  subcultures and, 207, 210, 212–214
  transgression of norms as, 253
Reynolds, Larry T., 318
Richards, Ernest, 148
Richardson, Glenn W., Jr., 287
Richardson, Laurel, 62
Ridgeway, Cecilia, 410
Riggins, Stephen H., 152
Rinaldi, Cirus, 19, 425
risk, perceptions of, 163, 497, 536–538, 540–541
Risman, Barbara, 410
Ritchey, Ferris: Statistical Imagination, 116

572   INDEX

Roberts, J. Timmons, 523
Robinson, Laura, 305
Rock, Paul, 37–38
role-taking. *See also* gender roles; social roles
  benefits of, 94
  generalized other in, 279
  in healthcare, 479, 482, 485
  lack of skills for, 95, 98
  language of, 165
  religion and, 322
  in research process, 54
Romero, George Andrew, 243
Rosa, Hartmut, 83
Rose, Arnold, 134
Rosenberg, Morris, 304
Ruiz-Junco, Natalia, 134, 370
rules
  digital technologies and, 88, 97
  of impression management, 306
  localized interpretation of, 35
  normative, 374–375, 378, 381, 382
  in performances, 153, 154
  in power relationships, 128
  procedural, 374, 375, 378, 381, 382
  quantitative measurement and, 106
  of racial ancestry, 337
  religious, 320–322, 327
  as shared meaning structures, 197
  in shopping malls, 250–252
  social constructionism and, 167
  social scenes and, 150
  strain theory on, 208
  subcultures and, 260
Rushkoff, Douglas, 88, 94
Russell, John D., 134
Rutter, Jason, 305

S

Sabetta, Lorenzo, 19, 350
Saguy, Abigail C., 415
Salcedo, Rodrigo, 252
Salvini, Andrea, 10, 15–16, 18, 49, 134, 314
same-sex relationships. *See* LGBTQ+
  community
Samuel, Sajay, 134
Sandstrom, Kent, 129
Sartre, Jean-Paul, 34

Sauder, Michael, 135
Schechner, Richard, 147
Schilt, Kristen, 416
Schippers, Mimi, 413
Schmidt, Eric, 95
Schneider, Christopher J.: Policing and Social
  Media: Social Control in an Era of New
  Media, 458–459
Schneider, Joseph W., 157
Schneider, L.: The Scottish Moralists on
  Human Nature and Society, 40
schools, as sites for socialization, 133, 393–394,
  406
Schroeder, Julianna, 94
Schur, Edwin M.: The Politics of
  Deviance, 453
Schütz, Alfred, 35, 38, 76, 151, 187, 221–222, 230
Schwalbe, Michael, 12, 19, 135, 368
Scott, Susie, 3, 16, 146, 154, 319
Scottish Enlightenment, 39–42
Seamster, Louise, 339
secret exhibitions (SEs), 354–356, 358
self. *See also* identity; sense of self; social self
  balanced, 263
  becoming of, 266, 270
  cyber, 286, 305
  deemphasization of, 3
  dialogical and semiotic, 10
  digital, 285, 302–303
  double consciousness of, 14
  eco-self, 516, 522
  existential, 262–263
  looking glass self, 41, 149, 297, 449
  marginal, 263–264
  mass-media influences on, 280
  moral, 459, 461
  music and, 262–264, 270
  narrative studies of, 179–186
  new-media influences on, 285–286
  performance of, 3, 8, 16, 149
  postmodern, 285–286, 305
  reflexive, 2, 3, 11, 149, 188, 262
  religion and, 319–325
  sexual, 435–439
  situated, 285
  social construction of, 3, 166–167
  social genesis of, 223, 224

terminal, 261, 286
virtual, 285, 372–373, 376, 377, 381, 382
self-consciousness, 9, 223, 224, 231
self-esteem, 86–87, 390, 434, 456, 460, 480
self-knowledge, 231, 305
self-perception, 35, 449, 461
self-presentation
  in dramaturgical perspective, 152–154, 157
  moral character and, 449
  in narrative studies, 179, 180
  in online interactions, 302–306, 309, 311
self-surveillance, 280, 479
self-triangulation, 305
semiotics
  consumption and, 243
  culture and, 228
  encoding/decoding model and, 210
  inner speech and, 10
  marked/unmarked identities and, 336–338, 344
  Marxism and, 211
  music criticism and, 267
  online interactions and, 299
  sexuality and, 431
  subcultures and, 217
sense of place, 18, 249, 250, 265
sense of self
  creation of, 29, 41, 43, 81
  digital technologies and, 98
  disease and, 469, 474
  interpersonal relationships and, 2
  racism's effects on, 395
  in shopping situations, 249
sensitizing concepts
  Blumer on, 11, 16, 71, 258, 336
  in concept-driven research, 16, 71–72, 74–76
  in empirical research, 54, 65
  formal sociology and, 11
  in grounded theory research, 60
  in marked/unmarked identities, 336–338
  meaning and meaning-making as, 196
  in mesodomain analysis, 127, 139n3
  music and, 259, 270
  religion and, 328
  social organization and, 126, 127, 136, 138, 139n1
sensory incongruity, 89–90

SEs (secret exhibitions), 354–356, 358
sex and sexuality, 425–441. *See also* LGBTQ+
  community
  cultural influences on, 434
  emotions and, 436–437
  gender and, 433, 435–438
  identity based on, 402, 405, 413–415, 429, 438–439
  inequality and, 412
  language of, 403–406, 404f, 429–433
  marked/unmarked identities and, 337, 346
  meaning and, 425–432, 436, 440–441
  naming and labeling practices, 429–433
  nature and, 425–426, 430
  performances of, 8, 19, 437, 438
  pragmatism and, 427–428
  quantitative measurement of, 112
  rape, 434, 459–460
  scripts related to, 427–428, 433, 436
  situations involving, 434–435
  socialization and, 435–439
  standpoint theories and, 339–340
  stigmatization and, 440, 450
  subcultures and, 213, 426, 439–440
  transsexuals, 182–183, 403–404, 416–417, 419n5 440
sex differences, 163–164, 409
sexual-emotional capital, 437
sexual self, 435–439
Shank, Barry, 264
Shankar, Avi, 309
shared meaning
  contextual influences on, 276
  generalized other and, 7
  interpretivist approach to, 4
  language and, 163, 278
  of mass-media messages, 278
  in new-media interactions, 284
  pragmatism and, 223
  quantitative measurement and, 12, 110
  reflexive self and, 2
  religion and, 327
  rules as structure for, 197
  subcultures and, 216, 281
Sharp, Shane, 326
Shaw, Clifford: *The Jack Roller*, 177
Shibutani, T., 29

574 INDEX

shopping and shopping malls. *See also* consumption
  contextual and negotiated practice of, 247–252
  customer and clerk interactions in, 250–251
  emancipatory vs. manipulative nature of, 246
  feminism and, 248–249
  globalization of, 251–252
  identity construction and, 8, 246–251
  inequality reproduced through, 250–251
  private ownership of, 252, 253, 253n1
  rules in, 250–252
  as spaces of consumption, 17, 242–246, 251–252
Shore, Marlene, 31
Short, John, 298
Shupe, A., 318
Shuter, Robert, 282
SI. *See* symbolic interactionism
Simmel, Georg
  on consumption, 242
  cultural sociology and, 221, 222
  Kantian framework and, 38
  lectures given by, 37
  on patterned interactions, 11
  quantification of ideas, 119
  on social relations, 247
Simon, William: *Sexual Conduct: The Social Sources of Human Sexuality*, 427–428
situated self, 285
situational analysis, 60
Sjoberg, Gideon, 129
Skaggs, Rachel, 267
Skipper, James, 117
Small, Albion W., 32, 33, 36–37, 39–41
smartphones, 83–84, 86, 281–284, 286
Smith, Adam
  Lectures on Jurisprudence, 42–43
  Small on moral philosophy of, 39–40
  Theory of Moral Sentiments, 41, 43
  Wealth of Nations, 41–42
Smith, Christian, 197
Smith, Dorothy E., 407, 418
Smith, Greg, 178, 305
Smith, Kate, 353
Smith, Philip, 198

Smith-Lovin, Lynn, 410
Snead, David, 233
Snorton, C. Riley, 416
Snow, David, 65, 166–167, 319, 512
social actors. *See also* performances
  actor-network theory, 495, 503, 540
  cultural pragmatics and, 8
  in dramaturgical perspective, 3, 146–158
  in everyday life, 221–222, 224
  facework by, 153, 155, 157
  life contingencies of, 316
  meaning assigned by, 243
  in research process, 50–54
  social scientists as, 105, 110
  in subcultures, 211, 215
social arenas theory, 128
social change
  ASA's commitment to, 5
  gender and, 407, 410
  in macro phenomena analysis, 135, 139
  new media and, 283–284
  theoretical and methodological implications of, 64
social constructionism, 162–172
  analytic bracketing and, 168–169
  communicative, 539
  critiques of, 167–171
  culture and, 7, 8, 164–165, 225
  disasters and, 532–535, 540
  disease and, 19, 471, 472
  emotions and, 17, 225–228, 232
  gender and, 13, 171
  grounded theory research and, 60
  knowledge and, 162–164, 167, 169, 225
  language of, 170–171, 232
  lived experiences and, 16, 172
  ontological gerrymandering in, 168, 169
  politics of, 169–172
  postmodernism and, 34
  race and, 14, 171, 172, 386–389
  reality and, 162–170, 225
  religion and, 320, 326–327
  selective relativism in, 167–169
  self and, 3, 166–167
  strict vs. contextual, 168
  subjectivity and, 169, 226, 230
Social Darwinism, 31

social ecology, 3, 12, 30–33
social forces, 5, 19, 83, 125–126, 137, 196
social identity
  in becoming of self, 270
  intersectionality and, 345, 346
  moral career and, 157
  performance of, 149
  power and inequality in shaping of, 336
  religion and, 316, 319
social interactions. *See also* communication;
    online interactions
  analytic bracketing and, 168–169
  celebrity sightings and, 202
  contextual influences, 3, 387
  in conversational narratives, 176
  dynamic nature of, 199
  environment and, 3, 39
  in everyday life, 201–203
  generic social processes of, 11
  in healthcare, 469–470, 475–483
  meaning-making through, 4, 18–19, 109,
    276, 296
  music and, 266–267
  narrative studies and, 183, 185
  power in, 372–379
  quantitative measurement and, 109
  racism in, 343, 344
  religion and, 323–326
  research data generated through, 53
  rituals and routines of, 152
  signifying in, 228, 373
socialization
  attentional, 76–77, 336
  cultural, 165
  educational, 133, 393–394, 406
  gender and, 392, 406–407
  of healthcare professions, 472
  interaction orders and, 150
  marked/unmarked identities and, 343–344
  meta-power and, 128
  in norm acquisition, 7
  passive view of, 391
  perceptions and, 163
  politics and, 392
  professional, 35, 77, 133
  racial, 14, 19, 343–344, 390–396
  religion and, 314, 320, 323

sexual, 435–439
  in subcultures, 281
  transactional nature of, 391
social life
  co-construction of meaning in, 2
  culture in relation to, 197
  dimensions of, 4, 12, 19, 165
  dramaturgical perspective and, 146–148
  ecologies of, 3
  eco-uncertainty in, 20
  as emerging process, 426
  ethnic cleavages in, 208
  institutional management of, 186
  material reality and, 163–164
  measurement and, 109, 119
  mesostructure as realm of, 126
  music's role in, 18, 258, 271
  of nothingness, 352
  organization of, 123
  rapid pace of, 16
  religion in, 315
  signifying in, 228
  social psychological foundations of, 166
  survey research on, 51
  theatre as metaphor for, 146, 152, 158
social meaning. *See* shared meaning
social media. *See also* online interactions;
    specific platforms
  communication through, 93
  cultural scripts and, 148
  disasters and, 542
  feedback channels on, 288
  global rates of use, 284
  in healthcare, 476
  influencers on, 216, 287, 353
  as news source, 90–91
  policing incidents on, 458–459
  user types, 301
social networks
  bot searches of, 96–97
  interactionist analysis of, 133–134
  of internet users, 284
  in mesodomain analysis, 127
  research methodology and, 64–66
  sexuality and, 439
  in sociology world, 113
  in subcultures, 211, 216

INDEX

social norms
    deviation from, 395
    hegemonic, 212
    internalization of, 389
    resilience and, 494
    sensitization to, 76
    in social roles, 308
    structural functionalism on, 2
social objects, 224, 231–232, 326, 352, 427
social order
    classical writings on, 42
    ecological thinking and, 30
    interactional creation of, 368
    latent power of, 209
    subcultures and, 213, 214
    of values and classification, 243
social organization, 122–133
    analysis of, 129–133, 136, 138, 139n1 267
    contemporary views of, 125–132
    of COVID-19 response, 139–140n3
    in deemphasization of self, 3
    disassociation of culture from, 139n1
    ecological thinking and, 31
    future research directions, 129–131, 139
    historical views of, 122–125
    of inequality, 130
    lack of interest in study of, 131–132, 138
    mesodomain analysis of, 127–128, 133, 138
    mesostructures and, 126–127, 129
    music and, 267–268
    negotiated orders and, 124, 126–127, 129, 133
    sensitizing concepts and, 126, 127, 136, 138, 139n1
    social psychology and, 124
    social worlds/social arenas theory of, 128
    temporal structure of, 72–73, 75
social pattern analysis, 71
social performances, 13, 16, 146, 148–149, 226
social power, 12, 209, 335, 338, 345, 347
social pragmatism, 1, 17, 221, 223–224
social presence theory, 298
social psychology
    Blumerian, 28–30
    constructionism and, 226
    culture and, 7
    emotions and, 17, 377
    foundations of, 2

Meadian, 4, 29–30, 166, 223–225
    on mental-moral evolution, 94
    on power, 373
    pragmatism and, 221
    social organization and, 124
social reality
    communication of, 63
    de-realization and, 81
    essentialistic vision of, 51
    interactional reproduction of, 336
    knowledge of, 64
    mass media in construction of, 278–280
    measures of, 112
    moral panics and, 451
    nothingness and, 350, 358
    perceptions of, 278, 280
    selective attention to, 72
    semiotics and, 228
    subcultures and, 207
    unmarked identities and, 337, 338
social research. *See* research methodology
social roles
    mass-media use and, 277
    new-media use and, 285
    pragmatism and, 428
    religion and, 322
    sexuality and, 427, 428
    social norms in, 308
    structural functionalism on, 2
social scenes, 146, 150–151, 264–265
social self
    Black, 342
    in communities, 264
    constructionism and, 226
    reflexive, 2, 3, 149, 188
    religion and, 325
    sexuality and, 429
social status. *See* class
social worlds/social arenas theory, 128
Society for the Study of Symbolic Interaction
    (SSSI), 4, 52, 137
sociology. See also specific theorists and
        theoretical orientations
    Birmingham School, 207–213, 217
    Chicago School (*see* Chicago School)
    cognitive, 11, 77, 104, 204n1 516
    concept-driven, 16, 70–78

cultural, 5, 7–8, 196–204, 221–222, 228, 538
of disasters, 20, 529, 532–533
ecological thinking in, 30–33
of emotions, 11, 17, 229, 381
environmental, 493, 514, 516
epistemic exclusion in, 13, 338–340
formal, 11–12, 14
Frankfurt School, 197
gender theory in, 406–409, 411, 415, 416
of identity, 2, 337
interpretive, 179, 533
of knowledge, 223
language of, 63, 113, 137
of occupations, 31–32, 42
phenomenological, 221
of religion, 314–316, 320, 322, 326, 327
of storytelling, 178–179
theoretical disputes with psychology, 29
verstehen, 2, 36, 221
sociology world, 105, 113–116, 118, 119
software mindset, 90–91
Sohn, Dongyoung, 302
Sokal, Alan: "Transgressing the Boundaries:
Toward a Transformative Hermeneutics
of Quantum Gravity," 169–170
Sokolowski, Peter, 195
Sombart, Werner, 242
Sorokin, Pitirim, 76, 115–117
spatial detachment, 88–89
Spector, Malcolm, 534
Spencer, Herbert, 31, 32, 37
Spillman, Lyn, 199
spirituality. *See* religion and spirituality
spontaneous order, 33, 36, 40
SSSI (Society for the Study of Symbolic
Interaction), 4, 52, 137
Staffen, Lisa, 474
standpoint theories, 12–13, 19, 335, 339–342, 347
Stark, Rodney, 321
statistics. *See* quantitative measurement
Stevens, Wallace: *The Snow Man*, 352
Stewart, David C., 472
Stewart, Dugald, 40
stigmatization
dramaturgical perspective and, 156–157
labeling and, 453
of LGBTQ+ community, 453

marked positions and, 336
moral degradation and, 449
in narrative studies, 178
of pariah femininities, 413
religion and, 323–326
of rule avoidance, 374
sexual, 440, 450
virtual self and, 373
Stillerman, Joel, 252
stimulus-response model, 29
Stoicism, 43
stories and storytelling. *See also* narrative studies
counter-narratives, 186
life stories, 56, 177, 417
master narratives, 186
in performances, 147, 148
popularity of, 175
recipient-designed, 177
of self and group identity, 180–182
sociology of, 178–179
strain theory, 207, 208
Strauss, Anselm L.
on conceptual ordering, 55–56
ethnomethodology and, 35
grounded theory research and, 20n2 60
Hughes as influence on, 32
on initiation processes, 326
on interaction tactics, 354
Mirrors and Masks, 29–30, 124
on negotiated orders, 151, 200, 474
on patients, 469, 471–473
on social organization, 128, 129
Strawson, Galen: "Against Narrativity," 188
Stretesky, Paul B., 458
Stroud, Angela, 345
structural functionalism
in British social anthropology, 35
critiques of, 166
on disasters, 530, 532
feminist challenges to, 5
gender theory and, 406
macro-deterministic biases, 2
on religious worship, 148
on sexuality, 436
SI as alternative to, 1, 2, 137, 335, 347
on socialization, 391
theoretical principles, 1–2

578   INDEX

structural inequality, 12, 134, 347, 373, 394, 532–533, 543
Stryker, Sheldon, 322, 340, 496
subcultures, 207–217
    authenticity and, 214, 216
    Birmingham School on, 207–213, 217
    Chicago School on, 3, 7, 207–209, 211, 213, 217
    definitions of, 211, 259
    demise of, 207, 215–217
    deviance and, 208–209, 262, 440
    ethnographic study of, 208, 211–212, 217
    hegemony and, 212–214
    hierarchies and, 214
    identity and, 213, 346–347
    marketization of, 215, 216
    mass media and, 215–216
    meaning-making and, 17, 207, 211
    music and, 259–262
    resistance and, 207, 210, 212–214
    sexuality and, 213, 426, 439–440
    shared meaning and, 216, 281
    socialization in, 281
subjectivity. *See also* intersubjectivity
    culture and, 229–234
    defined, 149, 224–225
    emotions and, 230, 231, 234
    postmodern, 242
    pragmatism and, 223, 224
    of religious experiences, 317
    social constructionism and, 169, 226, 230
subordinate masculinity, 411
suicide, 111, 115, 450
Sullivan, Thomas J., 472
Sumerau, J. Edward, 323, 326, 346
Sunstein, Cass, 352, 356–359, 363nn9–10
surveillance
    by digital technologies, 95–96, 98
    gender and, 403, 406
    of masculinity, 412
    self-surveillance, 280, 479
survey research, 50–51, 77, 393, 497
Sutherland, Edwin, 3
Sweeney, John A., 97
Swistun, Debora A., 498, 513–516, 521–522, 537
symbolic interactionism (SI). *See also specific theorists*

Blumer's premises of, 2, 4, 19, 64, 109, 125, 137, 361
classical heritage of, 42–43
on consumption, 246–253
critiques of, 12, 32, 125–126, 132, 137, 164, 335, 370
culture and (*see* culture)
dichotomies of attention and interpretation in, 136–138
disasters and (*see* disasters)
emotions and (*see* emotions)
environment and (*see* environmental issues)
expansive vision of, 6–15
formal, 11–12, 16
gender issues and (*see* gender)
German influences on, 34, 36–39
on healthcare, 470–475
historical foundations, 1–4, 27–44
holistic approach of, 468, 471, 474–475
identity in (*see* identity)
inequality and (*see* inequality)
intellectual sectarianism and, 4–6
intersectional, 338, 343–348
macro phenomena in (*see* macro phenomena)
meaning in (*see* meaning)
on media, 276–286, 288–289
micro phenomena in, 122, 125–127, 129, 136–139
music and (*see* music)
origins of term, 2, 4, 27–28, 388, 419n1
performances in (*see* performances)
politics of, 32
power and (*see* power)
pragmatism and (*see* pragmatism)
racial/ethnic issues and (*see* race and ethnicity)
religion and (*see* religion and spirituality)
research in (*see* research methodology)
resilience and (*see* resilience)
Scottish influences on, 39–42
self in (*see* self)
sexuality and (*see* sex and sexuality)
social organization and (*see* social organization)
subcultures and (*see* subcultures)

technologies and (*see* technologies)
theoretical expansion, 4–6
traditionalist perspective, 2–4
sympathy, 29, 32, 36, 41, 155, 179
syntactic model of interaction, 302
systems theory, 530, 532

T

Tamir, Diana I., 284
Tan, Joo Ean, 129
Tannenbaum, Frank, 448
Tavory, Iddo, 10, 20n2 137, 202–203, 343–344, 361
Taylor, Dorceta, 514
technologies. *See also* digital technologies
    artificial intelligence, 97, 98, 361
    GPS, 89, 92, 358
    in healthcare, 476–479
    ICTs, 18, 296–301, 303
    occupational structures and, 42
    for statistical computations, 115
temporal disorganization, 85–87
temporality, 127, 130, 133, 453, 496–498, 500
Ten Have, Paul, 351
terminal self, 261, 286
texting, 86, 90, 93, 276, 282, 288
Thaler, Richard, 352, 356, 359, 363n10
theatre, 146–148, 152, 156, 158
theodicy, defined, 315
theoretical sampling, 61
Thirlaway, Kate, 309
Thomas, Dorothy Swaine, 8, 227
Thomas, William I.
    Chicago School and, 2, 208
    on definition of the situation, 165
    Four Wishes concept, 29
    The Polish Peasant in Europe and America, 177
    role in invention of SI, 28, 124
    situation concept of, 227
    structural interactionism of, 30
    subculture studies by, 208
Thomas theorem, 8, 388, 449
Thomson, William (Lord Kelvin), 118
Thorne, Barrie, 391
Thornton, Sarah, 214
thought communities, 76, 106, 516–517
Thrasher, Frederic, 3

Tian, Xiaoli, 9, 18, 296, 308
Tierney, Kathleen, 529, 530, 532–534
time, experience of, 9, 164
Timmermans, Stefan, 10, 20n2 343, 344
Toffolon-Weiss, Melissa, 523
Tohoku-Fukushima nuclear disaster (2011), 532
transgender persons. *See also* LGBTQ+ community
    children as, 416, 418
    identity of, 170–171, 416–417
    interactional practices and, 346
    storytelling tools of, 183
    violence against, 416
translational science movement, 262–263
transportation (immersed media experience), 280
transsexuals, 182–183, 403–404, 416–417, 419n5 440
trauma, collective, 539
Trautner, Mary Nell, 414
Trump, Donald, 170
Turkle, Sherry, 86, 94, 95
    Simulation and Its Discontent, 85
Tuvel, Rebecca, 170–172
Twitter, 276, 306, 310
Tyler, Imogen, 148–149

U

unmarked identities, 335–348
    epistemological concerns and, 335, 338–342
    intersectionality and, 338, 343–348
    power and, 338–340, 343, 345, 346
    sensitizing concepts and, 336–338
    socialization and, 343–344
upshifting, 344
urban ecology, 207–209
urban ethnography, 3, 339, 449
uses and gratifications theory, 277

V

Van Ausdale, Debra, 395
Van Maanen, John, 154
Vannini, Phillip
    on authenticity, 268
    on life-as-music approach, 270
    Popular Culture in Everyday Life, 201
    on semiotics and music criticism, 267

Vaughan, Diane, 539
Veblen, Thorstein, 242
Vera, Héctor, 12, 16, 104
Veyne, Paul, 359–360
vicarious masculinity, 412
Vidal-Ortiz, Salvadore, 416
Vincent, G. E., 32, 33, 41
violence
    dehumanization and, 93
    domestic, 453–454, 457
    gang-related, 199
    as labeling, 456–458
    language of, 437
    political, 213
    racial, 172, 340, 390
    rape, 434, 459–460
    sex offenders and, 178, 183–184
    symbolic, 171–172
    against transgender persons, 416
virtual self, 285, 372–373, 376, 377, 381, 382
voice over internet protocol (VoIP) services,
    281–282
Voltaire: *The Henriade*, 118
vom Lehn, Dirk, 260

W

Wachinger, Gisela, 536–537
Wang, Dawei, 288
Ward, Adrian F., 284
Ward, Jane, 412
Warikoo, Natasha K., 395
Warner, Lloyd: "Communication Conduct in
    an Island Community," 34–35
Waskul, Dennis, 270, 327
    Popular Culture in Everyday Life, 201
Watson, J. B., 29
Watzlawick, Paul, 92
Waugh, Linda, 337
Weaver, Gary R., 322
Weber, Marianne, 37
Weber, Max
    on bureaucracy, 502
    culture in work of, 221, 222, 230
    on force of ideas, 340
    on meaning-adequate concepts, 222
    Parsons influenced by, 2
    on power, 368, 373

on religion, 38, 314, 315
    visit to United States, 37
Weigert, Andrew J., 516
Weiss, Jane, 135
Weizenbaum, Joseph, 86
West, Candace, 13, 211, 408–410, 415, 416
Westbrook, Laurel, 416
White, Hayden, 11
whiteness
    in concept-driven research, 73
    misrepresentations of, 213
    privilege and, 171, 213, 343, 395
    of queer scholarship, 405
    as unmarked identity, 345–346
Whittaker, Elvi, 27, 30, 35
Whyte, William Foote, 114, 208
Widavsky, Aaron, 538
Wieder, Lawrence, 184
Wiest, Julie B., 9, 18, 275
Wiley, Norbert, 10
Williams, Christine L.: Inside Toyland:
    Working, Shopping, and Social
    Inequality, 250
Williams, Ederyn, 298
Williams, J. Patrick, 213, 216, 259–261, 268, 269
Williams, James Mickel, 124
Williams, Juliet A., 415
Williams, Raymond, 209, 233
    Keywords, 196
Willman, Rebecca K., 412
Wilshire, Bruce W., 262
Wimberley, Dale W., 321
Winant, Howard, 388, 396n1
Windelband, Wilhelm, 38
Winkler, Erin, 392, 393
Wirth, Louis, 28
Witherspoon, John, 40
Wittgenstein, L., 36, 38
women. *See also* femininity; feminism; gender
    Chicago School and, 32, 341
    cultural production by, 213
    domestic violence against, 453–454
    gender roles for, 406–407
    marginalization as theorists, 339
    marriage for, 135, 407
    media images of, 280
    rape and, 434, 459–460

shopping malls as public sphere for, 245
suffrage movement for, 402
Woolgar, Steve, 167–168
work. *See* labor; occupations
Wynn, Jonathan R., 200, 267

Y

Yatim, Sammy, 459
Yeadon-Lee, Tracey, 414
Yee, Aubrey M., 97
Yoels, William, 269
Young, Iris, 413
YouTube, 276, 459

Z

Zayts, Olga, 513
Zeno, 43
Zerubavel, Eviatar
    Ancestors and Relatives, 73, 76
    on concept-driven research, 16, 70
    The Elephant in the Room, 73, 75
    The Fine Line, 72, 73

Generally Speaking: An Invitation to
    Concept-Driven Sociology, 78
Hidden in Plain Sight, 74, 76
"If Simmel Were a Fieldworker," 11
Patterns of Time in Hospital Life, 75
on sensitizing concepts, 336
The Seven-Day Circle, 74
Social Mindscapes, 76
Taken for Granted, 73, 76
on temporal orders, 164
on thought communities, 516–517
Time Maps, 73, 76
Zhao, Shanyang, 285, 301–303, 307
Zimmerman, Don H., 13, 211, 408–410, 415, 416
Znaniecki, Florian
    on definition of the situation, 165
    The Polish Peasant in Europe and America,
        177
    role in invention of SI, 28, 124
    on sexuality, 427
    subculture studies by, 208
Zuboff, Shoshana, 97